# Fifty Years of the Law Commissions

## The Dynamics of Law Reform

Edited by
Matthew Dyson
James Lee
Shona Wilson Stark

·HART·

OXFORD · LONDON · NEW YORK · NEW DELHI · SYDNEY

HART PUBLISHING
Bloomsbury Publishing Plc
Kemp House, Chawley Park, Cumnor Hill, Oxford, OX2 9PH, UK

HART PUBLISHING, the Hart/Stag logo, BLOOMSBURY and the Diana logo are
trademarks of Bloomsbury Publishing Plc
First published in Great Britain 2016

First published in hardback, 2016
Paperback edition, 2019

A catalogue record for this book is available from the British Library.

**Library of Congress Cataloging-in-Publication Data**

Names: Dyson, Matthew, 1982– editor. | Lee, James, 1983– editor. | Wilson Stark, Shona, editor.

Title: Fifty years of the Law Commissions : the dynamics of law reform / Edited by Matthew Dyson,
James Lee, Shona Wilson Stark.

Description: Portland, Oregon : Hart Publishing, 2016. | Includes bibliographical
references and index.

Identifiers: LCCN 2016016067 (print) | LCCN 2016016212 (ebook) | ISBN 9781849468572
(hardback) | ISBN 9781849468596 (Epub)

Subjects: LCSH: Law reform—Great Britain. | Great Britain. Law Commission.

Classification: LCC KD654 .F54 2016 (print) | LCC KD654 (ebook) | DDC 340/.30941—dc23

LC record available at https://lccn.loc.gov/2016016067

ISBN: HB: 978-1-84946-857-2
PB: 978-1-50992-791-3
ePDF: 978-1-84946-858-9
ePub: 978-1-84946-859-6

Typeset by Compuscript Ltd, Shannon

To find out more about our authors and books visit www.hartpublishing.co.uk. Here you will find
extracts, author information, details of forthcoming events and the option to sign up for our
newsletters.

# FIFTY YEARS OF THE LAW COMMISSIONS

This book brings together past and present law commissioners, judges, practitioners, academics and law reformers to analyse the past, present and future of the Law Commissions in the United Kingdom and beyond. Its internationally recognised authors bring a wealth of experience and insight into how and why law reform does and should take place, covering statutory and non-statutory reform from national and international perspectives. The chapters of the book developed from papers given at a conference to mark the fiftieth anniversary of the Law Commissions Act 1965.

# Acknowledgements

This book arises out of a conference to mark the fiftieth anniversary of the Law Commissions Act 1965, on 10–11 July 2015, at the United Kingdom Supreme Court. It was an event to mark that special anniversary and to look back, around and forward; we hope that this collection of the papers from the conference provides the same opportunity to others.

However, nothing would have been possible without the generous support the event received from a number of sources. We gratefully acknowledge the support of the Modern Law Review Seminar Series, the Society of Legal Scholars, the Dickson Poon School of Law at King's College London, the Clark Foundation for Legal Education, Hart Publishing and the Honourable Society of the Inner Temple.

We also should like to thank Hector MacQueen, who was a major support throughout the project and was our liaison at the Scottish Law Commission, and David Ormerod, who assisted us greatly as our liaison with the Law Commission. The then Chairmen and Chief Executives of each Commission, Lord Pentland and Sir David Lloyd Jones, and Malcolm McMillan and Elaine Lorimer respectively, were enthusiastic in ensuring the Commissions' collective engagement with the event, and we thank them. We are also very grateful for the efforts and insights of all of our contributors, and everyone who attended the conference over its two days.

The administration of the conference was greatly facilitated by many people, including David Caron, David Nelken, Amanda Willmott, Anna Wood, Gemma Noyce, Leonie Taylor, Sara Bladon, Sally Thomson, Jenny Rowe, Albinist Llugiqi and David Mills.

We should also like to thank all of the team at Hart Publishing for their support through the editorial and publication process, especially Bill Asquith, Annie Mirza, Mel Hamill, Emma Platt, John Hort and Tom Adams.

The book endeavours to state the law as of 1 December 2015.

Matthew Dyson, James Lee and Shona Wilson Stark

# Table of Contents

*Acknowledgements* .................................................................................. v
*Table of Law Reform Reports and Papers* ........................................ xi
*Contributors* ...................................................................................... xvii

### Part 1: Introduction

1. Introduction ................................................................................... 3
   *Matthew Dyson, James Lee and Shona Wilson Stark*

2. Fifty Years of the Law Commissions: The Dynamics of Law
   Reform Now, Then and Next ..................................................... 17
   *Lady Hale*

### Part 2: The First Half-Century of the Commissions

3. Introduction ................................................................................ 29
   *Lord Hodge*

4. Strategies of the Early Law Commission ................................. 31
   *Paul Mitchell*

5. Fifty Years of Law Reform—A Note on the Northern
   Ireland Style ............................................................................... 46
   *Neil Faris*

6. Working on the Larger Canvas—Law Reform in a Federal
   System: Thoughts on Forty Years of the Australian
   Law Reform Commission ......................................................... 55
   *Kathryn Cronin*

7. Law Reform and Social Policy ................................................. 64
   *Eric Clive*

### Part 3: Institutions, Commissions, Committees, Codifiers

8. Introduction ................................................................................ 75
   *Lord Beith*

9. Memoir of a Reforming Chairman .......................................... 76
   *Sir Terence Etherton*

10. The Duty to Make the Law More Accessible?
    The Two C-Words .................................................................... 89
    *George L Gretton*

11. The Former Law Commission of Canada: The Road
    Less Travelled ............................................................................. 97
    *Yves Le Bouthillier*

12. The Law Commission and the Criminal Law: Reflections
    on the Codification Project .................................................... 108
    *Ian Dennis*

**Part 4: The Many Faces of Law Reform**

13. Introduction .............................................................................. 125
    *Lord Carnwath*

14. Democracy, Law Reform and the Rule of Law ......................... 127
    *Lord Toulson*

15. Promoting Law Reform: By Means of Draft Bills or Otherwise ................. 139
    *Shona Wilson Stark*

16. Law Commissions, Courts and Society: A Sceptical View ........................ 151
    *William Binchy*

17. A Good Name, a Long Game ................................................... 159
    *Laura Dunlop*

**Part 5: Implementation by Statute**

18. Introduction .............................................................................. 173
    *Dame Mary Arden*

19. The Legislative Implementation of Law Reform Proposals ....................... 175
    *Sir Grant Hammond*

20. Post-legislative Scrutiny, Legislative Drafting and
    the 'Elusive Boundary' ............................................................ 189
    *Andrew Burrows*

21. Reflections on Statutory Implementation in the Law Commission ............. 198
    *Nicholas Paines*

22. Implementation by Statute: What the Future Holds ................................ 201
    *Hector MacQueen*

**Part 6: How Law Commissions Work**

23. Introduction .............................................................................. 217
    *Sir James Munby*

24. The Law Commission Method: Exportable to the EU? ............................. 219
    *Hugh Beale*

25. How Law Commissions Work: Some Lessons from the Past ..................... 235
    *David Johnston*

26.   Challenges for Independent Law Reformers from Changing
       External Priorities and Shorter Timescales ................................. 245
       *Sir Jack Beatson*

27.   The Bill's Progress ..................................................................... 266
       *Stephen Lewis*

### Part 7: Courts and Commissions

28.   Introduction ............................................................................. 273
       *Lord Drummond Young*

29.   The Etiquette of Law Reform .................................................... 274
       *James Lee*

30.   Law Reform in Private Law: The Role of Statutes in
       Supplementing or Supplanting the Common Law ......................... 297
       *Barbara McDonald*

31.   The Refiner's Fire ..................................................................... 310
       *Charles Harpum*

32.   Reflections on the Courts and the Commission ............................ 326
       *David Ormerod*

### Part 8: Commissioning the Future

33.   Introduction ............................................................................. 339
       *Elizabeth Cooke*

34.   The Scottish Law Commission and the Future of
       Law Reform in Scotland ............................................................ 340
       *Lord Pentland*

35.   Looking to the Future ............................................................... 355
       *Sir David Lloyd Jones*

36.   Commissioning the Future—A Chief Executive's Perspective ........ 365
       *Elaine Lorimer*

37.   Implementation of Law Reform Reports: Developments
       in Scotland .............................................................................. 369
       *Malcolm McMillan*

38.   The Future is a Foreign Country, They Do Things
       Differently There ...................................................................... 380
       *Matthew Dyson*

39.   Making Law—Who, How and What? .......................................... 400
       *KJ Keith*

Index ................................................................................................ 413

# Table of Law Reform Reports and Papers

**Law Commission Reports**

LC 1, *First Programme of Law Reform* (1965) ............................................... 13, 20, 34, 391
LC 3, *Proposals to Abolish Certain Ancient Criminal Offences* (1966)............................ 39
LC 4, *First Annual Report* (1966) ........................................................................ 34, 39, 43
LC 5, *Landlord and Tenant: Interim Report on Distress for Rent* (1966) ................... 40, 43
LC 6, *Reform of the Grounds of Divorce: The Field of Choice* (1966)............................ 37
LC 8, *Report on the Powers of Appeal Courts to Sit in Private and the
    Restrictions upon Publicity in Domestic Proceedings* (1966) ........................................ 40
LC 9, *Transfer of Land: Interim Report on Root of Title to
    Freehold Land* (1966)...................................................................................................... 36, 40
LC 10, *Imputed Criminal Intent (Director of Public Prosecutions v Smith)* (1966)............ 35
LC 11, *Transfer of Land: Report on Restrictive Covenants* (1967) ...................18, 24–25, 40
LC 12, *Second Annual Report* (1967) ................................................................................. 36, 38
LC 13, *Civil Liability for Animals* (1967) ............................................................................... 35
LC 14, *Second Programme of Law Reform* (1968) ................................................. 13, 20, 108
LC 15, *Third Annual Report* (1968) ....................................................................... 38, 39, 41
LC 16, *Blood Tests and the Proof of Paternity in Civil Proceedings* (1968) .............. 43, 393
LC 19, *Proceedings against Estates* (1969)........................................................................... 36
LC 20, *Administrative Law* (1969) .................................................................................... 37, 43
LC 40, *Civil Liability of Vendors and Lessors for Defective Premises* (1970).................. 143
LC 54, *Third Programme of Law Reform* (1973) .................................................................. 21
LC 104, *Insurance Law: Non-Disclosure and Breach of Warranty* (1980) ...................... 266
LC 110, *Breach of Confidence* (1981).................................................................................. 149
LC 123, *Offences Relating to Public Order* (1983)............................................................. 280
LC 143, *Codification of the Criminal Law:
    A Report to the Law Commission* (1985)..................... 21, 108, 109, 112, 116, 117, 395
LC 145, *Criminal Law: Offences against Religion and Public Worship* (1985)................ 146
LC 152, *Liability for Chancel Repairs* (1985) ..................................................................... 260
LC 154, *Law of Contract: The Parol Evidence Rule* (1986)............................................... 252
LC 164, *Formalities for Contracts for Sale etc of Land* (1987)......................................... 312
LC 177, *A Criminal Code for England and Wales* (1989) .................54, 55 70–72, 108, 111,
    113–15, 117, 302, 395
LC 185, *Fourth Programme of Law Reform* (1989)....................................................... 21, 249
LC 192, *Ground for Divorce* (1990) .................................................................................... 253
LC 200, *Fifth Programme of Law Reform* (1991)......................................................... 22, 249
LC 205, *Rape within Marriage* (1992) .................................................................................. 24
LC 207, *Domestic Violence and Occupation of the Family Home* (1992) ...................... 247
LC 208, *Landlord and Tenant: Business Tenancies—A Periodic Review of
    the Landlord and Tenant Act 1954 Part II* (1992)....................................................... 143
LC 216, *The Hearsay Rule in Civil Proceedings* (1993) ..................................................... 393

LC 218, *Legislating the Criminal Code: Offences against the
Person and General Principles* (1993)........................ 14, 111, 117, 146
LC 219, *Contributory Negligence as a Defence in Contract* (1993) ................. 283
LC 224, *Structured Settlements and Interim and Provisional Damages* (1994) ............... 246
LC 225, *Personal Injury Compensation: How Much is Enough?* (1994)......................... 249
LC 226, *Administrative Law: Judicial Review and Statutory Appeals* (1994)................... 281
LC 227, *Restitution: Mistakes of Law and Ultra Vires
Public Authority Receipts and Payments* (1994)................... 144, 163, 164, 241, 252, 395
LC 231, *Mental Incapacity* (1995) ........................................................ 253
LC 232, *Twenty-Ninth Annual Report: 1994* (1995) ......................247–48, 258
LC 234, *Sixth Programme of Law Reform* (1995) ................................... 22
LC 236, *Fiduciary Duties and Regulatory Rules* (1995)........................... 149, 252
LC 237, *Legislating the Criminal Code:
Involuntary Manslaughter* (1996)........................ 14, 111, 118, 146
LC 239, *Thirtieth Annual Report: 1995* (1996) ...................................... 247
LC 242, *Privity of Contract: Contracts for the Benefit of Third Parties* (1996)............... 304
LC 245, *Evidence in Criminal Proceedings: Hearsay and
Related Topics* (1997)........................................................ 292, 393
LC 247, *Aggravated, Exemplary and Restitutionary Damages* (1997) ........................... 145
LC 248, *Legislating the Criminal Code: Corruption* (1998) ........................... 255
LC 249, *Liability for Psychiatric Illness* (1998).................................... 306
LC 251, *The Rules against Perpetuities and Excessive Accumulations* (1998)................... 82
LC 253, *The Execution of Deeds and Documents by or on behalf of
Bodies Corporate* (1998) ........................................................ 143
LC 254, *Land Registration for the Twenty-First Century:
A Consultative Document* (1998)........................................ 314, 323
LC 255, *Consents to Prosecution* (1998).......................................... 396
LC 257, *Damages for Personal Injury:
Non-Pecuniary Loss* (1999)........................ 28, 136, 193, 246, 249, 395
LC 259, *Seventh Programme of Law Reform* (1999) ....................... 14, 19, 22
LC 265, *Thirty-Fourth Annual Report: 1999* (2000).......................... 144
LC 267, *Double Jeopardy and Prosecution Appeals* (2001) ...................... 393
LC 270, *Report on Limitation of Actions* (2001),..................... 238, 282, 393
LC 271, *Land Registration for the Twenty-First Century:
A Conveyancing Revolution* (2001) ....................314–15, 317–19, 320, 339
LC 273, *Evidence of Bad Character in Criminal Proceedings* (2001) ........................... 393
LC 274, *Eighth Programme of Law Reform* (2001).................................. 22
LC 275, *Thirty-Sixth Annual Report: 2001* (2002) ............................. 143
LC 276, *Fraud* (2002) ........................................................ 118
LC 280, *Annual Report 2002–03* (2003) ...................................... 149
LC 293, *Ninth Programme of Law Reform* (2005).................................. 22
LC 295, *The Forfeiture Rule and the Law of Succession* (2005)....................... 391
LC 297, *Renting Homes: The Final Report* (2006)................................ 360
LC 301, *Trustee Exemption Clauses* (2006) ........................... 25, 113, 305, 395
LC 302, *Post-Legislative Scrutiny* (2006) ........................... 135, 190, 395
LC 303, *Termination of Tenancies for Tenant Default* (2006)....................... 260
LC 307, *Cohabitation: The Financial Consequences of Relationship
Breakdown* (2007)........................................................ 284, 300
LC 309, *Housing: Proportionate Dispute Resolution* (2008) ........................... 395
LC 311, *Tenth Programme of Law Reform* (2008) ...................... 22, 109

LC 312, *Housing: Encouraging Responsible Letting* (2008) ................................. 395
LC 313, *Reforming Bribery* (2008) ................................................ 255
LC 314, *Intoxication and Criminal Liability* (2009) ................................. 8, 122
LC 315, *Capital and Income in Trusts: Classification and Apportionment* (2009) ............ 83
LC 320, *The Illegality Defence* (2010) ...................................25, 133, 145, 252, 286–87
LC 321, *Protocol between the Lord Chancellor (on behalf of the
   Government) and the Law Commission* (2010) ...................... 22, 248, 256, 275
LC 322, *Administrative Redress: Public Bodies and The Citizen* (2010) ......................... 260
LC 325, *Expert Evidence in Criminal Proceedings in
   England and Wales* (2011) ............................ 120, 144, 333, 361, 394
LC 328, *Annual Report 2010–11* (2011) ............................................... 356
LC 330, *Eleventh Programme of Law Reform* (2011) .............................. 23, 327
LC 331, *Intestacy and Family Provision Claims on Death* (2011) ............................ 83, 361
LC 335, *Contempt of Court: Scandalising the Court* (2012) ............................... 263
LC 337, *Renting Homes in Wales/Rhentu Cartrefiyng Nghymru* (2013) ....................... 360
LC 338, *Annual Report 2012–13* (2013) ............................................. 149
LC 340, *Contempt of Court (1): Juror Misconduct and
   Internet Publications* (2013) ............................................. 263, 332
LC 342, *Wildlife Law: Control of Invasive Non-native Species* (2014) ...................... 361
LC 343, *Matrimonial Property, Needs and Agreements* (2014) ............................. 361
LC 344, *Contempt of Court (2): Court Reporting* (2014) .............................. 263
LC 346, *Patents, Trade Marks and Design Rights: Groundless Threats* (2014) ............... 361
LC 347, *Taxi and Private Hire Services* (2014) ...................................... 361
LC 348, *Hate Crime: Should the Current Offences be Extended?* (2014) ..................... 361
LC 349, *Conservation Covenants* (2014) ........................................... 361
LC 350, *Fiduciary Duties of Investment Intermediaries* (2014) .............................. 299, 361
LC 351, *Data Sharing between Public Bodies* (2014) ................................. 361, 394
LC 352, *Annual Report 2013–14* (2014) ............21, 33, 39, 50, 133–34, 144, 146, 148, 254
LC 354, *Twelfth Programme of Law Reform* (2014) ......11–12, 23, 109, 120, 262, 357, 362
LC 355, *Simplification of Criminal Law: Kidnapping and
   Related Offences* (2014) .......................................... 121, 357, 361
LC 356, *Rights to Light* (2014) ................................................. 361
LC 358, *Simplification of Criminal Law: Public Nuisance and
   Outraging Public Decency* (2015) ................................. 121, 357
LC 361, *Reform of Offences Against the Person* (2015) ................................. 117

## Scottish Law Commission Reports

SLC 1, *First Programme of Law Reform* (1965) .............................. 7, 13, 69
SLC 3, *First Annual Report* (1966) .............................................. 67
SLC 4, *Proposal for Reform of the Law of Evidence Relating to
   Corroboration* (1967) ................................................... 344
SLC 5, *Reform of the Law Relating to Legitimation* per Subsequens
   Matrimonium (1967) ................................................... 345
SLC 6, *Divorce: The Grounds Considered* (1967) .............................. 70, 345
SLC 8, *Second Programme of Law Reform* (1968) ............................... 69
SLC 15, *Report on Reform of the Law Relating to Prescription and
   Limitation of Actions* (1970) ............................................. 236
SLC 30, *Report on Liability for Antenatal Injury* (1973) ............................ 161
SLC 31, *The Law Relating to Damages for Injuries Causing Death* (1973) .................... 346
SLC 41, *Tenth Annual Report* (1976) .............................................. 370

SLC 43, *Eleventh Annual Report* (1977) ............................................................... 370

SLC 57, *Report on Lost and Abandoned Property* (1980) ............................................. 160

SLC 60, *Report on Occupancy Rights in the Matrimonial Home and Domestic Violence* (1980) ............................................................................ 346

SLC 67, *Report on Aliment and Financial Provision* (1981) ........................................... 346

SLC 68, *Report on Bankruptcy and Related Aspects of Insolvency and Liquidation* (1981) ........................................................................ 143

SLC 76, *Report on Outdated Rules in the Law of Husband and Wife* (1983) .................. 346

SLC 82, *Report on Illegitimacy* (1984) ................................................................. 346

SLC 86, *Report on Matrimonial Property* (1984) ....................................................... 346

SLC 102, *Child Abduction* (1987) ......................................................................... 346

SLC 118, *Recovery of Possession of Heritable Property* (1989) .................................... 144

SLC 122, *Report on Prescription and Limitation of Actions (Latent Damage and Other Related Issues)* (1989) ............................................... 237–38

SLC 124, *Report on Succession* (1990) ............................................................ 146, 346

SLC 125, *Report on the Evidence of Children and Other Potentially Vulnerable Witnesses* (1990) ........................................................... 161

SLC 126, *Fourth Programme of Law Reform* (1990) ................................................... 69

SLC 135, *Report on Family Law* (1992) ................................................................. 285

SLC 146, *Twenty-Eighth Annual Report 1992–93* (1993) ............................................ 162

SLC 149, *Evidence: Report on Hearsay Evidence in Criminal Proceedings* (1995) ........... 143

SLC 152, *Report on Three Bad Rules in Contract Law* (1996) ...................................... 346

SLC 154, *Multi-Party Actions* (1996) .................................................................... 167

SLC 168, *Abolition of the Feudal System* (1999) ............................................... 70, 346

SLC 169, *Report on Unjustified Enrichment, Error of Law and Public Authority Receipts and Disbursements* (1999) ........... 145, 163, 165, 201, 241

SLC 174, *Report on Remedies for Breach of Contract* (1999) ...................................... 346

SLC 196, *Report on Damages for Psychiatric Injury* (2004) ........................................ 346

SLC 209, *Rape and Other Sexual Offences* (2007) .................................................... 347

SLC 214, *Annual Report 2008* (2009) .................................................................... 372

SLC 215, *Report on Succession* (2009) ...................................................... 209, 346, 376

SLC 217, *Unincorporated Associations* (2009) ......................................................... 204

SLC 218, *Double Jeopardy* (2009) ......................................................................... 347

SLC 222, *Land Registration* (2010) ....................................................................... 246

SLC 224, *Report on Criminal Liability of Partnerships* (2011) ........................ 83, 211, 373

SLC 228, *Prescription and Title to Moveable Property* (2012) ..................................... 211

SLC 229, *Report on Similar Fact Evidence and the* Moorov *Doctrine* (2012) ......... 143, 347

SLC 231, *Review of Contract Law—Report on Formation of Contract: Execution in Counterpart* (2013) .................................................. 11, 202, 375

SLC 232, *Report on the Consolidation of Bankruptcy Legislation in Scotland* (2013) ....... 92

SLC 233, *Judicial Factors* (2013) .......................................................................... 210

SLC 236, *Annual Report 2013* (2014) .................................................................... 148

SLC 239, *Trust Law* (2014) ................................................................................ 211

SLC 240, *Report on Adults with Incapacity* (2014) ............................................. 210, 346

SLC 242, *Ninth Programme of Law Reform* (2015) ................................... 11, 20–21, 210

**Joint Reports**

LC 11A and SLC 6A, *Sea Fisheries (Shellfish) Bill: Report on the Consolidation of Certain Enactments Relating to Shellfish Fisheries and Shellfish* (1967) ............... 37, 44

LC 21 and SLC 11, *Interpretation of Statutes* (1969) ..................................................391–92
LC 82 and SLC 45, *Liability for Defective Products* (1977) .............................................. 140
LC 137 and SLC 88, *Recognition of Foreign Nullity Decrees
   and Related Matters* (1984) ..................................................................................................... 346
LC 138 and SLC 91, *Custody of Children—Jurisdiction
   and Enforcement within the United Kingdom* (1985) ......................................... 283, 346
LC 193 and SLC 129, *Private International Law: Choice of Law in
   Tort and Delict* (1990) ............................................................................................................. 248
LC 196 and SLC 130, *Rights of Suit in Respect of Carriage of
   Goods by Sea* (1991) ................................................................................................................. 249
LC 215 and SLC 145, *Sale of Goods Forming Part of a Bulk* (1993) ............................. 249
LC 261 and SLC 173, *Company Directors: Regulating Conflicts of
   Interests and Formulating a Statement of Duties* (1999) ....................................................... 92
LC 266 and SLC 180, *Damages Under the Human Rights Act* (2000) ........................... 280
LC 272 and SLC 184, *Third Parties—Rights against Insurers* (2001) ............... 82, 209, 373
LC 283 and SLC 192, *Partnership Law* (2003) ........................................ 143, 147, 204, 346
LC 292 and SLC 199, *Unfair Terms in Contracts* (2005) ........................................ 261, 361
LC 298 and SLC 202, *Parliamentary Costs Bill: Report on the
   Consolidation of Legislation Relating to Parliamentary Costs* (2006) ........................... 92
LC 317 and SLC 216, *Consumer Remedies for Faulty Goods* (2009) .............. 222, 261, 361
LC 319 and SLC 219, *Consumer Insurance Law: Pre-Contract
   Disclosure and Misrepresentation* (2009) .............................................................. 82, 268
LC 332 and SLC 226, *Consumer Redress for Misleading and
   Aggressive Practices* (2012) .................................................................... 261, 361, 395
LC 341 and SLC 235, *Co-operative and Community Benefit Societies Bill:
   Report on the Consolidation of Legislation Relating to Co-operative
   and Community Benefit Societies* (2013) ..................................................................... 92
LC 345, SLC 237 and NILC 18, *Regulation of Health Care
   Professionals: Regulation of Social Care Professionals in
   England* (2014) ............................................................................... 50, 360, 361, 363
LC 353 and SLC 238, *Insurance Contract Law: Business Disclosure;
   Warranties; Insurers' Remedies for Fraudulent Claims;
   and Late Payment* (2014) ........................................................................... 83, 361
LC 357 and SLC 243, *Statute Law Repeals: Twentieth Report:
   Draft Statute Law (Repeals) Bill* (2015) ...................................................... 93, 347

## Law Commission Consultation and Working Papers

LC WP 1, *Law Commission First Programme, Item IX—Transfer of
   Land, B—Root of Title to Freehold Land* (1966) .......................................................... 36
LC WP 2, *Law Commission's Draft Proposals on Powers of the
   Court of Appeal to Sit in Private and Restrictions upon Publicity in
   Legitimacy [ sic] Proceedings* (1966) .......................................................................... 40
LC WP 3, *Restrictive Covenants* (1966) ........................................................................ 40
LC WP 4, *Should English Wills be Registrable?* (1966) .................................................. 36
LC WP 12, *Family Law: Proof of Paternity in Civil Proceedings* (1967) ........................... 43
LC WP 13, *Exploratory Working Paper on Administrative Law* (1967) ...................... 36, 44
LC WP 112, *Rights to Goods in Bulk* (1989) .................................................................. 249
LC WP 116, *Rape within Marriage* (1990) ............................................................... 24, 246
LC CP 120, *Restitution of Payments Made Under a Mistake of Law* (1991) ........... 162, 241

LC CP 124, *Fiduciary Duties and Regulatory Rules* (1992) ............................................. 149
LC CP 126, *Administrative Law: Judicial Review and Statutory Appeals* (1993) ............. 143
LC CP 127, *Intoxication and Criminal Liability* (1993) .................................................... 111
LC CP 131, *Assisting and Encouraging Crime* (1993) ...................................................... 111
LC CP 151, *Limitation of Actions* (1998) ........................................................180–240, 237
LC CP 154, *Illegal Transactions: The Effect of Illegality on
  Contracts and Trusts* (1999) ................................................................................. 25, 252
LC CP 160, *The Illegality Defence in Tort* (2001) ............................................................. 25
LC CP 178, *Post-Legislative Scrutiny* (2005) .................................................................. 190
LC CP 189, *The Illegality Defence* (2009)................................................................. 25, 252
LC CP 190, *The Admissibility of Expert Evidence in Criminal Proceedings
  in England and Wales* (2009)..................................................................................... 333
LC CP 197, *Unfitness to Plead* (2010)............................................................................ 359
LC CP 209, *Contempt of Court* (2012)........................................................................... 295
LC CP 217, *Reform of Offences against the Person: A Scoping Consultation
  Paper* (2014).............................................................................................. 117, 329
LC CP 222, *Mental Capacity and Deprivation of Liberty* (2015)................................... 200
LC CP 223, *Form and Accessibility of the Law Applicable
  in Wales* (2015) .................................................................................. 355–57, 360
LC CP 224, *Firearms Law: A Scoping Consultation Paper* (2015) ................................. 358

## Scottish Law Commission Discussion Papers and Memoranda

SLC Memorandum 9, *Prescription and Limitation of Actions* (1968) ............................. 236
SLC Memorandum 74, *Prescription and Limitation of Actions
  (Latent Damage)* (1987)............................................................................................ 237
SLC DP 83, *Bulk Goods* (1989) ..................................................................................... 249
SLC DP 95, *Recovery of Benefits Conferred under
  Error of Law* (1993)................................................................ 145, 163, 165, 201, 241
SLC DP 99, *The Judicial Abolition of the Error of Law Rule
  and its Aftermath* (1996) ........................................................................ 163, 165, 241
SLC DP 100, *Recovery of Ultra Vires Public Authority Receipts
  and Disbursements* (1996).......................................................................................... 201
SLC DP 113, *The Law of the Foreshore and Seabed* (2001)........................................... 167
SLC DP 133, *The Nature and Constitution of Trusts* (2006)......................................... 166
SLC DP 136, *Discussion Paper on Succession* (2007)..................................................... 146
SLC DP 154, *Discussion Paper on Formation of Contract* (2012)................................. 376
SLC DP 157, *Third Party Rights in Contract* (2014)...................................................... 202

## Joint Consultation, Working and Discussion Papers

LC WP 87 and SLC DP 62, *Private International Law:
  Choice of Law in Tort and Delict* (1984)................................................................. 248
LC CP 182 and SLC DP 134, *Misrepresentation, Non-Disclosure
  and Breach of Warranty by the Insured* (2007)......................................................... 268
LC CP 201 and SLC DP 152, *Insurance Contract Law: Post Contract
  Duties and other Issues* (2011) ................................................................................. 268
LC CP 204 and SLC DP 155, *The Business Insured's Duty of Disclosure
  and the Law of Warranties* (2012).............................................................................. 268
LC CP 218, SLC DP 158 and NILC 20, *Electoral Law:
  A Joint Consultation Paper* (2014) ................................................................ 52, 359, 363

# Contributors

Mary Arden (The Rt Hon Lady Justice Arden DBE) is a member of the Court of Appeal of England and Wales, a former Chairman of the Law Commission of England and Wales, Head of International Judicial Relations for England and Wales, a UK ad hoc judge of the European Court of Human Rights and a Member of the Permanent Court of Arbitration in The Hague.

Hugh Beale QC FBA is Professor of Law at the University of Warwick, and Senior Research Fellow at Harris Manchester College and Visiting Professor at the University of Oxford. He was a Law Commissioner at the Law Commission of England and Wales from 2000 to 2007, with responsibility for the Commercial and Common Law Team.

Jack Beatson FBA (The Rt Hon Lord Justice Beatson) is a member of the Court of England and Wales. He was a member of the Law Commission of England and Wales between 1989 and 1994 and Rouse Ball Professor of English Law at the University of Cambridge between 1994 and 2003.

Alan Beith, Baron Beith, is a member of the House of Lords. He was a Member of Parliament for Berwick-upon-Tweed between 1973 and 2015 and is a former Chairman of the House of Commons Justice Select Committee.

William Binchy is a practising barrister, Fellow Emeritus and Emeritus Regius Professor of Trinity College, Dublin. He was formerly a special legal adviser on family law reform to the Irish Department of Justice and Research Counsellor to the Law Reform Commission of Ireland and was a Commissioner with the Irish Human Rights Commission from 2000 to 2011.

Andrew Burrows QC, FBA, DCL, is Professor of the Law of England at the University of Oxford, a Fellow of All Souls College, and an Honorary Bencher of the Middle Temple. He was a Law Commissioner for England and Wales from 1994 to 1999.

Lord Carnwath CVO is a Justice of the Supreme Court of the United Kingdom; from 1998 to 2002 he was Chairman of the Law Commission for England and Wales and from 2007 to 2012 he was appointed as the first Senior President of Tribunals.

Eric Clive is an Honorary Professor at the University of Edinburgh Law School and was a full-time member of the Scottish Law Commission from 1981 to 1999.

Elizabeth Cooke is the Principal Judge of the Land Registration Division of the First-tier Tribunal (Property Chamber); from 2008 to 2015 she served as a Law Commissioner for England and Wales.

Kathryn Cronin is a barrister and Joint Head of Chambers at Garden Court Chambers. From 1996 to 2001, Kathryn was commissioner and then deputy president of the Australian Law Reform Commission.

Ian Dennis is Emeritus Professor of Law and Director of the Centre for Criminal Law, University College London, and a Barrister of Gray's Inn.

Laura Dunlop is in practice as a QC at the Scottish Bar, and was a part-time Commissioner in the Scottish Law Commission between 2009 and 2014.

Matthew Dyson is a Fellow and Director of Studies at Trinity College, University of Cambridge.

Sir Terence Etherton is the Chancellor of the High Court and was Chairman of the Law Commission from 2006 to 2009.

Neil Faris is an adviser in public and commercial law in Belfast, principally working with solicitors' firms. He was Commissioner at the Northern Ireland Law Commission from 2008 to 2012.

George Gretton holds the Lord President Reid Chair of Law at the University of Edinburgh and was a Commissioner at the Scottish Law Commission from 2006 to 2011.

Brenda Hale (Baroness Hale of Richmond, DBE, LLD, FBA) is Deputy President of the Supreme Court of the United Kingdom. She was a Law Commissioner from 1984 to 1993. She is Chancellor of the University of Bristol, Visitor of Girton College, Cambridge, and Visiting Professor of Law at King's College London.

Sir Grant Hammond was President of the New Zealand Law Commission from 2010 to 2016. He is a former Judge of the New Zealand Court of Appeal.

Charles Harpum is a barrister at Falcon Chambers and Emeritus Fellow of Downing College, Cambridge. He was a Law Commissioner from 1994 to 2001.

Lord Hodge JSC is a Justice of the United Kingdom Supreme Court. From 1997 to 2003, he was a part-time Law Commissioner at the Scottish Law Commission.

David Johnston is a QC practising in Scotland, an honorary professor at Edinburgh Law School, and a part-time Commissioner of the Scottish Law Commission.

Sir David Lloyd Jones (The Rt Hon Lord Justice Lloyd Jones) is a member of the Court of Appeal of England and Wales. He was Chairman of the Law Commission of England and Wales from 2012 to 2015.

Sir Kenneth Keith is Professor Emeritus, Victoria University of Wellington, Wellington, New Zealand. He is a former Judge of the International Court of Justice and former President of the New Zealand Law Commission.

Yves Le Bouthillier is Full Professor in the Common Law Section of the Faculty of Law of the University of Ottawa. He is also currently Executive Director of the IUCN Academy of Environmental Law. He was President of the Law Commission of Canada in 2005–2006.

James Lee is Senior Lecturer in Private Law at the Dickson Poon School of Law, King's College London, and an Associate Academic Fellow of the Honourable Society of the Inner Temple.

Stephen Lewis is a current Law Commissioner for England and Wales and a solicitor. He has been a member of the Committee of the British Insurance Law Association since 1995 and was its Chairman from 2010–12.

Elaine Lorimer was the Chief Executive of the Law Commission of England and Wales from 2012 to 2016.

Hector MacQueen FBA FRSE has been the Professor of Private Law at the University of Edinburgh since 1994 and a full-time Commissioner, Scottish Law Commission, since September 2009.

Barbara McDonald is Professor of Law at the University of Sydney. She served as a Commissioner of the Australian Law Reform Commission, heading the Inquiry into Serious Invasions of Privacy in the Digital Era (published 2014).

Malcolm McMillan is the Chief Executive of the Scottish Law Commission.

Paul Mitchell is Professor of Laws at University College London.

Sir James Munby is President of the Family Division of the High Court of Justice and Head of Family Justice for England and Wales (and has been since January 2013). He was Chairman of the Law Commission of England and Wales from 2009 to 2012.

David Ormerod QC is a Law Commissioner for England and Wales, Professor of Criminal Justice at University College London and a practising barrister.

Nicholas Paines QC is a Law Commissioner for England and Wales. He also sits as a Deputy High Court Judge in the Administrative Court, a Deputy Judge of the Upper Tribunal (Administrative Appeals Chamber) and the First-tier Tribunal (Tax Chamber) and a Recorder in the Crown Court.

The Honourable Lord Pentland is a Senator of the College of Justice in Scotland. He is Chairman of the Scottish Law Commission.

Shona Wilson Stark is a College Lecturer and Fellow in Law at Christ's College and an Affiliated Lecturer in the Faculty of Law, both University of Cambridge.

Lord Toulson JSC is a Justice of the United Kingdom Supreme Court. He was Chairman of the Law Commission of England and Wales between 2002 and 2006. He has also served on the Judicial Appointments Commission for England and Wales.

James Drummond Young (The Rt Hon Lord Drummond Young) is a judge of the Inner House of the Court of Session. From 2007 to 2012 he was Chairman of the Scottish Law Commission.

# Part 1

# Introduction

# 1

# *Introduction*

MATTHEW DYSON, JAMES LEE AND SHONA WILSON STARK

This collection arises from a conference held at the United Kingdom Supreme Court in July 2015 which marked the fiftieth anniversary of the Law Commissions Act 1965. The book celebrates fifty years of institutional law reform in the United Kingdom, embracing the Law Commission of England and Wales and the Scottish Law Commission, as well as the Northern Ireland Law Commission. Law reform bodies are not a new concept in England. Attempts were made to tidy the statute book as far back as 1593,[1] and Sir Matthew Hale's seventeenth century commission has been described as the 'first law commission'.[2] Law reform bodies have at least as long a history in Scotland. As long ago as 1425, an Act sought to appoint a commission to 'examyn the bukis of law of this realme ... and mend the lawis that nedis mendment'.[3] In the event, this early commission was 'fruitless', and over the years many other similarly unsuccessful attempts were made.[4] The Law Commissions of 1965 appear to have been planted in more fertile soil.

The book is divided into eight parts reflecting the panels at the conference combined with the introductory and concluding keynote addresses. Each panel was chaired by a distinguished law reformer who has also written a brief introduction to that panel for this volume. The panels were selected to frame key aspects of the Commissions' role in law reform:

1. Introduction

2. The First Half-Century of the Commissions
   *Reflecting on the origins and development of the Commissions*

3. Institutions, Commissions, Committees, Codifiers
   *Analysing the legal actors and configurations of reformers and their work*

4. The Many Faces of Law Reform
   *Surveying and critiquing the non-legislative means of law reform*

---

[1] For a summary of previous English law reform bodies, see M Kerr, 'Law Reform in Changing Times' (1980) 96 *LQR* 515, 518–521.

[2] S Sedley, *Lions under the Throne: Essays on the History of English Public Law* (Cambridge, Cambridge University Press, 2015) 92.

[3] Statute Law Revision Act 1425 (APS II 10, c 10).

[4] See HRM Macdonald, JC Mullin, TB Smith and JF Wallace, *The Laws of Scotland: Stair Memorial Encyclopaedia*, vol 22, (Edinburgh, 1987) para 627, and see paras 627–664 for a summary of the pre-1965 Scottish law reform bodies.

5.  Implementation by Statute
    *Examining the role of statute in calculating the success of reform*

6.  How Law Commissions Work
    *Exploring the ways the Commissions do, could and should function*

7.  Courts and Commissions
    *Studying the relationship between the Commissions' work and the courts*

8.  Commissioning the Future
    *Looking forward to the challenges and reforms of the future*

This Introduction will pick out some of the themes that have emerged across the parts of the book. For the sake of convenience, when we refer here to 'the Commissions', we mean both the Law Commission of England and Wales (Law Commission) and the Scottish Law Commission.

The collection brings together judicial and academic perspectives with commentary from past and current Commissioners on the issues relating to law reform. Thus we have essays from those who have served as Chairs of the Law Commission (Etherton, Carnwath, Toulson, Arden, Munby, Lloyd Jones) and the Scottish Law Commission (Drummond Young and Pentland). In addition, there are essays by former and serving individual Commissioners from England and Wales (Hale, Burrows, Paines, Beale, Beatson, Lewis, Harpum, Ormerod, Cooke) and from Scotland (Hodge, Clive, Gretton, Dunlop, MacQueen, Johnston). The Chief Executives at the time of the conference (Lorimer and McMillan) offer comments on the operation of the Commissions today. There are external perspectives, from academics and parliamentarians independent of the Commissions (Mitchell, Beith, Dennis, Stark, Lee and Dyson) and from law reformers from other legal systems drawing comparisons on a wider scale: Northern Ireland (Faris), Australia (Cronin and McDonald), Canada (Le Bouthillier), Ireland (Binchy) and New Zealand (Hammond and Keith).[5]

## I  WHOSE ROLE IS LAW REFORM?

Lord Reid once opined that '[p]eople want two inconsistent things; that the law shall be certain, and that it shall be just and shall move with the times'.[6] The need for a legal system to be both predictable and certain as well as to develop and adapt to societal changes is one of the fundamental tensions the Commissions were created to ease. The creation of statutory bodies to review law and recommend reform clearly raised questions of their relationships with other reforming bodies and which matters the Commissions are best suited to examine and on which to propose reform. Here we briefly consider the Commissions' relationship with four bodies: government, Parliament, the courts and the wider reform community.

---

[5] See section IV below.
[6] Lord Reid, 'The Judge as Law Maker' (1972–73) 12 *Journal of the Society of Public Teachers of Law* 22, 26.

**Government.** The Commissions are advisory bodies and the primary addressee of their advice is the government. The government is vital in approving programmes of reform and indicating willingness to reform in the areas examined in specific projects, as well as playing a role in the Commissions' long-term funding. The relationship between the Law Commission of England and Wales and government has seen significant changes recently, with the Law Commission Act 2009 and the protocol made under it, as discussed in, for instance, Sir Terence Etherton's chapter, and our section II below. Recent changes made by the Wales Act 2014 have increased the Welsh Government's stake in Commission-driven law reform, as discussed in Sir David Lloyd Jones' chapter.

While the legal framework may be different, the Scottish Law Commission too has been nurturing its relationship with the Scottish Government, as the chapters by Hector MacQueen and Malcolm McMillan demonstrate. In fact, these relationships have changed and developed over time, however much it is easy to imagine the events of today are particularly important or novel. The relationships depend strongly on the actors involved at the relevant time. The cycle of re-negotiating the formal and institutional connections can also function as a strengthening of the underlying personal relationships and their legacies. The Commissions' relationships with government require a careful balancing of the need to maintain implementation rates with the need for independence in project selection and reform proposals. That balance is explored in various essays in this volume, particularly those by Sir Terence Etherton and Sir Jack Beatson.

**Legislators.** Even if the government is the first addressee of the Commissions' work, the Westminster and Scottish Parliaments and the Welsh Assembly are key to the success of the Commissions' goals. The governmental duty to lay Commission reports before the legislatures is crucial in disseminating the Commissions' work to a wider audience. This volume contains numerous examples of the importance of parliamentary support and supporters. Just like government, this relationship requires care and respect, as well as periodic renewal. As Sir Terence Etherton notes, reform of the governmental mechanisms for law reform naturally dovetail with giving Parliament greater oversight of the work of the Commission in England. The relationship with Parliament is also a two-way street, independent lanes but ideas moving in both directions. On the one hand, the Law Commission's Bills must go through Parliament, surviving whatever changes are made or attempted during that passage. The Law Commission also needs more general political support for its mission. Going even further, Kathryn Cronin in her chapter stresses the need for reformers to attend to delegated legislation, especially in a federal system. On the other hand, parliamentarians recognise the expertise of both Commissions and the quality of their work. Lord Beith provides good examples of the problems and possibilities of parliamentary engagement. As chairman of the House of Commons Justice Committee, he himself had called for the Law Commission to examine or re-examine areas of law.[7] Competition for parliamentary time and attention has led to procedures where uncontentious Commission Bills can more easily

---

[7] eg House of Commons Justice Committee, *Joint Enterprise: Follow-up* (2014–15, HC 310) 20.

find a place in the parliamentary timetable. This procedure is used carefully, for fear of one even mildly contentious Bill being met with a backlash and the closing of the route altogether. Further innovation for more than completely uncontroversial Bills could well be important for the future. The possibilities are fascinating: Sir Grant Hammond considers some alternatives in parliamentary practice, and Matthew Dyson considers comparisons in law making both internationally, and between Commission proposals and the quality of non-Commission proposals. Similarly, the story does not end with legislation: as Andrew Burrows notes, post-legislative scrutiny is an important part of gauging the success of a law reform enterprise, and it is one that the legislator could meaningfully be involved in.

**Courts.** The Commissions and the courts are engaged in, as Lord Drummond Young puts it in his paper, a 'continuing dialogue'. Several chapters throughout the volume consider when it is appropriate for the courts to develop the law and when reform should be enacted by legislation, what Andrew Burrows calls the 'elusive boundary'.[8] Lady Hale and Sir Kenneth Keith each argue for flexible approaches, depending upon the context. As James Lee points out, there are many reasons why Commission material might be used, let alone why it might be decisive. For his part, Burrows' view is that the Commissions should focus their energies on areas which the higher courts cannot realistically be expected to reform. For the future, English higher courts will hopefully continue to receive the cases that allow difficult areas to come to light and then be resolved, but that is not certain. Movements away from expensive litigation, whether towards arbitration or mediation, or other forms of resolution, may deprive courts of the material. The lack of material is a problem known well to the Scottish legal system. As Hector MacQueen notes, Scotland lacks the 'steady stream and quality of case law' which might give judges the opportunity to develop the law and this, he argues, contributes to the distinctive role of the Scottish Law Commission. Lord Pentland also sees the Commission's role as par-ticularly important in contrast with the constraints and political priorities affecting government departments.

Occasionally, a Commission may appeal directly to the courts to develop the law. In certain cases, the courts do pick up Law Commission recommendations and run with them, as happened in respect of damages for personal injury, as Lords Toulson and Carnwath note. In Lee's essay, the recent history of the illegality defence in pri-vate law is given as an unfortunate example of the Law Commission deferring to the courts but the judges only muddying the waters further. Charles Harpum's chapter details the uncertainty over the extent to which a Commission report which led to legislation may be used by the courts when it comes to statutory interpretation. Harpum uses the Land Registration Act 2002 as a case study, but his analysis has application well beyond that landmark statute.

One part of the relationship between courts and the Commissions is the role performed by the apex court, now the Supreme Court. The Commissions were

---

[8] Chapter 20 (Andrew Burrows). See also AS Burrows, 'The Relationship between Common Law and Statute in the Law of Obligations' (2012) 128 *LQR* 232.

created one year before the House of Lords Practice Statement on Judicial Precedent, in which their Lordships adopted the power to depart from their own previous decisions.[9] The Practice Statement was a direct result of the establishment of the Commissions. The subject of precedent was a topic in the Scottish Law Commission's *First Programme of Law Reform*.[10] The project was no doubt selected by one of the first Commissioners, TB Smith, who had previously criticised the prospect of English rules of precedent creeping into Scots law.[11] Lord Gardiner who, as it is widely known, was instrumental in the establishment of the Commissions, was alerted to the project and devised the Practice Statement on the back of the 'Scottish initiative'.[12] Such a move was crucially linked to the Commissions' duty to codify the law. Precedent could no longer be allowed to be 'sovereign' if codification was to be pursued and so the 'rigidities' of the House of Lords being bound by its own decisions had to be removed.[13]

The close relationship between the Commissions and the courts continues today. Of our 12 current Supreme Court Justices, four have previously held roles at the Commissions.[14] They, and the other Justices, make reasonably frequent use of materials published by both the Law Commission and the Scottish Law Commission,[15] as well as recommending that certain areas of law are studied by the Commissions.[16] It is not just a matter of the Supreme Court. Sir Jack Beatson discusses his long-lasting connections with the Law Commission's work in his contribution. Elizabeth Cooke details her own personal experience of this in her paper. A former Commissioner of the Law Commission of England and Wales, she is now Principal Judge of the Land Registration Division of the First Tier Tribunal (Property Chamber)—a post created by legislation based on a Law Commission proposal.

**The wider community** is also vital for many aspects of the Commissions' work. One obvious form of this is in terms of personnel. While the Chairman of each Commission is a senior judge, the bulk of the Commissions is made up of practitioners and academics, in roughly equal measure. Another important form of this connection is in the consultees who give their time and expertise without remuneration, not

---

[9] In *Austin v Southwark London Borough Council* [2010] UKSC 28, [2011] 1 AC 355 Lord Hope confirmed that the Supreme Court had inherited the power to use the Practice Statement if it so wished (at [25]).

[10] SLC 1 (1965) paras 16–19.

[11] TB Smith, *The Doctrines of Judicial Precedent in Scots Law* (Edinburgh, W Green and Son, 1952); TB Smith, *British Justice: The Scottish Contribution (The Hamlyn Lectures)* (London, Stevens, 1961) 84–85.

[12] L Blom-Cooper, '1966 and All That: The Story of the Practice Statement' in L Blom-Cooper, B Dickson and G Drewry (eds), *The Judicial House of Lords 1876–2009* (Oxford, OUP, 2009) 134.

[13] L Scarman, 'A Code of English Law?', Lecture given at the University of Hull (1966) 14; L Scarman, 'Codification and Judge-made Law: A Problem of Co-Existence', University of Birmingham Lecture (1966) 17.

[14] Lady Hale DPSC was in 1984 the first woman to be appointed as a Law Commissioner in England and Wales, Lord Carnwath JSC (1999–2002) and Lord Toulson JSC (2002–06) were Chairmen of the Law Commission of England and Wales, and Lord Hodge JSC was a part-time Commissioner for the Scottish Law Commission (1997–2003).

[15] See, eg, *Granatino v Radmacher* [2010] UKSC 42, [2011] 1 AC 534; *HM Advocate v P* [2011] UKSC 44, 2012 SC (UKSC) 108; *Gow v Grant* [2012] UKSC 29, 2013 SC (UKSC) 1.

[16] See, eg, *Joseph v Spiller* [2010] UKSC 53, [2011] 1 AC 852; *Jones v Kaney* [2011] UKSC 13, [2011] 2 AC 398.

just the legal profession but other interested parties. Depending on the project such parties could include Land Registry, banks, insurance companies, other businesses, victims' groups, charities and even the general public. In this volume, Lord Hodge praises the Commissions' practice of consultation as greatly enhancing the authority of their reports and it is easy to see why. The Commissions are trusted to consult widely, listen carefully and reform appropriately and the whole endeavour marks them out in legislation and law reform. The role of the wider community is vital, as Stephen Lewis so ably shows in reference to the reform of various aspects of the law of insurance. Indeed, Lewis shows how the congruence of different communities, where individual interests align and ideally even where they do not, is a powerful force for reform.

However, as Sir Jack Beatson notes, 'all worthwhile law reform has winners and losers'. Certain objections will simply be that developing a more nuanced position may be too difficult or not a priority. As former Scottish Law Commission Chairman Lord Davidson remarked, '[m]any lawyers are cool, or even hostile, to large-scale law reform' simply because 'they regard it as an intolerable extra burden to have to learn a whole new scheme of law'.[17] Indeed, such hostility has been advanced by the government as one reason to reject a Law Commission proposal.[18] The task of the Commissions is to engage all sides throughout the process of reform and implementation, which is clearly a tall order. Beatson suggests 'education and persuasion' as the tools of the Commission(s). The Commissions succeed in producing incredibly valuable and educational materials in their consultations and their reports, as is evident from the perusal of any law library shelf. However, behind the scenes *persuasion* must be far more nuanced and flexible, with the Commissions constantly seeking to understand a proposal from the stakeholder's perspective and to persuade all and sundry about its overall benefits. This process starts, as David Johnston notes, from the very conception of a project, and continues after implementation. The task of engaging with stakeholders merges with the task of persuading government and Parliament, who will also react to and be lobbied by the same stakeholders in due course. Such coalition building, previously rare amongst British political parties, is certainly the reality of the Commissions as law reformers, as Sir James Munby points out.

While all of these four groups—government, legislators, courts and the wider community—each combine with the Commissions in law reform, the Commissions are perhaps in a special position in rarely being directly blamed when reforms do not occur. It may be that we have not reached the position when the Commissions are thought to have the obligation to make change happen, such that a failure to reform can be pinned on them. Clearly such a label would be unfair given the complexity of the law reform process, but the need to do, or be seen to do, 'something' in the face of a legal problem is a problem for many of the Commissions' partners.

---

[17] Lord Davidson, 'Law Reform—Who Cares?' (1992) 37(4) *Journal of the Law Society of Scotland* 130, 132.

[18] Ministry of Justice, *Report on the Implementation of Law Commission Proposals* (HC 1900, 2012) para 50, where the government rejected LC 314, *Intoxication and Criminal Liability* (2009) on the basis that (inter alia) it would replace 'a complex but well understood process with a complicated new test which practitioners would need to master'.

The Commissions have, as yet, rightly been given the benefit of the doubt in taking some time to craft most of their proposals. Of course, there are exceptions, whether by very fast turnaround, such as the urgent work Beatson has noted, or by delayed results which are no less important for being delayed, as Hale and Stark note. The result has also been that sending a matter to the Commissions can be doing 'something' and, it should be said, one of the better forms of 'something' that could be done. Projects should not, however, be referred to the Commissions simply as a way of kicking difficult issues into the long grass. The protocols in England and Wales should ensure this does not happen, together with the project-selection criteria used by both Commissions (importance, suitability and resources) which should ensure that the Commissions' finite resources are targeted towards the most deserving projects.

In what areas should the Commissions propose reform? Given what has just been said, it will come as no surprise that this is in part a question of relative competence. That is, based on the relationship enjoyed at that time between the Commissions and the other bodies just mentioned, who should propose law reform? This is a matter addressed head on by Sir Kenneth Keith, who notes that matters to consider include the constitutional importance of the issue, any international dimension and whether a practical answer, without legislation, would be more effective or whether it could lead to a fudge. He concludes with a functional question: 'which body or combination of bodies, is best qualified, following what procedures and with what principles and product in mind to undertake the task?'

One of the questions arising repeatedly in this volume is how the Commissions should prioritise their resources. In particular, the question of whether the Commissions should be limited to 'lawyers' law', focusing on technicalities otherwise unlikely to be examined, is raised by numerous contributors. This question was addressed shortly before our conference by Sir Geoffrey Palmer in his Scarman Lecture, where he put forward the view that the Commissions should not shy away from 'big policy' issues.[19] Such a view may not be widely shared in the British jurisdictions despite experiences of law commissions elsewhere having responsibility for such topics. For example, Dame Mary Arden highlights that the South African Law Commission has dealt with euthanasia, a topic which is instinctively not one with which the Great British Commissions might deal. It is striking that Palmer is both former Prime Minister of New Zealand and former President of the New Zealand Law Commission. Such a mixture of politics and law reform would be unlikely to be seen in Commissions on these shores and may have influenced Palmer's perspective. Contrary to Palmer, Sir David Lloyd Jones argues that the Commissions may be at their best when delivering on lawyers' law. But there is no universal formula. While accepting that there is no 'bright line', Lloyd Jones indicates his view that the more politically controversial a topic, the less likely it is to be appropriate for the Commissions.[20] Lord Toulson offers an examination of the role for the

---

[19] G Palmer, 'The Law Reform Enterprise: Evaluating the Past and Charting the Future' (2015) 131 *LQR* 402, 414.

[20] See also chapter 7 (Eric Clive).

Commissions in a legislative system of what he identifies as ever-increasing complexity, complemented on this point by Barbara McDonald's insights from her involvement in the Australian attempts at privacy reform. Similarly, Yves Le Bouthillier frames the discussion of the work of a Commission not just in terms of its successes, but in its role in bringing together disparate legal actors and examining social issues rather than 'lawyers' law'. Le Bouthillier has defended the now defunct Law Commission of Canada from those who have suggested that its broad remit caused its demise. As Le Bouthillier argues, the first Law Reform Commission of Canada had a more 'traditional' remit yet it too was abolished. In creating the second Law Commission of Canada, a different approach was deliberately chosen. Le Bouthillier ends with the hope that a new Commission for Canada will be established—and that hopefully the third time will be the charm. Dyson discusses the objects of law reform, particularly outside of the classic domain of substantive law and in the light of what the law will need to be in the future.

William Binchy's provocative chapter argues that Commissions need carefully to consider their independence, not only from the branches of government, but also from external bodies. Le Bouthillier's essay also emphasises the importance of the independence of a Commission for the authority which its recommendations may command.

## II  THE BUSINESS OF LAW REFORM: IMPLEMENTATION AND BEYOND

Many of the essays in this collection engage with the idea of implementation. Stark's essay offers a detailed assessment of implementation rates for the Law Commission and Scottish Law Commission, and suggests revisions to how the Commissions themselves should calculate their rates, in terms of both what counts as 'implementation', and the applicable timeframe. Dunlop, in her chapter, details the 'value added' by the Commissions beyond implementation by primary legislation. Hammond's paper provides a statistical analysis of implementation rates across a range of 12 law reform bodies: Sir Grant concludes that the failure of some reports to be implemented tends to lie at the feet of parliamentary processes, rather than in inherent deficiencies of Commission proposals.

In the 50 years of the Commissions, lessons have been learned. It is instructive to trace the evolution of the Commissions' roles and positioning through their first 50 years. Paul Mitchell's essay details the strategy of the Law Commission in its early years. The Commissions now occupy an established space in our machinery of law reform and appear to behave slightly differently. Similarly, Lord Pentland's essay contextualises the challenges faced by the Scottish Law Commission in establishing itself as an independent driver of law reform in Scotland. He argues that the early Scottish Law Commission demonstrated its independence immediately by tackling the controversial topic of corroboration, a 'sacred icon' of Scots law. In so doing, the Scottish Law Commission set the tone for the decades which have followed. Sir Jack Beatson's chapter gives a survey of the many practical intricacies of the work of the Law Commission in the late 1980s and early 1990s.

As noted already, the fiftieth anniversary came at a time of evolution for the Commissions in the nature of their work and their relationships with government. Many of the chapters engage with this evolution. For the Law Commission of England and Wales, the new regime is detailed in the chapter by Sir Terence Etherton, who was Chairman at the time of the changes. The changes are potentially far-reaching and set the format for Commission work for decades to come.

On the one hand, there have been fears that the Law Commission Act 2009 focuses any assessment of the Law Commission on the implementation of reports, rather than seeing any value in the extensive research, consultation, drafting and promulgation of reports.

On the other hand, the 2009 Act and its accompanying protocol are silent on these issues, and the Law Commission itself disputes this effect. The 2009 Act introduces new governmental accountability for the implementation of Law Commission reports, in that an annual report must be issued by the Lord Chancellor, indicating what decisions have been made about proposals submitted to him during that year. Political considerations, both practical and policy-based, are given a specific role in shaping Law Commission policy: there is also now an agreed protocol between the government and the Law Commission (and a separate protocol between the Law Commission and Welsh Ministers), which requires the specific endorsement of a government department before the Law Commission can even begin a project. Although ministerial approval has always been required before embarking on a project,[21] the 2009 Act arguably brings the Law Commission closer to government. As noted above, the question considered at various points in this volume is whether that compromise in independence is necessary to improve implementation rates. In the summer of 2014, the Law Commission published its *Twelfth Programme of Law Reform*, which was the second to be developed under the new scheme.[22] Given that neither the production of Commission reports nor their implementation can necessarily be expected quickly, it is too soon to tell whether the Law Commission's compromise has been worthwhile.

In February 2015, the Scottish Law Commission began its *Ninth Programme of Law Reform*.[23] Although the 2009 Act does not apply to the Scottish Law Commission, both Commissions benefit from a separate new House of Lords procedure for their most technical and uncontroversial Bills. Such Bills can be introduced in the Lords and their second reading is then debated in a Committee, rather than on the floor of the House. Since 2008, seven Bills have been passed using this new procedure. A similar Committee-based procedure has recently been introduced in the Scottish Parliament for technical and uncontroversial Scottish Law Commission proposals on devolved issues, with the first Bill having been introduced on 14 May 2014.[24] These reforms are considered in detail by Hector MacQueen and Malcolm McMillan in their chapters.

---

[21] Law Commissions Act 1965, s 3(1)(b) and (c).
[22] LC 354, (2014).
[23] SLC 242 (2015).
[24] The Legal Writings (Counterparts and Delivery) (Scotland) Act 2015 implemented SLC 231, *Review of Contract Law—Report on Formation of Contract: Execution in Counterpart* (2013).

The essays by current members of the Commissions contain many insights into the operation of these revised procedures, with Nicholas Paines and Stephen Lewis offering examples from their own experiences of the challenges of implementation. The evolution of the Commissions' work can also be seen in reflection over their engagement with other parties. The efforts to change the working relationships of the Commissions with governments can be understood from this perspective. Several essays also emphasise the efforts of the Commissions to engage more widely: a feature which emerges particularly in the contributions from Chief Executives Elaine Lorimer and Malcolm McMillan. David Johnston of the Scottish Law Commission stresses the need for Commissions to engage with those directly interested in the area of law under reform. For its *Twelfth Programme of Reform*, the Law Commission received 'over 250 proposals from 180 consultees',[25] demonstrating the extent of stakeholder engagement in potential reforms.

It is also strongly argued by contributors that there are other roles which the Commissions might assume. As mentioned above, Burrows' essay makes a compelling case for greater attention to be paid to the quality of legislation once implemented. Post-legislative scrutiny is also mentioned by Sir Grant Hammond, who gives the example of the New Zealand Evidence Act 2006, which provides its own mechanism for quinquennial review by the New Zealand Law Commission. It remains to be seen whether the Commissions develop a more rounded approach to scrutiny, what we might call an 'after sales' service as part of their obligations, in addition to the after sales services already provided by both Commissions to help generally with their draft Bill's onward journey.

## III CODIFICATION

Numerous chapters take as their starting point section 3 of the Law Commissions Act 1965, which lists the functions of the Commissions. The Commissions' duties are 'to take and keep under review all the law with which they are respectively concerned with a view to its systematic development and reform, including in particular the codification of such law'.[26] Codification was an attractive proposition when the Commissions were established. Thankfully long gone was what one of the criminal code commissioners of the nineteenth century had called English lawyers' and government's 'codiphobia'.[27] It was even believed that codification would be 'essential' for the United Kingdom's entry into what is now the European Union.[28] The Commissions began their codification task with 'enthusiastic innocence'.[29]

---

[25] LC 354, n 22 above, para 1.8.

[26] The section continues with 'the elimination of anomalies, the repeal of obsolete and unnecessary enactments, the reduction of the number of separate enactments and generally the simplification and modernisation of the law'.

[27] A Amos, *Ruins of Time: Exemplified in Sir Mathew Hale's History of the Pleas of the Crown* (London, V and R Stevens, 1856) xvi, xix.

[28] LCB Gower, 'A Comment' (1967) 30 *MLR* 259, 260.

[29] TB Smith, 'Law Reform in a Mixed "Civil Law" and "Common Law" Jurisdiction' (1974–75) 35 *Louisiana Law Review* 927, 942.

In its *First Programme of Law Reform*, the Law Commission set out ambitious plans for a contract code, a code of landlord and tenant law and a code of family law,[30] followed in its *Second Programme* by a criminal code.[31] In its *First Programme of Law Reform*,[32] the Scottish Law Commission proposed to codify the law of evidence and the law of obligations. The two Commissions worked together on a joint contract code, which was later abandoned. Most of the Commissions' other attempts at codification were divided up into less ambitious projects. In fact, the Commissions have been said to have had a 'disastrous' record of codification,[33] and have steadily moved away from explicitly pursuing it. In 2011, while still Chairman, Sir James Munby remarked that codification was 'little more than a distant memory' for the Commissions.[34]

In his Scarman Lecture, however, Sir Geoffrey Palmer argued that the Law Commission's interest in codification should be revived.[35] The Scottish Law Commission's track record in codification (as well as consolidation) is examined by George Gretton in his chapter. He laments the fact that codification and consolidation are not governmental priorities. On balance, he thinks the Commissions are doing the right thing in not pursuing work that is unlikely to be enacted. He nonetheless encourages the Commissions not to abandon completely their duties under the 1965 Act.

The tale of codification for the Law Commission has been primarily limited to criminal law, and the particular challenges of codification in that field are explored in the chapters by Ian Dennis and David Ormerod. Ormerod sets out the Commission's new approach as being to consider codification of particular areas rather than an overall rationalisation or restatement of the law. The approach of dividing up the aim of codification into 'manageable chunks' is endorsed by Clive in his essay, while Lloyd Jones notes that codification 'may be coming back into fashion'. McDonald's chapter provides valuable reflections on the differences of more systematic reform of private law and the limits of what legislation can reasonably be expected to achieve.

Codification is a good example of the intricate nature of the Commissions' work. It is easy to criticise the Commissions for seeming to have given up on the task of codification. Their reform programmes no longer have the scope in codification they once did, nor does it appear that they push hard for that codification behind the scenes. This may be the result of being pragmatic about what can be legislated on effectively, given that codification will require significant legislation. It is also a shift in principle and it is here that criticism of the Commissions can be undermined. There is no reason why codification should be brought in at once, even though that is the norm in most other countries. Even where that does happen,

---

[30] LC 1 (1965), items I, VIII and X respectively.
[31] LC 14 (1968), item XVIII.
[32] SLC 1 (1965).
[33] F Bennion, 'Additional Comments' in G Zellick (ed), *The Law Commission and Law Reform* (London, Sweet & Maxwell, 1988) 63.
[34] J Munby, 'Shaping the Law—the Law Commission at the Crossroads', Denning Lecture (2011) 11.
[35] Palmer, n 19 above, 412.

there are usually a series of codes for different core components of the law, such as procedure, civil law and criminal law. The purpose of codification, creating a highly coherent and interrelated set of norms, expressing concepts through consistent terms does not require just one, or a small group of statutes. It could be carried out over a longer time, in a decidedly British model of codification.

A piecemeal approach itself is not new, as the furious effort towards codification in England in the nineteenth century led not to a criminal code, but did lead to the Bills of Exchange Act 1882, the Partnership Act 1890, the Sale of Goods Act 1893, the Arbitration Act 1889 and the Marine Insurance Act 1906. These provisions were easier to legislate and avoided the apparent finality of codification, particularly as contrasted with the earlier judicial power to develop law.[36] The difficulty is in drawing the right line between codification and, in effect, suggesting that any single provision is itself 'a code', any more than these 'mini codes' to use Dennis' language, are really codes. As Scarman noted, codification is not a 'term of art' in this country.[37] The term 'code' is, however, harder to substantiate the narrower its scope, since codification does imply some level of generality or universality. However, individual provisions getting the law right can always be aggregated later in what would in effect be a further step in the long tradition of consolidation, rather than codification. So long as a clear intellectual thread links each area set of proposals, it can do so across many fields of law and across decades of enactments. Indeed, the Law Commission has aimed to do just that, by breaking up its criminal code into smaller enactments with the view that they can eventually be 'welded together into a Code'.[38] The difficulty with that approach is that certain of the Law Commission's criminal reforms were implemented in small parts only.[39] Any resultant code would thus not be as comprehensive as one might hope for.

Nevertheless, the Commissions are willing to work, patiently and far-sightedly, towards codification; indeed, perhaps the less obviously that codification work is done, the more successful it will be. That is a troubling statement for a legal system, but if true, renders the Commissions' change of language significantly less problematic to those willing to bend to the pressures of real life. Just like any effect from the new protocols on reducing the independence or wider utility of the Commissions' work in England and Wales, it may well be that a strong and able Commission is the best hope for any legislative environment.

---

[36] See, eg, A Braun, 'The English Codification Debate and the Role of Jurists in the Development of Legal Doctrines' in M Lobban and J Moses (eds), *The Impact of Ideas on Legal Development* (Cambridge, CUP, 2012).

[37] L Scarman, 'A Code of English Law?', Lecture given at the University of Hull (1966) 4; L Scarman, 'Codification and Judge-made Law: A Problem of Co-Existence', University of Birmingham Lecture (1966) 3.

[38] LC 259, *Seventh Programme of Law Reform* (1999) 19.

[39] eg LC 218, *Legislating the Criminal Code: Offences against the Person and General Principles* (1993) (only one recommendation implemented by the Domestic Violence, Crime and Victims Act 2004) and LC 237, *Legislating the Criminal Code: Involuntary Manslaughter* (1996) (partially implemented by the Corporate Manslaughter and Corporate Homicide Act 2007).

## IV BROADER HORIZONS

Another theme running through the essays is the question of comparative experience. In this connection, we include, as noted above, contributions from a variety of common law jurisdictions: Northern Ireland, Australia, Canada, Ireland and New Zealand. Lord Neuberger PSC recently, on behalf of the Supreme Court, has extolled the virtues of common law jurisdictions 'learning from each other'.[40] Le Bouthillier commends the British procedures for any resurrected Canadian Commission. The chapters by Dyson and Beale point to experience of civilian jurisdictions, and more broadly pan-European efforts at law reform. In his chapter, Sir Kenneth Keith addresses the work of international law commissions. The courts and Commissions also readily recognise the value of comparing the positions as between England and Scotland when proposing reforms.[41] The Commissions' duty to 'act in consultation with each other' facilitates the sharing of lessons and laws between the British jurisdictions.[42] Clive in his chapter calls for the Commissions to undertake more comparative work—examining the law of other jurisdictions is, after all, one of the Commissions' explicit duties.[43] Johnston, by contrast, urges caution in the deployment of scarce resources. Beatson's essay further illustrates the difficulties of changing governmental priorities. The fates of the Commissions in Northern Ireland, where the commission is currently suspended, and Canada, which is currently without a federal commission, serve as timely reminders that the existence of law reform commissions cannot be taken for granted, not least in terms of financial restrictions on governmental spending. On the Northern Ireland and Canadian experiences, see the chapters by Faris and Le Bouthillier respectively.

An area of future development for the Law Commission's work will be a renewed focus on Wales, which is increasingly a different legal system to that in England, as Sir David Lloyd Jones considers.[44] Section 25 of the Wales Act 2014 provides for a direct relationship between the Welsh Ministers and the Law Commission, so that the Ministers can now refer matters to the Commission. It also imposes an obligation on the Ministers to report to the National Assembly for Wales in respect of Commission proposals relating to Welsh devolved matters.

## V CONCLUSION

One of the themes in this book is how the work and successes of the Commissions come in cycles, making a conclusion somewhat artificial. The relationships the

---

[40] 'As overseas countries secede from the jurisdiction of the Privy Council, it is inevitable that inconsistencies in the common law will develop between different jurisdictions. However, it seems to us highly desirable for all those jurisdictions to learn from each other, and at least to lean in favour of harmonising the development of the common law round the world.' *FHR European Ventures LLP v Cedar Capital Partners LLC* [2014] UKSC 45, [2014] 3 WLR 535, [45].

[41] See, eg, Lord Neuberger in *Marley v Rawlings* [2014] UKSC 2, [2015] AC 129, [87].

[42] Law Commissions Act 1965, s 3(4).

[43] Law Commissions Act 1965, s 3(1)(f).

[44] See section III of chapter 35 (Sir David Lloyd Jones).

Commissions must nurture require constant care and periodic renewal, the process of implementation feeds back into future projects, codification has become a long game of subtle form and any aspect of national reform has increasingly wide and international dimensions. The statute book gets ever larger, so the task of pruning it of legal curiosities is always a game of catch-up and returning to the same material, returning to the same subject matters over the years.[45] Perhaps this volume can best be seen as a chance to return to some of the most important aspects and themes in the Commissions' work, easily lost sight of in the drive to perfect or comment on the next report. It is a chance to reflect and plan for the future, informed by expert insights and scholarly debate.

Another cycle to which the Law Commission of England and Wales, as an Advisory Non-Departmental Public Body, is subject is a Triennial Review, with the next due to begin as this volume hits the bookshelves. We hope this book might be read by stakeholders and particularly the government, and that it may therefore be of benefit in supporting the vital role of the Commissions.

When the Law Commissions Bill was passing through Parliament in 1965, Lord Reid remarked that the Commissions could do 'five or ten years of really useful work' by which time 'lawyers' law ought to be in pretty good shape'.[46] That the Commissions have not achieved that ambitious target is neither a criticism of them, nor of Lord Reid. Neither could have predicted the continued growth in legislation, nor was the role that the Commissions would play really clear at that stage—indeed the debate between Palmer and Lloyd Jones highlighted above shows that it is still not settled. The Commissions continue to provide a valuable service of proposing reforms to lawyers' law and beyond. This volume is not, therefore, a eulogy for the Commissions. Indeed, Part 8 of the volume specifically looks to the future. It is hoped that the essays in this collection demonstrate the vitality of institutional law reform in Great Britain, with different ways of conceiving the contributions made by the Commissions to law reform then, now and next.

---

[45] See, eg, Law Commission Statute Law Repeals Team, 'Legal Curiosities: Fact or Fable?' www.lawcom.gov.uk/wp-content/uploads/2015/03/Legal_Oddities.pdf.

[46] HL Deb 1 April 1965, vol 264 col 1201.

# 2

# *Fifty Years of the Law Commissions: The Dynamics of Law Reform Now, Then and Next*

LADY HALE

My role, I believe, is to set the scene for the multitude of more learned contributions to follow, beginning at the beginning. I do not think that there is anything particularly radical about the idea that law reform is too important to be left to the judges, indeed that law reform is not for the judges at all. There are some very conservative judges across the Atlantic who purport to think just that. Nor could anyone, left or right, have thought that the state of the common law, let alone the statute book, was perfect in every way. But it does so happen that the idea of the UK Law Commissions came from two books edited and largely authored by Labour lawyers.

It began with *The Reform of the Law*, edited by Professor Glanville Williams, published under auspices of the Haldane Society in 1951, just before the post-war Labour government came to an end. The 'reason why so much of our English law is out of date, some of it indeed quite antediluvian', they said, 'is that nobody has ever been entrusted with the job of looking after it'. Hence there was a need for a Minister of Justice, 'to keep under review the whole field of our law, to take arrangements for investigating and reporting on any section of it which seemed not to be fulfilling the present needs of the community, and to see that in due course proposals for legislative reform were brought before Parliament'.[1] But there was a scathing review by Arnold Goodman in the *Modern Law Review*: 'there is a fine muster of names—enough to encourage high hopes of an exciting and provocative book, hopes which, alas, are by no means fully realised'.[2] The main problem was that 'no real thought was given to the precise extent of the legal topics which are appropriate for law reform *through the intervention of lawyers*'.[3]

That has been the conundrum ever since. Despite this, however, Goodman played a crucial role in the next phase of the story. In the early 1960s, Gerald Gardiner QC, who had long been a member of the Law Reform Committee, was approached to edit a similar but updated collection. The result was *Law Reform Now*, edited

---

[1] G Williams (ed), *The Reform of the Law* (London, Victor Gollancz, 1951) 9.
[2] A Goodman, 'Review of *The Reform of the Law* Edited by G Williams' (1952) 15 *MLR* 378, 378.
[3] ibid, emphasis in original.

by Gerald Gardiner and Andrew Martin, published in July 1963.[4] The chapter by Gardiner and Martin on 'The Machinery of Law Reform' contained the blueprint for setting up the Law Commission. Otherwise the book was still something of a ragbag of proposals for the reform of the substantive law.

Shortly afterwards, Gardiner was invited to dinner by Goodman. The other two guests were Harold Wilson, leader of the Opposition, and George Wigg, MP for Dudley and (according to Wikipedia) very influential behind the scenes, particularly with Harold Wilson. Gardiner was offered a Life Peerage in the next New Year Honours and promised that, if Labour won the next general election, he would be made Lord Chancellor. Apparently he made it a condition of accepting this offer that his ideas on law reform would be adopted. Sure enough, after Labour won the election in October 1964, Gardiner became Lord Chancellor and the appointment of Law Commissioners to advance the reform of the law was heralded in the Queen's Speech, a White Paper was published in January 1965[5] and the Law Commissions Act enacted in June 1965.

Some important principles were established:

*(1) Independence of Government*

In fact, Gardiner and Martin had proposed a body headed by a 'Vice Chancellor' who would hold the rank of Minister of State, be exclusively concerned with law reform, and sit in the House of Commons. Their vision was of a law reform unit located within the Lord Chancellor's Department (LCD) (just as Glanville Williams had envisaged that Department developing into a Ministry of Justice, but a very different one from the one we have today). However, they also proposed that the Vice Chancellor would preside over a body of not less than five highly qualified full-time Commissioners, who would not be ordinary civil servants, but who would enjoy a high degree of independence, and serve for a minimum of three to five years.

It turned out, of course, that the Commission was even more independent than that. It was not headed by a Minister but by a High Court judge, latterly an Appeal Court judge. I cannot imagine that an up-and-coming House of Commons Minister would want to be exclusively concerned with law reform. But it might have been a direct line to implementation, which has been a recurring problem for the Commission.

*(2) Diversity of Legal Expertise*

From the start the object has been to include each branch of the legal profession within membership—judges, barristers, solicitors, academics. Five minds may be better than one, but only if they bring a variety of perspectives and expertise to bear on the problem. As Cardozo put it, 'out of the attrition of diverse minds there is beaten something which has a constancy and uniformity and average value greater than its component elements'.[6] But unlike some other law reform bodies (eg the

---

[4]  G Gardiner and A Martin (eds), *Law Reform Now* (London, Victor Gollancz, 1963).
[5]  *Proposals for English and Scottish Law Commissions* (Cmnd 2573, 1965).
[6]  BN Cardozo, *The Nature of the Judicial Process* (New Haven, Yale University Press, 1921) 177.

Irish Law Reform Commission) it has always been legal expertise—reinforcing the point that it should be concerned with law reform which is properly the business of lawyers.

Recruitment has not always been easy. Apart from the sheer fascination of the task, the reality is that a judicial chair can be attracted by the prospect (and now the certainty) of promotion to the Court of Appeal; a barrister can be attracted by prospect of promotion to the High Court bench; an academic can be attracted by all sorts of things, including a much better salary, but also the enticing prospect of changing one's own subject for the better; but for a solicitor it is rather more difficult to see the attractions unless he or she is an unusual person who is not worried about what to do next. Hence when the Commission started there was not a solicitor Commissioner, but Arthur Stapleton Cotton was recruited as a consultant.

*(3) Mission*

As Gardiner and Martin put it:

> The chief responsibility of the Law Commissioners would be to review, bring up to date and keep up to date what may be called 'the general law': the common law and equity, and also that part of the statute law which does not fall within the province of any government department.[7]

In other words, lawyers' law. But even then, the Commissioners should be consulted by the departments about proposed reforms to 'administrators' law' and should not be debarred from taking the initiative themselves if there was a need for reform and none of the administrators seemed interested.

Along with law reform came codification, and consolidation, already being done by Parliamentary Counsel in consultation with the relevant government departments, and statute law revision, cleaning up the statute book, already being done by a unit in the LCD. As translated into section 3(1) of the Law Commissions Act 1965, the mission is:

> To take and keep under review all the law, with a view to its systematic development and reform, including in particular the codification of such law, the elimination of anomalies, the repeal of obsolete and unnecessary enactments, the reduction of the number of separate enactments, and generally the simplification and modernisation of the law.

Obviously, this is mission impossible and gets more impossible year on year, as the law gets ever more complicated. The challenge is to work out the most valuable tasks the Commission can accomplish.

*(4) Implementation*

The Commission may not have had the advantage of a ministerial chair, but it has had the huge advantage of Parliamentary Counsel on secondment, not only to deal with consolidation and statute law revision, but also bringing with it the privilege of

---

[7] See n 4 above, 9.

direct access for drafting law reform measures. This means that the Commissioners and their teams have to work hard with Parliamentary Counsel to produce recommendations which might actually be legislated. This is so even if, when the measure is put before Parliament, another draftsman is assigned who almost always rewrites it. Our direct access to Parliamentary Counsel was, for example, extremely important in securing the passage of the Children Act 1989, as a complete code of private and public law, rather than only as a solution to the important but particular problems thrown up by the child abuse enquiries of the 1980s.

*(5) Methods*

The original idea was that the Law Commissions would take a strategic view. They would identify what needed to be done and who should do it. It was not intended that a Law Commission would do it all. Hence the idea of programmes. The Commissions have the duty to prepare and submit to Ministers from time to time programmes for the examination of different branches of the law with a view to reform, including recommendations as to the body by which it should be done,[8] and then to undertake that examination themselves if so recommended and approved by the Minister.[9] The reality in England and Wales for many years was very different. The Law Commission secured approval early on for some very wide-ranging programmes, within which it could pick and choose what to do.

The first programme in 1965[10] contained a list of items mainly derived from *Law Reform Now*. It included codification of the law of contact (item I) and of the law of landlord and tenant (item VIII), along with the recognition of 'a new branch of the law, embracing all matters which directly affect the family as such, whether they concern property, status, or otherwise, and contemplates the eventual enactment of a code of family law' (item X). I am not sure why they thought it a new branch of law, when it was already sufficiently recognised to be a subject in the Cambridge Tripos (which I was studying myself at the time) and Professor Bromley's major academic textbook on *Family Law* had been published in 1957 (perhaps it indicates a time-lag before the practitioners' and judicial thinking catches up with the academics').[11] At that stage, the Commission's role was to make a preliminary examination of three topics 'with a view to proposing, in the light of their social implications, the agencies to which they should be referred'. This was alongside such specific items as civil liability for animals (item V) and the implications of the decision in *DPP v Smith* (item XIII).[12]

The second programme in 1968[13] added codification of the general principles of the criminal law (item XVIII) and 'a comprehensive examination of family law with a view to its systematic reform and eventual codification' (item XIX), both to be done by the Law Commission (plus a specific item on the interpretation of wills

---

[8] 1965 Act, s 3(1)(b).
[9] 1965 Act, s 3(2)(c).
[10] Law Commission, LC 1, *First Programme of Law Reform* (1965).
[11] P Bromley, *Family Law* (London, Butterworths, 1957).
[12] *DPP v Smith* [1961] AC 290 [HL].
[13] Law Commission, LC 14, *Second Programme of Law Reform* (1968).

to be done by the Law Reform Committee). The third programme did not turn up until 1973[14] and simply added virtually the whole of private international law, to be undertaken in co-operation with the Scottish Law Commission (item XXI).

That was how things stood in 1984 when I joined the Commission. By that stage it was clear that codification of contract law and the law of landlord and tenant were not going to happen. Codification of criminal law was also not going to happen if left to the Law Commission's unaided efforts, but an academic team headed by Professor John Smith had offered their services,[15] and a great deal of work was done during my time towards trying to achieve that admirable objective.

But that was why I was able to tackle more or less what I pleased within the area of family law, beginning with the public and private law relating to children, moving on to the ground for divorce, then domestic violence and abuse, and then adoption. Two of these, public child care law and adoption, were undertaken as joint projects with the Department of Health and Social Security (as it was then). Despite the fact that the 1965 Act did not envisage the Commission doing everything itself, this was controversial on two counts: first, the expenditure of Law Commission resources on a project that was not 'their' project and second, the necessarily limited involvement of the other Law Commissioners in deciding upon the eventual recommendations. But it was hugely productive, and I believe a feather in the Law Commission's cap: working with government meant that the public law could become government policy and our direct access to Parliamentary Counsel meant that we could draft a composite Children Bill covering both public and private law without prior approval.

The family lawyers could never really complain about implementation rates. Over the years, the Commission has done a great deal of family law. This might be thought odd, because it is not exactly 'lawyers' law'. But in those days it was mainly the responsibility of the LCD, and they seemed happy to have someone else do it. Hence the Commission was responsible for the revolution in matrimonial law which came into force in 1971 and in children's law which came into force 20 years later. My theory is that it worked well then because we were mainly dealing with remedies and not rules. It is easy to get rules wrong but discretionary remedies are more flexible and less controversial. This is one of the reasons why the Commission's proposals for automatic joint ownership of the matrimonial home were never adopted.

The fourth programme of law reform did not arrive until 1989[16] and was still on the same model. It consolidated all the previous items without giving anything up unless it had been completed and it added the Law of Trusts and Mentally Incapacitated Adults. I am particularly proud of the latter report, which was completed under the skilful direction of Henry Brooke after I had left, because the government consulted and considered but eventually adopted something very much the same, which became the Mental Capacity Act 2005 ten years later. In my view,

---

[14] Law Commission, LC 54, *Third Programme of Law Reform* (1973).
[15] Law Commission, LC 143, *Codification of the Criminal Law: A Report to the Law Commission* (1985).
[16] Law Commission, LC 185, *Fourth Programme of Law Reform* (1989).

it is not always desirable to press government too hard for an answer. They may get round to it in the end. Better late than never.

The fifth programme in 1991[17] followed a similar pattern in not giving anything up but adding two new items, based on what the new Commissioner (Jack Beatson) wanted to do.

It was the sixth programme in 1995,[18] when Henry Brooke was still Chairman, which marked a new departure—cutting down the breadth of the previous programmes and identifying specific items which would constitute the law reform agenda for next three years. It did not abandon codification of family law (item 8) but the Commission did not have anyone to do it. By the seventh programme in 1999,[19] while Robert Carnwath was chairman, the Commission had discontinued work on family law unless it was related to other law reform work. The eighth programme in 2001[20] does not mention it at all. Nor does the ninth programme in 2005, under Roger Toulson,[21] but it announces a new item, requested by government, on cohabitation. By the tenth programme in 2008,[22] under Terence Etherton, the Commission had abandoned codification altogether, in favour of specific law reform projects (marital property agreements being one of them).

Between the tenth programme and the next, there were three significant changes. First, the Law Commission Act 2009 required the Lord Chancellor to lay an annual report before Parliament on the extent to which Law Commission proposals had been implemented by the government. Of the five so far,[23] the 2013 report stands out, explaining that no proposals had been implemented, none rejected and 18 had not yet been implemented. Second, there was to be a new procedure for handling Law Commission Bills in the House of Lords. And third, a Protocol was agreed between the Lord Chancellor and the Law Commission on how they would work together.[24] The aim was to ensure that government departments are supportive of the Law Commission's proposed work in terms of future implementation, including providing staff to liaise with the Commission during the project and undertaking that there is a serious intention to take forward law reform in the area.[25] Interestingly, this includes providing views on the most appropriate output for a project—whether simply making policy recommendations, providing a draft Bill, or recommending guidance.[26]

---

[17] Law Commission, LC 200, *Fifth Programme of Law Reform* (1991).
[18] Law Commission, LC 234, *Sixth Programme of Law Reform* (1995).
[19] Law Commission, LC 259, *Seventh Programme of Law Reform* (1999).
[20] Law Commission, LC 274, *Eighth Programme of Law Reform* (2001).
[21] Law Commission, LC 293, *Ninth Programme of Law Reform* (2005).
[22] Law Commission, LC 311, *Tenth Programme of Law Reform* (2008).
[23] Ministry of Justice, *Report on the Implementation of Law Commission Proposals* (HC 719, 2011); (HC 1900, 2012); (HC 908, 2013); (HC 1237, 2014); (HC 1062, 2015).
[24] Law Commission and Ministry of Justice, LC 321, *Protocol between the Lord Chancellor (on behalf of the Government) and the Law Commission* (2010).
[25] ibid para 6.
[26] ibid para 7.

The eleventh[27] and twelfth[28] programmes have been agreed under these new arrangements. I fully understand the attractions on both sides, but it must lead to a very different relationship, and the abandonment of some of the advantages of the old. I have a real regret about abandoning the codification of family law, because I think that that was a doable project, and one which would have been immensely valuable in this new world, where so many family litigants do not have access to legal advice and help and are having to represent themselves. Whether the reward will be, as hoped, an increased rate of implementation, remains to be seen. It may even have been the price of the Commission's survival.

The other big change from the olden days has been in the range of methods of bringing about legal change. The assumption used to be that reform would always be by statute, including codification by statute rather than by restatement. After all, the judges were the ones who had got the common law into a mess, and sometimes the statute book too, and someone else had it sort it out. This brings me to the debate about the judicial role and how far the judges can go in reforming the law. We ought to distinguish between judicial law reform and judicial development of the law, but the two cannot always be so easily separated.

There are several strong arguments against judicial law reform: (1) The law should be clear and predictable. (2) The judges should be, and be seen to be, impartial and not to have an agenda of their own. (3) Well-meaning judicial law reform may plug the worst holes and thus hold up more systematic statutory reform. (4) Litigation is not a suitable tool for law reform. Too much is under the control of the parties, especially in our adversarial system, where even in the Supreme Court we debate whether it would be proper to decide the case on a basis not put forward by either party. (5) Judges by themselves are not well equipped to do law reform—they cannot do the empirical research, the public and professional consultation, the deep consideration of several options that the Law Commissions can do. (6) Once judges step out of the realm of applying legal principles to particular facts, and start considering policy and even common sense, subjectivity and inconsistency are bound to creep in. (7) The judges lack the seal of approval from the people that elected politicians enjoy.

On other hand, there are many disadvantages in relying on Parliament to reform the law: (1) It freezes the law in a particular place, when the evolutive development of the common law would have been more adaptable to new situations and new problems. For example, it would probably not have been possible to develop the law of privacy had the Law Commission's 1981 *Report on Breach of Confidence*[29] been implemented. (2) Parliamentary intervention may deter judges from further sensible developments. A prime example is *OBG Ltd v Allan*.[30] One of the reasons why the majority were unwilling to extend the tort of conversion to choses in action was the Torts (Interference with Goods) Act 1977, the result of a perfectly sensible

[27] Law Commission, LC 330, *Eleventh Programme of Law Reform* (2011).
[28] Law Commission, LC 354, *Twelfth Programme of Law Reform* (2014).
[29] LC 110 (1981).
[30] *OBG Ltd v Allan* [2007] UKHL 21, [2008] 1 AC 1.

report by the Law Reform Committee on reforming the law of conversion and deti-nue.[31] Both the Committee and Parliament had assumed that these torts were con-fined to chattels. Lord Nicholls took the view that 'Parliament cannot be taken to have intended to preclude the courts from developing the common law tort of con-version if this becomes necessary to achieve justice',[32] but he was in the minority. (3) Parliament may mess up a perfectly sensible scheme by well-meaning but less than fully thought-through amendments. I am tempted to give Part II of the Family Law Act 1996 as an example, because it did not take long for everyone to realise that the amendments to the Law Commission's simple scheme for a new divorce law had made the Act unworkable. (4) There are some things that Parliament is most reluctant to touch, however strongly it is urged to do so by the courts, who are only too aware of the problems of making law on the subject. The best example is their Lordships' unanswered plea in the case of Tony Bland.[33] (5) Parliament may do nothing, but a judge must always do something, even if it is not at all clear what he or she should do.[34] Cardozo, in his discussion of 'The Judge as Legislator',[35] quotes article 4 of the French Code Civil:

> Le juge, qui refusera de juger, sous prétexte du silence, de l'obscurité ou de l'insuffiance de la loi, pourra être poursuivi comme capable de déni de justice.[36]

So it is a fascinating idea that the Law Commission itself could stimulate judicial law reform, by a providing fully researched, reasoned and consulted upon policy case for developing the law in a particular area in a particular way.

It may be that our working paper on *Rape within Marriage*[37] was the first, albeit unwitting, example of this. Somehow or other, between the publication of the working paper in October 1990, and our report in January 1992,[38] both the Court of Appeal and the House of Lords had persuaded themselves that they could abolish the marital rape exemption without parliamentary intervention.[39] Neither judgment mentions the powerful case made in the working paper, a joint effort between the criminal and family law teams, but it is difficult to believe that their Lordships had not read it.

A better example, because it was deliberate, is the Commission's 1998 report on *Damages for Personal Injury*.[40] This proposed that the Court of Appeal and House of Lords use their existing powers to raise the level of general damages in accord-ance with the Commission's recommendations, with legislation only if they had not done so within, say, three years. As is well known, the Court of Appeal sat as a

---

[31] Law Reform Committee, *Eighteenth Report (Conversion and Detinue)* (Cmnd 4774, 1971).
[32] *OBG* [234].
[33] *Airedale NHS Trust v Bland* [1993] AC 789 (HL), 880 and 890.
[34] See, eg, *Jones v Kernott* [2011] UKSC 53, [2012] 1 AC 776, [47].
[35] BN Cardozo, *The Nature of the Judicial Process* (Yale, Yale University Press, 1921) Lecture III, 134–35.
[36] 'A judge who refuses to decide a case on the pretext that the law is silent, unclear or insufficient, can be prosecuted as liable for a denial of justice' (editors' translation).
[37] Law Commission, LC WP 116, *Rape within Marriage* (1990).
[38] Law Commission, LC 205, *Rape within Marriage* (1992).
[39] *R v R* [1991] 2 WLR 1065 (CA) and [1992] 1 AC 599 (HL).
[40] LC 257 (1999) paras 5.8–5.13.

bench of five to do this, but after an adversarial hearing in which the research relied upon by the Commission was subject to intense forensic examination on behalf of the insurance industry, the result was a lower increase than the Commission had recommended.[41]

Another example is the illegality defence. This was a project that ran and ran. The Commission published consultation papers on *The Effect of Illegality on Contracts and Trusts* in 1999[42] and *The Illegality Defence in Tort* in 2001.[43] Then, in 2009, it took the unusual step of publishing a further 'Consultative Report',[44] because it was finding the subject so difficult. This was partly because it would be difficult to draft a statutory scheme which did not introduce new uncertainties, and partly because it seemed to the Commission that it was open to the courts to develop the law in ways which would make it 'considerably clearer, more certain and less arbitrary'. So in its 2010 report,[45] it recommended statutory reform in the area of trusts but not in the areas of contract and tort. Given the mess which the Supreme Court has now got itself into on this subject,[46] I am not sure that this was a wise solution. Frankly, however, I think this is more a criticism of the Court than of the Commission. Arguably at least, the Court should have paid more attention to the arguments of the Commission, and to its own previous decisions, than it did.

Other solutions are also available. Thus in its report on *Trustee Exemption Clauses*,[47] the Commission rejected a statutory scheme prohibiting the exemption of professional trustees from liability in negligence, in favour of a rule of professional conduct requiring paid trustees to take reasonable steps to ensure that the settlor is aware of the meaning and effect of such a clause. Some reliance was placed in argument before the Privy Council in the case of *Spread Trustee Co Ltd v Hutcheson*[48] on the fact that the Commission had not, in its report, even recommended banning clauses exempting trustees from gross negligence.

I sum up with four concluding questions, some of which I know will be further addressed in later chapters in this volume:

(1)  Is the Law Commission model—five distinguished and diverse lawyers with independent status—a good model? Should there be a greater range of expertise in this day and age? Or can the Commission discover the relevant information for itself, just as the courts have to do?

(2)  If it is the right model, what should its mission be? Should it include the overall oversight contemplated by the founding fathers? Should it include large projects such as the codification of a whole area of law? If it should stick to defined

---

[41]  *Heil v Rankin* [2001] QB 272 (CA).
[42]  LC CP 154 (1999).
[43]  LC CP 160 (2001).
[44]  Law Commission, LC CP 189, *The Illegality Defence* (2009).
[45]  Law Commission, LC 320, *The Illegality Defence* (2010).
[46]  cf *Hounga v Allen* [2014] UKSC 47, [2014] 1 WLR 2889; *Les Laboratoires Service v Apotex* [2014] UKSC 55, [2015] AC 430; and *Bilta (UK) Ltd v Nazir (No 2)* [2015] UKSC 23, [2015] 2 WLR 1168. See further chapter 29 (James Lee).
[47]  LC 301 (2006).
[48]  *Spread Trustee Co Ltd v Hutcheson* [2011] UKPC 13, [2012] 2 AC 194.

projects, how should these be chosen? Should the government have a veto? Should the defining criterion be a topic that is well suited to reform by lawyers and for which there is an obvious need, whether or not the government wants it done?

(3)   How independent should the Law Commission be of government? Does the protocol strike the right note? Can we distinguish between what the Commission should tackle, over which government should have some influence or even control, and what the Commission proposes, over which it should not?

(4)   What is the most suitable means of tackling a problem? Should statute be the method of choice, or should the Commission be thinking of a range of solutions, including judicial development of the law, and softer law such as guidance or Codes of Practice?

Despite the changes over the last 50 years, I remain convinced that the Law Commissions can be very proud of their achievements to date; that there is still a strong case for having such institutions, especially in common law countries; and that is a case which governments of all political persuasions can recognise and support.

So back to where I began. The Society of Labour Lawyers returned to the fray 20 years after *Law Reform Now*, with *More Law Reform Now*, published in 1983 and edited by Peter Archer and Andrew Martin,[49] and again with *Law Reform for All*, published in 1996 and edited by none other than David Bean,[50] whose appointment as the latest Chairman of the Law Commission is so welcome. That was a very different book from its predecessors (being mostly about access to justice and human rights) and somehow I do not think that the Law Commission will be tackling the agenda which it set!

---

[49]   P Archer and A Martin (eds), *More Law Reform Now* (Chichester, Barry Rose, 1983).
[50]   D Bean (ed), *Law Reform for All* (London, Blackstone Press, 1996).

# Part 2

# The First Half-Century of the Commissions

# 3

# *Introduction*

LORD HODGE

The discussion of the first half-century of the Commissions raised questions of policy which the various Law Commissions have faced since their initial establishment. The questions included: (i) what was the place of such law reform bodies in relation to Parliament and the executive branch of government; (ii) from where did those bodies obtain their political (rather than legal) authority to make policy recommendations; (iii) how to conduct effective consultation; and (iv) how to encourage governments to implement their reports.

Law Commissions do not operate in a political vacuum. In some jurisdictions politicians have sought to exercise close control over law reform bodies. At the outset, as Paul Mitchell showed, the influence of Lord Gardiner in the UK Cabinet got the Law Commissions on the mainland off to a good start. But, as Neil Faris explained, a wish by politicians in Northern Ireland for control over law reform delayed the creation of a Law Commission there for over 40 years. Periodically, Law Commissions have had to fight off proposals by the executive to take law reform 'in house' by replacing a Law Commission with a departmental law reform body. I recall that there was talk of such a proposal in London when I served at the Scottish Law Commission.

The authority of the work of a Law Commission is derived in part from the agreement of its programme by the government and the presentation of the programme to the legislature. The negotiation with the executive of the programme and terms of reference of a particular project is a critically important process by which Commissioners can seek to promote a coherent approach to law reform. In part authority flows from the reputation of the Commissioners as lawyers and the skill with which they present their arguments. But the principal source of authority for a Commission's proposals comes from the quality of the consultation. If a Commission engages the correct people in the consultation, prevents parties with an agenda from selecting themselves, and uses the consultation responses wisely to justify its recommendations after thorough debate within the Commission, it greatly enhances the authority of its reports.

Consultation can involve the creation of working groups as advisers, the production of a consultation paper and also the use of the media, including, more recently, social media. Different views were expressed on the merits of press conferences. Some reforms, however, are so technical that consultation may add little and the Commission has to rest on the credibility of its own members for the authority of its recommendations.

The continuing difficulty of persuading governments to implement Commissions' recommendations for law reform was a common theme throughout the papers in this section.

# 4

# *Strategies of the Early Law Commission*

### PAUL MITCHELL

It is our hope that those amendments will be as acceptable to Parliament as they
have been to those whom we have consulted.

Law Commission and Scottish Law Commission, *Report on the Consolidation of
Certain Enactments Relating to Shellfish Fisheries and Shellfish* (1967)

I

Writing in the year that the statute was passed, Lord Chorley and Gerald Dworkin
observed that the Law Commissions Act 1965 'may well prove a landmark in the
history of English law'.[1] As their cautious phrasing suggested, they had their doubts.
Some of their concerns related to the failure to integrate the Law Commission into
the machinery of government: there was, for instance, no intention to give the
Commission's proposals any special status in the parliamentary process, and the
provision for the involvement of Parliamentary Counsel looked worryingly sketchy.[2]
Perhaps more damagingly, Chorley and Dworkin also pointed to what they saw as
problems with the constitution of the Commission itself. All the Law Commissioners were to be lawyers, and the two authors echoed a point made by WT Wells (in
the parliamentary debates) that years 'in the higher reaches of the legal profession'
might not be the best way to learn where 'the shoe pinches the foot of the ordinary
man'.[3] Chorley and Dworkin also both reported and shared in the widespread appre-
hension about the political leanings of the first Law Commissioners; their widely
known sympathy with the Labour Party, it was feared, might lend the Commission's
proposals a political slant that would provoke parliamentary resistance.[4] WT Wells,
writing an 'interim appraisal' of the Law Commission as early as 1966, put the point
more starkly: the Commissioners' fixed terms of office were due to expire around the
time of the next General Election, and a future Conservative government might be

---

[1] R Chorley and G Dworkin, 'The Law Commissions Act, 1965' (1965) 28 *MLR* 675, 675.
[2] ibid 681–82 and 683 respectively.
[3] ibid 683.
[4] ibid 684–85.

'not only critical, but hostile' in assessing the Commission's performance.[5] The Law Commissioners, Wells pointed out, had a 'general image ... of being rather to the left of centre, and this fact could, conceivably, after 1970, operate to the detriment of the Commission and their work'.[6]

A vivid illustration of how deeply these difficulties were felt by those involved is provided by a public lecture given by Lord Kilbrandon, the Chairman of the Scottish Law Commission, in 1966.[7] He began his lecture by acknowledging that the phrase 'law reform' suggested change 'after some immense popular outburst having radical, revolutionary or even Marxist characteristics. In fact we think of something like the constitutional changes of the years 1832, 1867 and 1918'.[8] Kilbrandon was quick to distance both himself and (implicitly) his Commission from this conception of law reform; the Law Commission's remit must be narrower, but he struggled to define it:

> [I]s there any dividing line which can be discerned between law reform and social legisla-tion? In practice, the answer to this question must be in the affirmative, otherwise the Law Commissions would never have been set up. If all law is social legislation, then all law reform is social reform. You would not set up commissions consisting exclusively of legally-qualified persons in order to investigate matters of that kind and to report thereon.[9]

This tortured passage, full of self-doubt and circularity, set the scene for Kilbrandon's attempt to identify what, exactly, the Law Commissions should be looking at. He started with 'lawyers' law', but quickly found this 'an expression which seems to be full of epigrammatic meaning when you hear it first, but the more you think about it the less attractive it becomes'.[10] He put forward his own version of 'lawyers' law' as the law concerned with the transfer (as opposed to the establishment) of rights; but then, almost immediately, he undermined it by propos-ing that a no-fault compensation scheme for personal injury would be a matter of 'lawyers' law'.[11] This was an extraordinary public crisis of confidence, purpose and identity to be experiencing at such an early stage.

The English and Welsh Law Commission's experience, however, seems to have been happier—or, at least, its crises less public. Its first Commissioners, led by Lord Scarman (the Commission's first Chairman), were prolific and highly effec-tive: all the reports produced during Scarman's tenure were implemented.[12] The first Commissioners also established methods and patterns of working that remain funda-mental to the Commission's role and identity today. How did they do it? This essay examines the Commission's earliest publications—its programmes, annual reports, working papers and reports on individual legal topics—to identify and analyse some of its strategies.

---

[5] WT Wells, 'The Law Reform Commission: An Interim Appraisal' (1966) 37 *Political Quarterly* 291, 292.

[6] ibid 294.

[7] On the founding history of the Scottish Commission, see chapter 34 (Lord Pentland), especially sections II, III and V.

[8] Lord Kilbrandon, 'The Prospects of Law Reform' (1966) 17 *NILQ* 484, 484.

[9] ibid 485.

[10] ibid 486.

[11] ibid 486–87.

[12] S Sedley, 'Scarman, Leslie George' in *Oxford Dictionary of National Biography* (online edn).

II

In asking ourselves 'how they did it' some stress must be placed on 'they'. It seems clear that that no one individual was the dominating or driving force. Indeed, it is quite striking that in the *Oxford Dictionary of National Biography*'s entries on the only two early Law Commissioners it includes, both biographers emphasise that their subjects suppressed or concealed their true views when working at the Law Commission.[13] The implicit suggestion here that both Lord Scarman and LCB Gower recognised that they had roles to play, and adapted their activities accordingly, could be equally applied to other leading figures. Lord Gardiner, whose energetic advocacy of a permanent law reform body had put law reform on the political agenda,[14] and who was rumoured to have insisted on the creation of the Law Commission as a condition of accepting the Lord Chancellorship,[15] characterised the Commission's work as 'part of that process on which we are now engaged, the modernization of Britain'.[16] To proclaim the Commission as an agent of modernisation was very much to align both the institution and its aims with a central theme of political discourse in 1960s Britain. The Labour Party had come to power in 1964 following an election campaign in which it had dwelt on the unrealised potential of the British economy and the urgent need to make more use of new technology. Once in power, the drive to modernise inspired a wealth of policies beyond industry including new road signage, postcodes and decimalisation.[17] A Law Commission that said it was setting out to modernise the law was, therefore, very astutely positioning itself in the prevailing political landscape.

It was also possible for the Commission to draw on two related, dominant political values: professionalism and planning. An appeal to professionalism had been an important aspect of the argument for creating a Law Commission in the first place, with Lord Gardiner making much of the limited achievements of the Commission's part-time predecessors;[18] it remained central to the Commission's identity.[19] Professionalism was a particularly powerful concept to invoke at that time as it was one of the factors that the Labour Party had used to differentiate itself from the Conservatives, and was something which the Prime Minister, Harold Wilson, took great personal pride in.[20] The full-time nature of a Law Commissioner's role,

[13] ibid; S Cretney 'Gower, Laurence Cecil Bartlett [Jim]' *Oxford Dictionary of National Biography* (online edn).

[14] See, particularly his co-editorship of, and contribution to, G Gardiner and A Martin (eds), *Law Reform Now* (London, Victor Gollancz, 1963).

[15] Chorley and Dworkin, n 1 above, 679.

[16] G Gardiner, 'Comparative Law Reform' (1966) 52 *American Bar Association Journal* 1021, 1023.

[17] D Sandbrook, *White Heat: A History of Britain in the Swinging Sixties* (London, Abacus, 2007) 167–69.

[18] Chorley and Dworkin, n 1 above, 680–81; J Farrar, *Law Reform and the Law Commission* (London, Sweet & Maxwell, 1974) 13.

[19] See, eg, the emphasis given to professionalism by the Commission's first Chairman in lectures to international audiences: L Scarman, 'The Work of the Law Commission for England and Wales' (1969) 8 *University of Western Ontario Law Review* 33, 33–34; L Scarman, 'Inside the English Law Commission' (1971) 57 *American Bar Association Journal* 867, 867.

[20] Sandbrook, n 17 above, 41. Edward Heath, the Leader of the Opposition in the same period also emphasised his professionalism (ibid 164).

and the Commission's practice of submitting annual reports were reflections of professionalism, as also, perhaps, was the Commission's over-ambitious *First Programme of Reform*[21] (Wilson was notorious for his conflation of professionalism and overwork).[22]

The importance of planning in government policies of the period was embodied in the creation of a new government ministry, the Department of Economic Affairs, which was designed to formulate strategic economic policy.[23] The Department's main role proved to be the creation of a National Plan for economic growth, which would achieve a 25 per cent increase in output by 1970. As it turned out, the government had been wildly optimistic about its ability to control the economic conditions that would have made such extraordinary growth possible, but, in 1965, planning was still seen as the route to modernisation. The centrality of planning can be seen immediately in the Law Commission's first published document, its *First Programme*.[24] By identifying the areas that it proposed to examine, the Commission was obviously engaging in making a plan; but how it explained the choice of those topics, and how it proposed that they should be examined, revealed a different dimension of the Commission's strategy. Right at the outset there was an emphasis on 'practical considerations': 'we have excluded those projects on which we cannot hope to make an immediate start'.[25] There was also, equally prominently, an insistence on co-ordination between the Commission and other agencies: alongside the exclusion of projects on which an immediate start could not be made, the Commission stated that for the 'avoidance of duplication of effort' it had excluded matters already under consideration by other agencies, and that it proposed to give active consideration to studies by other reform bodies that had not yet been implemented.[26] The Law Commission had instantly adopted the mentality and language of an efficiency-driven public body—the 'immediate start' implicitly promised prompt conclusions[27]—but it was not seeking to dominate. The themes of collaboration and co-ordination were carried through in the individual programme items: for instance, item II, on contractual exemption clauses in general, explained that it was building on the work of an earlier committee, and proposed dividing up the new investigation between an interdepartmental committee and the Commission.[28] Item V proposed to revisit the vexed question of civil liability for animals, which had been the subject of an unimplemented report in 1953.[29] The programme also called for

---

[21] LC 1 (1965).

[22] The annual reports began with Law Commission, LC 4, *First Annual Report* (1966). The amount of work that the *First Annual Report* described alarmed CP Harvey: see 'The Law Commission: First Annual Report 1965–1966' (1966) 29 *MLR* 649, 650: 'it fairly staggers one with the revelation of the amount of work that the Commission have already got through, are currently getting through and are proposing to get through in the immediate future'.

[23] Sandbrook, n 17 above, 170–77.

[24] See n 21 above.

[25] ibid para 1(ii).

[26] ibid paras 1(i) and 1(iii).

[27] Some topics were added in the hope that they would yield impressively speedy recommendations: LCB Gower, 'Reflections on Law Reform' (1973) 23 *University of Toronto Law Journal* 257, 263.

[28] *First Programme*, n 21 above, 6–7.

[29] ibid 8.

the creation of new ad hoc committees—on jurisdiction and procedure in personal injury litigation, on financial limits on magistrates' orders in domestic and affiliation proceedings, and on the Judicature Act in its application to Northern Ireland.[30] What this approach suggested, in addition to the importance of planning, was that the Commission was being very careful about relying on its own status and authority in bringing about legal change.

III

The anxieties about authority implicit in the Law Commission's *First Programme* were made explicit in the Commissioners' later unofficial writings. Both LCB Gower and Norman Marsh explained that 'as a new and untried body' the Commission had not felt able to do battle with vested professional interests by pushing for widespread procedural reforms.[31] Marsh's essay also contained a very eloquent passage explaining why judicial development of the common law was no longer adequate:

> [I]t is no longer possible for the judge in modern English society to make those bold assumptions about family life and about relations between landlord and tenant, employer and employee, citizen and State which underlie many reforms of a seemingly legal character. On the one hand, he lives in an era where many value assumptions are being challenged; on the other he does not enjoy quite the unquestioned privilege, the charismatic authority, enjoyed by his Victorian forebearers.[32]

A footnote to this passage identified the dethronement of the father-figure as one of several reasons for this development. What is particularly striking about Marsh's comments, for our purposes, is that they apply equally forcefully to attempts at law reform by four late-middle aged lawyers led by a judge. What moral authority, what credibility could such figures lay claim to? It is one of the most remarkable features of the early Law Commission publications that they hardly ever make such claims.

In the first 20 publications, only once, in its report on civil liability for animals, does the Commission unapologetically rely on its own judgement about social conditions mandating legal change.[33] More characteristic is the report on imputed criminal intent, where the Commission's discomfort in having to advance its own test (consultees having disagreed) is palpable.[34] The Commission's preferred approach, however, was to either play down or minimise its own agency, and to depict the true impetus for change as emanating from elsewhere.

'Elsewhere' might be taken literally—the working paper on administrative law, for instance, cast envious glances towards France, and suggested that we needed

---

[30] ibid 9, 12 and 14 respectively.

[31] Gower, n 27 above, 266 (from which the quotation is taken); N Marsh, 'Law Reform in the United Kingdom: A New Institutional Approach' (1971–72) 13 *William & Mary Law Review* 263, 275 n 31.

[32] Marsh, n 31 above, 266.

[33] Law Commission, LC 13, *Civil Liability for Animals* (1967) para 40.

[34] Law Commission, LC 10, *Imputed Criminal Intent (Director of Public Prosecutions v Smith)* (1966) para 20.

to be keeping up with the neighbours[35]—but even representations from a single solicitor could trigger an investigation.[36] More significantly, the Commission might seek to arrogate an external body's authority when taking up that body's reform proposal. In its report *Proceedings against Estates*, the Commission supported a proposal from the Law Society to abolish a special limitation rule that applied only in respect of such proceedings.[37] The Commission reported the Law Society's view that the existing rule was failing to achieve its intended policy purpose, and added that 'solicitors are more likely to be familiar with the practical consequences and those whom we consulted did not believe that the abolition of the rule would cause serious delay'.[38] This was, of course, technically the Law Commission's proposal; but the Law Commission was presenting itself as little more than an obliging intermediary.

The Commission's publications on the reform of root of title to freehold land provide a particularly vivid illustration of its enthusiasm for depicting itself as a messenger.[39] Both the working paper (the Commission's first) and the report proposed that vendors of freehold land should only need to prove that they had good title that could be traced back for a minimum of 15 years (the requirement at the time was 30 years), but the working paper was quick to acknowledge that any such reform must have the support of conveyancers: 'it would ... be realistic to propose a reduction only if it would be acceptable generally to the public and to those in the legal profession on whom the public normally rely for guidance in land purchase'.[40] The Commission went out of its way to gain the support of the conveyancing profession by publishing the paper in the *New Law Journal*, and the confident reiteration of the 15-year proposal in its subsequent report showed that the Commission had received the responses it had hoped for.[41] The report went even further than the working paper in its extravagant deference to conveyancers—'we appreciate' the Commission gushed, 'that, on a question such as this, it is easier for experts to know the answer than to prove it'[42]—and it also offered a much more elaborate, historical account of conveyancers as agents of legal change. In this account, the statutory reduction in root of title effected by the Vendor and Purchaser Act 1874 was partly attributable to the changing practices of conveyancers;[43] in the same way, current conveyancing practice could be seen as 'repeating the historical pattern whereby a move to reduce the period has been preceded by the voluntary adoption of a shorter period'.[44] The reform was presented as having an inevitability about it, and the Law

---

[35] Law Commission, LC WP 13, *Exploratory Working Paper on Administrative Law* (1967) paras 6 and 9. The Commission's *Second Annual Report* (LC 12, 1967) para 25 recorded that a member of the Commission's staff had been to see the Conseil d'Etat at work. See also Law Commission, LC WP 4, *Should English Wills be Registrable?* (1966) which gave striking prominence to Dutch law.

[36] *Should English Wills be Registrable?*, n 35 above, para 1.

[37] Law Commission, LC 19, *Proceedings against Estates* (1969).

[38] ibid para 18.

[39] Law Commission, LC WP 1, *Law Commission First Programme, Item IX—Transfer of Land, B—Root of Title to Freehold Land* (1966); Law Commission, LC 9, *Transfer of Land: Interim Report on Root of Title to Freehold Land* (1966).

[40] WP 1, n 39 above, para 11.

[41] LC 9, n 39 above, para 31 records the publication; the 15-year recommendation is at para 36.

[42] ibid para 28.

[43] ibid para 17.

[44] ibid para 26.

Commission as being little more than the amanuensis of a cyclical historical process. The last thing the Commission could have been accused of was acting on its own initiative.

IV

Invoking the external sources of reform proposals glossed over the Law Commission's own limitations; but sometimes those limitations could not be avoided. In such circumstances the Commission went out of its way to signal that it fully appreciated where the line was. Thus, where its researches brought to light an indefensible disparity between the level of fines for selling lobsters carrying spawn and for selling crabs in the same condition, the Commission proposed assimilating the penalties, but refused to be drawn on what the appropriate fine should be: 'we do not think that Parliament would look to us for advice on the proper level of a fine'.[45] An appreciation of its own limitations also seems to have motivated the Commission's proposals to allocate certain law reform tasks to entities other than itself (as we saw in the *First Programme*),[46] and was expressly given as its reason for entrusting the reform of administrative law to a Royal Commission or similar body.[47]

These public demonstrations that the Commission was aware of the limitations of its role and functions may well have had the paradoxical general effect of increasing its standing—a confident understanding of the limits of one's role might, after all, imply a confident understanding of the role itself. But in one particularly significant instance the Commission went further, and exploited its own self-proclaimed limitations to create a uniquely authoritative and influential position for itself. This was its report *Reform of the Grounds of Divorce: The Field of Choice*,[48] which was the Commission's response to *Putting Asunder*, a report by a group appointed by the Archbishop of Canterbury.[49]

The opening paragraphs of *Reform of the Grounds of Divorce* suggested an acute self-consciousness. 'It is not, of course, for us but for Parliament to settle such controversial social issues as the advisability of extending the present grounds of divorce', said the Commission.[50] 'Our function ... must be to assist the Legislature and the general public in considering these questions by pointing out the implications of various courses of action'.[51] This 'limited task' had an apparently modest ambition:

> As lawyers we recognise that the improvement of the divorce law is too important a matter to be left to specialists, whether they be churchmen, sociologists or lawyers. Nevertheless public discussion of the subject should be more constructive and fruitful if it can be focussed

---

[45] Law Commission and Scottish Law Commission, LC 11A and SLC 6A, *Sea Fisheries (Shellfish) Bill: Report on the Consolidation of Certain Enactments Relating to Shellfish Fisheries and Shellfish* (1967) para 7.

[46] See text accompanying nn 27–30 above.

[47] Law Commission, LC 20, *Administrative Law* (1969) para 10.

[48] LC 6 (1966).

[49] Church of England Group on Divorce Law, *Putting Asunder: A Divorce Law for Contemporary Society* (London, SPCK, 1966).

[50] *Reform of the Grounds of Divorce*, n 48 above, para 2.

[51] ibid.

on practical possibilities. We have therefore tried to restrict this Report to a consideration of what appears from a lawyer's point of view to be practicable.[52]

However, when the report turned to consider the proposals advanced by the *Putting Asunder* committee, the analytical and persuasive power of the practical lawyer's perspective became apparent. The *Putting Asunder* report had called for the replacement of matrimonial offences as grounds of divorce with a sole ground of breakdown of marriage. So far as the principle was concerned, the Law Commission was quick to acknowledge its own incompetence to judge: 'many of the arguments for and against the breakdown test', it commented, 'depend on judgments of personal and social morality. To these we can only draw attention; it is not for us to determine their validity'.[53] But what the Law Commission emphatically did feel itself competent to evaluate was the adjudicatory mechanism proposed in *Putting Asunder*. This required positive proof of breakdown, to the satisfaction of the judge, in every case whether defended or not. In the Law Commission's view, this made the proposals impractical: litigation would take longer and cost more.[54] A more practical solution, the Commission suggested, would be 'Breakdown without Inquest', in which an investigation of the marriage would not be mandatory, and breakdown could be assumed on proof of a six-month separation.[55] The Commission portrayed itself as helpfully proposing alternative legal machinery to give effect to the same principle—of matrimonial breakdown as the ground of divorce—that *Putting Asunder* had adopted. But the reality was that, in its application to ordinary litigants, this was an entirely different system: the paternalistic, invasive procedure required by *Putting Asunder* was being replaced by an approach in which the parties' own feelings, desires and evaluations—in short, their autonomy—was determinative. The Commission's sardonic observation that 'The parties are likely to be better judges of the viability of their own marriage than a court can hope to be' underlined its awareness that its proposals would shift the balance of power in divorce litigation away from (professional) judges, thereby giving the parties control.[56] The Commission's proposal formed the basis of subsequent reforms,[57] and the strategy it employed in its report illustrated the advantages that could be gained by (paradoxically) emphasising its own limited expertise. For here professions of limited expertise served *both* as expressions of appropriate modesty, and, simultaneously, as peculiarly compelling demands to be listened to on the self-identified specialism.

V

The Law Commission's response to *Putting Asunder* was a compelling illustration of the way that, by claiming to speak *as lawyers*, the Law Commission could fashion for itself a position of authority and influence in a debate with wide-ranging

---

[52] ibid para 3.
[53] ibid para 59.
[54] ibid paras 62, 70.
[55] ibid paras 71–72, 76.
[56] ibid para 71; the point is repeated at para 73.
[57] See Law Commission, LC 12, *Second Annual Report* (1967) para 75 and Law Commission, LC 15, *Third Annual Report* (1968) paras 50–51 and app III (30–32).

social and political dimensions. The Commission also had notable success, as we have seen in the previous section, when it depicted itself as speaking *for lawyers*— as, for instance, when it supported the Law Society's proposal to amend the limitation period for claims against estates. In order to adopt this position it had to be *representative* of the legal profession, and the way it did this was by using the fundamentally important process of consultation.

Contemporaries had absolutely no doubt about the significance of consultation in the early Law Commission's activities. Gower described it as 'vital',[58] and Marsh went so far as suggesting that 'the techniques of consultation which the Law Commissions have developed are at least as important as the actual reforms which they have proposed'.[59] As the Commission explained in its *First Annual Report*, it envisaged an integral role for consultation as part of a structural process: the Commission first undertook research, which yielded a working paper, and this paper was then put out for consultation.[60] In the *First Annual Report* this account of the Commission's working methods was preceded by the *caveat* that '[f]rom the outset we have taken the view that it would be inexpedient to lay down hard and fast rules of procedure'.[61] By the *Third Annual Report* the tone had changed: 'Our role in law reform demands research and then consultation', it proclaimed. 'The working paper marks the transition from research to consultation'.[62] This striking self-confidence about the demands of the Law Commission's role had a certain irony, for the *Third Annual Report* highlighted that the attractive simplicity of the binary model under which the Commission worked up its ideas first, before bringing in external consultees later, was already starting to unravel. Thus, the project on personal injury damages had involved circulating a paper 'to a limited number of experts' which was then being developed into a working paper; the project on appurtenant rights to land had made use of 'a consultative group of lawyers and surveyors with expert knowledge', whose responses to preparatory studies would inform a forthcoming working paper; and the land registration project had also undertaken an extraordinarily wide consultation in advance of producing a working paper.[63] Consultation was becoming all-pervasive.

It is also clear that the Commission regarded consultation as having a substantive contribution to make—it was never a case of simply going through the formal motions for the sake of appearances. The point is made negatively in *Proposals to Abolish Certain Ancient Criminal Offences*, where the obsolescence of the offences proposed for abolition led the Commission to explain that 'their abolition, as now proposed, is more akin to statute law revision than to law reform. It is for this reason that the Commission has not thought it necessary to consult the profession formally on the proposal'.[64] In other words, it was only where consultation had something to add that it would be undertaken.

---

[58] Gower, n 27 above, 262.
[59] Marsh, n 31 above, 278.
[60] Law Commission, LC 4, *First Annual Report* (1966) paras 15–16.
[61] ibid para 14.
[62] Law Commission, LC 15, *Third Annual Report* (1968) para 4.
[63] ibid paras 18, 29 and 34 respectively.
[64] Law Commission, LC 3, *Proposals to Abolish Certain Ancient Criminal Offences* (1966) para 7. The sentence went on to report that there had been 'informal reference' to the profession.

What consultation did add varied across the range of projects. Sometimes its contribution could be modest yet subtle. A good example can be seen by comparing
the Commission's working paper on powers of the Court of Appeal to sit in private in legitimacy proceedings with its report on the same subject.[65] The substantive proposals and arguments of principle advanced in support of those proposals
were essentially the same in both documents. But the report gave a sense of being
grounded in practicalities, which the working paper lacked; for instance, it drew on
judges' impressions of the 'acute and stultifying embarrassment' of parties who were
required to give evidence about their sexual behaviour in open court, and proposed
making use of the Bar Library to disseminate judgments on important points of principle that had been delivered in closed proceedings.[66] Consultees' approval might
also be relied on as, in itself, an additional reason to proceed with a reform. As we
saw earlier, as part of its strategy to minimise assertions of its own (fragile) authority, the Commission attributed the initiative for its proposals to reform the rules on
root of title to freehold land to the conveyancing profession; when conveyancers
responded positively to the consultation paper this was, in itself, a strong reason to
implement the proposal.[67]

Perhaps the most powerful illustrations of the centrality of consultation,
however, could be seen where the consultation process changed the substantive content of reform proposals. In its project on restrictive covenants, for instance, the
Commission had initially proposed abolishing the need to register such covenants
affecting unregistered land on the Land Charges Register; it had also proposed
allowing the legal member of the Lands Tribunal to adjudicate on the validity of
restrictive covenants.[68] Both proposals were abandoned following consultation.[69]
More dramatically, the consultation process might persuade the Commission to
abstain from intervention altogether, as occurred with its *Interim Report on Distress
for Rent*.[70]

It was not necessary to read beyond the second page of this report to find out
what the Commission thought of a landlord's right to seize his tenant's goods to
satisfy a demand for rent: distress was 'a relic of feudalism', and the self-help remedy 'an obvious anachronism'.[71] Readers of these opening pages must have felt
that they could see what was coming. But then the mood shifted, as the Commission recounted the results of its extensive consultations, which showed that '[t]here
is no evidence that wrongful distress is at all widespread'; that there was 'little

[65] Law Commission, LC WP 2, *Law Commission's Draft Proposals on Powers of the Court of Appeal to Sit in Private and Restrictions upon Publicity in Legitamacy [sic] Proceedings* (1966); Law Commission, LC 8, *Report on the Powers of Appeal Courts to Sit in Private and the Restrictions upon Publicity in Domestic Proceedings* (1966).
[66] LC 8, n 65 above, paras 11 and 24 respectively.
[67] Law Commission, LC 9, *Transfer of Land: Interim Report on Root of Title to Freehold Land* (1966) para 34.
[68] Law Commission, LC WP 3, *Restrictive Covenants* (1966) paras 8(ii)–(iii) and 22 respectively.
[69] Law Commission, LC 11, *Transfer of Land: Report on Restrictive Covenants* (1967) 18 and 24–25 respectively.
[70] Law Commission, LC 5, *Landlord and Tenant: Interim Report on Distress for Rent* (1966).
[71] ibid para 5.

indication' of the threat of distraint being abused, and that 'the practice of most landlords [was] to stay their hand'.[72] Landlords, indeed, deserved more sympathetic treatment, said the report, since, unlike other creditors, they were forced to continue giving credit until they could recover possession of the premises.[73] What was needed, the Commission concluded, was a better system of remedies; but, pending that, and 'in view of the state of opinion emerging', the remedy of distress should be retained.[74] Here, then, consultation had been determinative, and it is worthwhile pausing for a moment to register quite how powerful its effects had been. For, if ever a legal doctrine invited sweeping, ideologically-inspired abolition by a left-leaning law reform agency, surely it was distress for rent. It needed very little imagination to see this doctrine as dramatising, and furthering, the effects of unequal distribution of wealth, yet the Law Commission was making very clear that it was not partisan: it had its views, of course (which were expressed at the start of the report), but the responses and experiences of consultees could dissuade the Commission from following its instincts.

## VI

If the Commission's publications give ample illustrations of the importance and influence of consultation, they are perhaps less forthcoming in explaining its significance. Why was it, exactly, that the Commission had felt able to assert, in its *Third Annual Report*, that its 'role ... demands ... consultation'?[75] Some rationales can, perhaps, be inferred from the use of consultation in the Commission's reports, but more explicit discussions can be found in lectures given by the first Commissioners, particularly by the Commission's first Chairman, Lord Scarman. Scarman gave a series of lectures in Canada in the autumn of 1967;[76] in a chilling reminder of the limitations of in-flight entertainment of that era, he told one lecture audience that he had spent the journey pondering the ambiguities in the following sentence: 'That fellow Thomas, whenever he met his uncle in the street, he removed his hat'.[77] He had also, evidently, been thinking about the Law Commission's operations, and about the functions of consultation. He told his audience in Manitoba that 'consultation is vital'. 'It means', he explained:

[K]eeping in touch with the social realities around us, finding out what interested people want, finding out their criticisms and their views, going to the practising profession, seeing where the shoe pinches, seeing what's wrong and how it can be put right.[78]

---

[72] ibid paras 14–15.
[73] ibid para 18.
[74] ibid para 24.
[75] Law Commission, LC 15, *Third Annual Report* (1968) para 4.
[76] ibid para 95.
[77] L Scarman, 'Law Reform by Legislative Techniques' (1967) 32 *Saskatchewan Law Review* 217, 221.
[78] L Scarman, 'Law Reform—Lessons from English Experience' (1968–69) 3 *Manitoba Law Journal* 47, 58.

'Controversy disappears', he added, 'largely in the process of consultation'.[79] In Western Ontario, a rather more muted account of the benefits of consultation was offered:

> [P]rovided the Law Commission remains aware of its limitations as a specialist body it can make a valuable contribution to the resolution of social problems ... through the processes of consultation and research, as a medium for the collection and assimilation of information gleaned from other fields such as the social and economic sciences.[80]

Scarman was back in North America in 1971, when he put forward a rather different justification for consultation in the *American Bar Association Journal*: 'The Law Commission sees the ultimate object of the elaborate process of consultation as assisting Parliament on matters often of great technical detail which can seldom be adequately investigated in the course of Parliamentary debate.'[81] A year later, in the pages of the *Anglo-American Law Review*, he offered his most elaborate account:

> I have already mentioned one of the advantages of open consultation: it enables the layman's voice to be heard in the process of law reform and it ensures that the Commission's first tentative proposals are subject to the criticism of those who know where the shoe pinches. But consultation offers other advantages. It helps to dispose of possible misconceptions regarding the possible effects of the Commission's proposals and thus improves the chance of our recommendations, when finally put forward, being acceptable to a large section of the informed public. Further, it helps to stimulate interest in law reform. And last, but not the least of the advantages of open consultation: it helps the legislature in the field of law reform. The Law Commission is an advisory body and if it is to render effective assistance to Parliament it must consult widely and set out in its final report the scope and nature of the consultation.[82]

What is immediately striking about these passages is their shifting contents and emphases—Scarman did not have one simple, stable rationale in mind that underpinned the Commission's commitment to consultation. In effect he describes a cluster of substantively and functionally distinct techniques having in common only the formal procedures of consultation. To take the narrowest first: consultation as a method of casting light on technical details calls for the involvement of specialists, typically professionals but not necessarily lawyers, whose expertise gives them a heightened alertness to the likely consequences and side-effects of reforms. An illustration of this kind of consultation at work can be seen in *Blood Tests and the Proof of Paternity in Civil Proceedings*, where the Commission withdrew its earlier suggestion that the law should permit a person to refuse a blood test on health grounds, because medical respondents to the working paper had said that blood tests posed

---

[79] ibid.
[80] L Scarman, 'The Work of the Law Commission for England and Wales' (1969) 8 *University of Western Ontario Law Review* 33, 41.
[81] L Scarman, 'Inside the English Law Commission' (1971) 57 *American Bar Association Journal* 867, 869.
[82] L Scarman, 'The Law Commission' (1972) 1 *Anglo-American Law Review* 31, 36.

no risk to health.[83] Crucially, what makes this kind of consultation valuable is that it is targeted at experts.

Broader, more representative consultation had different merits. Scarman spoke of 'keeping in touch with the social realities',[84] just as the *First Annual Report* had claimed that 'whenever any proposed reform of the law originates from social or economic considerations or is likely to have social or economic consequences, it is imperative to consult with those qualified to speak for the social and economic interests concerned'.[85] The *Interim Report on Distress for Rent* provided a model example here, having involved 'Government Departments which have proprietary interests, housing authorities, professional bodies, and organizations representing landlords on the one hand and tenants on the other'.[86] For this kind of consultation to be valuable, it was essential to involve representatives of all those potentially affected by the reform.

A third form of consultation practised by the Commission involved a hybrid of the two forms already discussed. This consultation of representative groups of specialists was particularly useful to the Commission in its dealings with lawyers. Two of the first Commissioners expressed in print the view that the greatest obstacle to law reform was often lawyers themselves,[87] and it is tempting to see the Commission's strenuous efforts to involve the legal profession, to flatter it, to defer to it, and to publicise reform projects in the legal press as a way of managing an inherently conservative and potentially hostile group. Thus, when Gower wrote that 'The main reason [for consultation] is that if all those who think they ought to be consulted have not had an opportunity of objecting, they will take umbrage when the report is presented and be sure to raise objections then', we might suspect that he had primarily in mind lawyers, whom he described a couple of pages later as 'react[ing] violently against changes in their professional organization and methods'.[88] The pomposity, self-importance and pettiness that his description implied was hardly a compliment, and we can only speculate about how he endured consultative events like the 'widely representative Seminar on Administrative Law, organised by All Souls College' in December 1966.[89] Connoisseurs of irony can enjoy the conjunction of 'widely representative' and All Souls College under the Wardenship of John Sparrow,[90] and the event in many ways enacts the contradictory impulses underlying the Commission's

---

[83] Law Commission, LC 16, *Blood Tests and the Proof of Paternity in Civil Proceedings* (1968) para 40; the earlier proposal was made in Law Commission, LC WP 12, *Family Law Proof of Paternity in Civil Proceedings* (1967) para 36.

[84] Scarman, n 78 above, 58.

[85] Law Commission, LC 4, *First Annual Report* (1966) para 16.

[86] Law Commission, LC 5, *Landlord and Tenant: Interim Report on Distress for Rent* (1966) para 8.

[87] Marsh, n 31 above, 264; Gower, n 27 above, 266.

[88] Gower, n 27 above, 262–63, 266. The sweeping nature of this judgement does not seem to be borne out by, for instance, the conveyancing profession's response to the Commission's proposals to halve the period for root of title (see above, text at nn 39–44).

[89] Law Commission, LC 20, *Administrative Law* (1969) para 2.

[90] J Lowe, *The Warden: A Portrait of John Sparrow* (London, HarperCollins, 1999) gives a sympathetic account of Sparrow. Stefan Collini's review, 'From Bar to Bar-room Floor' *Times Higher Education Supplement* (18 January 1999) gives an invaluable account of the book's value and limitations.

consultation exercises. For this seminar was 'widely representative' only in the narrow sense of bringing together 'a number of lawyers and administrators'[91]—no further information was given as to who had been invited, or why they were considered to be representative—and there is nothing to suggest that any section of the public *affected* by administrative law attended. Viewed as an exercise in 'keeping in touch with social realities' the exercise was a failure; but seen in terms of embracing those interest groups who were articulate, organised and powerful enough to derail future proposals, one could not fault its strategy.

Finally, we might turn to consider why the Law Commission set such store by consultation. Was it really, as Gower argued, little more than a strategy for drawing out the sting of opposition before the proposals reached a delicate stage? My sense is that there was more to it, and that the Law Commission regarded consultation as giving its proposals an authority and legitimacy that they would otherwise have lacked. One clue is in the form of words used by Leslie Scarman, that enthusiast for ambiguity, when he spoke of consultation being valuable because 'it helps the legislature in the field of law reform'.[92] Helps it to do what? The obvious answer is: to do what legislatures do—legislate. 'The assistance will be ineffective', he wrote, 'unless on the face of the report the scope and nature of the consultation are clearly set out'.[93] Again, we might ask why this should make a difference if the primary aim of consultation is to anticipate objections? The success of that more cynical strategy had to be judged by its results (the neutralisation of objections) not by the quality of the consultation. The answer must be that Scarman envisaged that Parliament should use the evidence of consultation as a *reason* to legislate. The Commission itself captured the potential symmetry between consultation and parliamentary decision-making in the sentence used as an epigraph to this chapter: 'It is our hope that those amendments will be as acceptable to Parliament as they have been to those whom we have consulted'.[94] Consultation was so important because it was a mimesis of democratic decision-making.

## VII

At exactly the same time that the Law Commission was being created, Michel Foucault was writing *Les Mots et Les Choses*, a work in which he explored, among many other issues, questions about the authority and authorship of texts. One commentator has paraphrased part of Foucault's concerns in a way that is particularly suggestive for this chapter: it was, he said, 'the importance of always asking of a text, "Who is speaking? (who—from what historical position, with what particular interests—is claiming the authority to be listened to?)"'[95] As we have seen,

[91] Law Commission, LC WP 13, *Exploratory Working Paper on Administrative Law* (1967) para 2.
[92] Scarman, n 82 above, 36.
[93] Scarman, n 81 above, 869.
[94] Law Commission and Scottish Law Commission, LC 11A and SLC 6A, *Sea Fisheries (Shellfish) Bill: Report on the Consolidation of Certain Enactments Relating to Shellfish Fisheries and Shellfish* (1967) 5.
[95] G Gutting, *Foucault: A Very Short Introduction* (Oxford, OUP, 2005) 12.

trying to think about this question in respect of the texts created by the early Law Commission gives a peculiarly rich and complex answer, for the circumstances of the Commission—as a newly-created, unrepresentative, advisory body operating in a sphere already densely populated by well-established, organised, authoritative and articulate actors—drove it in search of strategies that would lend its operations and proposals persuasive power. The success of those proposals, and the longevity of the Commission itself, reflect the sophistication, imagination and ingenuity of the strategies it chose.

# 5

# *Fifty Years of Law Reform—A Note on the Northern Ireland Style*

NEIL FARIS[*]

## I FIFTY YEARS AGO?

Possibly, at the time, there was a *Guardian* reader in the Northern Ireland Cabinet Secretariat. Its 'law reform' files are held in the Public Record Office of Northern Ireland (PRONI)[1] and the first file[2] opens with a neatly-pasted 18-inch column from the paper's edition of 20 October 1964: 'Many Law Reforms Expected'. This extolled the law reforming ambitions of the new Labour administration, especially Lord Gardiner's scheme for new law reform machinery.

The Attorney-General for Northern Ireland, and the Stormont Parliamentary Draftsmen, seized on these proposals with a fair degree of dynamism. There is substantial archival material held by PRONI dealing with the consideration of the matter by the Northern Ireland law officers, the Cabinet Secretariat and the Ministers of the then Northern Ireland Government (albeit no record of any consultation outside those circles) and there is not space in this essay to do any justice to that.[3] But a brief summary can be given.

In correspondence and memoranda between these Law Officers and the Minister of Home Affairs, they canvassed proposals for Northern Ireland and argued in particular for a 'Law Commissioner for Northern Ireland'.[4] Papers were prepared

---

[*] I was Commissioner in the Northern Ireland Law Commission from 2008–12. The views here expressed are solely my own and cannot be taken to represent the Commission—even if it still exists, which, as I suggest later in this essay, is moot. I also gratefully acknowledge help from George Woodman, formerly Librarian at the Northern Ireland Assembly, who has informed my understanding of the various documents, Cabinet re-shuffles and Stormont personalities of the 1960s. I also gratefully acknowledge Brian Garrett, Solicitor of Belfast, who has laboured to achieve law reform for Northern Ireland over the past 50 years and who has helpfully discussed these matters with me. Dr Shona Wilson Stark and Ronan Cormacain have kindly commented on a draft of this essay. Responsibility rests with me.

[1] I gratefully acknowledge the agreement of the Deputy Keeper of Records of the Public Record Office of Northern Ireland to cite the relevant records in this essay.

[2] PRONI CAB/9B/241/1.

[3] For more detail on this and other areas touched upon in this essay, see SW Stark and N Faris, 'Law Reform in Northern Ireland: Cheshire Cat or Potemkin Commission?' forthcoming October 2016 *Public Law*.

[4] Letter from the Attorney-General to the First Parliamentary Draftsman, 18 January 1965, PRONI CAB/9B/241/2A.

for the Northern Ireland Cabinet proposing there should be such an officer with a degree of independence to match the Law Commission being established in London. But this met with resistance, first from the then Lord Chief Justice of Northern Ireland, Lord MacDermott (who was reported to be 'lukewarm' about the project)[5] and particularly from Ministers in the Northern Ireland Cabinet for a variety of reasons, briefly summarised as follows:

— Some were reluctant that work could be taken from their ministries. Perhaps there was a degree of ministerial rivalry as the proposed Law Commissioner would formally be under the aegis of the Minister of Home Affairs who put forward the proposal to the Cabinet.
— There was also a view that such law reform as was needed could be adequately carried out as part of each ministry's work: this was indignantly repudiated by the First Parliamentary Draftsman who expressed himself in pungent terms on the indifference to any law reform of the various ministries.
— Finally, there was a suspicion abroad in the Cabinet that an independent officer reporting directly to the Stormont Parliament could cause embarrassment to Ministers by reporting adversely on the work of their ministries.

But an olive branch was offered: it was agreed that a new law reform unit could be created within the Parliamentary Draftsmen's Office. This would be headed by a 'Director of Law Reform' and the Second Parliamentary Draftsman was already ear-marked for the role. It was also agreed that the status of the Director would be that of a civil servant of senior status but carefully stipulated to be subordinate to the Permanent Secretary of the Ministry of Finance. Thus there would be no danger of 'embarrassing' reports being issued.

That compromise ended for almost half a century the prospects for commissioner-led independent law reform in Northern Ireland.

## II DIRECTOR AND OFFICE OF LAW REFORM

The arrangements persisted (with some modifications) until the formation of the Northern Ireland Law Commission (NILC) in 2007. One modification arose in the arrangements for the 'power-sharing' executive of 1974. Sir Oliver Napier (as the leader of the Alliance Party of Northern Ireland—and a prominent Belfast solicitor) had the post of Legal Member of the Executive and Head of the Office of Law Reform but the remit of the Office was confined to civil law with responsibility for criminal law residing in the Northern Ireland Office. Then under 'direct rule' from mid-1974 onwards, the Office of Law Reform was placed within the Department of Finance and Personnel where it continued until its demise on the formation of the NILC in 2007.

In the late 1980s, it was the Law Society of Northern Ireland who took the initiative to point out the lack of any independent element for law reform within Northern

---

[5] Letter from the Attorney-General to the Minister of Home Affairs, 9 March 1965, PRONI CAB/9B/241/2A.

Ireland. (There were no standing committees for any aspect of law reform within Northern Ireland.) The representations led to the formation of the Law Reform Advisory Committee for Northern Ireland in March 1989[6] chaired by a High Court Judge, with volunteer members from both branches of the legal profession and the universities as well as a lay member, with a secretary and some research and administrative services from the Office of Law Reform.[7]

Further historical detail is contained in the research report by Brice Dickson and Michael Hamilton published in March 2000, *Re-forming Law Reform in Northern Ireland*, forming part of the Review of Criminal Justice.[8]

### III THE ROLE OF THE LAW COMMISSION OF ENGLAND AND WALES

One should not overlook the role that the Law Commission in London played in regard to law reform in Northern Ireland in the period until the inception of the NILC. This is because section 1(1) of the Law Commissions Act 1965 (the 1965 Act) declared that 'for the purpose of reforming the law' there should be (constituted in accordance with the section) 'a body of Commissioners, to be known as the Law Commission'. Then section 1(5) declared that in the section, '"the law" does not include the law of Scotland or any law of Northern Ireland which the Parliament of Northern Ireland has power to amend'. Thus, the Law Commission in London retained the right to exercise for Northern Ireland its reforming powers in respect of the law of the United Kingdom, other than where the Northern Ireland Parliament could legislate.

This arrangement continued until the formation of the NILC when the legislation constituting the NILC, the Justice (Northern Ireland) Act 2002 (the 2002 Act) specifically limited the remit of the Law Commission under section 1(1) of the 1965 Act to 'the law ... of England and Wales'[9] and repealed section 1(5) of the 1965 Act.[10]

### IV NILC: 2007 TO 2015

I do not purport to speak on behalf of the NILC, and in any case it is for others to judge the success or otherwise of the work of the Commission during my period of office from 2008 to 2012.[11] However, some brief detail on the NILC may be helpful.

---

[6] This was led by Brian Garrett, Solicitor of Belfast, who proposed the matter to the Society's Parliamentary and Law Reform Committee. I was also then a member of the Committee. Further details will be given in the text referred to in n 3 above.

[7] Albeit this was established by decision of the Secretary of State for Northern Ireland, rather than being given a legislative basis as some of us at the time hoped for.

[8] B Dickson and M Hamilton, *Re-forming Law Reform in Northern Ireland* (Belfast, The Stationery Office, 2000) ch 2.

[9] 2002 Act, sch 12 para 8.

[10] 2002 Act, sch 13.

[11] See N Faris, 'Law Commissions—What is the Essence of Their Law Reform Role?' (2014) 2 *IALS Student Law Review* 52.

The original legislative base for the NILC was in sections 50–52 of the 2002 Act. This was an Act enacted by Parliament at Westminster for Northern Ireland because at the time 'direct rule' for Northern Ireland was in place and, even in the event of devolution returning, powers over policing and justice were not at that time in the devolution package—see further below. The 2002 Act established the NILC as a body corporate and the Secretary of State for Northern Ireland had the duty to appoint a Chairman (a High Court judge) and four other Commissioners. Matters took their due course and the relevant provisions of the 2002 Act were commenced on 16 April 2007.[12] The Chairman was appointed in 2007 and the Commissioners were appointed in 2008.

As indicated above, the Secretary of State for Northern Ireland originally had her role, under the 2002 Act, to appoint the Commissioners, since the functions of policing and justice had not been devolved to Northern Ireland. By the time of the commencement of the NILC's work in 2008, the devolved institutions in Northern Ireland, Assembly and Executive, were fully functioning, but the political parties in the Assembly did not agree on the terms for the devolution of policing and justice until 2011. Therefore it was only in 2011 that the relevant powers and duties of the Secretary of State for Northern Ireland were transferred to the new Department of Justice for Northern Ireland (DoJNI) and the 2002 Act was duly amended.[13]

The remit of the NILC was, under section 51 of the 2002 Act, 'to keep under review the law of Northern Ireland'. This included power in respect of reserved or excepted matters (where the Parliament at Westminster retains legislative powers). But the DoJNI was required to consult with the Secretary of State before approving any such project for inclusion in the NILC's programme of work.

This scheme allowed for law reform on a United Kingdom-wide basis to continue by means of agreement on 'joint projects' between the three Commissions (with the requisite governmental approval in each of the jurisdictions). Unfortunately, this is currently jeopardised by reason of the DoJNI's withdrawal of funding and its other measures taken in respect of the NILC which are set out later in this essay.

In any event, the NILC's work from 2008 to 2015 included:

— A major project of reform of Northern Ireland's land law;[14]
— Reform proposals for aspects of Northern Ireland's business tenancy protection law;[15]
— Proposals for protection for vulnerable witnesses in civil litigation;[16]
— Proposals for reform of bail law in criminal proceedings in Northern Ireland;[17]
— A report on unfitness to plead;[18] and
— Review of the law on apartments in Northern Ireland.[19]

---

[12] Justice (Northern Ireland) Act 2002 (Commencement No 12) Order 2007/237.
[13] Northern Ireland Act 1998 (Devolution of Policing and Justice Functions) Order 2010/976.
[14] NILC 8, *Report on Land Law* (2010).
[15] NILC 9, *Report on Business Tenancies* (2011).
[16] NILC 10, *Report on Vulnerable Witnesses in Civil Proceedings* (2011).
[17] NILC 14, *Report on Bail in Criminal Proceedings* (2012).
[18] NILC 16, *Report on Unfitness to Plead* (2013).
[19] NILC 17, *Report on Apartments* (2013).

In addition, the NILC worked with the Commissions in Great Britain on the *Regulation of Health Care Professionals*.[20] The joint electoral law project (with the other Commissions) and the reform of defamation law project are discussed later in this essay.

A Commissioner (or, in certain cases, the Chief Executive) headed the work on each project aided by staff members. The staff members comprised a small number of established legal researchers, some of whom had transferred across from the Office of Law Reform. Each project also had the assistance of a number of junior researchers, recruited directly by the NILC for fixed terms such as three years, generally recent law graduates or postgraduates. The land law project had the benefit of the services of a senior academic consultant, and the NILC also retained from time to time a legislative drafter consultant.

The NILC was served by a Chief Executive, a qualified lawyer, who had also served in senior positions in the Northern Ireland Civil Service. She was a board member of the NILC and its Accounting Officer, responsible to the Northern Ireland Office and then, after devolution of policing and justice, to the DoJNI. The Chief Executive was also Director of Legal Research and led the development of the NILC's programmes of law reform. She was the ultimate line manager for all members of staff and she engaged in the supervision of some of the projects.

While the staff members were all full-time, the Commissioners were all part-time, in the case of two at two days per week and the other two served for one day per week only. In addition, it was originally intended that the Chairman, as High Court Judge, would devote two days per week to the NILC. But early on this was reduced to one day per week, primarily because of pressure on the NILC's budget. In any assessment of the NILC and its work, this 'part-time' element must be taken into account.

It may be thought that the institution of the NILC:

— was a 're-forming'[21] of the law reform institutions of Northern Ireland; and
— subsumed the role and duties of both the Office of Law Reform and the Advisory Committee; and
— had, as its main institutional change, that it was under the wing of, and reported to, first the Northern Ireland Office and then, on the devolution of policing and justice, to the DoJNI instead of the supervision (of the Office of Law Reform) which had been carried out by Department of Finance and Personnel.

However, this view fundamentally misunderstands the particular role that should be performed by a Law Commission (for independent, commissioner-led law reform), as compared with the institutional arrangements for law reform which prevailed in Northern Ireland from 1965 to 2007. I have set out my views on that elsewhere, and will not repeat them here.[22]

---

[20] LC 345, SLC 237, NILC 18 (2014).
[21] Note the hyphen in the title of n 8 above.
[22] See n 11 above.

## V NILC: 2015 ONWARDS

The following statement appeared in the 'Welcome' section of the NILC's website in March 2015:

> The Minister for Justice has decided to reduce significantly funding to [the NILC] from April 2015 in response to budget pressures within [the DoJNI]. This will allow only essential law reform to continue. Until further notice any enquiries should be directed to ...[23]

It does not appear that there is any other public statement relating to this ministerial decision. By the end of March 2015, the NILC had terminated or made alternative arrangements for all its staff and it closed its doors. Only a few projects were in progress at the time of closure and some of the work was transferred to other departments.[24]

Certainly, all departments of the Northern Ireland Executive labour under severe financial pressures.[25] So it is not the purport of this essay to argue for the NILC alone to be ring-fenced. But it is the method of, in effect, usurpation of the NILC into the DoJNI which does require comment, if one believes that all executive power should be exercised under lawful authority.

There are various statutory duties imposed on the DoJNI and on the NILC under the 2002 Act; I give some examples:

— There is to be a body corporate known as the Northern Ireland Law Commission:[26] can such body corporate properly reside as a mere contact point within the DoJNI?

— The NILC is to consist of a Chairman (who holds the office of High Court judge) and four Commissioners all to be appointed by the DoJNI:[27] a Chairman has apparently been appointed—though without any public announcement (see further below). There are currently no appointments of Commissioners.

— The NILC must keep under review the law of Northern Ireland:[28] how can that statutory task be performed within the DoJNI in accordance with the terms of the 2002 Act?

— The NILC is to prepare law reform programmes for approval of the DoJNI:[29] how can any further programme be prepared for adoption from April 2015 onwards?

---

[23] The contact details of the DoJNI 'Strategy and Secretariat Branch' are given, including the email: 'NILC@dojni.x.gsi.gov.uk'.

[24] The project on defamation law reform, as to whether Northern Ireland should enact legislation along the lines of the reform contained in the Defamation Act 2013, is in a particular limbo.

[25] See DoJNI, 'Ford Outlines Cuts to Justice Budget', 3 December 2014, www.dojni.gov.uk/index/media-centre/news-archive/december-2014/ford-outlines-cuts-to-justice-budget.htm, which reports that the starting point in the Department's 2015–16 Budget was 15.1% lower than the previous year's provision—amounting to a budget cut of £164m.

[26] 2002 Act, s 50(1).

[27] 2002 Act, s 50(2) and (3).

[28] 2002 Act, s 51(1).

[29] 2002 Act, s 51(2)(b). The *First Programme of Law Reform* (2009) ran from 1 June 2009–31 March 2011. NILC 11, *Second Programme of Law Reform* (2012) ran from May 2012–March 2015. In NILC, *Annual Report for the Year Ended 31 March 2014* (2014) it is recorded that preparation for a third programme began during the year and positive proposals were received from Northern Ireland departments in response to the initial call for proposals: 3.

— The NILC must make an annual report on the performance of its duties and present annual accounts;[30] the Annual Report for the year ended 31 March 2015 was issued in September 2015 (the 2015 Annual Report), signed by the then sole surviving Commissioner. (His term of office has since expired.) How then can any further annual reports be issued and how can annual accounts be properly prepared and delivered by the NILC?

There are also particular legal problems in regard to the NILC's current projects.

First, the review of defamation law project is in serious difficulty. The project originated in a request from the Department of Finance & Personnel (the DFP) on 23 November 2013 that the NILC should examine whether the Defamation Act 2013 should be extended to Northern Ireland. The request was approved by the Minister of Justice on 7 January 2014 and the project included in the NILC's work programme. However, the NILC's work had not proceeded beyond the preparation and issue of a consultation paper,[31] with submissions to be made by 20 February 2015. The NILC in current circumstances is not in a position to formulate any proposals on defamation law reform. Accordingly, there cannot be any report from the NILC to be laid before the Assembly. The 2015 Annual Report states that the NILC provided a summary of the responses to the consultation to the DFP 'who will progress through to the final stages of the project as appropriate'.[32]

Second, there are wide ranging complications for the future of the electoral law reform project. This is being carried out as a joint project of the Law Commissions in Great Britain and the NILC: a joint consultation paper was issued on 9 December 2014 with submissions to be made by 31 March 2015, and on 4 February 2016 a joint interim report on Electoral Law was published by the three Commissions.[33] An associated press release referred to Mr Justice Maguire as Chairman of the NILC. However, there is no announcement of his appointment on the NILC website, nor has the DoJNI issued any press release on its website to announce the appointment. Curiouser and curiouser.[34]

A further issue is that, the NILC apart, the DoJNI does not have any statutory responsibility or vires for law reform in Northern Ireland. That is because, as indicated above, under the previous arrangements for law reform in Northern Ireland, responsibility for civil law reform resided with the Department of Finance and Personnel and responsibility for criminal law reform resided with the Northern Ireland Office. Under the arrangements for the devolution of policing and justice to Northern Ireland, responsibility for the NILC devolved to the DoJNI but it did not assume any other role or responsibility for law reform as such.[35] Thus, unless the NILC is duly constituted, it appears to me that the DoJNI has no proper role in the conduct of law reform for Northern Ireland and, of course, if the NILC is duly constituted,

[30] 2002 Act, s 51(5) and sch 9 para 6.
[31] NILC 19, *Consultation Paper: Defamation Law in Northern Ireland* (2014).
[32] NILC, *Annual Report for the Year Ended 31 March 2015*, 9.
[33] Law Commission, Scottish Law Commission and NILC, LC CP 218, SLC DP 158, NILC 20, *Electoral Law: A Joint Consultation Paper* (2014); Law Commission, Scottish Law Commission and NILC, *Electoral Law: A Joint Interim Report* (2016).
[34] *cf* chapter 35 (Sir David Lloyd Jones).
[35] See n 3 above.

then the role of the DoJNI is simply that as set out in the 2002 Act as amended. I cannot solve these various conundrums but make the following final comments.

## A Pre-emption of Parliament

Could the DoJNI be lawfully acting under a Northern Ireland version of the doctrine of 'pre-emption of Parliament' where 'the interests of efficient and cost-effective public administration require that the Government pre-empt Parliament by undertaking preparatory work in anticipation of a bill becoming law'?[36] However, I cannot see that any version of the doctrine could apply, given there is no Bill before the Northern Ireland Assembly on the topic and the Minister has not evinced any intention to promote such a Bill.[37]

## B The Belfast Agreement

The proposal for independent commissioner-led law reform in Northern Ireland had its origins in the *Belfast Agreement*.[38] This, among very many other matters of course, obliged the UK Government to carry out a 'wide ranging review of criminal justice ... through a mechanism with an independent element'.[39] That resulted in the *Review of the Criminal Justice System in Northern Ireland*,[40] which, among many other recommendations, proposed that:

> [A] Law Commission for Northern Ireland be established by statute to keep under review criminal and civil law, including practice and procedure and to make recommendations to Government on whatever changes it considers necessary or desirable.[41]

Under Article 2 of the related British–Irish Agreement[42] 'the two governments affirm their solemn commitment to support, and where appropriate implement, the provisions of the ... Agreement'. Thus the enactment by Parliament of the 2002 Act was in pursuance of this element of the Belfast Agreement.

So it is a moot point—and may turn out to be a political one in the Northern Ireland Assembly—as to whether the Minister for Justice may on his own motion, or the Assembly by legislation, dismantle, by termination of the NILC, this particular part of the justice structures erected pursuant to the Belfast Agreement.

---

[36] House of Lords Select Committee on the Constitution, *The Pre-emption of Parliament* (HL 2012–13, 165) 4.

[37] Even though a Justice Bill was at the time before the Northern Ireland Assembly and opportunity could have been taken to amend or repeal the NILC provisions in the 2002 Act.

[38] *The Belfast Agreement: An Agreement reached at the Multi-Party Talks on Northern Ireland* (Cm 3883, 1998).

[39] ibid strand 3, 'Policing and Justice' para 5.

[40] Criminal Justice Review Group (2000).

[41] ibid para 244. The Review based its recommendations on n 8 above.

[42] Done at Belfast on 10 April 1998.

## C 'Warm Storage'

There is an argument that, in the undoubtedly fraught financial circumstances, it is more politic for the future survival of the NILC not to seek its legislative abolition, but to be in a position to revive it as soon as the financial position improves. Of course, that could be achieved in legislation suspending the NILC's work with proper transitional arrangements and provision for the DoJNI by Order to commence again the work of the NILC in happier times.

That seems to me to be a more proper way to proceed, rather than ministerial protective custody of Northern Ireland's law reformers.

# 6

# *Working on the Larger Canvas—Law Reform in a Federal System: Thoughts on Forty Years of the Australian Law Reform Commission*

KATHRYN CRONIN

The Australian Law Reform Commission (ALRC) is one agency in a 'crowded field' of Australian law reformers[1] which includes permanent, semi-permanent and ad hoc commissions, committees and inquiries charged with examining and recommending reform of Commonwealth and state laws. I served for a time as a Commissioner and Deputy President of the ALRC, but also spent some six years closer to the coal face of law making, in the role of counsel assigned to assist the Joint Standing Committee on Migration in the Australian federal Parliament. The Standing Committee had oversight and scrutiny of the drafting and implementation of immigration regulations. My experience in these two roles highlighted the particular role of a Law Commission working in a federal system and aptly demonstrated the real need for law reformers to focus on delegated legislation which now forms so much of a working legal discourse. I feature these two themes in turn.

The ALRC was established in 1975 as one of the last reforms introduced by the Whitlam Labour Government. As that inauguration date makes clear, 2015 marked the ALRC's fortieth anniversary. The ALRC was the second Australian Law Reform Commission to be established. The New South Wales Law Reform Commission began advising on laws in its state jurisdiction in 1966. In subsequent years—and for varying terms—there were Law Reform Commissions in each of the Australian states and the Northern Territory. The Law Commission of England and Wales was the model, but not the exact template, for all of these Law Commissions.

---

[1] D Weisbrot, 'The Future for Institutional Law Reform' in B Opeskin and D Weisbrot (eds), *The Promise of Law Reform* (Sydney, Federation Press, 2005) 20. See also R Sackville, 'Law Reform Agencies and Royal Commissions: Toiling in the Same Field?' [2005] *Federal Judicial Scholarship* 10. The additional law reform agencies include the National Health and Medical Research Council, ad hoc Legislation Review Committees, the Australian Human Rights and Equal Opportunity Commission and the Productivity Commission whose law reform reports range from gambling, to disability care and support, to international trade, and to climate change.

Justice Sackville (of the Federal Court) speaking at the ALRC's thirtieth anniversary symposium on 'Law Reform Agencies and Royal Commissions: Toiling in the Same Field?'[2] noted the five characteristics, apart from their focus on law reform, shared by Australia's law reform agencies: they are permanent statutory bodies; they consult widely among interest groups and provide opportunities for community participation in shaping reform proposals; much of their work is carried out in public and, in particular, their reports are tabled in Parliament; they are independent, in the sense that their members exercise their own judgement in weighing up policy issues and formulate recommendations free from governmental interference or direction; and since their members are appointed and their programmes are largely determined by elected governments, and since implementation of their recommendations usually requires legislation, the agencies enjoy a degree of democratic legitimacy. Those characteristics could be said to apply to all Commonwealth Law Reform Commissions.

As this chapter focuses on the work of the ALRC, it is important to note the federal context within which it works. The Commonwealth of Australia Constitution Act 1900 outlines specific powers given to the federal Parliament by the states—some of which are exercised exclusively by the federal Parliament but many are exercised concurrently with the states.[3] Thus the federal Parliament has power to legislate concerning, for example:

— external affairs;
— trade and commerce with other countries;
— taxation;
— postal, telegraphic, telephonic and similar services;
— marriage/divorce/matrimonial causes (including the custody and guardianship of children);
— foreign corporations, and trading or financial corporations formed within the limits of the Commonwealth;
— military defence;
— citizenship and immigration;
— pensions;
— 'special laws' for people of any race;
— copyright, patents and trademarks;
— banking and insurance (other than state banking and insurance); and
— the conciliation and arbitration of industrial disputes.

Where subjects are not specifically allocated as powers to the federal Parliament, these 'residual' powers lie in state jurisdiction. Thus the states retained power to make laws concerning law and order, education, housing, child care, public health and social welfare issues. The Constitution Act provided that if in areas of concurrent jurisdiction the state and federal laws are inconsistent (such that it is impossible to obey both laws) the federal laws prevail over state law and, to the extent of the

---

[2] Sackville, n 1 above.
[3] Commonwealth of Australia Constitution Act 1900, ss 51–52.

inconsistency, the state law is invalid.[4] These constitutional provisions point to some of the complexities of law reform in a federal system.

The ALRC was established as an independent statutory authority with a mandate to provide the federal Attorney-General (the Minister responsible for the ALRC) with reports on law reform. It is responsible to Parliament through the Attorney-General. The ALRC President, full- and part-time Commissioners are appointed by the Attorney-General. The candidates for these posts are generally judges, academics or senior administrators. Certain of the Commissioners are chosen because of their particular expertise in the subject matter of a reference.

The ALRC's role and functions are now set down in the Australian Law Reform Commission Act 1996 (Cth) (the ALRC Act), the Financial Management and Accountability Act 1997 (Cth) and the Public Service Act 1999 (Cth). Unlike the Law Commission of England and Wales, the ALRC cannot self-initiate an inquiry. It has been, and remains, dependent on references from the Attorney-General. While certain of the Commission's early reports were nominated by government departments other than the Attorney-General's, this was rare, and the vast bulk of ALRC work concerns matters within the Attorney-General's ministerial brief. While the Attorney-General chooses the reference, once an inquiry has been assigned to the ALRC the government has no capacity to direct the Commission on its performance, functions, findings or recommendations.

The primary function of the ALRC, as set out in section 21 of the ALRC Act, is to report to the Attorney-General on the results of any review of Commonwealth laws relevant to those matters referred by the Attorney-General for the purposes of 'systematically developing and reforming the law' and to include in the report its recommendations. The ALRC is required to undertake its review by:

— bringing the law into line with current conditions and ensuring that it meets current needs;
— removing defects in the law;
— simplifying the law;
— adopting new or more effective methods for administering the law and dispensing justice; and
— providing improved access to justice.

Once tasked with a review, the ALRC is required to consider proposals for making or consolidating Commonwealth laws, and must consider proposals for: the repeal of obsolete or unnecessary laws; uniformity between state and territory laws; and complementary Commonwealth, state and territory laws with reference to those matters referred to it. In the context of Australia's federal jurisdiction, the ALRC's brief requires it to work on an Australia-wide legal canvas but to maintain oversight of relevant state and territory laws.

The ALRC is also required by section 24 of the ALRC Act to ensure that proposed laws and recommendations do not trespass unduly on personal rights and liberties or

---

[4] Commonwealth of Australia Constitution Act 1900, s 109.

make the rights and liberties of citizens unduly dependent on administrative, rather than judicial decisions; to have regard to any relevant international obligations; and as far as practicable, to take into account the potential impact of its recommendations on the costs of getting access to and dispensing justice and the persons and businesses affected by the recommendations (including the economic effects). The Law Reform Commission Act 1973 (Cth), which set the functions for the ALRC at its inception, also noted in section 7(b) the requirement to bring Australian law and practice as far as practicable in conformity with the standards set by the UN International Covenant on Civil and Political Rights. As this was the first Australian statutory reference to this human rights instrument, Michael Kirby, the first ALRC Chair, remarked that '[i]nternational human rights law had at last reached Australia in a practical way'.[5]

The broad framework provided to the ALRC allows for references on topics ranging from the specifically legal or forensic, such as the civil admiralty jurisdiction, marine insurance or uniform evidence law, costs shifting in litigation or client legal privilege in federal investigations to more wide-ranging inquiries addressing issues such as gene patenting and human health or equality before the law for women, children, indigenous communities, the old or the disabled. As detailed below, much of the ALRC's work has had a wide-ranging rather than a particular statutory focus.

Michael Kirby (later a Justice of the High Court) was Chair of the ALRC from 1975 until 1984. Along with co-Commissioners he was responsible for the nine-year study, the *Recognition of Aboriginal Customary Laws*.[6] This respected and much cited study set the model for the ALRC's wider reports and its procedures. Kirby's approach to law reform in practice was, as he has said, 'significantly different from overseas commissions'.[7] His objective was to provide, through the processes of consultation, an 'institutional voice' for those beyond 'the big end of town', particularly 'the poor and the powerless',[8] to take the ideas to the public, and ensure that all the public was included; and to develop recommendations for reform in accord with international human rights law.[9]

When undertaking the Aboriginal customary law reference, the Commission nominated for appointment by the Attorney-General a group of honorary consultants, including knowledgeable Aborigines and other experts in the relevant disciplines, who were to provide advice on the legal, social, administrative and anthropological issues. This tradition of appointing honorary consultants, advisory committees or expert panels has been followed in many later ALRC inquiries. In addition the

---

[5] M Kirby, 'The ALRC — A Winning Formula' (2003) 82 *Reform* 58, 60.

[6] ALRC 31 (1996).

[7] M Kirby, 'ALRC, Law Reform and Equal Justice under Law', ALRC's 25th Anniversary Dinner (2000). This address was cited by Rosalind Croucher, President of the ALRC, in the Michael Kirby Lecture, 'Re-imagining Law Reform—Michael Kirby's Vision, Human Rights and the Australian Law Reform Commission in the 21st Century' (2015).

[8] Kirby, n 7 above.

[9] See I Freckelton and H Selby (eds), *Appealing to the Future: Michael Kirby and His Legacy* (Sydney, Thomson Reuters, 2009) 14. In the introduction to this study marking Justice Kirby's retirement from the High Court in 2009, Freckelton said that 'law reform Kirby-style was different'. It was 'more inclusive, more energetic and with a broader vision'.

Commission examining customary law used interdisciplinary and field research and investigations, had extensive discussions with anthropologists, sociologists, historians, judges, lawyers, magistrates and the police, with Aboriginal communities, many individual Aborigines, and organisations such as the Aboriginal legal services, Aboriginal child care agencies and land councils, and with government departments both at the state and federal level. It produced and widely distributed three discussion papers and numerous field trip reports and research papers (which were translated into recordings in the Eastern Arrente, Warlpiri and Pitjantjatjara languages), made research or field trips to most parts of Australia, especially to remote areas where the more traditionally-oriented Aborigines lived, and held public hearings at 32 venues in all parts of Australia. The Commission took particular care to provide an opportunity for Aboriginal people to express their views on the general legal systems, and on the continued existence and importance to them of their customary laws.

The same empirical methodology was adopted in the ALRC's 1975 investigation into police complaints and investigation, during which Commissioners accompanied police and travelled to remote areas to observe law enforcement first-hand;[10] in the extensive case file and case cost analysis undertaken for the ALRC's *Managing Justice* inquiry into the federal civil justice system;[11] and in the consultations of teenage detainees and school children surveying their experiences of criminal justice or their parents' divorce, used in the inquiry into children in the legal system.[12] The ALRC routinely arranges public and private hearings and consultations in all parts of Australia.

There is no doubt that the customary law report set a blueprint for many subsequent 'large canvas' reports by the ALRC. The long list of such wide ranging reports adopting its empirical methodology[13] includes:

— *Serious Invasions of Privacy in the Digital Era*;[14]
— *Equality, Capacity and Disability in Commonwealth Laws*;[15]
— *Access All Ages—Older Workers and Commonwealth Laws*;[16]
— *Family Violence and Commonwealth Laws—Improving Legal Frameworks*;[17]
— *Family Violence—A National Legal Response*;[18]
— *Secrecy Laws and Open Government in Australia*;[19]
— *Genes and Ingenuity: Gene Patenting and Human Health*;[20]

[10] ALRC 2, *Criminal Investigation* (1975).
[11] ALRC 89, *Managing Justice: A Review of the Federal Civil Justice System* (2000).
[12] ALRC 84, *Seen and Heard: Priority for Children in the Legal Process* (1997).
[13] The ALRC annual report for 2014 records that the Commission is working on Commonwealth Legal Barriers to Older Persons Participating in the Workforce (the Age Barriers Inquiry) and the Copyright in the Digital Economy Inquiry and anticipates being asked to undertake a future study into Legal Barriers for People with Disability: ALRC 125, *Annual Report 2013–14* (2014).
[14] ALRC 123 (2014), for some reflections on which see chapter 30 (Barbara McDonald).
[15] ALRC 124 (2014).
[16] ALRC 120 (2013).
[17] ALRC 117 (2011).
[18] ALRC 114 (2010).
[19] ALRC 112 (2010).
[20] ALRC 99 (2004).

— *Essentially Yours: The Protection of Human Genetic Information in Australia;*[21]
— *Principled Regulation: Federal Civil and Administrative Penalties in Australia;*[22]
— *Managing Justice: A Review of the Federal Civil Justice System;*[23]
— *Seen and Heard: Priority for Children in the Legal Process;*[24]
— *Making Rights Count: Services for People with a Disability;*[25]
— *Legal Risk in International Transactions;*[26]
— *Integrity: But Not by Trust Alone;*[27]
— *Equality before the Law: Women's Equality;*[28] and
— *Multiculturalism and the Law.*[29]

This is not to say that the ALRC has neglected the scrutiny of particular statutes,[30] rather that the many layered arrangements in federal legal systems necessitate a focus on access to justice and the implementation and 'fit' of federal and state laws. This appears to be one of the key reasons why Australian governments of different political persuasions have continued the practice of selecting broad socio-legal references for the ALRC.

In his analysis of the 'Citation Practices of the Australian Law Reform Commission in Final Reports 1992–2012',[31] Kieran Tranter noted that in this period the ALRC 'had few references that could be characterised as "technical law reform"'.[32] He continues:

> An explanation for this can be seen in the federal jurisdiction of the ALRC. In Australia, technical law reform tends to be a state responsibility and the state law reform commissions often produce short reports on narrow topics such as vicarious liability or time limits on loans payable on demand … most of the references to the ALRC involve broader social, political and economic considerations … Common to all these references was a requirement that the ALRC understand law and the process of law reform 'in context'.[33]

Because of the devolved jurisdictions in a federal system, federal governments may be unaware of deficits in shared administrative arrangements, or may be aware of such deficits and want to prompt a solution from all parties in shared administrative fields, or may see a need to mark out a national approach on key matters such as the response to new technology or demographic changes. These can be seen to

---

[21] ALRC 96 (2003).
[22] ALRC 95 (2003).
[23] ALRC 89 (2000).
[24] ALRC 84 (1997).
[25] ALRC 79 (1996).
[26] ALRC 80 (1996).
[27] ALRC 82 (1996).
[28] ALRC 69 (1994).
[29] ALRC 57 (1992).
[30] See, eg, the following ALRC reports: ALRC 91, *Review of the Marine Insurance Act 1909 (Cth)* (2001); ALRC 92, *The Judicial Power of the Commonwealth: A Review of the Judiciary Act 1903 and Related Legislation* (2001); ALRC 87, *Confiscation that Counts: A Review of the Proceeds of Crime Act 1987* (1999); ALRC 77, *Open Government—A Review of the Federal Freedom of Information Act 1982* (1996); and ALRC 61, *Administrative Penalties in Customs and Excise* (1992).
[31] K Tranter, 'Citation Practices of the Australian Law Reform Commission in Final Reports 1992–2012' (2015) 38 *University of New South Wales Law Journal* 323.
[32] ibid 337.
[33] ibid 337–38.

be the motivations behind a number of recent references referred to the ALRC. The Commission serves a useful purpose in mapping—if not improving—the complex federal system.

Two recent ALRC references reflect this continuing broad interest and focus. The 2013 terms of reference for an ALRC inquiry into specific areas of native title law required a review of the connection requirements for the recognition and scope of native title rights and interests. It also required examination of any barriers to access to justice for claimants, potential claimants and respondents imposed by the Native Title Act's authorisation and joinder provisions. The terms of reference directed the ALRC to consider the Act and any other relevant legislation, including how laws and legal frameworks operate in practice; any relevant case law; relevant reports, reviews and inquiries regarding the native title system and the practical implementation of recommendations and findings; the interests of key stakeholders; and any other relevant matter concerning the operation of the native title system. Similarly the 2014 terms of reference to the ALRC for a review of Commonwealth laws for consistency with traditional rights, freedoms and privileges asked the Commission to identify any Commonwealth laws that encroach upon traditional rights, freedoms and privileges and to consider how laws are drafted, implemented and operate in practice; and any safeguards provided in the laws, such as rights of review or other scrutiny mechanisms and to focus particularly on commercial and corporate regulation, environmental regulation, and workplace relations.[34]

The ALRC's now 40-year practice in federal law reform is generally highly regarded. The Commission itself estimates that some 88 per cent of its reports have been substantially or partially implemented by governments.[35] The high number of individuals and groups making submissions to or consulting with the ALRC suggests that it is seen to be a body with the capacity to influence change. However there is some criticism of its community-focused research, its 'relatively passive; targeted consultations with identified stakeholders' and 'the channelling of vested and mainstream opinions ... giving the appearance of a particular version of agency capture'.[36] Tranter notes that some of the most controversial and wide-ranging reforms to Commonwealth law over the past decades have not been from ALRC reports but from bodies such as the Australian Human Rights and Equal Opportunity Commission (on recognition of same-sex relationships by the Commonwealth)[37] or the Productivity Commission—which, funded from within the Treasury department, has produced and analysed its own data and economic modelling supporting the recommendations in reports on gambling, disability care and support, international trade and climate change.[38]

---

[34] ALRC 125, *Annual Report 2013–14* (2014) 22–23.
[35] ibid 27.
[36] Tranter, n 31 above, 354.
[37] Same-Sex Relationships (Equal Treatment in Commonwealth Laws—General Law Reform) Act 2008 (Cth).
[38] Productivity Commission, *Gambling*, Inquiry Report 50 (2010); Productivity Commission, *Disability Care and Support*, Inquiry Report 54 (2011); Australian Productivity Commission and New Zealand Productivity Commission, *Strengthening Trans-Tasman Economic Relations* (2012); Productivity Commission, *Barriers to Effective Climate Change Adaptation*, Inquiry Report 59 (2012).

This anniversary year lends itself to considerations of the future of the ALRC and Law Commissions generally in Australia. The current ALRC President, Rosalind Croucher, warns that the Commission must be 'constantly vigilant against the threat of … extinction'.[39] Western Australia's Law Reform Commission was absorbed into that state's Attorney-General's department in 2013. In 2014, the National Commission of Audit, initiated by the Treasurer, included in its report a list of 'Principal bodies for rationalisation', which included bodies that were to be abolished, those to be merged and those that were to be consolidated into departments. The ALRC appeared in the last category.[40] The ALRC has already had its budget significantly reduced and changes made in the governance structure and financial management from 1 July 2011. In the face of these actual or suggested changes, the Commission has been robustly defended by other reform agencies, courts and tribunals and the legal profession. In a short piece endorsing its 40 years of law reform, the winner of an ALRC essay competition, law student Justin Pen argued that the ALRC's work served to:

> improve the ongoing dialogue 'between government and its constituents' concerning the economic, social and political challenges of the day. Given the increasingly fragile state of public trust in the government's ability to consult and engage with the public, there is a clear and pressing need for intermediaries such as the ALRC.[41]

My own experience suggests that the ALRC needs to reshape its role if it is to remain viable and relevant. There may be, as Justin Pen suggests, a pressing need for intermediaries between public and politicians, but this is not the core skill or responsibility of a Law Commission. The ALRC was founded to assist in bringing the law into line with current conditions and ensuring that it meets current needs and to adopt new or more effective methods for administering the law and dispensing justice. My experience in the controversial area of delegated immigration legislation suggests that the law most in need of scrutiny, reform and simplification is delegated legislation—the array of regulations and rules which receive limited parliamentary scrutiny and often take the form of conditional legislation, leaving it to some specified authority to determine the circumstances in which the law shall be applied, or to what its operation shall be extended, or the particular class of persons or goods to which it shall be applied. In Australia as elsewhere the array of delegated legislation includes regulations, determinations, declarations, approvals, principles and notices, ordinances of territories, plans of management, for example, for fisheries or navigation and aviation orders or directives, by-laws of statutory authorities, notices or standards such as broadcasting service notices and accounting standards or guidelines, such as aged care and child care guidelines. *Odgers' Australian Senate Practice* estimates that about half of the law of the Commonwealth by volume consists of delegated legislation rather than Acts of Parliament.[42]

---

[39] R Croucher, 'Re-imagining Law Reform—Michael Kirby's Vision, Human Rights and the Australian Law Reform Commission in the 21st Century' Michael Kirby Lecture (2015).

[40] National Commission of Audit, *Towards Responsible Government—Phase One* (2014) annex C.

[41] J Pen, '"Without Fear or Favour": 40 Years of Independent Law Reform', Winning Entry of ALRC fortieth anniversary essay competition (2015).

[42] H Evans (ed), *Odgers' Australian Senate Practice*, 12th edn (Canberra, CanPrint, 2008) ch 15.

There are several roles the ALRC could undertake concerning delegated legislation. Within set and relatively short time lines—and with some minor adjustment of its functions—the Commission could supplement Parliament's own scrutiny of disallowable instruments, the Standing Regulations and Ordinances Committee by examining proposed delegated legislation. Within its existing functions the Commission could undertake to examine particular delegated legislation or sets of delegated legislation. Frequently such legislation is drafted by departmental officers and can comprise complex provisions directly affecting the rights of individuals and entities. The disallowance or committee scrutiny arrangements do not allow consideration of such legislation in its working context. Immigration law is a telling example showing the volume, complexity and incoherence of delegated legislation. The Commission's own skill base, its ability to involve relevant experts and stakeholders and its reporting role make it an ideal entity to undertake the scrutiny and assessment of this—Parliament's high volume legislative output. There may be some resistance to such a proposal from government, as delegated legislation is often seen to serve practical needs for speed of implementation and ease of amendment. However in many instances these claimed benefits are overridden because delegated legislation is amended too often, is left unconsolidated and is impenetrable or inaccessible to users. Given the volume, reach and importance of such legislation, there is much to be said for crafting a role for established Law Commissions overseeing or examining delegated legislation.

This is one suggestion for the ALRC's future. If the ALRC is to reach the 50 years of the Law Commission of England and Wales it will have to critically examine its continuing relevance and adapt to changing legislative and governmental functioning. As Tranter's study of the Commission makes clear, its community research focus may have less value now than in the past. This is particularly so today, where the internet allows for direct dialogue between government and communities. The value of the ALRC lies in its own legal expertise and its ability to involve those with specialist skills in the subject areas. It may need to develop more of the data analysis functions of competitor entities such as the Productivity Commission. If the 'threat of extinction' involves the Commission's incorporation in the Attorney-General's department, its survival depends upon it demonstrating the value of its legal analysis and reform skills, its ability to co-opt and build upon relevant expertise and to show these are outside the functions and the skill set of a government department.

# 7

# *Law Reform and Social Policy*

ERIC CLIVE

## I INTRODUCTION

In Sir Geoffrey Palmer's 2015 Scarman Lecture, there is a section headed 'Lawyers' Law v Big Policy'.[1] Later in his lecture, Sir Geoffrey said that 'Law Commissions should be entrusted with wider responsibilities and their remits broadened to include big projects with social implications.'[2] The questions I would like to consider are the extent to which the UK Law Commissions can take on such projects, the extent to which they have taken on such projects over the past 50 years, and the extent to which they should take on such projects. In concentrating on these questions, I do not wish in any way to suggest an undervaluing of the Law Commissions' work in areas with few social implications, such as their work on consolidation, on statute law revision, and on the actual drafting of the draft Bills attached to their reports.

## II WHAT CAN THE COMMISSIONS DO?

### A The Cabinet Meeting

On 15 December 1964 there was a meeting of Harold Wilson's Cabinet at 10 Downing Street. That meeting considered a memorandum by the Chancellor of the Duchy of Lancaster on the setting up of the Law Commissions. The minutes (technically 'conclusions') of the meeting contain three points of particular interest.[3]

First, the overlap of law and policy was clearly recognised. The minutes note that '[i]n many fields issues of law and of policy were closely related' and that:

> [I]t might be desirable on occasion to ensure that particular topics were not examined at a time which might be inopportune in relation to the development of Government policy and that questions involving important political and social issues were examined by an appropriately constituted body.

---

[1] G Palmer, 'The Law Reform Enterprise: Evaluating the Past and Charting the Future' (2015) 131 LQR 402, 414.

[2] ibid 423.

[3] The conclusions can be viewed on the website of the National Archives at www.discovery. nationalarchives.gov.uk/.

The use of the words 'on occasion' is intriguing. Does this imply that on many occasions it would be acceptable for the Commissions to deal with particular topics at a time which might be politically inopportune or to deal with questions involving important social and political issues? Or does it mean that the Commissions might on occasion want to stray into such areas and that it would then be desirable to head them off? The second meaning seems more likely, unless this is just tactful language designed to placate both those who favoured Commissions with maximum independence and those who wanted adequate governmental control.

Secondly, the technique suggested for keeping the Law Commission of England and Wales away from inappropriate topics or questions was not to be a provision in the constituting Act expressly limiting its powers, but a political mechanism whereby the Commission would submit programmes 'for the detailed examination of particular aspects of the law' to the Lord Chancellor who 'would consult the Ministers concerned, and any proposals on which agreement could not be reached would be submitted to the Cabinet'. Later in the minutes, it was noted specifically that Departmental Ministers 'would not be in a position to prevent particular projects from being undertaken unless the Cabinet were prepared to support their objections'. The position in Scotland would be similar but would involve the Secretary of State for Scotland and the Lord Advocate 'who would consult the appropriate English [*sic*] Ministers on any proposals affecting the law with which they were concerned'.

Thirdly, the government seems to have seen the Commissions' advisory function, as opposed to their 'own initiative' functions, as a rather limited one of a non-policy nature. The minutes say that the Law Commission was to have the task of 'providing Departments with a research and advisory service, particularly on Commonwealth and foreign law'.

The problem of the overlap between law reform and social policy seems to have been considered only from the governmental or departmental point of view. There is no suggestion of any awareness that it might have been useful for a body of responsible Commissioners, who would be anxious to keep within a remit and not misuse public money, to have an indication of what they could not properly do as well as an indication of what they could properly do. The mechanism of requiring programmes to be submitted from time to time and approved turned out to be not very effective in providing this boundary.

## B  The Law Commissions Act 1965

The Law Commissions Act 1965 followed this scheme. It gave the Commissions a very wide remit. It is certainly not restricted to matters with little social or political content. Section 1 says that the Commissions are constituted 'for the purpose of promoting reform of the law'. That is clear enough. Section 3 is less clear. It is headed 'Functions of the Commissions'. Subsection (1) provides as follows:

> It shall be the duty of each of the Commissions to take and keep under review all the law with which they are respectively concerned with a view to its systematic development and reform, including in particular the codification of such law, the elimination of anomalies,

the repeal of obsolete and unnecessary enactments, the reduction of the number of separate enactments and generally the simplification and modernisation of the law, and for that purpose—

(a)   to receive and consider any proposals for the reform of the law which may be made or referred to them;

(b)   to prepare and submit to the Minister from time to time programmes for the examination of different branches of the law with a view to reform, including recommendations as to the agency (whether the Commission or another body) by which any such examination should be carried out;

(c)   to undertake, pursuant to any such recommendations approved by the Minister, the examination of particular branches of the law and the formulation, by means of draft Bills or otherwise, of proposals for reform therein;

(d)   to prepare from time to time at the request of the Minister comprehensive programmes of consolidation and statute law revision, and to undertake the preparation of draft Bills pursuant to any such programme approved by the Minister;

(e)   to provide advice and information to government departments and other authorities or bodies concerned at the instance of the Government [of the United Kingdom or the Scottish Administration][4] with proposals for the reform or amendment of any branch of the law;

(f)   to obtain such information as to the legal systems of other countries as appears to the Commissioners likely to facilitate the performance of any of their functions.

The key function of the Commissions is to 'take and keep under review all the law with which they are respectively concerned with a view to its systematic development and reform'. What does this mean?

There does not seem to be much independent significance in the words 'take and'. Presumably the Commissions took the law under review as soon as they started their work. My suspicion is that the operative words are 'keep under review' and that someone with a logical mind thought that a body could not keep something under review unless it already had it under review.

But how, precisely, does a body keep all the law under review? I am not aware that either Commission has ever said how this has been done or is being done. Of course, the Commissions consider areas of the law which might be in need of reform in formulating their law reform programmes from time to time, but that is not quite the same as keeping all of the law under review all of the time. The words sound good but are not very clear. What is clear is that the words 'take and keep under review all the law with which they are respectively concerned' do not limit the Commissions to lawyers' law. They do not prevent the Commissions from dealing with matters with big social policy implications. The 'law with which they are respectively concerned' is all the law of England and Wales for the Law Commission and all the law of Scotland for the Scottish Law Commission. This was spelled out very clearly by the Scottish Law Commission in its first annual report. This is what they said:

We are concerned with all the law of Scotland, and we do not consider that we are in any way confined to what is loosely referred to as 'lawyers' law'. All law has social implications,

---

[4] Words in s 3(1)(e) inserted by Scotland Act 1998 (Consequential Modifications) (No 2) Order 1999/1820, sch 2(I) para 36(3)(a).

and it is impossible to draw any dividing line between 'social law' and 'lawyers' law'. We interpret the terms of the Act as imposing on us a duty to see to the development and reform of *all* the law systematically. Our intention is that when any question of social policy arises in connection with any branch of the law with which we are dealing, we shall draw attention to it and express our views on it so far as it affects the legal point under consideration. The decisions upon it will be a matter for others—ultimately for the Government of the day.[5]

Can any limitation be read into the words 'with a view to its systematic development and reform'? So far as I know nobody has ever said what system the Commissions should use. There is perhaps an indication in the references to 'branches of the law' in section 3(1) that the Commissions should not adopt, say, an alphabetical or chronological system and there is perhaps an indication that the Commissions should not just cherry-pick topics of particular interest at the time. But this is a mere indication. It is difficult to read any real limitation into the words 'with a view to its systematic development and reform'. A topic with very big social or political implications could well fit within a programme of systematic development and reform.

The remaining words in the first part of section 3(1)—'including in particular the codification of such law, the elimination of anomalies, the repeal of obsolete and unnecessary enactments, the reduction of the number of separate enactments and generally the simplification and modernisation of the law'—are just examples of the sort of work the Commissions are expected to do. They provide a powerful indication of the type of work the Commissions can appropriately do. They do not introduce any limitation on the Commissions' remit.

The particular duties in the lettered paragraphs of section 3(1) are introduced by the words 'and for that purpose'. What do these words mean? No purpose has been mentioned earlier in the section. Perhaps the meaning is 'for the purpose of fulfilling their duty to take and keep under review all the law with which they are respectively concerned', etc, but that does not make a lot of sense. The particular duties are for the purpose of promoting reform of the law, not for the purpose of taking and keeping it under review. The drafting is not very happy.

The particular duties in the lettered paragraphs themselves do not appear to impose any *legal* limitation on the type of law reform projects the Commissions can undertake under their programmes of law reform or on a reference from a Minister under section 3(1)(e).[6]

Might it be argued that the remit is confined to topics which can be regarded as fitting into a system based on branches of the law, rather than areas of life covered by many branches of the law? The 1965 Act refers to branches of the law in several places. Section 3(1)(b) refers to examining 'different branches of the law with a view to reform'; section 3(1)(c) refers to 'particular branches of the law'; and

---

[5] Scottish Law Commission, SLC 3, *First Annual Report* (1966) para 9.

[6] Here it is worth noting that although, as mentioned earlier, the Wilson government seems to have seen the section 3(1)(e) function as a rather limited non-policy one, the provision has in fact been widely used to refer whole law reform projects to the Commissions. It has also been used to justify making Commissioners available, at the request of the government, to represent the United Kingdom in legal projects of bodies like the Hague Conference on Private International Law or the Council of Europe. See n 5 above, para 33.

section 3(1)(e) refers to 'any branch of the law'. Could it therefore be argued that a big project involving an examination of an area of life covered by many different branches of the law would not be within the scope of the 1965 Act? At first I was tempted by this argument, but the difficulty with it is that there is nothing fixed or scientific about the notion of 'branches of the law'. It cannot be said to be confined to traditional branches of a conceptual nature—like the law of obligations, or contract law, or tort and delict, or property law, or succession law. A branch of the law could be defined by reference to an area of life. Family law is a prime example. Within that area you could have a book on the law of husband and wife which covered all rules of law affecting husbands and wives as such, including not only private law rules on marriage, divorce, contract, property, evidence, succession and so on, but also public law rules on such matters as tax, social security, nationality and immigration. You could have a book on the law relating to children which did the same, covering whole areas of private and public law, including the law on education and on the powers and duties of local authorities in relation to children. Commercial law is another wide-ranging branch of the law, capable of including any aspect of the law likely to affect commercial activity. A branch of the law could be any reasonably packaged set of legal rules which anyone chooses to call a branch of the law. So probably the references to 'branches of the law' in the 1965 Act do not impose a limit on the type of project which could be undertaken. They do, however, convey an impression that the Commissions were expected to operate within, rather than across, branches of the law.

So, the conclusion on the 1965 Act is that the Commissions' remit is wide. Indeed, the only legal limitation on it is that it is confined to the law and law reform. The Commissions could not undertake a project which was concerned purely with non-legal matters. They could probably not undertake a project which was in reality a social policy project even if it had some minimal legal aspect and was dressed up as a request for law reform advice, but the line between a genuine law reform project with big social policy implications and a project which was not a genuine law reform project but was simply a social policy project presented as a law reform project would be very difficult to draw. Most legal matters have some social impact[7] and many social matters have some law regulating some part of them. The most that can be said is that the Act contains indications of the kind of law reform work appropriate for the Commissions and, because of the very nature and composition of the Commissions, embodies some assumptions about the kind of project that they should not undertake. The real brake was to be political, via the mechanism for the approval of programmes by the Minister.

In fact, the system of approval of programmes has not worked effectively as a limitation on the Commissions' freedom of action because the programmes, which were duly approved, contained some very widely-defined topics. A great deal was therefore left to the Commissions' own self-restraint and sense of their own

---

[7] Some might say 'all' but it seems to me that some questions of pure drafting, like whether to use 'omit', 'delete' or 'are repealed' in a repealing section, do not have any social policy implications. The same might be said of much consolidation and statute law revision work.

proper purpose. Again, this was clearly recognised from the beginning by the Scottish Law Commission. In their first programme, they proposed to examine the following topics: evidence; obligations; prescription and the limitation of actions; and interpretation of statutes. They said that 'the examination of these branches of the law may involve questions of social policy appropriate for consideration by more widely representative bodies, but we take the view that our preliminary work will enable us at least to supply valuable information derived from other systems of law'.[8] Later programmes contained topics with even more potential for projects with big social implications. The second programme had, among other topics, insolvency, bankruptcy and liquidation, succession and diligence (ie the enforcement of court decrees and related matters).[9] The fourth programme had property law, a potentially vast and explosive subject in relation to which the Commission noted that 'our first objective is the consideration of land tenure law reform with a view to the completion in due course of statutory reform of feudal tenure'.[10]

## C The Protocol of 2010

The Protocol of 2010[11] agreed between the Lord Chancellor and the Law Commission under the Law Commission Act 2009 does not affect the Scottish Law Commission directly and it does not affect the legal scope of the 1965 Act. But it is of some interest in the present context. One of its purposes was to set out 'principles and methods to be applied in deciding the work to be carried out by the Law Commission and in the carrying out of that work'.[12]

Paragraph 5 of the Protocol provides that in deciding whether to include a project in its programme, the Commission is to take account, among other things, of 'whether the independent non-political Commission is the most suitable body to conduct a review in that area of the law' and 'whether the Commissioners and staff have or have access to the relevant experience'. Paragraph 8 provides that where a Minister asks the Commission to take on a new project, he or she must among other things 'explain why the law in that area is unsatisfactory' and 'give an undertaking that there is a serious intention in the department to take forward law reform in this area (if applicable in the case of the particular project)'. Paragraph 9 provides that, in deciding whether or not to accept a referral, the Commission will take account, among other things, of 'the extent to which the law in that area is unsatisfactory', 'whether the independent non-political Commission is the most suitable body to conduct a review in that area of the law' and 'whether the Commissioners and staff have or have access to the relevant experience'.[13] Notice the references to areas of the law. Notice too that the Protocol seems to envisage that one department

---

[8] Scottish Law Commission, SLC 1, *First Programme of Law Reform* (1965) para 4.
[9] Scottish Law Commission, SLC 8, *Second Programme of Law Reform* (1968).
[10] Scottish Law Commission, SLC 126, *Fourth Programme of Law Reform* (1990) 1.
[11] Law Commission and Ministry of Justice, LC 321, *Protocol between the Lord Chancellor (on behalf of the Government) and the Law Commission* (2010).
[12] Law Commission Act 2009, s 2 (inserting a new s 3B into the 1965 Act).
[13] The acknowledgement that the Commission can refuse to accept a referral is interesting.

will be involved. It could be quite difficult to operate if multiple departments were involved.

All of this seems to confirm the impression given by the 1965 Act itself that projects of social policy reform, with little legal content, or law reform projects of a highly political nature, would not be within the type of work envisaged by the 1965 Act, even although they might not be strictly excluded by its terms.

### III  WHAT HAS BEEN DONE IN THE LAST FIFTY YEARS?

The Commissions' remit has not prevented them from undertaking law reform projects of great social interest and importance.[14] They have undertaken many such projects over the past 50 years. Important areas of the law affecting the lives of people directly have been transformed and modernised. This is true of family law, property law, the law on children, the law on adults with incapacity, the law on the enforcement of debts, the law on bankruptcy and the law on succession. The Law Commission, to a much greater extent than the Scottish Law Commission, has done highly impressive work of great public interest in the area of criminal law.

But the Commissions have been very conscious of the indications in, and assumptions behind, the 1965 Act. Professor Mitchell's chapter explains how the Law Commission for England and Wales justified their first intervention in the matter of the grounds for divorce.[15] The Scottish Law Commission were invited under section 3(1)(e) of the 1965 Act to review, in relation to Scotland, the ground covered by the Law Commission in its report. They also displayed a proper hesitation when it came to recommending a precise period of separation which might constitute a ground for divorce even against the wishes of an innocent spouse. They said:

> We have not, however, made any recommendation as to the length of period of separation appropriate in the case in which one of the parties does not consent or acquiesce since we think that this is a policy question for Parliament.[16]

There is another, more recent, example of remit consciousness in the Scottish Law Commission's report on the feudal system of land tenure.[17] This report, which led to the abolition of the feudal system of land tenure in Scotland, had social implications for ordinary home owners because the old system was being abused by some feudal superiors. Some campaigners for land law reform in Scotland nevertheless argued that the Commission should have gone much further. This is what the Commission said in the report:

> It is important to be clear about our remit. Some of those who commented on our earlier discussion paper on the feudal system criticised us for taking a narrow and rather technical

---

[14] Both Commissions have also undertaken many projects, often big projects, on law reform matters of more interest to lawyers, or specific sections of society, than to the general public. The Commissions have also done extremely valuable, and often sadly underrated, work on consolidation and statute law revision. But these areas are not the main concern of this chapter.

[15] See chapter 4 (Paul Mitchell).

[16] Scottish Law Commission, SLC 6, *Divorce: The Grounds Considered* (1967) para 39.

[17] Scottish Law Commission, SLC 168, *Abolition of the Feudal System* (1999).

approach and for not dealing with more wide-ranging aspects of land law reform. That, however, is not our role. We are a non-political advisory body acting under statutory powers and subject to statutory restraints. Our governing statute is the Law Commissions Act 1965 and our main function is to keep the law of Scotland under review 'with a view to its systematic development and reform, including in particular the codification of such law, the elimination of anomalies, the repeal of obsolete and unnecessary enactments, the reduction of the number of separate enactments and generally the simplification and modernisation of the law'.

It is against that background that the item relating to feudal tenure in our Fifth Programme has to be read. It is not our function to consider or make recommendations on more wide-ranging aspects of Scottish land law which might well be politically controversial.

This report provides a good example of the type of law reform envisaged in the Law Commissions Act. It is concerned with the reform of a legal institution which has fallen into disrepair and disrepute. It paves the way for the systematic development and reform of related areas of the law, including in particular the law on non-feudal real burdens. It eliminates the anomalies which result from having several different forms of ownership-like land tenure. It recommends the repeal of 45 whole Acts, as well as 246 sections, 56 schedules and many obsolete and unnecessary words in other Acts. It would lead to a simplification and modernisation of an important branch of the law of Scotland.[18]

Here we get the impression that the Commission was glad to be able to refer to the 1965 Act and glad to leave the more political aspects of land law reform to others. In fact, the wider question of land law reform was referred to another body,[19] and a large Bill on the topic is currently before the Scottish Parliament.[20]

## IV SHOULD THE REMIT BE WIDENED?

In the light of what has been done in other parts of the Commonwealth, where bolder views have prevailed,[21] it might be asked whether the existing legal regime or, perhaps more accurately, the assumptions underlying it and the understandings which have developed as to the proper role of the Commissions, should be changed so as to clearly give the Commissions an even wider area of operation.[22] Should they be regarded as standing Royal Commissions available for governments to use for the production of recommendations, without draft Bills, on big controversial issues of social policy even if they do not have much legal content and would not involve the Commissions in doing the kind of law reform work they are used to doing? It could be attractive for a government to have such a resource. There would be no need to

---

[18] ibid paras 1.2–1.4.

[19] The Land Reform Review Group. See www.gov.scot/About/Review/land-reform/ReviewGroup.

[20] Land Reform (Scotland) Bill 2015. The long title of the Bill sets out the very many things it is designed to achieve.

[21] On the experiences of law reform bodies in Australia and Canada, see chapter 6 (Kathryn Cronin) and chapter 11 (Yves Le Bouthillier) respectively.

[22] Technically, there would be no need to widen the remit of the Law Commissions to enable them to deal with law reform matters with big social implications. Their remit is already wide enough to enable them to do that.

cast around for a Chair and for members or for premises or staff. A difficult problem could be referred in hours and shelved for years. And there might seem to be a gap in the market because Royal Commissions have fallen out of favour in recent years.

My own view is that such a development would not be desirable even if adequate funding was made available. The main reason is that, insofar as a project involved non-legal matters, the Commissions are not appropriately constituted and it would be an inappropriate use of the Commissions' specifically legal expertise. Insofar as a project involved an examination of many different areas of law, it might involve a clash of systems and potentially result in a clash of recommendations. I would also worry about the long-term effects on the Commissions' general law reform work. Failure or success could be equally dangerous. Failure would be immediately damaging to the reputation of the Commissions and this could have serious effects. Success might be even worse because the Commissions might be asked to do more and more big social policy projects to the obvious detriment of their more traditional law reform work. They could become a dumping ground. And I would be concerned that if the Commissions were regularly involved in matters of sensitive social policy there could be a more intense scrutiny of the values and political views of individual Commissioners. There could be pressure from within governments to make appointments more political. I do not think that this sort of thing would be good for law reform in the long run.

## V CONCLUSION

Of course, it might be said that traditional law reform of the kind done by the Commissions over the last 50 years has little value and no future and that they should do less of it and more of the other thing. I do not share that view. Indeed I think they should do more of what they are asked by the 1965 Act to do. In particular, they should try to do more codification—in manageable chunks—and more comparative law. These are the two areas where they have significantly failed to live up to the expectations embodied in their founding statute. In all other respects they have fully lived up to those expectations and have done a superb job.

I am not against the use of powerful, independent Commissions to examine enormous issues of pressing social importance. Indeed there is an obvious need for such work. It could act as a counter to the pernicious short-termism inherent in our political system. But it seems to me that differently constituted Commissions specially adapted to each challenging task would be the better way forward.

# Part 3

# Institutions, Commissions, Committees, Codifiers

# 8

# *Introduction*

LORD BEITH

Politics and law reform rarely meet on the same terms or the same timescale. Parliaments and Law Commissions have a common interest in ensuring that laws fulfil their intended purpose, are capable of being understood and enforced, and are reviewed when they may have ceased to satisfy these tests. But, as Professor Gretton puts it, government is not interested in codification and not much interested in consolidation of laws. It is a rare event indeed for law reform to rise up the political agenda in its own right, as it did during Lord Gardiner's exceptional term as Lord Chancellor. However, Sir Terence Etherton sets out that there has been progress, even in these less reform-minded times. New procedures since 2009 have facilitated uncontroversial revising legislation. Furthermore, guidelines and codes such as the Police and Criminal Evidence Act 1984 have achieved a measure of codification without the criminal code which some law reformers advocated. Another example is provided by the Sentencing Guidelines, which are subject to statutory consultation with the House of Commons Justice Committee. As the Committee's chairman until May of this year, I also sought to provide the Law Commission with a route for communication with the elected House. It was a two-way process: we learned more about the high quality of work done by the Commission, but we also had to explain to them not only the low level of interest in law reform among MPs, but also the extent to which their efforts were likely to be frustrated by the desire of governments and backbench MPs to use law making as a form of political signalling, especially, but not exclusively, in the field of criminal law. Ineffective or counterproductive legislation remains on the statute book because governments or oppositions are fearful of appearing 'soft on crime', and misconceived new provisions are hastily added to Bills so that politicians can be seen to be 'doing something' about a problem which has hit the headlines. But we should count ourselves fortunate that neither in England and Wales nor in Scotland has the work of law reform been closed down. Professor Le Bouthillier sets out how this happened in Canada to both the federal Law Commission which he chaired and to provincial law commissions where they existed. In an earlier chapter, Neil Faris made clear that the Northern Ireland Law Commission is effectively suspended.

There will never be a completely coherent, internally consistent corpus of statute law which accommodates changing circumstances. Even if it were possible, it would not be a priority for parliamentarians over their day-to-day concerns. But that does not mean that the improvement of law should be abandoned. Law Commissions are now a necessary and, to a significant degree, an effective part of our constitutional arrangements. Legislators should be challenged to make more use of their work.

# 9

# *Memoir of a Reforming Chairman*

SIR TERENCE ETHERTON*

The topic of law reform and law reform agencies has become the subject of widespread academic study. This is unsurprising. What began as a European movement in the nineteenth century based on philosophical and political ideas for codification of the law has matured into a standard objective of many democracies to promote better and fairer laws through sustained programmes of law reform. That is promoted across the globe in a myriad of different ways, from permanent independent bodies staffed by full-time researchers and other employees—via multi-agency arrangements centred around a university law faculty—to proposals generated and promoted entirely within government.[1]

The advantages and disadvantages of the different models are rightly the subject of investigation and scrutiny for many reasons, not least because access to justice, the coherence and accessibility of the law and the fairness of laws matter to all of us. The aims and concerns of those who promoted the creation of the Law Commission of England and Wales and the Scottish Law Commission in 1965 are timeless: the need for laws which are just, up-to-date and accessible to all who are affected by them.[2] One of the consequences of the academic study of law reform and law reform agencies is that there is no shortage of detailed and excellent analysis across many countries and models. I asked myself, when invited to participate in this conference, whether there was actually anything useful that I could add as a non-academic, past Chairman of the Law Commission of England and Wales and now a full-time senior judge.

There are many common features of the history of law of reform agencies in different countries, including the rise and fall of their existence and effectiveness. The Law Commission of England and Wales (the Law Commission) stands out, not merely because of its survival despite attacks on its budget and threats to its very existence,[3] but because it has over the 50 years of its existence pragmatically adapted and evolved its relationship with government, the legislature and (to a lesser

---

* I am very grateful to Daniel Robinson and James Linney of the Law Commission and Daria Popescu, my judicial assistant, for their assistance in the preparation of this chapter.

[1] See, eg, some examples collected in chapter 38 (Matthew Dyson).

[2] White Paper, *Proposals for English and Scottish Law Commissions* (Cmnd 2573, 1965); Law Commissions Act 1965, s 3.

[3] Highlighted by Sir James Munby in 'Shaping the Law—the Law Commission at the Crossroads', Denning Lecture (2011).

extent) the judiciary. What I can offer is a personal perspective on the most important changes in those relationships since 1965 which were conceived during my time as Chairman of the Law Commission. Some of them have been the subject of academic commentary but not all. The background to them, the objectives intended to be attained by them, and the ways in which they came about may hold some wider lessons.

Every independent law reform body is concerned with its 'strike' record—the proportion of its reports which are accepted and implemented in whole or part. This is rightly so. If the rationale for the existence of such a body is the reform of the law then the best indicator that its existence is justified is the implementation in whole or in part of its recommendations for law reform. Like all other public organisations, an independent law reform body must compete for public resources and that requires some objective measure of value. Acceptance of recommendations and their implementation are not the entire story, as has been pointed out many times. The report of an independent law reform body on a given topic, even if it is not immediately accepted by government, may make an important contribution to debate within society. It may provide a more comprehensive view of the relevant legal principles and history than is to be found elsewhere and, for that reason, be of value in judicial decision-making, academic research and informed debate. The value of contributions of that kind are not, however, practically measurable. It may be possible, with modern technology, to track references to the recommendations of an independent law reform body in parliamentary debates, scholarly works, lectures and other publications, but a mere numerical exercise says little or nothing about value: the references could all be criticisms and denunciations.

When I became Chairman of the Law Commission in 2006, I instigated an analysis of successive governments' responses to the Law Commission's recommendations. Taking successive five-year periods from 1965, the statistics showed that since 1990 there had been a marked decline in the percentage of reports which had been accepted by government and an increase in the number accepted but not implemented. There was also a significant percentage of reports which had neither been accepted nor rejected for more than two and a half years.[4]

I tried to understand the reasons for that declining record of success and effectiveness. I identified the following causes.

First, no period matched the success of the first five-year period[5] because the person then politically responsible for the Law Commission, the Lord Chancellor, Lord Gardiner, was a passionate supporter of independent law reform,[6] was the person directly responsible for the creation of the Law Commission itself, held a senior constitutional role as Lord Chancellor and was a highly respected member of

[4] T Etherton, 'Law Reform in England and Wales: A Shattered Dream or Triumph of Political Vision?' (2008) 10 *European Journal of Law Reform* 135.
[5] During its first five years the Law Commission published 24 law reform reports, 22 of which were accepted and implemented in their entirety and the remaining two in part.
[6] See further, Lady Hale's insights into his role (chapter 2).

the Cabinet,[7] and was the head of a small department of state and so able to take a close personal interest in the work of the Law Commission.

Second, by contrast with that situation at the Law Commission's inception, the Lord Chancellor, whose role became coloured in the eyes of many by his more recent second political office of Secretary of State for Justice, had become over time a fully fledged party politician. Indeed, he now has no judicial or legislative role and his political influence is measured by the relative size and importance of his department and his personal political standing.[8] Much of that change is reflected in the provisions of the Constitutional Reform Act 2005, which moreover does not require the Lord Chancellor to be a lawyer.

Third, the Lord Chancellor's department, which has mutated from the Lord Chancellor's Office, to the Department for Constitutional Affairs, to the Ministry of Justice, has grown exponentially in its range of responsibilities, with a particularly marked expansion since 1971. In that year the Lord Chancellor took over the running of the court service. The department then took on responsibility for criminal and civil legal aid and, more recently, the magistrates' courts, criminal law policy, the prison service and probation services. It has a United Kingdom-wide remit in relation to EU and international justice policy, freedom of information and data protection, human rights and civil liberties, the Supreme Court and the National Archives. There has been a commensurate increase in its budget. When I took on the Chairmanship of the Law Commission in 2006–07 the departmental expenditure (other than for Scotland and Wales) was £3.7 billion, of which the Law Commission's £4 million budget was 0.11 per cent. The affairs of the Law Commission are now, therefore, in budgetary, administrative and political terms a tiny feature of the department's work.

Fourth, unsurprisingly in the circumstances, responsibility for the Law Commission is entrusted to one of several junior Ministers in the department and is just one of several matters of which that junior Minister has charge. Moreover, there have been periods when there has been a rapid turnover of junior Ministers. In the 15 months following my appointment as Chairman of the Law Commission, there were no fewer than four junior Ministers in the department with responsibility for the Law Commission, that is to say, averaging less than four months each. By contrast, it would be difficult for a Law Commission project to be completed, accompanied by a draft Bill, in under three years. This meant that there could be no assumption that a project supported, and even promoted, by a department would continue to receive that support by its conclusion.

Fifth, in the period since the establishment of the Law Commission there has been a remarkable increase in legislation. The number of pages of legislation nearly trebled in the 40 years 1965–2005 from 7,567 pages in 1965 to approximately

---

[7] The Lord Chancellor then combined the roles of head of the judiciary, the speakership of the House of Lords, membership of the executive and holder of a senior Cabinet position.

[8] He does, of course, have a constitutional role under the Constitutional Reform Act 2005 and his oath (pursuant to the 2005 Act, s 17) which requires him to respect the rule of law, defend the independence of the judiciary and ensure the provision of resources for the efficient and effective support of the courts.

20,800 pages in 2005. In addition to this increase the size of each page of legislation has also increased by 11 per cent.

This has inevitably restricted the parliamentary time available for enactment of non-political, non-party Law Commission reports. With Ministers and departments competing vigorously for a share of the limited parliamentary time available each session, priority is understandably claimed for those initiatives which will best secure votes and the political support of the electorate.

An understanding of the last point in terms of Cabinet and legislative process is central to an appreciation of the practical difficulties in securing implementation of Law Commission recommendations even where the government has accepted the recommendations in principle.[9] Parliamentary time available for government Bills is extremely limited. No more than one third of time in the Commons, for example, tends to be available for scrutiny of government legislation. Governments normally introduce a programme of legislation in each session of Parliament consisting of up to 30 Bills. Each is part of the wider legislative programme. The Parliamentary Business and Legislation Committee (the PBL Committee)[10] of the Cabinet Office, which plays a critical role, manages the government's current legislative programme on behalf of the Cabinet and advises the Cabinet on the strategic management of its forthcoming programme. It is chaired by the Leader of the Commons and its membership includes various Ministers and the chief Whips in the Commons and the Lords.

Departments must bid for a slot in the legislative programme for any Bills they wish to introduce.[11] The PBL Committee usually receives around twice as many bids for legislative slots as there are available. This is normally through the annual bidding round when the Leader of the House Commons, as chair of the PBL Committee, invites Cabinet colleagues to submit Bills for the following session of Parliament. The PBL Committee will assess bids on their political importance, urgency and state of preparation. It will then advise Cabinet on the contents of the programme. The content of the government's legislative programme is decided by Cabinet on the basis of the PBL's proposals. The Cabinet will finalise the programme about a month before the start of the parliamentary session. The PBL Committee reviews the programme throughout the year.[12]

A number of initiatives were put in hand to address these various obstacles to the effectiveness of the Law Commission as a law reform body. Those initiatives would not have come to fruition without the active support and political determination and skill of two successive Ministers responsible for the Law Commission, Baroness

---

[9] Cabinet Office, *Guide to Making Legislation* (2015).

[10] It was formerly called the Ministerial Committee on Legislative Programme until 2007, and then became the Ministerial Committee on Legislation. It took its current name in 2010.

[11] This short account does not deal with Finance Bills, Consolidated Fund Bills, Appropriation Bills and some other special categories of primary legislation. Consolidation Bills (which include Statute Law Revision Bills and Statute Law Repeal Bills) recommended by the Law Commission must also be approved by the PBL Committee before introduction but they are subject to special procedures in Parliament and are addressed as a separate category of legislation in the PBL Secretariat's guidance: see n 9 above, ch 44.

[12] The PBL Committee also decides whether the Bill should be introduced in the House of Lords or the House of Commons.

Ashton[13] and Michael Wills.[14] They had to confront and overcome the caution, and occasionally the hostility, of civil servants and to persuade and engage the support of other politicians for bold action. Another important factor in the success of the initiatives I describe below was that during the critical years 2007–10 Jack Straw was Lord Chancellor and Secretary of State for Justice. He had studied law, was a strong supporter of the Law Commission and the principles which inspired its establishment, and he could remember when, as a student actively engaged with politics, he was aware of the establishment of the Law Commission.

The initiatives to improve the effectiveness of the Law Commission can be categorised broadly in the following way: (1) giving Parliament itself greater oversight of the work of the Law Commission and the government's response to it and so enabling it to hold the government to account; (2) creating greater space in the legislative programme for Law Commission Bills; (3) providing a better working framework between the Law Commission and departments for engaging the support of a department and sustaining that support throughout the duration of the project; and (4) enhancing the standing of the Law Commission in its relations with government, the executive, the legislature and the judiciary. There is inevitably some overlap in these initiatives.

The Law Commission Act 2009 (the 2009 Act) sought to achieve the first of those objectives. The Bill was not a government Bill but it could not have succeeded without the support of Michael Wills and Jack Straw. Lord Lloyd of Berwick, a former Law Lord and a tremendous long-term supporter of the Law Commission in the House of Lords, agreed to introduce the Bill in the House of Lords as a private peer's Bill. It was taken through the House of Commons by Emily Thornberry, a barrister with a human rights practice and subsequently a shadow Attorney-General in the last Parliament.

The 2009 Act amended the Law Commissions Act 1965 (the 1965 Act) in two respects. The first respect, relevant to the issue I am now addressing, was to impose an obligation on the Lord Chancellor to lay a report before Parliament every year stating which Law Commission proposals had been implemented in whole or in part during the year and, where proposals had not been implemented as at the end of the year, giving details of the plans for dealing with those proposals and, if a decision had been taken not to implement the proposals in whole or in part, the reasons for that decision.

In introducing the second reading of the Bill in the House of Lords, Lord Lloyd said of clause 1 (which became section 1 of the 2009 Act):

> Clause 1 imposes the statutory duty on the Lord Chancellor to report annually to Parliament … This will enable Parliament for the first time to hold the Government to

[13] Baroness Catherine Ashton, GCMG, PC, subsequently became the European Union Trade Commissioner in 2008 and then the High Representative of the European Union for Foreign Affairs and Security Policy and the First Vice President of the European Commission from 2009–14.

[14] Now Lord Wills, PC. He did not have the usual precursor to a political career as an MP. Having graduated with a double first in history from the University of Cambridge, he joined the diplomatic service where he worked from 1976–80. He then became a researcher for London Weekend Television from 1980–84. From 1984–97 he was a director of a television production company. He was then elected an MP.

account in relation to the important subject of law reform ... I cannot do better than quote the words of the Lord Chancellor: 'Good law is imperative for accessible and modern constitutional arrangements. For 40 years the Law Commission has played a vital role in that respect, but I intend to strengthen its role by placing a statutory duty on the Lord Chancellor to report annually to Parliament on the Government's intentions regarding outstanding Law Commission recommendations, and providing a statutory backing for the arrangements underpinning the way in which Government should work with the Law Commission'.[15]

The 2009 Act provided the legislative and procedural mechanism by which it will be possible in an appropriate case for questions to be asked in Parliament holding the government to account for its reaction, or lack of reaction, to recommendations made by the Law Commission. That possibility has indeed been given practical effect since the 2009 Act came into force.[16]

The second objective I have mentioned was the creation of space within the legislative programme for Law Commission Bills. As I have said, the practical difficulties with implementation of Law Commission recommendations are that they are unlikely to find their way into a political party's manifesto or be of vote-catching political interest; there is great competition for slots in the government's legislative programme, and the amount of parliamentary time available for new legislation is limited. My predecessor as Chairman of the Law Commission, Sir Roger Toulson (now Lord Toulson), had begun to explore the possibility of an expedited procedure in the House of Lords for appropriate Law Commission Bills. There was some caution, even opposition, to the idea in a number of quarters, and there was the difficulty of having to satisfy the powerful Procedure Committee of the House of Lords and the government's business managers in the House of Lords that any such new procedure was both practical and desirable.

The idea was that uncontroversial Law Commission Bills would be started in the House of Lords and a significant part of their progress would be taken off the floor of the House and dealt with in committee. Once approved, they would expect to have a speedy passage through the House of Commons.

Baroness Ashton, as Minister responsible for the Law Commission from 2004 to 2006, was an enthusiastic supporter of the proposal for the new procedure. By a stroke of good fortune, she was appointed Leader of the House of Lords and Lord President of the Council shortly after my appointment. With her political skills and influence, and her robust determination not to be deflected by some civil servants, the proposal was ultimately considered by the House of Lords' Procedure Committee and approved in the 2007–08 session for a trial period of two years.[17] Following a second report by the Procedure Committee,[18] the new procedure was made permanent by the House of Lords on 7 October 2010.[19]

---

[15] HL Deb 24 April 2009, vol 709, col 1735.
[16] See the questions asked in the House of Lords of the Minister for the Law Commission Lord Faulks: HL Deb 12 May 2014, vol 753, cols GC435–GC452.
[17] House of Lords Procedure Committee, *Law Commission Bills* (2007–08, HL 63).
[18] House of Lords Procedure Committee, *Law Commission Bills* (2010–11, HL 30).
[19] HL Deb 7 October 2010, vol 721 col 224.

The procedure is intended only for Law Commission Bills that are generally agreed to be uncontroversial.[20] Before the introduction of any such proposed Bill there must be full consultation within 'the usual channels' to determine whether or not it is suitable for the procedure. On introduction, the Bill is identified as a Law Commission Bill in House of Lords' Business. Following first reading a motion is tabled, with at least three sitting days' notice, to refer the Bill to a 'Second Reading Committee'. This was an innovation for the Lords. It functions like a Grand Committee, with unlimited membership, and takes place in the Moses Room. Any member can speak and there is no time limit on the debate. However, as in Grand Committee, there is no provision for divisions. The Second Reading Committee only debates the Bill; it would not itself decide on the motion for second reading. The Second Reading Committee simply reports that it has considered the Bill, and the motion for second reading is formally taken in the House at a later date. Assuming the Bill has been given a second reading, the next stage is a motion to commit the Bill. The Special Public Bill Committee's procedure is then followed. The Bill is considered in Committee, which is empowered to take written and oral evidence. Having taken evidence, the Committee considers the Bill clause by clause and decides whether there should be amendments. Once the Committee has completed its work the Bill is reprinted as amended. Written and oral evidence, and a verbatim report of proceedings, are also published. The remaining stages, report and third reading, follow in the usual way, on the floor of the House and on separate days.

The special House of Lords procedure has been an undoubted success in securing the enactment of Law Commission recommendations that would otherwise have stood no or little prospect of becoming law. The very first piece of legislation which was passed using the new procedure, the Perpetuities and Accumulations Bill in 2009 gave effect to recommendations in a report of the Law Commission published as long ago as 1998[21] and which had been accepted by government but had never found its way into the government's legislative programme. I am quite certain that, but for the new procedure, it would never have found its way on to the statute book because it was highly technical, had no political appeal whatsoever and related to a specialist area of the law of little interest to the general public even though of real importance in relation to lifetime transactions (both private and commercial) and testamentary dispositions.

A number of other statutes have now been enacted using the new House of Lords procedure: the Third Parties (Rights against Insurers) Act 2010;[22] the Consumer Insurance (Disclosure and Representations) Act 2012;[23] the Trusts (Capital and

---

[20] See also chapter 19 (Sir Grant Hammond).

[21] Law Commission, LC 251, *The Rules against Perpetuities and Excessive Accumulations* (1998).

[22] This was introduced on 23 November 2009 and received Royal Assent on 25 March 2010. It implements Law Commission and Scottish Law Commission, LC 272 and SLC 184, *Third Parties—Rights against Insurers* (2001).

[23] This was introduced into Parliament on 16 May 2011 and received Royal Assent on 8 March 2012. It implements Law Commission and Scottish Law Commission, LC 319 and SLC 219, *Consumer Insurance Law: Pre-Contract Disclosure and Misrepresentation* (2009).

Income) Act 2013;[24] the Inheritance and Trustees' Powers Act 2014;[25] and the Insurance Act 2015.[26] One Scottish Law Commission Bill, the Partnerships (Prosecution) (Scotland) Act 2013 has followed the special procedure.[27]

A particular advantage of the House of Lords special procedure for Law Commission Bills is that, even though such Bills must be approved by the PBL Committee, departments do not need to bid for slots forgotten in the government's legislative programme in that there is an understanding that up to two Law Commission Bills can proceed under the special procedure in each parliamentary session.

Furthermore, the special procedure has not curtailed the possibility of Law Commission Bills being promoted by departments and introduced into Parliament following normal procedures. The PBL Secretariat's Guidance specifically states that departments should consider whether Law Commission recommendations accepted by the government could be included in their bid to the PBL Committee as a standalone measure or part of a larger Bill and that, when bidding for legislation, departments should make clear whether the Bill implements Law Commission recommendations as well as whether it is suitable for the special parliamentary procedure.[28]

This brings us to the third objective mentioned earlier, that is the provision of a working framework between the Law Commission and departments best calculated to engaging the sustained support of the relevant department throughout the duration of the project. When I became Chairman of the Law Commission there was already in existence a protocol setting out the way in which the Law Commission and government should work together to achieve the objectives in the 1965 Act and the White Paper that preceded it.[29] The drawing up of such a protocol was one of the recommendations of the report of John Halliday in March 2003 as part of the quinquennial review of the Law Commission.[30] The protocol had the title 'The Law Commission and Government—Working Together to Deliver the Benefits of Clear, Simple and Modern Law'. It was a detailed, thoroughly worthy and appropriate document. The problem was that civil servants within departments were generally unaware of its contents, or at least content to proceed without regard to them—not least the requirements that departments should aim to respond to reports within six months of publication and should in any event give a definitive decision on

---

[24] This was introduced into Parliament on 29 February 2012 and received Royal Assent on 31 January 2013. It implements Law Commission, LC 315, *Capital and Income in Trusts: Classification and Apportionment* (2009).

[25] This was introduced into Parliament on 30 July 2013 and received Royal Assent on 14 May 2014. It implements, in part, Law Commission, LC 331, *Intestacy and Family Provision Claims on Death* (2011).

[26] This was introduced into Parliament on 18 July 2014 and received Royal Assent on 12 February 2015. The main provisions of the Act give effect, with some modifications, to the recommendations in a joint report of the Law Commission and the Scottish Law Commission, LC 353 and SLC 238, *Insurance Contract Law: Business Disclosure; Warranties; Insurers' Remedies for Fraudulent Claims; and Late Payment* (2014). It also amends the Third Parties (Rights against Insurers) Act 2010 (mentioned in n 22 above).

[27] This was introduced into Parliament in November 2012 and received Royal Assent on 25 April 2013. It implements Scottish Law Commission, SLC 224, *Report on Criminal Liability of Partnerships* (2011).

[28] Cabinet Office, *Guide to Making Legislation* (2015) para 5.22.

[29] White Paper, *Proposals for English and Scottish Law Commissions* (Cmnd 2573, 1965).

[30] J Halliday, *Quinquennial Review of the Law Commission* (2003).

whether they intended to implement the report within two and a half years of its publication.

As appears from what Lord Lloyd said when introducing the second reading of the Bill which became the 2009 Act, part of which I have quoted earlier, the 2009 Act sought to address this problem by giving statutory backing to an appropriate protocol of working relations between the Law Commission and departments. This was achieved by section 2 of the 2009 Act, which inserted a new section 3B in the 1965 Act providing for the Lord Chancellor and the Law Commission to agree a protocol to be laid before Parliament (and any revisions to it) and to which Ministers and the Law Commission must have regard. The section stipulated that the protocol could include, among other things, provisions about: (a) principles and methods to be applied in deciding the work to be carried out by the Law Commission and in the carrying out of that work; (b) the assistance and information that Ministers and the Law Commission are to give each other; and (c) the way in which Ministers are to deal with the Law Commission's proposals for reform, consolidation or statute law revision.

Discussions and negotiations about the terms of the protocol were continued and concluded during the Chairmanship of my successor, Sir James Munby. The Protocol agreed between him and the Lord Chancellor, Jack Straw, was laid before Parliament and published in March 2010.[31] There has been some published commentary on the Protocol.[32] In broad terms the Protocol covers the various stages of a project— before the Law Commission takes the project on; at the outset of the project; during the currency of the project; and after the project. It sets out the matters the Law Commission must take into account in deciding whether to include a project as part of its three-yearly programme of law reform and, where the Law Commission is considering including a project, requires notification to, and discussion with, the department having relevant responsibility. It sets out the steps to be taken and the matters to be taken into account where a Minister asks the Law Commission to take on a new project. Whichever of those two routes is taken, if the project is taken on with ministerial consent, the Protocol provides that the department is expected to provide sufficient staff to liaise with the Law Commission and to undertake that there is a serious intention to take forward law reform in the area in question. The Protocol provides for the agreement, at the outset of a project, of terms of reference, review points and an overall timescale. It provides for communication and review during the currency of a project, the preparation by the Commission of an impact assessment to accompany the final report and the assistance and, where possible, the agreement of departmental officials in respect of that impact assessment. The Protocol stipulates that the relevant Minister will provide an interim response to the Law Commission as soon as possible and, in any event, within six months of the publication of the report unless otherwise agreed with the Law Commission,

---

[31] Law Commission and Ministry of Justice, LC 321, *Protocol between the Lord Chancellor (on behalf of the Government) and the Law Commission* (2010).

[32] M Partington, 'Law Reform: The UK Experience' in M Tilbury, S Young and L Ng (eds), *Reforming Law Reform: Perspectives from Hong Kong and Beyond* (Hong Kong, Hong Kong University Press 2014) 77–78; and R Croucher, 'Defending Independence' (2014) 34 *Legal Studies* 515, 523–24.

and a full response as soon as possible after delivery of the interim response and in any event within one year of publication unless otherwise agreed with the Law Commission. If applicable, the Minister is to provide the timescale for implementation and the Law Commission and the Minister will agree what additional support the Law Commission will provide to assist implementation.[33]

The Protocol applies only to projects which the Law Commission has taken on after the date on which it was agreed.[34] Bearing in mind the length of time a Law Commission project normally takes to complete, it may be too early to pass a definitive judgement on the way the Protocol has worked across government. There can be no doubt, however, that its statutory backing by primary legislation provides the best opportunity for a practically enforceable framework for effective and efficient collaboration between departments and the Law Commission for law reform.[35]

I turn to the fourth of the objectives mentioned earlier, that is enhancing the standing of the Law Commission with government, the legislature and the judiciary. I am not referring here to the Law Commission's general reputation, which has always been high. That general reputation would in any event inevitably be enhanced by achievement of the other objectives I have already discussed and any increase in the effectiveness of the Law Commission in consequence of them. What I am concerned with at this point are two particular and connected issues that were of importance when I became Chairman of the Law Commission.

They both relate to the Chairmanship of the Law Commission. From the establishment of the Law Commission up to and including my own appointment, the Chairman of the Law Commission had always been a High Court judge on full-time secondment to the Law Commission (usually for three years but occasionally extended to a longer period). This was a powerful symbol both of the independence of the Law Commission from the executive and of the standing of the Law Commission itself. Moreover, the convention was that, following the end of a judge's Chairmanship, he or she would sooner or later be appointed to the Court of Appeal.

At the beginning of the century there was a growing recognition that the traditional 'tap on the shoulder' approach to senior judicial appointments, including Court of Appeal appointments, was no longer acceptable.[36] There was also a growing recognition that a similar approach in relation to the appointment of the Chairman of the Law Commission, as a non-departmental public body, was also unacceptable. As to the first of those matters, the Judicial Appointments Commission (JAC) was established following the enactment of the Constitutional Reform

---

[33] The Protocol is supplemented in practice by a Memorandum of Understanding agreed between the Law Commission and the department in relation to each project.

[34] Protocol, n 31 above, para 3. Government departments and the Law Commission agreed, however, to take it into account, so far as practicable, in relation to projects which were ongoing as at that date. The Protocol does not apply to Commission proposals for consolidation or statute law revision.

[35] For the perspective of a Chairman of the Law Commission on the working of the Protocol, see D Lloyd Jones, 'The Law Commission and the Implementation of Law Reform' (2013) 15 *European Journal of Law Reform* 333.

[36] That is to say an invitation by the Lord Chancellor to a particular practitioner to become a High Court judge after taking soundings from other senior judges and without any formal selection process or invitations to all those interested to apply for appointment.

Act 2005. It is an independent body which set up and administers formal processes for selecting (among others) High Court and Court of Appeal judges. As to the appointment of the Chairman of the Law Commission, for the first time on the occasion on which I was appointed, it was decided that there should be an invitation to existing High Court judges of expressions of interest and an interview of the shortlisted applicants by a panel comprising the Lord Chief Justice, the Permanent Secretary of the Department for Constitutional Affairs (now the Ministry of Justice) and a lay person.[37]

Those arrangements posed a number of practical difficulties from the perspective of the Law Commission. The involvement of the JAC in Court of Appeal appointments meant that there could no longer be any expectation that past Chairmen of the Law Commission would in due course be promoted to the Court of Appeal. That posed a practical problem for recruitment of the most able and suitable High Court judge to chair the Law Commission. Not only would High Court judges have to compete with each other for appointment as Chairman of the Law Commission, but they could no longer have any confidence that in all likelihood, if they became Chairman, they would at some point be promoted to the Court of Appeal. That would depend on the outcome of a JAC competition in due course. Appointment as Chairman of the Law Commission could, on the contrary, damage their prospects of future or at any event timely appointment to the Court of Appeal since they might be overtaken by more junior colleagues during the three years on permanent secondment to the Law Commission when the Chairman would not be available for judicial promotion and would be away from the judicial 'coal face' giving judgments and enhancing their reputation. There was a real prospect that no High Court judge, other possibly than one coming up to retirement, would apply in the future to become Chairman of the Law Commission.

The problem was first identified by Sir Roger Toulson, when he was Chairman of the Law Commission, but he had not been able to make any progress with a solution by the time his appointment came to an end. The issue became live again as I entered the second year of my Chairmanship and the question of my successor came into focus. I raised with the then Lord Chief Justice, Lord Phillips, the possibility of appointing an existing Court of Appeal judge to the Chairmanship of the Commission or appointing a High Court judge to the Court of Appeal on his or her becoming Chairman. This would have several advantages. It would make appointment as Chairman of the Law Commission more attractive to able High Court judges and encourage competition for appointment. It would enhance the reputation and standing of the Law Commission if the Chairman was a Court of Appeal judge. That would also meet the second problem, to which I was alluding earlier, namely the increasing difficulty in securing answers to correspondence from the Law Commission generally, and the Chairman in particular, as to the intentions of the government with regard to accepting and implementing Law Commission recommendations. The reason the appointment of

---

[37] In my case, I then had a further interview by the Lord Chancellor, Lord Falconer.

a Court of Appeal judge to the Chairmanship of the Law Commission would help assist that problem was not merely because of the standing of such a judge within the judicial hierarchy but also because Court of Appeal judges are members of the Privy Council and the constitutional convention is that Ministers must reply in person to correspondence from Privy Counsellors.

Lord Phillips, who was very supportive of the work of the Commission, was agreeable in principle to my proposal but the then Master of the Rolls, Sir Anthony Clarke (now Lord Clarke), had a practical problem that the Court of Appeal could not afford to lose one of its judges full-time for three years in view of the Court of Appeal's notoriously heavy workload. The only solution would be to secure an enlargement of the Court of Appeal (then 37 members) to accommodate the appointment to the Court of Appeal of the Chairman of the Law Commission (if not an existing Lord or Lady Justice). This would require a positive resolution of both Houses of Parliament, a somewhat daunting requirement.

With the blessing of Lord Phillips, there began a lengthy and time-consuming process of securing the support of the government, the principal opposition parties and cross-bench peers to an increase of the numbers in the Court of Appeal from 37 to 38 in order that the Chairman of the Law Commission would, on appointment as Chairman, be made a member of that Court if not already a member of it. The support of Ministers and, above all, the high reputation of the Law Commission among parliamentarians eventually secured the positive resolution of both Houses, with a number of peers and MPs making speeches in support.[38]

Following the positive resolution a protocol was entered into between the Ministry of Justice, the JAC and the judiciary for the appointment of the incoming Chairman of the Law Commission (if not already a member of the Court of Appeal) to fill the next vacancy in the Court of Appeal. That protocol was implemented on the appointment of Sir James Munby, who succeeded me as Chairman, and then Sir David Lloyd Jones, who succeeded him.

In conclusion, I would like to make the following general observations about the initiatives I have described. The first is that none of them would or could have been achieved unless the Law Commission had been an independent body. They all involved at one stage or another cross-party parliamentary support. If the work of the Law Commission had been carried out wholly within the executive, I believe it is inconceivable that such support could have been obtained.

Secondly, none of the initiatives would have been successfully achieved without the fact that the Law Commission is respected among parliamentarians. Its reputation for excellence in the quality of its reports and in the Bills which accompany its recommendations (drafted by the Parliamentary Counsel seconded to it) and for its non-political and independent stance were brought home to me in my engagement with politicians of all colours throughout my Chairmanship. The greatest reflection

---

[38] Maximum Number of Judges Order 2008, SI 2008/1777. HL Deb 12 June 2008, vol 702, cols 746–52; HC Deb 10 June 2008, vol 477, col 279; Draft Maximum Number of Judges Order 2008 Deb 9 June 2008, cols 3–8. The first ever appointment of a sitting Court of Appeal judge to be Chairman of the Law Commission was Lord Justice Bean, whose appointment as the successor to Sir David Lloyd Jones was announced on 27 March 2015 and took effect in August 2015.

of that is, to my mind, the securing of a positive resolution of both Houses to increase the size of the Court of Appeal to accommodate the appointment to the Court of the new Chairman of the Law Commission.

Thirdly and finally, regular engagement with Ministers, opposition spokespersons, parliamentary committee chairs and other parliamentarians promoted the goodwill, interest and knowledge on their part which made possible all the reforms I have mentioned. All three of those general observations must surely have lessons for the future.

# 10

# *The Duty to Make the Law More Accessible? The Two C-Words*

GEORGE L GRETTON

## I INTRODUCTION

What are the Law Commissions supposed to do? What is their job? When I was appointed,[1] I assumed that I knew the answer. The job was law reform—law reform in the sense of examining an area of law to see what was wrong with it, and coming up with recommendations for improvement. I did not study the Law Commissions Act 1965 at that time. (A shameful admission, I know.) I took it for granted that I knew what it said. It was only after I had been a Commissioner for some time that I began to look at the Act seriously.[2]

Here is the core of what the Commissions were told to do, by the Queen's most Excellent Majesty, with the advice and consent of the Lords Spiritual and Temporal, and the Commons:

> It shall be the duty of each of the Commissions to take and keep under review all the law with which they are respectively concerned with a view to its systematic development and reform, including in particular the *codification* of such law, the elimination of anomalies, the repeal of obsolete and unnecessary enactments, the reduction of the number of separate enactments and generally the simplification and modernisation of the law … [and] to prepare from time to time … *comprehensive programmes of consolidation* … and to undertake the preparation of draft Bills pursuant to any such programme.[3]

No doubt the first cohort of Law Commissioners reflected diligently on what the Act said. But thereafter the Commissions developed their remit in their own way[4] and it seems, to me at least, that the actual terms of the legislation drifted to the back of the drawer. Consolidation was for a time carried out with some energy, but later went into decline. Codification was, with some qualifications, largely abandoned by the mid-1970s.

---

[1] As a Scottish Law Commissioner, in 2006.

[2] In many ways it is a strange text (though the same could be said of many enactments), and would merit, what I think it has never received, a detailed critical commentary. Perhaps it should be a candidate for reform. (A joint project for the Commissions?) But these issues cannot be pursued here.

[3] Law Commissions Act 1965, s 3, emphasis added. The Act goes on to give further detail.

[4] And on the whole there has not been much difference, in this respect, between London and Edinburgh.

Let it be said at once that what the Commissions have done has been valuable and successful. Neither the general public, nor those active politically,[5] nor lawyers in general, nor even academic lawyers, really understand how much the law has been changed by the work of the two Commissions.[6] 1965 is one of the most important dates in the whole of English legal history, and likewise of Scottish legal history. But what the Commissions have done is not precisely what they were supposed to do. This paper looks back to the 1965 Act and reflects a little on aspects of the original vision, a vision which, in theory at any rate, remains legally binding, and to raise the question of whether the de facto approach, good and effective as it has generally been, should perhaps be freshened up with a little of the romantic idealism of youth.

One word that does not appear in the Act is 'accessibility'. It should have done so. Accessibility was part of the conception. The White Paper that led to the Act said: 'It is today extremely difficult for anyone without special training[7] to discover what the law is on any given topic … English law[8] should be capable of being recast in a form which is accessible'.[9] Is there a problem about accessibility? Whilst the law can never be fully accessible, is the *degree* of accessibility unacceptably low? There is no way of settling this: I know of no metric for degrees of accessibility of legal rules. It is a matter of impression, and in forming that impression one must of course be aware of the position in other countries. In my view the position was unacceptable in 1965 and it is unacceptable now. Some progress has been made, in part by the work of the Commissions, but at the same time there have been contrary forces. The *overall* position is probably no better than it was in 1965 and arguably it is worse. We have been swimming, but we have been swimming upstream. From the standpoint of an observer on the river bank, the results do not look good.

## II UNDERESTIMATING THE PROBLEM

Many of us underestimate the problem of accessibility. Why? Because each of us specialises. Naturally, in our own fields we seldom have much difficulty in tracking down legal norms, statutory or otherwise. When I was a law student I made an intense study of the Scottish statutes about property and conveyancing and trusts and succession. I remember—my name's George and I'm a nerd—*reading them in bed.*

---

[5] A candidate might be Jack Straw, author of *Aspects of Law Reform: An Insider's Perspective* (Hamlyn Lectures 2012) (Cambridge, CUP, 2013). But as far as I can see the book does not mention the Commissions.

[6] This is a by-and-large statement. Of course, there are individuals who are exceptions.

[7] The implication is that those without 'special training' *should* be able 'to discover what the law is on any given topic'. But the idea that all statutes (not to broach the issue of case law) could be written so as to be read and understood by the intelligent non-lawyer strikes me as an impossibility. A very desirable impossibility, as so many impossibilities are, but an impossibility nonetheless.

[8] And what of Scots law? Either it was thought not to stand in need of a 'recast', or the writer had forgotten it. The former explanation would work out as a compliment. The latter would work out as the opposite.

[9] White Paper, *Proposals for English and Scottish Law Commissions* (Cmnd 2573, 1965) 2.

I knew my way around them as I knew my way around the streets of Edinburgh. And I still do. But when I step back and reflect, the truth cannot be denied: legislation is too often a mess, a teenager's bedroom. It needs to be sorted out. And the same is true of so many other fields of law, though those who are experts in those areas too seldom notice that fact. Thus those of us with influence in the development of the law tend, by the very nature of the case, to underestimate the degree to which the law is inaccessible, simply because we are so familiar with our own fields. And it is not only legislation that is too often a teenager's bedroom. So too, all too often, is law based on decided cases.

## III MAKING THE LAW MORE ACCESSIBLE

How can the law be made more accessible? Not easily. Inaccessible law arises almost spontaneously and without effort, like the messy bedroom. Accessible law is hard to make. It is like keeping a room clean and tidy. It is hard and unglamorous and it is a job that needs doing repeatedly. As to the causes of inaccessibility, they are many. One issue concerns the way statutes are drafted, about which nothing will be said here.[10] Another concerns the simple question of the public availability of legislative texts. Here things have improved since 1965. The idea that legislation should be available in anything more than a formal sense was then an alien one. Statutes were printed and could be bought but only at a high price. One might have thought that the government would have at least provided public libraries with them. Not so. People were bound by legislation whose existence they could in practice not discover. Even if you had access to the raw materials—the primary and secondary legislation[11]—working out the current version of a legislative text could be extraordinarily slow. First you had to track down the amendments through the citators.[12] Then there was the slow business of photocopying and assembling with scissors and paste.[13] Before the advent of photocopying it was even worse than that. You were lucky if the topic was one where a commercial publisher had already done the work, as with, say, the companies legislation.

Since then, the digital revolution. New legislative texts are placed free on the internet, and there is an official database providing legislative texts as amended,[14] albeit that updating can be slow. (The commercial providers are quicker.) But databases are

---

[10] Except that I will, briefly. Many legal rules can hardly be understood when expressed abstractly. They need examples. That is how we teach students. 'Section 86 says ... So, eg, suppose that Jack's the registered owner of Blackmains. He decides to sell to Jill ... and then ...'. The obscurity of UK legislation would be much lessened were examples to be used, but this is always rejected on the specious sophism that if an example says the same as the abstract formulation it is superfluous, and if it does not the result is contradiction. Some legislatures, more enlightened than our own in this matter (and Holyrood is as bad as Westminster) use examples in legislative texts.

[11] Many law firms—but, horrifyingly, far from all—had a standing subscription to the statutes, which arrived fairly promptly. But secondary legislation was almost completely inaccessible. The statutory instruments were published in annual volumes but these came out years in arrears.

[12] Which of course had to be paid for.

[13] To use the standard phrase, but in fact latterly it was usually scissors and Sellotape.

[14] www.legislation.gov.uk.

not always accurate: people have been sent to prison on the basis of legislation that had been repealed and not replaced.[15] Of course, editorial errors cannot be wholly avoided. My point is that the error rate in statute databases will tend to be higher, the messier the underlying data. Which leads to the subject of consolidation.

## IV  CONSOLIDATION

Given the digital revolution, it might be asked whether consolidation actually serves much purpose today. The answer is that, though much less important, it is still important. It remains the case that relevant legislation that should really be in a single statute is scattered over several statutes. And even individual statutes can become so heavily amended that whilst the amended text is available it is a headache to work with. An example familiar to me is the Bankruptcy (Scotland) Act 1985, for while I was at the Scottish Law Commission we worked on a consolidation of it.[16]

In the early years of the two Commissions there was a good deal of consolidation work. The Renton Report listed an impressive 61 consolidation statutes that resulted from the first ten years (ie 1965–74 inclusive) of the work of the two Commissions.[17] Today consolidation work is just a trickle. In the ten years from 2005 to 2014 inclusive the number of consolidation reports by the Scottish Law Commission was three.[18] It would be nice to think that consolidation is being carried out by other agencies, but in fact not much of that happens.[19] The consolidation problem is going from bad to worse. The legislative slum goes from bad to worse.

It might be argued that consolidation is unsuitable work for the Commissions because their expertise lies in substantive law reform. It is true that the individual Commissioners do not have expertise in consolidation. But a Law Commission is

[15] *R v Chambers* [2008] EWCA Crim 2467, discussed by Lord Toulson (chapter 14). (And also discussed in G Gretton, 'Of Law Commissioning' (2013) 17 *Edinburgh Law Review* 119, 133.) Lord Toulson's excellent chapter merits the careful attention, but will receive, no doubt, the careless neglect, of politicians.

[16] The result being Scottish Law Commission, SLC 232, *Report on the Consolidation of Bankruptcy Legislation in Scotland* (2013). The report was implemented by the Bankruptcy (Scotland) Act 2016.

[17] The Renton Committee, *The Preparation of Legislation* (Cmnd 6053, 1975) app C. I say 'ten' years but in fact it was less because in 1965 itself there was, of course, no consolidation arising from the work of the Commissions.

[18] Law Commission and Scottish Law Commission, LC 298 and SLC 202, *Parliamentary Costs Bill: Report on the Consolidation of Legislation Relating to Parliamentary Costs* (2006); LC 341 and SLC 235, *Co-operative and Community Benefit Bill: Report on the Consolidation of Legislation Relating to Co-operative and Community Benefit Societies* (2013); Scottish Law Commission, SLC 232, *Report on the Consolidation of Bankruptcy Legislation in Scotland* (2013). The first two were joint with the London Commission.

[19] A special case is the 'tax law rewrite'. Another special case is the companies legislation, with some of the statutes since the nineteenth century being pure consolidation and others a mixture, including the Companies Act 2006. It could be argued that both these areas are codal. The consolidation/codification distinction is not precise. It may be noted that whilst for the most part the two Commissions have had little involvement in these two areas, the 2006 Act contains codal or quasi-codal provisions (s 170 ff) on directors' duties that derive from Commission work: Law Commission and Scottish Law Commission, LC 261 and SLC 173, *Company Directors: Regulating Conflicts of Interests and Formulating a Statement of Duties* (1999).

not only a set of five jurists: it is an organisation. Moreover, Commissioners may still be able to tender useful advice in consolidation projects.[20] And the Commissions do in fact carry on with the repeal of enactments that are 'spent, obsolete, unnecessary or otherwise not now of practical utility',[21] to which the same argument could be applied. Useful though statute law revision is, it seems to me less important than consolidation, so perhaps priorities need to be reviewed.[22]

## V CODIFICATION

There is a literature on the various meanings of 'codification' and I do not wish to add to that literature here. Codification can be narrow (eg the Bills of Exchange Act 1882) or broad (eg the German Civil Code).[23] It can restate the law without major change (the Bills of Exchange Act 1882 again) or it can reform the law (the German Civil Code again). Restatement codification is like consolidation, only that it supersedes common law rather than superseding prior legislation. The celebrated mini-codes of the late nineteenth and early twentieth centuries were, by and large, restatement codes rather than reform codes.[24]

Prominent as codification was in the 1965 vision, the achievement of the Commissions has been not been good. '[C]odification is a dead issue in England today' pronounced Kötz in 1987.[25] That is slightly too sweeping. Some Commission projects have resulted in legislation of a quasi-codal nature,[26] but even here what has tended to happen has been that reform projects have generated semi-codification as a spin-off of reform, codification not having been the main objective. And there have been some code-like spasms and twitches in the body politic, arising from non-Commission work, such as the Arbitration Act 2006 and the Arbitration (Scotland) Act 2010.[27]

---

[20] I made some contributions to the Scottish Law Commission project to consolidate the bankruptcy legislation. It is true that Commissioners will not always be familiar with the area to be consolidated, but sometimes they will.

[21] These reports make fascinating reading. The latest, Law Commission and Scottish Law Commission, LC 357 and SLC 243, *Statute Law Repeals: Twentieth Report: Draft Statute Law (Repeals) Bill* (2015), is no exception.

[22] Perhaps I should confess that while at the Scottish Law Commission I decided against a consolidation of the conveyancing legislation. My reason was pragmatic. The work would not have been just a technical consolidation, and so would have involved more time than I had available.

[23] What did those responsible for the 1965 Act have in mind? CGB Nicholson thought that the narrow approach was intended ('Codification of Scots Law: A Way Ahead, or a Blind Alley?'1987 *Statute Law Review* 173, 175). My own view, for what it is worth, is that there probably was no definite policy on the matter.

[24] There are some qualifications here. Perhaps most obviously, whilst the Sale of Goods Act 1893 was a restatement code for England, it was (alas) a reform code for Scotland.

[25] H Kötz, 'Taking Civil Codes Less Seriously' (1987) 50 *MLR* 1, 2.

[26] In the Scottish context the examples that come to my mind are the Family Law (Scotland) Act 1994, the Title Conditions (Scotland) Act 2003 and the Tenements (Scotland) Act 2004.

[27] For the 'tax law rewrite' and the companies legislation, see above. Outside officialdom there are those who would like to see something broadly comparable to the Uniform Commercial Code of the USA enacted. (The obvious name here is that remarkable figure, RM Goode.) Incidentally, the idea that one often encounters that codification is in some mystical way incompatible with a common law system,

Why is the statutory command to codify ignored? In the early years it was not ignored. The London Commission began with plans to codify contract law, the law of landlord and tenant, criminal law and family law. The Edinburgh Commission (always less well-resourced, of course) began with plans to codify contract law and the law of evidence. The contract project was joint, and famously failed. Partly that was because it was a joint project, and joint projects are often problematic.[28] But the other projects failed too. Within less than ten years of the 1965 Act the idea of codification was more or less dead,[29] the main exception being the codification of criminal law in England and Wales. That has not been achieved, but the ideal continues.[30]

There are two main reasons why codification has been virtually abandoned, a minor reason and a major reason, though they interact. The minor reason is the problem of resources. Codification is difficult and it is time-consuming.[31] But that is only the minor reason because if codification were thought important, resources could be found. The reality is that it is not thought important—and that is the second and major reason. I recall once mentioning the topic to a Minister in the Scottish Government, and his response, in a sceptical tone of voice that communicated more than the words themselves, was: 'how would that benefit the Scottish economy?' Most politicians are indifferent. Influential sections, to say the least, of the legal profession are not indifferent: they are actively opposed. Even if Law Commissioners thought codification to be a good idea—and my impression is that on the whole there is not much support for it among Commissioners themselves[32]—there would not be much point in preparing codifying texts whose chances of enactment would be so low.

It would be tempting to expatiate on codification: I will resist. But one comment I must make, concerning the 'how would that benefit the economy?' question. More than 60 years ago there appeared in the USA the Uniform Commercial Code, one

as well as being disproved by the commercial codifications of the late nineteenth and early twentieth centuries, is also disproved by the US experience, where the codification movement did not die, but continues today, and not only in the field of commercial law.

[28] A large subject that awaits scholarly study, which, I suspect, it will not receive.

[29] For valuable reflections on this subject by Commissioners, appearing in the 1980s, see M Kerr, 'Law Reform in Changing Times' (1980) 96 *LQR* 515; AE Anton, 'Obstacles to Codification' 1982 *Juridical Review* 15; PM North, 'Problems of Codification in a Common Law System' (1982) 46 *Rabels Zeitschrift* 390; and Nicholson, n 23 above. A recent paper of interest is C Skinner, 'Codification and the Common Law' (2009) 11 *European Journal of Law Reform* 225.

[30] For the position in England and Wales see chapter 12 (Ian Dennis). The Edinburgh Commission has not pursued criminal codification. To some extent the difference here between London and Edinburgh may be one of resources. The Edinburgh Commission has always been much smaller. The Edinburgh Commission did however publish the fruits of an independent initiative: E Clive, P Ferguson, C Gane and A McCall Smith, *A Draft Criminal Code for Scotland with Commentary* (2003). But, alas, we are no nearer a criminal code now than we were then.

[31] Yet Mackenzie Chalmers did the Bills of Exchange Act 1882 and the Sale of Goods Act 1893 single-handed. Thomas Macaulay did the original draft of the Indian Penal Code virtually single-handed. Are legislative drafts the easier, the fewer the people involved? Discuss (20 marks).

[32] Of course, this is not true of all. A particularly notable exception is Eric Clive, a Commissioner in Edinburgh from 1981–99, who was one of the leading figures behind the Draft Common Frame of Reference (DCFR). One of his publications worth mentioning in the present context is 'A Scottish Civil Code' in H MacQueen (ed), *Scots Law into the 21st Century: Essays in Honour of WA Wilson* (Edinburgh, W Green, 1996).

of the leading promoters of which was Karl Llewellyn. 'No one,' wrote Llewellyn, 'who has never seen a puzzled Continental lawyer turn to his little library and then turn out at least a workable understanding of his problem within half an hour will really grasp what the availability of the working leads packed into a systematic Code can do to cheapen the rendering of respectably adequate legal service.'[33] The costs of legislative failure are dumped by government on to the individuals and businesses who, because of that failure, end up paying higher fees: cost externalisation. Codification and consolidation are economically efficient. The current situation is economically inefficient. I say this on the assumption that the net savings to government, in not undertaking consolidation and codification, are much less than the costs imposed on individuals and businesses by the chaotic state of the law. I cannot prove that. But it seems to me obviously true.[34]

All law reform proposals nowadays have to be accompanied by 'impact assessments' setting out the expected economic consequences, in pounds, shillings and pence. In practice these are often works of fiction. But consolidation and codification would bring real, not fictional, benefits.[35]

Why does government[36] get away with it? Government gets away with it because it is a monopoly supplier. If government were a supermarket, it would have gone bankrupt long ago. Imagine a supermarket in which in every aisle there are jumbles of wares, the tins of baked beans sitting in disorderly heaps among the lettuces and the detergents, a supermarket in which some goods have no labels, and others misleading labels, so that only experts know what they contain, a supermarket in which much of the food is stale or downright off. So disorderly is the supermarket that customers have to hire expert shoppers, but even those experts, who of course are expensive, can never know more than small parts of the supermarket: one specialises in kitchen cleaning materials and another in free-from foods. It might be objected that if English law is so bad, why is it so commonly adopted in international commercial contracts? That is too large a question to discuss here; here all that can be said is that the adoption is not of English law in general, but of a narrow slice of it, contract law, and, indeed, more narrowly still, business-to-business contract law.

---

[33] K Llewellyn, 'The Bar's Troubles, and Poultices—and Cures?' (1938) 5 *Law and Contemporary Problems* 104, 118. Lord Reid's view was different: 'It is a delusion that codification will bring about any substantial saving. A competent counsel can find the relevant cases very quickly' ('The Law and the Reasonable Man' (1968) 54 *Proceedings of the British Academy* 189, 194.) Lord Reid could find the relevant cases very quickly. Suppose that all counsel are Lord Reids, which alas is not so, why is the need to employ counsel, so as to discover what the law is, evidence of the cheapness of the existing system? Even the greatest of judges can on occasion say silly things. (For more misunderstanding of codification, see what he says near the end of the previous page.)

[34] I do not suggest that there exists codal heaven. Codes have grave drawbacks, drawbacks that are often pointed out, not least by those who live in strongly codified systems. Opponents of codification dwell on these drawbacks *as if that settled the question*. But the question is not whether codification has grave drawbacks. It does. The question is whether, *on a fair balance taken*, codification is beneficial.

[35] To cut spending, governments often externalise costs. That is not necessarily inefficient. It all depends. It seems to me obvious that the total costs imposed on individuals and businesses by the legislative slum must be much greater than what the costs would be to government of clearing the slum.

[36] I write with a small rather a capital G because culpability is shared between London, Edinburgh, Cardiff and Belfast. I will not mention Br*ss*ls because reflecting on the technical quality of EU legislation is bad for the cardiovascular system.

## VI  WHAT IS TO BE DONE?

Government is not much interested in consolidation and even less in codification.[37] It is not easy to see this indifference changing, and I do not see that the Commissions can do much, and I could not recommend that they spend time doing work that is unlikely to be enacted. But what could be done is to keep these issues on the agenda. For instance, every annual report could have a 'consolidation and codification' section. Perhaps one day the educated public might start to make a fuss and demand that the requirements of the 1965 Act be once again taken seriously.[38] You may say I'm a dreamer. But I'm not the only one.

[37] Let me make it clear that I do not accuse government in the United Kingdom of exceptional inaction. What would need a book-length study is how matters fare round the world. In that book it would, no doubt, be noted that article 44 of the Constitution of India calls for a Civil Code. Nearly 70 years later the train has yet to arrive.

[38] Let me admit that while a Commissioner I did very little about all this.

# 11

# *The Former Law Commission of Canada: The Road Less Travelled*

YVES LE BOUTHILLIER

## I INTRODUCTION

Canada has a rich and long, but also somewhat troubling, experience with law reform Commissions both at the federal and provincial levels. Since I had the honour to preside over the Law Commission of Canada in 2005 and 2006, this chapter focuses on the role and the work of Law Commissions at the federal level. However, the reader should keep in mind that a comprehensive study of the nature of Law Commissions in Canada, as well as their contribution to the common good, would necessarily encompass the work of the many provincial Law Commissions over the years.[1]

In the poem by Robert Frost 'The Road Not Taken',[2] there are two unknown roads for the traveller to choose from and he chooses the road less travelled. The Law Commission I presided over took the road less travelled because Canada had

---

[1] Currently, six of the ten Canadian provinces have entities that can be considered as Law Commissions. Starting from the west of the country and going east, these provinces are: British Columbia (the British Columbia Law Institute); Alberta (the Alberta Law Reform Institute); Saskatchewan (Law Reform Commission of Saskatchewan); Manitoba (Manitoba Law Reform Commission); Ontario (Law Commission of Ontario); and Nova Scotia (Law Reform Commission of Nova Scotia). Of the remaining four provinces, two, Newfoundland and Labrador (1981–92) and Prince Edward Island (1976–83) established Law Commissions but later abolished them, in both cases apparently because of needed fiscal restraint. New Brunswick has never had a Law Commission. The Department of the Attorney-General has a Legislative Services Branch which solicits comments on initiatives by the government of the day. As for the province of Quebec, while it enacted legislation in 1992 to create a Quebec Law Reform Institute that would have played a role similar to Law Commissions in common law provinces, the Institute has not yet been created. This is not surprising as Quebec has a civil law regime for private law matters and traditionally civil law states have not opted for Law Commissions to reform the law. The province has found other means to proceed with modernising its laws. Despite the absence of a Commission, the province of Quebec, after years of studies and reports produced by experts appointed by the province, adopted a new Civil Code in 1991. International meetings of law reform Commissions are, therefore, essentially a meeting of common law countries. Finally, none of the three Canadian territories (Northwest Territories, Yukon and Nunavut) have established Law Commissions although it has been discussed at the policy level in some territories.

[2] R Frost, 'The Road Not Taken' in R Frost, *Mountain Interval* (New York, Henry Holt, 1916).

already experimented with the other road. Canada, to my knowledge, is the only common law country that has created and closed a national Law Commission, not only once but twice. That, in itself, is unusual. But what is even more unusual and little appreciated is that, as I will explain, there were great differences between the first Law Commission, called the Law Reform Commission of Canada, created in 1971 and closed in 1993, and its successor, created in 1997 and closed in December 2006.[3] What they have in common is that despite these differences, both came to a dead end. This means that political actors, in different periods of our history, have decided (at least at the national level) not to do law reform through legislatively mandated Commissions. As we know, law evolves all the time, through various means, as a result of actions of various actors and despite the wishes of others. Fundamental changes to the law can result from initiatives taken by the government of the day as when in 1982, the Prime Minister at the time, Pierre-Elliott Trudeau, acted to repatriate the Canadian constitution from the United Kingdom with a constitutional Act that included both a Charter of Rights and Freedoms and a Canadian amending formula.[4] Reforms can result from the pressure and demands (and often thoughtful proposals) from external actors such as NGOs, professional groups, scholars, international organisations and so on. What is unique, however, to a Law Commission is that it is a permanent entity created by the will of elected representatives and that it has the sole mandate to question the continuing relevance of existing law and to study new directions that the law could take. It does not prevent reform of the law through other avenues. It adds another means to do it and, in my view, in doing so, it enriches the overall law reform process.[5]

## II  A BROAD MANDATE

To what extent did the mandate of the Law Commission of Canada differ from the older Law Reform Commission of Canada? The first Commission did what is more commonly expected from such entities. It took as a starting point existing legislation and asked how it could be modernised to account for a changing society.[6] For instance, that Commission took a detailed look at various provisions of the then existing Criminal Code and made important and detailed recommendations to

---

[3] On 25 September 2006, the President of the Treasury Board at the time, John Baird, announced cuts to a long list of federal programmes in order to save over a billion Canadian dollars a year. Included among these cuts was the entire budget of the Law Commission of Canada. The Commission ceased its operations at the end of that year. Among one of numerous comments at the time on the elimination of funding for the Commission see J Ibbitson, 'Fatal Cuts to Law Panel Deeply Ideological', *The Globe and Mail* (Toronto, 28 September 2006) A4.

[4] Enacted as schedule B to the Canada Act 1982 (UK), which came into force on 17 April 1982.

[5] For the unique functions carried out by Law Commissions, see G Murphy, *Law Reform Agencies* (Ottawa, Department of Justice Canada, 2004).

[6] On the mandate and work of the Law Reform Commission of Canada see, among others, N Lyon, 'Law Reform Needs Reform' (1974) 12 *Osgoode Hall Law Journal* 421; A Macklin, 'Law Reform Error: Retry or Abort?' (1993) 16 *Dalhousie Law Journal* 395; T Scassa, 'A Critical Overview of the Work of the Law Reform Commission of Canada: Learning from the Past', in Atlantic Institute of Criminology (ed), *Federal Law Reform Conference: Final Report* (Halifax, Atlantic Institute of Criminology, 1993); RA MacDonald, 'Recommissioning Law Reform' (1996–97) 35 *Alberta Law Review* 831.

modify it, some of which were acted upon. In other cases, a ruling by a court would include a comment on the need to fix the law and the Commission would seize itself of the matter. Similarly, in the past it was not infrequent, and it still happens today for various courts in Canada, including the Supreme Court of Canada, to refer to the work of that Commission, given the very high quality of its legal analysis.

Arguably, the approach of the most recent Commission was much broader than a focused attention on legislative reform. In taking this new approach, this Commission simply fulfilled the mandate conferred to it by Parliament. Section 3 of the Law Commission of Canada Act 1996[7] sets the mission of the Commission. Here are some of the key elements in this provision:

(a)   the development of new approaches to, and new concepts of, law;
(b)   the development of measures to make the legal system more efficient, economical and accessible;
(c)   the stimulation of critical debate in, and the forging of productive networks among academic and other communities in Canada in order to ensure co-operation and co-ordination; and
(d)   the elimination of obsolete laws and anomalies in the law (more commonly expected from a Law Commission).

Embracing this mission, the Commission, at the outset, determined to question the role of law in our modern society where relationships in various spheres are constantly evolving. It identified categories of relationships (personal, social, economic and governance) and then asked what role law played in these. In other words, it first looked at a concept broader than law, namely relationships, and then situated the law within this concept.[8] One of the consequences of this wide approach was that, in some of its reports, the Commission examined issues that were partly within the sphere of competence of provincial governments. For instance, in its reports on policing, the Commission addressed both the work carried out by police forces, some of which are under the federal jurisdiction (for instance, the Royal Canadian Mounted Police), and private security agencies, which fall under provincial jurisdiction.[9] Likewise, its numerous studies to clarify 'what is a crime?' led to the examination of a number of provincial laws.[10] The first President of the Commission, the late and much missed Professor Roderick MacDonald, made the following observation on this broad approach:

> [S]ome provincial governments mistrusted the Commission's decision to attack 'problems' rather than legally-labelled issues, and explore subjects (like institutional child abuse) that could not be pigeon-holed into 'water-tight' constitutional areas of jurisdiction.[11]

---

[7]  This law is still in force despite the fact that the Commission was closed in December 2006.
[8]  See the statement by the second President of the Law Commission of Canada: 'It was not a question of simply keeping the law up to date; it was necessary at times to rethink its role': N Des Rosiers, 'The Law Commission of Canada and its Role in the Development of Policy' (2003 speech).
[9]  Law Commission of Canada, *In Search of Security: The Future of Policing in Canada* (2006).
[10]  Law Commission of Canada, *What is a Crime? Challenges and Alternatives: Discussion Paper* (2003).
[11]  RA MacDonald, 'Jamais Deux Sans Trois … Once Reform, Twice Commission, Thrice Law' (2007) 22(2) *Canadian Journal of Law and Society* 117, 120. Given the foray of the Commission in matters of provincial jurisdiction, it is not surprising that subsequently the Ontario Law Commission did, in turn, refer to the work of the Law Commission of Canada. See for instance Law Commission of Ontario,

In sum, if law remained at the heart of the Commission's mission, the Commission was nevertheless situating law within larger issues, of interest to both levels of governments but more generally to the Canadian public, and that law could help to address. Again, MacDonald was of the view that this mindset of the Commission rankled some legal minds, used to reigning unchallenged in their fields:

> Even law teachers were sceptical, and a number did not like the Commission's decision to frame issues in unorthodox ways; as experts in particular fields—criminal law, marriage and divorce, intellectual property, labour law—they resisted any research agenda that did not automatically acknowledge their superior intellectual capital.[12]

Some also criticised the fact that reports from the Commission did not usually include proposed draft provisions or draft Bills but instead laid out a number of recommendations that could be transposed in appropriate legal wording.

Again, if the approach of the Commission suggested a break with the traditional view one has of law reform Commissions, the fact is that the Commission was simply fulfilling the wishes of those drafters who, having witnessed the dismantlement of the first Commission, had wanted to offer a new, fresh, different outlook. In this regard, in addition to section 3 of the 1996 Act, it is also worth mentioning elements of the preamble to the Act and, in particular the following paragraphs:

> [T]he commission should adopt a multidisciplinary approach to its work that views the law and the legal system in a broad social and economic context... the commission should take account of cost-effectiveness and the impact of the law on different groups and individuals in formulating its recommendations.[13]

To get a good grasp of the consequences of legal norms on affected individuals and groups, one cannot rely solely on legal experts, but must also seek the views of experts in other fields such as economists, sociologists, criminologists and others depending on the nature of the topic. Moreover, one does not want to rely solely on experts. One wants to hear from, and listen to, those directly affected. Again, I will leave it to MacDonald, the real visionary behind this Commission, to explain the rationale for this approach:

> [U]ltimately, the source of inspiration is the forms and processes of social ordering in everyday life—since, after all, law is inextricably connected with everyday life. For a Law Commission, this is a fundamental and sobering thought. If one (wrongly) conceives law as separate from human action, as an external force that imposes itself relentlessly on social and economic relations, anything is possible ... Over and again we ignore Portalis' wisdom: 'les lois proposent; les hommes disposent'.[14]

In almost all cases, the topics selected by the Commission were not part of the government short-term priorities. Its role was to take a long view of legal issues, and not to pursue or complement a government agenda.

---

*Vulnerable Workers and Precarious Work: Final Report* (2012) 31; Law Commission of Ontario, *A Framework for the Law as it Affects Older Adults: Advancing Substantive Equality for Older Persons through Law, Policy and Practice: Final Report* (2012) 27.

[12] MacDonald, n 11 above, 120–21.
[13] Law Commission of Canada Act 1996, preamble.
[14] MacDonald, n 11 above, 133.

## III INDEPENDENCE

One fundamental feature of the Commission was its independence. It was left to the Commission, save where the Minister of Justice specifically referred a matter since responding to such references was obligatory, to determine its research programme as well as its activities. While section 5 of the 1996 Act provides that '[t]he Commission shall consult with the Minister of Justice with respect to the annual program of studies that it proposes to undertake', this provision, far from constraining the independence of the Commission, was rather a means to ensure an exchange between the Commission and a key actor that could implement changes proposed by the Commission.

With respect to a reference, the Act did provide that the Minister could request that the Commission 'shall prepare such reports as the Minister, after consultation with the Commission and taking into consideration the workload and resources of the Commission, may require'.[15] However, how this report would be developed and what its recommendations would be was a matter solely for the Commission to determine. In the early days of the Commission, the Minister did indeed request the Commission to prepare a report on institutional child abuse which was duly delivered by the Commission.[16] It is worth noting that this report of the Commission, its first one, was very recently referred to in the report tabled by the Truth and Reconciliation Commission of Canada on the treatment of Aboriginal children in residential schools:

> A statute of limitation defence has to be raised by the defendant. In its 2000 report on responding to child abuse in institutions, the Law Commission of Canada recommended that the federal government should not rely solely on statute of limitation defences. Nevertheless, the Government of Canada and the churches have frequently and successfully raised these defences in residential school litigation. The Commission believes that the federal government's successful use of statute of limitation defences has meant that Canadian courts and Canadians in general have considered only a small part of the harms of residential schools, mostly those caused by sexual abuse. Some provinces have amended their limitation statutes to enable civil prosecutions for a wider range of offences. We urge others to follow suit.[17]

Views of those who followed closely the work of the Commission differ as to whether the Department of Justice supported the work of the Commission after this initial and last request.

## IV STRUCTURE

The structure of the Commission to meet its objectives was as follows:

— Five Commissioners, including a President, were appointed by the federal Cabinet, which means in practice by the Prime Minister on the recommendation

---

[15] Law Commission of Canada Act 1996, s 5(1)(b).
[16] Law Commission of Canada, *Restoring Dignity: Responding to Institutional Child Abuse* (2000).
[17] Truth and Reconciliation Commission of Canada, *Honouring the Truth, Reconciling the Future: Summary of the Final Report of the Truth and Reconciliation Commission of Canada* (2015) 214.

of the Justice Minister. Section 7(3) of the 1996 Act provides that: 'As a group, the Commissioners should be broadly representative of the socio-economic and cultural diversity of Canada, represent various disciplines and reflect knowledge of the common law and civil law systems.'

— During my term, the five Commissioners were from different regions of Canada (two from the west, one from the east and two from the centre). The Commission was composed of two Francophones, two Anglophones and one Aboriginal; of four men and one woman; of three jurists trained in common law and one in civil law and one from a discipline other than law. Scholars formed the majority of the Commission with three Commissioners active as professors. To ensure continuity instead of a complete turnover on the Board, the Commissioners were not appointed all at the same time. This means that a new Commissioner, including a new President, would join an already existing team, with its own group dynamic and its ongoing projects. This could prove to be challenging for a new Commissioner. While the nominations were at the discretion of the federal Cabinet, I can truly say that I did not perceive political partisanship from other Commissioners.

— The Act also provided for the creation of an Advisory Committee to be composed of at least 12 persons and a maximum of 24. People on the Committee represented different components of society—whether it was older persons, unions, business, the police forces and so on. These persons, however, participated in this Committee in their personal capacity and not to voice the concerns of specific groups. The Commission would meet members of this Committee at least once a year to report on the progress of its work and to ask for their reactions to proposed new projects. Moreover, during the year, the Commission also asked for the views of various members of this group if needed. These members, although acting in their personal capacity, served as links between their community of interest and their regions and the Commission. They could provide points of view that otherwise would not have been voiced by other actors. The obvious enthusiasm, over the years, from members of this Committee for the initiatives taken by the Commission was of course welcomed by the Commission. The composition of the Committee was another signal that law reform was no longer the preserve of jurists and judges.

— Only the President of the Commission, typically a university professor, held a full-time position at the Commission. He or she, as well as the part-time Commissioners, were supported by a team at the national office located in the capital, Ottawa. It was a small team, approximately 12 employees, including an executive director and three researchers. Given the multidisciplinary approach of the Commission, some of these researchers as well as the executive director were not jurists.

The budget of the Commission remained more or less the same over the years.[18] An important portion of this budget was used to support the cost of public consultations

[18] The budget was approximatively CAN$ 3m annually. See Law Commission of Canada, *Report on Plans and Priorities: 2006–2007 Estimates* (2006).

and other means of consultation, including the cost of translation. Given its limited resources, the Commission worked with various partners in order to reach a larger audience. Through these partnerships the Commission was able to support research projects that could not have happened otherwise and also to do more outreach.

## V  EXPERTISE AND PUBLIC INPUT

As already alluded to, one key role of the Commission was to involve members of the public in its programme of actions. As the second President of the Commission, Nathalie Des Rosiers, wrote: one of the objectives of the Commission was to modernise law reform, to make it a more democratic exercise,[19] and, in doing so, to enrich in turn our democratic system.

For a vast country like Canada, the second largest one in terms of land mass in the world, it is not easy to engage the public from all corners of the country. Nevertheless, the Commission attempted to promote, through all kinds of means, the largest possible participation in its work. First, shortly after its creation in 1997, it asked Canadians to identify the most pressing problems that needed to be addressed by the Law Commission. This was before e-mails were used regularly and certainly pre-Skype. The Commission received hundreds of suggestions and, given its limited resources, had to identify a set of priorities. In doing so, the Commission consulted its Advisory Committee.

The means by which the Commission conveyed information, provoked reactions and invited dialogue were through a great diversity of activities, some of which were novel for a Law Commission. For instance, while the Commission set up a number of panels for in-depth discussion of issues, it also produced brochures in accessible language, sponsored the production of documentary films as well as plays, and created partnerships with public radio. In particular, the Commission was keen to reach out to the most vulnerable persons, including by working with support groups for these persons. Once again, in doing so, the Commission was acting in conformity with its mandate. Section 4 of the 1996 Act provides that the Commission could, among other things:

(a)  undertake, promote, initiate and evaluate studies and research;
(b)  support, publish, sell and otherwise disseminate studies, reports and other documents;
(c)  sponsor or support conferences, seminars and other meetings;
(d)  facilitate and support co-operative efforts among the Commission, governments, the academic community, the legal profession and other organisations and persons interested in the Commission's work.

I was particularly pleased that through its action the Commission empowered various groups and institutions as well as experts from various disciplines to work

---

[19] N Des Rosiers, 'In Memoriam: La Commission du Droit du Canada/The Law Commission of Canada, 1997–2006' (2007) 22(2) *Canadian Journal of Law and Society* 145.

together and to publish the results of this work in both official languages of Canada. Over the years the Commission was able to develop links with, and count on the support of, various groups interested in the work being carried out by the Commission as well as on the participation of many scholars that would answer in great number the request for proposals by the Commission to realise scholarly work at a modest cost. In my view, this support for the work of the Commission was due to its independence and, consequently, its credibility. As well, the opportunity for scholars from various disciplines to work together on a topic of common interest was certainly a draw.

It is interesting to note that for some themes, for instance one that concerned relationships between generations, there were very few jurists working on these issues compared to other disciplines such as sociology, economy, or psychology to name but three. However, this did not deter the Commission from pursuing this issue.

The publication of a Commission report was the result of, usually, a long process of consultations and research. One key step in this process was the publication of a discussion paper in which the Commission would identify a series of questions raised by the topic under consideration. Since this document, by its nature, identified many of the key issues that would need to be addressed, its content would be debated at length before its publication. Over time the Commission tried to further refine this document so as to make it easier to use in all kinds of fora and by the general public. The last discussion paper published, on indigenous legal traditions, included not only a list of issues to be discussed as well as an in-depth scholarly paper, but also a film documentary that gave voice to Aboriginal people from various regions of the country.[20]

## VI  A SUBSTANTIVE PROGRAMME BUILT ON THE CONCEPT OF RELATIONSHIPS

In terms of substance, the problems considered by the Commission during its nine years of existence were varied, each one fitting within one of the four relationships mentioned previously (personal, social, economic and governance). For instance:

— Regarding 'personal relationships', the Commission published a report in 2001 titled *Beyond Conjugality*.[21] It noted that Canadians participate in a diversity of close personal relationships with other adults and that the nature of these relationships was becoming even more diversified. While many have a conjugal partner, others live with their parents, brothers, sisters, their caregivers or others. The Commission asked the following question: 'Since there are many kinds of personal relationships between adults, why is the law focused almost exclusively on conjugal relationships?' Based on this question, the Commission proposed to rethink entirely the manner in which governments regulate

---

[20] Law Commission of Canada, *Justice Within: Indigenous Legal Traditions: Discussion Paper* (2006).
[21] Law Commission of Canada, *Beyond Conjugality: Recognizing and Supporting Close Personal Adult Relationships* (2002).

relationships between adults. The Commission recommended, among many things, that government support equality in relationships. The Commission did suggest modifying a number of laws to apply this approach. It is very likely that the legislature will want to revisit this approach as relationships of all kinds are forming, notably with a population getting older and young adults staying with their parents longer.

— In 2004, in the category of social relationships, the Commission published a report on electoral reform titled *Voting Counts: Electoral Reform for Canada*.[22] It concluded that more and more Canadians hope for a renewal of democratic institutions, starting with the electoral system of first past the post. The report helped shape debate that followed on this issue, notably in a few provinces where reforms were proposed but ultimately rejected by the population. This issue did not go away in any event since electoral reform was part of the policy platform of the two main opposition parties for the federal election in October 2015 and the newly elected government is committed to electoral reform.

— Another project that was initiated by the Commission in the governance relationship and that led to a discussion paper was on the topic of *Law in a Globalized World*.[23] The Commission looked at a number of issues, including the relationship between national and international law and extraterritoriality. The first of these touched on democracy, transparency and public participation. The starting premise was that international law had an increasing influence on domestic law.[24] As for the concept of extraterritoriality, the Commission asked a number of questions that are certainly still relevant today. For instance, should the state criminalise the actions of Canadians who support insurgents in armed conflicts? Should the purchase of organ transplants abroad that cannot be purchased in Canada be criminalised? However, the project reached well beyond criminal law. To encourage new thinking on the matter the Commission issued a request for proposals with the proviso that the only proposals that would be considered would be those put forward by a team of legal scholars. In addition, each member of the team had to be an expert in an area of law different from the area of expertise of other members. It is worth noting that teams of scholars from various regions of the country put forward proposals, and this despite the fact that the amount paid for the research was rather modest. Also interestingly, the team that was ultimately selected produced a paper, published by the Commission in both official languages, which was later published in a law review and cited by the Supreme Court of Canada.[25] That paper was also

---

[22] Law Commission of Canada, *Voting Counts: Electoral Reform for Canada* (2004).

[23] Law Commission of Canada, *Crossing Borders: Law in a Globalized World: Discussion Paper* (2006).

[24] In that regard the Commission asked the following three questions: (1) What should be the respective roles of Parliament, of the executive and of civil society in the negotiation and ratification of treaties? (2) How can we achieve a more transparent and efficient implementation of international obligations? (3) How much weight should administrative tribunals and courts give to international law?

[25] See the reference to S Coughlan et al, 'Global Reach, Local Grasp: Constructing Extraterritorial Jurisdiction in the Age of Globalization' (2007) 6 *Canadian Journal of Law and Technology* 29 in *R v Hape* [2007] 2 SCR 292.

a launchpad for this team for a much more ambitious project that was the recipient of a major grant by a public funding agency and led to the publication of a volume on the topic.[26] As this example demonstrates, a project that originated from the Commission could be successfully pursued later through other means.

VII CONCLUSION

The second Law Commission of Canada, from its mandate and the way it went about implementing it, was not only different from the first Commission but also from other Commissions at the provincial level or in other countries. For the traveller in Robert Frost's poem, in the end the road chosen made all the difference. I leave it to others to determine if the novel approach adopted by the second Law Commission did make a difference.

Some critics have argued that this model was so far removed from what is expected from a Law Commission that its closure was only a matter of time.[27] These critics fail to appreciate a number of considerations.

First, although the Law Commission did not usually submit draft Bills, it nevertheless made a number of suggestions to amend laws, and, in some cases, specific provisions. In other words, it did not shy away from in-depth studies of legislation when needed.

Second, the Law Commission acted pursuant to the mandate conferred to it by Parliament. As mentioned previously, the Act creating the second Law Commission was putting forward a new approach to law reform.[28]

Third, for those who find comfort and security in the percentage of proposed legislation subsequently implemented by a legislature, the reality is that there is no cover when the government of the day wants to put an end to the operation of a Law Commission. The first Law Commission of Canada, as noted earlier, was closed despite the fact that its approach was more in keeping with the traditional model. Moreover, the same is true of the first Law Commission of Ontario. These responses to critics are not meant to defend or promote the model embraced by the second Law Commission in Canada but rather to warn against complacency whatever the model is.

Looking ahead, I am convinced that there will be, one day, a new national Law Commission in Canada. However, having demonstrated that there is not one way

[26] S Coughlan, RJ Currie, HM Kindred and T Scassa, *Law Beyond Borders: Extraterritorial Jurisdiction in an Age of Globalization* (Toronto, Irwin Law, 2014).
[27] At the conference in London, one scholar opined that the Law Commission looked more like a cross-disciplinary research centre; he was not sure it should be called a law reform body.
[28] See the statement of Richard Mosley (Assistant Deputy Minister, Criminal Policy, Department of Justice) to a parliamentary committee when the second Law Commission was proposed. The Commission was to adopt 'a new approach to law reform, namely openness, inclusiveness, responsiveness: a multidisciplinary approach; along with innovation and cost effectiveness': Standing Committee on Justice and Legal Affairs, Law Commission of Canada Bill, 7 December 1995.

to design a Law Commission, Canada will not want to revisit the same paths. Therefore, a new Commission is likely to be different from the first two on the basis of lessons learned from our past experience. A Commission could pursue both more traditional law reform (commonly called 'lawyers' law') as well as looking, through a multidisciplinary approach, at the role of law in social issues of importance to the public. A number of measures could be taken to ensure that both the Department of Justice and Parliament engage meaningfully and regularly with the Commissioners. For instance:

— The Minister of Justice could be required to meet at least once a year with the Commission and the Deputy Minister to meet with the Commission on a quarterly basis.
— The Minister of Justice could be required, within six months of the release of a report, to respond to it, in a similar vein to the new protocol in England. The Minister should also be expected to appear in front of a relevant parliamentary committee to explain his or her response.
— If a report has not been implemented, the Minister of Justice could be required, every year, to restate her/his position and justification for not acting.
— The Commission could appear at least once a year in front of relevant parliamentary committees.
— Relevant parliamentary committees could be entitled, in addition to the Minister of Justice, to refer a matter to the Commission.
— When submitting a final report, the expectation could be that the Commission would submit a draft Bill and, if no draft is submitted, to explain why.
— A specific process could be set up for the consideration by Parliament of a draft Bill.

Readers will recognise in this list of plausible measures, a number of practices adopted in other jurisdictions. Canada should carefully consider successful models adopted by other countries if it were to create, once more, a new Commission. On the other hand, other countries may want to look carefully at the accumulated experience of Canada. After all, Canada, '*par la force des choses*' is developing an expertise in reforming Law Commissions. Other countries may want to draw lessons from that experience and adopt some of the key features found in the first and/or second Law Commission.

# 12

# The Law Commission
# and the Criminal Law: Reflections
# on the Codification Project

IAN DENNIS*

## I INTRODUCTION

The criminal law provides an instructive case-study for the debate about codification in a common law jurisdiction. Many common law jurisdictions have succeeded in codifying their criminal law, but in England and Wales, the home of the common law, there has never been a penal code. Of course efforts have been made, but the attempts to codify English criminal law via the work of law reform commissions have a 'long but chequered history'[1] of repeated failure. The collapse of two major projects in the nineteenth century[2] took the subject of codification off the law reform agenda for decades, but it was revived in the second half of the twentieth century following the establishment of the Law Commission of England and Wales in 1965. The Law Commissions Act 1965 assigned to each of the Law Commissions for England and Wales, and for Scotland, the duty:

> to take and keep under review all the law with which they are respectively concerned with a view to its systematic development and reform, including in particular the codification of such law, the elimination of anomalies, the repeal of obsolete and unnecessary enactments, the reduction of the number of separate enactments and generally the simplification and modernisation of the law.[3]

Pursuant to this duty the Law Commission of England and Wales embarked in 1968 on a project of a comprehensive examination of the criminal law with a view to its codification.[4] Some 20 years later the Commission, with the assistance of a team of academic lawyers,[5] published a Draft Criminal Code Bill and accompanying report.[6]

---

* I am grateful to Professor David Ormerod QC for helpful suggestions. The usual disclaimer applies.
[1] Law Commission, LC 143, *Codification of the Criminal Law: A Report to the Law Commission* (1985) Introduction by the Law Commission, para 3.
[2] The history is briefly summarised in Introduction by the Law Commission, n 1 above, paras 3–6.
[3] Law Commissions Act 1965, s 3(1).
[4] Law Commission, LC 14, *Second Programme of Law Reform* (1968) item XVIII.
[5] The team consisted of the late Professor Sir JC Smith, the late Professor EJ Griew and myself.
[6] Law Commission, LC 177, *A Criminal Code for England and Wales* (1989).

The draft Bill was never enacted, but the Commission continued to work on the codification project for another two decades until it announced the effective abandonment of the project in 2008.[7] After 2008, the Commission carried on work on specific topics in criminal law and made important recommendations for reform, but codification of the criminal law once again appeared to be off the agenda. However, the project may not be completely dead and buried. The Law Commission's recent initiative on sentencing procedure[8] may signal a partial revival of the original scheme and could conceivably lead to the resuscitation of the whole scheme. Ironically though, the strategy for achieving codification might now be the exact reverse of what the Commission envisaged 25 years ago.

The purpose of my chapter is to revisit the 1989 attempt at codification of the criminal law. First, from the standpoint of someone who was closely associated with the Law Commission's project for much of its existence, I will offer some reflections[9] about what the draft code of 1989 achieved and why it ultimately failed. Secondly, and in some contrast, I will suggest that the values which underpinned the codification project have to some extent been promoted in other forms, notably the development of what might be called 'mini-codes' in a number of areas. Thirdly, I will conclude with some comments on the sentencing initiative and an assessment of its implications for the codification project as a whole.

## II  THE CODIFICATION PROJECT: SUCCESS AND FAILURE OF THE DRAFT CODE

### A  Objective and Theory of the Draft Code

In evaluating the codification project it is essential to appreciate its objective. Different conceptions of codification are possible. These range from a pure consolidation of existing sources of the law with no changes at all to a new model code incorporating extensive changes to previous law or recasting the law completely.[10] For the purposes of its codification project, the Law Commission accepted the academic team's proposition that sought to distinguish codification from both consolidation and the creation of a new model code. According to this proposition the aim of codification was to set out the criminal law in a 'single, coherent, consistent, unified and comprehensive piece of legislation'.[11] In the team's view achieving this aim would not necessarily require reconsideration of all the relevant law with a view to reform. Much of the law might simply require the restatement of existing principles. However, some reform might be necessary to achieve the objectives of codification and to that extent

---

[7] Law Commission, LC 311, *Tenth Programme of Law Reform* (2008) para 1.6.

[8] Law Commission, LC 354, *Twelfth Programme of Law Reform* (2014) para. 2.29. See also chapter 35 (Sir David Lloyd Jones).

[9] The paper draws on ideas sketched in two previously published papers: I Dennis, 'The Critical Condition of Criminal Law' (1997) 50 *Current Legal Problems* 213 (hereafter Dennis, CLP); I Dennis, 'Codifying the Law of Criminal Evidence' (2014) 35 *Statute Law Review* 107 (hereafter Dennis, SLR).

[10] As George Gretton has also noted in his contribution to this volume (chapter 10).

[11] LC 143, n 1 above, Introduction by the Law Commission, para 16.

the project could not be one of pure consolidation of existing law in a single statute. We should note that the team's conception of codification was founded on a set of values which it was thought the criminal law should embody; these were the values of accessibility of the law, its comprehensibility, its consistency and its certainty.[12] I will return to these values in section III below.

The team and the Commission envisaged a code in four parts. Part I would contain general principles of criminal liability, Part II specific offences, Part III the rules of criminal evidence and procedure, and Part IV provisions relating to sentencing and the disposal of offenders. The Draft Criminal Code Bill appended to the Commission's 1989 report contained a reasonably complete draft of Part I and a draft of a substantial Part II covering some 90 per cent of the offences regularly tried in the criminal courts. No work at that stage had been done on Part III or IV.

The academic team made it clear that most of their work had gone into the drafting of the provisions in Part I. The general principles of criminal liability, most of which were wholly or partly to be found in the common law, were thought to present the biggest challenges to the values on which the code should be based. Accordingly, most of the examples used to illustrate problems of obscurity, inconsistency and uncertainty in the law were taken from the general part of criminal law. The specific offences included in Part II were originally selected to test the adequacy of the provisions in Part I; as the team put it, '[i]t would be impossible to see how Part I would function unless specific offences were drafted in the light of the principles therein stated'.[13]

It is worth emphasising that this approach to codification was founded on a distinct conception of the criminal law itself. According to this conception substantive criminal offences should be interpreted and applied within a theoretical and doctrinal framework supplied by the general principles of liability. The general part thus provides the starting-point for an inquiry into individual guilt of specific offences. The priority and importance of the general part was signalled in the 1989 draft code by its placing in Part I and by its length of 52 clauses. These covered an extensive range of topics: preliminary matters; interpretation; procedural issues relating to alternative verdicts and double jeopardy; proof; external elements of offences; fault and fault terms; ignorance or mistake of law; intoxication; parties to offences; corporate liability; incapacity and mental disorder; defences; and preliminary offences.

The normative theory of liability on which many of the provisions were based was what Duff has described as 'orthodox subjectivism'.[14] This theory was 'defendant-centred', meaning that the theory focused on a defendant's culpability. At its core were the principles that a person should not in general be liable for an offence unless he or she intended or was (subjectively) reckless as to the conduct or harm in question, and that he or she had the capacity and a fair opportunity to act otherwise.

---

[12]  ibid paras 1.3–1.9.
[13]  ibid para 0.3.
[14]  RA Duff, *Intention Agency and Criminal Liability* (Oxford, Blackwell, 1990). For a brief summary of the theory see Dennis, CLP, 236–38.

The theory had been developed and refined as the foundation of the general part by some of the most distinguished scholars of the twentieth century, most notably HLA Hart,[15] and Glanville Williams.[16] The second edition of Williams' seminal treatise *Criminal Law: The General Part* had appeared in 1961 and in the decades that followed it had a profound and lasting influence on the way that scholars and law reform bodies thought about the criminal law. Williams himself was both a founder member of the Criminal Law Revision Committee and the Law Commission's original working group, the two key bodies concerned with the implementation of the codification project until the end of the 1970s. Much of the analysis and argument in the treatise had found its way into Smith and Hogan's textbook,[17] unsurprisingly a principal source for the academic team working on the project in the 1980s.

## B Successes of the Draft Code

The Draft Criminal Code Bill was never introduced into Parliament, even in an amended form. What then did the 1989 draft code achieve, in spite of not being enacted? I suggest that we can make three claims for it. First, and most importantly, it demonstrated that the codification project was feasible. It showed that it was possible, more than a century after James Fitzjames Stephen's great work,[18] to draft a coherent and workable code of modern English criminal law. While there was disagreement about the content of some of the draft code (see below), the foundation values which inspired it were widely accepted, and the arguments of critics opposed to the goal of codification were thought to carry little conviction.[19] Second, although the Law Commission accepted in the early 1990s that it could not take forward the draft code as a whole,[20] it was able to use the draft as the basis for further work. The reports on offences against the person,[21] and involuntary manslaughter[22] were explicitly aimed at refining and carrying forward the provisions in the draft code relating to those topics. The cogency of those reports has not diminished with time.

---

[15] HLA Hart, *Punishment and Responsibility* (Oxford, Clarendon, 1968).

[16] G Williams, *Criminal Law: The General Part*, 2nd edn (London Stevens, 1961); G Williams, *Textbook of Criminal Law*, 2nd edn (London, Stevens, 1983).

[17] JC Smith and B Hogan, *Criminal Law*, the first edition of which appeared in 1965 (London, Butterworths). The text, now known as *Smith and Hogan's Criminal Law*, is currently in its 14th edition, edited by D Ormerod and K Laird (Oxford, OUP, 2015).

[18] See his Criminal Code (Indictable Offences) Bill 1878. It was this Bill which was referred to a Royal Commission, composed of Stephen and three High Court judges, which presented a revised version of the Bill in 1879, the Draft Code (Indictable Offences) Bill.

[19] See LC 177, n 6 above, vol 1, paras 2.12–2.26.

[20] This acceptance followed a conference in Cambridge at which a number of difficulties and reservations about the draft code were discussed (see Editorial, 'Codifying English Criminal Law' [1990] *Crim LR* 141). Within the Law Commission there was a feeling on the part of new members that the law on certain topics in the draft code needed a rethink, notably intoxication (Law Commission, LC CP 127, *Intoxication and Criminal Liability* (1993)) and complicity (Law Commission, LC CP 131, *Assisting and Encouraging Crime* (1993)).

[21] Law Commission, LC 218, *Legislating the Criminal Code: Offences against the Person and General Principles* (1993).

[22] Law Commission, LC 237, *Legislating the Criminal Code: Involuntary Manslaughter* (1996).

Third, the draft code has exerted considerable influence as an authoritative restatement of common law principles of criminal liability. Many university courses on criminal law have exposed students to the draft code. It has been discussed in all the leading textbooks on criminal law,[23] and it has been cited to and by courts on a number of occasions.[24]

## C Failure of the Draft Code

With those points in mind we can now turn to consider how to account for the failure of the draft code to make legislative progress. It is not possible to point to any single factor as the reason for failure. A number of factors played a role, most of which were clearly apparent at the time but others less so. Pre-eminent was the lack of interest in Westminster and Whitehall in a criminal code. It had been more than 20 years since a Home Secretary had publicly expressed support for codification,[25] and when the draft code was published the subject did not form part of the programme for any political party. The Home Office, which at the time would have had responsibility for introducing a Criminal Code Bill, was known to be at best lukewarm about the codification project. It was almost certainly unenthusiastic about the academic team's draft because of the amount of reform it contained, particularly in areas likely to be controversial, such as sexual offences and mental disorder. Legislation in those areas could probably not have been brought forward without further extensive consultation.

Also lacking was professional support for the draft code, in the sense that there was no powerful judicial or practitioner constituency pressing for its implementation. In later years senior judges expressed themselves strongly in favour of codification,[26] but that level of support was not apparent in 1989. One can only speculate why that was so, but at least one influential member of the House of Lords was a critic of codification, and it may be that the amount of reform in the draft code caused as much unease to practitioners and the judiciary as it did to the politicians. Further problems arose from the principle of restatement of existing law. The draft came under fire from two different groups of academic critics. One group argued that in some areas the code did not state the existing law accurately.[27] The other group argued that insofar as the code did state the law accurately it had merely succeeded

---

[23] See Smith and Hogan, 14th edn, n 17 above, 30–31; AP Simester, JR Spencer, GR Sullivan and GJ Virgo, *Simester and Sullivan's Criminal Law*, 5th edn (Oxford, Hart Publishing, 2013) 44–45; W Wilson, *Criminal Law*, 5th edn (Harlow, Pearson, 2014) 32–33.

[24] A leading example is *R v Hasan* [2005] UKHL 22, [2005] 2 AC 467, [34] (Lord Bingham), [67] (Lady Hale).

[25] Rt Hon Roy Jenkins, in a speech in 1967: Law Commission, LC 143, *Codification of the Criminal Law: A Report to the Law Commission* (1985) Introduction by the Law Commission, para 7.

[26] H Brooke, 'The Law Commission and Criminal Law Reform' [1995] *Crim LR* 911; T Bingham, 'A Criminal Code: Must We Wait for Ever?' [1998] *Crim LR* 694; M Arden, 'Criminal Law at the Crossroads: The Impact of Human Rights from the Law Commission's Perspective and the Need for a Code' [1999] *Crim LR* 439.

[27] See, eg, G de Burca and S Gardner, 'The Codification of the Criminal Law' (1990) 10 *OJLS* 559; G Williams, '*Finis* for *Novus Actus?*' (1989) 48 *CLJ* 391.

in replicating existing confusions, contradictions and unsound policy embodied in the law.[28]

This last point leads us to consider two less obvious and more deep-seated factors. The first is one to which I drew attention some years ago. As I put it:

> The restatement principle had been the foundation on which the original ... proposal to the Commission had been constructed. It made coherent sense in 1980, which was probably the high water-mark of the acceptance of orthodox subjectivism by the courts and the legislature. At that stage it certainly looked feasible to construct a code based on subjectivist principles and to claim fairly that it represented the fundamental principles of English law. By 1989 this claim was more controversial. The courts had moved off in different directions in a number of areas: intention, recklessness, duress, parties, and so on. Criticism of orthodox subjectivism was beginning to make itself felt on several fronts.[29]

The academic debate about the draft code's underlying theory of liability did not target the aim of codification as such. Rather it called into question the desirability of a code incorporating a cluster of subjectivist principles which would have the effect of limiting a defendant's culpability and restricting liability for serious harms. The draft code would, for example, have eliminated constructive liability in the law of homicide and non-fatal offences against the person,[30] and would have retained the highly controversial rule that an honest but unreasonable belief in consent is a defence to rape.[31] The theoretical debate has continued in the 25 years since the publication of the draft code, and has been sharpened by two further developments. The first of these is the greatly increased importance now attached to the victims of crime and the need for the criminal law to provide appropriate degrees of protection to victims. Such protection may well take the form of 'objective' fault elements, as in the modern law of rape,[32] or the extensive use of constructive liability, as in the law of driving offences causing death.[33] The other related development derives from human rights jurisprudence and the doctrine of positive obligations under the European Convention on Human Rights. This may require member states to make changes to their criminal laws to safeguard the Convention rights of victims. An example is the limitation of the common law defence of reasonable chastisement of a child effected by section 58 of the Children Act 2004 in response to the decision of the European Court of Human Rights in *A v United Kingdom*.[34]

The final factor which may help to account for the failure of the draft code derives from one of the arguments against codification. This is the argument that the enactment of a code would lead to ossification of the law and close down the opportunity

---

[28] See, eg, A Norrie, *Crime Reason and History* (London, Weidenfeld and Nicolson, 1993); PR Glazebrook, 'Structuring the Criminal Code: Functional Approaches to Complicity, Incomplete Offences and General Defences' in AP Simester and ATH Smith (eds), *Harm and Culpability* (Oxford, OUP, 1996) 195.

[29] Dennis, CLP 243–44.

[30] Law Commission, LC 177, *A Criminal Code for England and Wales* (1989) vol 1, Draft Criminal Code Bill, cll 54, 55, 70–72.

[31] ibid cl 89.

[32] Sexual Offences Act 2003, s 1.

[33] Road Traffic Act 1988, ss 1, 2B, 3ZB.

[34] *A v United Kingdom* (1999) 27 EHRR 611.

for gradual development of the law which the flexibility of the common law would otherwise allow. The Law Commission thought there was some force in this view, but went on to reject it as founded on a number of misconceptions.[35] However, it now seems to me that there is a dimension to the argument that was not sufficiently appreciated at the time by either its advocates or by the Commission. The point is concerned with codification of the general principles of liability and the relationship of the general part of a code to substantive offences. I mentioned above that the conception of the criminal law embodied in the draft code was that of an overarching framework of general principles within which substantive offences are to be interpreted and applied. The general part is thus at the heart of the code. However, it is possible to contrast this conception with an older alternative view of the criminal law. This view regards the law as largely consisting of a collection of free-standing specific offences, each with separate elements which require separate interpretation. This was in essence the nineteenth-century view of the law, and was exemplified in *Tolson* in the form of Stephen J's well-known denial of the existence of general principles of *mens rea*.[36] The view was reflected in Stephen's draft code,[37] which formed the basis of the draft code appended to the Report of the Royal Commissioners in 1879.[38] On this view the roles of the general and special parts of the code are effectively reversed. The primary task is the interpretation of the specific offence. The interpretation is subject to limited and miscellaneous common law rules, such as those relating to parties or intoxication, which apply generally to supplement or modify offence definitions. There are also certain exculpatory principles, such as the limited number of general defences or the novus actus doctrine of causation, which may be invoked by way of defence in appropriate cases. Overall then the role of the general part is to be a resource, to be called on by the prosecution or the defence as and when an offence definition requires to be modified or supplemented in order to do justice in the instant case.

It may well be that it was this conception of the criminal law which continued to be the dominant mindset of the majority of the judiciary and the legal profession throughout the twentieth century, certainly up to the time of the appearance of the Law Commission's draft code. If this is right, it may follow that when critics of codification complained of the loss of flexibility in a code their target was not statutory definitions of common law offences but the codified framework of general principle. Their concern may have been the loss of the courts' ability to reinterpret general principles in difficult individual cases to enable justice to be done. It seems clear that this flexibility had become well-established at the time of the draft code, witness the number of leading cases on issues of general principle decided in the period between

---

[35] LC 177, n 30 above, paras 2.16–2.18.

[36] *R v Tolson* (1889) 23 QBD 168, 185.

[37] See S Kadish, 'Codifiers of the Criminal Law: Wechsler's Predecessors' (1978) 78 *Columbia Law Review* 1098, 1121–30.

[38] *Report of the Royal Commission on the Law Relating to Indictable Offences* (C 2345, 1879). The draft contained a Part I consisting of just six preliminary provisions, compared with 52 in the 1989 draft code.

the early 1960s[39] and the late 1980s. And with hindsight it is clear that the process of settling common law general principles had not reached full maturity at the time of the draft code. There is no doubt that the process of judicial development of general principles has continued since the draft code. A prominent example of the expansion of liability via general principles is the growth of the controversial doctrine of joint enterprise for use in cases of serious crimes committed by members of groups. In the area of defences the courts have usefully clarified the scope of duress[40] but have proved unable to do so in the case of necessity. Pleas of necessity have given rise to some particularly interesting and tricky issues,[41] and it is still impossible to state confidently whether a defence of necessity exists outside the parameters of duress of circumstances, and, if it does, what its elements are.

I conclude this part of the chapter therefore with a speculation. It may be that the combination of theoretical uncertainty and scepticism about the case for codification of the general part reinforced concerns on the part of politicians, civil servants and some of the legal profession about the pragmatic difficulties of taking forward the draft code, particularly given the controversial nature of a significant part of its content.

### III PROMOTING THE VALUES OF CODIFICATION

It was noted above that the draft code sought to promote via codification the values of accessibility, comprehensibility, consistency and certainty of the criminal law. To this list we now need to add the value of efficiency in the operation of the criminal process, a value increasingly emphasised in debates on criminal justice reform since the appearance of the draft code. Although the 1989 draft code has not been enacted, several developments over the last quarter of a century bear on these values. We can now turn to consider how far these developments have furthered the codification agenda.

### A Accessibility

The first rather obvious point is that the availability of much of the law has been greatly improved by the computer revolution. At the time of the draft code in 1989

---

[39] In 1960 the requirement for the Attorney-General's fiat to take a case to the House of Lords was abolished and replaced by the requirements for certification and leave (Administration of Justice 1960, s 1). Issues of general principle in the criminal law were almost certain to be points of law of general public importance and hence eligible for certification.

[40] See in particular the judgment of Lord Bingham in *R v Hasan* [2005] UKHL 22, [2005] 2 AC 467.

[41] See the well-known conjoined twins case of *Re A (Children)* [2001] Fam 147 (CA). See also *R v Quayle* [2005] EWCA Crim 1415, [2005] 1 WLR 3642. The issues are discussed in I Dennis, 'On Necessity as a Defence to Crime: Possibilities, Problems and the Limits of Justification and Excuse' (2009) 3 *Criminal Law and Philosophy* 29. It should be noted in this context that the draft code codified only the form of necessity called duress of circumstances and left open the possibility that other forms of the defence might be held to exist at common law: Law Commission, LC 177, *A Criminal Code for England and Wales* (1989) vol 1, Draft Criminal Code Bill, cl 4(4).

personal computers were in their infancy and the internet was not much more than a gleam in the eyes of its inventors. Its widespread commercial and domestic use did not get under way until the 1990s. Now, thanks to public access websites such as www.legislation.gov.uk and www.bailii.org, most of the primary sources of the criminal law are freely available online to any inquirer.[42] In addition legal professionals have access to numerous general and specialised legal databases which have greatly facilitated the task of researching the law on virtually any given topic. However, improved availability of the law is only a partial answer to the problem of accessibility. The code team's aspiration was that an inquirer should not have to search the statute book and hundreds of volumes of law reports to find the criminal law. As the team put it in relation to Part I of the draft code, an effect of codification would be that:

> The source of the general principles of liability would be found in little more than 50 sections of an Act of Parliament instead of many statutes, thousands of cases and the extensive commentaries on them to be found in the textbooks.[43]

This aspiration has not yet been realised, but some piecemeal progress has been made. The Serious Crime Act 2007 recast the law of facilitating and encouraging crime and abolished the common law offence of incitement. Section 76 of the Criminal Justice and Immigration Act 2008 partly codified the common law of self-defence. In relation to specific offences, the old common law defence to murder of provocation was abolished by the Coroners and Justice Act 2009 and replaced by a new statutory partial defence of loss of control. Other topics in the common law have received important judicial consideration which has improved the accessibility of the law; I have already mentioned *Hasan*, with Lord Bingham's review of the defence of duress,[44] and we should add two leading decisions of the House of Lords which respectively clarified the meaning of intention, *Woollin* in 1999,[45] and recklessness, *G* in 2003,[46] in the criminal law.

## B Comprehensibility

The second value which the draft code sought to promote was that the law, when found, should not be incomprehensible or misleading. To quote the code team again:

> The second aim of codification must be to ensure that the law is as intelligible as possible. Ideally, it should be capable of being readily understood not only by lawyers but also by lay magistrates, police and, indeed, the ordinary intelligent citizen.[47]

---

[42] Though note Lord Toulson's and Matthew Dyson's comparisons of the effectiveness of these sources, in their contributions to this volume (chapters 14 and 38 respectively).
[43] Law Commission, LC 143, *Codification of the Criminal Law: A Report to the Law Commission* (1985) para 1.4.
[44] *R v Hasan* [2005] UKHL 22, [2005] 2 AC 467.
[45] *R v Woollin* [1999] 1 AC 82 (HL). See also the judgment of the Court of Appeal in *R v Matthews and Alleyne* [2003] EWCA Crim 192, [2003] 2 Cr App R 30.
[46] *R v G* [2003] UKHL 50, [2004] 1 AC 1034, overruling *R v Caldwell* [1982] AC 341 (HL).
[47] LC 143, n 43 above, para 1.5.

The code team recognised that achievement of this aim would involve difficult issues of drafting, given the inevitable complexity of doctrine in a developed and sophisticated system of criminal law. Nevertheless we thought that much could be done by stating rules as concisely as possible, using consistent terminology, avoiding legal jargon and using familiar words as nearly as possible in their ordinary sense.[48]

It is debatable whether the comprehensibility of the law has improved since the draft code. Some of the developments just mentioned in relation to accessibility have helped to make the law clearer to lawyers, although Part II of the Serious Crime Act is a notable exception.[49] But there is much work still to be done. To take an obvious example, we are unfortunately still living with the Offences against the Person Act 1861 as the main source of our law on non-fatal violence. Critics have repeatedly pointed out the many flaws of the Act, not least in this context its use of the term 'malicious' to describe the mental element of a number of key offences. This term is highly misleading; its technical meaning of intention or recklessness as to the causing of a specific type of harm bears no relation to its ordinary meaning of actions founded on emotions of spite or ill-will. Any competent law reform exercise would eliminate this anomaly and define the relevant mental element more accurately and precisely. Fortunately there is some reason for optimism that this might finally happen. Following a reference by the Ministry of Justice, the Law Commission issued in November 2014 a scoping paper on reform of the 1861 Act.[50] This has now been followed by a report in which the Commission has been sufficiently encouraged by a positive response to its consultation to make a strong case for a new law.[51] This could be based on the draft Bill appended to a Home Office paper in 1998 discussing offences against the person;[52] the origins of which can be traced to the provisions in the 1989 draft code.[53]

## C Consistency and Certainty

The haphazard development of the criminal law through the accidents of litigation and piecemeal legislation may have significant adverse consequences. Inconsistencies of terminology and substance may result, or there may be gaps where it is quite unclear what the law is. Alternatively a statute or case may state the law obscurely, so there is uncertainty as to the law to be applied to a particular problem.[54] A further related issue is that changes in social attitudes or political priorities or international

---

[48] ibid para 1.7.

[49] See D Ormerod and R Fortson, 'Serious Crime Act 2007: The Part 2 Offences' [2009] *Crim LR* 389.

[50] Law Commission, LC CP 217, *Reform of Offences against the Person: A Scoping Consultation Paper* (2014).

[51] LC 361, *Reform of Offences Against the Person* (2015).

[52] Home Office, *Violence: Reforming the Offences against the Person Act 1861: Consultation Document* (1998).

[53] Via Law Commission, LC 218, *Legislating the Criminal Code: Offences against the Person and General Principles* (1993).

[54] See LC 143, n 43 above, paras 1.8–1.9; Law Commission, LC 177, *A Criminal Code for England and Wales* (1989) vol 1, paras 2.8–2.11.

obligations may mean that older law is no longer 'fit for purpose'. The policies or
principles that it embodies may require at least updating and possibly discarding
altogether if they are thought no longer to be appropriate as the basis for the law in
question. Codification is capable of addressing all these concerns, although it will
be necessary to undertake substantial consultation exercises where the code will
contain extensive reforms.

It is in this connection that I want to draw attention to an important development that has taken place since the publication of the 1989 draft code. This is the
increasing use of what may be called new 'mini-codes'. These are pieces of legislation designed to recast the law in particular areas and to provide a reasonably
clear and consistent statement of the law based on coherent principles and policies.
A key feature of such mini-codes is that they make a fresh start.[55] They provide a
new authoritative text which does not usually require interpretation by reference to
previous law, and indeed the courts will generally discourage attempts to revive law
which they think Parliament has rejected.[56] The process of creating these mini-codes
has been particularly marked in relation to Parts II and III of the full code envisaged
by the Law Commission in 1989.

Dealing then with the substantive offences likely to be included in Part II, we can
note first the enactment of the Fraud Act 2006. This replaced the various offences
of deception in the Theft Acts 1968 and 1978. The new fraud offence has a number
of forms, all founded on a distinct conception of fraudulent conduct as a wrong
that does not require proof that the defendant made any particular gain from his
dishonesty.[57] Secondly, the Bribery Act 2010 was a landmark piece of legislation. It
replaced a mix of old and unsatisfactory common law and statutory offences with
a comprehensive new scheme designed at least in part to satisfy the UK's international obligations to have in place clear and effective laws to combat bribery and
corruption.[58] Thirdly, the Sexual Offences Act 2003 was a major reforming statute.
It revised and updated nearly all the law relating to sexual offences, much of which
dated back to the nineteenth century. If the Offences against the Person Act 1861
can be revised as the Law Commission has recommended that will mean that almost
all the major criminal offences in regular use will be contained in modern statutes.
The major exceptions will of course be the common law offences of murder and
manslaughter. As a matter of principle these ought to be in statutory form, and in
relation to manslaughter I have already mentioned the good report from the Law
Commission some years ago which contained a draft Bill.[59]

The development of mini-codes is even more marked in relation to the proposed
Part III of the code. The law of criminal evidence has been transformed over the last

[55] For examples see *R v Singh* [2006] EWCA Crim 660, [2006] 1 WLR 1564 and *R v Hanson* [2005]
EWCA Crim 824, [2005] 1 WLR 3169, dealing respectively with the new law of hearsay evidence and
bad character evidence set out in part 11 of the Criminal Justice Act 2003.
[56] See, eg, *R v Somanathan*, reported with *R v Weir* [2005] EWCA Crim 2866, [2006] 1 WLR 1885,
dealing with the new law on evidence of bad character set out in ch 1 of part 11 of the Criminal Justice
Act 2003.
[57] See further Law Commission, LC 276, *Fraud* (2002).
[58] See further GR Sullivan, 'The Bribery Act 2010: (1) An Overview' [2011] *Crim LR* 87.
[59] Law Commission, LC 237, *Legislating the Criminal Code: Involuntary Manslaughter* (1996).

30 years by a series of reforming statutes. The process began with the Police and Criminal Evidence Act 1984 which partly codified the law of police powers, including the obtaining of evidence such as confessions and identification evidence. Twenty years later the Criminal Justice Act 2003 recast the law on the major topics of hearsay evidence and bad character evidence; in the case of hearsay evidence Thomas LJ (as he then was) has described the new regime as a 'comprehensive statutory code'.[60] In between these two major statutes the Youth Justice and Criminal Evidence Act 1999 recast important parts of the law relating to witnesses; the topics covered included the competency of witnesses, special measures directions for vulnerable witnesses, cross-examination of vulnerable witnesses by defendants in person, and the controversial issue of evidence of a complainant's sexual history. The Criminal Justice and Public Order Act 1994 made significant modifications to the common law right to silence. In a paper in 2014,[61] I suggested that the process of statutory reform had reached the stage where codifying the law of criminal evidence would be appropriate and not an unduly difficult exercise. The majority of the general principles are now set out in modern statutes and the remaining common law principles are relatively well settled. In my view there are very few rules of evidence which would require difficult decisions of policy before codification could be achieved. In fact one such issue was resolved shortly after the paper was published. This issue concerns expert evidence which was dealt with by using a further development to which I now turn.

So far I have considered only primary legislation as the vehicle for codification. But the aim of making the law more accessible, comprehensible, consistent, certain and efficient, does not necessarily always require the use of primary legislation. Much can be achieved through the use of different forms of secondary legislation or 'soft law'. There are prominent examples in the law of criminal process. Codes of Practice now supplement statutory powers and duties at many stages of the investigative and prosecutorial process, from stop and search,[62] to the questioning of suspects,[63] to the use of surveillance and undercover agents,[64] to prosecutorial decisions,[65] and disclosure.[66] The style and detail of much of this material means that it is not appropriate for a code of primary legislation. As I commented in the earlier paper, 'The PACE codes of practice ... with their combination of rules, instructions, notes of guidance and explanatory material, would look very odd in a statute, even in a schedule'.[67] However, in terms of clarifying in detail how statutory powers should be exercised and statutory duties discharged, the codes provide essential information for lawyers, courts and the general public. The other example is the Criminal

---

[60] See *R v Horncastle* [2009] EWCA Crim 964, [2009] 4 All ER 183, [10].

[61] Dennis, SLR.

[62] PACE, code A.

[63] PACE, code C.

[64] Regulation of Investigatory Powers Act 2000.

[65] Code for Crown Prosecutors.

[66] Code of Practice issued under the Criminal Procedure and Investigations Act 1996. There is an abundance of further guidance on the operation of the statutory disclosure provisions which could usefully be consolidated.

[67] Dennis, SLR, 114.

Procedure Rules, first introduced in 2005 and now updated every six months. These provide extensive guidance for case management, including some issues of evidence. They have been used creatively in the last year to effect significant reform of the law governing the admissibility of expert evidence. The government had indicated that it did not wish to bring forward primary legislation to implement the Law Commission's recommendations on the subject,[68] but suggested that the substance of the recommendations should be incorporated in the Criminal Procedure Rules and/or a Practice Direction. This has now happened,[69] and the signs are that the courts will treat the new requirements almost as if they were in primary legislation.[70] It is worth concluding this brief glance at the Rules with a reminder that they begin with a statement of their 'overriding objective' that includes the proposition that the Rules are a 'new code'.

Finally, we should note the Law Commission's very recent initiative on sentencing procedure. The *Twelfth Programme of Law Reform*[71] drew attention to the complexity and confusion of modern sentencing legislation which creates many problems for courts and lawyers and results in a disturbing number of unlawful sentences that have to be corrected by the Court of Appeal.[72] The Commission announced a project to:

> introduce a single sentencing statute that will, thereafter, be the first and only port of call for sentencing tribunals. It will set out the relevant provisions in a clear and logical way. Just as importantly, any changes to sentencing procedure that Parliament wishes to make will be made to that Act and to no other. This will ensure that there is no need for judges and practitioners to look anywhere else.[73]

This welcome development would represent a major step forward in the promotion of codification values. In the first of the follow-up issues papers it is notable that the Commission refers expressly to the aim of the project as 'to codify sentencing procedure' and to produce a 'New Sentencing Code'.[74]

This aim has the explicit support of the senior judiciary. The Law Commission's website quotes the Lord Chief Justice, Lord Thomas of Cymgiedd: 'the Law Commission's project to codify sentencing law is a valuable and long-overdue stepping stone in the process of the rationalisation and clarification of the criminal law'.[75] A similar quote comes from Lord Justice Treacy, Chairman of the Sentencing Council:

> A sentencing code, containing a single comprehensive statement of the procedure to be followed after an offender's conviction, would greatly increase the accessibility and clarity

---

[68] Law Commission, LC 325, *Expert Evidence in Criminal Proceedings in England and Wales* (2011).

[69] See Editorial, 'Tightening the Law on Expert Evidence' [2015] *Crim LR* 1.

[70] *R v H* [2014] EWCA Crim 1555, (2014) 140 BMLR 59, [44] (Sir Brian Leveson P); J Thomas, 'The Criminal Procedure Rules: 10 Years On' [2015] *Crim LR* 395.

[71] LC 354 (2014).

[72] In the first of the follow-up issues papers, the Law Commission cites a figure of no less than 95 unlawful sentences in a randomly selected sample of 262 cases in 2012: Law Commission, *Sentencing Procedure: Issues Paper 1: Transition* (2015) para 1.9. This is an astonishing error rate.

[73] LC 354, n 71 above, para 2.29.

[74] *Sentencing Procedure Issues Paper*, n 72 above, para 1.1.

[75] Law Commission, 'Sentencing Procedure' www.lawcom.gov.uk/project/sentencing-procedure/#sentencing-procedure-issues-paper.

of the law in this area. This would reduce the potential for confusion which may create real problems in practice. This in turn would help promote fairness and consistency in sentencing.[76]

Such support, and it is further bolstered by quotations on the website from the President of the Law Society, the Chairman of the Bar Council and the Director of Public Prosecutions, provides strong grounds for optimism that a sentencing code has a good chance of enactment. Moreover, the promise of eliminating errors in sentencing and reducing the costs of appeals ought to attract the kind of political and executive support that the 1989 draft code sadly lacked.

## IV  CONCLUSION

It seems therefore that, despite the failure of the 1989 draft code, developments in the criminal law over the 25 years since the draft code was published show significant progress in promoting the values on which it was based. In my view there remains a strong case in principle for the enactment of the large-scale code envisaged in the Law Commission's 1989 report, but the strategy for achieving codification needs a further rethink. I have previously argued[77] that the most promising starting-point would now be Part III of the code given the transformation of the law of criminal procedure and evidence in the intervening period. There is every reason to think this would attract widespread support in the judiciary and the legal profession, and possible efficiency gains would make it appealing to politicians and civil servants also. However, given that the Commission has since taken up the sentencing initiative with good prospects of success, we should treat the initiative as providing both the clue and the impetus for a new strategy.

The new strategy would retain the four-part code envisaged in the 1989 report. But the order of enactment would be reversed. The first stage would be Part IV, the code of sentencing procedure. The second stage would be Part III, the code of procedure and evidence. Much of the relevant law in this Part is already effectively codified. The third stage should be Part II, the code of substantive offences. There is surely an unanswerable argument in principle that all substantive offences should be in statutory form.[78] In the twenty-first century there can be no case for retaining common law definitions of offences, particularly the very serious offences of murder and manslaughter. I suspect though that comprehensive legislation to replace common law offences will not happen any time soon. It seems safe to assume that politicians and policymakers will be reluctant to let Parliament debate the substantive law of homicide. The definition of murder in particular is likely to prove highly controversial, and of course there would almost certainly be attempts, encouraged by sections of the media, to reintroduce capital punishment for some categories of

[76] ibid.
[77] Dennis, SLR.
[78] The Law Commission has recently published two important reports in this connection: LC 355, *Simplification of Criminal Law: Kidnapping and Related Offences* (2014); LC 358, *Simplification of Criminal Law: Public Nuisance and Outraging Public Decency* (2015).

murder. Political considerations, coupled with the pragmatic view that 'the present law works, so why change it?' seem likely therefore to stymie efforts to complete a comprehensive Part II.

If, however, it could be achieved then attention could finally return to Part I. The way forward here might be to separate out those general rules which supplement offence definitions by enlarging the scope of liability. These are principally the rules governing complicity in crime and the effect of a defendant's voluntary intoxication by drink or drugs. They ought to be codified along with the substantive offences.[79] Exculpatory rules, such as the various general defences, might be left largely to the common law if it is thought desirable to preserve some inherent flexibility for deserving cases. It would not be an ideal solution for Part I, but might have some pragmatic appeal.[80]

To end on a positive note, as the fiftieth anniversary of the codification project approaches in 2018, all of us who have supported and continue to support the Commission's work on the project have some cause for optimism. There is momentum once again and it is to be hoped that it can finally produce real results.

---

[79] The difficulty of doing so should not be under-estimated. The law on both topics is notoriously complex and the Law Commission's most recent report on intoxication (LC 314, *Intoxication and Criminal Liability* (2009)) has not found favour with government.

[80] It will be interesting to see what happens to the Law Commission's current project on insanity, automatism and unfitness to plead: see Law Commission, *Criminal Liability: Insanity and Automatism: A Discussion Paper* (2013).

Part 4

# The Many Faces of Law Reform

# 13

# *Introduction*

### LORD CARNWATH

The Law Commission has come a long way from Lord Gardiner's splendidly ambitious mission, encapsulated in the 1965 statute, for the 'systematic development and reform' of 'all the law'. Experience, and the realities of the political process, have shown that large-scale law reform projects require large resources, human and financial, widespread support in the legal world, and very powerful friends in government to achieve success. During my time as Chairman of the Commission, the best example was the land registration project, which was not only badly needed, but also had the full support of the then Lord Chancellor, Lord Irvine. Less successful was the partnership law project, which in retrospect may have been too ambitious. The policy support was also weakened by the arrival of limited liability partnerships. A more targeted, piecemeal reform might have had a better chance of acceptance.

Against this background there has been increasing emphasis on smaller scale projects, and alternatives to statutory reform—'the many faces' of law reform, which were explored in this session. A good example from my time, mentioned by Lord Toulson, was our 1999 report on non-pecuniary damages for personal injury, in which we recommended against legislation, and in favour of guidelines laid down by the courts. In *Heil v Rankin*,[1] a five-judge Court of Appeal, led by Lord Woolf MR, responded positively to that challenge. Laura Dunlop shows in her paper how the Scottish Law Commission has been able to contribute to the development of the law by the courts, notably in relation to the law of unjust enrichment. Of special interest to me is her reference to their report on the foreshore and seabed, on which I drew in my judgment in the recent *Newhaven* case.[2] Shona Wilson Stark's fascinating analysis demonstrates convincingly the many ways in which Law Commission reports, with or without draft Bills, can influence the law. As she says, we must not write off unimplemented reports as failures; they may push the boundaries of law reform, and 'shine light into corners of the law which might otherwise be

---

[1] *Heil v Rankin* [2001] QB 272 (CA).
[2] *R (on the application of Newhaven Port and Properties Limited) v East Sussex County Council and another* [2015] UKSC 7, [2015] 2 WLR 601.

left in the shadows'. William Binchy, from an Irish perspective, expresses a similar idea: the best Commissions are those that nurture rather than suppress the 'quirky, contrary independence of mind' that, in the long term, carries the prospect of quality and substance.

At the end of the day, the success of a Law Commission depends on the quality of its work, more than the precise method of implementation. As Lord Toulson said, one hallmark has been the 'broad and inclusive consultation followed by rigorous and unrelenting analysis'. I am happy that this aspect of the Commissions' work has not changed over the 50 years of their lives, and this should ensure their continued place at the heart of the UK legal system.

# 14

# *Democracy, Law Reform and the Rule of Law*

LORD TOULSON

> English policy is to float lazily downstream, occasionally putting
> out a diplomatic boathook to avoid collisions.
>
> Lord Salisbury (1877)

## I INTRODUCTION

Lord Salisbury's words could be applied to our approach to the legal system. Particular problems lead to piecemeal adjustments. As a result the statute book resembles a sea of floating objects of bewildering number and complexity. My aim in this chapter is to consider what the rule of law in our democracy means, or should mean, for law making and law reform. I would like to look at the lessons to be gained from the 50 years since the passage of Law Commissions Act 1965 and their application for the future. The Act established both the Law Commission of England and Wales and the Scottish Law Commission, and the Commissions have worked in good harmony. I believe that most of what I have to say would apply equally both sides of the border, and when referring, as I shall, to the Law Commission I do not wish to seem narrowly parochial.

## II RULE OF LAW

For reasons ancient and modern, the rule of law was the subject of much public discussion in 2015. Books, exhibitions and celebrations marked the 800th anniversary of Magna Carta. Simultaneously the government announced that it is going to propose the introduction of a new Bill of Rights, referred to in short as a British Bill of Rights although the intention is that it should apply to all parts of the United Kingdom.

We are not the only country reflecting on what the rule of law should mean for us. In October 2014 the fourth plenum of the Eighteenth Central Committee of the Chinese Communist Party (CCP) took place. Its central focus was 'the rule of law'. At the plenum's closing the CCP's Central Committee issued a communique on 'comprehensively moving governing the country according to the law'.[1] The communique made it clear that the Central Committee's concept of the rule of law was the 'Socialist rule of law with Chinese characteristics'.[2] One way in which this differs from our conception of the rule of the law is that the ruling party is not subordinate to the law. Lest there be any doubt of that, the communique stated that 'Party leadership and Socialist rule of law are identical'.[3]

As every student of law or politics knows, our concept of the rule of law is closely wedded to our democratic form of government and increasingly to the recognition that our constitution embodies certain fundamental rights, partly developed by the common law and partly contained in charters of rights, of which Magna Carta has come to be hallowed as the first. That characterisation of Magna Carta may contain a large element of myth made by Coke and his contemporaries in the seventeenth-century struggle between Parliament and the Stuarts, but myth can acquire a force of its own. In an introduction to Sir Matthew Hale's *The History of the Common Law of England*, published by the University of Chicago Press in 1971, Professor Charles Gray wrote:

> The late Elizabethan generation, to which Sir Edward Coke, the greatest lawyer in English history, belonged, achieved an unanticipated consciousness of the legal past … Coke and his contemporaries were mythmakers and practical men, antiquaries stronger on ancestor worship and patriotism than on realistic perspective, polemical and political users of the legal history they discovered or invented … Nevertheless … [t]hey transformed the law from a craft to a liberal art—a focus for social thought, including historical thought.[4]

Historical consciousness is an essential factor for anyone taking a serious interest in the development of our law. For this reason it is imperative that we never lose sight of the common law principles and methods which provide our legal soil and bedrock, while recognising that they have been and are capable of accommodating cultivars from elsewhere.

By those sentiments I do not mean to give a misty-eyed impression that everything about the common law is a model of perfection. I shall have something to say about reform of the common law, but first I would like to share some thoughts about the state of the statute book 50 years on from the establishment of the Law Commission.

In our jurisdiction Parliament is recognised to be the supreme law maker, the interpretation of the law is recognised to be the function of the courts and the executive branch of government is recognised to be subject to the law, but the way in which the law is shaped is more complex than those simple statements might suggest. Many modern statutes give powers to the executive including delegated legislative powers. Moreover if the government has a working parliamentary majority it is in a strong position to change the law, including in ways which may be popular at large but discriminatory and oppressive towards unpopular minorities. Much of the

---

[1] CCP Central Committee, *Decision Concerning Some Major Questions in Comprehensively Moving Governing the Country According to the Law Forward* (2014).
[2] ibid.
[3] ibid.
[4] C Gray (ed), *Sir Matthew Hale: The History of the Common Law of England* (Chicago, University of Chicago Press, 1971) 12.

development of constitutional law and of the concept of the rule of law over the last 70 years has been concerned with ways of handling the conflict between the democratic power of an elected Parliament to make laws as it thinks fit, and the protection of rights which have come to be regarded as fundamental for all members of society.

In his seminal book, *The Rule of Law*, Lord Bingham described the core of the principle of the rule of law in these words:

> [T]hat all persons and authorities within the state, whether public or private, should be bound by and entitled to the benefit of laws publicly made, taking effect (generally) in the future and publicly administered in the courts.[5]

This formulation was not intended to be rigid or comprehensive but to capture the central concept, which he supplemented with a number of supporting propositions or principles. The first is of particular interest: 'The law must be accessible and so far as possible intelligible, clear and predictable'.[6]

The idea is scarcely new or revolutionary. Among earlier eminent scholars, Professor Lon L Fuller of Harvard Law School set out a number of necessary elements of the rule of law in his book, *The Morality of Law*, published in the year before the passage of the Law Commissions Act. They included requirements of reasonable clarity to avoid unfair enforcement[7] and the need to avoid contradictions.[8]

Nor is the idea unique to western democratic society. The communique from the Chinese fourth plenum stated:

> To construct a Socialist legal system with Chinese characteristics, we must persist in giving precedence to legislation, giving rein to the guiding and driving role of legislation, and grasp the crucial matter of raising legislative quality ... We must let the principles of fairness, justice and transparency penetrate into the entire process of legislation, perfect legislative systems and mechanisms, persist in simultaneously carrying out legislation, revision, abolition and interpretation, strengthen the timeliness, systemic nature, focus and effectiveness of laws and regulations.[9]

Compare those objectives, particularly the references to fairness, transparency, revision and systemic nature, with the words of section 3(1) of the Law Commissions Act:

> It shall be the duty of each of the Commissions to take and keep under review all the law with which they are respectively concerned with a view to its systematic development and reform, including in particular the codification of such law, the elimination of anomalies, the repeal of obsolete and unnecessary enactments, the reduction of the number of separate enactments and generally the simplification and modernisation of the law.

Like the Chinese, we have a problem and it is serious. In 2013 the Office of Parliamentary Counsel (OPC) and the Cabinet Office began a 'good law initiative' with the publication of a report entitled *When Laws Become Too Complex*.[10] The OPC

---

[5] T Bingham, *The Rule of Law* (London, Penguin, 2011) 8.
[6] ibid 17.
[7] L Fuller, *The Morality of Law* (New Haven, Yale University Press, revised edn, 1969) 63–65.
[8] ibid 65–70.
[9] See n 1 above.
[10] Office of the Parliamentary Counsel and Cabinet Office, *When Laws Become Too Complex: A Review into the Causes of Complex Legislation* (2013).

identified the qualities of good law as law which is 'necessary, effective, clear, coherent and accessible'.[11] But there is a gulf between how the law should be and how it is. The OPC correctly observed that the problem is not new, but it continues to grow with the ever-increasing volume of legislation. The OPC acknowledged that the volume of statutes and regulations, and their level of detail and frequent amendments, make legislation hard to understand and difficult to comply with. It recognised that 'there is no compelling incentive [within government or Parliament] to create simplicity or to avoid making an intricate web of laws even more complex',[12] and that every addition has the potential to cause an exponential increase to the overall complexity. Good law requires us to consider how the situation can be reversed, for as the OPC candidly recognised, inability to access and understand the law 'undermines the rule of law'.[13]

The case of *R v Chambers* provides an example of how justice can miscarry.[14] Mr Chambers pleaded guilty to a tobacco smuggling offence under section 170(1)(b) of the Customs and Excise Management Act 1979. He was an accomplice in the venture and was sentenced to community service. A confiscation order was also made against him under the Proceeds of Crime Act 2002 in the sum of £66,210, with a sentence of 20 months' imprisonment in default of payment.

Mr Chambers appealed against the confiscation order to the Court of Appeal. The panel included myself. The appeal turned on the question of what personal benefit he obtained within the meaning of the 2002 Act. The prosecution's case was that he benefited by the amount of the duty which was evaded, but that depended on showing that under the appropriate Regulations he was himself liable for payment of the amount of the duty.

Throughout the case, the prosecution had relied on the Excise Goods Regulations 1992. On the basis of these Regulations, we concluded that Mr Chambers was liable for the payment of the duty and we prepared a judgment dismissing his appeal. As is customary, the draft judgment was sent to the lawyers on both sides a few days before the intended hand down so that they could check for any minor errors. On this occasion, fortuitously, the draft judgment caught the eye of a lawyer in the Asset Forfeiture Division of the Revenue and Customs Prosecutions Office, who was aware that the 1992 Regulations no longer applied to tobacco products. She saw to it that the Court was immediately alerted to this embarrassing discovery.

It turned out that the relevant parts of the 1992 Regulations had been replaced by the Tobacco Product Regulations 2001, which had come into force some five years before Mr Chambers' offence. Importantly, the 2001 Regulations were materially different from the 1992 Regulations, and Mr Chambers' liability under the 2001 Regulations required the prosecution to establish matters about which they had never produced evidence. There was no way in which the trial judge or the Court of Appeal could have known of the mistake. Nor was it the fault of counsel who appeared for the prosecution. In preparing the case he checked the wording of the

---

[11] ibid 1.
[12] ibid.
[13] ibid.
[14] *R v Chambers* [2008] EWCA Crim 2467.

Regulations on the government's information website, but the website was inaccurate. The upshot was that we allowed Mr Chambers' appeal and quashed the order, which might otherwise have resulted in him being wrongly sent to prison.

After drawing out the serious consequences that might well have been created by the prosecution's ignorance of the 2001 Regulations in this and similar cases, I said in the judgment:

> This case also provides an example of a wider problem. It is a maxim that ignorance of the law is no excuse, but it is profoundly unsatisfactory if the law itself is not practically accessible. To a worryingly large extent, statutory law is not practically accessible today, even to the courts whose constitutional duty it is to interpret and enforce it. There are four principal reasons.

> First, the majority of legislation is secondary legislation.

> Secondly, the volume of legislation has increased very greatly over the last 40 years. The Law Commission's Report on Post-Legislative Scrutiny, (2006) Law Com 302, gave some figures in Appendix C. In 2005 there were 2,868 pages of new Public General Acts and approximately 13,000 pages of new Statutory Instruments, making a total well in excess of 15,000 pages (which is equivalent to over 300 pages a week) excluding European Directives and European Regulations, which were responsible for over 5,000 additional pages of legislation.

> Thirdly, on many subjects the legislation cannot be found in a single place, but in a patchwork of primary and secondary legislation.

> Fourthly, there is no comprehensive statute law database with hyperlinks which would enable an intelligent person, by using a search engine, to find out all the legislation on a particular topic. This means that the courts are in many cases unable to discover what the law is, or was at the date with which the court is concerned, and are entirely dependent on the parties for being able to inform them what were the relevant statutory provisions which the court has to apply. This lamentable state of affairs has been raised by responsible bodies on many occasions, including the House of Lords Committee on the Merits of Secondary Legislation.[15]

I use the example to highlight a systemic problem. If a government department, advised and represented by lawyers, does not know what the law is or where to go to find it, what hope is there for the ordinary citizen? Lord Bingham referred to Mr Chambers' case in his book. He noted that in 1988 and again in 1995 the Italian Constitutional Court ruled that ignorance of the law may constitute an excuse for the citizen when the formulation of the law is such as to lead to obscure and contradictory results. With studied moderation he observed that '[i]t must be questioned whether the current volume and style of legislation are well suited to serve the rule of law even if it is accepted, as it must be, that the subject matter of much legislation is inevitably very complex'.[16]

The problem for law reformers today is a combination of an avalanche of primary and secondary legislation and a shortage of parliamentary time allocated to law reform.

---

[15] ibid [64]–[68].
[16] Bingham, n 5 above, 42.

It is important that we recognise the consequences of this. Anybody with experience of the process of legislative drafting can testify that it takes more time to produce a shorter and clearer Bill than it does to produce one which is longer and more complex. It can also result in an ultimate saving of time and cost. Poorly drafted legislation brings costs in terms of time spent by officials and others, litigation costs to sort out its meaning and sometimes the need for further corrective legislation. If a prime aim of government is to improve the quality of government legislation, it should reduce the volume and allow more time for preparation and scrutiny. The problem is political. Although not all departments are responsible for introducing large quantities of legislation, it is generally true that in recent years government departments have wanted to introduce as much legislation as can be squeezed into the parliamentary timetable.

A vicious cycle is created whereby, because Westminster is spending more time producing ever more legislation, with insufficient time for its proper digestion, it has less time to consider Law Commission proposals (which are becoming more and more necessary). Unfortunately, there is little political will to use scarce parliamentary time for a Bill whose purpose is merely to simplify and clarify the law.

Evidence of this is the proliferation of legislation on the same, or similar topics. In the area of education, the Butler Act (the Education Act 1944) stood for over 30 years. In the last 20 years there have been 10 Education Acts: the Education Act 1996; Education Act 1997; Teaching and Higher Education Act 1998; School Standards and Framework Act 1998; Learning and Skills Act 2000; Education Act 2002; Higher Education Act 2004; Education Act 2005; Education and Skills Act 2008; and the Education Act 2011.

Asylum and immigration cases produce a constant flow of appeals to the Court of Appeal and the Supreme Court. They only reach that level if they involve a difficult point of law. The law is complex because it is to be found in a confusing mosaic of Acts, regulations, rules and departmental statements. The Acts include the Nationality, Immigration and Asylum Act 2002, the Asylum and Immigration Act 2004, the Immigration, Asylum and Nationality Act 2006, the UK Borders Act 2007, the Borders, Citizenship and Immigration Act 2009 and the Immigration Act 2014. What has been created is a pile of Acts amending or replacing parts of earlier Acts, interspersed with secondary legislation and soft law in the form of departmental statements. The courts have the task of trying to digest the equivalent of a multi-decker partly eaten sandwich.

Things do not have to continue in the same way. First, there is too often an untested assumption that legislation is needed to remedy an ill, especially one which has attracted media attention and prompted demands for government action. A legislative response can give the appearance of action, whether or not it is likely to have practical results which could not be achieved without it. In recent years parliamentary time has been spent creating a truly vast number of criminal offences covering conduct which in the main was already criminal. In contrast, the Law Commission deserves congratulation for its reluctance to propose legislation where it considers that there is a realistic prospect of achieving necessary reform by other means. Its reports on *Trustee Exemption Clauses*,[17] and on *The Illegality Defence* are examples.[18]

Second, the proper purpose of legislation is to make new law or repeal or amend the existing law, or to make the law clearer and simpler where there is legal uncertainty or the existing law is needlessly complex. In other words, its proper purpose is to have legal effect. It is not its proper purpose merely to create publicity where the law is sufficiently clear. There are plenty of other ways of publicising the law or making political statements about it.

Third, good law requires good housekeeping by consolidation and by the removal of legislation which is obsolete or duplicative. This is not a new idea. The Statute Law Revision Act 1867 repealed over a thousand statutes. The Law Commission has taken over this task. Since 1965 it has drafted 19 Statute Law (Repeals) Acts, repealing 3,000 whole Acts and thousands of other Acts in part.[19] It has also been responsible for drafting more than 200 consolidation Acts. The work is unglamorous but important.

The Law Commission's current project on sentencing procedure well illustrates the problems which I have been discussing and the value of the Commission.[20] It is worth quoting at some length from the issues paper published by the Commission on 1 July 2015:

> [T]he aim of the project is to introduce a single sentencing statute that will act as the first and only port of call for sentencing tribunals regarding the procedure to be followed at the sentencing hearing. It will set out the relevant provisions in a clear, simple and logical way, and will allow for all updates to sentencing procedure to be made in a single place.
>
> This will represent a sharp contrast to the current state of the law in this area. The current law is an impenetrable thicket, contained in hundreds of separate provisions scattered across dozens of statutes. The provisions are often overlapping, technical and complex. They have different commencement and transition dates.
>
> The confused state of the current law has concrete negative effects in practice. It is extremely difficult even for an experienced judge to identify the correct sentencing procedure applicable to any case. The impact of this is that judges spend more time on the sentencing process than ought to be needed, which adds cost and delay to sentencing determinations and can have knock-on effects on the punctuality of other trials. Practitioners are also forced to spend more time assisting the judge on these issues.
>
> This complexity leads to error. That causes additional cost and delay with additional court hearings under the 'slip rule' to remedy minor errors and more appeals to the Court of Appeal (Criminal Division) (CACD). These unnecessary appeals on sentence are expensive and time consuming, and delay other appeals. An analysis of 262 randomly selected cases in the CACD in 2012 showed that the complexity of the legislation is resulting in an extraordinary number of wrongfully-passed sentences: there were 95 *unlawful* sentences passed in the sample [almost 40%] …

---

[17] LC 301 (2006).
[18] LC 320 (2010).
[19] Law Commission, LC 352, *Annual Report 2013–14* (2014) 50.
[20] See also chapter 12 (Ian Dennis).

The complexity also impedes the rational development of the law. According to policy officials, the landscape has become so confused that they cannot always be confident when advising on the likely effects of proposed sentencing initiatives. Unintended consequences of new statutory procedures cannot reliably be identified and guarded against. We have now reached the point at which it is difficult to see how the existing morass of legislation can effectively be amended.[21]

In a recent annual report, the Law Commission recorded that as of May 2014 it had published 202 reports recommending statutory reform of which 135 had been implemented in whole or in part.[22] It has achieved some important reforms and it has also been a beacon of good legislation. It has achieved that by three practices which are core to its method of operating: open consultation; involvement of the drafter at an early stage; and taking the time needed to produce a clear and satisfactory Bill. It does not have the luxury of comforting itself that problems which may later appear can be ironed out by amending legislation.

Sir Geoffrey Palmer, former Minister of Justice and Prime Minister of New Zealand, Court of Appeal judge and President of the New Zealand Law Commission, said in his 2015 Scarman Lecture that:

> The great expectations of 1965 have not been realised. The Commissions have added value. They have promoted, and quite often achieved, important legal reforms. But progress is not of the sort that would have impressed someone like Jeremy Bentham. No coherent philosophy for the law reform enterprise has emerged. Probably none can be devised because the Commissions occupy an awkward space between principle and expediency. We are still awaiting the golden age of law reform. While law commissions lifted law reform to a professional full time activity, the vision has stalled.[23]

Sir Geoffrey advocated reform thereby 'upending the whole method by which law is made by the executive and parliaments now', so that all legislation should follow a process of consultation and preparation on the Law Commission model.[24] He was correct to admit that such reform would be a 'formidable undertaking'.[25]

I belong temperamentally to the 'glass half full' school of thought, but I do think that the contribution of the Law Commission cannot be measured only in terms of the reforms contained in Law Commission Bills which have reached the statute book but also by its processes from which there are wider lessons about how to make good law. If governments could be persuaded to exercise self-discipline in legislating less; to spend more time on genuine consultation and preparation; and to make a higher priority of simplifying and consolidating the law which their predecessors have produced, the aspirations which have prompted the good law initiative could be converted into real and lasting achievements. The increased use of pre-legislative scrutiny is a healthy development, as is the OPC's examination of how the process of scrutiny could be improved by more informative explanatory notes. Post-legislative

---

[21] Law Commission, *Sentencing Procedure: Issues Paper 1: Transition* (2015) paras 1.6–1.10.
[22] LC 352, n 19 above, 33.
[23] G Palmer, 'The Law Reform Enterprise: Evaluating the Past and Charting the Future' (2015) 131 *LQR* 402, 420.
[24] ibid 421.
[25] ibid.

scrutiny, about which the Law Commission produced a report in 2006,[26] could provide a useful means of evaluating legislation against good law targets.

I turn to problems with the common law. It has not been the sole prerogative of Parliament to produce complex and obscure law. In a memorably disrespectful and often very funny book about the legal system under the title *The Advocate's Devil*, CP Harvey QC stated:

> It is fatally easy to mistake the ingenuity of practitioners for legal genius, to attribute to society itself some kind of deep-seated talent for jurisprudence, to attach a mystical significance to ridiculous figures like 'the Casual Ejector,' and ultimately to regard the whole hotchpotch of barbarities, accidents, fictions, customs, prejudices, rituals, horse-sense and nonsense which we call the common law as a sort of super-natural seedling which somehow planted itself in the soil of England at the dawn of modern history and found such nourishment in the underlying humus that it grew up and flowered and fruited and enlarged itself until it provided shelter and refreshment for a whole Empire of freedom-loving people.[27]

Harvey had a valid point and it remains true that there are plenty of areas of the common law which merit simplification, clarification or reform. The Law Commission has a statutory responsibility to keep the law under review and produce proposals for its systematic development and reform, but this need not necessarily be through legislation.

In a book of essays in honour of the former Law Commissioner, Professor Hugh Beale, Professor Andrew Burrows chose the subject 'Alternatives to Legislation: Restatements and Judicial Law Reform'. He wrote:

> Perhaps oddly for a former Law Commissioner, I have never been a great fan of legislative reform of the non-criminal common law. Indeed, my years at the Law Commission merely served to reinforce my legislative scepticism. That scepticism is built on two main concerns about legislative law reform. The first is that the vagaries of the legislative process mean that whether time is found for legislation depends almost entirely on whether one can fit one's law reform within the political imperatives of the day and has little or no relationship to the quality of, or necessity for, the reform proposed. The second is that, while legislative drafting and progressive judicial interpretation can overcome the difficulties, there is some risk that legislative reform, as opposed to judicial reform, may freeze the law in a way that makes desirable change, and the correcting of mistakes, difficult.[28]

I agree with his first concern and can see the force of the second, although much depends on the subject-matter and the proposed form of legislation. I certainly agree that there are some areas in which reform may be better achieved by other means than legislation, including a non-statutory industry code enforceable by industry regulators or reform led by judicial decisions. In relation to the latter, the Commission can perform an invaluable role by carrying out a panoramic analysis of the law and a consultation process on a scale which a court hearing an individual case would not be able to do.

---

[26] Law Commission, LC 302, *Post-Legislative Scrutiny* (2006).
[27] CP Harvey, *The Advocate's Devil* (London, Stevens, 1958) 78–79.
[28] A Burrows, 'Alternatives to Legislation: Restatements and Judicial Law Reform' in L Gullifer and S Vogenauer (eds), *English and European Perspectives on Contract and Commercial Law: Essays in Honour of Hugh Beale* (Oxford, Hart Publishing, 2014) 37, 43.

One such area which the Law Commission examined over a period of 14 years is the doctrine of illegality in the law of contract. It concluded that judicial reform was the best way forward and it made recommendations to that end. Whether it guessed right in its optimism about the possibilities of judicial reform remains to be seen. Three recent decisions of the Supreme Court have revealed a sharp divergence of views on the subject.[29] It may be that the Law Commission will need to go back to the drawing board and propose some form of statutory reform, but I am in no doubt that since the Commission believed that the law in this area, being judge made, was best left to the courts to reform, it was correct to say so.[30] Leaving aside the merits of this particular subject, I agree firmly with Professor Burrows that the work of the Law Commission can be of real help to the courts in improving the common law where it has become unsatisfactory. The reluctance of governments to legislate for pure law reform makes the need all the greater.

Another example of the valuable dialogue that can exist between the Law Commission and the judiciary—which Professor Burrows sets out in his essay[31]— relates to the level of damages for pain, suffering and loss of amenity (PSLA) in personal injury cases. In 1999, the Law Commission published a report titled *Damages for Personal Injury: Non-Pecuniary Loss*.[32] It concluded that the level of damages awarded for PSLA had not kept up with the times and should be increased. As to how this change should be achieved, the Law Commission stated:

> We recommend that, at least initially, legislation imposing an increase in the level of damages for non-pecuniary loss in personal injury cases should be avoided. Instead we hope that the Court of Appeal and the House of Lords will use their existing powers to lay down guidelines, in a case or series of cases, which would raise damages in line with the increases recommended.[33]

The Law Commission, no doubt, felt confident in making this recommendation due to the advice given to it by Lord Woolf MR and Lord Bingham CJ,[34] but it should not feel any need to have such judicial encouragement.

### III FUNDAMENTAL RIGHTS

Lord Bingham's fifth principle was that the law must afford adequate protection of human rights, and no discussion of the rule of law today would be complete without some reference to this vital topic.

Over the last 70 years there have been four major developments. First, there has been a great increase in powers of the state, whether through central government, local government or a myriad of public agencies and regulatory authorities. There

---

[29] *Hounga v Allen* [2014] UKSC 47, [2014] 1 WLR 2889; *Les Laboratoires Servier v Apotex Inc* [2014] UKSC 55, [2015] AC 430; and *Jetivia SA v Bilta (UK) Ltd* [2015] UKSC 23, [2015] 2 WLR 1168.
[30] Note also chapter 29 (James Lee).
[31] Burrows, n 28 above, 45–47.
[32] Law Commission, LC 257, *Damages for Personal Injury: Non-Pecuniary Loss* (1999).
[33] ibid para 5.10.
[34] ibid para 3.156.

has been a corresponding development in our domestic public law as a check on the exercise of such powers. This has been largely the work of the courts.

Second, the principle referred to by Lord Hoffmann in *R v Secretary of State for the Home Department, ex p Simms*[35] as the principle of legality has received increased prominence. He set out this principle in the following terms:

> [T]he principle of legality means that Parliament must squarely confront what it is doing and accept the political cost. Fundamental rights cannot be overridden by general or ambiguous words. This is because there is too great a risk that the full implications of their unqualified meaning may have passed unnoticed in the democratic process. In the absence of express language or necessary implication to the contrary, the courts therefore presume that even the most general words were intended to be subject to the basic rights of the individual. In this way the courts of the United Kingdom, though acknowledging the sovereignty of Parliament, apply principles of constitutionality little different from those which exist in countries where the power of the legislature is expressly limited by a constitutional document.[36]

The principle itself is not new. In *United States v Fisher* in 1805 Chief Justice Marshall wrote:

> Where rights are infringed, where fundamental principles are overthrown, where the general system of the laws is departed from, the legislative intention must be expressed with irresistible clearness to induce a court of justice to suppose a design to effect such objects. But where only a political regulation is made, which is inconvenient, if the intention of the legislature be expressed in terms which are sufficiently intelligible to leave no doubt in the mind when the words are taken in their ordinary sense, it would be going a great way to say that a constrained interpretation must be put upon them, to avoid an inconvenience which ought to have been contemplated in the legislature when the act was passed and which, in their opinion, was probably overbalanced by the particular advantages it was calculated to produce.[37]

Thirdly, equality of the treatment of individuals by public bodies has received much closer scrutiny by the courts and by Parliament. The judicial oath contains an affirmation of the duty of every judicial office holder to do right to all manner of people, and the courts have always had a special duty (although it has not always been honoured) to fight against unjust discrimination towards minorities. We now also have a substantial body of equality legislation, well-intentioned but not always well drafted.

Fourthly and most controversially, the European Convention on Human Rights has been incorporated in our domestic law by the Human Rights Act 1998. Things would have taken a rather different course if past governments had followed the suggestion of the Law Commission's first Chairman, Lord Scarman, in his 1974 Hamlyn Lectures. He called for a United Kingdom Bill of Rights. He stated that:

> It is no longer enough to say, with Magna Carta, 'no free man shall be taken or imprisoned ... or any otherwise destroyed, nor will we pass upon him nor deal with him but

---

[35] *R v Secretary of State for the Home Department, ex p Simms* [2000] 2 AC 115 (HL).
[36] ibid 131.
[37] *United States v Fisher* 6 US (2 Cranch) 358, 390 (1805).

by lawful judgment of his peers, or by the law of the land'. The legal system must now ensure that the law of the land will itself meet the exacting standards of human rights declared by international instruments, to which the United Kingdom is a party, as inviolable. This calls for entrenched or fundamental laws protected by a Bill of Rights—a constitutional law which it is the duty of the courts to protect even against the power of Parliament. In other words, there must be a constitutional restraint placed upon the legislative power which is designed to protect the individual citizen from instant legislation, conceived in fear or prejudice and enacted in breach of human rights.[38]

It is interesting that 40 years on, the government is intending to implement Lord Scarman's recommendation. This should provide some comfort and encouragement to later Chairmen of the Law Commission as an illustration of the words of the philosopher author of the book of Ecclesiastes: 'Cast thy bread upon the waters for thou shalt find it after many days'.[39]

Lord Scarman spoke in general terms, and it would be right for the judges to speak from their experience if there were a proposal to remove the substance of rights now regarded as fundamental. However, there has been no suggestion to that effect of which I am aware, and in those circumstances I do not consider that it would be appropriate for me to speculate or enter the political debate about the detailed form of any future human rights legislation.

## IV CONCLUSION

I began this chapter with the rule of law and I end it with the role of the Law Commission. That is no coincidence. The Law Commission plays a vital role as a champion of accessibility and modernisation of the law. Its work can affect millions of people. The Children Act 1989 and the Renting Homes (Wales) Act 2016 are examples.

Law reform has never enjoyed much popularity with most lawyers. Practically every worthwhile reform has been opposed, sometimes for reasons which afterwards seem bizarre. The establishment of a Court of Criminal Appeal was successfully resisted until 1907 on the ground, among others, that juries would not take their jobs seriously if they knew that wrong convictions could be quashed on appeal.

The Law Commission should therefore be proud of what it has achieved and not be too despondent where it has failed to persuade the government of the day. There are always voices for leaving things as they are, save for putting out the occasional boathook, but on no account should the Law Commission shrink its horizons. Its method of broad and inclusive consultation followed by rigorous and unrelenting analysis is sound. There is much more which needs to be done in order to improve the present state of the law, but the Commission has proved itself to be an exemplar of the promotion of the rule of law.

[38] L Scarman, *English Law—The New Dimension* (Hamlyn Lectures 1974) (London, Stevens, 1974) 19–20.
[39] Ecclesiastes 11:1, King James version.

# 15

# Promoting Law Reform: By Means of Draft Bills or Otherwise

SHONA WILSON STARK[*]

Any assessment of a law reform body's success must be based on more than a simple calculation of implementation rates. Furthermore, those implementation rates must include more than just primary legislation, and should be calculated in a way which removes the expectation of immediate implementation. This chapter will concentrate on the Law Commission of England and Wales (LCEW) and the Scottish Law Commission (SLC)—together 'the Commissions'—as examples which show that the proper function of independent law reform bodies does, and should, entail much more than legislative enactment of their proposals. The Commissions have already shown significant success in promoting law reform through other methods, such as by way of statutory instruments, court rules, or the common law. Such alternative methods address the difficulty of finding the opportunity to implement law reform proposals. Implementation (statutory or otherwise) may not always happen quickly. Those alternative implementation methods, and the delay between proposals and implementation, must be taken into account when assessing implementation rates. Furthermore, it should not be forgotten that even unimplemented reports can promote law reform.

## I THE INSUFFICIENCY OF PRIMARY LEGISLATION

Primary legislation can be said to have two specific deficiencies in relation to the Commissions. First, it will be argued that primary legislation alone is insufficient as a tool of law reform in the British jurisdictions. Second, it will be argued that, partially as a consequence, simply counting how many Commission recommendations have been enacted in primary legislation is an insufficient indicator of the Commissions' success.

[*] The title of this chapter incorporates the motto of the Scottish Law Commission: 'promoting law reform'. The Law Commission's motto is 'reforming the law'. I am grateful to Findlay Stark and those who attended the conference marking the Commissions' fiftieth anniversary for helpful comments on earlier drafts.

## A Insufficiency as a Tool of Law Reform

We need look no further than the Law Commissions Act 1965 (the 1965 Act) to see that the Commissions need not solely propose reforms by way of primary legislation. The Commissions' duties can be split into two main areas of law reform: consolidation and repeals; and substantive law reform. On the former, the 1965 Act is clear that the Commissions' proposals for reform must be submitted to government by way of draft Bill.[1] On the latter, the 1965 Act is equally clear, as Beale has pointed out, that the proposals can be made 'by means of draft Bill or otherwise'.[2] The draftsman of the 1965 Act may have intended simply to allow the Commissions to be able to choose whether or not to draft their own Bill, or to leave the Bill to be drafted in the usual manner. But the perhaps unintended consequence of the drafting of the 1965 Act is that it allows flexibility in how the Commissions' proposals are both presented and implemented.

In practice, it is often helpful for the Commissions to present their work in a draft Bill, because it 'provides Parliament with as much help as possible' if the suggestions are taken forward.[3] Furthermore, if the same draftsman can be recruited to make amendments to the Bill if it is introduced, any 'unnecessary delay and duplication of resources' can be avoided.[4] The production of draft Bills also allows those reading the proposals to see how they translate into law,[5] and ensures that the Commissions do not produce 'theoretical' work.[6] Miller has described the draft Bill procedure as 'valuable' in allowing 'points of difficulty' to be identified at an early stage.[7] In certain instances, however, a draft Bill may not be thought to be appropriate. In at least one case, a Bill was not drafted in order to speed up publication of a report.[8] In other cases, draft Bills have not been prepared where another mechanism of reform (such as judicial development) is recommended.[9]

In addition, the 1965 Act states that the Commissions are to 'take and keep under review *all* the law' of their jurisdictions.[10] That law will consist of common law, secondary legislation and European Union law, as well as primary legislation, and the Commissions have not only the *power*, but the *duty* to review it all. The Commissions are, therefore, not limited to either examining primary legislation, or to proposing reforms by way of primary legislation.

---

[1] 1965 Act, s 3(1)(d). The Commissions have in-house Parliamentary Counsel to fulfil the drafting function.

[2] 1965 Act, s 3(1)(c); H Beale, 'The Law Commission and Judicial Law Reform' (2001) 35 *The Law Teacher* 323, 335.

[3] P Gibson, 'Law Reform Now: The Law Commission 25 Years On', Denning Lecture (1991) 11.

[4] H Brooke, 'The Role of the Law Commission in Simplifying Statute Law' (1995) 16 *Statute Law Review* 1, 3.

[5] DM Walker, 'The Second Annual Report of the Scottish Law Commission' 1968 *Scots Law Times (News)* 2, 3.

[6] M Arden, 'The Work of the Law Commission' (2000) 53 *Current Legal Problems* 559, 565.

[7] K Miller, 'Legal Change: The Social Dimension' (1998) 3 *Scottish Law and Practice Quarterly* 117, 119.

[8] See, eg, LC 82 and SLC 45, *Liability for Defective Products* (1977) para 18.

[9] See n 51 below.

[10] 1965 Act, s 3(1) (emphasis added).

At the time of the Commissions' establishment, however, it would have been foreseen that they would propose most (if not all) of their reforms by way of draft Bills designed to be implemented by Parliament. In the 1960s, the judiciary were widely perceived to be inadequate law reformers. The first Chairman of the LCEW, Lord Scarman, was particularly vehement that the courts were not suitable as a tool of law reform for various reasons. Scarman noted in 1966 that the common law 'stands little chance of survival to-day. Speed, accessibility, and convenience are ... powerfully demanded of the law'.[11] Scarman also felt that 'law made by lawyers' was no longer acceptable because modern society had an increasingly diverse and 'wide-ranging social structure' for which judges could no longer speak.[12] Codification became seen as a suitable alternative—the polar opposite to the common law in terms of its accessibility, legitimacy and modernity, motivated particularly by entry into the then Common Market.[13]

Developments since 1965 have, however, reinvigorated the common law, and codification is now 'little more than a distant memory' for the Commissions.[14] Judicial law reform is still piecemeal, but is aided at the Supreme Court level by the Practice Statement,[15] and by an increasing tendency for collegiate decision-making and therefore an ability to hear more cases.[16] A trend has been observed for the Court of Appeal to give 'single or collective' judgments,[17] and indeed it is obliged to do so (with rare exceptions) in criminal cases.[18] The judiciary may not be fully diverse, but things have improved,[19] plus training is more thorough,[20] and selection more transparent.[21] Judges have shown an increased tendency to reform the

[11] L Scarman, 'Codification and Judge-made Law: A Problem of Co-Existence', University of Birmingham Lecture (1966) 2.

[12] ibid 18.

[13] LCB Gower, 'A Comment' (1967) 30 *MLR* 259, 260.

[14] J Munby, 'Shaping the Law—the Law Commission at the Crossroads', Denning Lecture (2011) 11.

[15] Where the House of Lords decided that it would no longer be bound by stare decisis: [1966] 1 WLR 1234. In *Austin v Southwark London Borough Council* [2010] UKSC 28, [2011] 1 AC 355, the Practice Statement was not used, but Lord Hope confirmed that the Supreme Court did have the power to use it if it so wished: [25]. The endorsement of the Practice Statement in *Austin* is now incorporated into the Supreme Court's Practice Directions, Direction 3.1.3: see further, J Lee, 'Fides et Ratio: Precedent in the Early Jurisprudence of the United Kingdom Supreme Court' (2015) 21(1) *European Journal of Current Legal Issues*.

[16] Of the 58 cases heard by the Supreme Court in the 2011–12 legal year, 18 cases (31%) had only one written judgment, whereas only ten cases (17%) had a separate written opinion from every Justice: author's own research. A huge increase was seen in 2012–13, when 83 cases were heard. See generally A Paterson, *Final Judgment* (Oxford, Hart Publishing, 2013) ch 4.

[17] P Darbyshire, *Sitting in Judgment: The Working Lives of Judges* (Oxford, Hart Publishing, 2011) 324.

[18] Senior Courts Act 1981, s 59.

[19] Judges may still tend to be 'old, white and male', but are now far less likely to be 'privileged, elitist, insensitive and out-of-touch': Darbyshire, n 17 above, 42.

[20] By the Judicial Institute in Scotland and the Judicial College in England.

[21] In Scotland, the Judicial Appointments Board was introduced in 2002 'to create a more open and accessible system for judicial appointments in Scotland that could be readily understood and so command the respect of the legal profession and the general public': Judicial Appointments Board website, www.judicialappointments.scot/about-us/history. In England, the Constitutional Reform Act 2005, s 61 established the Judicial Appointments Commission, which is now responsible for recommending judges (except Supreme Court judges) for appointment. The selection of new judges was previously within the remit of the Lord Chancellor, who made his decisions based on the 'soundings' of existing judges: Darbyshire, n 17 above, 97.

law, starting with the reforming judges of the mid- to late-twentieth century,[22] and later with the rise of 'jurists' as judges.[23] Issues of accessibility of the law have been alleviated by the increase in online legal databases. Therefore we need no longer put all our law reform hopes into the hands of Parliament. The courts can, and do, perform a law reform function too—as will be argued below, often in conjunction with the Commissions.

In addition, the problem of finding parliamentary time for law reform has been notorious throughout the Commissions' histories. Even before they were established, concerns were voiced about the obstacle parliamentary time would be to law reform—even from the Commissions' founding father, Lord Gardiner.[24] It has been queried whether parliamentary and governmental apathy is more of a problem than parliamentary time per se.[25] Either way, the problem of a lack of parliamentary implementation of Commission proposals has had to be addressed. Certain methods of addressing that problem have concentrated on finding more parliamentary time,[26] whereas others have focused on finding alternative avenues for law reform. Both methods are valuable ways of increasing the implementation of Commission proposals, although only the latter is the focus of this chapter.

## B Insufficiency as a Measure of Success

In the light of what has been said above, it follows logically that simply looking at the Commissions' success rate in terms of primary legislation resulting from their proposals is insufficient as a measure of their success—examining, or proposing reforms by way of, primary legislation is not the Commissions' only function under the 1965 Act. It will be demonstrated below that the Commissions' implementation figures do include proposals implemented by less-orthodox means—as is entirely proper. It will be argued, however, that the method of calculating implementation rates could be improved, both in how implementation is calculated, and in the transparency of those calculation methods. More realistic (and healthier) implementation figures may take some pressure off the Commissions to allow them to take risks on reports which may not be implemented immediately, if ever. The benefits of taking such risks are advanced below.

In addition, mere implementation figures alone cannot give an accurate picture of the valuable role the Commissions play because they assess only quantity, not

---

[22] A Lester, 'English Judges as Law Makers' [1993] *PL* 269, 278, citing Lords Reid, Denning and Wilberforce in particular.

[23] D Hope, 'Law Reform: Alternative Strategies to Legislation', *Law Reform: Catching the Eye of Government*, Papers from a joint seminar presented by the Law Commission and UCL Faculty of Laws (2001) 36–37, citing Lord Goff, Lord Hoffmann, Buxton LJ and Lady Hale.

[24] HL Deb 1 April 1965, vol 264, col 1154 (Lord Chancellor (Gardiner)). See also, eg, HC Deb 8 February 1965, vol 706, cols 60, 64–65 (Sir John Hobson); col 88 (Sir David Renton); col 107 (Charles Fletcher-Cooke).

[25] See, eg, DJ Cusine, 'Law Reform—Who Cares?' (1993) 38(3) *Journal of the Law Society of Scotland* 101, 102–03.

[26] Such methods include (most recently) the new House of Lords and Scottish Parliament procedures for the more technical and uncontroversial Commission Bills. Private Members' Bills have also made a significant contribution to Commission implementation rates, but discussion of these is beyond the scope of this chapter.

quality. Criticism of Commission proposals is ubiquitous in the academy,[27] and not unheard of in Parliament,[28] or the courts.[29] An implemented Commission proposal is not necessarily a good Commission proposal. As Lord McCluskey put it: '[h]owever much we may admire the Scottish Law Commission ... we must not just look at those decisions and say that because the Scottish Law Commission did it, it is good'.[30]

It therefore seems illogical to automatically count an implemented proposal as a success, and an unimplemented report as a failure. Consequently, this chapter will also assess the potential value of unimplemented Commission reports.

## II IMPLEMENTED REPORTS

Beyond primary legislation, Commission reports can be (and have been) implemented in a number of ways. One method is by delegated legislation. The potential for Commission proposals to be implemented by delegated legislation has been increased, initially by Regulatory Reform Order (RRO) under the Regulatory Reform Act 2001 and now by Legislative Reform Order (LRO) under the Legislative and Regulatory Reform Act 2006 (the 2006 Act). Only the most technical and uncontroversial Commission recommendations qualify for the procedure, and so it does not cover all Commission work.[31] Furthermore, LROs can only make amendments to existing legislation[32] and the LRO must have the effect of removing or reducing a 'burden' rather than simply removing inconsistencies or anomalies.[33] So far, three RROs/LROs have been made.[34]

---

[27] Examples are too numerous to provide a comprehensive list, but include P Cane, 'The Law Commission on Judicial Review' (1993) 56 *MLR* 887, which criticises LC CP 126, *Administrative Law: Judicial Review and Statutory Appeals* (1993); WW McBryde, 'Law Reform: The Scottish Experience' (1998) 3 *Scottish Law and Practice Quarterly* 86, which describes how SLC 68, *Report on Bankruptcy and Related Aspects of Insolvency and Liquidation* (1981) 'contained an error which cost taxpayers millions of pounds' (93); F Stark, 'Wiping the Slate Clean: Reforming Scots Law's Approach to Evidence of the Accused's Bad Character' (2013) 76 *MLR* 346, which argues against the proposals in SLC 229, *Report on Similar Fact Evidence and the* Moorov *Doctrine* (2012).

[28] eg the description of the LCEW as an 'unrepresentative quango' by Lord Rawlinson of Ewell: HL Deb 11 January 1996, vol 568, col 290.

[29] See, eg, *Rimmer v Liverpool City Council* [1985] QB 1 (CA), which described one provision of the Bill attached to LC 40, *Civil Liability of Vendors and Lessors for Defective Premises* (1970) and the Defective Premises Act 1972 which implemented it as being 'imperfectly' drafted (15); and *N v HM Advocate* 2003 JC 140, where Lord Justice Clerk Gill ([25]) had 'strong reservations about the policy recommendation' in SLC 149, *Evidence: Report on Hearsay Evidence in Criminal Proceedings* (1995) which led to the Criminal Justice (Scotland) Act 1995, which amended the Criminal Procedure (Scotland) Act 1995.

[30] HL Deb 4 December 1984, vol 457, col 1268.

[31] LC 275, *Thirty-Sixth Annual Report: 2001* (2002) para 2.15.

[32] 2006 Act, s 1(2); *Thirty-Sixth Annual Report*, n 31 above, para 2.16.

[33] 2006 Act, s 1(2); *Thirty-Sixth Annual Report*, n 31 above, para 2.16.

[34] The Regulatory Reform (Business Tenancies) (England and Wales) Order 2003, which implemented LC 208, *Landlord and Tenant: Business Tenancies—A Periodic Review of the Landlord and Tenant Act 1954 Part II* (1992); the Regulatory Reform (Execution of Deeds and Documents) Order 2005, which implemented LC 253, *The Execution of Deeds and Documents by or on behalf of Bodies Corporate* (1998); and the Legislative Reform (Limited Partnerships) Order 2009, which implemented part of LC 283 and SLC 192, *Partnership Law* (2003).

As originally drafted, the Legislative and Regulatory Reform Bill gave Ministers the power to implement Commission[35] recommendations by order 'with or without changes'.[36] This power, however, proved highly controversial, because it would have allowed any non-contentious Commission proposal to be implemented without parliamentary scrutiny.[37] The provision was removed before the legislation was enacted, because Parliament ultimately felt that it could not 'leave it to the Law Commission, good though it undoubtedly is, to legislate on our behalf'.[38] As well as the fact that it cannot be assumed that all Commission proposals are good, a total lack of scrutiny propagates the myth that the Commissions only examine uncontroversial and technical areas. Therefore although the LRO procedure has added another avenue for law reform, it will not be suitable for many Commission proposals.

The Commissions can also implement their proposals by Court Rules. For example, the SLC's *Recovery of Possession of Heritable Property* report[39] was implemented by the addition of Chapter 45A to the Rules of the Court of Session.[40] Such implementation shows that the Commissions can have impact beyond legislation— something the Commissions themselves should (and do) bear in mind both before and after drafting Bills.[41] For example, in *Expert Evidence in Criminal Proceedings in England and Wales*, the LCEW made recommendations both by way of a draft Bill (which was rejected by government) and by proposed amendments to part 33 of the Criminal Procedure Rules 2010 (which were accepted by the Criminal Procedure Rules Committee).[42] In addition, the LCEW 'actively [pursued] alternative methods of implementation', resulting in the adoption of the proposals by the Advocacy Training Council,[43] and a Practice Direction by the Lord Chief Justice.[44]

The common law is another source by which the Commissions' proposals can be implemented. For example, in 1998, the House of Lords in *Kleinwort Benson Ltd v Lincoln City Council*[45] implemented the main recommendations in the LCEW's *Restitution: Mistakes of Law and Ultra Vires Public Authority Receipts and Payments* report.[46] *Heil v Rankin*[47] partially implemented *Damages for*

---

[35] Either the LCEW, SLC or the Northern Ireland Law Commission.

[36] Legislative and Regulatory Reform Bill (as introduced), cl 1(1)(b).

[37] The Bill itself made no distinction between 'contentious' and 'non-contentious' Commission proposals, but parliamentary debates confirmed that the procedure was not intended to be used for contentious proposals. See, eg, HC Deb 9 February 2006, vol 442, cols 1048–49 (Jim Murphy and David Howarth).

[38] HL Deb 13 June 2006, vol 683, col 146 (Lord Lloyd of Berwick). See also, eg, JR Spencer et al, 'Legislative Reform' *The Times* (London, 16 February 2006) and D Howarth, 'Who Wants the Abolition of Parliament Bill?' *The Times* (London, 21 February 2006).

[39] SLC 118 (1989).

[40] Act of Sederunt (Rules of the Court of Session Amendment No 4) (Miscellaneous) 1996/2168, r 2(12).

[41] The *Recovery of Possession of Heritable Property* report (n 39 above) did contain a draft Bill, but also recommended that certain issues should be prescribed by Act of Sederunt.

[42] LC 325, *Expert Evidence in Criminal Proceedings in England and Wales* (2011) apps A and B respectively. See chapter 32 (David Ormerod).

[43] LC 359, *Annual Report 2014–15* (2015) 47.

[44] Criminal Practice Directions Division V, Evidence 33A: Expert Evidence.

[45] *Kleinwort Benson Ltd v Lincoln City Council* [1999] 2 AC 349 (HL).

[46] LC 227 (1994). See LC 265, *Thirty-Fourth Annual Report: 1999* (2000) para 1.10.

[47] *Heil v Rankin* [2000] EWCA Civ 84, [2001] QB 272.

*Personal Injury: Non-Pecuniary Loss*,[48] and *Kuddus v Chief Constable of Leicestershire Constabulary*[49] partially implemented *Aggravated, Exemplary and Restitutionary Damages*.[50] The Commissions themselves have occasionally decided that legislation would be inappropriate and have left an area of law for the courts to develop.[51]

Precedent also exists for SLC proposals shaping judicial opinions and being partially implemented through the common law. For example, the Inner House of the Court of Session in *Morgan Guaranty Trust Company of New York v Lothian Regional Council*[52] reached substantially the same conclusion as the SLC's *Discussion Paper on Recovery of Benefits Conferred under Error of Law*,[53] thus negating the need for the project to proceed to report stage. The Court did not cite the SLC, but the discussion paper had been cited in the lower Court,[54] and the SLC claimed the appellate Court was 'assisted by [the SLC's] research and the discussion set out in that Paper'.[55]

Judicial development of the law can be controversial, particularly among politicians.[56] The traditional belief is that judges only 'interpret and apply' the law rather than developing it,[57] although that belief was decried by Lord Reid as a 'fairy tale'.[58] Two objections are commonly advanced to judicial law reform: judges lack democratic accountability, and they lack information.[59] Reliance on Commission materials may not cure the former objection, but the vast amount of highly-respected research carried out by the Commissions certainly cures the latter. The Commissions also aid the dialogue between the branches of the legal professions.[60] In particular, when former Commissioners or Chairmen join or rejoin the judiciary, they are particularly inclined to make reference to Commission material. For example, of our 12 current Supreme Court Justices, four have previously held roles

---

[48] LC 257 (1999). The LCEW specifically recommended that legislative reform of certain aspects should be postponed pending judicial development: see paras 3.165, 3.170, 3.176 and 3.188.

[49] *Kuddus v Chief Constable of Leicestershire Constabulary* [2001] UKHL 29, [2002] 2 AC 122.

[50] LC 247 (1997).

[51] See, eg, LC 320, *The Illegality Defence* (2010), where it was recommended that 'no legislative reform is needed in relation to the illegality defence as it applies to claims other than those arising under a trust' (para 1.18). Instead, the LCEW recommended it should be 'open to the courts to develop the law in ways that would render it considerably clearer, more certain and less arbitrary' (para 3.37). See also *ParkingEye Ltd v Somerfield Stores Ltd* [2012] EWCA Civ 1338, [2013] QB 840, and see generally, chapter 29 (James Lee).

[52] *Morgan Guaranty Trust Company of New York v Lothian Regional Council* 1995 SC 151 (IH).

[53] SLC DP 95 (1993).

[54] *Morgan Guaranty Trust Company of New York v Lothian Regional Council* 1994 SCLR 213 (OH).

[55] SLC 169, *Report on Unjustified Enrichment, Error of Law and Public Authority Receipts and Disbursements* (1999) para 1.3. See also D Hope, 'Law Reform: Alternative Strategies to Legislation', *Law Reform: Catching the Eye of Government*, Papers from a joint seminar presented by the Law Commission and UCL Faculty of Laws (2001) 40.

[56] See, eg, T May, '"It is Not for Judges to be Legislators": Home Secretary's Public Attack on Rebel Judges' *Mail on Sunday* (London, 17 February 2013).

[57] Hope, n 55 above, 36.

[58] J Reid, 'The Judge as Law Maker' (1972–73) 12 *Journal of the Society of Public Teachers of Law* 22, 22.

[59] Hope, n 55 above, 36.

[60] ibid 37.

at the Commissions.[61] They, and the other Justices, make reasonably frequent use of materials published by both the LCEW and the SLC,[62] as well as recommending that certain areas of law are examined by the Commissions.[63]

Finally, it is also important to consider Commission proposals which are implemented (by primary legislation or otherwise), but only after a long time has passed. The starkest example is the LCEW's proposal to abolish the crime of blasphemy which took almost 23 years to be implemented.[64] The importance of such proposals is that they challenge the orthodoxy by pushing the boundaries of law reform— one of the real benefits of having an independent law reform body. It is crucial that implementation is not expected to occur too quickly, otherwise we risk losing the Commissions' ability to examine areas and draft proposals which a body closer to government might not be able to do.

## III  DEFINING IMPLEMENTATION

Calculation of implementation rates requires consideration of what to class as 'implemented', and the outcome of such consideration should be transparent. In terms of what to class as 'implemented', both Commissions currently calculate implementation so as to include not only proposals implemented by primary legislation, but also by the alternative routes considered above.[65] Both also include consolidation and repeals reports. Again, this is quite proper because it is part of the Commissions' remit under the 1965 Act. Furthermore, because the implementation rate for consolidation and repeals is 100 per cent,[66] it would give a decreased and inaccurate picture of implementation rates to exclude such projects. Both Commissions also include partially implemented reports in their implementation figures, although the SLC may be less generous in not including reports where only one or two recommendations have been implemented,[67] as compared to the LCEW.[68] This

---

[61] Lady Hale (LCEW Commissioner 1984–93); Lord Hodge (SLC Commissioner 1997–2003); Lord Carnwath (LCEW Chairman 1999–2002); and Lord Toulson (LCEW Chairman 2002–06).

[62] See, eg, *Granatino v Radmacher* [2010] UKSC 42, [2011] 1 AC 534; *HM Advocate v P* [2011] UKSC 44, 2012 SC (UKSC) 108; *Gow v Grant* [2012] UKSC 29, 2013 SC (UKSC) 1. See also in the Court of Appeal, former LCEW Chairman Sir Henry Brooke's reliance on Commission material in the infamous *Re A (Children)* case: [2001] Fam 147 (CA).

[63] See, eg, *Joseph v Spiller* [2010] UKSC 53, [2011] 1 AC 852; *Jones v Kaney* [2011] UKSC 13, [2011] 2 AC 398.

[64] LC 145, *Criminal Law: Offences against Religion and Public Worship* (1985) implemented by the Criminal Justice and Immigration Act 2008.

[65] For information regarding how the Commissions calculate implementation rates, I am grateful to Malcolm McMillan (SLC) and Catherine Vine (LCEW).

[66] Author's own research, June 2012.

[67] eg only two of the 68 recommendations contained in SLC 124, *Report on Succession* (1990) were implemented (by the Family Law (Scotland) Act 2006, s 19 and sch 3) and the report is described as 'almost entirely unimplemented': SLC DP 136, *Discussion Paper on Succession* (2007) para 1.2.

[68] eg LC 237, *Legislating the Criminal Code: Involuntary Manslaughter* (1996) is classed as 'implemented in part' (LC 352, *Annual Report 2013–14* (2014) app A) even though the Corporate Manslaughter and Corporate Homicide Act 2007 enacted just a small part of the proposed reforms. LC 218, *Legislating the Criminal Code: Offences against the Person and General Principles* (1993) is also classed as 'implemented in part' (*Annual Report 2013–14*, ibid) despite only one of its recommendations being implemented by the Domestic Violence, Crime and Victims Act 2004.

difference in approach can produce anomalies when the Commissions have worked jointly on a project.[69] It is argued that all partially implemented projects should be included in implementation figures because it is difficult to draw a line otherwise between what is implemented and what is not. For example, if a report contains ten recommendations, is it 'implemented' if five recommendations are taken forward, but 'not implemented' if four are taken forward, or if two are taken forward? The better solution, it is argued here, is to be more transparent in how implementation figures are calculated. Such transparency could help us to understand better what we should actually expect of our Commissions. It is currently impossible to find out, without contacting the Commissions directly, how their figures are arrived at. Instead, the Commissions should explicitly and publicly state that their implementation figures include: reports implemented by any means whatsoever; consolidation and repeals reports; and partially implemented reports, no matter how small the implemented part.

In addition, the Commissions should make a further change as to how implementation rates are calculated. Currently, the Commissions include reports in implementation figures as soon as they are published—but of course these reports are unimplemented, and may continue to be unimplemented for some time. The average time for an LCEW proposal to be implemented is two years and eight months.[70] With that in mind, Cretney recommended that proposals should not be counted in implementation figures until two years have passed from the date of publication,[71] and that recommendation is endorsed here. By taking such an approach, implementation figures would more realistically reflect the Commissions' track record. For example, recent figures suggest an LCEW implementation figure of 68 per cent.[72] Using the definition of implementation advanced here, that figure is actually 80 per cent.[73]

We need to move away from an expectation that Commission proposals should be implemented immediately. One way of doing this is by not discharging government from their duty to consider Commission proposals so easily. For example, under the Law Commission Act 2009, the Lord Chancellor must report to Parliament on how he has dealt with, or intends to deal with, LCEW proposals from the previous year.[74] Once reported on, a proposal need not be reported on again.[75] That is the case even if the Lord Chancellor's finding is that the LCEW's proposal is simply not

---

[69] eg the Legislative Reform (Limited Partnerships) Order 2009 implemented a small part of LC 283 and SLC 192, *Partnership Law* (2003). The LCEW classes the report as 'implemented in part' (*Annual Report 2013–14*, n 68 above, app A) and the SLC as unimplemented (SLC website, 'Table of Implementing Legislation' www.scotlawcom.gov.uk/publications/implementing-legislation).

[70] Author's own research of all LCEW reports published between 1965 and 2009, conducted in June 2012. The shortest length of time before implementation occurred was one month and the longest was 22 years 11 months. The figure includes both consolidation and repeals projects and projects proposing substantive reform, and projects implemented either fully or substantially, or partially.

[71] S Cretney, 'The Politics of Law Reform—A View from the Inside' (1985) 48 *MLR* 493, 498, n 23.

[72] Munby, n 14 above, 3.

[73] Calculated by the author.

[74] 2009 Act, s 1, which inserted s 3A into the 1965 Act. Scottish Ministers have undertaken to respond to SLC proposals within three months of their publication: Scottish Parliament Official Report, Written Answer, 12 February 2010 (S3W-31752) (Kenny MacAskill).

[75] 1965 Act, s 3A(4).

a priority at present.[76] It is recommended here that the Lord Chancellor should be obliged to reconsider rejected reports annually. That might seem like a huge burden, but considering the LCEW currently only produces an average of four reports per year, it is entirely manageable.[77] The reconsideration need not be laborious, but simply to remember that the LCEW's work is there, should it become more palatable, or if parliamentary space can more easily be found for it in subsequent years. It is highly undesirable that a perfectly good Commission proposal may continue to gather dust simply because the time was not ripe to implement it within the first year of its publication.

In summary, we need to consider implementation broadly, we need to be more transparent about how it is calculated, and we need to move away from the notion of immediate implementation. By fixating too much on immediacy in particular we run the real risk that the Commissions are unable to undertake certain important and suitable projects.[78]

## IV  UNIMPLEMENTED REPORTS

In addition to proposals which are implemented by means other than primary legislation, certain Commission proposals remain unimplemented. It is submitted, however, that even unimplemented proposals can contribute to the Commissions' function to promote law reform. In the words of former SLC Chairman, Lady Clark of Calton, Commission work is 'never work wasted' because of its potential utility beyond primary legislation.[79] The LCEW appears to agree, having taken the opportunity in its latest Annual Report to note, for example, citations in academic journals, in Hansard, and in court judgments in the United Kingdom and abroad.[80]

Unimplemented Commission proposals can have a number of uses. Academic endorsement of a Commission proposal can show its utility, even if it is not implemented—or at least not implemented quickly. Such proposals can generate debate and inform legal thinking. For example, a European Court of Human Rights ruling in relation to a lack of Swedish privacy law led one author to argue that the United Kingdom may be compelled to enact a privacy law.[81] Despite the time since its publication, James Michael argued that there was a 'ready-made bill' for this

---

[76] As is often the case. See, eg, Ministry of Justice, *Report on the Implementation of Law Commission Proposals* (HC 719, 2011) paras 50 and 56.

[77] Calculated from the number of reports (excluding consolidation and repeals) published between 1 January 2009 and 31 December 2013 inclusive. During the same time period, the SLC produced an average of three reports per year.

[78] Both Commissions use the project-selection criteria of resources, suitability and importance when embarking upon new projects: see, eg, LC 352, *Annual Report 2013–14* (2014) 21 and SLC 236, *Annual Report 2013* (2014) 13.

[79] J Forsyth, 'Interview: Lady Clark, First Female Chairman of the SLC' *The Scotsman* (Edinburgh, 24 September 2012).

[80] LC 359, *Annual Report 2014–15* (2015) 11.

[81] J Michael, 'UK May Need Law against Secret Filming and Photography after European Court Ruling' (*UK Human Rights Blog*, 21 November 2013) www.ukhumanrightsblog.com/2013/11/21/uk-may-need-law-against-secret-filming-and-photography-after-european-court-ruling-james-michael/. I am grateful to Neil Faris for referring me to this piece.

purpose in the form of an unimplemented LCEW report published in 1981.[82] This example demonstrates that Commission work, even if not immediately (or ever) implemented, may stand the test of time and be used in academic discourse, in this case some three decades later.

Unimplemented Commission reports can also be cited in in judicial opinions. For example, in *Prince Jefri Bolkiah v KPMG*,[83] the definition of 'Chinese Walls' was lifted from a consultation paper on *Fiduciary Duties and Regulatory Rules*.[84] The project's eventual report was rejected by government.[85]

Commission reports may also be used by legal practitioners or law students for their useful summaries of what the law is, let alone how it may be reformed.[86] Such use must be ancillary to the Commissions' statutory duty to promote law reform—although it may contribute towards it in a more indirect way.

We should value the Commissions' independence and, as such, we should not expect them to have 100 per cent implementation rates. Not only would such an implementation rate be unlikely to be achieved, it would also be undesirable, reflecting a Commission too close to government to be truly independent. Of course, we cannot allow implementation rates to drop too low. Low implementation rates would likely be seen by government as an indicator of poor value for money. In the light of the Commissions' recent experiences of budget cuts,[87] and surviving so-called quangocide,[88] it would be foolhardy to allow implementation rates to drop too low.[89]

The Commissions are often critical of their own implementation rates.[90] Such criticism is the natural reaction of individuals who suffer 'wastage and frustration' if their proposals are not taken forward.[91] In Oerton's candid words: 'I think I might have been willing in the end to work happily on a project to prescribe the size of the wire mesh on chicken runs if only its implementation had been guaranteed'.[92] But we, as outsiders and stakeholders in the Commissions, might prefer the Commissions to take a gamble on a more important project, which is why we must take stock and reappraise what we expect of our Commissions.

A significant minority of Commission proposals can remain unimplemented without threatening the Commissions' reputation or very existence. From a brief

---

[82] ibid; LC 110, *Breach of Confidence* (1981).

[83] *Prince Jefri Bolkiah v KPMG* [1999] 2 AC 222 (HL).

[84] LC CP 124 (1992).

[85] LC 236, *Fiduciary Duties and Regulatory Rules* (1995).

[86] D Hope, 'Do We Still Need a Scottish Law Commission?' (2006) 10 *Edinburgh Law Review* 10, 21.

[87] eg, the funding received by the LCEW in 2012–13 was over £1.8 million less than in 2002–03: Compare LC 280, *Annual Report 2002–03* (2003) app F with LC 338, *Annual Report 2012–13* (2013) app B.

[88] The LCEW was one of the bodies at risk of abolition in the coalition government's 2010 review of so-called 'quangos': Public Bodies Bill as introduced, sch 7.

[89] Abolition of Law Commissions is not unheard of. For example, in 1993, the Law Reform Commission of Canada (established in 1971) was abolished. Its successor, the Law Commission of Canada, was established in 1997. In 2006, the Canadian Government withdrew funding, forcing the Law Commission of Canada to close. See chapter 11 (Yves Le Bouthillier).

[90] See, eg, Sir James Munby's assertions that implementation has been a 'grave concern' to successive LCEW Chairmen, and that although the LCEW has a 'good [implementation] record ... we believe it could—and should—be considerably better': n 14 above, 3–4.

[91] M Kerr, 'Law Reform in Changing Times' (1980) 96 *LQR* 515, 531.

[92] RT Oerton, *A Lament for the Law Commission* (Chichester, Countrywise Press, 1987) 106.

survey of other Commissions, an implementation rate of 75–85 per cent seems desirable.[93] Such a figure demonstrates that the majority of Commission proposals are implemented (by whatever means) whereas a minority of proposals may not be implemented, but may promote law reform in other ways. Furthermore, it may be entirely possible that those unimplemented reports do eventually become law, many years—or even decades—after publication.

## V CONCLUSION

After a successful start,[94] implementation rates for both Commissions have dropped almost every decade since 1965.[95] It is understandable and desirable that efforts have been made to combat those falling implementation rates. We must, however, be more explicit and certain about what we mean when we calculate implementation rates. It is reassuring that the Commissions already include less orthodox means of implementation in their implementation rates. That inclusion should be more open in order to re-educate us about what we should expect from our Commissions. Our expectation of a draft Bill appended to a report followed by introduction into Parliament may still be strong. We must assess the Commissions' output holistically to include other methods of implementation. Equally importantly, we must not write off unimplemented reports as failures. Like dissenting judgments, they may be the reports which push the boundaries of law reform in a climate which is not yet ready for change. The Commissions are not, and should not be, academic institutions. They are, after all, publicly-funded bodies and they should do public good. But there is little public good in an implemented but unimportant or flawed Commission proposal. We should value the independence of our Commissions to challenge the orthodoxy, to push the boundaries of law reform, and to shine light into corners of the law which might otherwise be left in the shadows.

---

[93] For example, the current implementation figure for the Australian Law Reform Commission (ALRC) is 'over 85 per cent': ALRC website, 'About' www.alrc.gov.au/about. The method of calculation is not specified beyond the fact that the figure includes both substantial and partial implementation (and has not been discovered despite attempted correspondence with the ALRC). It cannot therefore be known how accurate a comparison between this figure and the SLC/LCEW figures is. The implementation rate of New Zealand Law Commission (NZLC) proposals from its establishment in 1986 until 2006 was 66%: M Thompson (Special Projects Adviser, NZLC) to M McMillan (Chief Executive, SLC), 'Implementation of Law Reform Recommendations', 19 February 2009, SLC file. The exact method of calculation is not specified, although the phrase 'some legislative implementation' is used, suggesting that partial implementation is included, but judicial implementation is not. It is unclear, however, whether immediately published reports are classed as 'not implemented' and this has not been discovered despite attempted correspondence with the NZLC. See also, Sir Grant Hammond's contribution in this volume (chapter 19) for a recent survey of figures. The figures given there are very similar, though there is always a question of counting rules and rounding in such an exercise.

[94] During the Commissions' first ten years of operation, only one SLC project and three LCEW projects were not implemented: author's own research, June 2012.

[95] Implementation rates by decade for the LCEW, including consolidation and repeals and partially implemented projects, are: 96% (1965–74); 86% (1975–84); 83% (1985–94); and 67% (1995–2004). The corresponding figures for the SLC are: 96% (1965–74); 97% (1975–84); 89% (1985–94); and 74% (1995–2004). Percentages calculated by the author using the method of calculation advanced in this chapter.

# 16

# Law Commissions, Courts and Society: A Sceptical View

## WILLIAM BINCHY

Whilst the title of this chapter speaks of scepticism, my argument is in no way designed to offer scepticism about the whole, noble, venture of law reform, but rather to express doubt as to the merits of certain tendencies in recent years to integrate Law Reform Commissions more closely into the agendas of others—most obviously the legislature, but less obviously also the judiciary, human rights bodies and philanthropists with agendas. I am seeking to make a call for a reaffirmation of the principle of maximum independence for Law Reform Commissions, which animated the movement for the establishment of the Law Commissions 50 years ago.

## I THE PRINCIPLE OF INDEPENDENCE

Independence is the fundamental bedrock of a Law Reform Commission. This is well captured by the Commonwealth Secretariat in its paper, 'Law Reform Agencies: Their Role and Effectiveness', presented at the Meeting of the Commonwealth Law Ministers and Senior Officials in Accra, 17–20 October 2005:

> An essential feature and a key advantage of an LRA is its independence, especially from government but also from all others. This independence has a particular value as it demonstrates that the LRA's views are objective and impartial and are not dependent on others' views. The Executive and the Legislature frequently need and value specialist advice in the planning and formulation of law reform. This advice is best provided by an independent body. An LRA is independent in the recommendations it makes as to the reform of any particular area of law. An LRA should have no preconceptions and no in-built bias. It should therefore be composed of Commissioners and staff who do not have strong allegiances, who have open minds and who are sufficiently resilient not to be persuaded by any pressure other than sound argument. It is a body that has nothing to fear from expressing its views, after a sound law reform process.[1]

---

[1] Commonwealth Secretariat, 'Law Reform Agencies: Their Role and Effectiveness' (2005), executive summary, para 13.

In echoing this call for independence for Law Reform Commissions, I am fully aware of the need for practicality. Law Reform Commissions should not exist in a political vacuum. They are generally creatures of the legislative process; a government Minister, Attorney-General or the legislature will have some say over their programme for reform; perhaps most importantly, whether their recommendations are translated into law depends on the goodwill and positive actions of the legislature (and, realistically, in most countries, the government). No sensible Law Reform Commission, however conscious of its independence, can ignore these realities. Prudent Commissions will seek to smooth the lines of communication with the other organs of government. But there is a difference between doing that and transforming the role of Law Reform Commissions into one of alliance with the government, legislature and judiciary, all marching in the common direction of law reform. Unless we were to work on the premise that what constitutes law reform has an agreed normative content, necessarily shared by all of these separate bodies, it would be wrong to set out on such a shared journey.

## II  AN AGREED NORMATIVE CONTENT?

There is a certain reticence among Law Reform Commissions, and Law Reform Commissioners, about engaging in frank public discussion of the normative content of law reform. It is very easy for all to agree that some ancient law dealing with matters that have long since been overtaken by technological changes, or reflecting social attitudes that command no contemporary support, should be abolished. But there is a considerable range of law where there is no universal agreement as to whether it should stay or go, and, if it is to go, what should replace it. It would be odd for a Law Reform Commission to share the philosophy of Burke but is it required to concur with Marx? Or Mill? How left-wing and liberal must it be if it is to fulfil its proper role?[2] Would there be something prima facie illegitimate in a Law Reform Commission's recommendation of a complete prohibition of surrogacy, for example; or the retention of the parental prerogative to administer physical discipline to their children; or a change in the law of landlord and tenant premised on naked free market economic principles rather than social justice? Each of these recommendations might be considered contrary to the views of bodies monitoring the implementation of the international human rights instruments, as well as national human rights bodies. Must Law Reform Commissions get in line, at peril of having the very legitimacy (as opposed to the merit) of their recommendations called into question?

These questions have become sharper in recent years because of the greater penetration of human rights rhetoric into areas traditionally considered (wrongly, of course) simply as 'lawyers' law'. No-one today believes that any area of law,

---

[2] I do not here refer to pragmatic reasons why a Law Reform Commission might be better to avoid the perception of having a specific political perspective, *cf* JS Ziegel, 'Editorial: Law Reform Commissions: A Haven for Left Wing Ideologues?' (2006–07) 44 *Canadian Business Law Journal* 325; M Tilbury, 'Why Law Reform Commissions?: A Deconstruction and Stakeholder Analysis from an Australian Perspective' (2005) 23 *Windsor Yearbook of Access to Justice* 313, 327; G Gretton, 'Of Law Commissioning' (2013) 17 *Edinburgh Law Review* 119, 129.

however dry and technical, is exclusively 'lawyers' law'. Equally, it is not a sufficient resolution of the question of the normative content of law reform to recommend that Law Reform Commissions steer clear of politically controversial topics. The worst—certainly the least honest—strategy is for a Law Reform Commission to bury important normative preferences in a sea of technical procedural recommendations, designed to reduce the risk of public debate.

## III INDEPENDENCE OF MIND, NOT NORMATIVE ORTHODOXY: THE PROPER TEST

It is true that some great law reformers who have led their Law Reform Commissions to do great things were unambiguous advocates of radical normative changes in the law; but commitment to such a radical philosophy is not a term of employment as a Law Reform Commissioner. Instead, a less prescriptive approach has tradition-ally been adopted, which emphasises the intellectual strength and scholarship of Commissioners rather than the extent of their radicalism or the orthodoxy of their philosophy from the standpoint of liberalism.

It is this element of chance, I suggest, that is part of the strength of Law Reform Commissions. The recommendations that emerge from a group of independently-minded, intellectually gifted people are not predictable. They may, or may not, appeal to the legislature of the day, or of some future day. That is as it should be. Once Commissioners regard their task as serving the agenda of others, their inde-pendence is compromised and their very rationale subverted. I stress again that Law Reform Commissions should retain a sound appreciation that the prospect of imple-mentation of law reform proposals is a relevant consideration, but it should not be a dominant consideration and it certainly should not induce in Commissioners a sense that making strategic alignments with politicians, civil servants or judges is the proper way to proceed.

## IV RELATIONS WITH THE LEGISLATURE AND EXECUTIVE

Law Reform Commissions, of course, have certain inevitable connections with the legislature and the executive. They are, after all, generally creatures of legislation and the subject matter of their law reform proposals is generally circumscribed by either or both of these organs of government. Equally obviously, the precise way in which the relationship between the Law Reform Commission and the executive and legislature is calibrated will have a significant effect on the content and thrust of the recommendations for law reform that emerge. If too close a relationship is prescribed, or simply develops over time, there is a danger that the Law Reform Commission will become more akin to a law reform division of the Ministry for Justice—an arm of the legislature and executive rather than an independent agency.[3]

---

[3] *cf* P North, 'Law Reform: Problems and Pitfalls' (1999–2000) 33 *University of British Columbia Law Review* 37, 44–45: 'I believe that the law reform process lacks credibility if a report is prepared in terms of a dialogue with politicians.'

Law reform divisions of Ministries can perform valuable work, but they lack the spark of independence that should animate a Law Reform Commission.

## V RELATIONS WITH THE JUDICIARY

What relationship should exist between a Law Reform Commission and the judiciary? Let us begin with matters that can scarcely be controversial.

### A Judges as Commissioners

The first is that of direct judicial participation in the law reform process. It can enhance the prestige of a Law Reform Commission to appoint a leading member of the judiciary as its President, Chairman or similar. Judges, of their very being, confer legitimacy on an enterprise. Moreover, judges might be considered likely to have particular understanding of the areas of law calling for reform.

The process of selecting a judge to be President is, however, not quite as straight-forward as it may look. Some judges of the first rank intellectually may have no great commitment to the desirability of reform. Others may be reformist but prefer to see reform implemented through the judicial rather than legislative process. Still others may simply be *too* reformist (or too reformist to generate any real prospect of having their ideas implemented through legislation). Moreover, it will not always be possible to find a judge of the first order: there will naturally be a demand for such judges to continue in their judicial role and part-time Presidents cannot always provide the necessary leadership for the task.

There is also a potential difficulty of culture: many judges are not used to working in teams (though appellate judges will have experience of having to negotiate with others of equal rank). A judge who has had years of receiving and adjudicating on submissions may find it difficult to adjust to the more level relationships of decision-making that presidency of a Law Reform Commission requires.

### B Consulting with the Judiciary

A second area surely of no controversy is that of consultation. Law Reform Commissions, in the process of preparing reform proposals, obviously benefit from consulting with a range of people[4] and groups. Among these is the judiciary. There

---

[4] Some Commissions engage in what is represented as democratic consultation. One has to be a little doubtful as to the extent to which a professed attempt to reflect the popular will is entirely sincere. The public has the tendency, distressing to many Commissioners, to baulk at particularly radical proposals for law reform. On occasion, Commissions frankly acknowledge that their proposals may conflict with public opinion. For example the Law Commission of India, Report 262, *The Death Penalty* (2015), proposes the general abolition of the death penalty (save for terrorist offences), conscious that this may not coincide with public opinion, but confident, on the basis of experience elsewhere, that, after abolition, public opinion would in due course come to support this.

is much to gain from having judges contribute to seminars and working groups and offering their own observations on proposals as they go through the consultative process. Even informal consultation with judges can be justified. But there are limits. Law Reform Commissions, and Law Reform Commissioners, should not become allies of the judiciary or of any particular member of the judiciary who has not been openly and formally appointed to a position within the Commission. They certainly should not seek to garner judicial support for their proposals. There is no legitimate basis for forming an alliance between a Law Reform Commission and members of the judiciary. Any perception of a commonality of interest is misconceived. It is the function of Law Reform Commissions to propose, not to become political players, forming alliances with judges to strengthen the prospects of legislative implementation of their proposals.

It is an aspect of human nature that a positive experience on a single shared project with others can encourage one to seek to develop the relationship more broadly. From time to time, Law Reform Commissions closely consult with judges on a particular project, where it is entirely reasonable, in the light of the nature of the project, that the judicial perspective should be heard and given weight. Having had this single success, Commissioners may think it only sensible to go back again, and yet again, to the same judicial well. Something like an alliance may build up, which can be rationalised fairly easily. Surely it is only reasonable that the opinions of judges, who implement and, realistically if not formally, create law, should have a say in its future development? The answer to that argument has to be that, however reasonable it may appear, it is not desirable, or at least should be assessed with complete frankness, as it carries the risk of partial surrender of the independence of the Commission to the perspective of a powerful outsider.

## C Proposing Changes within the Remit of the Judiciary

Let us now consider the question of the extent to which the recommendations of a Law Reform Commission may trench upon the exercise of the judicial power. Of course, it is the nature of Law Reform Commissions that they are entitled to recommend the statutory abolition or modification of legal rules articulated by judges—indeed, potentially the entire corpus of the common law—including a rule specifically articulated in a particular judgment—the rule in *Searle v Wallbank*,[5] for example, or even the rule in *Rylands v Fletcher*.[6] Statutory reform of this kind is entirely non-problematic, but what about a recommendation directed, not to the legislature, but to the judiciary? Is it desirable, or even legitimate, for a Law Reform Commission formally to recommend to the courts that they develop the law in a particular way?

A direct recommendation of this kind could be regarded as too confrontational, inconsistent with the separation of powers. Instead, Commissions tend to prefer to

---

[5] *Searle v Wallbank* [1947] AC 341 (HL).
[6] *Rylands v Fletcher* (1868) LR 3 HL 330 (HL).

hint, sometimes broadly, as to how they would wish to see the common law develop in a particular area. Perhaps it could be argued that, since Law Reform Commissions are perfectly entitled to recommend the statutory reversal of a specific judicial decision, their less intrusive suggestions or expressions of hope that courts develop the law in a particular direction create no problem. Yet I suggest that they do. Judges have the sole responsibility to develop the law, subject only to constitutional and legislative constraints. They should not be the object of attempts to influence them in this way by any external body, however eminent.

### D  Influencing Judicial Reform through Recommendations for Statutory Reform

It seems entirely legitimate that particular recommendations by a Law Reform Commission for statutory reform might, on occasion, inspire a court to take the initiative and develop the law itself on the lines recommended by the Commission.[7] Frequently, Law Reform Commission recommendations address areas of law where the most recent judicial pronouncement was some time ago and the principles are clearly in need of modernisation. In such circumstances, a court, freed from the shackles of stare decisis, is perfectly free to update the law, without having to wait for possible future legislation. If it considers that the Law Reform Commission recommendations are the most sensible way forward, it is entitled to gain inspiration from them. A court that thus follows the path proposed by a Law Reform Commission is doing no more than it would if it found inspiration in an article by an academic writer in the *Law Quarterly Review*. It owes no a priori respect to recommendations emanating from Law Reform Commissions, which, formally at least, it should treat with neutrality. Thus, for example, in the Irish Supreme Court decision of *CC v Ireland*,[8] striking down as unconstitutional a strict liability statutory offence of having sexual relations with underage girls, Hardiman J observed:

> It might, for example, be thought desirable to have a law on this subject along the lines proposed by the Law Reform Commission in 1990. But for present purposes it is sufficient to say that there is, obviously, more than one form of statutory rape provision which would pass constitutional muster, and it does not appear to be appropriate for the Court, as opposed to the legislature, to choose between them.[9]

Similarly, in the Irish High Court decision of *Byrne v Director of Public Prosecutions*,[10] where the question arose as to the relevance of a recently published Law Reform Commission of Ireland consultation paper on jury service,[11] in which the Commission had recommended the creation of an offence for jurors to conduct

---

[7] For one aspect of this relationship, who should act out of the Commissions and the Supreme Court, see chapter 29 (James Lee). More generally, see chapter 15 (Shona Wilson Stark).

[8] *CC v Ireland* [2006] 4 IR 1.

[9] ibid 86.

[10] *Byrne v Director of Public Prosecutions* [2010] IEHC 382.

[11] Law Reform Commission of Ireland, LRC CP 61, *Jury Service* (2010).

independent internet inquiries outside the courtroom, Charleton J considered the proposals to be sensible but added:

> The Court has no entitlement, however, with a view to enforcing a recommendation, to make a ruling in favour of an applicant; O'Higgins CJ put the principle thus in *Norris v AG*[12]: –

> 'Judges may, and do, share with other citizens a concern and interest in desirable changes in reform in our laws; but, under the Constitution, they have no function in achieving such by judicial decision. It may be regarded as emphasising the obvious but, nevertheless, I think it proper to remind the plaintiff and others interested in these proceedings that the sole and exclusive power of altering the laws of Ireland is, by the Constitution, vested in the [Parliament]. The Courts declare what the law is—it is for the [Parliament] to make changes if it so thinks proper.'

> It follows that the merits of each application are to be judged individually and without regard to any view that a court may have as to whether the law is sensible, might be changed, or that a provisional recommendation of the Law Reform Commission is or is not correct.[13]

## VI RELATIONS WITH NATIONAL HUMAN RIGHTS INSTITUTIONS

In many countries the last couple of decades have seen a mushrooming of national human rights institutions. The relationship between Law Reform Commissions and these bodies is still evolving, politely, but carries real challenges for Law Reform Commissions.

The Paris Principles[14] set out the gold standard for national human rights institutions. Under the heading 'Competence and Responsibilities', principle 3(a)(1) of the Paris Principles provides that the national institution:

> shall examine the legislation and administrative provisions in force, as well as bills and proposals, and shall make such recommendations as it deems appropriate in order to ensure that these provisions conform to the fundamental principles of human rights; it shall, if necessary, recommend the adoption of new legislation, the amendment of legislation in force and the adoption or amendment of administrative measures.

What is this if not law reform, albeit law reform imbued with a very specific normative perspective?

Human Rights Commissions differ from Law Reform Commissions in the clarity and specificity of their normative agenda, which is to advocate for a maximalist legal implementation within their own countries of the international human rights jurisprudence developed through Conventions, magnified in turn by the very broad

---

[12] *Norris v AG* [1984] IR 36, 53.
[13] *Byrne*, n 10 above, [25]–[26].
[14] *Principles Relating to the Status of National Institutions (The Paris Principles)*, adopted by the United Nations Human Rights Commission in Resolution 1992/54 of 1992 and by the General Assembly in Resolution 48/134 of 1993.

interpretations given by the personnel of the bodies monitoring the Conventions. Of course Law Reform Commissions when making their recommendations on any subject will have regard to human rights and to the extent to which their national domestic order has incorporated international human rights treaties, but this does not require Law Reform Commissions to adopt the latest dicta of the most radical monitoring body. Liaising with Human Rights Commissions needs to be carefully carried out as Human Rights Commissions properly advocating for law reform are tied to a specific normative perspective whereas it is the essence of Law Reform Commissions that they preserve their independence as to their normative premises.

## VII RELATIONS WITH PHILANTHROPISTS

How should a Law Reform Commission respond to the offer of benefaction from a philanthropist? I suggest that it should do so with the very greatest of caution. Philanthropists have no doubt done much good in the world but their benefaction can come at a price, at least to the extent of suggesting, if not actually calling, the tune. Philanthropists have the luxury of choosing whom to benefit and with what intended outcome. Money brings with it power and power need not always be exercised even-handedly. Philanthropists have no obligation to be politically neutral: they are free to fund projects, or institutions, that appeal to them. The recipients of their munificence tend to develop a sophisticated capacity to work out what pleases them most, and least. Of course, there will often be times where the values of the philanthropist and the beneficiary completely coincide. That is absolutely fine where these values relate to some universally acknowledged social goal, such as the advancement of education or the relief of poverty. But where law reform is concerned, the philanthropist's payment of money carries the risk of compromising the independence of the Law Reform Commission that receives it. Even to accept research money to advance a reform to which the Commission is already independently fully committed is problematic: in taking this money, the Commission is skewing the process of law reform in its country by acquiescing in the selective advancement of one possible reform over another.

## VIII CONCLUDING OBSERVATIONS

Those who have been involved in law reform know that measurement of success and failure is not reducible to the extent of implementation of Law Reform Commission recommendations, by legislatures or courts. It would be possible for a Commission to tailor its recommendations to achieve complete implementation but we can say with confidence that such a Commission would have lost sight of its mandate. The best Commissions are those that nurture rather than suppress the quirky, contrary independence of mind that, in the long term, carries the prospect of quality and substance.

# 17

# *A Good Name, a Long Game*

LAURA DUNLOP

## I INTRODUCTION

In the autumn of 2009, shortly after I had been appointed to the Scottish Law Commission as a part-time Commissioner, I was stopped in the Advocates Library by one of the judges of the Court of Session. He asked me for information about the Law Commission's coat of arms. I knew nothing about any heraldry at my new base, the Commission's offices in Causewayside, on the south side of Edinburgh. So I promised to find out.

On my next visit to the Commission, I studied the crest above the entrance. It is possible to make out two owls, some quill pens, what might be a set of scales, and some wording beneath. Bits of the shield and bits of the motto are missing—not the venerability attributable to years of weathering, but the chipping off of 1960s concrete. I managed to work out that the motto was '*In trutina ponentur eadem*', which everyone will immediately recognize as a line from the Roman poet Horace.[1]

Roughly translated as 'Let all be weighed in the same balance', you might think it a good enough motto for the occupants of the building, with its implications of objectivity and measured consideration. But Iain Ritchie in the General Office of the Commission threw me off track, when I sought further information there. He asserted that these were not arms of the Scottish Law Commission, but of the examination board which was previously housed in the building. I reported back to the judge. 'No no', he said, 'it must belong to the Law Commission. It includes the scales of justice.'

But the judge was wrong, and Iain was right. Although the motto refers to weighing, the scales of justice were in the eye of the beholder. (In relation to seeing what one expects to see, it is noteworthy that, when it visited the site, the Public Monuments and Sculpture Association thought it saw a wig.)[2] The exam board wanted to show that it would assess everyone in the same way, candidate to candidate and year on year. Nowadays, they exist in a different form, and they have a new motto. Could the Scottish Law Commission justify appropriating their old one?

---

[1] Horace, *Satires*, book I satire III line 72, changed from singular to plural.
[2] Public Monuments and Sculpture Association: Edinburgh, *Field Visit* (1999) www.canmore.org.uk/event/612268.

Tempting as it is to take that as an excuse to digress into the Scottish Law Commission's 1980 *Report on Lost and Abandoned Property*,[3] I must stay on topic—'the many faces of law reform' or, as was suggested to me by the organisers of this conference, 'to consider the value of the Law Commissions beyond mere primary legislative implementation'. This session is to be in contrast to the next one, which will concentrate on implementation as more traditionally defined, that is by legislation. So I am required to look elsewhere than at primary legislation, and elsewhere than at the use of Commission materials by courts for the purposes of interpretation. A general heading might appropriately be 'Impact—other'.

There was a danger of this being an odd sock drawer of a chapter, so I decided to revisit the three elements of the crest—the owls, the weighing and the quills. The symbolism is not hard to interpret: wisdom or learning, balancing, and the written word. How well do these symbols match the activities of the organisation which happens to be displaying them above its entrance? In answering this question, I will concentrate on the Scottish Law Commission (because I know more about it) and I should reassure you that I have been selective, not comprehensive. There are only a few socks in the drawer.

## II DILIGENCE

I begin with an example from the 1980s of the Commission playing a direct role in the justice system. It is apparent from a case called *Roboserve Ltd v Akerman*,[4] a dispute concerning the former debt recovery process of poinding, that is, attachment of goods. Poinding in practice involved a type of audit of the debtor's moveable property, when sheriff officers would present the required documentation of debt and then identify property which appeared to have a sale value sufficient to clear the sum due. That property was then poinded, that is, set apart to be sold. The next step involved obtaining a warrant for sale from the sheriff. In the *Roboserve* case, a warrant had been obtained and a sale arranged, but the debtor had paid some money so the sale had been cancelled. Promised further payments by the debtor not having materialised, the question arose of whether a second sale could be warranted without a fresh poinding. Under the law then in force, this depended on whether there had been 'undue delay' in applying for a second warrant. In referring to recent difficulty with this concept, Sheriff Principal O'Brien said:

> It was because of the changing attitude by the courts to what would amount to undue delay in the context of present day conditions that all the sheriffs principal, after consulting the Scottish Law Commission, issued practice notes, the gist of which was to indicate that a period of up to six months would not call for inquiry into whether the delay was undue.[5]

Of course, the whole topic of diligence was on the agenda of the Commission from the late 1970s, so that helps to explain why its involvement was thought

[3] SLC 57, (1980).
[4] *Roboserve Ltd v Akerman* 1987 SLT (Sh Ct) 137.
[5] ibid 138.

apposite. Even allowing for the element of topicality, however, the fact that a section of the judiciary collectively sought such advice is eloquent of the standing of the Commission. It was therefore able to contribute to the process of formulating a balanced approach on a difficult issue.

## III DELICT

Next, I turn to a case of my own, from the early 1990s. The topic was injury sustained *in utero*, and the case was *McWilliams v Lord Advocate*.[6] A child had died as a result of injuries sustained during his birth, and his parents sought damages for their loss. The death was proved to have been due to obstetric negligence on the part of personnel in the Royal Army Medical Corps. The defenders argued that the parents were presenting a claim based on the *nasciturus* fiction (the fiction that in all matters affecting its interests at a given moment in time, the unborn child *in utero* should be deemed to be already born) and that, since the fiction could not be invoked to benefit third parties as distinct from the child, the claim must fail. That argument had recently been sustained in another case involving antenatal injury, so we were facing an uphill climb. The Scottish Law Commission provided the necessary lift.

In the early 1970s, both Commissions had examined the law on antenatal injury, the Law Commission in consequence of a reference from the Lord Chancellor in November 1972 and the Scottish Law Commission in consequence of a reference from the Lord Advocate in December 1972. Interestingly, the first question in that reference was 'What is the present law of Scotland regarding liability to make reparation … in respect of injury caused to a child before birth?'

As would be expected, the question was answered. In paragraphs 11 and 12 of its report,[7] the Commission set out the present law, concluding that the right of a child to sue for injuries sustained during the antenatal period and, where the child has died of such injuries, its parents, does not depend on the *nasciturus* fiction but on ordinary principles of the law of delict. The Lord Ordinary set out these paragraphs from the report in his judgment, commenting: 'I consider that that passage which I have quoted at length is a correct statement of the law of Scotland … and I gratefully adopt it as a clear statement of the law'.[8] The Commission's advice was that existing law was adequate to cover the situations to which its remit was related.

## IV EVIDENCE

I mention now a recommendation addressed to the judiciary directly. Towards the end of the 1980s, the Scottish Law Commission undertook a law reform project on the evidence of children and other vulnerable witnesses. In its report,[9] when

---

[6] *McWilliams v Lord Advocate* 1991 SLT 1045 (OH).
[7] Scottish Law Commission, SLC 30, *Report on Liability for Antenatal Injury* (1973).
[8] *McWilliams*, n 6 above, 1047–48.
[9] Scottish Law Commission, SLC 125, *Report on the Evidence of Children and Other Potentially Vulnerable Witnesses* (1990).

commenting on the practices to be adopted in courts when children were testifying, the Commission observed:

> It does occur to us ... that some desirable uniformity of approach in the exercise of judicial discretion would be likely to be achieved if some authoritative guidance could be provided for all judges. Some years ago that was achieved in relation to the matter of contempt of court when, in 1975, a memorandum of guidance was issued to all judges by the Lord Justice General. We respectfully suggest that the Lord Justice General might consider the preparation and circulation of a similar memorandum in relation to the matters which we have just been discussing.[10]

The report was published in February 1990, and that particular recommendation was effected by the Lord Justice General's memorandum of 26 July 1990, which governed the position for the next 15 years.[11] This may be the swiftest ever implementation of a Scottish Law Commission recommendation.

## V  UNJUSTIFIED ENRICHMENT

No account of the contribution represented by the published legal research of the Commissions would be complete without mention of the work of both Commissions in the 1990s on unjustified enrichment.[12] Major developments of the law were effected by the courts, first in the *Woolwich* case,[13] concerning the recovery of monies paid to the Inland Revenue under regulations subsequently declared to have been ultra vires and, secondly, in the cases of *Morgan Guaranty v Lothian Regional Council*[14] and *Kleinwort Benson Ltd v Lincoln City Council*[15] which, for Scotland, and England and Wales respectively, abrogated the rule precluding the recovery in an enrichment claim of money paid under a mistake of law. The context of both *Morgan Guaranty* and *Kleinwort Benson* was the participation by local authorities in the United Kingdom in 'interest rate swap' schemes in the 1980s. The House of Lords having held that participation in these schemes was ultra vires,[16] restitutionary claims were raised by the banks. The legal difficulty in their way was the rule that money paid under a mistake of law could not be recovered.

A timeline illustrates the sequence of proposals by the Commissions and relative judicial decisions:

1991: The Law Commission publishes a consultation paper on restitution of mistaken payments,[17] following a reference in March 1990 from the Lord Chancellor.

---

[10]  ibid para 2.5.

[11]  See *McGinley v HM Advocate* 2001 SLT 198 (JC) and High Court of Justiciary Practice Note, *Child Witnesses: Discretionary Powers*, No 2 of 2005, available on the Scottish Courts website: www.scotcourts.gov.uk/rules-and-practice/practice-notes/criminal-courts-practice-notes-and-directions.

[12]  It is apparent from the annual reports of the SLC that this was stimulating work. See, eg, Scottish Law Commission, SLC 146, *Twenty-Eighth Annual Report 1992–93* (1993) para 2.25: 'We are pleased to note that after a long period of academic and official neglect, a new and lively interest in the Scots law on unjustified enrichment can be detected.'

[13]  *Woolwich Equitable Building Society v Inland Revenue Commissioners* [1993] AC 70 (HL).

[14]  *Morgan Guaranty Trust Company of New York v Lothian Regional Council* 1995 SC 151 (IH).

[15]  *Kleinwort Benson Ltd v Lincoln City Council* [1999] 2 AC 349 (HL).

[16]  In *Hazell v Hammersmith and Fulham London Borough Council and Others* [1992] 2 AC 1 (HL).

[17]  Law Commission, LC CP 120, *Restitution of Payments Made Under a Mistake of Law* (1991).

1992: The House of Lords recognises a right of recovery in restitution where money has been paid as a result of an ultra vires demand by a public authority (*Woolwich*).[18]

1993: The Scottish Law Commission publishes a discussion paper on recovery of benefits conferred under error of law.[19]

1994: The Law Commission publishes a report on mistakes of law.[20]

1995: The Inner House of the Court of Session abrogates the error of law rule in Scots law (*Morgan Guaranty*).[21]

1996: The Scottish Law Commission publishes two discussion papers, the first concerning the aftermath of the judicial abolition of the error of law rule and the second addressing the potential recovery of ultra vires public authority receipts and disbursements.[22]

1998: The House of Lords abrogates the error of law rule in the law of England and Wales (*Kleinwort Benson*).[23]

1999: The Scottish Law Commission publishes its report on error of law and recovery of public authority receipts and disbursements.[24]

In this area of law in the 1990s, the strands of Law Commission thinking and analysis by the courts were interwoven. Each was taken into account by the other. In the *Woolwich* case, Lord Goff reflected on this positioning:

> It is a reflection of this fact [the relevance of the case to the future of the law of restitution] that there have been cited to your Lordships not only the full range of English authorities, and also authorities from Commonwealth countries and the United States of America, but in addition a number of academic works of considerable importance. These include a most valuable Consultation Paper (Law Com No 120) published last year by the Law Commission, entitled *Restitution of Payments Made Under a Mistake of Law*, for which we owe much to Mr Jack Beatson and also, I understand, to Dr Sue Arrowsmith; and a series of articles by academic lawyers of distinction working in the field of restitution. I shall be referring to this academic material in due course. But I wish to record at once that, in my opinion, it is of such importance that it has a powerful bearing upon the consideration by your Lordships of the central question in the case.[25]

In Scotland, the involvement of the Commissions was acknowledged in an article by Lord Rodger of Earlsferry, published in 1993. He referred to the 1990s (up to that point) as 'a remarkable period of creativity by English and Commonwealth courts and legal scholars in building up the law of restitution'. In relation to the possibility that the courts would reform the law to remove the mistake of law rule, he said:

> The fact that the Scottish Law Commission has been looking at this area of the law would not seem in itself to be a barrier to the courts taking such a step. On the contrary, the fruits

---

[18] See n 13 above.

[19] Scottish Law Commission, SLC DP 95, *Recovery of Benefits Conferred under Error of Law* (1993).

[20] Law Commission, LC 227, *Restitution: Mistakes of Law* (1994).

[21] See n 14 above.

[22] Scottish Law Commission, SLC DP 99, *The Judicial Abolition of the Error of Law Rule and its Aftermath* (1996) and SLC DP 100, *Recovery of Ultra Vires Public Authority Receipts and Disbursements* (1996).

[23] See n 15 above.

[24] Scottish Law Commission, SLC 169, *Unjustified Enrichment, Error of Law and Public Authority Receipts and Disbursements* (1999).

[25] *Woolwich*, n 13 above, 163–64.

of the commission's work would almost certainly be of the greatest assistance to the courts when considering the issue. Indeed the growing importance of the Scottish Law Commission's papers and reports in informing debate in our courts should be acknowledged.[26]

He led by example: at the end of the chapter on unjustified enrichment in the tenth edition of Gloag and Henderson's, *The Law of Scotland*,[27] which chapter Lord Rodger rewrote from scratch, the reader is referred to the Scottish Law Commission discussion paper of 1993.[28] When the Inner House came to address the mistake of law rule in Scots law, in the *Morgan Guaranty* case, the contribution made by Niall Whitty of the Scottish Law Commission in his writing was expressly acknowledged.

Although there was consensus on the need to remove the error of law rule, controversy developed on the issue of a particular consequential provision. Both Commissions initially proposed that payments made on the basis of a 'settled view of the law' should be exempted from recovery. In essence, the controversy surrounding this issue depended upon the characterisation of the court's action. Was the law being changed, or should the declaratory theory of judicial decision-making be fully respected, with the result that prior transactions, based on a view of the law seen as settled at the time but now mistaken, could be opened up?

On this important question, the two Commissions ultimately diverged. The Law Commission, in its report, stated:

> The Commission's provisional view was that it should not matter whether a change occurs through legislation or judicial decision: the payment should not be recoverable because in substance there has been no mistake.[29]

It adhered to this provisional view, recommending that:

> [A] restitutionary claim in respect of any payment, service or benefit that has been made, rendered or conferred under a mistake of law should not be permitted merely because it was done in accordance with a settled view of the law at the time, which was later departed from by a subsequent judicial decision.[30]

This recommendation underlay the secondary argument for the bank in the *Kleinwort Benson* case—that if the House abrogated the mistake of law rule, it should provide a defence in cases in which money had been paid in accordance with a settled view of the law (such as had occurred in this case). In disposing of this argument, Lord Goff concluded:

> The question then arises whether ... it would be appropriate for your Lordships' House so to develop the law on the lines of the Law Commission's proposed reform as a corollary to the newly developed right of recovery. I can see no good reason why your Lordships' House should take a step which, as I see it, is inconsistent with the declaratory theory of judicial decision as applied in our legal system, under which the law as declared by the judge is the

[26] A Rodger, 'The Bell of Law Reform' 1993 *Scots Law Times (News)* 339, 345.
[27] WM Gloag and RC Henderson, *Gloag and Henderson: The Law of Scotland*, 10th edn (WA Wilson and A Forte eds, Edinburgh, W Green, 1995).
[28] See n 19 above.
[29] LC 227, n 20 above, para 5.3.
[30] ibid para 5.13.

law applicable not only at the date of the decision but at the date of the events which are the subject of the case before him, and of the events of other cases *in pari materia* which may thereafter come before the courts.[31]

Lord Goff was able to base his rejection of the Law Commission's proposal for a 'settled law' exemption in part on a *volte face* which the Scottish Law Commission had performed.

In its 1993 discussion paper, the Scottish Law Commission had recommended legislating to create a change in the defence to an enrichment claim. In so recommending, the Commission was expressly following the course proposed by the Law Commission in its consultation paper. The Scottish Law Commission recognised that this position was at odds with the declaratory theory of judicial decision-making, but was not deterred on that ground, briskly rejecting its supposedly conclusive effect: 'We agree however, with the Law Commission's observation that the declaratory theory is "a mere fiction and should not be allowed to affect substantive rights"'.[32]

As already noted, the Law Commission adhered to its proposal for a legislative provision protecting payments made in accordance with 'a settled view of the law'. The Scottish Law Commission, however, changed its mind, making in its later discussion paper the provisional proposal 'that a statutory bar precluding the re-opening of settled payment transactions following a change in the settled view of the law effected by judicial decision should not be introduced'.[33] This enabled Lord Goff to observe:

> In Scotland, as I have already recorded, the Scottish Law Commission at first recommended its adoption [a 'settled understanding of the law' defence], but later resiled from that recommendation. That this whole topic is one of great difficulty can perhaps best be seen in the Scottish Law Commission's Discussion Paper No 99, in which the rival arguments for and against legislative reform are rehearsed in some detail, and the difficulties exposed. This division of opinion does not encourage statutory adoption of a provision in these or comparable terms, still less its recognition as part of the common law of this country.[34]

The Scottish Law Commission, with the benefit of publishing its report after the *Kleinwort Benson* case, was able to cite Lord Goff's approval of its change of position.[35] It is evident that the explanation for the change of view by the Commission concerned the force of comments made in response to its earlier proposal.[36]

It may be that the gold standard for the Commissions is a project which achieves, within a reasonable time, the milestones of research, consultation, proposals, legislation. Unjustified enrichment did not complete this process. But the scholarship

---

[31] *Kleinwort Benson*, n 15 above, 381.
[32] SLC DP 95, n 19 above, para 2.116.
[33] SLC DP 99, n 22 above, para 3.51.
[34] *Kleinwort Benson*, n 15 above, 384.
[35] SLC 169, n 24 above, para 2.14.
[36] ibid; see also SLC DP 99, n 22 above, para 3.14, where the views of Lords Coulsfield and Prosser are set out. Lord Coulsfield described the declaratory theory as 'a fundamental working assumption or basis for the legal system'. Lord Prosser doubted that the issue of whether the court has changed the law is, itself, a justiciable question.

brought to the topic on the part of both Commissions was undoubtedly of benefit to the courts in reshaping the law in this previously neglected area.

## VI TRUSTS

The topic of unjustified enrichment is a good illustration of how the Commission has been able to marry its Commissioners and legal staff to projects reflecting their individual interests and expertise (or, on occasions, the other way around). Another such illustration is provided by the more recent work of the Commission in supplying a conceptual basis for the protection of the personal property of a trustee from creditors of the trust.

The recent case of *Glasgow City Council v Springboig St John's School Managers*[37] concerned the council's administration of a pension scheme, to which employees of the defenders had belonged. After the closure of the school, its managers became liable to make payment into the pension fund, in respect of the fund's liabilities to former employees of the school. The only remaining substantive asset was the school itself. It was in the names of trustees, who held it for the religious and educational purposes of the Archdiocese of Glasgow. The council attempted to inhibit (attach) the property pending resolution of their case against the board. Given that a trust is not, in Scots law, a separate legal person, when a trustee is sued, what property is available to satisfy a judgment against him: everything he owns or something less than that?

In resolving this question, Lord Malcolm found assistance in a Scottish Law Commission discussion paper:[38]

My attention was drawn to the Scottish Law Commission's discussion paper on the *Nature and the Constitution of Trusts* (October 2006). The suggestion is that much of our law can be explained on the basis of a trustee acquiring a patrimony, which is separate from his personal patrimony, consisting of the trust fund and any obligations incurred in the proper administration of the trust. The paper states: 'If, as will usually be the case, there are two or more trustees, the trust patrimony is owned by them jointly.' It is noted that Professor Reid has expressed the view that 'a private creditor must claim from the private patrimony and a trust creditor from the trust patrimony'. At paragraph 2.22 the Commission observes that 'where obligations have been incurred in the trust patrimony, for example by the trustee in the course of the administration of the trust, the claims of the trust creditors have to be satisfied before the trust purposes can be fulfilled.' It is part and parcel of this that personal claims against a trustee can only be satisfied from his personal patrimony, that is from the assets which he owns as an individual ... In my view, the notion of a trustee's dual patrimony is helpful and can assist in an understanding of many of the implications and consequences of our law of trusts. It has been described by Professor Gretton as an 'organising concept' which can be employed to the extent that it is useful.[39]

---

[37] *Glasgow City Council v Springboig St John's School Managers* [2014] CSOH 76.
[38] Scottish Law Commission, SLC DP 133, *The Nature and Constitution of Trusts* (2006).
[39] *Glasgow City Council*, n 37 above, [12] and [16].

## VII PROPERTY

As recently as February 2015, research by the Scottish Law Commission featured in the Supreme Court. In an appeal concerning a dispute about the foreshore at Newhaven, issues arose about the rights enjoyed by the public to use the foreshore for recreation, and the relationship between the principles of law underlying such rights, and the parallel regime whereby a port authority holds and uses land for its statutory purposes. Lord Carnwath was interested in comparative law regarding public rights to the foreshore. Both in its account of the position under Scots law and in its narration of the position in other jurisdictions, the Scottish Law Commission's discussion paper on the foreshore and seabed,[40] proved a useful source of such material.[41]

## VIII PROCEDURE—A LONG GAME

In 1996, the Scottish Law Commission published a report on court actions involving multiple parties.[42] This was in response to a reference from the Lord Advocate:

(a)   to consider the desirability and feasibility of introducing in Scottish civil court proceedings arrangements to provide a more effective remedy in situations where a number of persons have the same or similar rights;
(b)   to consider how such arrangements might be funded; and
(c)   to make recommendations.[43]

The report was long and detailed. The project followed not only the usual method of consulting via a discussion paper, but also the establishment by the Scottish Law Commission of a working party. The rationale for that step was said to be that because implementation would be likely to be by subordinate legislation (rules of court or legal aid rules), the design of a process would be complemented by a separate study of court procedures and legal aid. Thus, a body comprising Commission personnel, advocates, solicitors and officials of the Scottish Office, the Courts Service and the Legal Aid Board was established. It reported in 1994. The 1996 report by the Commission recommended introduction of a multi-party procedure for situations where a number of persons have the same or similar rights. Elements of a suggested procedure were set out. In 2000, the recommendations were considered by the Court of Session Rules Council. It decided not to take the recommendations forward on the grounds that informal mechanisms for handling multi-party actions appeared to be working satisfactorily in Scotland and that the introduction of a formal procedure would give rise to 'serious and complex' questions.[44]

---

[40]   Scottish Law Commission, SLC DP 113, *The Law of the Foreshore and Seabed* (2001).
[41]   *Regina (Newhaven Port & Properties Ltd) v East Sussex County Council* [2015] UKSC 7, [2015] 2 WLR 601 [119]–[121].
[42]   Scottish Law Commission, SLC 154, *Multi-Party Actions* (1996).
[43]   ibid para 1.1.
[44]   Court of Session, *Report of the Scottish Civil Courts Review* (2009) vol 2, ch 13, para 12.

In 2009, the Scottish Civil Courts Review published its views on the civil justice system, and its proposals for reform. One of the issues addressed was the question of multi-party actions. The Commission's report on the matter was considered in detail, and the reasons for non-implementation by the Rules Council recorded. The Review Group agreed with the Commission, however, and adopted its recommendation that there should be a special multi-party procedure. Many of the individual aspects of the process devised by the Commission were also incorporated into the Review Group's proposals. Thereafter, the Scottish Government accepted in principle the recommendation that there should be a special multi-party procedure.[45]

This was going to be my example of recommendations being implemented entirely by secondary legislation, but I note that the Scottish Government now thinks that primary legislation will be required. In January 2015, the matter was included in a government consultation. So it may be that implementation will be achieved around 20 years after these proposals were made—a long game indeed.

## IX CONCLUSIONS

To revert to my instructions (ingrained habits are hard to break), this session involves a consideration of the value of the Law Commissions beyond mere primary legislative implementation. None of the examples I have discussed involves primary legislative implementation; all of them reflect value added by one or other of the Commissions. There are examples of recommendations as to practice and procedure in the courts, on one occasion in response to a request for help. There are landmark cases where the Commission's exposition of the common law in a particular area and options for its improvement have assisted judges engaged in law reform. More generally, there are instances of judges gladly having resort to written accounts by the Commission of existing law on a subject, even occasionally accounts of law from beyond British shores. Work which may seem to pass unremarked at the time may feature years later—perhaps in ways the team responsible would not have predicted.

Moreover, there will be countless other occasions where Commission publications, although unattributed, have shaped a submission in court.[46] Their legendary balance may militate against their acknowledgement by the advocate—they do rather tend to set out both sides of an argument.

As this miscellany of cases has shown, the influence of the Commissions can be identified across many different areas of law. With their blend of practitioner, academic and judicial input, the Commissions bring a perspective on the law and its reform not offered by any other institution. Whilst the primary measure of the success of a law reform body must be the extent to which it has generated reform of

---

[45] Scottish Government, *Response to the Report and Recommendations of the Scottish Civil Courts Review* (2010) para 166.

[46] For an illustration of the Law Commission's work being used in this way, see the example given in J Beatson, 'Legal Academics: Forgotten Players or Interlopers?' in A Burrows, D Johnston and R Zimmermann (eds), *Judge and Jurist, Essays in Memory of Lord Rodger of Earlsferry* (Oxford, Oxford University Press, 2013) 524, n 4.

the law, to measure the Commissions' impact solely by enumerating recommendations which have been enacted would yield an inadequate account of their influence. There have been reports which have concluded that no reform was necessary,[47] and reports which have contributed to the shaping of litigation practice.[48] Regularly throughout the last 50 years, the publications of the Commissions have been taken into account in court, their scholarship respected by both the Bar and the Bench. The fact that Commission publications are seen as providing a reliable account of the current law in an area is, unequivocally, a major strength. Such a reputation cannot do other than enhance the respect with which reform proposals made by the Commission are considered.

Finally, let me return to the heraldry with which I began. Conscious of the eminence of the audience, I decided that speculation about what was in the arms above the entrance was not good enough. I contacted the office of the Lord Lyon, and as a result am able to advise that what is shown is a combination of: (1) a Saltire, for Scotland; (2) owls, to signify learning; (3) quills, to denote the written word; and (4) a book with the sun emerging from clouds behind it, to denote enlightenment. It transpires that the symbols are even more appropriate than I suspected. Rather a pity, then, that the Scottish Law Commission can make no legitimate use of them—unless, that is, the law were to be reformed?

---

[47] Such as the *Report on Liability for Antenatal Injury*, n 7 above.
[48] Such as the recommendations on diligence and evidence, referred to above.

# Part 5

# Implementation by Statute

# 18

## *Introduction*

### DAME MARY ARDEN

It is not much good having a Law Commission that produces reports which are never implemented. Nor should a democratic society automatically enact such reports. The best solution is that advocated by Lord Mackay of Clashfern LC whose normal assumption on reports on matters within his responsibilities was that one would wish to give effect to it. Let other government Ministers take note!

In his chapter, Sir Grant Hammond shows that (with one exception) the majority of recommendations from Law Commissions around the world are advanced into legislation but there is a question of how long that process takes. Sir Grant describes techniques for enhancing implementation by legislation, but, on some occasions, a bold judicial development of the law will do the trick. Professor Andrew Burrows discusses the 'elusive boundary' between courts and the legislature but his broad message is that courts should be bold in making new law in line with Law Commission reports. The subject of assisted dying is one which the Supreme Court of the United Kingdom has recently held is a matter for Parliament.[1] By contrast, in South Africa, the South African Law Commission[2] wrote a relevant report,[3] and that was one of the factors taken into account in a recent decision in the High Court which decided that there was a right to physician-assisted dying under the South African Constitution.[4]

As Nicholas Paines QC, points out, a Law Commission report can be of great value in influencing judicial development of the law. The great American judge, Benjamin Cardozo, wrote that, if there was no prior case law on a point, he would consult 'the social mind'.[5] Where better to find such information than in a report of a Law Commission, on which the public and professions have been consulted?

Professor Hector MacQueen is realistic about reform through new decisions of the courts when he makes the point that courts may only be able to deal with parts

---

[1] *R (on the application of Nicklinson) v Ministry of Justice* [2014] UKSC 38, [2015] AC 657.

[2] The South African Law Commission was renamed the South African Law Reform Commission by the Judicial Matters Amendment Act 2002, s 4.

[3] South African Law Commission, Project 86, *Euthanasia and the Artificial Preservation of Life* (1998).

[4] *Stransham-Ford v Ministry of Justice and Correctional Services* (27401/15) [2015] ZAGPPHC 230 (4 May 2015) (North Gauteng High Court).

[5] B Cardozo, *The Paradoxes of Legal Science* (New York, Columbia University Press, 1928) 37.

of the law in any given case. His focus is on legislation and he tells an encouraging tale of the effectiveness of high quality work in the Scottish Law Commission.

Experience shows that there are a number of things which can slow up the process of implementation. They include pressure of business in Parliament. I share Sir Grant Hammond's frustration when the government department, for which a Law Commission report was carefully produced, decides that it is necessary for it to do a new consultation on the same proposals and then consider what emerges from its own consultation. That ought not to happen in a well-organised society. The Commission and the 'commissioning' department should liaise during the project to ensure that all the concerns of the department have been addressed. That would narrow delays to those caused by unforeseen events which happen after the report has been produced. Issues such as these must be practical concerns for the Law Commission from the very start of a project.

In summary, the problems discussed in this Part are of vital importance to every well-run Law Commission.

# 19

# The Legislative Implementation of Law Reform Proposals

## SIR GRANT HAMMOND*

### I INTRODUCTION

Law Commissions are applied research institutions. They examine a given body of law to form a view as to whether they should recommend to Parliament that the existing law be modified, or some new area of human endeavour legislated for. Such Commissions are in the business of legal change. There are two ways change can be brought about: directly, by legislation, or more indirectly, by influencing the general climate of informed legal opinion so that individuals, courts or other entities can change their views or practices. We should not underestimate the importance of this second role, in which the Commissions' endeavours are somewhat closer to a 'primary' research role and add to the general pool of human knowledge.

That said, the structure of the relevant statutes is clear. For instance, the New Zealand Law Commission Act 1985—which borrowed heavily from the legislation in Great Britain promoted by Lord Gardiner—provides that it is '[a]n Act to establish a Law Commission as a central advisory body for the review, reform, and *development* of the law of New Zealand'.[1] That is an affirmative statement, couched in instrumental terms.

The duties of the Law Commission of England and Wales are:[2]

— to consider any proposals for law reform given or directed to them;
— to prepare recommendations for programmes of law reform;
— to prepare draft Bills or other documents for such programmes;
— to prepare statute law revision or consolidation programmes;
— to provide legal advice to government departments concerning law reform; and
— to examine the legal systems of other nations to obtain any information that would facilitate programmes of law reform.

---

* Thanks go to Henry Hillind, the New Zealand Law Commission Law Clerk who provided valuable research assistance for this chapter.
[1] Law Commission Act 1985 (NZ), preamble, emphasis added. The UK legislation is the Law Commissions Act 1965.
[2] See generally R Chorley and G Dworkin, 'The Law Commissions Act, 1965' (1965) 28 *MLR* 675.

To nail down the lid on the coffin of practicality, section 5 of the New Zealand Act provides that the principal functions of the Commission are:

to take and keep under review in a systematic way the law of New Zealand;

to make recommendations for the reform and development of the law of New Zealand;

to advise on the review of any aspect of the law of New Zealand conducted by any government department or organisation... and on proposals made as a result of the review; and

to advise the Minister of Justice and the responsible Minister on ways in which the law of New Zealand can be made as understandable and accessible as is practicable.

In New Zealand there is required to be a Minister responsible for the Law Commission.[3] The Commission must submit to the responsible Minister every report prepared on any aspect of the law of New Zealand, and publish it.[4] The Minister is to lay a copy of that report before Parliament as soon as practical after the receipt of the report by him or her.[5] There is a like, if slightly less sharp, duty cast on the Great British Commissions.

Accordingly, one point of measurement for the work of such Commissions could be how many reports, and of what quality, have been laid before Parliament over a given period of time. However, a very real difficulty in all jurisdictions which utilise a Commission model is that it is only that capricious beast, Parliament, which can bring about direct change.

Those who evolved the idea of standing Commissions and the ways in which they should work were not entirely unaware of the difficulties which might be faced in implementation. So many things compete for a place in the Queen's Speech and an always congested parliamentary timetable, the material is often unappetisingly technical and has generally 'low political sex appeal'.[6] The large and always pressing preoccupations of unlawful immigrants, firefights threatening to break into full scale wars, and the ever increasing complexity of financial and economic affairs, take precedence in Parliament. They always will.

The early institutional law reformers thought there was a case for a Commission being able to introduce Bills directly into a House of Parliament. Indeed Sir Owen Woodhouse, always a shrewd legal tactician beneath a socially benign exterior, almost managed to smuggle such a proposal into the draft of the New Zealand legislation, but that was 'spotted' and turned back.[7]

So the Commissions, somewhat against the odds and not without a good deal of frustration, have, over the last few years had to set about trying to find ways, sometimes with help from progressive Ministers and senior members of the judiciary, of getting their legislative proposals into and through a crowded and increasingly complex parliamentary process.

---

[3] Law Commission Act 1985 (NZ), s 3A, meaning of 'responsible Minister'.

[4] Law Commission Act 1985 (NZ), s 16(1).

[5] Law Commission Act 1985 (NZ), s 16(2).

[6] G Drewry, 'The Legislative Implementation of Law Reform Proposals' (1986) 7 *Statute Law Review* 161, 163.

[7] See G Hammond, 'The Challenge of Implementation: Getting Law Reform Reports onto the Statute Book' (2013) 13 *Oxford University Commonwealth Law Journal* 239, 244. Sir Owen Woodhouse ONZ, KBE, DSC was the first Chairman of the New Zealand Law Commission.

In this essay I tackle two specific questions. First, the law reform literature, Commission annual reports, and observations by judges and academics alike are replete with discussion of 'the implementation problem' relating to law reform reports. But we should ask: empirically, is it correct that the Commissions have in fact fared so badly? That raises an interesting sub-question: given the Commissions are no more than advisory bodies, in the terminology of the new public management with which we now live, and will continue to be so for the foreseeable future, what is a 'benchmark' that Commissions should aspire to? My second question is, what means might be open to the Commissions to improve legislative uptake? And, do we need alterations to the machinery of Parliaments themselves?

## II TAKE-UP RATES

On the published information it is not possible to establish a 'scientific' implementation rate for all the established Law Commissions. But it is possible to get a reasonable picture as to the lie of the land, or an overall pattern.

Table 1 summarises the published statistics on websites or from annual reports of 12 Commissions, in the closest years they could be assembled. The first column shows the total number of reports advanced. The second column records the total number of those reports which recommended some legislative change. The third column indicates the number of those reports recommending legislative change that have been advanced into legislation, in whole or part. The fourth column is then expressed in percentage terms.

Table 1

| Commission | Total Number of Reports | Number of Reports Recommending Legislative Change | Number of Reports Recommending Legislative Change Substantially Advanced into Legislation | Percentage of Reports Advanced into Legislation |
|---|---|---|---|---|
| South African Law Reform Commission | 148 (2011 annual report) | 118 | 87 | 73.7% |
| Law Commission of England and Wales | 202 (May 2014) | 202 | 135 | 66.8% |
| Scottish Law Commission | 87 (October 2014) | 84 | 56 | 66.7% |
| Law Reform Commission of the Republic of Ireland | 111 (October 2014) | 99 | 76 | 76.7% |

*(continued)*

Table 1: *(Continued)*

| Commission | Total Number of Reports | Number of Reports Recommending Legislative Change | Number of Reports Recommending Legislative Change Substantially Advanced into Legislation | Percentage of Reports Advanced into Legislation |
|---|---|---|---|---|
| Australian Law Reform Commission | 83 (2014 annual report) | 83 | 73 | 88.0% |
| Law Reform Commission of Hong Kong | 64 (2014 annual report) | 63 | 41[8] | 65.1% |
| Malawi Law Commission | 23 (2011 annual report) | 23 | 14 | 60.9% |
| Ghana Law Reform Commission | 42 (1968 to 2000) | 42 | 29 | 69.0% |
| Law Commission of India | 167 (1992 to 2000) | 167 | 80[9] | 47.9% |
| **State Commissions** | | | | |
| Queensland Law Reform Commission | 69 (2013 annual report) | 67 | 48 | 71.6% |
| Manitoba Law Reform Commission | 128 (2014 annual report) | 122 | 79 | 64.8% |
| Alberta Law Reform Institute | 106 (March 2015) | 106 | 72 | 67.9% |
| **AVERAGE implementation across these Commissions (sample size: 12 Commissions)** | | | | 68.3% |

These figures are somewhat raw.[10] I have not attempted the difficult, if not impossible, task of accounting within those figures for the precise percentage of recommendations within a report which are taken up. In other words, if even one of say 20 recommendations was adopted, that counts as a whole 'success' for that report. I have not attempted to factor in the size or complexity of particular reports, or the time taken to complete them. It is therefore tempting to dismiss averages thrown up by the table as 'hopelessly crude'. They are certainly simplistic! But as so often

---

[8] Including 3 rejected, 2 no intention to implement, 17 under consideration.
[9] Including 17 rejected, 70 in different stages of consideration.
[10] *cf* chapter 15 (Shona Wilson Stark) for analysis of counting methods.

in matters of this kind, the outcome of the exercise is at least some confirmation of what one's common sense would likely suggest. That is, a very respectable number of recommendations are advanced into legislation. The average figure of nearly 70 per cent across those Commissions over many years is a substantial contribution to the development of the law in those various jurisdictions. The greater problems lie in the slow, oftentimes tortuous pace of change.[11]

### III THE FIELD PROBLEMS IN GREATER REFINEMENT

I am in a position to look more deeply into these sorts of statistics in my own jurisdiction, to endeavour to identify systemic problems. First, the percentage of Law Commission reports advanced into legislation on a rolling five-year average since 1991, in New Zealand, is as follows:

Table 2

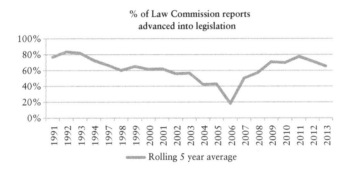

Second, the broad categories of work undertaken to date in New Zealand Reports have been as follows. These categories overlap at times.

Table 3

| Justice: Criminal | 28 | 26% |
|---|---|---|
| Justice: Civil | 16 | 15% |
| Business | 15 | 14% |
| Land and Property | 8 | 7% |
| Social and Family | 8 | 7% |
| Justice: Legislation | 7 | 6% |
| Information and privacy | 6 | 6% |
| Justice: Courts | 5 | 5% |

*(continued)*

---

[11] This appears to be a common problem. See A Burrows, 'Some Reflections on Law Reform in England and Canada' (2003) 39 *Canadian Business Law Journal* 320.

Table 3: *(Continued)*

| Government | 4 | 4% |
|---|---|---|
| Health/Mental Health | 4 | 4% |
| Treaty of Waitangi and Māori | 3 | 3% |
| Accident Compensation | 2 | 2% |
| International | 1 | 1% |
| Justice: Other | 1 | 1% |
| **Grand Total** | **108** | **100%** |

Third, the times taken to complete these reports were as follows:

Table 4: Time from commencement of project to the publication of report

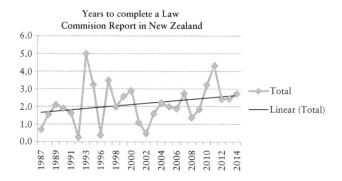

Fourth, since the adoption of mandatory Cabinet responses post-2004 by the Cabinet Manual provisions, the legislative response over 29 measures has risen to 79 per cent. This strongly suggests that the phenomenon of reports being simply 'left on the shelf' as opposed to distinctly rejected can be addressed by such measures. I will describe the way in which these measures work later in this essay.

More broadly, enactment clearly turns on a number of factors, not least the 'weight' of a given reference. Some matters go to the core of the legal infrastructure; others to only one or two amending sections to a measure. Examples of the first in New Zealand are the Companies Act 1993 and perhaps above all, the Evidence Act 2006. This was very much a Commission 'baby' as an evidence code in all but name. The extent of that commitment is shown by the fact that the statute contains a provision that it is to be reviewed every five years (presumably into infinity!) by the Commission and a report provided to the responsible Minister for tabling in Parliament.[12] Amendments to the Evidence Act based on the Commission's ongoing

---

[12] Evidence Act 2006, s 202.

work have been made from time to time. At the other end of the scale there is currently before the Justice Select Committee in the House of Representatives two short amendments to the Coroners Act 2006 (in itself largely Commission-derived) as to when reporting of the details of a suicide are permissible. To the persistent fury of the press, New Zealand has some restrictions in that respect.

These sorts of statistics suggest that on average it seems to have taken New Zealand two to two and a half years to produce a report from the date the project is commenced. There was a period from 2000 through to 2007 when it was then taking up to five years to get a Bill introduced. That has been improved since that time by a combination of the Cabinet procedures adopted and, it has to be said, the political drive for legislation. In particular, a number of references given to the Commission in that period were born out of urgent requests by senior Ministers, some as high as the Prime Minister. Instances of that kind included the request for cyber-bullying legislation and improvements to the coronial legislation.

To revert to the wider picture, an average around the jurisdictions surveyed of something near 70 per cent enactment can hardly be considered a failure. Given the nature of the beast it may even be regarded as pretty respectable, given the competing demands on the parliamentary process. The difficulties which have arisen have done so, with respect, primarily at the parliamentary implementation end rather than the Commission production end, and may suggest that it is the overhauling of parliamentary processes which is most pressing.

## IV IMPLEMENTATION TECHNIQUES

Given the concerns which continue to be raised about implementation of Law Commission reports, what techniques and mechanisms have been adopted in recent years to address this problem?

### A Securing Prompt Government Consideration and Endorsement

Parliaments are reluctant to give up time for consideration of law reform measures, let alone even a sliver of their 'jurisdiction'. But some Parliaments have agreed to publicly *report* their responses and prospective steps with respect to Law Commission reports.

For instance, when the Law Commissions Act 1965 was amended in 2009, the amendment Act provided a number of provisions which are aimed at increasing implementation of law reform reports. One of these places a duty on the Lord Chancellor to report to Parliament each year on the extent to which Law Commission of England and Wales proposals have been implemented by the government during the particular year. The fifth such report, covering the period 12 January 2014 to 11 January 2015, saw the then Lord Chancellor, the Rt Hon Chris Grayling MP, noting the implementation of law reform proposals into legislation, including the Consumer Protection (Amendment) Regulations 2014, the Insurance Act 2015 and a consolidation of the legislation concerning the Co-operative and Community Benefit

Societies.[13] Proposals that were still under consideration were also listed, including proposals relating to hate crimes, rights to light, property rights for cohabitants and termination of tenancies. The report further noted recommendations that were not to be implemented, such as the 'Administrative Redress: Public Bodies and the Citizen' proposals.[14]

New Zealand had accumulated a number of significant measures which had not been advanced. For instance, a revised Property Law Act 1952 sat on the shelf for far too long. The then President of the Commission, The Rt Hon Sir Geoffrey Palmer QC, as a former Prime Minister was able to speak directly with the then New Zealand Prime Minister, The Rt Hon Helen Clark. New provisions were adopted and inserted in the Cabinet Office Manual, which is required to be observed by all Ministries.[15]

Under the protocol set out in that Manual, once a Portfolio Minister has received a Law Commission report, a draft Cabinet Paper is required to be prepared as soon as reasonably practicable, which reflects the views of the Minister and all relevant agencies and incorporates staff recommendations where there is no consensus.[16] The Portfolio Minister decides on a case by case basis which agency will prepare the draft Cabinet Paper on the Minister's behalf. It is possible for the Law Commission to prepare the Cabinet Paper in consultation with all relevant agencies or it can jointly prepare the Cabinet Paper with another agency. The relevant Minister is required to submit the paper to a Cabinet Committee and seek Cabinet approval of the recommendations in the Law Commission report so far as the Minister considers it appropriate. If Cabinet accepts the recommendations, then a Bill must be prepared, if one was not submitted with the report. Cabinet then adds the Bill to the legislative programme with an appropriate priority.

Where Cabinet accepts the recommendations in the Law Commission report, there is no need for a formal government response to the report to be presented to the House of Representatives. If Cabinet rejects the Law Commission's recommendations, or some of them, the government is required to respond, by way of a paper presented to the House of Representatives, within 120 working days of the presentation of the Law Commission's report to the House. So the problem of reports simply being 'pigeon holed' is no longer possible in New Zealand. Either the government has to get on with introducing legislation, or if it rejects the Law Commission proposals in whole or in part, it has to say why, in face of the House.

That is the principle, and mainly, the practice. But regrettably, particularly the Ministry of Justice has, on occasion, reported back that it supports the recommendations in principle but 'more work' is required in some respect. Sometimes that is coupled with an expression that Ministry staff must report to the Minister not later than a stated date, but often that is some months hence. It would be wrong

[13] Ministry of Justice, *Report on the Implementation of Law Commission Proposals* (HC 1062, 2015).
[14] ibid 22.
[15] Cabinet Office Circular, 'Law Commission: Processes for Setting the Work Programme and Government Response to Reports' (24 April 2009) CO 09/1.
[16] Cabinet Office, *Cabinet Manual* (2008) para 7.18.

to suggest, at least in my experience, that this is a deliberate evasive tactic. The real problem is that the Ministry, which becomes responsible for the majority of the Commission's reports, is sometimes hard pressed for available staff, or does not have instant expertise, and similar reasons.

Nevertheless for government to have to acknowledge overtly that it has had the report and what has or is to become of it, in face of the House is, with respect, a distinct step forward for the Commission. The technique prevents reports being advertently or inadvertently swept under the carpet. Members of the Opposition take an interest in these sorts of reports and of course can use them to make political weather out of New Zealand being less than progressive in dealing with identified injustices.

## B Distinct Implementation Units within Justice Sector Ministries

Although I am not familiar with any jurisdiction which has set up a distinct implementation unit as such in the public sector for Commissions, there may be something to be said for such a device. The unit need not be a large one and could be under the aegis of the Attorney-General or a senior Minister. There is something to be said for it being separate from the Ministry of Justice or another justice sector agency because of the tensions which can arise as to whether a particular measure should go forward or not at that particular time. This would enlarge the reporting to Parliament function. The unit would have the role of stirring things along, where appropriate. Final responsibility for priority must of course rest with the administration of the day, but having reports languish (whatever is ultimately to happen to them) for undue time is highly inefficient.

## C Parallel Chambers

In some jurisdictions the notion of a parallel chamber with suitable interface provisions to the main Chamber of Parliament has proved fruitful. The central concept is that a new 'lower Chamber' should be established in Parliament or a legislature. When introduced, Bills are referred to it.[17] This would be an 'all member' Chamber. That is, any member of Parliament could attend at any time and debate the matter before it. It would not be restricted just to considering the law reform reports introduced before it. It could also consider highly technical and non-controversial Bills or amendment Bills from any Ministry. If there proved to be support for the measure it can then advance through an expedited process in Parliament for enactment.

There are of course advantages and disadvantages to a mechanism of this kind. The principal problem is identifying what kind of legislation should go through such a process. But there are very real advantages too. As has been widely remarked around the Commonwealth there is today much public criticism and diminishment

---

[17] *cf* chapter 22 (Hector MacQueen), discussing a 'second' chamber.

of the stature of Parliaments. Their 'doings' are not infrequently somewhat rambunctious and self-serving, and the advancement of the rule of law, and its content by which citizens are expected to live, is harmed. There are many able and somewhat disaffected backbenchers who could be drawn on more directly and usefully into the advancement of truly informed parliamentary business. In short the prestige of the critical democratic institution of Parliaments can also be advanced by a new 'lower' or otherwise ancillary chamber.

To take only one example, there is a Federation Chamber in the Australian Parliament. Once called the Main Committee, it is really a second Debating Chamber. It considers relatively uncontroversial matters in political terms. These can be referred by the entire House to the Federation Chamber where substantive debate can take place. The Chamber cannot initiate or make a final decision on any parliamentary business, although it can perform all the tasks in between. The Chamber was created in 1994 to relieve some of the burdens on the entire House. It is a less formal body. The quorum can be as low as three members: the Speaker of the House, one government member, and one non-government member. Decisions must be unanimous. Any divided question is required to be referred back to the House at large. The creation of this Chamber is through the House's own Standing Orders, so it is a subordinate body of the House. It can only be in session while the House itself is in session. It is housed in one of the House's Committee Rooms which has been customised and laid out to somewhat resemble the Chamber of the House.

The existence of this body was one of the factors noted during the creation of Westminster Hall in the United Kingdom Parliament.[18] The Modernisation Committee which promoted the creation of that Chamber was keen to avoid simply providing an outlet for more government business, and Parliament as such should remain clearly preeminent. It was against that background that in 2008 the House of Lords trialled its new procedure to fast track 'uncontroversial' Law Commission and Scottish Law Commission Bills through the House, and the changes became permanent in 2010.[19]

In essence, under the new procedure a Law Commission Bill is introduced to the House of Lords and passes through the first reading in the normal way. The House then tables a Bill to a Second Reading Committee with at least three sitting days' notice. The Second Reading Committee takes place in the Moses Room and functions like a Grand Committee, in that all decisions must be unanimous. There is unlimited membership and no time limit on debates or speakers.

The formal motion for Second Reading takes place in the House and the House could vote it down just as it could with any other measure. The Bill is then committed to a Special Public Bill Committee. That Committee can take written and oral evidence before considering the Bill. It has a membership of nine to ten, including the relevant Minister and spokespersons from Opposition parties. Members of the House who are not on the Special Public Bill Committee may attend public meetings

---

[18]  See also chapter 9 (Sir Terence Etherton).
[19]  House of Lords Procedure Committee, *Law Commission Bills* (2010–11, HL 30).

and suggest amendments, but cannot vote. The process for reporting and Third Reading is unchanged, as is the process in the House of Commons.

The House of Lords Procedure Committee has indicated that there will be adequate consultation on whether the streamlined approach is appropriate for each particular Bill. If what seemed an uncontroversial Bill should later spark controversy, its passage can be stopped. The Government Business Managers will decide whether the normal procedures will apply to that Bill.

This is a welcome mechanism which can happily be adopted with respect to reports that do not address significant issues of social policy. It could readily be adopted in other jurisdictions.

## D Revised Parliamentary Committee Structures

Scotland has recently taken a distinct and welcome step forward in the advancement of law reform reports.[20] There is now a committee in the Scottish Parliament specifically focused on law reform. It is called the Delegated Powers and Law Reform Committee. Many Scottish Law Commission Bills will now come under the Committee's remit, and the Committee will take the lead in scrutinising such Bills. These are very important changes. The Scottish Parliament, with respect, rightly recognised the nature of the problem of slow implementation. In May 2013 it decided to make changes to its Standing Orders to provide for this Committee and its law reform remit. More specifically, the changes distinctly recognise 'Commission Bills'.

A Scottish Law Commission Bill is one within the legislative competence of the Scottish Parliament:

— where there is a wide degree of consensus amongst key stakeholders about the need for reform and the approach recommended;
— which does not relate directly to criminal law reform;
— which does not have significant financial implications;
— which does not have significant European Convention on Human Rights (ECHR) implications; and
— where the Scottish Government is not planning wider work in that particular subject area.

The general sense of the Scottish proposal reflected Parliament's wish to find a way forward for some Commission Bills; particularly updating the law to keep in step with changes in society to develop the common law, rather than Bills which were contentious or had a political profile. A respectable number of Commission Bills are likely to qualify for the process, which is subject to the proviso that on consultation, consultees must generally agree that reform is needed and on the proposed approach to reform.[21]

---

[20] See particularly chapter 37 (Malcolm McMillan).
[21] See Scottish Parliament Standards, Procedures and Public Appointments Committee, *Implementing Scottish Law Commission Reports* (SP 307, 18 April 2013).

It is useful to note the first Bill to use this procedure as an example. This was the Legal Writings (Counterparts and Delivery) (Scotland) Bill 2014 which was introduced into the Scottish Parliament on 14 May 2014. It was referred to the Delegated Powers and Law Reform Committee. That Committee approved the principles of the Bill in its Stage One report which was published on 14 November 2014.[22] The Bill proposed two significant improvements to Scots law in practice, relating to the execution of documents. One encompassed, amongst other things, delivery of legal documents by electronic means. The Scottish Commission had carried out extensive consultation (as is its usual practice) which had shown there was widespread support for the Bill, particularly amongst solicitors. After a seminar on execution in counterpart at the University of Edinburgh Centre for Private and Commercial Law, some modifications were made. The matter related to civil law, not criminal law reform; it had no significant social implications, and it did not have European Convention on Human Rights implications. Imagine if this Bill had needed to march to a funereal beat under the 'old system'![23]

## V THE COMPLEXITIES OF BIGGER REFERENCES

Most of the references given to Commissions are not what might be termed 'mega projects'. What is such a project may be a matter for debate. Perhaps we might agree that a new criminal code, or an evidence code, would fall under that rubric. Occasionally Commissions have been given such an enterprise. Generally they struggle with them. These are longer term projects extending over several years. There are then the problems of changing Commissioners and personnel, and the ground moving beneath the Commission's feet in a fast moving world. Such projects have their own constraints and technical problems of interface with administrations, which may change. Apart from anything else, sheer stamina is required.

I am here referring to what might be termed 'legal infrastructure' projects, with a respectably heavy legal content. Quite when Commissions should have their 'remits broadened to include big projects with social implications' as Sir Geoffrey Palmer has recently suggested[24] is beyond my task in this paper. Whatever one's views on role, tasks in this area give rise to even more difficulties of implementation. Assuming the administration of the day can be persuaded, or willingly accepts the work output, getting it into a determined legislative programme is, in these crowded times, even

---

[22] Scottish Parliament Delegated Powers and Law Reform Committee, *Report on the Legal Writings (Counterparts and Delivery) (Scotland) Bill at Stage 1* (SP 612, 14 November 2014).

[23] See M McMillan, 'Law Reform: A New Era?' (2015) 60(1) *Journal of the Law Society of Scotland* 22.

[24] G Palmer, 'The Law Reform Enterprise: Evaluating the Past and Charting the Future' (2015) 131 *LQR* 402, 423. On the whole, I am with Professor Burrows (A Burrows, 'Some Reflections on Law Reform in England and Canada' (2003) 39 *Canadian Business Law Journal* 320); they should be stable, highly regarded bodies, ideally suited to lawyers' law reform.

more of a challenge. Here more of a 'task force' approach is helpful. There must be a lot of work done to persuade the administration of the day that this is truly an infrastructure type measure; its importance of a central kind must be clearly established and it is with legislation of this kind that the Select Committee process has so much to contribute and commend it.

Can it be done? The latest example in New Zealand is the Judicature Modernisation Bill. New Zealand has a courts structure distinctly like that in England: District Court; High Court; Court of Appeal; and Supreme Court. The somewhat challenging enterprise was to devise one court statute with the various bumps and problems that had come about over the years involving these courts smoothed out. Holding a unified model together proved no easy task. In the end the administration agreed to a unitary Senior Courts Act and a new District Courts Act. The legislation progressed through the Justice and Electoral Select Committee to a successful Second Reading. There was wide recognition and support for the measures by all parties. At the moment it is awaiting a Third Reading, a little way down the Order Paper, because some really pressing matters have had to sail pass it, but it will advance.

## VI LOBBYING

I have elsewhere addressed the long standing issue of how far Law Commissions should lobby or promote their proposals.[25] I expressed the view that the essential difficulty in such an approach:

> is surely that the law reform agency is independent of the political process. Once it starts to meddle in it, there is a real danger of becoming politicised. A law reform agency occupies a somewhat delicate position. The more a law reform agency is seen as a threat, or to suggest pressure to take a matter outside the Executive Government, the more it will have difficulties with that body.[26]

Another perspective valuing independence above implementation can be seen in chapter 16 (William Binchy) in this volume. Sir Peter North also grappled with this problem. Whilst Commissions should be independent advisory bodies, he appears to have come gradually to the view that they should do what they can to promote their own causes in Parliament and elsewhere.[27]

Whatever one's views are on this point, there is surely great force in the proposition that getting greater engagement between Commissions and legislatures is terribly important at the *early* stages of the legislative process. Inevitably, such an approach will occasionally put a Commission more into the political arena. But does that necessarily even impact on, let alone endanger, independence?

---

[25] G Hammond 'The Challenge of Implementation: Getting Law Reform Reports onto the Statute Book' (2013) 13 *Oxford University Commonwealth Law Journal* 239, 251.

[26] ibid 252.

[27] P North, 'Law Reform: Processes and Problems' (1985) 101 *LQR* 338.

## VII CONCLUSION

The statutory Commissions have travelled some distance from their beginnings half a century ago. They have become part of the constitutional landscape. If they did not exist, they would have to be 'reinvented' in some form.[28] Inevitably, as agents of legal change, they have to work closely with the mechanics of Parliament. New ideas are evolving on that issue, and are having a welcome impact.

---

[28] See the discussion in chapter 11 (Yves Le Bouthillier) for a stark example from Canada, *cf* the current position in Northern Ireland, as chapter 5 (Neil Faris) shows.

# 20

# *Post-legislative Scrutiny, Legislative Drafting and the 'Elusive Boundary'*

ANDREW BURROWS

There are three issues that I would like to address in this short chapter: first, post-legislative scrutiny of Law Commission-inspired legislation; secondly, legislative drafting and what has been happening to the Office of Parliamentary Counsel; and thirdly, identifying when implementation of law reform is better carried out by the judges than by legislation and vice versa.

## I POST-LEGISLATIVE SCRUTINY

The first issue I would like to discuss, post-legislative scrutiny, relates to a very interesting point made by Sir Grant Hammond in his chapter in this book. He is there talking about the New Zealand Evidence Act 2006 which he describes as an evidence code in all but name. He writes:

> The extent of [the Law Commission's] commitment is shown by the fact that the statute contains a provision that it is to be reviewed every five years (presumably into infinity!) by the Commission and a report provided to the responsible Minister for tabling in Parliament. Amendments to the Evidence Act based on the Commission's ongoing work have been made from time to time.[1]

This is especially interesting because, at least in this jurisdiction, there has been very little, if any, post-legislative scrutiny of Law Commission-inspired legislation. It is surely true—and certainly we were told this time and time again by senior civil servants during my time at the Law Commission—that the Law Commission stands or falls on the quality of its work and hence, one would have thought, in large measure on the quality of the legislation brought in to implement its proposals. Yet

---

[1] See chapter 19 (Sir Grant Hammond). I understand from Sir Grant that this is not the only example of required 'follow-ups' by the New Zealand Law Commission. Other examples are the legislation on privacy and search and surveillance; and the same will apply with the Judicial Modernisation Bill presently going through the New Zealand Parliament.

as far as I am aware, no-one in this jurisdiction over the 50 years of the Law Commission's existence has ever tested, or even attempted to test, the quality of Law Commission work by comparing the success or failure of Law Commission legislation with what we might call 'standard' legislation.

In his superb Scarman Lecture earlier this year, 'The Law Reform Enterprise: Evaluating the Past and Charting the Future',[2] Sir Geoffrey Palmer asserted that Law Commission Bills were superior to other Bills:

> I assert that they are superior to those usually adopted by the executive government for the legislative projects it promotes ... Systematic methods of problem definition, research and public consultation on the basis of carefully researched issues papers are vital. The law commissions produce legislation that is better thought through than that produced by governments, it is more likely to work and it has been rigorously tested before enactment.[3]

He went on to say:

> The take-away message is that law commissions have forged superior methods of designing law compared with those employed by executive governments and parliaments. A robust set of transparent processes is bound to produce a better outcome that has been better tested than plans hatched by ministers and officials working behind closed doors. Furthermore, when the product comes to be considered by Parliament, there is a great deal more relevant information available to MPs and the public than is usually available on government bills.[4]

It may well be, and I very much suspect and hope that it is, that Sir Geoffrey is correct. But he is relying simply on assertion and on what he thinks is likely to be the case and not on evidence.

There was a Law Commission report in 2006 on post-legislative scrutiny generally.[5] That revealed that there was very wide support for enhancing post-legislative scrutiny. While the government rejected the Law Commission's recommendation of a new Joint Committee for Post-Legislative Scrutiny, it did accept that departments should generally produce a memorandum, within three to five years of Royal Assent, on the post-legislative review of an Act which the relevant select committee could then take further in a full review.[6] Unfortunately, on the latest figures that I can find (up until January 2013),[7] while this initiative has led to 58 such memoranda, only three of those have subsequently been the subject of reports by select committees.[8] The position appears to remain, therefore, one of non-systematic and ad hoc post-legislative scrutiny.

However, my point is the narrower one that, after 50 years, there should by now have been a more focused post-legislative study of Law Commission Acts. Then one

---

[2] G Palmer, 'The Law Reform Enterprise: Evaluating the Past and Charting the Future' (2015) 131 *LQR* 402.

[3] ibid 415.

[4] ibid 416.

[5] Law Commission, LC 302, *Post-Legislative Scrutiny* (2006). This followed LC CP 178 (2005).

[6] Office of the Leader of the House of Commons, *Post-Legislative Scrutiny—The Government's Approach* (Cm 7320, 2008).

[7] House of Commons Library, *Post-Legislative Scrutiny* (SN/PC/05232, 2013).

[8] There have also been some post-legislative reviews by committees not prompted by post-legislative memoranda (eg the Gambling Act 2005).

really can speak with confidence about the merits of the Law Commission's work and process. Without such a study it seems to me that much of what we have been discussing at this conference rests on hunch and assertion and not good evidence. Why has this not been done?

One answer may be thought to be that it is very difficult to formulate reliable criteria to test how successful any Act of Parliament is. Certainly I would not under-estimate those difficulties. However, I am unconvinced that they are overwhelming.[9] If one were to undertake this task, factors that will surely be relevant include the numbers of cases coming to court based on uncertainties in the Act, the extent to which those directly affected consider that the Act has dealt satisfactorily with the underlying mischief, the extent to which those affected by the Act or lawyers advising on it can easily understand it, whether there have been any unfortunate unintended consequences, and the extent to which amending legislation has proved necessary. Indeed if we cannot devise criteria for assessing the success of an Act it seems to me that we are incapable of forming an evidence-based view as to whether any law, whether judge-made or legislative, is good or bad.

Another answer may be that, even if the criteria can be devised, the results are certain to be inconclusive so that the whole exercise is destined to prove nothing. That harbinger of doom approach goes too far. I think it will prove possible, even if very difficult, to distinguish good and bad legislation and surely it is an exercise worth trying.

It may well be that, not least given the need for the Law Commission to prioritise its limited finances, a study of this kind would best be carried out by an academic or academic team rather than by the Law Commission itself. Indeed, it may be thought that a report by an outside body would be preferable in ensuring objectivity. After all, the Law Commission may feel somewhat hampered in potentially praising or criticising its own work. Alternatively it may be that, because some of the issues may require help from those inside the Law Commission, an academic or academic team working with, or in consultation with, the Law Commission would provide the best way forward. The input of MPs and officials who have been involved in parliamen-tary post-legislative scrutiny generally would also seem to be invaluable.

It was in the light of this background that I found so interesting Sir Grant Hammond's observation that the New Zealand Law Commission is required to go back every five years to look at its Evidence Act 2006; and that amendments have already been made to it. In other words, post-legislative scrutiny of that Act is built into the Act. Such a quinquennial review can be expected to produce considerable useful information about the merits or defects of that Act. Closer to my own exper-tise, I am also conscious that the New Zealand Law Commission did carry out in 1993 a very interesting review of various statutes on contract law that had been largely enacted as a result of the recommendations of a very similar law reform body to the Law Commission, namely the Contracts and Commercial Law Reform Committee.[10]

---

[9] Indeed some criteria for judging the success of an Act have been formulated in the context of advising departments on the content of a post-legislative memorandum that departments may be required to produce.

[10] New Zealand Law Commission, NZLC 25, *Contract Statutes Review* (1993).

There are also likely to be useful consequential spin-offs from this type of study. So another question about legislation that I have long pondered over is this: are certain types of clause or drafting more or less effective than others? Most obviously, are clauses giving discretion to the courts better or worse than those which lay down clear rules or principles? To give a well-known concrete example, within the Limitation Act 1980, sections 2 and 5 present clear rules for claims in tort and contract. Section 2 provides that:

> An action founded on tort shall not be brought after the expiration of six years from the date on which the cause of action accrued.

For contract, section 5 provides that:

> An action founded on simple contract shall not be brought after the expiration of six years from the date on which the cause of action accrued.

Section 11 provides a special regime for personal injury (generally a three-year limitation period), but subject to a discretion under section 33:

> (1)   If it appears to the court that it would be equitable to allow an action to proceed having regard to the degree to which—
>    (a)   the provisions of section 11 or 11A or 12 of this Act prejudice the plaintiff or any person whom he represents; and
>    (b)   any decision of the court under this subsection would prejudice the defendant or any person whom he represents;
>    the court may direct that those provisions shall not apply to the action, or shall not apply to any specified cause of action to which the action relates.[11]

But is the discretionary approach under section 33 better than the clear rules of sections 2 and 5? Post-legislative scrutiny of Law Commission Acts can be expected to help to answer that type of question.

## II LEGISLATIVE DRAFTING

That leads me conveniently on to my second issue, legislative drafting. One of the greatest pleasures of my life as a Law Commissioner was working with Parliamentary Counsel. I am sure all former Law Commissioners would agree that it is imperative that legislation is skilfully drafted. Again to quote Sir Geoffrey Palmer's Scarman Lecture: 'The most critical legal skill without which nothing else is possible is the drafting of a bill.'[12] He goes on to argue that working out policy at a Law Commission is a reflexive process that depends on the wording of a Bill. Almost always one has to have the draft Bill in order to test the policy. Put another way, when dealing with law reform the devil is often in the detail: 'No policy proposal can be properly understood and tested unless there is a bill drafted by parliamentary

---

[11]   Under s 33(3), the court shall have regard to all the circumstances and six, for particular attention, are specified.

[12]   Palmer, n 2 above, 413.

counsel. Embedding parliamentary counsel in the Commission in London was a stroke of genius.'[13]

In the light of the importance of Parliamentary Counsel to all Law Commission legislation, as well as to the internal work of a Law Commission, I regard us as duty bound to consider what has happened to the Office of Parliamentary Counsel in this jurisdiction. As I understand it, the recent story has not been an entirely happy one.

In particular, over the last few years, in a supposed cost-cutting exercise, many of the top and most experienced Parliamentary Counsel have been encouraged to leave the Office. So since approximately 2011, it would appear that the number of senior Parliamentary Counsel has been halved from about 16 to eight. Even in an age of austerity, some may think it obvious that this is not a sensible way to proceed and will inevitably lead to inferior quality legislation. At the very least, one might have thought that there would have been some open debate about this. Yet this potential attack on the quality of our laws appears to have happened under the radar. For example, I have seen nothing about it in the legal press.

## III THE 'ELUSIVE BOUNDARY'

Finally, I turn to my third issue: when is it that implementation of law reform is better carried out by the judges than by legislation and vice versa? In shorthand terms, this is the question of the 'elusive boundary'. In itself, this is plainly a more wide-ranging question than the more specific issue, which we often had to think about as Law Commissioners especially in recommending new projects, which is whether the Law Commission should embark on a legislative project or should leave reform to the judges (or, albeit rare, should take a middle course of making recommendations for judicial law reform as in our project on levels of damages for non-pecuniary loss in personal injury cases).[14] But whether one is a Supreme Court judge or a Law Commissioner the underlying issue is similar subject to three major differences. The first is that a judge is faced immediately with having to decide in a case whether to develop the law whereas the Law Commission may take on a project precisely because it is unknown when, if ever, the appellate courts will have the opportunity to develop the law. Secondly, a judge can of course take the view that it is better to leave matters to the Law Commission and Parliament and that precise argument has indeed sometimes been used.[15] Thirdly, as the judges are themselves effecting the

---

[13] ibid 413–14.

[14] Law Commission, LC 257, *Damages for Personal Injury: Non-Pecuniary Loss* (1999) which was partly implemented by the Court of Appeal's decision in *Heil v Rankin* [2001] QB 272 (CA). I discussed this in 'Alternatives to Legislation: Restatements and Judicial Law Reform' in L Gullifer and S Vogenauer (eds), *English and European Perspectives on Contract and Commercial Law: Essays in Honour of Hugh Beale* (Oxford, Hart Publishing, 2014) 37, 45–47.

[15] See, eg, *Kleinwort Benson v Lincoln City Council* [1999] 2 AC 349 (HL) (restitution for mistake of law) 364 and 398 (Lords Browne-Wilkinson and Lloyd of Berwick dissenting); *Radmacher v Granatino* [2010] UKSC 42, [2011] 1 AC 534 (weight to be given to pre-nuptial agreements in deciding ancillary relief) [133]–[137] (Lady Hale dissenting); *Jones v Kaney* [2011] UKSC 13, [2011] 2 AC 398 (expert witness immunity in the tort of negligence) [173] and [190] (Lord Hope DPSC and Lady Hale dissenting).

reform, there is more of an issue about the process being non-democratic: in contrast the Law Commission is merely making a recommendation which the government and Parliament can choose to accept or reject.

In thinking about this question, we are able to turn for help to probably the two greatest English judges of the last 25 years, Lord Goff and Lord Bingham.

In *Woolwich Equitable Building Society v Inland Revenue Commissioners*,[16] Lord Goff was faced with the argument that it would be preferable to rely on legislation rather than to develop the common law so as to grant restitution of money paid to a public authority acting ultra vires. The minority Lordships thought that one should wait for legislation not least because the Law Commission was already working on the topic. Lord Goff giving the leading speech for the majority disagreed and turned the latter argument on its head by saying that it strengthened the case for judicial law reform in this area that the Law Commission was already looking at the area. In a classic statement he said the following:

> [It is argued that] for your Lordships' House to recognise such a principle would overstep the boundary which we traditionally set for ourselves, separating the legitimate development of the law by the judges from legislation. It was strongly urged by [counsel for the Revenue] in his powerful argument ... that we would indeed be trespassing beyond that boundary if we were to accept the argument of Woolwich. I feel bound however to say that, although I am well aware of the existence of the boundary, I am never quite sure where to find it. Its position seems to vary from case to case. Indeed, if it were to be as firmly and clearly drawn as some of our mentors would wish, I cannot help feeling that a number of leading cases in your Lordships' House would never have been decided the way they were. For example, the minority view would have prevailed in *Donoghue v Stevenson*;[17] our modern law of judicial review would have never developed from its old, ineffectual, origins; and *Mareva* injunctions would never have seen the light of day.[18]

And later he went on to point out that the opportunity for the judges to develop a particular area of the law rarely arises and should be seized where it does arise; and that in some areas, where central government has a vested interest in maintaining the present law, there is no practical prospect of legislation:

> [T]his opportunity will never come again. If we do not take it now, it will be gone forever. [Moreover,] I fear that, however compelling the principle of justice may be, it would never be sufficient to persuade a government to propose its legislative recognition by Parliament; caution, otherwise known as the Treasury, would never allow this to happen.[19]

The reason why, perhaps counter-intuitively, Lord Goff thought that the fact that the Law Commission was working on the area strengthened the case for judicial law reform was that, if the judicial law reform was thought to be going too far, and that, for example, defences should be modified or adapted to curb claimants' rights against the executive, that could be quickly recommended by the Law Commission in its then ongoing project.

[16] *Woolwich Equitable Building Society v Inland Revenue Commissioners* [1993] AC 70 (HL). See chapter 17 (Laura Dunlop).
[17] *Donoghue v Stevenson* [1932] AC 562 (HL).
[18] *Woolwich*, n 16 above, 173.
[19] ibid 176.

Lord Bingham extra-judicially analysed this question in his inimitable succinct and penetrating style in his essay 'The Judge as Lawmaker: An English Perspective'.[20] Even accepting, as Lord Bingham thought most judges now do, that appellate judges can and indeed should make law by developing the common law, he suggested that caution has to be exercised. There are, he suggested, 'a range of different road signs [which] may in different situations be appropriate, ranging from "No entry" and "Stop" to "Give way" and "Slow"'.[21]

He gave five examples of situations where the judges must move ahead carefully if at all:

(1)   Where reasonable and right-minded citizens have legitimately ordered their affairs on the basis of a certain understanding of the law ...

(2)   Where, although a rule of law is seen to be defective, its amendment calls for a detailed legislative code, with qualifications, exceptions and safeguards which cannot feasibly be introduced by judicial decisions ...

(3)   Where the question involves an issue of current social policy [eg a controversial issue within family law] on which there is no consensus within the community ...

(4)   Where an issue is the subject of current legislative activity ...

(5)   Where the issue arises in a field far removed from ordinary judicial experience [ie one is a long way from 'lawyers' law reform'].[22]

He concluded by saying that even where a judge recognises that a change in the law is called for, it is better to proceed incrementally.[23] Hence judicial law reform should be:

> by small steps, not by giant bounds. Many Judges will seek to adopt the approach of Bacon, in his declaration that 'The work which I propound tendeth to pruning and grafting the law, and not to ploughing up and planting it again'.[24]

Another approach to drawing the 'elusive boundary' is to think of the advantages and disadvantages of legislative as against judicial law reform. So the advantages of legislative law reform include that:

(1)   one can deal with a wide area in precisely the way one wishes;

(2)   the change can be, and almost always is, non-retrospective;

(3)   the reform can be fully informed by differing points of view, research and consultation; and

(4)   difficult decisions are ultimately legitimised because the process can be seen to reflect the democratic will.

---

[20] T Bingham, 'The Judge as Lawmaker: An English Perspective' in T Bingham, *The Business of Judging: Selected Essays and Speeches* (Oxford, OUP, 2000) 25–34. For a further penetrating analysis, building from Lord Bingham's propositions, see J Dyson, 'Where the Common Law Fears to Tread' (2013) 34 *Statute Law Review* 1: he regarded Lord Bingham's propositions (1), (3) and (4) as relatively uncontroversial and therefore concentrated on propositions (2) and (5). See also, eg, M Kirby, *Judicial Activism* (Hamlyn Lectures 2003) (London, Sweet & Maxwell, 2004); R Walker, 'Developing the Common Law: How Far is Too Far?' (2013–14) 37 *Melbourne University Law Review* 232, esp 250–53.

[21] Bingham, n 20 above, 31.

[22] ibid 31–32.

[23] One might say that Lord Bingham's approach reflects a distinction between the (acceptable) application of principle and the (dangerous) creation of policy. But of course the distinction between principle and policy is itself a controversial one.

[24] Bingham, n 20 above, 32.

The disadvantages of legislative law reform as against judicial law reform include that:

(1)   it is difficult to find time in the legislative programme for 'non-sexy' lawyers' law reform;
(2)   there is a danger of legislation freezing the law so that 'mistakes' cannot be corrected so easily or, perhaps expressed more accurately, the law cannot be so easily adapted to changing circumstances and values;
(3)   the very process of a Bill going through Parliament can undermine and complicate its drafting and structure thereby producing law that is irrational and incoherent; and
(4)   legislation can produce a clash between the common law and the statutory inroad which may produce costly and problematic boundary issues.

If one concludes that, in general, it is a finely balanced argument as to whether to proceed by judicial law reform or legislation, there are two pragmatic reasons why at least Supreme Court Justices (and parallel arguments can apply to the Law Commission taking on a project) should almost always (outside the context of criminal and family law or other areas requiring a wide-ranging policy choice)[25] reject the argument of waiting for legislation in a situation where they have an opportunity to develop the law in a desired direction.[26]

First, one can never predict what the legislature will do. Many of those at this conference know this only too well. To refuse to develop the law judicially on the ground that the legislature can deal with the issue is to forgo an opportunity to improve the law on the basis of the lottery that is parliamentary law reform. In any particular case, to reject judicial law reform in favour of legislation, may be thought to be an irresponsible gambling away of an opportunity that may never arise again.

Secondly, if what the courts do by way of judicial law reform is regarded as undesirable by the legislature, it is always open to the legislature to reverse that reform by legislation.

---

[25] For a good recent example of the Supreme Court debating this issue in the context of a challenge under the Human Rights Act 1998 to the criminal law on assisted suicide, see *R (Nicklinson) v Ministry of Justice* [2014] UKSC 38, [2015] AC 657. By a 5:4 majority it was held that it was institutionally legitimate for the courts to make a declaration that the Suicide Act 1961, s 2 was incompatible with Article 8 of the ECHR. But of the majority, only Lady Hale and Lord Kerr would have gone ahead and immediately made such a declaration: Lords Neuberger, Mance and Wilson preferred to defer making such a declaration until the legislature had had a chance to consider the matter. The minority (Lords Sumption, Clarke, Reed and Hughes) reasoned that it was institutionally inappropriate for the courts to make such a declaration because, inter alia, it was a matter raising a fundamental moral and social dilemma on which Parliament had already made a choice. In the Divisional Court, [2012] EWHC 2381 (Admin), [2012] 3 FCR 233, Toulson LJ said that, for reasons of 'competence, constitutionality and control of the consequences', it was a matter for Parliament not the courts whether to amend the law to legalise voluntary euthanasia: [75].

[26] For a similar approach, see A Burrows, 'The Relationship between Common Law and Statute in the Law of Obligations' (2012) 128 *LQR* 232, 247–48. It is important to stress that I was there arguing that, in the context of the law of obligations and provided the judges are deploying traditional incremental reasoning rather than making a wide-ranging policy choice, it should be rare for them to refuse to develop the common law in deference to legislative reform. *cf* J Lee, 'The Doctrine of Precedent and the Supreme Court' (Inner Temple Lecture, 2012) 2, 17–18. See also chapter 2 (Lady Hale).

My conclusion, therefore, is that putting to one side some clear exceptions, such as criminal law and family law, the default position should be that, where there is the possibility of making a desirable change to the law judicially, the judges should seize that chance in line with the common law's incremental tradition. It is normally an unacceptable denial of justice to refuse to develop the law on the argument that reform is best left to the legislature.[27] Indeed one suspects that deference to possible legislation may often be used by judges, who for other good reasons, do not favour the development in question. If so, it would be better to rely rationally and openly on those other reasons.

Consistently with this, my own view is that the Law Commission should tend to steer clear of areas where one can realistically expect the judges themselves, acting progressively, to correct errors or to bring the law into line with modern conditions and values. This meant that in relation to, for example the law of obligations, I tended to the view during my time as a Law Commissioner that legislative reform (and hence Law Commission projects in that area) ought normally to be confined to lawyers' law reform[28] and to situations either where the law was already based on statute (eg the law of limitation or the Fatal Accidents Act 1976) or where the common law was so entrenched that even the highest court would be likely to take the view that judicial law reform would be too radical (eg the law on privity of contract).[29]

---

[27] For a disappointing relatively recent example of this sort of reasoning see some of the majority's reasoning in *R (Prudential plc) v Special Commissioner of Income Tax* [2013] UKSC 1, [2013] 2 AC 185 (majority deciding against extending legal professional privilege to accountants giving legal advice).

[28] On lawyers' law reform, see A Burrows, 'Some Reflections on Law Reform in England and Canada' (2003) 39 *Canadian Business Law Journal* 320, 330–32.

[29] See also, eg, chapters 2 (Lady Hale) and 16 (William Binchy).

# 21

# *Reflections on Statutory Implementation in the Law Commission*

NICHOLAS PAINES

My strong impression when I read the papers prepared for this conference, which was reinforced by hearing the day's discussion, was of having been thrown among a group of people who have thought more deeply, and informed themselves more thoroughly, than I have succeeded in doing about the perennial issues facing institutions such as the one of which I am a member. So it was with some trepidation that I raised my voice in this gathering.

I consoled myself by bearing in mind that I was billed as offering 'reflections', rather than a cogently reasoned analysis of the problems and their solutions; if I could not match the depth of the thinking of others, I could at least offer the impressions of a relative newcomer (of some one and a half year's standing) as to the situation that the Law Commission faces currently in comparison with periods in its previous five decades. I have confined my reflections to the topic of implementation, a topic which, as the contributions to this volume show, has both a quantitative and a qualitative dimension.

Regarding the quantitative aspect—the rate of implementation—I was struck, but not surprised, by the frequency with which that issue cropped up in this conference, by no means confined to the contributions to the present panel. Rates of implementation are a difficult thing to measure, as Shona Wilson Stark has demonstrated.[1] I tried to do some calculations of my own, but failed to reach any very clear conclusions. I suspect the best, but very rough, estimate that can be given is that the rate of legislative implementation of our reports, taking the last 50 years as a whole, stands at about two thirds—the figure including some reports that will be too recent to expect implementation; Sir Grant Hammond's research suggests that that is about the norm for Law Commissions in the common law world.[2]

Turning to the qualitative aspects of the issue—by which I mean the nature or type of implementation—Shona Wilson Stark and Baroness Hale have given us

---

[1] See chapter 15 (Shona Wilson Stark).
[2] See chapter 19 (Sir Grant Hammond).

timely reminders that giving rise to legislation is not the only way in which our reports can contribute to law reform. They may assist the judiciary in the development of judge-made law—a topic that Professors Binchy and Burrows and Laura Dunlop QC[3] have also discussed—and, more widely, may influence thinking not only amongst practising and academic lawyers and judges but also outside the world of the law. Sometimes, as the Law Commission is currently doing in our project on the form of the statute book as it applies to Wales, we undertake an advisory project in which we do not aim to make 'hard' law reform proposals.

Where the development of law is best carried out by the judiciary, I would expect us to recognise that and recommend accordingly. But where we have proposed legislation, only achieving those other results strikes me as at best a consolation prize. I cannot help thinking of the non-implementation of our proposals for legislative reform as a failure: either our reform proposals were not satisfactory, which is a failure by us, or—as we inevitably tend to view the situation—a set of worthwhile proposals have come to nothing, which is a failure elsewhere. It is not the sort of failure for which it is fruitful to apportion blame, though it is worth exploring and addressing its causes; this has been done in recent years with the procedures introduced pursuant to the Law Commission Act 2009 (though Sir Jack Beatson has reminded us that these are to a large extent a formalisation of practices adopted to address similar problems in earlier decades of the Commission's existence).[4] Non-implementation is at least a failure of the system; as Sir Terence Etherton has observed,[5] it leaves the citizen, who has paid mine and my colleagues' salaries and possibly contributed to our work as a stakeholder, with nothing to show for that investment.

Professor Mitchell offers an enlightening chapter about the early years of the Law Commission,[6] and Sir Terence Etherton has pointed to a number of respects in which the Commission's position has subsequently been weakened by changes in the structure of government. It is tempting to see the Gardiner–Scarman years as a heyday, but pointless to regret their passing. We are less well funded than previously, as has also been pointed out, but that again only reflects a fact of modern economic life.

We are less proactive than our early predecessors were allowed to be; the Lord Chancellor's approval of programmes of projects is no longer there for the asking. We are in some other respects less ambitious but, I think, only as regards the pace at which we can improve the law and not as regards the extent of the improvement that we can make. We are doing less consolidation work than previously, but that reflects a dramatic cut in the number of Parliamentary Counsel seconded to us. We have not given up on consolidation; our consultation paper on the form of the law in Wales[7] contains extensive discussion both of consolidation

---

[3] See chapters 16 (William Binchy), 17 (Laura Dunlop) and 20 (Andrew Burrows).
[4] See chapter 26 (Sir Jack Beatson).
[5] See, eg, chapter 9 (Sir Terence Etherton).
[6] See chapter 4 (Paul Mitchell).
[7] LC CP223, *Form and Accessibility of the Law Applicable in Wales* (2015).

and of codification; but we have come to appreciate that in many areas law reform is a necessary precursor to consolidation.

We have to cut our coats according to the currently available amount of cloth, but I believe that we can still produce attractive and serviceable garments. May I advertise a couple of them? I shall explain later why I am doing so.

In July 2015 we published a consultation paper[8] in relation to a project to improve the way in which people who lack mental capacity to take decisions, such as the growing number of elderly people with dementia, are treated with regard to the arrangements made for their care and treatment; this is at the request of the Department of Health and follows the widespread criticism of a scheme the Department brought in a few years ago. My colleague Stephen Lewis is supervising a project to reform the antiquated law of bills of sale, this time at the request of the Treasury. The impetus for that project is the fact that those Victorian legal instruments are increasingly being used today by moneylenders who lend money to subprime borrowers on the security of their motor vehicles; the borrowers have to sign a document that opens with the words 'This indenture witnesseth' and, more seriously, they lack many of the protections of the Consumer Credit Act.

I have chosen those two projects because they illustrate a positive point about prospects of implementation: we are often better placed than government, and are recognised by the government as better placed than them, to devise law reform of a sort that makes an immediate contribution to improving people's lives. We always have been. In our current mental capacity project we are standing on the shoulders of our predecessors whose recommendations gave rise to the original Mental Capacity Act, to which Lady Hale refers in her chapter.[9] The current projects to which I have referred are less high-flown than codifying the entire law of contract, for example, but are nevertheless both interesting and challenging, and also very worthwhile. For as long as there remain areas of the statute book that require the sort of attention that we are the best people to give to them, the prospects of legislative implementation, in my view, remain good.

A final thing I would mention in the context of statutory implementation is the work we have in hand and in prospect in relation to the future form of legislation. It is a major feature of our Welsh project that I have mentioned; my colleague David Ormerod's project on sentencing law will also consider novel approaches to the presentation of the law in that area, to prevent repeated amendment from bringing that area of the law back into its current sorry state. As regards effective law reform, our ambitions remain high.

[8] LC CP222, *Mental Capacity and Deprivation of Liberty* (2015).
[9] See Chapter 2.

# 22

# *Implementation by Statute: What the Future Holds*

HECTOR MACQUEEN

## I INTRODUCTION

There is no doubt in my mind that the Law Commissions Act 1965 anticipated passage of statutes as the primary method by which the proposals of the bodies it created would be carried out. Equally I have no doubt that Law Commission work can lead at least to development of the law in the courts. But in my view the 'systematic development and reform' which the 1965 Act envisages is not something which can be done by courts deciding particular cases.[1] The perspective given by the particular facts of a case, or even a group of cases, is not necessarily, or even often, a sound basis on which to generalise or go very far beyond whatever may be the present state of the law. To give an example, 20-odd years ago the Scottish Law Commission began a detailed review of the whole law of unjustified enrichment. The publications which emerged from that were undoubtedly influential in a subsequent shift of direction in the Scottish courts; but there has been insufficient case law since, especially appellate case law, to consolidate the details of the 'enrichment revolution'.[2] That task has fallen instead to writers on the law, who have fortunately shown a fair degree of consensus as to what the outcomes are, or should be;[3] but much of this still awaits the imprimatur of high-level judicial confirmation, and

---

[1] Law Commissions Act 1965, s 3(1).

[2] See the following Scottish Law Commission Discussion Papers: SLC DP 95, *Recovery of Benefits Conferred under Error of Law* (2 vols, 1993); SLC DP 99, *Judicial Abolition of the Error of Law Rule and its Aftermath* (1996); SLC DP 100, *Recovery of Ultra Vires Public Authority Receipts and Disbursements* (1996); also Scottish Law Commission, SLC 169, *Unjustified Enrichment, Error of Law and Public Authority Receipts and Disbursements* (1999). The major cases manifesting the influence of the Commission's work on the subject are *Morgan Guaranty Trust Co of New York v Lothian Regional Council* 1995 SC 151 (IH) and *Shilliday v Smith* 1998 SC 725 (IH). See also chapter 17 (Laura Dunlop).

[3] R Evans-Jones, *Unjustified Enrichment*, 2 vols (Edinburgh, W Green for the Scottish Universities Law Institute, 2003, 2013); Lord Eassie and HL MacQueen (eds), *Gloag and Henderson: The Law of Scotland*, 12th edn (Edinburgh, W Green, 2012) ch 24; M Hogg, *Obligations*, 2nd edn (Edinburgh, Avizandum, 2006) 201–41. It is to be anticipated that Niall Whitty's treatment of the subject within the forthcoming *Laws of Scotland: Stair Memorial Encyclopaedia Reissue Obligations*, will also follow a similar general approach.

meanwhile a degree of confusion and uncertainty remains apparent in at least some of the first instance lower court decisions.[4]

Again, one of my present projects in contract law in the Scottish Commission is third party rights, where Scots law went badly wrong in a House of Lords decision in 1920.[5] It is possible that if the right case were to come along and go all the way to the UK Supreme Court, the difficulties could be sorted out, not least with the help the Scottish Law Commission has already offered in its publications on the subject; but meanwhile contracts that are 'naturally' Scots law are made subject to English law instead in order to use the Contracts (Rights of Third Parties) Act 1999, or, where that option is not possible or impracticable, go through horrible drafting contortions in order to negotiate the hairpin bends and skid pans which the House of Lords put in their path nearly a century ago.[6] In a system which lacks a steady stream and quality of case law, law reform by statute is actually critical to its health and well-being, and perhaps the only way it can respond quickly enough to changing social and economic conditions as well as to the correction of the errors of the past. Indeed it can sort out the errors of the present. The Legal Writings (Counterparts and Delivery) (Scotland) Act 2015, which completed its passage through the Scottish Parliament at the end of February 2014, received Royal Assent on the auspicious date of 1 April 2015, and came into force on 1 July, reintroduced execution in counterpart into Scots law. This was made necessary by the general belief in the Scottish legal profession that such execution was not possible. The researches of the Scottish Law Commission, based on the advanced technique of searching on 'execution in counterpart' amongst Scottish cases on Westlaw, showed that in fact counterpart execution had been recognised and widely practised in Scotland before the Anglo–Scottish Union of 1707, and had indeed been accepted in Glasgow Sheriff Court as recently as 1957.[7] But such research alone was never going to be enough to shake the entrenched opinion of the profession, and in any event legislative modernisation was certainly needed to recognise electronic transmission of facsimiles of signed paper documents as delivery of these documents for the purpose of making them legally effective. Hence the Act.

Later in this volume, Elaine Lorimer and Malcolm McMillan, former and current Chief Executives of the Law Commission and the Scottish Law Commission, respectively, describe and discuss still new procedures in each of the Westminster and Holyrood Parliaments for the implementation of certain kinds of Commission proposals for law reform.[8] I will leave the detail to them; the chapters by Sir Terence Etherton

---

[4] See, eg, *Corrie v Craig* 2013 GWD 1-55 (Sheriffdom of South Strathclyde, Dumfries and Galloway at Kirkcudbright), criticised by M Hogg, 'Continued Uncertainty in the Analysis of Unjustified Enrichment' 2013 *Scots Law Times (News)* 111; *Virdee v Stewart* [2011] CSOH 50 (criticised by M Hogg, 'Unjustified Enrichment Claims: When Does the Prescriptive Clock begin to Run?' (2013) 17 *Edinburgh Law Review* 405).

[5] *Carmichael v Carmichael's Executrix* 1920 SC (HL) 195.

[6] See generally Scottish Law Commission, SLC DP 157, *Third Party Rights in Contract* (2014).

[7] See generally Scottish Law Commission, SLC 231, *Formation of Contract: Execution in Counterpart* (2013); *Wilson v Fenton Brothers (Glasgow) Ltd* 1957 SLT (Sh Ct) 3.

[8] See chapters 36 (Elaine Lorimer) and 37 (Malcolm McMillan). See also M McMillan, 'Law Reform in the Scottish Parliament: A New Process—A New Era?' (2014) 3 *Scottish Parliamentary Review* 95.

and Sir Grant Hammond have already touched on some of it.[9] The critical point for my purposes is that the Bills taken through under them must not be of even a potentially political controversial nature, and their substance must have widespread support in the stakeholder communities primarily affected by the measures.[10] I have been lucky enough to be involved in legislation of the relevant kind going through Westminster, the subject-matter being the law of insurance; and also to be the Commission's lead in the first Bill under the Holyrood procedure, the Legal Writings Bill already mentioned. As I have also seen the passage of Commission legislation outside the procedures in both Parliaments, I have had plenty of opportunity to reflect on implementation of law reform by statute, and what follows gives the present state of those reflections, driven by the thought that the best way of predicting the future is by means of extrapolation from the most recent past. After some thoughts on Westminster, this chapter focuses mainly on the recent Scottish experience.

## II THE WESTMINSTER PROCEDURE

The initiation of a Special Public Bill procedure for uncontroversial Law Commission Bills was largely the result of pressure applied by the Scottish Law Commission's sister body, the Law Commission for England and Wales, but it can be—and has been—used to implement joint reports of the two bodies and also reports brought forward by one of them alone. The details of the procedure have been set out fully in other contributions to this volume.[11] The features to which I would draw particular attention here are that the membership of the Special Public Bill Committee is ad hoc, determined in relation to each Bill; that the Committee can (and generally does) take evidence; and that the Bill receives the usual clause-by-clause scrutiny. Despite the membership's ad hoc composition, scrutiny in a Special Public Bill Committee may even be more rigorous than usual because at least some of the committee members will already have knowledge and understanding of the Bill's subject matter. The hollow-square table arrangements and wood-panelled atmosphere of a House of Lords committee room also lend themselves to expert seminar-style discussion of technical issues between committee members and witnesses. The procedure is not in any way 'fast-track': the process takes as long as it needs to take, although that will be controlled by the managers of parliamentary business. After this procedure, the House of Commons has not tended to spend very much time over the Bill once it has been scrutinised and passed in the House of Lords Committee.

---

[9] See chapters 9 (Sir Terence Etherton) and 19 (Sir Grant Hammond).

[10] For Westminster, see House of Lords Procedure Committee, *Law Commission Bills* (2007–08, HL 63) and (2010–11, HL 30); House of Lords, *Companion to the Standing Orders and Guide to the Proceedings of the House of Lords* (2013 edn) paras 3.16, 8.43, 8.112. For Holyrood, see Standing Orders of the Scottish Parliament, 4th edn (2014) rule 9.17A ('Scottish Law Commission Bills'); and further criteria for the procedure set down by the Presiding Officer and published on 6 June 2013: Scottish Parliament Business Bulletin (93/2013) 1.

[11] See above, notes 8–10. See also E Cooke and H MacQueen, 'Law Reform in a Political Environment: The Work of the Law Commissions' in D Feldman (ed), *Law in Politics, Politics in Law* (Oxford, Hart Publishing, 2013) ch 9.

Of the seven Law Commission Bills (just about one a year) that have gone through the procedure to date, three were the product of joint English and Scottish Law Commission reports, with the resultant legislation applying throughout the United Kingdom: the Third Parties (Rights Against Insurers) Act 2010, the Consumer Insurance (Disclosure and Representation) Act 2012 and the Insurance Act 2015. The four other Bills were either England and Wales only (the Perpetuities and Accumulations Act 2009, the Trusts (Capital and Income) Act 2013 and the Inheritance and Trustees' Powers Act 2014) or Scotland only (the Partnerships (Prosecution) (Scotland) Act 2013). In each of these four cases, therefore, the Bill was the result of one Commission's work only. Given the extent to which matters of purely Scots law are reserved under the devolution settlement, the procedure's capacity to deal with Scotland-only Bills remains significant. The Partnerships (Prosecution) (Scotland) Bill had to go through Westminster because the law of partnership is not devolved even in those aspects which are peculiar to Scotland, such as the juristic personality of the partnership.[12] Another possible future candidate for a Scottish Bill at Westminster arises from the Scottish Law Commission's as yet unimplemented report on unincorporated associations, another matter reserved under the Scotland Act 1998 even though Scots law in this area is much more distinct from its English counterpart than is true for partnership.[13]

As the Scottish Commissioner responsible from late 2009 in the joint project on insurance law, I was closely involved with all the insurance Bills throughout, although I gave oral evidence only in relation to what became the 2015 Act.[14] The progress of that Bill was an excellent illustration of some of the major features of the special procedure. As initially presented to the committee by the government, the Bill was not wholly un-amended from its original form as appended to the relevant Law Commissions report. Two clauses were omitted: one on warranties (although others on the same subject were retained) and the other on damages against insurers guilty of late payment of claims. The argument against their inclusion was that both were controversial in the sense that there was no consensus of support amongst stakeholders, that is, the insurance industry. Although the Special Public Bills Committee showed some initial inclination to seek to include the clause on late payment damages in the Bill, in the end this did not happen. The concern about it expressed in evidence to the committee by significant parties such as the Lloyds Market Association—namely that it would expose UK insurers to speculative litigation, especially from foreign policy-holders—was sufficient to confirm the government's position. The clause on warranties was eventually reinstated, however, after some redrafting by the Law Commissions was taken to have removed the controversy.[15] This shows that a Bill can be subject to substantive amendment during

---

[12]   Scotland Act 1998, sch 5, part 2, head C1; and see further the unimplemented report by the Commissions: Law Commission and Scottish Law Commission, LC 283 and SLC 193, *Partnership Law* (2003).

[13]   Scotland Act 1998, sch 5, part 2, head C1; and see further Scottish Law Commission, SLC 217, *Unincorporated Associations* (2009).

[14]   See House of Lords Special Public Bill Committee, *Insurance Bill* (2014, HL 81) 2–11.

[15]   For the parliamentary debates on the passage of the Bill, see www.services.parliament.uk/bills/2014-15/insurance/stages.html.

its progress without thereby falling outside the scope of the special procedure. But an amendment to introduce something that had not been in the Law Commissions' report would clearly have meant the Bill being moved to ordinary legislative procedures, or failing altogether.

It is not known, however, how far the process of updating and adjustment, whether by the government before introduction or during a Bill's parliamentary progress, can go before it ceases to be a Law Commission Bill and so ineligible for the procedure. Certainly a Bill going through this procedure cannot be a vehicle for a piece of non-Law Commission policy. Hence, for example, although the government's Consumer Rights Bill 2014 implemented two sets of Law Commission recommendations, one on remedies in the supply of goods and the other on protection against unfair contract terms, it could not be a Law Commissions Bill, since it additionally provided in considerable detail for implied terms in contracts for the supply of services as well as goods, for rules on the supply of digital content, and for various other aspects of consumer protection.[16] It further seems that where a Bill is dealing with English law alone, it must not seek to impact also upon Scots law without any prior consultation in Scotland. The Inheritance and Trustees' Powers Bill 2013 as originally laid before Parliament contained a provision (*not* recommended by the Law Commission in the relevant report, a fact by itself possibly making the Bill unsuitable for the procedure) that would have allowed English and Welsh courts to undo the outcomes of Scottish succession law in certain circumstances, at least insofar as they took effect in England and Wales. The provision was withdrawn without ever reaching the Special Public Bill Committee after fierce opposition from Scottish interests.[17]

Finally, my experience of giving evidence before the Special Public Bill Committee contrasted rather sharply in some ways with my earlier appearance before the House of Commons Committee appointed to consider the Consumer Rights Bill in February 2014.[18] Both the membership of the latter committee and the room in which it sat in Portcullis House were much larger and less intimate than the House of Lords. The committee members had been gathered together only the day before they began to hear evidence, and it was fairly clear from the questioning that few had had time to acquaint themselves with the content of the Bill (admittedly a much larger text than the Insurance Bill). A number did, however, have knowledge of consumer affairs and resultant agendas which they wished to pursue, even though there was nothing relevant in the Bill and little prospect of persuading the government to take action by means of this vehicle. The initial discussion was thus less focused than was later to be the case with the Insurance Bill in the House of Lords. But in due course the Consumer Rights Bill was subjected to such detailed line-by-line scrutiny and amendment in both Commons and Lords that it was virtually the last Act to be passed before Parliament rose for the May 2015 General Election.[19]

---

[16] For the Consumer Rights Bill 2014 in Parliament, see www.services.parliament.uk/bills/2014-15/consumerrights.html.

[17] For the progress of the Inheritance and Trustees' Powers Bill 2013, see www.services.parliament.uk/bills/2013-14/inheritanceandtrusteespowers.html.

[18] Consumer Rights Bill Deb 11 February 2014, cols 16–24.

[19] The Bill received Royal Assent on 26 March 2015, the same day on which the prorogation of Parliament took place, with dissolution following on 30 March.

### III PARLIAMENTARY RECOGNITION OF THE IMPORTANCE
### OF LAW REFORM LEGISLATION

It is evident that the Westminster special procedure has been successful. Important reforms have been carried through even though at least some of the Bills attracted discussion and debate en route. The procedures are not 'fast-tracks' or rubber stamps for the Commissions' proposals. The Bills are as subject to the democratic process as any others, albeit the bulk of the work is done in the unelected second chamber. But the procedure seems to have established its credentials with government and parliamentarians, and its future thus seems assured for at least the lifetime of the 2015–20 Westminster Parliament.

The first experience of the parallel process at Holyrood in 2014–15 led the Scottish Parliament as a whole—that is, across party divides—to acknowledge the significance of its own a- or non-political role in keeping the Scottish legal system and Scots law up-to-date and not too drastically out of line with developments elsewhere. In the Scottish Law Commission's fiftieth year, its role as a public but independent body charged with making recommendations for simplifying, updating and improving the law was also significantly enhanced by an increased visibility in the Scottish parliamentary and governmental processes.

So, for example, in a Stage 1 debate on the Legal Writings Bill held on 25 November 2014, a Labour MSP, Richard Baker, said:

> I reflect on the fact that dealing with bills introduced by the Scottish Law Commission will be beneficial generally to legislative reform in the Parliament … Too many bills on important issues, which could have been equally as beneficial as the one that we are considering, were not progressed, so it is good that with our committee's parliamentary consideration, we can look forward to more progress with such legislation … In this process, the committee's work will be beneficial not just to Parliament but to the quality of law.[20]

An SNP MSP, John Mason, added another general observation in the same debate:

> As a non-lawyer, I have to ask where Scotland is positioning herself in the global market. The legal system is not just another product such as whisky or cheese. It is much more than a product, but it is a product nonetheless. If Scotland is to compete on quality with the best food and drink, top-of-the-range engineering and one of the cleanest environments in the world, similarly we want one of the best legal systems in the world. From that perspective, I do not see today's debate as being of narrow interest only to the legal profession. It has a much wider economic impact. If this Parliament cannot fight the corner of Scots law, I do not know who can.[21]

The concluding Stage 3 debate on the Bill took place in the full Scottish Parliament on 24 February 2015.[22] There were no amendments to discuss, and the debate largely consisted of speeches from the Minister and the spokespersons for the various parties, along with contributions from the members of the committee (the Delegated Powers and Law Reform Committee (DPLRC)) which had worked on the Bill.

---

[20] Scottish Parliament Official Report 25 November 2014, cols 52–53.
[21] ibid col 56.
[22] Scottish Parliament Official Report 24 February 2015, cols 8–28.

These speeches included a number of general statements about the significance of the Scottish Law Commission Bill procedure. Opening the agenda item, the Presiding Officer, Tricia Marwick, declared:

> I put on record my gratitude to the committee for the work that it has carried out on the bill and for its contribution to improving the Parliament's capacity to legislate. I expect further Law Commission bills to be considered in this way.[23]

This was picked up straightaway by the Minister Fergus Ewing, in his opening statement:

> [I]t is an important new development of our parliamentary procedure, and I am extremely grateful to the Scottish Law Commission for its work in providing us with the legislation … I hope and expect that the new process, which we see coming to its conclusion in respect of the first bill today, will go some way towards increasing the implementation rate of commission reports … I was particularly impressed with the way in which the committee took on its new role, so I look forward to successive commission bills being considered in this way. To use a non-parliamentary expression, bring them on.[24]

Opening for Labour, Lewis MacDonald noted a devolved Scottish Parliament provided greater opportunities for keeping Scots law up to date than had been available at Westminster pre-devolution:

> It is fair to say that this devolved Parliament has taken a little time to work out the best way to deliver that objective, but there is no need to apologise for that. This is, after all, a maturing institution … However, we are now moving on to a new phase, and I think that the committee's focus on law reform will prove useful to both the Parliament and the legal profession, while the whole Parliament remains responsible—as it is today—for the final outcome.
>
> The bill is useful, not because it will bring businesses flocking to these shores, but because it will ensure that Scotland and Scots law do not get left behind. The process of law reform as it is exemplified by today's debate does not give Scotland a novel competitive advantage, but ensures that we are not at a disadvantage and that our Parliament delivers on one of the purposes of devolution … The bill can help to ensure that we also have a legal system that is modern, up to date and fit for purpose.[25]

For the Conservatives, Annabel Goldie associated herself with the tributes to the work of the Scottish Law Commission and the DPLRC, and their 'important functions'.[26] In her closing speech, she again added her acknowledgement of 'the need to adapt and change our centuries-old legal system to meet the exigencies of the modern age'.[27] Nigel Don, the SNP convener of the DPLRC, laid especial emphasis upon this aspect of the significance of the Law Commission Bill procedure as a response to changing socio-economic conditions:

> Parliament has historically never found enough time for the repair and maintenance of Scottish law. We now have the opportunity to do that … I suggest that we will need to do

[23] ibid col 8.
[24] ibid.
[25] ibid cols 12–13.
[26] ibid col 13.
[27] ibid col 22.

more of the kind of thing that we have done … I therefore suggest to you, Presiding Officer, and the chamber that we need to start thinking about whether there should be a wider remit for my committee or any other; I would not want to say what the process should be. We need to ensure that we can look after the repair and maintenance of Scots law—in particular, perhaps, private law.[28]

Fergus Ewing picked this point up in his closing statement:

I can say that the Scottish Government echoes the sentiment that he expressed and which I think underlay his criticism, which is that we require to have a process for the repair and maintenance of Scots law. That was a prudent comment and one on which it may be sensible to ponder further.[29]

The significance of this and the other contributions quoted lies, as it seems to me, in the acceptance that the Scottish Parliament's function in passing legislation is not only to deal with the political issues of the day, but also to engage with the care and maintenance of the law and the legal system of Scotland to ensure that as far as possible it keeps pace with the basic requirements of contemporary life, including those of legal and business practice. For the moment, the new procedure represents the Parliament's best attempt to get to grips with this function, but it is possible to see, especially in Nigel Don's speech and the Minister's direct response, that there may still be room for further development in the not too distant future.

It is also worth noting that members of the DPLRC suggested that they would not object to a more active role in developing Bills brought before them under the procedure. An SNP member, Stewart Stevenson, expressed a modicum of concern during the Stage 3 debate on the Legal Writings Bill:

[T]he danger with the process that the Law Commission undertakes—it involves a rigorous examination before fully developed proposals are brought to Parliament, which is extremely helpful—is that all the contentious and difficult bits have been removed from the proposals, so we end up with something that is the lowest common denominator, to some extent.[30]

This concern was probably shared at least by his convenor, who remarked early on in the progress of the Bill: 'I suspect that there are few bills before the Parliament that have been consulted on quite so much and have been so consensually put together.'[31] It was certainly true that a great deal of effort went into the preparation of the Legal Writings Bill as the pilot for the new procedure; but the effort on the part of the Scottish Law Commission at least would have been no less, since at the time of most of its substantive work on counterpart execution, the new procedure was by no means certain to come about. Nor was there an absence of contentious or difficult elements, as, for example, the Faculty of Advocates undoubtedly brought out in its written and oral submissions to the DPLRC, which dealt with the possibility of increased risk of fraud and error if counterpart execution was used.[32] So the

---

[28]  ibid cols 20–22.
[29]  ibid col 26.
[30]  ibid col 17.
[31]  Scottish Parliament Official Report (DPLRC) 17 June 2014, col 1510.
[32]  See further H MacQueen, C Garland and L Smith, 'Law Reform in the Scottish Parliament' (2015–16) 3(2) *Scottish Parliamentary Review* 3.

Commission at least should not be deterred by contention or difficulty in bringing forward its recommendations; and the result put before the DPLRC should therefore not be the minimum that all stakeholders involved are prepared to accept. With future Bills under the procedure there will surely be opportunities for the DPLRC to play a more creative role, while remembering that from the perspective of those bringing legislative proposals forward, Bills are made to pass as razors are to sell.[33] Whether, however, present Holyrood procedures could ever match the multi-level line-by-line scrutiny to be observed at Westminster is unclear to me; certainly the text of the Legal Writings Bill received nothing like the attention I have seen with, not only the insurance Bills, but also the Consumer Rights Bill, at Westminster.

## IV WHAT NEXT?

The agreement by which the Scottish Parliament's Law Commission Bill procedure was set up provides for a review after either two Bills had gone through it or, in any event, two years. The Legal Writings Bill was the first Bill. The question of which is to be the second has now been answered. The Succession (Scotland) Bill, introduced to the Parliament on 16 June 2015, was referred to the DPLRC. The Bill implements some of the more technical aspects of the report on succession published by the Scottish Law Commission in April 2009.[34] The committee began its Stage 1 processes in September 2015 and the Bill was passed on 28 January 2016.[35] Meantime, the Scottish Parliament's Standards, Procedures and Public Appointments Committee completed a review of the procedure begun in August 2015 in accordance with the two-year provision made at the time of its introduction, with a recommendation dated December of no change meantime.[36]

The Succession Bill presented a number of important differences from the Legal Writings Bill, and not just in its subject-matter. First, where the latter Bill implemented a report made the year before it was introduced, it was more than six years since the Scottish Law Commission reported on succession. There have also been long gaps after the relevant report in relation to certain Bills going through the Westminster special procedure, including the very first, the one on third party rights against insurers in 2009–10, where the joint report had been published in 2001.[37] So how this works out now is bound to be of interest, if only with regard to other older unimplemented reports in both Commissions. Second, whereas the Legal Writings Bill was only seven sections long, the Succession Bill

---

[33] The famous aphorism attributed to the great Parliamentary Counsel of the Victorian era, Sir Henry Thring; found quoted in A Rodger, 'The Form and Language of Legislation' in D Feldman (ed), *Law in Politics, Politics in Law* (Oxford, Hart Publishing, 2013) 65, 80.

[34] Scottish Law Commission, SLC 215, *Succession* (2009).

[35] See the websites of the DPLRC: www.scottish.parliament.uk/parliamentarybusiness/Current Committees/90922.aspx; and for the Bill: www.scottish.parliament.uk/parliamentarybusiness/Bills/90123. aspx.

[36] See   www.scottish.parliament.uk/S4_StandardsProceduresandPublicAppointmentsCommittee/ NoteOfReview.pdf.

[37] Law Commission and Scottish Law Commission, LC 272 and SLC 183, *Joint Report on Third Parties—Rights against Insurers* (2001). See also chapter 9 (Sir Terence Etherton).

had 27 sections when introduced, covering a fairly wide and rather miscellaneous range of matters. On the other hand, the Bill affects potentially everyone living in Scotland, and not just the business and legal profession communities. It is about wills, survivorship of potential heirs, forfeiture for parricide, gifts made in contemplation of death, and mourning expenses; so it has plenty of human interest to put alongside the more technical issues also covered, such as estate administration, liferents and destinations giving rise to conditional institutes. The Bill thus provided a helpful test of the DPLRC's capacity to deal, not only with a longer Bill, but also one touching on diverse matters. Successful completion by the Committee and the Parliament, despite making 51 amendments altogether, encourages the bringing forward of further more substantial Bills in future.

Finally, one of the criteria which a Scottish Law Commission Bill has to meet to go to the DPLRC is that the Scottish Government must not be planning wider work in that particular subject area.[38] But it was already clear at the time of the Succession Bill's introduction that the Scottish Government is planning further legislation on succession in implementation of those parts of the Commission's 2009 report not covered by the Bill. A consultation indicating the government's intention so to legislate was published on 26 June 2015.[39] It covers intestate succession (including the abolition of the distinction between heritable and moveable property in that context), the scope for disinheritance (to be less restricted than in the present law, especially in relation to children), and the protection of cohabitants. This can be read as broadly covering succession where there is no will, and the extent of a testator's power to override these rules in a will, whereas the Succession Bill is primarily about cases where there is a will and about the system by which a deceased person's executor is authorised to administer the estate. So there is a distinction to be drawn, even if the overall substance of the two pieces of prospective legislation comes from a single Scottish Law Commission report. The crucial point is that the relevant criterion has been read as narrowly as possible, although the development suggests that this particular restriction is a candidate for reconsideration in any further review of the procedure.

If the other existing criteria continue to apply, a 2013 report on judicial factors[40] and forthcoming work on contract[41] and negative prescription[42] seem likely candidates for the procedure. There are however other topics on the current Scottish Law Commission agenda likely to fall foul of one or other of the criteria. Amongst more recent, as yet, unimplemented reports, the one concerning adults with incapacity seems not to be a candidate for the DPLRC procedure since it involves significant engagement with human rights, indeed is really about the application of Convention rights in the context of care arrangements for incapable persons.[43] Also likely to be

[38] For the criteria see n 10 above.
[39] Scottish Government, *Consultation on the Law of Succession* (2015).
[40] Scottish Law Commission, SLC 233, *Judicial Factors* (2013).
[41] eg the work on third party rights mentioned above, text accompanying nn 5–6.
[42] See Scottish Law Commission, SLC 242, *Ninth Programme of Law Reform* (2015) 20–21, for negative prescription as an agenda item.
[43] Scottish Law Commission, SLC 240, *Adults with Incapacity* (2014).

of this nature is the new project on defamation (because it relates significantly to freedom of expression).[44] At least for the moment, it is clear that the Scottish Law Commission is not putting all its law reform eggs into the DPLRC basket. In my view, it would be inappropriate and unwise to do so.

A question may be raised about whether criminal law reform should continue to be excluded, given that at Westminster the Partnerships (Prosecution) (Scotland) Act 2013 has been put through the equivalent process. But that Act is the only criminal law statute to go through the Westminster procedure so far; all the other Acts under it have related to non-criminal law. Nor was the 2013 Act entirely uncontroversial, despite its being a response to an outrageous case which had attracted much public attention and criticism of the law;[45] the Law Society of Scotland, worried about the consequences for solicitors' partnership arrangements, expressed difficulties with the Bill in its evidence, albeit these were eventually overcome.[46]

The second Succession Bill is, however, thought unlikely to be put to the DPLRC, even if (improbably) the Scottish Government's consultation shows a wide degree of consensus as to how the law should be reformed. Given that everyone dies but only a minority make wills, the social significance of the distribution of estates on intestacy, the extent to which the family of the deceased should be protected against disinheritance, and the mutual claims of cohabitants, means that these are bound to be matters on which MSPs in general have views, often based on the difficulties experienced by constituents and on personal, social and moral positions. Because the proposed Bill would also abolish the distinction between moveable and heritable property for the purposes of succession, it has been linked by the SNP Government with its highly controversial land reform agenda. The Scottish Parliament and others of its committees will want to hold a detailed public debate on all these matters, of a kind probably making it unsuitable for the relatively low-key DPLRC procedure, even with its Stage 1 and Stage 3 full parliamentary debates. Whether or not the reports on trust law[47] and on positive prescription in relation to moveable property,[48] and the forthcoming report on transactions secured over moveables will be viewed similarly remains to be seen.[49]

Even in its more technical aspects, therefore, reform of private law by statute often involves the sorts of issue in which MSPs are generally interested and want to have a say. Nigel Don's idea of a law reform committee limited to private law matters may also leave uncontroversial reforms of non-criminal public law in an awkward limbo. While it would be wrong to suggest that lack of general interest should be the basis

---

[44] See the *Ninth Programme*, n 42 above, 19, for defamation as an agenda item.

[45] *Balmer v HM Advocate* [2008] HCJAC 44, 2008 SLT 799.

[46] See generally Scottish Law Commission, SLC 224, *Criminal Liability of Partnerships* (2011); and for the relevant committee proceedings and evidence see House of Lords Special Public Bill Committee, *Partnerships (Prosecution) (Scotland) Bill* (2013, HL 119).

[47] Scottish Law Commission, SLC 239, *Trust Law* (2014).

[48] Scottish Law Commission, SLC 228, *Prescription and Title to Moveable Property* (2012). The Scottish Government published a consultation on this report on 1 July 2015: Scottish Government, *Prescription and Title to Moveable Property (Scotland) Bill Consultation* (2015).

[49] For the progress of this project see its website: www.scotlawcom.gov.uk/law-reform/law-reform-projects/security-over-corporeal-and-incorporeal-moveable-property/.

for the division of law reform labour in the Scottish Parliament, it is also important to recognise that not all Scottish Law Commission work can be generally privileged in its access to legislative processes. What may be most important for the future development of special law reform procedures is not so much revision as generous interpretation of their criteria such as has been seen with the first Succession Bill, along with acceptance that there may be controversy about provisions within a Bill upon which the DPLRC will have to pass judgment (whether that involves rejecting criticism of the Bill, amending the Bill, or rejecting it completely as unsuitable for the procedure). There will have to be acceptance as well of the possibility of a full-scale parliamentary debate and vote at Stage 1 of the process when the DPLRC reports on the general principles of the Bill, recommending acceptance or rejection. The managers of parliamentary business will also have to be prepared to take these matters on board.

A final point is that there is much to be said in principle for a *standing* committee dealing with appropriate Law Commission Bills under special procedures.[50] My impression of Westminster was that Special Public Bill Committee members, appointed ad hoc for one Bill only, had to get up to speed with what the procedure did and did not enable them to do with it. The Holyrood committee (and, importantly, its supporting clerks) might in contrast be expected over a parliamentary session to develop a certain expertise in the procedure and matters of non-political law reform generally, always provided that its membership remained constant (which in fact it did not, even between the Legal Writings and the Succession Bills). Perhaps in both instances a satisfactory compromise might be to have some permanency in the committee's convenership over time, with strong leaders committed to law reform (as with Nigel Don of the DPLRC) being appointed or elected to the position. Were the Scottish Parliament ever to gain a second chamber, being the main forum for Scottish Law Commission Bills (whether through a committee or otherwise) might be one appropriate function for it.[51]

## V SELLING THE LAW REFORM

With the Legal Writings Bill, the Scottish Law Commission has found itself more in the business of 'selling' its recommendations both before and now after passage of the Bill. Extensive consultation with the legal profession was of course carried through during the preparation of the report and accompanying draft Bill published in 2013, but to adapt Thring's already mentioned aphorism, Acts must be made to work as razors are to give a clean shave.[52] Aware of the need to ensure at least majority stakeholder consensus, the Commission team gave numerous presentations on the proposed Bill at professional CPD and other events in the run-up to, and during the course of, the parliamentary stages, and indeed on the very eve of the Act

---

[50] *cf* the discussion in chapter 19 (Sir Grant Hammond).
[51] See further H MacQueen, 'A Second Chamber for the Scottish Parliament?' (2015) 24 *Scottish Affairs* 432.
[52] See text accompanying n 33 above.

coming into force. That close identification with the Bill had other consequences after it passed. The Commission engaged with a reaction triggered by a remark of Annabel Goldie in the Stage 3 debate, to the effect that practice guidance notes on the Act would be necessary to ensure that practitioners did not go wrong in applying it.[53] The comment, made in the context of worries about the likelihood of fraud and error, has been taken up by a group of the Scottish commercial law firms who will be amongst the most regular users of execution in counterpart. The group is working on a mutually agreed protocol on how to apply the Act in the execution of documents, and sought the Commission's (readily given) advice in its discussions.[54] The Commission team has also prepared articles and comments for professional journals with the aim of helping practitioners in general to understand the Act and the steps needed to make proper use of it.[55] The hope is to help develop a professional consensus as to how the Act operates and indeed should be operated. That ought at least to reduce the possibility of professional error, even if it will not stop those determined to commit fraud. A measure of the success of these efforts will be the number—or rather lack—of cases about the Act coming into court.

VI CONCLUSION

Opening the Stage 3 debate on the Legal Writings Bill, Fergus Ewing, the responsible Minister, opined that 'we are creating a piece of history today, albeit one that I suspect will appear in the minor footnotes rather than the front pages or forewords'.[56] While in general that is probably a fair assessment, the first steps under the new Scottish Law Commission Bill procedure have shown that it has at least some wider significance for the Scottish Parliament and legal system. The Parliament has manifested cross-party acceptance of the significance of its non-political role as the principal guardian of the well-being of the legal system. Scotland is a small legal system. Despite the strength of its common law, or precedent-based, dimensions, it simply does not generate enough cases to permit judicial development of the law to meet changing social and economic conditions, even if the judges felt inclined to try and do so. Legislation therefore provides the likeliest way forward. But it is critical that the legislation is as well prepared as it possibly can be; otherwise the cure may be worse than the disease. There is also a need to ensure as far as possible that those who will have to use and apply the Act do understand what it is meant to do, and

---

[53] Scottish Parliament Official Report 24 February 2015, col 23.

[54] See A Stewart, 'Are You Ready for Counterpart Signing?' (2015) 60(7) *Journal of the Law Society of Scotland* 33. In August 2015, the Law Society of Scotland also prepared a practice note update on the application of the Act to conveyancing missives, accessible only online: see Law Society of Scotland, 'Profession Practice Updates, August 2015, Electronic Delivery of Paper Documents', www.lawscot.org.uk/members/member-services/professional-practice/professional-practice-updates/#Electronic.

[55] Scottish Law Commission, 'Writings Redefined' (2015) 60(3) *Journal of the Law Society of Scotland* 4, published in full online only at www.journalonline.co.uk/Magazine/60-3/1019015.aspx; H MacQueen, C Garland and L Smith, 'The Legal Writings (Counterparts and Delivery) (Scotland) Act 2015' 2015 *Scots Law Times (News)* 103.

[56] Scottish Parliament Official Report 24 February 2015, col 8.

how the statutory language achieves that. It is further significant that perceptions of the value of the Scottish Law Commission have been enhanced by a legislative procedure bringing the nature of its work to the attention of a widening group of MSPs and others. How far this will help improve implementation of Commission recommendations remains to be seen. If the possibilities can seem daunting at a time of ever-dwindling resources, they are also exciting, at least for an elderly Scottish Law Commissioner.

# Part 6

# How Law Commissions Work

# 23

# *Introduction*

SIR JAMES MUNBY

Four issues underlie these papers and were given emphasis in the discussion that followed.

First, there is the question of at whom a Law Commission report is aimed. On one level the answer might be thought obvious: government and the legislature. But lurking behind this are more teasing points. Is this a report written for the here and now, or is it a report written rather with an eye to the more or less distant future? Is this a report written to encourage a legislative solution or rather to persuade the judges to come up with a judicial solution? Is this a report written to provide possible arguments to be deployed by advocates in court? Is it grist for the academic mill? Why is any of this important?

That leads on to the second point. How should a Law Commission balance principle and pragmatism? To what extent should intellectual purity be sacrificed for pragmatic advantage? If there are two principled solutions, is it right to select the one which will generate the least opposition? If the pursuit of principle means that nothing will be achieved, what course should be adopted? Can a desire to overcome opposition justify pursuit of an unprincipled solution?

The third point flows from the second. Consultation for the modern Law Commission means much more than merely canvassing the views of lawyers. Consultation must embrace a very wide range of stakeholders. Crucially, it means, if at all possible, carrying them along, especially where powerful commercial interests are engaged. Successful implementation may require the painstaking building of a coalition even of those whose interests seemingly conflict. But a Law Commission must not allow itself too easily to be deflected by commercial, industrial or professional lobbying.

The fourth point connects with the third. How should a Law Commission best go about creating potentially productive relationships with officials (both officials who serve Ministers and those who serve the legislature), with Ministers and with members of the legislature?

I pose questions. There are no easy answers. Probably there are no answers of universal application. As so often, whether in law or in politics, or, here, at the interface, it all depends ... Law Commissions, unlike judges, have to be attuned to the art of the possible. One key message emerges however: the central importance of the relationships which a Law Commission must create if it is to be successful; relationships with the potential opponents as well as the potential supporters of a particular project; and relationships with the officials, Ministers and legislators upon whose final decision implementation or non-implementation will usually depend.

# 24

# The Law Commission Method: Exportable to the EU?

HUGH BEALE

## I INTRODUCTION

There is a widespread perception that the quality of European Union (EU) legislation leaves a lot to be desired. Part of the problem is that the legislation is often fragmentary. For example, the directives affecting consumer contracts are sector specific (eg the directives on package travel,[1] timeshare contracts,[2] or the sale of goods),[3] deal only with particular methods of selling (doorstep sales,[4] distance sales,[5] and so on) or cover only specific legal issues (such as unfair terms).[6] To some extent fragmentation may be inevitable, given that the EU can act only where there is a legal base within the Treaty and that consumer protection is not itself a legal base,[7] so that the consumer directives have been based on promotion of the Internal Market—the Commission's approach having been to build the confidence of consumers to 'shop abroad' by ensuring that, wherever in the EU the consumer made his or her purchase, he or she would have a set of minimum rights—and only particular issues may be seen as sufficiently serious to justify intervention. But there are other problems. One is that provisions have not been consistent: for example, the consumer's right to withdraw from a doorstep transaction was measured in calendar days,[8] while the right to withdraw from a distance contract was measured in working days.[9]

---

[1] Council Directive 90/314/EEC of 13 June 1990 on package travel, package holidays and package tours [1990] OJ L158/59.

[2] Directive 94/47/EC of the European Parliament and of the Council of 26 October 1994 on the protection of purchasers in respect of certain aspects of contracts relating to the purchase of the right to use immovable properties on a timeshare basis [1994] OJ L280/83.

[3] Directive 1999/44/EC of the European Parliament and of the Council of 25 May 1999 on certain aspects of the sale of consumer goods and associated guarantees [1999] OJ L171/12.

[4] Council Directive 85/577/EEC of 20 December 1985 to protect the consumer in respect of contracts negotiated away from business premises [1985] OJ L372/31.

[5] Directive 97/7/EC of the European Parliament and of the Council of 20 May 1997 on the protection of consumers in respect of distance contracts [1997] OJ L144/19.

[6] Council Directive 93/13/EEC of 5 April 1993 on unfair terms in consumer contracts [1993] OJ L95/29.

[7] See S Weatherill, 'Reflections on the EC's Competence to Develop a "European Contract Law"' (2005) 13 *European Review of Private Law* 405.

[8] Directive 85/577, n 4 above, art 5.

[9] Directive 97/7, n 5 above, art 6.

Another problem is that legal terms are frequently used without definition. On occasion the meaning of a legal term is left to national law,[10] but frequently it appears that the term must be given an 'autonomous European legal meaning'.[11] The classic example is the *Simone Leitner* case.[12] The Court of Justice (ECJ) had to decide whether the damages to which a consumer was entitled under the provisions of the Package Travel Directive must include compensation for non-pecuniary loss suffered when the holiday was not as promised. This head of damages is recognised by many national laws but was not recognised by Austrian law.[13] The ECJ held that 'damage' in the Directive must be given an autonomous, 'European', legal meaning—and that in this context 'damage' is to be interpreted as including non-pecuniary loss.

Further, the individual provisions of Directives are often difficult to take in because they are in the form of long lists without any apparent logic to the order. Lastly, the provisions are sometimes very hard to interpret because they have not been well drafted.[14]

I have heard many English colleagues ask informally whether it would not be possible to improve this sorry state of affairs by setting up something like a European Law Commission, or by employing some of the law reform methods developed by the Law Commissions in the United Kingdom and in New Zealand.[15] In this chapter, I consider whether it would be feasible for Europe to adopt the methods developed by the Law Commissions or to establish a European Law Commission of some sort, and whether the European Law Institute, a body recently set up by a group of academics, judges and professional lawyers, may be able to perform this role. I will seek to illustrate my arguments by considering the fate of two proposals made by the European Commission: the attempt to replace four existing Directives with a single new Consumer Rights Directive; and the proposal, subsequently withdrawn but possibly to be replaced, for a Common European Sales Law.

## II  THE CONSUMER RIGHTS DIRECTIVE

In part the proposal for a Consumer Rights Directive was intended to address some of the issues to which I have referred. In 2001 the European Commission published a consultation paper[16] which provisionally proposed, among other things, to 'improve the quality of legislation already in place'.[17] Subsequently the Commission published an *Action Plan on Contract Law*, which proposed the creation of a Common Frame

---

[10] eg Case C-203/99 *Veedfald v Århus Amtskommune* [2001] ECR I-03569, para 27: content of 'damage' in art 9 of Directive 85/374/EEC concerning liability for defective products [1985] OJ L210/29, left to national law.

[11] See H Beale (ed), *Chitty on Contracts*, 32nd edn (London, Sweet & Maxwell, 2015) vol II, para 38-014.

[12] Case C-168/00 *Simone Leitner v TUI Deutschland* [2002] ECR I-2631.

[13] Outside of cases of deprivation of liberty.

[14] Examples of both these issues will be given below.

[15] I am not suggesting a body that should tackle the broad social issues previously taken on by the Law Commission of Canada: for detail on which see chapter 11 (Yves Le Bouthillier).

[16] Commission, 'European Contract Law' (Communication) COM (2001) 398 final.

[17] ibid paras 57–60, which refer to various earlier initiatives to simplify European legislation.

of Reference[18] in order to provide 'fundamental principles, definitions and model rules' that could assist in the improvement of the existing *acquis communautaire*.[19] Meanwhile a parallel review of eight consumer Directives was to be carried out.[20] In 2007 the Commission published a *Green Paper on Review of the Consumer Acquis*,[21] and in 2008 a proposal for a new Directive on Consumer Rights.[22] This would have replaced four of the existing Directives.[23]

The proposed Directive[24] would have made some improvements to the quality of the legislation, for example by simplifying the consumer's right to withdraw from distance and what were by then called 'off-premises' contracts.[25] There would also have been some modest further protections for consumers, such as a general information duty;[26] rights in the case of delay in delivering goods;[27] protection from the passing of risk;[28] and a right to damages for non-conformity.[29] The most significant change, however, would not have been to increase consumer protection but to require full harmonisation of many of the existing rules;[30] and it was this that led to the failure of the proposal in its original form.

I have noted that the Commission's original approach was to try to build the confidence of consumers to 'shop abroad' by providing them with minimum rights. But in the *Action Plan* documents there were clear indications[31] that the approach was changing. The approach was now about encouraging cross-border sales by removing the barriers faced by businesses. In particular, the Commission wanted to tackle what it perceived to be a major problem for traders wanting to sell to consumers in another Member State, arising from what is now art 6 of the Rome I Regulation on the law applicable to contractual obligations.[32] Under the Regulation, the parties to a consumer contract may choose which law is to apply to the contract but the consumer cannot be deprived of the protection of the mandatory rules of the State

---

[18] See Commission, 'A More Coherent European Contract Law: An Action Plan' (Communication) COM (2003) 68 final (hereafter Action Plan); and Commission, 'European Contract Law and the Revision of the *Acquis*: The Way Forward' (Communication) COM (2004) 651 final (hereafter The Way Forward).

[19] It was suggested also that the CFR might form the basis of an Optional Instrument if it was decided to create one: Action Plan, n 18 above, 2 and 23–24; The Way Forward, n 18 above, 8–9. For a fuller discussion of the purposes of the CFR, see H Beale, 'The Future of the Common Frame of Reference' (2007) 3 *European Review of Contract Law* 257.

[20] The Way Forward, n 18 above, 3. The Directives to be reviewed were: 85/577 ('Door-step Selling'); 90/314 ('Package Travel'); 93/13 ('Unfair Terms'); 94/47 ('Timeshare'); 97/7 ('Distance Selling'); 98/6 ('Unit Prices'); 98/27 ('Injunctions'); and 99/44 ('Consumer Sales').

[21] COM (2006) 744 final.

[22] Commission, 'Proposal for a Directive of the European Parliament and of the Council on Consumer Rights' COM (2008) 614 final.

[23] Directives 85/577 ('Door-step Selling'), 93/13 ('Unfair Terms'), 97/7 ('Distance Selling') and 99/44 ('Consumer Sales').

[24] On the proposed directive generally see G Howells and R Schulze (eds), *Modernising and Harmonising Consumer Contract Law* (Munich, Sellier, 2009).

[25] COM (2008) 614 final, n 22 above, arts 12–20.

[26] ibid art 5.

[27] ibid art 22.

[28] ibid art 23.

[29] ibid art 27.

[30] ibid art 4.

[31] eg Action Plan, n 18 above, para 4.2.2.

[32] Regulation (EC) 593/2008 of 17 June 2008 on the law applicable to contractual obligations.

in which the consumer is habitually resident if the contract resulted from the trader directing its activities to consumers in that State. This means that a trader who is seeking to sell across borders may need to know the mandatory rules of each country towards which it directs its activities. An internet shop which runs a website which appears to invite customers from all over the EU may therefore have to know 30 or more different laws.

The answer to this found in *The Way Forward*[33] was that there might be a move from minimum harmonisation to full harmonisation[34]—so that, within the fields covered by the directives, the substance of the law would be the same in each Member State. Therefore the proposed Consumer Rights Directive would have been a full harmonisation Directive. This would have meant that consumers in Member States that give their consumers more extensive rights than provided for by the Directive would suffer a reduction in protection. For example, in the United Kingdom this would have meant abolishing the consumer's right to reject goods without first going through the 'hierarchy of remedies';[35] a restriction of the implied terms to non-conformities which appear within the first two years;[36] and the imposition of a requirement to notify the seller of any non-conformity within a two-month period.[37] It was the requirement for Member States to give up higher levels of consumer protection than those contained in the draft directive that led to the rejection of the full proposal by the Council of Ministers. In the end, the Consumer Rights Directive[38] was adopted but in a much more restricted version, replacing only the doorstep and distance selling Directives and adding a few provisions on disclosure of information in 'on-premises' contracts,[39] delay in delivering goods,[40] and the passing of risk.[41]

Even in its restricted final version, the drafting of the Consumer Rights Directive is far from satisfactory. For example, the information that traders have to provide is in a long list[42] when it would be much easier to follow had it been sub-divided;[43] some of the provisions are hard to understand;[44] and the legal effect of the some of the provisions seems not to have been thought out.[45]

---

[33] See n 18 above.

[34] The Way Forward, n 18 above, 4.

[35] COM (2008) 614 final, n 22 above, art 26; compare Sale of Goods Act 1979, ss 11 and 14. The value of the consumer's right to reject was stressed by the Law Commission and the Scottish Law Commission in LC 317 and SLC 216, *Consumer Remedies for Faulty Goods* (2009), though they recommended changes that have been implemented in the Consumer Rights Act 2015, esp ss 19 ff.

[36] COM (2008) 614 final, n 22 above, art 28(4).

[37] ibid art 28(1).

[38] Directive 2011/83/EU of the European Parliament and of the Council of 25 October 2011 on consumer rights [2011] OJ L304/64.

[39] ibid art 5.

[40] ibid art 18.

[41] ibid art 20.

[42] ibid art 6.

[43] Compare arts 13–19 of the proposed Common European Sales Law: see below.

[44] eg the second sentence of art 20 of the Directive (n 38 above): 'the risk shall pass to the consumer upon delivery to the carrier if the carrier was commissioned by the consumer to carry the goods and that choice was not offered by the trader, without prejudice to the rights of the consumer against the carrier'. It took me hours to work out what 'choice' is being referred to.

[45] eg ibid art 6(5), which provides that the information that the trader gives under the requirements of the article 'shall form an integral part of the distance or off-premises contract and shall not be altered

## III THE PROPOSED COMMON EUROPEAN SALES LAW

Some time before the Consumer Rights Directive was finally adopted, the European Commission had decided to try to tackle the 'Rome I' problem by a different approach. This was to not to seek further harmonisation of Member States' laws for all 'B2C' transactions, but to create an optional law which could be used for cross-border contracts. The proposed Regulation on a Common European Sales Law (the CESL) would have inserted into each Member State's law a separate set of rules which the parties could choose to use for cross-border contracts instead of the 'pre-existing' or 'domestic' rules. If the parties had chosen the CESL, its rules would have applied to any issues that fell within its scope, not the rules of the 'domestic' law. Most importantly, this included mandatory rules. The CESL contained its own set of mandatory rules for consumer contracts and, within the scope of its application, it is these that would have applied, not the mandatory rules of the 'pre-existing' domestic law. These mandatory rules provided a high level of consumer protection.[46] In an attempt to encourage small and medium-sized enterprises (SMEs) to sell also to businesses in other Member States, the CESL could also have been used for 'B2B' contracts where one of the parties was an SME.[47] For B2B contracts the CESL contained provisions that were designed to protect the SME in ways that many national laws do not, for example by controlling unfair terms that were not individually negotiated.[48]

To be fair, the European Commission made real efforts to produce a well-drafted proposal. It appointed an expert group to produce the first draft of the detailed rules that formed the annex to the Regulation; and this group included two ex-Law Commissioners[49] who were brought onto the group specifically to provide help in drafting. The group met regularly for a year and members did a great deal of work between meetings. I do not claim that the drafting of the proposed text produced by the group[50] was perfect but it was pretty good. Unfortunately, however, the final proposal was less than perfect, for a number of reasons.

First, the rules governing when and how the CESL might be used (often referred to as the 'chapeau' rules), which were set out in the proposed Regulation itself,[51] were

unless the contracting parties expressly agree otherwise'. As the trader has to give information both relating to its own performance (eg the main characteristics of goods to be supplied) and to other people such as the whether the producer of the goods offers a commercial guarantee, the effect in terms of the consumer's rights is very hard to work out. I believe that it is correctly captured by the complex provisions in the Consumer Rights Act 2015, ss 11(4), 12 and 19(3) and (5).

[46] For a consumer contract, art 8(3) of the Regulation provided that the CESL could only be adopted in its entirety: see below, text before n 52.

[47] CESL Reg art 7. Member States would have had an option to allow use of the CESL where neither trader was an SME: Reg art 13(b).

[48] CESL art 86. For the possible advantages of the CESL to SMEs, see H Beale, 'A Common European Sales Law (CESL) for Business-to-Business Contracts' in L Moccia (ed), *The Making of European Private Law: Why, How, What, Who* (Munich, Sellier, 2013) 65.

[49] Professor Eric Clive and myself.

[50] *A European Contract Law for Consumers and Businesses: Publication of the Results of the Feasibility Study Carried out by the Expert Group on European Contract Law for Stakeholders' and Legal Practitioners' Feedback* (May 2011) (hereafter *Feasibility Study*).

[51] The substantive rules were mainly in an annex, though definitions were uncomfortably placed, some in the Regulation and some in the annex. Articles of the Regulation are referred to here as 'Reg art x'; those of the annex as 'art x'.

not circulated in draft to the expert group or stakeholders in advance and contained serious mistakes. For example, article 8(3) of the Regulation provided that *in a B2C contract*, the CESL 'may not be chosen partially, but only in its entirety'. This was to prevent the trader from 'cherry-picking' just those parts of the CESL that might be more favourable to it than the otherwise-applicable law. The obvious implication is that in a B2B contract the CESL could be adopted in part. This would have the unfortunate effect that a trader who was dealing with another business could avoid any provision that it did not like—for example, control over its standard terms—by the simple expedient of including in its standard terms a provision that the relevant article of the CESL should not apply, so effectively rendering the controls nugatory. This was apparently not the Commission's intention[52] and is the sort of error that a better process of drafting would have picked up.

Secondly, and for much the same reason, some of the provisions of the proposed Regulation would have made the CESL risky to use. For example, it applied only to contracts of sales and 'related services', which were narrowly defined and specifically excluded 'telecommunication support services'.[53] Any contract that included other elements was deemed to be a 'mixed purpose' contract and, rather than providing that the CESL would not apply to the elements of the contract other than sales or related services, article 6 of the Regulation provided that the CESL could not be used for mixed purpose contracts. This might well have resulted in a trader who intended to use the CESL to sell sophisticated goods but who offered a 'telephone help-line' finding that the CESL did not apply after all.

Thirdly, when the Commission published its proposal, it emerged that the rules now contained in the annex to the Regulation contained significant changes from what had been proposed by the expert group. Some were changes of policy, which of course is a matter for the Commission, but others were of drafting. Some of them had been discussed with members of the expert group or others, but some apparently had not and again mistakes were made. To give just one example, the *Feasibility Study* contained a rule that when the business takes the initiative of contacting the consumer by telephone with a view to concluding a distance contract, the consumer would not be bound until he or she had received a confirmation from the business and had signed the offer or had sent written consent.[54] This reflects an option given to Member States by the Consumer Rights Directive.[55] In the Commission's

---

[52] Commission officials told me that they thought Reg art 8(3) did not allow a business, even in a B2B contract, to exclude the rules which CESL states are mandatory. They relied on Reg art 1(2), which provided that 'Parties may exclude the application of any of the provisions of the Common European Sales Law, or derogate from or vary their effects, unless otherwise stated in those provisions'. Unfortunately, their interpretation was almost certainly incorrect. Article 1 bit only where there was a provision elsewhere in the CESL making a particular article mandatory. Article 81, which provided that the rules on unfair terms are mandatory, was contained in the chapter on unfair terms. So if the CESL were adopted without that chapter, there would have been nothing to make the rules mandatory and they would have been excluded.

[53] CESL Reg art 2(m).

[54] *Feasibility Study*, n 50 above, art 20(6).

[55] Directive 2011/83/EU of the European Parliament and of the Council of 25 October 2011 on consumer rights [2011] OJ L304/64, art 8(6).

proposal, this was re-drafted to say until the consumer had signed the offer or had sent written consent, the contract would not be 'valid'.[56] It is easy to see that what was intended to be a rule to protect the consumer would have become a trap for consumers who might rely on the contract made over the phone being binding; and this provision did not comply with the Directive.

A last problem was that when the proposal was made, it was published without detailed explanatory notes or 'comments'. Originally the expert group was asked to produce not only articles but 'short comments … In the comments, reporters should state their main sources of inspiration and set out the policy reasons of their choice, as well as illustrations as to how the rule works'.[57] However, partly because the Commission Legal Services pointed out that comments could not form part of any legislation (which can include only Articles and Recitals) and partly because of pressure of time, the Commission did not insist on comments being produced. So neither the *Feasibility Study* nor the proposed CESL itself were accompanied by any commentary save the limited amount that is to be found in the Recitals and the Explanatory Memorandum to the proposal. These are much less detailed than the comments provided in, for example, *The Principles of European Contract Law*[58] or the Explanatory Notes attached to Bills in the United Kingdom. Commission officials found that the lack of comments made it hard to explain to stakeholders and members of the working group in the European Council how the various rules were to work or why certain choices had been made. As a consequence, the life of the expert group was extended so that comments could be produced. Comments were written on many of the chapters and delivered to the Commission. Officials report that they used these comments to help them explain the provisions to stakeholders and the working group, but the comments have not been made public.

To cut a long story short: the CESL proposal was adopted by the European Parliament, subject to a number of (mainly very helpful) amendments, by a substantial majority.[59] However, in the European Council the proposal was much less well received and in December 2014 it was withdrawn by the Commission.[60] There were many reasons for the Council's lack of enthusiasm. Reasons of substance are not relevant here, but I am sure that the weaknesses in drafting and the lack of explanatory comments must have made it harder for Commission officials to convince the Council working group of the merits of the proposal.

---

[56] CESL art 19(4).

[57] EU Commission, *Working Method for the Group of Experts on a Common Frame of Reference in the Area of European Contract Law* (12 May 2010) para 1(b).

[58] O Lando and H Beale (eds), *Principles of European Contract Law*, parts I and II (The Hague, Kluwer, 2000); O Lando, E Clive, A Prüm and R Zimmermann (eds), *Principles of European Contract Law*, part III (The Hague, Kluwer, 2003).

[59] European Parliament legislative resolution of 26 February 2014 on the proposal for a regulation of the European Parliament and of the Council on a Common European Sales Law COM (2011) 0635, C7-0329/2011, 2011/0284 (COD).

[60] European Commission, annex 2 to the Commission Work Programme 2015 COM (2014) 910 final, 12. The Commission announced that it would forward a modified proposal 'to unleash the potential of e-commerce in the digital Single Market.' See also the Commission, A Digital Single Market Strategy for Europe (Communication) COM (2015) 192 final, 4–5; and the questionnaire, Public consultation on contract rules for online purchases of digital content and tangible goods: www.ec.europa.eu/justice/newsroom/contract/opinion/150609_en.htm.

One cannot justly blame the Commission officials responsible for the shortcomings in the proposal. The unit responsible is small and its junior staff turn over regularly, so that although they are very talented people, few of them acquire much experience of drafting or even detailed knowledge of the developing 'European' contract law. They also had to work under great time pressure. It is the system that is at fault.

## IV  THE PROCESS OF CONSULTATION

It is hard not to be critical of the process of consultation that preceded the formal proposal for the CESL. First, the earlier *Action Plan* documents[61] were often in very vague terms. For example, when the Commission proposed the Common Frame of Reference (CFR) it was unclear what form of document it had in mind. Even the group charged with producing the draft CFR was left unsure what was meant by 'fundamental principles', 'definitions' and 'model rules' and how, if at all, these differed from one another.[62] Nor was it clear how the CFR might be used. How would legislators use the 'toolbox' that was asked for? The idea of an 'optional instrument' was left even vaguer even though, as we have seen, this was what ultimately was proposed. Too often, rather than set out clearly the various possibilities, the documents resorted to generalities from which the reader got little idea of what was really intended. That breeds doubt if not suspicion.

Secondly, the timings were askew. The expert group was set up in April 2010,[63] some months before the European Commission published a Green Paper[64] setting out various options. These ranged from merely publishing the results of the work of an expert group,[65] through creating a CFR toolbox in various forms, a Recommendation to Member States on contract law, or an Optional Instrument to, at the extreme, a harmonising Directive on European contract law and even a full-blown European Civil Code. In reality, by the Commission's own account, the only viable options seemed to be a form of toolbox or the optional instrument; but it was not surprising if many stakeholders, and possibly MEPs and members of the Council working group, were unclear as to what the Commission was trying to achieve and therefore inclined to spend a disproportionate amount of time arguing over the basic concept once it emerged.

---

[61]  See n 18 above.

[62]  The task of producing a drafting CFR was given to a so-called Network of Excellence, comprising a number of mainly academic groups: for an account of the process and some of the uncertainties involved, see H Beale, 'European Contract Law: The Common Frame of Reference and Beyond' in C Twigg-Flesner (ed), *The Cambridge Companion to European Union Private Law* (Cambridge, CUP, 2010) 116, 122–29. A first draft was published in 2008 and the DCFR was finalised in 2009, in two forms: an Outline Edition containing just the articles and a full six-volume version containing comments and comparative notes: C von Bar, E Clive and H Schulte-Nölke (eds), *Principles, Definitions and Model Rules of European Private Law: Draft Common Frame of Reference* (Munich, Sellier, 2009).

[63]  Commission Decision of 26 April 2010 setting up the Expert Group on a Common Frame of Reference in the area of European contract law, (2010/233/EU), [2010] OJ L105/109.

[64]  Green Paper on Policy Options for progress towards a European Contract Law for consumers and businesses COM (2010) 348 final.

[65]  See below.

Third, there was too little time for consultation. There was an opportunity to comment on the *Feasibility Study*, but it was only about six weeks. Given the complexity of the questions—for example, the comparison to national law, the 'fit' with national law on questions that were outside the scope of the CESL and therefore still governed by the otherwise applicable law, the difficulty of identifying which matters were 'within' and which 'outside' the scope of the CESL, the meaning and import of new or foreign concepts like the duty of good faith—the time allowed was quite inadequate, especially when no detailed explanation of or comments on the text were made available.

Particularly if a proposal is likely to be controversial, proper groundwork beforehand is essential. The Law Commission methods of setting out clear and usually precise provisional proposals (often developed after informal discussions with stakeholders),[66] and of allowing a reasonable time for responses, is a much better model.

## V THE LEGISLATIVE PROCESS

Some of the problems are undoubtedly caused by the legislative process at the European level. In brief, the 'ordinary legislative process'[67] that enables legislation based on the needs of the Internal Market to be adopted by qualified majority voting is as follows:[68] the Commission makes a proposal to the Parliament and the Council; the Parliament adopts a position at first reading and communicates it to the Council; and if the Council does not approve the European Parliament's position, it shall adopt its position at first reading and communicate it to the European Parliament. Each body must then explain its reasons; and if necessary, a Conciliation Committee is set up to try to reach a common position. At this stage, the Commission should be involved, seeking to reconcile the positions of the European Parliament and the Council. If a joint text is agreed, the European Parliament, acting by a majority of the votes cast, and the Council, acting by a qualified majority, each has a period of six weeks in which to adopt the act in question in accordance with the joint text. If they do not do so, the proposed legislation will fail.

Within the Council, the matter is considered by a Working Group. This reports to the Permanent Representatives Committee (Coreper), which may 'approve the report or may try to negotiate a settlement itself; refer the proposal back to the working party, perhaps with suggestions for a compromise, or pass the matter up to the Council'.[69]

I believe there are at least two problems with these procedures. The first is that once the Commission has made a proposal, it is unable to accept amendments to

---

[66] The European Commission did hold monthly meetings with stakeholders to discuss the work of the expert group as it progressed.

[67] The procedure is set out in art 294 of the Treaty on the Functioning of the EU (TFEU). It was formerly called the 'co-decision procedure'.

[68] See TFEU, art 114.

[69] Council of the EU, 'The Decision-Making Process in the Council', www.consilium.europa.eu/en/council-eu/decision-making/.

it, even to correct mistakes or to remove provisions that are obviously not well received. All the Commission is able to do is to withdraw the proposal and replace it with a new one. The second is, I suspect, that particularly in the Council there may be last-minute proposals for amendments favoured by Member States' representatives and some 'horse-trading'—'we won't oppose your amendment if you won't oppose ours'—and that once an agreement has been reached there is a reluctance to raise questions about the drafting or even workability of the amendments.

How far these problems can be cured I do not know, but it does seem that there would be fewer problems if the initial proposal were better drafted and more fully explained in the documents, whether these be the formal proposal or 'informal' comments or explanatory notes.

## VI THE BETTER REGULATION AGENDA

The European Commission has been working for some time to improve its legislation,[70] and the current Commission has produced a welter of documents on the subject, including a Communication, *Better Regulation for Better Results—An EU Agenda*,[71] a *Proposal for an Inter-institutional Agreement on Better Regulation*,[72] and *Better Regulation Guidelines*.[73] These documents certainly make the right noises. For example, the first document states, under the heading 'Consulting more, listening better':

> First, stakeholders will be able to express their views over the entire lifecycle of a policy. 'Roadmaps' and 'inception impact assessments' will give stakeholders the chance to provide feedback and prompt them for relevant information, right from the very start of work on a new initiative.[74]

It also calls on the European Parliament and the Council to:

> [a]gree that legislation should be comprehensible and clear, allow parties to easily understand their rights and obligations include appropriate reporting, monitoring and evaluation requirements, avoid disproportionate costs, and be practical to implement.[75]

However, the *Better Regulation Guidelines* are primarily concerned with consultation and impact assessments,[76] not the drafting of legislation. And on consultation, the Commission is not proposing anything that seems very radical:

> For the first time the draft texts of delegated acts will be open to the public at large on the Commission's website for four weeks in parallel to the consultation of experts in the Member States. Important implementing acts which are subject to Committee opinion will

---

[70]  eg Commission, 'Better Lawmaking 2005', COM (2006) 289 final.
[71]  COM (2015) 215 final.
[72]  COM (2015) 216 final.
[73]  SWD (2015) 111 final.
[74]  COM (2015) 215 final, 5.
[75]  ibid 8.
[76]  So too the 400-odd pages of the Better Regulation Toolbox, which is primarily concerned with impact assessment.

also be made public for four weeks, allowing stakeholders to submit comments before any vote by Member States in the relevant Committee …

A new 'Lighten the Load—Have Your Say' feature on the Commission's better regulation website will give everyone a chance to air their views and make comments on existing EU laws and initiatives in addition to the formal consultations the Commission undertakes.[77]

The first change seems to be too little and too late in the day, as (as I understand it) national experts are normally consulted on a developed proposal.[78] The second seems to relate more to general comments than to specific proposals of targeted consultation. Neither change seems to come even close to the Law Commission consultation process.

As to amendments, the Commission remarks that '[p]roposals rarely emerge from the legislative process unchanged: amendments are made by the European Parliament and the Council'. However, the Commission seems interested in the substance not the drafting: it calls for impact assessments on substantial amendments.[79] So while we can hope for slightly improved consultation and perhaps better impact assessments,[80] there is little in the documents about drafting save references to existing arrangements—which do not seem to be doing the trick.

## VII COULD THE LAW COMMISSION MODEL HELP?

So the first question is whether the methods developed by the Law Commissions can help. It can be argued that some of the problems I have identified are really matters of drafting, and what is needed is not so much a European Law Commission as a European Office of Parliamentary Counsel that could do the initial drafting and also check the amendments, as and when they are proposed, for workability and fit. And indeed the Commission's Legal Service does have drafting experts, who did look at the *Feasibility Study* for the CESL. However, their input was limited to commenting on existing drafts, whereas one of the great strengths of the Law Commissions is that they have Parliamentary Counsel on whom they can call from the outset and who are involved in the drafting from the start.

When I first went to the Law Commission, I was warned that dealing with Parliamentary Counsel would be difficult. Absolutely all communication would have to be in writing; Commissioners were in no circumstances to draft, but only to state what result they wished to achieve; and the correspondence from Counsel would go something like this: (1) 'You have not told me what it is that you wish to achieve.' (2) 'I don't believe that that is really what you wish to achieve.' (3) 'If that is what you do wish to achieve, you are even more stupid than I thought.' I am happy to

[77] *Better Regulation Guidelines*, n 73 above, 5 and 6.
[78] Though they will also be consulted as part of the so-called Refit Programme, which aims to review existing legislation: see ibid 10–13.
[79] ibid 7–8.
[80] The Law Commissions also found impact assessment to be difficult to do (or get others to carry out) well, at least in my time as a Commissioner.

report that the warnings about the difficulties of the relationship turned out to be completely untrue. Writing instructions did indeed put my ideas to the test; but that was a very good thing. I found Parliamentary Counsel to be extremely helpful, flexible and constructive in any criticism. Working with them was one of the most enjoyable parts of the job. So it is not surprising that I would like officials at the European Commission to have the same kind of benefits of working with skilled draftsmen from the outset, if that could be somehow arranged.

It is not just drafting that is the issue, however. Whoever is to draft must be given adequate instructions. The kind of vagueness that infused some of the indications given to the expert group working on the draft of the CESL are surmountable when the expert group has members as experienced, wise and determined as Professor Eric Clive: the Commission would be pinned down very effectively. But not every group has such members. Even then, we were not always successful in discovering what it was the Commission thought, nor even in articulating why the expert group itself adopted a particular approach rather than another. The worst of all is when the Commission drafts its own provisions, apparently starting to draft without first settling the detail of the policy and the reasoning for it—tempting, as I know to my cost in helping to develop *The Principles of European Contract Law*, but very unwise. It is vital to have critics to look at, analyse and help to articulate the policy before turning it into legislative words. I strongly suspect that failure to do this was one reason why the 'chapeau' rules of the proposed Regulation on the CESL were so unsatisfactory.

However, with the Consumer Rights Directive and the CESL I think the problems lay even further back. If we assume acceptance of the broad aim, namely to improve the functioning of the Internal Market by reducing or removing differences between the laws of the Member States, there are still fundamental questions on which there should be much more detailed consultation than was ever carried out. What are the real legal hindrances? Is it really general contract law, or is it other legal issues affecting contracts but springing from other sources, such as different rules on how goods must be labelled, what kind of selling arrangements are permitted and indeed, with products like insurance, what cover is mandatory and what provisions are forbidden by national legislation? The *Communication on Contract Law* of 2001 did not identify the various different kinds of hindrance, and as a consequence many of the responses were also imprecise. Then, if general contract law is identified as a real hindrance, surely it would make sense to consult on whether the best solution is full harmonisation or an optional instrument, rather than go straight to legislative proposals, first on one approach and then on the other, with both ultimately failing. And once the preferred approach has been identified, surely there should be detailed consultation on how the instrument will work (eg how it fits with the requirements of the Rome I Regulation—many commentators were unsure that the Commission's proposal in this respect would work)[81] as well as on the substantive content and the drafting.

---

[81] eg S Whittaker, 'The Proposed "Common European Sales Law": Legal Framework and the Agreement of the Parties' (2012) 75 *MLR* 578.

Thus it would be much better were there to be a body to which the European Commission could entrust the task of consulting and drawing up proposals.

## VIII  A EUROPEAN LAW COMMISSION?

There are legitimate questions about how appropriate it would be for a 'Law Commission-type' body to be given the task I have described. On the one hand, the new body might appear to be no more than a servant of the Commission, wholly lacking in independence. However, the experience in the United Kingdom, described in other chapters in this volume, is that with care it is possible to work on tasks set by government and yet remain independent.[82] To use the stock phrase, 'they can tell us what to think about but they can't tell us what to think'. Conversely, the European Commission might feel that to entrust the development of legislative proposals, even on private law issues, to an independent body would weaken the Commission's own authority. Again our experience is that while government will always keep some topics to itself, there is much valuable work that can be done by an independent body. After all, the European Commission would have no obligation to accept any recommendations.

Is a 'European Law Commission' feasible? I think it is clear that the current European Commission, with its 'lean' approach, would refuse to sanction the establishment of a new physical institution, for budgetary and political reasons. The needs for flexibility to cover the wide range of potential subjects and for the ability to deal with 30 or more legal systems would require a large staff. That is out of the question. An institution of that kind is not what I have in mind. Rather, I am thinking of a network of scholars, judges and practitioners on whose expertise the Commission could draw as required. Judging by the enthusiasm I find among my colleagues in the field of 'European private law', much of the work would be done voluntarily. There would certainly be some cost: travelling and accommodation expenses for each project would have to be reimbursed, and a small central secretariat would be needed to co-ordinate things. I have not done the sums, but I suspect the cost—for the whole of Europe—would be no more than the costs of the Law Commissions in just the United Kingdom, and might well be less.

## IX  THE EUROPEAN LAW INSTITUTE

There is a possible candidate for this role already, the European Law Institute (ELI) that was established in 2011.[83] It now has a membership of over 1,000 individuals— judges, practitioners and academics from all over the EU, with the United Kingdom providing the fourth-largest national group—as well as 60 individual observers and 88 institutional observers. The secretariat is based in the University of Vienna, which

---

[82] See, eg, chapters 9 (Sir Terence Etherton), 16 (William Binchy) and 27 (Stephen Lewis).
[83] I should immediately declare an interest: I was one of the founder members and am currently a member of the ELI Council.

has provided a very generous subsidy. The first president was Sir Francis Jacobs, former Advocate-General of the Court of Justice; the current president is Diana Wallis, a solicitor who was for many years an MEP, ultimately having become Vice-President of the Parliament and being very active in the Legal Affairs Committee.

The ELI's website sets out its aims in the form of a manifesto, which is worth quoting:

> The European Law Institute (ELI) is an independent non-profit organisation established to initiate, conduct and facilitate research, make recommendations and provide practical guidance in the field of European legal development. Building on the wealth of diverse legal traditions, its mission is the quest for better law-making in Europe and the enhancement of European legal integration. By its endeavours, ELI seeks to contribute to the formation of a more vigorous European legal community, integrating the achievements of the various legal cultures, endorsing the value of comparative knowledge, and taking a genuinely pan-European perspective. As such its work covers all branches of the law: substantive and procedural; private and public.
>
> Among ELI's core tasks are:
>
> — to evaluate and stimulate the development of EU law, legal policy, and practice, and in particular make proposals for the further development of the acquis and for the enhancement of EU law implementation by the Member States;
> — to identify and analyse legal developments in areas within the competence of Member States which are relevant at the EU level;
> — to study EU approaches regarding international law and enhance the role EU law could play globally, for instance in drafting international instruments or model rules;
> — to conduct and facilitate pan-European research, in particular to draft, evaluate or improve principles and rules which are common to the European legal systems; and
> — to provide a forum, for discussion and cooperation, of jurists irrespective of their vocation or occupation, inter alia academics, judges, lawyers and other legal professionals, who take an active interest in European legal development and together represent a broad range of legal traditions.
>
> To accomplish its tasks, ELI operates on its own initiative. It is also, however, available for consultation by institutions involved in the development of law on a European, international or national level. As its perspective is not limited to the European experience, ELI is ready to seek cooperation with Non-European or international organisations such as the American Law Institute or UNIDROIT.[84]

A good indicator of the kind of assistance that I think that the ELI could provide is the working group it established to prepare a statement on the proposed CESL. The group, which was chaired by Lord Thomas of Cwmgiedd,[85] produced a *Statement on the Proposal for a Regulation on a Common European Sales Law*,[86] and two Supplements: a response to the European Parliament's proposed amendments to the

---

[84] ELI, 'About ELI' www.europeanlawinstitute.eu/about-eli/.
[85] Lord Thomas is currently the Lord Chief Justice of England and Wales.
[86] ELI, *Statement on the Proposal for a Regulation on a Common European Sales Law* (2012).

CESL,[87] and a response to the Commission's announcement, noted earlier,[88] that it will make a 'modified proposal in order to fully unleash the potential of e-commerce in the Digital Single Market'.[89]

The *Statement on the Proposal for a Regulation on a Common European Sales Law* is a very valuable critique of the proposal, and particularly of the 'chapeau' rules that were contained in the proposed Regulation itself. The Legal Affairs Committee of the European Parliament, which prepared the report ultimately adopted by the Parliament, relied heavily on the Statement and adopted many of its recommendations. I only wish that the ELI had been set up earlier, so that it could have commented on the *Feasibility Study* and could have been consulted by the Commission over the 'chapeau' rules before the formal proposal for a Regulation was made. But the question with which I end this chapter is whether the European Commission can be persuaded to delegate future projects to the ELI, much as government departments delegate them to the Law Commissions, so that it would be the ELI that would consult and make recommendations, preferably including draft legislation.

It seems certain that this cannot be achieved in the near future. First, some members of the ELI might be concerned about the body becoming 'too close' to the European Commission and losing its independence. Recently the ELI was told by the European Commission that an ELI project on European family and succession law may be awarded a grant under the Justice Programme,[90] and the project has also been included in a three-year framework agreement between the ELI and the European Commission (operating grant) under which the ELI hopes to receive funds also for 2016 and 2017. Though most members seemed to welcome this news, there were some who doubted that we should be accepting grants from the Commission. Secondly and more importantly, the ELI would first have to win the trust of the European Commission—and indeed, to be fully effective, of the Parliament and the Council. It would have to be trusted not only to do a competent job but also to do it impartially and quickly.

Speed is a problem. As we have seen with the new European Commission led by Mr Juncker, new Commissioners arrive with new or revised ideas, and they will want them implemented within their five-year term of office. Given the slowness of the legislative procedure, there will be little time for consultation and drafting—two or three years at most. So the ELI would not be able to adopt the measured pace that has characterised some Law Commission projects! But the Law Commissions are able to carry out projects quickly when the need arises, provided that the necessary resources are available; and the ELI ought to be able to achieve equally good outcomes.

---

[87] ELI, *First Supplement: Response to the EP Legislative Resolution of 26 February 2014* (2014).
[88] See n 60 above.
[89] *Second Supplement: Unlocking the Digital Single Market—An Instrument for 21st Century Europe* (2015). I was a member of the group that drew up this second supplement.
[90] Justice Programme, call for proposals JUST/2014/JCOO/AG/CIVI.

But the first thing is to build up trust in the ELI as competent and independent in the way that the Law Commissions are independent of government. The Statements on the CESL produced by the working party chaired by Lord Thomas have made an excellent start; and there are signs that the Commission wants to work with the group at an earlier stage of developing its new proposals for rules on contracts for online purchases of digital content and tangible goods.[91] So I am hopeful. Please watch this space!

---

[91] See n 60 above.

# 25

# *How Law Commissions Work: Some Lessons from the Past*

DAVID JOHNSTON

Many of the chapters in this volume are the fruit of long exposure to, and experience of, the tasks of law reform. This chapter, by contrast, is written after only six months' experience as a Law Commissioner. That makes for a change of perspective, since it is perhaps closer to a view from the outside than the inside. For a new Commissioner embarking on a project of law reform, it is clearly important to think about how projects have been carried out in the past and what can be learned from their success or lack of success. That is the modest aim of the present chapter.

It is necessary to restrict the material under scrutiny. All that can be provided here is a case study, which identifies some points that have emerged in the course of a current law reform project and, more tentatively, some of their wider implications. It is right, of course, to acknowledge that the conclusions derived from one case study may not be universal: different projects may call for different approaches.

It is obvious that one of the key challenges in achieving implementation of a law reform project is securing the political will to carry legislation forward. That is not discussed here. It can be taken for granted that a Law Commission needs to do what it can to develop and maintain good relations with Ministers and their officials and with those who schedule parliamentary business. This chapter, however, is mainly concerned with narrower but still important issues about the process of consultation and in particular the nature and scope of consultation papers and reports.

There is another important area which is not considered here, on the assumption that others will deal with it. When we consult nowadays we need to be thinking as much as possible about how to engage the public by using electronic communication and social media. It is direct, effective, economical and may be relatively undemanding for consultees. The points that follow about more traditional forms of consultation and publication need to be read with this gloss in mind.

## I  A CASE STUDY

The case study derives from a law reform project which began in 2015. It is concerned with possible reform of various aspects of the law of prescription, a term used in Scots law for what English law calls limitation of actions. The law is set out in the Prescription and Limitation (Scotland) Act 1973, which derives from one of the Scottish Law Commission's earliest reports.[1]

It is an area which seems promising as a case study. Why? Because this is the third time that the Scottish Law Commission has travelled over this terrain. That allows us to ask: what can we learn from our previous endeavours? It is true that Hegel declared that peoples and governments have never learned anything from history.[2] But that need not deter us from continuing to try.

In the project, one of the aspects under consideration is whether there is need for reform of the law about when the prescriptive period starts to run in claims for damage that was initially latent (eg defects in buildings which only emerge long after the buildings were completed). Most legal systems have some kind of so-called 'discoverability' provision which postpones the start of the prescriptive or limitation period until the claimant knew or ought to have known certain facts. Views differ on which facts are relevant for this purpose. In Scotland the issue is topical, since as a result of a decision in the UK Supreme Court in 2014 the general understanding about the knowledge relevant to discoverability has changed, and judgments in that case mention that this is an issue that the Scottish Law Commission might revisit.[3]

Even at this early stage the current project prompts some thoughts about issues that may be relevant to the general theme of the session of the conference in which it was presented, which was entitled 'How Law Commissions Work'. Here are six points.

First, in the background to the 1973 Act the initial consultation document issued by the Scottish Law Commission was entitled *Memorandum No 9: Prescription and Limitation of Actions*.[4] It is concerned with wholesale reform of the law of prescription and limitation of actions but nonetheless extends to only around 80 pages. Perhaps slightly oddly, the body of the memorandum does not make it very clear what those who read it are meant to do with it. But at the top of the first page there is a marginal note which says: 'NB This Memorandum is designed to elicit comments upon and criticism of the proposals which it contains. It does not represent the concluded views of the Scottish Law Commission.' It ends not with questions for consultees but with what are described as 'provisional proposals'.[5]

Second, the report which followed in 1970 is 75 pages long. It records that 23 organisations and 11 individuals had commented on the memorandum.[6] So far as discoverability is concerned, it is very brief: it does not spell out the various options; it does not consider the position in any other legal system; and it states only that 'the period should run from the date when the damage is, or could reasonably have been, ascertained by the aggrieved party'.[7] It does not contain a draft Bill.

---

[1] Scottish Law Commission, SLC 15, *Report on Reform of the Law Relating to Prescription and Limitation of Actions* (1970).

[2] GWF Hegel, *Lectures on the Philosophy of World History* (HB Nisbet tr, Cambridge, CUP, 1975) 21.

[3] *David T Morrison v ICL Plastics Ltd* [2014] UKSC 48, 2014 SC (UKSC) 222, [101] (Lord Hodge); cf [31] (Lord Reed).

[4] SLC Memorandum 9 (1968).

[5] ibid 58–67.

[6] SLC 15, n 1 above, annex A.

[7] ibid para 97.

Third, following enactment of the 1973 Act the issue of latent damage gave rise to various Scottish cases dealing with precisely what knowledge fell within the statutory provision on discoverability. More generally, the wider policy issues had attracted attention following the well-known English case of *Pirelli General Cable Works Ltd v Oscar Faber & Partners*.[8] That led in England to the enactment of the Latent Damage Act 1986. There was no legislation in Scotland, but the issue was referred back to the Scottish Law Commission for consideration. It published a consultative memorandum in 1987.[9] This memorandum contains both provisional proposals and questions for consultees. They are set out in a rather elaborate way, which makes it difficult to be precise even about how many questions there actually are—probably about ten main ones. The memorandum was followed by a report in 1989.[10] In this report there is a much fuller discussion of the various difficulties that had arisen in interpreting the relevant sub-section of the 1973 Act.[11] The Commission also observes that it is questionable whether the drafting of the sub-section accurately reflected the policy that the Commission had set out in its 1970 report.[12]

The 1989 report contains a draft Bill complete with explanatory notes. It also records that 23 organisations and nine individuals had submitted written comments.[13] Among those commenting were organisations representing insurers, architects, civil engineers, chartered surveyors, building employers and local authorities.

Fourth, the 1989 report has never been implemented. Some of its proposals gave rise to concerns, notably in the construction industry, with the result that the government was unwilling to take the proposals forward.

Fifth, it is worth moving out of Scotland for a moment but staying with the same subject-matter and comparing the style of a more modern consultation document, the Law Commission's 1998 consultation paper on limitation of actions.[14] It runs to 456 pages. There is an extremely full discussion of the various options and permutations for reform of the core limitation regime.

Another striking feature of that paper, with which we are nowadays familiar, is the extensive use of comparative material. That did not feature to any marked extent in the earlier Scottish Law Commission publications. The use of comparative material, however, is hardly a novelty: in the fifth century BC, for the purposes of compiling the Twelve Tables, the Romans allegedly sent a delegation to Athens to study the laws of Solon.[15] That was just one foreign system. In the modern day our preference is to study many different systems. Chapter 10 of the Law Commission of England and Wales' 1998 consultation paper consists of a remarkably lengthy but very useful survey of comparative legal material. It extends to 60 pages.[16] In recent times the

---

[8] *Pirelli General Cable Works Ltd v Oscar Faber & Partners* [1983] 2 AC 1 (HL).
[9] Scottish Law Commission, SLC Memorandum 74, *Prescription and Limitation of Actions (Latent Damage)* (1987).
[10] Scottish Law Commission, SLC 122, *Report on Prescription and Limitation of Actions (Latent Damage and Other Related Issues)* (1989).
[11] Prescription and Limitation (Scotland) Act 1973, s 11(3).
[12] SLC 122, n 10 above, para 2.8.
[13] ibid app B.
[14] Law Commission, LC CP 151, *Limitation of Actions* (1998).
[15] D.1.2.2.4, Pomponius, libro singulari enchiridii.
[16] LC CP 151, n 14 above, 180–240.

Scottish Law Commission too has come to make much greater use of comparative material, but it has never taken quite such an expansive approach to reporting on it in its publications.

Sixth, the 1998 paper was followed by a report in 2001. The same fate of non-implementation which had struck down the Scottish report of 1989 befell this report too.[17]

## II DIAGNOSIS

Does anything of wider significance emerge from these points? There are perhaps lessons to be drawn bearing on two main issues. First, effective engagement of interested parties in the process of consultation. Second, the content of Law Commission consultation papers and reports.

### A  Engagement in Consultation

Each of the Scottish consultation exercises just mentioned attracted about 30 responses (the English one attracted many more). That is not overwhelming but neither is it embarrassingly slight. Equally, the consultations evidently reached those with a particular interest in the issues, notably professionals in the construction industry.

The 1968 consultation and 1970 report were successful, inasmuch as they led to implementing legislation. The 1989 report was not and did not. Given the consultation that was carried out, it cannot be said that the Commission failed to engage with the right interested parties. In fact we know why the government decided not to proceed with the recommendations of the 1989 report, and this is quite instructive.

The construction industry strongly disagreed with the Commission's proposals on structuring the prescriptive period in relation to latent damage claims. It advocated something along the lines of what the Latent Damage Act 1986 had introduced for England. In particular it insisted that a long-stop prescription, which would cut off claims regardless of the claimant's knowledge of the facts, should run either from the date of the defendant's act or omission or else from the date of completion of the construction works. Both the industry and the Commission were content that an appropriate period for the long-stop was 15 years (which is the same as under the Latent Damage Act 1986). But the Commission maintained that the starting date ought to be the date on which loss had occurred as a result of the act or omission. There was a second issue. The Commission had considered whether the law prohibiting parties from entering into agreements purporting to lengthen the prescriptive periods should be revisited. It took the view that the prohibition should be retained.[18] The consequence was that there was no means

[17] Law Commission, LC 270, *Report on Limitation of Actions* (2001).
[18] SLC 122, n 10 above, paras 4.72–90.

for parties to employ an agreement in order to find their way round difficulties they might perceive in the starting date for the long-stop prescription. Ultimately in 1995 the government took the view that in these circumstances it could not take the recommendations forward.

It may be instructive to notice the Commission's reasons for holding to its recommendation on the appropriate starting date for the long-stop prescription. The report twice refers to the 'conceptual problem' and once to the 'conceptual difficulties' of having a long-stop prescription which could expire before the claimant's right had become actionable.[19] With the benefit of hindsight, it seems justifiable to assess this analysis and concern about conceptual problems as unfortunate. In general, while legal scholars rightly attach significance to the analytical and structural integrity of the law, they cannot expect those working in practice or in industry to be so impressed by it. Apart from this, there was no inevitability that conceptual problems would arise. Whether that was the case or not would depend on how the law was structured. It is, for example, possible to establish a rule that states that there is a maximum period within which a claim must be made, for instance 15 years from the date of an act or omission.[20] This involves a judgement about fairness and an assessment of whether a rule of that kind represents an appropriate balance between the interests of claimant and defendant. But it does not appear to involve conceptual difficulty.

What about the position in England? It is clear from the Law Commission's 2001 report on limitation of actions just how extensive their consultation exercise was; and indeed in 2002 the then government accepted the recommendations in principle. It was only in 2009 that the government of the day announced that following what was described as 'a recent consultation with key stakeholders' it had been demonstrated 'that there are insufficient benefits and potentially large-scale costs associated with the reform'. These were not further specified, but the result was clear: the government would not be taking the recommendations forward.[21]

Nowadays it is normal practice to carry out an impact assessment and to publish it with the report. (This was not the case as early as 2001.) The assessment addresses the costs and benefits of a proposed reform. From the point of view of implementation, it is no doubt as important as the soundness of the proposals for reform as a matter of law. It will be interesting to see in due course whether reports backed up by a thorough impact assessment fare better in terms of implementation.[22]

[19]  ibid paras 3.28, 3.31 and 3.33.

[20]  That is what happens under the Latent Damage Act 1986; and that is the approach set out in the Draft Common Frame of Reference III-7:307, where the maximum period is 10 years (30 years for personal injuries claims).

[21]  HC Deb 19 November 2009, Vol 501, col 13 WS (Bridget Prentice): 'The draft Bill will not now include provisions to reform the law of limitation of actions. These provisions were based on a Law Commission report of 2001. But a recent consultation with key stakeholders has demonstrated that there are insufficient benefits and potentially large-scale costs associated with the reform. In addition, the courts have remedied some of the most significant difficulties with the law that the Law Commission identified, for example, in relation to the limitation aspects of child abuse cases. The limitation reforms will therefore not now be taken forward.'

[22]  It is still early to draw firm conclusions on this point: the Scottish Law Commission appears first to have provided an impact assessment in 2010; and the Law Commission a couple of years earlier.

In the case of the 2001 report, in the absence of further information about the precise grounds on which the recommendations were not taken forward, all one may infer is that that outcome does not appear to reflect any deficiency in consultation or engagement with those affected. While a lack of engagement with those interested must carry a high risk that a project will not be implemented, engagement is itself no guarantee of success. Since parliamentary time is always short and the government's own legislative programme always takes priority, effective lobbying by those who do not support the policy aims of a law reform Bill may be enough to delay or impede implementation.

## B  Content of Commission Consultation Papers and Reports

What actually needs to be in a consultation paper or a report? We can approach the question from different perspectives. First, that of the consultation exercise. Second, that of the Commission seeking to advance the cause of implementation. Third, jumping ahead to the position after implementation, that of the lawyer or judge trying to construe the statute.

All four of the Scottish Law Commission publications mentioned earlier were, by contemporary standards, brief, even though they were dealing with many and complex issues. There is a lot to be said for brevity, which is the soul of wit. But can it perhaps go too far? The answer is surely 'yes'.

In its 1970 report the Scottish Law Commission actually did—in one sentence—clearly state its policy intention that time should start to run against a claimant once he or she knew or ought to have known of the fact of loss or damage (and nothing more). That is precisely what the UK Supreme Court decided in 2014 that the relevant sub-section meant. But in the previous 30 years or so, the Scottish courts had headed down an entirely different interpretative route. Probably there is no single explanation for that, but the following point may be important, namely that even if the single sentence in the 1970 report was clear, it was only a single sentence, easily missed. It would have been easy to miss because the report did not discuss what the various options were or articulate the reasoning for the particular policy choice. It may not even have been obvious that a choice had been made at all. So in this instance it might have been better for the report to say more. But how much more?

Nowadays perhaps we sometimes say too much more. The examples mentioned from Scotland are not particularly recent. As already noted, recent practice there and elsewhere has been to produce much longer and much more elaborate consultation papers and reports. There may be a tendency to overburden publications with fine points of analysis appropriate for academic monographs. That in turn may discourage or deter some who might otherwise engage with a consultation exercise.

Take—purely as an example—comparative law. For the purposes of a consultation exercise, it is clearly valuable (perhaps almost essential) for the Law Commissions themselves to have a broad understanding of how other legal systems deal with the same issues. It is useful and important for the purpose of informing the Commissions about options that have been tried more or less successfully elsewhere, and to limit the extent to which the wheel has to be reinvented. But it is far from obvious that the public at large (or the slightly smaller segment of the public who respond to consultations) needs to be burdened with all this material. Why is it there? It may well be that for the purposes of consultation little more is needed than a footnote about how things are done elsewhere.

It might reasonably be asked: does including this material do any harm? If not, why not just continue with the practice? Without advocating myopia, far less chauvinism, as the optimal path to reform of the law, one should perhaps recognise that there is a cost to comparative exercises in terms of resources. And there must also be a concern that, the more Law Commission publications become burdened with complexity, whether this derives from comparative law or elsewhere, the less it is possible to engage busy practitioners and members of the wider public in responding to consultation exercises.

There is a related point. Law Commission papers are rightly valued by those in legal practice and (no doubt) in the judiciary. Rightly, because of the thoroughness of the research on which they are based. This is invaluable, especially in areas teeming with arcane and seemingly inconsistent case law—an obvious example is the extraordinarily helpful Law Commission publications in the field of unjust enrichment.[23] But it is important always to focus on the purpose that Law Commission publications should serve. They should not be directed primarily, perhaps even at all, at seeking to resolve every point of legal controversy in the way that an academic work might. Nor should it be one of their main functions to provide practitioners with short cuts when carrying out legal research for their cases.

It is clearly vital that the high standards of Law Commission publications should be maintained, and that the views and proposals expressed in them should be soundly based on a grasp as complete as possible of all relevant law and policy. But it is surely not necessary to show all the working. Since in any project of law reform detailed research does need to be carried out, it may be that the best way of presenting it, providing the necessary underpinning for the Commission's proposals, and demonstrating that they are based on rigorous scrutiny of the law and the options for reform, would be to publish it separately. The possibility of online publication makes this straightforward.

From the perspective of the consultation exercise, the touchstone seems to be that a consultation paper should spell out sufficiently what the policy options are and the main consequences which are thought to flow from adopting one or another. A report, on the other hand, will need to spell out sufficiently the policy issues that arise and the reasons for the ultimate policy recommendation. In order to optimise the prospects for implementation within a reasonable period, it will no doubt also

---

[23] eg Law Commission, LC CP 120, *Restitution of Payments Made under a Mistake of Law* (1991); LC CP 227, *Restitution: Mistakes of Law and Ultra Vires Public Authority Receipts and Payments* (1994); Scottish Law Commission, SLC DP 95, *Recovery of Benefits Conferred under Error of Law* (1993); SLC DP 99, *Judicial Abolition of the Error of Law Rule and its Aftermath* (1996); SLC DP 100, *Recovery of Ultra Vires Public Authority Receipts and Disbursements* (1996); SLC 169, *Unjustified Enrichment, Error of Law and Public Authority Receipts and Disbursements* (1999). See further chapters 17 (Laura Dunlop) and 20 (Andrew Burrows).

be necessary for the report to convince government that the consultation has been extensive and thorough, and that the policy options have been adequately considered, balanced and assessed. It is far from clear that much more is required. It is, as the example of the single sentence in the 1970 report was intended to demonstrate, possible to say too little. But it is equally evident that it is possible to say so much that consultees lose the will to comment.

We can look at the same question from another perspective, when implementing legislation has followed on a Law Commission report.

Here too it is interesting to note how much has changed since the time of the Scottish publications mentioned earlier. Back in 1970 or even 1989 nobody in the Law Commission would have imagined that the courts would deploy Law Commission publications as an aid to interpreting legislation. Since *Pepper v Hart*[24] and many other subsequent cases, nobody can be in any doubt that they often will. Indeed, from the mass of extraneous material that the courts are now willing to consider, Law Commission publications must be among the most welcome, precisely because of their thoroughness and quality.

Statutory interpretation is frequently difficult. This is nothing new. The Roman jurists wrote quite a lot about it.[25] More recently, the key issue is captured in a single sentence from Hobbes, in his chapter 'Of civill lawes' in *Leviathan*:

> The written Laws, if they be short, are easily mis-interpreted, from the divers significations of a word, or two; if long, they be more obscure by the diverse significations of many words: in so much as no written Law, delivered in few, or many words, can be well understood, without a perfect understanding of the finall causes, for which the Law was made; the knowledge of which finall causes is in the Legislator.[26]

Perhaps the most valuable and thought-provoking point that this passage makes is that making statutes longer, more detailed or more elaborate does not entail that their meaning becomes clearer. The opposite may well be true. We cannot draft our way out of obscurity simply by drafting more. But the position of a person seeking to construe legislation would be much improved if he or she had an underlying Law Commission report which clearly articulated the relevant policy issues and the reasons for the ultimate policy recommendation.

It would, of course, be odd to say that the Law Commissions should in what they publish have at the forefront of their minds the question of statutory construction of eventual legislation following upon hypothetical implementation of their reports.[27] But—unlike the concerns mentioned earlier—if they did, it is difficult to see that that would distract them at all from their core functions. Quite the reverse. It would lead

---

[24] *Pepper v Hart* [1993] AC 593 (HL).

[25] Justinian's Digest preserves numerous observations on statutory interpretation. Some are concerned with the construction of particular statutes, such as the lex Aquilia (D.9.2). In addition, D.1.3 contains general observations on statutory interpretation, including such things as the impossibility of drafting a statute that does not require any interpretation (D.1.3.10–13); the dichotomy between literal and purposive construction (D.1.3.17); and the need to read statutes as a whole (D.1.3.24).

[26] T Hobbes, *Leviathan* (1651, repr New York, Penguin, 1968) 143.

[27] See too chapter 38 (Matthew Dyson).

them to articulate precisely the aims of the legislation; and Commission publications would explain, against the background of various possible policy options, why certain paths were rejected and particular policy recommendations were advanced. That in turn might inform the judges' understanding of what Hobbes calls the final causes for which a law was made.

There is a further point. At the moment it is normal practice in the United Kingdom for Law Commission reports to contain draft Bills. That does not happen everywhere, and so it is clearly possible to operate under a different system. Resource issues may no doubt place some strain on the practicability of always having a draft Bill to accompany a report. But, if at all possible, it is an extremely valuable—perhaps even a vital—element in the overall process. Again we may identify two different perspectives.

The first is that of the Commissioners, reviewing and signing off a report. Can there actually be a better means of close scrutiny of legislative proposals than seeing whether it is possible to encapsulate them in clear statutory language? That seems unlikely. This can be an extraordinarily valuable way of testing whether proposals appear to be workable.

The second perspective is that of the person seeking to construe the statute. A draft Bill can be a valuable tool for purposes of statutory construction. Recall the earlier example of the 1970 report, which did not contain a draft Bill. In its 1989 report, as already mentioned, the Commission doubted whether the implementing Act had correctly reflected the Commission's policy intentions. Had the report contained a draft Bill, that uncertainty might have been less likely to occur. As it is, if one finds a point of interpretative uncertainty in the 1973 Act, it is not always easy to link the terms of the Commission report with the way in which the Act is drafted. That seems unfortunate. Given the amount of detailed legal and policy work that goes into the production of a Law Commission report, it would surely always be preferable to have a draft Bill which made it possible to identify how the Commission crystallised its policy views and proposals in the crisp language of statute.

A final point is this: providing a draft Bill along with the report is an obvious strategy for seeking to smooth the path towards implementation of a Commission report. Without a draft Bill the report may simply take its place at the back of a long queue of drafting instructions to Parliamentary Counsel. With the Bill there must be at least a possibility that the report may move towards implementation at a brisker pace. Accordingly, in order for a Commission to fulfil its law reform promise, it is vital that it should enjoy proper support and resource for legislative drafting.

### III CONCLUSIONS

From this short case study we can draw the following main conclusions about conducting a law reform project with an eye to legislative implementation. Some of the points may perhaps resonate further.

First, it is crucial to engage closely with those directly interested in the subject-matter of a project. It is essential to understand the costs and benefits associated with proposals. It is important to be open-minded about the mechanisms that can be deployed to achieve practical improvement in the working of the law. Conversely, it is crucial not to be wedded to a Platonic form of legal purity if this stands in the way of practical workability.

Second, the optimal means of engaging with the interested public may well be to conduct rigorous research within the Commission but, at the stage of publication, to spell out only as much as is required in order to show the range of policy options and the main consequences that might flow from choosing one or another. This kind of focused consultation seems to stand the best chance of engaging, yet not overburdening, the interested public. A report, on the other hand, in order to maximise the prospects for implementation, will need to spell out sufficiently the policy issues that arise, the reasons for the ultimate policy recommendations, and it will need to make a cogent case for implementation. This is likely as a rule to require the preparation of detailed background research papers. If so, these papers too should be made available. But the emphasis should be on 'background': it should not be taken for granted that the product of this research has a place in the final report.

As noted at the outset, the views set out here have been shaped by only six months' experience as a Law Commissioner. Since the term of appointment is five years, there is plenty of time to learn more from the past about how best to reform the law in the future.

# 26

# Challenges for Independent Law Reformers from Changing External Priorities and Shorter Timescales

SIR JACK BEATSON[*]

## I SETTING THE SCENE

In this chapter, I seek to identify the challenges to Law Commissions that arise from changing external priorities and shorter timescales, and possible ways of addressing them. I hope I will be forgiven if, before turning to my topic, I set the context by reference to my own experience. I was a member of the Law Commission, the Commission with responsibility for the law of England and Wales,[1] although a number of the projects I was involved with were joint projects with the Scottish Law Commission.[2] I arrived at the Commission, then based at Conquest House, partly overlooking the leafy gardens of Gray's Inn, in July 1989. It is over two decades since, after five happy years, I left. But I venture to suggest that my experience is not only of historical interest.

After I left the Commission, at first I followed its work, particularly the projects I had started, such as those on contracts for the benefit of third parties and damages for personal injuries. I tried, and I hope that I succeeded, in helping where asked without stepping on the toes of my successors. But I did not have occasion to consider the Law Commission as an institution until early in 2012. Sir James Munby, then Chairman, had recently given his Denning Lecture.[3] His characteristic cheerfulness and ebullience were well hidden, and the lecture was rather depressing

[*] I am very grateful to Sir David Lloyd Jones for information about the current work of the Law Commission, and to those who contributed to the discussion at the panel at which I spoke, in particular Laura Dunlop QC and Sir Peter North.

[1] For the growing importance of the impact of devolution to Wales on the work of the Law Commission, see D Lloyd Jones, 'The Law Commission and the Implementation of Law Reform', Sir William Dale Annual Lecture (2012) (a revised and updated version of Sir David's Lecture has since been published: (2013) 94 *Amicus Curiae* 2) and Law Commission and Welsh Ministers, *Protocol between the Welsh Ministers and the Law Commission* (2015), Gen-LD10290.

[2] The statutory names of the three Law Commissions in the UK are the Law Commission, the Scottish Law Commission and the Northern Ireland Law Commission. The Northern Irish Commission was in substance 'mothballed' in April 2015: see chapter 5 (Neil Faris).

[3] J Munby, 'Shaping the Law—the Law Commission at the Crossroads', Denning Lecture (2011). See chapter 9 (Sir Terence Etherton).

to read. I wondered whether, despite the measures introduced by the Law Commission Act 2009 (the 2009 Act) and the invaluable work of the Commissions for almost half a century, in this country their time had run out. Would the Law Commission succumb to something similar to what public lawyers describe as 'regulatory capture'; effective control by those to whom the Commission was supposed to give independent advice? Would it become an outsourced research contractor for departments, which might be inclined or driven to take a short-term view of the needs of an area of the law and with some priorities reflecting the idea that legislation is enacted 'to send a message' rather than to change the law?[4] Would the Commission turn to clarifying the law by reports whose effect is likely to be as part of the rationale for doctrinal change by the courts, for example by the production of non-legislative restatements of an area, as one former Commissioner has been doing?[5] These can be valuable adjuncts to law reform by legislation,[6] but are unlikely to be seen as justifying the existence of a statutory body.

The picture drawn by Sir James was depressing because there remains a real need for a body which takes a long-term view when keeping our law under review and making proposals to modernise it, which become law rather than functioning as influential but not authoritative. We certainly need a mechanism to deal with crises which need to be addressed urgently. That is sometimes done by single-issue inquiries led by a judge or other public figure, and can sometimes be appropriately undertaken by a Law Commission. But we also need another type of body. We need one which is not buffeted by fashion and political pressure and which is concerned with having a principled and coherent body of law. It must be able to: (a) take on large and ambitious projects with social implications; (b) recommend legislative steps towards codification of an area; and (c) critically examine whether technical areas which may seem as dry as dust to the political and administrative classes are in fact 'fit for purpose' in the modern world or whether they harbour a latent legal crisis.[7] Borrowing the plumbing language that several Law Commissioners have used in the past,[8] do those areas contain pipes that are no longer adequate and just waiting to

---

[4] The Social Action, Responsibility and Heroism Act 2015 has been said to be an example of such legislation.

[5] See A Burrows, *A Restatement of the English Law of Unjust Enrichment* (Oxford, OUP, 2012) and *A Restatement of the English Law of Contract* (Oxford, OUP, 2016).

[6] Three notable examples are: (1) Marital rape: in *R v R* [1991] 2 WLR 1065 (CA) and [1992] 1 AC 599 (HL), although not cited, a pre-publication copy of Law Commission, LC WP 116, *Rape within Marriage* (1990) was before the Court of Appeal which was clearly influenced by it. (2) Multipliers in personal injuries damages: *Wells v Wells* [1999] 1 AC 345 (HL) reflected some of Law Commission, LC 224, *Structured Settlements and Interim and Provisional Damages* (1994). (3) Damages for non-pecuniary loss: *Heil v Rankin* [2001] QB 272 (CA) reflected some of Law Commission, LC 257, *Damages for Personal Injury: Non-Pecuniary Loss* (1999). See also chapters 2 (Lady Hale) and 20 (Andrew Burrows).

[7] See generally Sir Geoffrey Palmer's 2015 Scarman Lecture, 'The Law Reform Enterprise: Evaluating the Past and Charting the Future' (2015) 131 *LQR* 402 and his suggestions for how the tensions between government and Law Commissions should be addressed, including greater attention on links between Commissions and the legislature.

[8] See Scottish Law Commission, SLC 222, *Land Registration* (2010) para 1.1; P North, 'Is Law Reform Too Important to be Left to Lawyers?' (1985) 5 *LS* 119, 129; G Gretton, 'Of Law Commissioning' (2013) 17 *Edinburgh Law Review* 119, 127; E Cooke and H MacQueen, 'Law Reform in a Political Environment: The Work of the Law Commissions' in D Feldman (ed), *Law in Politics, Politics in Law* (Oxford, Hart Publishing, 2013) 148; (and, though not a Commissioner himself) S Sedley, 'Law and Plumbing' (2008) 28 *LS* 629.

burst, either because of technical developments or because of botch jobs undertaken at speed to deal with an emergency?

We also need a body which can try to make our statute law more accessible and accurate. The text of important statutes is not up to date on the statute law database. For example, when I consulted it last autumn in connection with a case before me, amendments made by the Finance Act 2005 to the VAT Act 1994 had not yet been made to the text displayed.[9] Sir Geoffrey Palmer has stated that 'it would be appropriate to redesign and reform the way statutes are made and promulgated to the public'.[10] At a time when citizens increasingly have to try to ascertain the law on a matter affecting them without professional assistance, the need for this is urgent.

For these reasons, when thinking about my contribution to the conference and this book, I was a tad gloomy. Closer examination of the position in July 2015 as Sir James's successor Sir David Lloyd Jones came to the end of a successful three years as Chairman of the Law Commission showed that, while law reform remains a cyclical process and we are making snail-like progress in putting our statute law into an accessible and accurate form, I was overly pessimistic. I consider that the fundamentals of the methods used by the Law Commission remain sound. The changes recently introduced, which some have criticised, reflect ways of doing things and aspirations that existed in the early 1990s, albeit in a modern guise and maybe not always exactly as past members of the Commission might have envisaged. A number of the current concerns about threats to the Commission's independence and difficulties with implementation existed in my time too. The suggestions for improvement that were made then and what was done also have similarities to more recent suggestions and developments.

I mention only two matters. First, a legislative procedure using special standing committees, known as 'Jellicoe Committees' was introduced in 1992, and used in 1994 and 1995[11] before disappearing mainly because Parliament turned to consider modernisation more generally, but possibly also because of the attempt to use it to implement a Law Commission report which proved controversial.[12] We also sought ways of getting commitment from government to projects undertaken and to require it to respond to Commission reports rather than let them gather dust. Under Sir Henry Brooke's chairmanship, the Law Commission sought to reach a wider audience in Whitehall, Westminster and elsewhere to explain the general nature and importance of its work and the reasons the problem of non-implementation was getting more serious. The first appearance of Law Commissioners before the Home

---

[9] Visitors to the website are, however, warned that there are outstanding changes not yet made to particular statutes, which can be found in the 'Changes to Legislation' area: www.legislation.gov.uk/ukpga/2005/7/contents. See also chapter 14 (Lord Toulson).

[10] Palmer, n 7 above, 421.

[11] See Law Commission, LC 232, *Twenty-Ninth Annual Report: 1994* (1995) paras 5.1–5.9, 5.14–5.15; Law Commission, LC 239, *Thirtieth Annual Report: 1995* (1996) para 1.10; H Brooke, 'Special Public Bill Committees' [1995] PL 351.

[12] Law Commission, LC 207, *Domestic Violence and the Occupation of the Family Home* (1992). What happened, or rather what did not happen, in relation to the special procedure is recorded in the Law Commission's annual reports for the rest of the 1990s. See also the judgment of Lady Hale in *Yemshaw v London Borough of Hounslow* [2011] UKSC 3, [2011] 1 WLR 433, at [21].

Affairs Committee to talk about these matters in general rather than as part of the consideration of a particular report occurred in May 1994.[13] The financial and non-financial cost of out-of-date laws and the merits and demerits of taking long-term and short-term views were canvassed at that hearing and in other fora.

Thanks to persistence by the Commission and many Commissioners over the years, and developments during and since Sir Terence Etherton's chairmanship, much has now been achieved. The 2009 Act enabled the Protocol between the Commission and the Lord Chancellor about principles to be applied in deciding the work to be carried out and a timetable for responses to reports in an annual report on implementation,[14] to which I will return. A special House of Lords procedure was adopted in October 2010, and its fruits are beginning to be seen. The comments and criticisms made about these developments and their implications for the independence of the Law Commission[15] have similarities to those made about what was going on in the early 1990s. As to independence, either the Lord Chancellor's consent to an item in a law reform programme or a specific reference by a government department has always been necessary. As to attitudes, part of the mood music in the late 1980s is illustrated by an encounter I had at the reception given in October 1989 by the Lord Chancellor after the service in Westminster Abbey to mark the beginning of the legal year. I was introduced to a senior Lord Chancellor's Department civil servant. His reaction was: 'Ah, new Law Commissioner; yours to propose, mine to dispose.'

## II  TIMESCALES: WAS THERE A PROBLEM?

On my second day at the Commission, its then Chairman, Sir Roy Beldam, told me that there were two main priorities for my Common Law team. The first was to finish two existing projects. One was a very long-standing joint project with the Scottish Law Commission as part of the Law Commission's item on private international law in its third programme of law reform.[16] Work had started in 1979, almost a decade earlier, initiated and led by Dr North (as he then was) in London and Professor Anton in Edinburgh. A consultation paper was published in 1984, almost five years earlier, but the project had been delayed. One reason for the delay was the complexity of the issue. But the really significant reason was that practitioners and academics

---

[13]  LC 232, n 11 above, paras 5.10–5.13.

[14]  Law Commission and Ministry of Justice, LC 321, *Protocol between the Lord Chancellor (on behalf of the Government) and the Law Commission* (2010).

[15]  See, eg, S Wilson, 'Reforming the Law (Commission): A Crisis of Identity?' [2013] *PL* 20.

[16]  Law Commission, LC 54, *Third Programme of Law Reform* (1973). The project grew out of a Joint Working Party set up by the two Commissions set up in 1979 to advise the UK Government about a proposed EEC Convention on contractual and non-contractual obligations. When it became clear that the Convention would only deal with contractual obligations (see *Convention on the Law Applicable to Contractual Obligations* (Cmnd 8489, 1980)), the Working Party took the work on tort and delict forward. A joint consultation document (Law Commission and Scottish Law Commission, LC WP 87 and SLC DP 62, *Private International Law: Choice of Law in Tort and Delict* (1984)) was published in September 1984. It was not until 1990 that the Commissions' joint report was published: Law Commission and Scottish Law Commission, LC 193 and SLC 129, *Private International Law: Choice of Law in Tort and Delict* (1990). It was implemented in the Private International Law (Miscellaneous Provisions) Act 1995, part III.

had radically divergent views about whether the problems of the law should be addressed by legislation, and, if they were to be so addressed, what model should be adopted.[17] There had also been similar differences between Commissioners, and between the two Commissions, although by the time I arrived those had largely been resolved.

The other project concerned rights to goods in bulk, and the operation of the Bills of Lading Act 1855 and section 16 of the Sale of Goods Act 1979. That project was referred to the Law Commissions by government after representatives of the leading international commodity trade associations approached the Law Commission in 1985, because of concerns about the state of the law in the light of recent decisions on the 1855 Act and difficulties that arose from transactions about undivided parts of bulk cargos in giant cargo vessels. The Commissions reported jointly on the 1855 Act in 1991 and on section 16 of the Sale of Goods Act in 1993. Although there were some difficulties,[18] there was no real delay in the conduct of the project or in the legislative implementation of the Commissions' recommendations. The proposals in both reports were implemented shortly after the report, in 1992 and 1995.[19]

The second priority was for me to identify, in consultation with government departments and non-governmental bodies, new common law and public law topics in need of reform which were suitable for the Law Commission to undertake. That process led to a number of new projects in late 1989, and in 1990 and 1991.[20] They included the item in its fifth programme on damages for personal injuries which I mention because the Lord Chancellor's Department made financial provision to allow empirical research. The result was the large-scale survey of victims of personal injury which was conducted for the Law Commission by Professor Hazel Genn which resulted in the report *Personal Injury Compensation: How Much Is Enough?*[21]

---

[17] The models for reform canvassed were: (1) a 'proper law' rule (which tended to be favoured by barristers and academics but not by those, including many solicitors, concerned with ex ante certainty); (2) a 'law of the place of the tort' rule; and (3) making the law of the place of the tort the default rule but capable of being displaced where this was just by the 'proper law' as an exception.

[18] The difficulties concerned the choice between two options for reform of the 1855 Act; one simply permitted the lawful holder of a bill of lading to sue, the other did so only if he was on risk in respect of the loss. The latter was rejected because 'risk' is not an easy concept to define, no other law explicitly used it, and some in the relevant market and some lawyers strongly opposed it as conducive to uncertainty, but one of the Scottish Law Commissioners favoured it and wrote a dissenting report.

[19] Law Commission, LC WP 112, *Rights to Goods in Bulk* (1989) and Scottish Law Commission, SLC DP 83, *Bulk Goods* (1989). The final joint reports were Law Commission and Scottish Law Commission, LC 196 and SLC 130, *Rights of Suit in Respect of Carriage of Goods by Sea* (1991) and LC 215 and SLC 145, *Sale of Goods Forming Part of a Bulk* (1993). The former report was enacted by the Carriage of Goods by Sea Act 1992. The latter was enacted by the Sale of Goods (Amendment) Act 1995.

[20] The common law and public law topics in the *Fourth* and *Fifth Programmes of Law Reform*, LC 185 (1989) and LC 200 (1991) respectively, were: judicial review and statutory appeals; contracts for the benefit of a third party; contributory negligence as a defence in contract; and damages for personal injuries. There were also references in 1989 and 1990 on: hearsay evidence in civil proceedings; mistakes of law and ultra vires public authority receipts; and fiduciary duties and regulatory rules.

[21] LC 225 (1994). The Commission's later work on personal injury damages for non-pecuniary loss was also informed by a large-scale survey conducted by the Office for National Statistics: see LC 257, *Damages for Personal Injury: Non-Pecuniary Loss* (1999).

I have referred to trying to help with the projects I had started after I left the Commission. My 'run-off service' included appearing before parliamentary committees and giving 'behind the scenes' help to civil servants when Bills based on projects which I had led were being considered by Parliament. I have particular memories of being cross-examined by Lord Wilberforce in January 1995 at a hearing of the Special Public Bill Committee on what became the Private International Law (Miscellaneous Provisions) Act 1995.[22] My files reveal that there were problems in the Law Commission affording me the support needed to prepare for the detailed questions on the way the Private International Law Bill would work for intellectual property torts and defamation.

I should mention that I also have experience, albeit a single experience, of what was virtually a single-person law reform project which produced recommendations for reform on a 'fast-track'. In mid-1999, I was asked by the then Lord Chancellor, Lord Irvine, to conduct a review of bailiff law for the Lord Chancellor's Department and to report in 12 months. I did so under the auspices of the University of Cambridge's Centre for Public Law with the help of a single very talented research assistant. The research was done in the second half of 1999. A consultation paper was published in March 2000 with a relatively short two-month period for responses. The final report was published at the end of June 2000, only just within the timetable set.[23] The recommendations generated an enormous amount of interest, but, apart from speaking at a couple of conferences, I had no involvement in the project after the report was published. The Lord Chancellor's Department, which stated it was committed to implementing the recommendations, conducted a consultation exercise on my proposals and ultimately, seven years later, the newly formed Ministry of Justice substantially implemented the report in part III of the Tribunals, Courts and Enforcement Act 2007.

I have three reasons for mentioning all this. The first is to show the contrast and similarities between recommendations by an independent individual on an ad hoc basis and those by a standing body bringing together different legal skills with the possibility of empirical research as well as doctrinal and policy analysis. While the work on bailiff law was undertaken on a fast track with a report within a year, the timescale for implementation was similar to that for some Law Commission reports. The second reason is that rigorous work on difficult topics by a standing body with a wide remit can take time and involve more than one lead Commissioner. Such work by two standing bodies is likely to take longer. There are a number of reasons for this, including the turn-over rate of civil servants and researchers. I consider the reasons that priorities change, and the problems of too short and too long a timetable, below. At this stage, it suffices to say that, in the case of some projects, and choice of law in tort and delict is a classic example, both Commissions could be criticised for letting the best be the enemy of the good.

---

[22] House of Lords Special Public Bill Committee, *Private International Law (Miscellaneous Provisions) Bill* (1994–95, HL 36).

[23] J Beatson, *Report of the Independent Review of Bailiff Law* (2000).

The third reason is to illustrate that, even where there is no delay, the need to identify and refine the problem, to conduct adequate consultation, to form policy, and to draft a high quality Bill means that 'carry over' from one Commissioner to another is usual for any project not started at the beginning of a Commissioner's tenure. Just as I had picked up and run with projects started but not completed by Sir Peter North and Brian Davenport, so Andrew Burrows picked up and ran with the projects on contracts for the benefit of a third party and personal injury damages, which I started. I should add that even in projects more narrowly focused, such 'carry over' was needed, because the work was meant to be part of a more systematic process.[24]

The strength of the Commissions is the fact that their recommendations are the product of a robust review of the work of the Commissioner leading a project by the four other Commissioners, each of whom is a very able lawyer. The rigour of their review enhances the quality of the finished product, but achieving consensus takes time. Sometimes there is difficulty in choosing between two models which are principled and possible in a purely doctrinal and technical sense, but one of which encounters strong opposition from some of those who will be affected.[25] In projects involving the two Commissions, there is the additional factor that the Commissioners come from different legal traditions. Sometimes participants from one tradition feel that there is insufficient understanding of or interest in their traditions by those in the other jurisdiction.[26] It is worth adding that in the 50 years of the Commissions, there have been very few dissents.

## III CHANGING PRIORITIES

To understand the benefits and challenges of shorter timescales, it is necessary to start by addressing the question of changing priorities. Why do they change so often? What does experience and an examination of the modern developments tell us about the ways of seeking to address the challenges that come from the fact that priorities are likely to change?

There are a number of reasons for priorities changing. The first is that the outcome of a law reform project may show that there is in fact no, or no longer, a need for reform. This may be either on legal grounds, for example a true understanding of the underlying common law shows that there is no need for legislation to address what had been perceived to be a problem. The signal example of that, in the

---

[24] The Law Commission's work on private international law led to a number of other statutes: the Matrimonial Proceedings (Polygamous Marriages) Act 1972; the Domicile and Matrimonial Proceedings Act 1973; the Matrimonial and Family Proceedings Act 1984; the Foreign Limitation Periods Act 1984 part III. L Collins et al, *Dicey, Morris and Collins on the Conflicts of Laws*, 15th edn (London, Sweet & Maxwell, 2015) para 1-019 describe these as prepared 'as part of a thoroughgoing and well-considered reform of the law'. On what North called 'codification—English style', see 'Problems of Codification in a Common Law System' (1982) 46 *Rabels Zeitschrift* 490.

[25] In his contribution to this volume (chapter 25), David Johnston suggests this was a factor in the non-implementation of the Scottish Law Commission's work on Prescription and Limitation of Actions.

[26] See, eg, G Gretton, 'Of Law Commissioning' (2013) 17 *Edinburgh Law Review* 119, 149–51.

halcyon days of the 1980s, was the Law Commission's work on the parol evidence rule. At the conclusion of its review, the Commission stated that there is no *rule of law* precluding the admissibility of evidence solely because a document exists which looks like a complete contract, that there is only a presumption that a document which looks like a complete contract is the whole document, and that, correctly applied, it is not possible for evidence to be unjustly excluded.[27]

Changes in the background or in perceptions about the law, for example as a result of developments in the case law while the project is underway, may also affect the case for legislative reform without removing it. This happened in the case of the Commission's mistake of law and ultra vires receipts project,[28] its work on fiduciary duties and regulatory rules,[29] and, more recently, its work on the illegality defence.[30] In none of these cases did the changes lead the Commission to conclude that legislation was no longer necessary. Might the Commission have been too quick to conclude that only very limited legislation was needed? In the case of illegality, the differing views of members of the Supreme Court in recent cases, and the conflict in the approach in two cases decided within three months of each other,[31] may be an indication that it was. Legal grounds for reassessing the need for reform may also arise as a result of changes in the underlying legislative structure because of domestic or EU legislation, or impending legislation.[32]

The second way in which priorities might change is because of a change in wider policy, as opposed to a change purely based on technical legal factors. Changes of policy can occur for a number of reasons. For example, a new government might take the view that a consumer protection proposal was proceeding on the wrong policy basis or that the resulting report recommended either too much or too little protection. Changes of policy may be the result of pressure by the public or by interest groups, as well as the result of changes within government and Parliament.

---

[27] Law Commission, LC 154, *Law of Contract: The Parol Evidence Rule* (1986) paras 2.7 and 2.17. This view has been approved in a number of decisions: see J Beatson, A Burrows and J Cartwright, *Anson's Law of Contract*, 29th edn (Oxford, OUP, 2010) 139 n 48. See also MP Furmston, 'Some Themes and Thoughts' (2005) 17 *Singapore Academy of Law Journal* 141, 144.

[28] Law Commission, LC 227, *Restitution: Mistakes of Law and Ultra Vires Public Authority Receipts and Payments* (1994) paras 1.9–1.10 as a result of the decision in *Woolwich Equitable Building Society v Inland Revenue Commissioners* [1993] AC 70 (HL).

[29] Law Commission, LC 236, *Fiduciary Duties and Regulatory Rules* (1995) para 1.12. The decisions of the courts, especially *Kelly v Cooper* [1993] AC 205 (PC), are discussed at paras 3.1–3.41.

[30] Law Commission, LC CP 154, *Illegal Transactions: The Effect of Illegality on Contracts and Trusts* (1999); LC CP 189, *The Illegality Defence* (2009); LC 320, *The Illegality Defence* (2010).

[31] See *Hounga v Allen* [2014] UKSC 47, [2014] 1 WLR 2889 and *Les Laboratoires Servier v Apotex Inc* [2014] UKSC 55, [2015] AC 430. See also *Jetivia SA v Bilta (UK) Ltd* [2015] UKSC 23, [2015] 2 WLR 1168 and *R (Best) v Chief Land Registrar* [2015] EWCA Civ 17 where a majority of the Court of Appeal preferred the approach in *Hounga v Allen*. See chapter 29 (James Lee).

[32] eg, the project on the private international law of tort and delict arose because it had become clear that the proposed EEC Convention would only deal with contractual obligations. But, had what ultimately became the Rome II Regulation ([2007] OJ L199/40 Regulation (EC) No 864/2007 of the European Parliament and of the Council on the Law Applicable to Non-Contractual Obligations) and The Law Applicable to Non-Contractual Obligations (England and Wales and Northern Ireland) Regulations 2008, SI 2008/2986 been completed before the Commission reported, although the reform contained in the Private International Law (Miscellaneous Provisions) Act 1995 would be relevant to torts falling outside the material temporal scope of Rome II, the case for legislation would have been significantly affected.

In a sense, this was the fate of the Law Commission's 1990 proposals on the grounds of divorce.[33] The re-assessment of policy came after enactment of the Family Law Act 1995, which was never brought into force. It could have happened before the Commission reported. Policy may also change because former pressure for change has dissipated by the time the Commission reports.

Thirdly, government priorities may change because of pressure on the legislative programme. Traditionally it was thought that this was most likely to be the case in the early stages of a new government and least likely to be the case in a period running up to a General Election. The rosier implementation scene in the period leading up to the 2015 election may reflect the fact that Parliament was not particularly busy with 'political' legislation.

A further reason for changing priorities, in some ways related to internal and external pressures on government, is an unwillingness by those responsible for deciding whether to bring forward legislative proposals to take responsibility for change in a particularly sensitive area, for example one involving difficult moral and ethical questions. The best example of this is an area which has not been the subject of projects by the Law Commissions, assisted suicide and other end of life issues. An example in an area in which the Law Commission has worked is the question of consent by or for a mentally incapacitated adult to medical treatment and to procedures such as sterilisation. Until a 1989 decision of the House of Lords,[34] there was no English authority on whether, as matter of common law and if so in what circumstances, such treatment could lawfully be given to such a person. This became part of the first of the Law Commission's projects on mentally incapacitated adults.[35]

Since 2010, the government has stated that the most important factor affecting priorities in practice is the financial climate. Whether or not there is particular financial stringency, other needs, such as those of the NHS or security, may be assessed as more pressing than law reform. The Lord Chancellor's annual reports on implementation since 2011 state that financial stringency is a major factor in not implementing law reform proposals.[36]

How, then, should the principled independent law reformer meet these challenges? As to other needs being more pressing and financial stringency, all that can, I believe, be done is to seek to educate those in government and elsewhere about the

[33] Law Commission, LC 192, *Ground for Divorce* (1990).

[34] On this, see *Re F (Mental Patient: Sterilisation)* [1990] 2 AC 1 (HL) [71]–[72] (Lord Goff).

[35] This was an item in the Commission's *Fourth Programme* in 1989 (n 20 above). The report was Law Commission, LC 231, *Mental Incapacity* (1995), which was enacted in substance ten years later by the Mental Capacity Act 2005 after extensive post-report consideration, a Green Paper in 1997 (Lord Chancellor's Department, *Making Decisions on Behalf of Mentally Incapacitated Adults: A Consultation Paper* (Cm 3808, 1997)), a White Paper in 1999 (Lord Chancellor's Department, *'Making Decisions': The Government's Proposals for Making Decisions on Behalf of Mentally Incapacitated Adults* (Cm 4465, 1999)) and pre-legislative scrutiny of a draft Bill in 2003 (see first report of Joint Committee on Draft Mental Incapacity Bill (2002–03, HL 189-I, HC 1083-I)). A new reference was needed to address the consequences of the Supreme Court's decision in *P v Cheshire West and Chester Council* [2014] UKSC 19, [2014] AC 896 about when living conditions made for a mentally incapacitated person amount to a deprivation of liberty.

[36] Ministry of Justice, *Report on the Implementaon of Law Commission Proposals* (HC 719, 2011); (HC 1900, 2012); (HC 908, 2013); (HC 1237, 2014); (HC 1062, 2015).

importance of keeping our body of law 'fit for purpose' and the cheapness of law reform conducted by an independent law reform body such as the three Law Commissions. In 2014, the cost of the Law Commission from core funding was £4.517 million.[37] Between 1989 and 1994 according to the Commission's annual reports, it rose from £2.248 million to £3.889 million. In today's values that is roughly the equivalent of £5.390 million in 1989 and £7.078 million in 1994, so the Commission is significantly less well off in real terms than it was then. The Commission is still expected to provide the taxpaying public with a standing service covering many areas of law.

£4.5 million for all this is very good value when compared with the cost of single-issue inquiries established under the Inquiries Act 2005 or other inquiries led by judges, senior lawyers and public figures. Although not entirely on all fours with Law Commissions because they generally involve investigating factual situations and taking evidence, some have also involved consideration of law reform issues. The Scottish Government's three and a half year fingerprint inquiry (2011) cost approximately £4.75 million.[38] The 16-month inquiry into the culture, practices and ethics of the press (2012) cost £5.4 million,[39] and the two and a half year inquiry into the Mid-Staffordshire NHS Foundation Trust (2013) cost an estimated £13.7 million.[40] It must be recognised that not all single-issue inquiries are expensive. The two-year inquiry into contaminated blood and blood products (2009) cost only £75,000. Such inquiries can, however, have other disadvantages.[41]

Again, borrowing and adapting the 'plumbing' analogy, the cost of the Law Commissions for their across the board service should be seen as roughly equivalent to the cost of an annual servicing contract for a household utility. While there are, no doubt, some greedy contractors, such a contract tends to be cheaper than the cost of calling out someone after an emergency has arisen and the house has flooded or the boiler blown up. The costs of the various inquiries to which I have referred, even excluding the really expensive inquiries, and before them Royal Commissions, bear this out.[42]

What has to be emphasised is that bad law costs money. While looking through my old files to refresh my memory, I found an item in the Sunday Times on 20 June 1993. The headline is 'Dangerous Dogs Law to Cost £10 million in Court Battles'. That was written only 19 months after the enactment of the Dangerous Dogs Act 1991. Throughout my time at the Law Commission we emphasised the cost of bad or uncertain law to government and legislators with less lurid figures. Some

---

[37] See Law Commission, LC 352, *Annual Report 2013–14* (2014) app B. The total includes the net cost of rent for accommodation which is met by the Ministry of Justice.

[38] Scottish Government Written Answers 6 October 2014, S4W-22594.

[39] Leveson Inquiry: Final Costs, October 2012 www.levesoninquiry.org.uk/about/inquiry-costs/.

[40] Mid-Staffordshire NHS Foundation Trust Public Inquiry Costs to date www.midstaffspublicinquiry.com/inquiry-costs.

[41] See below.

[42] The cost of many such inquiries is given in app A to my evidence to the House of Lords Select Committee on the Inquiries Act 2005, *The Inquiries Act 2005: Post-legislative Scrutiny* which is reproduced in app 4 to the committee's report (2013–14, HL 143).

concerned the annual cost of appeals in criminal cases on particular points where the law was unclear. Some were estimates of the loss of invisible exports if outdated commercial laws led commercial people to choose other legal systems to govern their transactions. The Carriage of Goods by Sea Act 1992 is an example of the latter as is, albeit based on a judge-led inquiry, the Arbitration Act 1996.[43]

I turn to the challenge of priorities changing as a result of changes in policy by government, dissipation of the pressure for reform during the life of a project, and the fact that a topic is placed in the 'too difficult' box because of its technical complexity or, as in the case of grounds of divorce or end of life questions, because it is inherently controversial. One way to seek to meet the first two of these challenges is for the Commission, before taking on a project, to try to assess whether the case for reform is based on durable or transitory factors. The position of those pressing for reform in a particular area may be thought to prove to be transitory because, for example, it is based on fear of legal uncertainty as a result of other changes or tied to the position of a particular political party or interest group. Such an assessment will often not be straightforward. Sometimes it is. For example, in the light of the position taken by a number of bodies, in particular the OECD, there was general recognition by government that the UK's bribery laws were inadequate. The Law Commission's first recommendations on the topic[44] were criticised by industrialists and politicians. The durability of the problem was, however, shown by a second reference in 2007, and the Commission's 2008 report[45] was (not without further difficulty) implemented by the Bribery Act 2010.

After the Commission has reported, it needs to do what it can to ensure that the constituency which has supported reform through the consultation process and has welcomed the proposals in the report remains active, and to try to address the concerns of those who do not support the proposals. The Commission must be careful to do this without becoming a mere lobbyist or joining what might be seen to be a single-issue lobby group. This is not an altogether easy task, because all worthwhile law reform has winners and losers. The losers will naturally resist reform. I vividly remember that, while cargo interests and their insurers and bankers strongly supported our proposals for reform of the Bills of Lading Act 1855, shipowners and their insurers and bankers were decidedly lukewarm and probably hostile. Similarly, in the early stages of the project on damages for non-pecuniary loss in personal injury cases, the claimants' lobby group, the Association of Personal Injury Lawyers, opposed any change which, however rational or principled, might result in a particular item in the list of recoverable losses being less well-compensated than it had previously been. As to the 'too difficult box', I have no solution other than education and persuasion.

---

[43] The Act was the result of a partnership between the public service and private initiative in drafting. The drive for reform was fear that support for the UNCITRAL *Model Law on International Commercial Arbitration* (1985) (www.uncitral.org/uncitral/en/uncitral_texts/arbitration/1985Model_arbitration.html) and concerns about the willingness of the English courts to grant permission to appeal against arbitration awards would lead to the choice of other jurisdictions as the seat and governing law of arbitrations.

[44] Law Commission, LC 248, *Legislating the Criminal Code: Corruption* (1998).

[45] Law Commission, LC 313, *Reforming Bribery* (2008).

Let us look at what has been done. My starting point is the effect of the 2010 Protocol to which I have referred. It provides that, where the Commission is considering including a project in one of its three-year programmes of law reform (whether it originates as part of such a three-year programme or is referred to the Commission by Ministers), it will notify the Minister with relevant policy responsibility about it. Before approving the inclusion of the project in the programme, the Lord Chancellor will expect the relevant Minister, with the support of his or her Permanent Secretary, to agree that the department involved will provide sufficient staff to liaise with the Commission during the project and give an undertaking that there is a serious intention to take forward law reform in this area. The Protocol also requires government to provide an interim response to every Law Commission report 'as soon as possible and in any event within six months'[46] and a final response as soon as possible after delivery of the interim response, and in any event within a year of publication of the report unless otherwise agreed. It should be remembered that sometimes, for example in the case of the project about the hearsay rule in civil proceedings, the department is the initiator.

What is the effect of pinning a government department down to accepting that there is a need for reform before work starts? My memory, particularly of the projects on fiduciary duties and regulatory rules, the tax aspects of the mistake of law rule, and the hearsay rule in civil proceedings, is that, before references were made to the Commission, there had been extensive discussion with officials in the departments, as well as with industry and what would today be called 'stakeholder groups'. Depending on the project there were differences as to the extent to which departments considered reform was needed. There were also topics on which there were differences between the department and the Law Commission as to the need for reform. It was not always the department which was the reluctant partner. The Commission has been alive to the danger of simply becoming the department's outsourced research arm or of a reference on a sensitive topic made in order to kick it into touch, although I do not think the latter was ever a problem while I was at the Commission save possibly at times in connection with work on the property rights of cohabitees.

Where the Commission initiated consideration of working in an area, in my time and in the period immediately beforehand, I do not believe it ever started work on a topic that fell within one of the items in an approved law reform programme against a background where the department responsible for the area stated that it considered there was no, or very little, need for reform. Nor was work started where it was stated that, because of the nature of a topic, it was unlikely that a Law Commission report would be implemented. In any event, as I have stated, either the Lord Chancellor's consent to an item in a law reform programme, or a specific reference by a government department has always been necessary. As Sir David Lloyd Jones stated in his Sir William Dale Lecture in 2012, the Protocol simply required the conversation on implementation to occur at an earlier stage in the process.[47]

---

[46] Law Commission and Ministry of Justice, LC 321, *Protocol between the Lord Chancellor (on behalf of the Government) and the Law Commission* (2010) para 18.

[47] D Lloyd Jones, 'The Law Commission and the Implementation of Law Reform', Sir William Dale Annual Lecture (2012).

Its formality will also help to avoid misunderstandings. It can thus be said that its effect is akin to requirements of form for certain contracts: evidential, rather than substantive.

As to the substance, in my assessment it is fundamentally necessary for the Commission to engage with all relevant external interests as well as government departments and Ministers before, during and after the project. I have referred to the need to ensure before taking on a project that the pressure for reform is not transitory. What needs to be done during the life of the project is now reasonably familiar. During my time at the Law Commission, as is the case today, all teams engaged in a range of public activities in connection with their projects in addition to the normal consultation process and meetings with key interest groups, Commissioners and teams organised conferences and seminars with practitioners, academics and other professionals from other relevant areas.[48] After the Commission has reported, what needs to be done is also reasonably familiar.[49] But the necessary engagement can be problematic where changes in personnel mean that the expertise required is no longer available within the Commission. The longer the time after the report, the more likely this will be. I have referred to the problems faced by the Law Commission in providing support to me as a former Commissioner in order to prepare for my appearance before the Jellicoe Committee considering the Private International Law Bill in 1995. Some of those who consider that the Protocol saps the independence of the Law Commission overlook the fact that there is an advantage in requiring active participation by those in the relevant department. Such participation may help to provide expertise within the department which will be required to take recommendations to the legislative stage where there is no longer expertise within the Commission.

The optimum position is for government departments to think of the Law Commission as part of the solution when they have a problem about the state of an area of law. I believe that the Lord Chancellor's Department generally did so in relation to family law in the period between 1978 and 1994. The confidence the Lord Chancellor's Department had in Stephen Cretney and Brenda Hale, then Hoggett, the Commissioners who would lead the work was an important part of this. There were similar relations between the Department of Health and Brenda Hale and her team in relation to mental incapacity, a project on which the Commission led on the purely legal aspects, and the department, assisted by contributions from the Law Commission's team, led on other aspects. Another example was the co-operation between the Land Registry and Charles Harpum and his team during his tenure. The result was the Land Registration Act 2002.[50]

---

[48] During the life of all Common Law projects, the team held or helped organise a number of seminars at various locations in London, conferences on fiduciary duties and judicial review respectively in Oxford and Cambridge and a two-day conference on damages in Manchester held jointly with the Society of Public Teachers of Law (now the Society of Legal Scholars) and Manchester University.

[49] In the case of carriage of goods by sea, events were organised with shipping and cargo interests and their insurers and bankers, and the assistance of the Confederation of British Industry (CBI) was enlisted. The latter, through the good offices of Howard Davies, then Director General of the CBI, was crucial to the swift implementation of the recommendations.

[50] See chapter 31 (Charles Harpum).

Other departments were less familiar with the Law Commission, but the way in which the Department of Trade and Industry (DTI) (as it was then called) became involved with it in the 1990s is instructive. The department approached the Commission about the interrelation of fiduciary duties and the new post-'Big Bang' regulatory rules, following financial de-regulation. The rules were designed for integrated businesses offering a range of services because it came under great pressure from city interests and the influential Company Law Committee of the Law Society to resolve what was seen as uncertainty about how that would work with the equitable duties of a fiduciary prohibiting conflicts of interest. It referred the matter to both Commissions because it was not able to devote adequate resources to address the complex technical legal issues involved. The lawyers and other officials in the DTI worked on the fiduciary duties project with the then Chairman, Sir Peter Gibson, who of course had unrivalled experience of the area from his time as Chancery counsel to the Treasury, me, and our consultant Professor Dan Prentice. I like to think that their experience and the quality of our work led them to decide to approach the Law Commission in 1993 about a reform project on aspects of company law.[51] It may, however, just have been their awareness that the Commission had access to the services of parliamentary draftsmen at an earlier stage than the department would have had. Whatever the reason, it led to references to the Commissions on shareholder remedies in 1995, and in 1997 on partnership law and directors' duties.

Pinning a government department down to accepting that there is a need for reform before work starts may reduce the risk of that department stating at the end of the process that there is no such need. It is, however, important to remember that it cannot eliminate it. After all, as my example of the report on the so-called parol evidence rule shows, the Commission itself may reach this conclusion. The cases of fiduciary duties and regulatory rules and restitution on the grounds of mistake of law are also useful but less dramatic examples.

When the Law Society's Company Law Committee and others approached the DTI and the Commission in 1990, their major concern was about uncertainty caused by the effect of the new regulatory system introduced by the Financial Services Act 1986, changes in the structure of financial markets and the range of services that a single financial service conglomerate would be able to provide. The concern in the case of mistake of law was not of uncertainty as to the legal position, but criticism of what appeared to be a clear and longstanding rule, albeit subject to many exceptions. That rule was considered by many to produce injustice.

By the time the Commission reported on mistaken payments and ultra vires payments, there had been a number of indications that the *Woolwich* case, which provided for a right of restitution in respect of ultra vires payments of tax,[52] might apply to other payments made under a mistake of law. In the case of fiduciary duties and regulatory rules, by the time the Law Commissions reported the market had a number of years' experience of working the new system and there had been a

---

[51]  See Law Commission, LC 232, *Twenty-Ninth Annual Report: 1994* (1995) para 2.19.
[52]  *Woolwich Equitable Building Society v Inland Revenue Commissioners* [1993] AC 70 (HL). See also chapter 17 (Laura Dunlop).

number of decisions in the courts which had a calming effect. Whereas in 1990, the market did not consider that mismatches between fiduciary duties and regulatory rules could be addressed adequately by contractual and structural techniques such as Chinese walls, by 1995 consultees and ultimately government were reasonably confident that the use of those techniques would avoid problems so that there was no longer a need for reform. Although the Commission concluded that, while those techniques assisted, they might not always work, the proposed legislation had little chance of being enacted. There was a similar process in the Law Commission's consideration of the effect of illegality.

Trespassing onto the shorter timetable point, in the case of the fiduciary duties project, had the Commission reported in 1991 or 1992, the perception of uncertainty would have been there and the pressure for reform would have been much greater. The lesson to be drawn from this is that sometimes a change of priority is fully justified. Additionally, although this only relates to a law reform project undertaken on the basis of uncertainty as to the law, a project which is completed too quickly may not produce sound recommendations. Such a project should perhaps only be pursued after a more robust demonstration of unacceptable uncertainty than existed in the case of the effect of the new regulatory regime.

An examination of the contents of the responses by the Lord Chancellor and his officials in the annual reports on the implementation of Law Commission proposals shows that the reasons for non-implementation, delay or change of priorities have not related to the view that developments have meant that reform is no longer needed. In his Denning Lecture, Sir James Munby was critical of what was said in the Lord Chancellor's first report on implementation in 2011.[53] It seemed that the problem at that stage was the time that a number of reports had lain on government shelves, during which time they had become out-of-date and would need considerable work, in Sir James's words, 'to refresh' them if the decision is ever taken to implement.[54] I doubt that he would have regarded the 2012 report as any better.

The reasons given in the first three reports were unparticularised and anodyne. Effectively, the main reason given for delay in considering whether to accept or reject a report and in implementing accepted reports was the financial situation in which the coalition government found itself. The 2013 report stated that 'less immediately pressing law reform proposals have, in some cases, been delayed'.[55] The position was more encouraging in the fourth report in 2014.[56] Six Commission reports were implemented or partially implemented in 2014. In 2015, the Charities Bill was before Parliament, and two reports on fiduciary duties of investment intermediaries and regulation of healthcare and social care professionals were accepted by government in whole or almost in whole. Additionally, the Commission's report on expert evidence in criminal proceedings has been implemented by secondary legislation, in particular, in the Criminal Procedure Rules.

---

[53] Munby, n 3 above.
[54] ibid 7.
[55] Ministry of Justice, *Report on the Implementation of Law Commission Proposals* (HC 908, 2013) 3.
[56] Ministry of Justice, *Report on the Implementation of Law Commission Proposals* (HC 1237, 2014).

Since none of the Lord Chancellor's reports on implementation suggest that priorities changed because of a changed perception as to the need for reform, the delays are depressing. For instance, nine years after the report on termination of tenancies,[57] the government was still having a discussion with 'stakeholders'. Again, over five years after the report on administrative redress,[58] the government is only beginning to do preliminary work to consider the feasibility of the Commission's proposals. There are two related reasons for a degree of depression. The first is that, as time passes, law reform proposals become more difficult to implement because, as many have observed, including Sir James Munby in his Denning Lecture, they will cost more to implement because of the work necessary to update them. The second is that mentioned above, that as time passes expertise in the particular area may no longer be available within the Law Commission.

Because much of the work of the two Commissions is about ensuring that the unseen parts of the law are up-to-date and work efficiently, what appears to allow the priorities to change is the absence of a crisis. In technical areas, a report may be left to gather dust because it is not seen as addressing an immediate and pressing problem by policy-makers and members of Parliament. The Commissions may, however, have identified a real but as yet latent problem. The best example of this, in my view, is the Commission's work on liability for chancel repairs.[59] The problem was that the purchasers of certain property could find themselves liable in respect of what could be very expensive repairs to churches in circumstances in which this liability was sometimes not discoverable from the Land Registry. The Law Commission became involved after concerns raised when a number of individuals were presented with large and unforeseen bills. But the problem was not seen as widespread or pressing, partly because parochial church councils were not generally zealous in enforcing their rights. When the Commission reported, some took the view that this was a dry and technical, and indeed theoretical, area. The Commission was criticised for reporting on what was largely an academic problem. Moreover, because the impact of any reform would have adversely affected church councils' rights, church interests, who of course are represented as such in the legislature, were generally opposed to the proposals. The report was shelved.

Things changed after, as a result of extensive dilapidations and a deteriorating financial position, the church became more zealous in enforcing the liability. The matter came to life again during my time at the Commission. As I recall, the reason was that a resident of Huntingdon, for which Mr John Major was then the MP, was faced with a large and unforeseeable bill. Despite the consequent pressure, there was no reform. The matter later came to life again in proceedings which unsuccessfully challenged the liability on human rights grounds.[60] It was, however, not until 2003,

---

[57] Law Commission, LC 303, *Termination of Tenancies for Tenant Default* (2006).

[58] Law Commission, LC 322, *Administrative Redress: Public Bodies and the Citizen* (2010).

[59] Law Commission, LC 152, *Liability for Chancel Repairs* (1985).

[60] *Wallbank v Aston Cantlow and Wilmcote PCC* [2003] UKHL 37, [2001] 1 AC 546. The Wallbanks, who were liable for £95,260, claimed that the liability was an indiscriminate form of taxation and violated ECHR Article 1 of Protocol 1. The merits of their case were perhaps not seen as compelling because they were aware of the potential liability at the time they acquired the rectorial property.

almost 20 years after the Law Commission's report, that the problem was addressed by a land registration solution.[61]

I have referred to the fact that the special legislative procedure that the Law Commission was seeking in my time now exists in the House of Lords. It does so as a result of the efforts of many over the years, and brought to fruition by Sir Terence Etherton when he was Chairman of the Commission. I do not consider the procedure is suitable for proposals raising very wide social and economic issues. This is because they are likely to lead to party-political controversy. But for many Law Commission recommendations, it is, in my view, an excellent way of seeking to meet some of the 'changed priorities' challenges. Its utility does, however, depend on the relevant government departments forming a view on a report relatively quickly. Its utility also depends on it not being used only for proposals that are completely uncontroversial. There are almost always winners and losers in changes in the law. There is accordingly likely to be some controversy in proposed reforms of the sort that there was in relation to the Commission's recent projects on insurance, which were enacted using the special procedure.[62] That was made possible because of a decision by the Treasury to shelve the recommendation that there be provision for damages for late payment of a claim.[63] Government had accepted this recommendation, but last minute opposition from a section of the industry meant that using the special procedure would risk losing the entire Bill. Some regard this as blackmail; others as a pragmatic and sensible decision not to risk the best imperilling the good.

My final suggestion about facing the risk that government's priorities will change and sound recommendations for reform will not be implemented concerns the part of Law Commissions' remit that I have not yet mentioned, consolidation. Consolidation is a central part of the duty of the Law Commissions under section 3(1) of the 1965 Act. They are required to 'simplify' the law inter alia by 'comprehensive programmes of consolidation'. Although law reform can address fundamental problems, and these are likely to be of greater interest to Commissioners, we should not lose sight of the benefits of consolidation. Where the problem with an area is lack of clarity because the law on a topic is spread over a large number of enactments areas that are confusing, and possibly inconsistent, consolidation can result in a substantial improvement and make a real difference.[64] The process of consolidation is also likely to highlight the parts of a topic where the problem is not simply lack of clarity and confusion because the law is spread over many statutes, but a bad rule.

[61] The Land Registration Act 2002 and the Land Registration Rules 2003, SI 2003/1417 provided that, unless registered by a parochial church council, the right lost its status as an overriding interest. Individuals may also take out chancel repair liability insurance.

[62] The following recent Acts implementing Law Commission reports used the procedure: Perpetuities and Accumulations Act 2009; Third Parties (Rights against Insurers) Act 2010; Consumer Insurance (Disclosure and Representations) Act 2012; Trusts (Capital and Income) Act 2013; Inheritance and Trustees' Powers Act 2014; and Insurance Act 2015. The Consumer Rights Act 2015 which implemented Law Commission recommendations in three reports conducted jointly with the Scottish Law Commission (LC 292 and SLC 199, *Unfair Terms in Contracts* (2005), LC 332 and SLC 226, *Consumer Redress for Misleading and Aggressive Practices* (2012); and LC 317 and SLC 216, *Consumer Remedies for Faulty Goods* (2009)) was a government programme Bill.

[63] See further chapter 27 (Stephen Lewis).

[64] See chapter 10 (George Gretton).

In that way it can assist in clearing the ground for a more focused law reform exercise which can be less difficult to implement. Moreover, the process of implementing a consolidation is faster. One obvious candidate for consolidation is immigration law. The lack of clarity in statutes, rules and guidance and the fact that a lot of the material is either inaccessible or difficult to access means that even the lawyers acting for the Home Secretary can be misled.[65] There is an urgent need for a consolidation of immigration legislation, although, perhaps given the sensitivity of the subject-matter, not solely by the Law Commission, but by a process involving it so that the Bill can include 'Law Commission style amendments' which reduce the inconsistencies and the obscure provisions.

It has to be recognised that deciding whether to proceed by consolidation or by law reform can, in a particular case, not be easy. For example, the Law Commission is currently examining sentencing law.[66] It has described the current law on sentencing as 'an impenetrable thicket, contained in hundreds of separate provisions scattered across dozens of statutes' and aims to introduce 'a single sentencing statute that will act as the first and only port of call for sentencing tribunals'.[67] Although it stated that it is not its aim to interfere with mandatory minimum sentences or with sentencing tariffs, and although the Lord Chief Justice described the need as for 'consolidation and simplification', the project is one of law reform rather than consolidation with 'Law Commission amendments'. This may be because it was considered that the 'simplification' required could not be accommodated comfortably within the constraints of a consolidation exercise. There is a real need for simplification and consistency in sentencing legislation, and a single Act would be a real boon. But, even if the recommendations of the Commission are implemented swiftly, unless Sir Geoffrey Palmer's suggestion that the way statutes are made and promulgated to the public is itself reformed, the experience of the Powers of Criminal Courts (Sentencing) Act 2000 suggests that the legislation would not remain in a single Act for long.

## IV  SHORTENING TIMESCALES?

I have stated that proper and rigorous consideration of problems and the solutions to them takes time. This is so even in this new age of instantaneousness. I referred to the difficulties posed by greatly delayed projects, the likelihood that a quick and imperfect fix will be made by another part of the system, or that the pressure for change will dissipate. There was no delay in the Commission's project on rape in marriage, and the decision of the House of Lords in *R v R* was a considered development of doctrine.[68] It was not a 'fix' that was either 'quick' or 'imperfect'. But the Lords'

---

[65] See *Singh v Secretary of State for the Home Department* [2015] EWCA Civ 74, [57] ff (Underhill LJ).
[66] Law Commission, LC 354, *Twelfth Programme of Law Reform* (2014) and Law Commission, *Sentencing Procedure: Issues Paper 1: Transition* (2015). See particularly chapter 12 (Ian Dennis).
[67] *Issues Paper*, n 66 above, paras 1.6–1.7.
[68] See n 6 above. See also chapter 2 (Lady Hale).

decision did not and could not deal with consequential questions such as whether the complainant should be compellable to give evidence for the prosecution.[69]

There is an understandable desire by those who wish to promote reform for it to be achieved as soon as possible. But producing recommendations quickly is not a guarantee of speedy implementation, even where government is fully in favour of them. That was the case in my one-man report on bailiff law where the legislation was enacted seven years after the report required within 12 months of the Lord Chancellor asking me to undertake it. Sir Peter North's review of drink and drug driving law provides another example. Sir Peter was appointed in December 2009, and asked to provide initial advice to the Secretary of State for Transport by 31 March 2010. The advice was provided on 29 March, and the review was submitted to Ministers in May and published on 16 June 2010.[70] The Select Committee on Transport conducted an inquiry into Sir Peter's recommendations, and published its report in December 2010.[71] The government published its response to the two reports in March 2011, stating that its first priority was to find an effective means of detecting and deterring drug-driving to enable a serious enforcement effort. It also stated that it accepted many of the recommendations, identified those which needed primary legislation, and stated it would seek a legislative slot for them.[72] Section 56 of the Crime and Courts Act 2013 created a new specific offence related to driving and drugs.[73]

There is also sometimes a clear need for urgency in addressing a pressing legal problem. In such a case, unless the problem is clearly self-contained and narrow, the question is whether the need to address it is so urgent that it is not suited to a Commission project. A second, and better, reason for a shorter or truncated timescale is the existence of an opportunity for legislation on a particular and defined issue which needs quick action. For example, part of the Commission's work on contempt, started in 2012, was accelerated at the request of the Attorney-General because a former Secretary of State for Northern Ireland was charged with the offence of 'scandalising the court' after criticising a Northern Irish judge in his memoirs. The Commission accelerated its work on that and reported on it in December 2012.[74] The offence was abolished by the Crime and Courts Act 2013. The remainder of the Law Commission's contempt project was completed in the spring of 2014,[75] and certain recommendations concerning juror misconduct and internet publications were enacted in the Criminal Justice and Courts Act 2015.

There is another danger of timetables that are too short. Law Commissions must not get themselves into a position where they take a short view in order to assist

---

[69] By the Police and Criminal Evidence Act 1984, s 80(2) a defendant's spouse is only compellable to give evidence on behalf of the defendant.

[70] P North, *Report of the Review of Drink and Drug Driving Law* (2010).

[71] House of Commons Transport Committee, *Drink and Drug Driving Law* (2010–11, HC 460).

[72] *The Government's Response to the Reports by Sir Peter North CBE QC and the Transport Select Committee on Drink and Drug Driving* (Cm 8050, 2011).

[73] See also schedule 22 of the 2013 Act.

[74] Law Commission, LC 335, *Contempt of Court: Scandalising the Court* (2012).

[75] See Law Commission, LC 340, *Contempt of Court (1): Juror Misconduct and Internet Publications* (2013), and LC 344, *Contempt of Court (2): Court Reporting* (2014).

in dealing with an urgent problem which is part of a larger topic, only to find that they have to revisit the matter or address another part of the topic soon afterwards. This has sometimes been a problem with single-issue inquiries set up to deal with a particular problem. More generally, in some areas, notably, in the last decade and a half, in the areas of criminal law and immigration to which I have referred, there has been a constant stream of legislation, regulation and guidance introduced quickly to address a particular problem. The result is not always happy.

If shorter timescales for projects become more common, there may be a number of consequences. The first is that there will be pressure on Commissions to undertake smaller-scale projects. Given present staffing levels, this would be inevitable unless members of staff are deployed disproportionately, or even exclusively, on a single project. That would imperil a Commission's ability to keep 'the general law' up-to-date, as its governing statute requires. It may also involve deploying staff with legal skills in one area to an area with which they are relatively unfamiliar. It might also leave the Commissioners who are not involved in the project benefiting from the extra resources with insufficient support for their projects.

The Commission has suffered numerous cuts since its foundation. The legal staff at first consisted of senior legal civil servants (assistant solicitors). They were removed long before my time.[76] In my time, the typical pattern was that a reform team consisted of three lawyers (a grade six team leader, and two grade seven lawyers), and two or three research assistants. Grade seven was the entry level rank so those lawyers were relatively junior. Each team would typically work on two or three projects at different stages. For any one project, typically, the responsibility for the first draft of a report or consultation paper lay with one of the legal civil servants, assisted by one or occasionally two research assistants, and under the supervision of the relevant Commissioner. The lawyer generally also had responsibility for another project. There was little scope to move staff to another team without slowing down or putting one of the other projects on hold. The privacy working party with which I was involved consisted of two more senior government lawyers and two other lawyers, together with me as a consultant. The Commission could not seek to work within shorter timescales on large-scale projects without a real risk of significantly prejudicing the quality of the finished product.

It is right for the Commission to seek to assist government with an urgent problem if it can. Sometimes, where the issue is clearly discrete, the assistance can be by a Commission project. But where it is not, as seen from some of the single-issue inquiries led by a judge or other public figure, the result will not be satisfactory because any solution will only be to part of the problem. Where the issue is intertwined with other issues which may not be suitable for a Law Commission inquiry, it will generally be better for one of the Commissioners and their team to assist the relevant department. There are many examples of this through the history of the Law Commission. They include the early stages of work on commonhold, Brenda Hale's work on mental incapacity, and the assistance I provided to Lord Mackay

---

[76] See RT Oerton, *A Lament for the Law Commission* (Chichester, Countrywide Press, 1987) ch 5.

and his department in 1993 in preparing a consultation paper on the infringement of privacy. It is, however, important for the Commissions to take a long view, even where that results in deciding not to take on an inappropriately designed project and to frustration in the short term.

To conclude, in his magisterial Scarman Lecture earlier this year, Sir Geoffrey Palmer stated: 'No coherent philosophy for the law reform enterprise has emerged. Probably none can be devised because the Commissions occupy an awkward space between principle and expediency.'[77] This applies as much to devising working methods for Commissions as to the identification of a mixture of appropriate topics for a Commission to work on at any time.

---

[77] G Palmer, 'The Law Reform Enterprise: Evaluating the Past and Charting the Future' (2015) 131 *LQR* 402, 420.

# 27

# *The Bill's Progress*

STEPHEN LEWIS

Like David Johnston, I have only been a Commissioner since January 2015. But while reading Sir Jack Beatson's contribution to this volume,[1] and in particular his reference to insurance law reform in this context, it struck me that, rather than give you my initial impressions of the way in which the Law Commission works, it might be more helpful to give you a thumbnail sketch of the history of one the Law Commission's more important recent projects—its extended programme of insurance contract law reform, against the background of the government's evolving priorities.

The starting point has to be the Law Commission's October 1980 *Report on Non-Disclosure and Breach of Warranty*,[2] in which the Law Commission concluded that the law in these areas was undoubtedly in need of reform, that reform had been far too long delayed—this was by no means the first report recommending reform of this area of the law—and recommended that several changes should be made to mitigate the harsh and one-sided nature of the law by, for example, narrowing the scope of the duty of disclosure and abolishing 'basis of the contract' clauses. This Report was accompanied by a draft Bill. The Law Commission was at that time chaired by Sir Michael Kerr—then a judge of the High Court—who had been an eminent practitioner in the field of insurance law. I happen to know that he wrote large chunks of the Report himself. And what happened to this comparatively modest, but well-thought-out package of reforms? The answer is: precisely nothing!

The historical background to what happened to the 1980 Report is succinctly set out in Lord Justice Longmore's Pat Saxton Memorial Lecture, 'An Insurance Contracts Act for a New Century?' given on 5 March 2001,[3] although reference can also usefully be made to Peter Tyldesley's excellent book on *Consumer Insurance Law*.[4] Suffice it to say that there was a great deal of procrastination by the government of the day which eventually provoked Peter North, who had been the Commissioner in charge of the project, to remark, somewhat cynically, 'the suspicious observer might conclude that the insurance industry lobby has been active behind closed doors and has in fact won'.[5] About a year later, the Secretary of State

---

[1] See chapter 26 (Sir Jack Beatson).
[2] Law Commission, LC 104 (1980).
[3] (2001) 3 *Lloyd's Maritime and Commercial Law Quarterly* 356; also at n 8 below, app A.
[4] PJ Tyldesley, *Consumer Insurance Law: Disclosure, Representations and Basis of the Contract Clauses* (Haywards Heath, Bloomsbury, 2013).
[5] P North, 'Law Reform: Processes and Problems' (1985) 101 *LQR* 338.

of the Department of Trade and Industry, Mr Channon, giving a written answer in the House of Commons,[6] confirmed that the Report had in effect been put 'on the back burner' pending the promulgation and bringing into effect of various voluntary Statements of Insurance Practice signed up to by the insurance industry, in which they basically promised not unreasonably to repudiate liability under insurance contracts. Indeed, nothing further happened until the turn of the century. In the meantime, the Australians had enacted an Insurance Contracts Act 1984 which was very much along the lines of the Law Commission's 1980 Report.

As indicated, Lord Justice Longmore gave his lecture in March 2001. This amounted to a clarion call for further consideration of reform. There was, in addition, an influential lecture from Lord Justice Rix,[7] also in support of reform.

In September 2002, a British Insurance Law Association (BILA) sub-committee chaired by Mr Adrian Hamilton QC, with the participation of academics, insurers, practising lawyers and loss adjusters, recommended the speedy implementation of the 1980 Report, with some revisions.[8] The sub-committee's view was that the Statements of Insurance Practice were not a sufficient protection to the insured. Nor was the establishment of the Financial Ombudsman Service, created by the Financial Services and Markets Act 2000, consolidating some existing schemes, a reason for not reforming the law. Lord Justice Mance—as he then was—who was at that time the BILA President, commended the Report to the attention of the Law Commission in his introduction to it.

The Law Commission was subsequently given a remit in 2006 to carry out a joint review, with the Scottish Law Commission, of insurance contract law. This project has spanned nine years and has culminated in the enactment of the Consumer Insurance (Disclosure and Representations) Act 2012, which replaced the consumer insured's duty of disclosure with a duty to answer the insurer's questions honestly and reasonably, and the Insurance Act 2015, which has preserved the business insurer's duty of disclosure but has provided a range of remedies for breach rather than only avoidance of the contract, has abolished 'the basis of the contract' clauses for all types of insurance contract, and has restricted remedies for breach of warranty, amongst many other things.

The history of our insurance project is not without interest. In very brief summary, the Commissions' initial views on issues ranging from misrepresentation and non-disclosure, breach of warranty, intermediaries, insurable interest, damages for late payment of claims, to broker's liability for premium, were set out in nine issues papers.[9] The project involved an enormous amount of research and consultation,

---

[6] HC Deb 21 Feb 1986, vol 92, cols 356–57.

[7] 'Good Faith: To Be or Not to Be?', delivered at BILA President's Lunch on 19 December 2001, reproduced in n 8 below, app B.

[8] British Insurance Law Association, *Insurance Contract Law Reform—Recommendations to the Law Commissions* (2002).

[9] Issues Papers on: (1) Misrepresentation and Non-Disclosure; (2) Warranties; (3) Intermediaries and Pre-Contract Information; (4) Insurable Interest; (5) Micro-Businesses; (6) Damages for Late Payment; (7) The Insured's Post-Contract Duty of Good Faith; (8) The Broker's Liability for Premium; and (9) The Requirement for a Formal Marine Policy are all available at www.lawcom.gov.uk/project/insurance-contract-law/#insurance-contract-law-issues-papers.

and benefitted from a great deal of help and support from a wide cross-section of the insurance market, together with legal practitioners and judges. As a result of this extensive consultation process, a widespread acceptance was secured from the insurance industry that legislative reform was needed. Eventually, the responses to the initial proposals in the nine issues papers were sufficiently refined and well-developed to be able to be included in a series of three consultation papers, making firm recommendations for reform.[10]

The wise decision was nevertheless taken by my predecessor, David Hertzell, to focus initially on the consumer's duty to disclose information to insurers, as this was the chief mischief in need of reform. In December 2009, a final report and draft Bill on consumer insurance was published.[11] The Bill was passed using the special procedure for non-controversial Law Commission Bills—about which more can be found elsewhere in this volume[12]—and this became the Consumer Insurance (Disclosure and Representation) Act 2012. The BILA has stated publically that throughout the consultation process, the Law Commission showed itself to be assiduously fair in its dealing with both policyholders and insurers and, as Sir David Lloyd Jones pointed out in his Sir William Dale Annual Lecture in 2012,[13] the work on this project provides a very good example of how the Commission is close enough to government to be able to influence outcomes, while at the same time being sufficiently removed from government to be able to act independently and to achieve balanced results.

The Law Commission's team then turned to work on the remaining issues of insurance contract law, including damages for late payment, remedies for fraudulent claims, insurable interest and broker's liability for premium. A further consultation paper was published in December 2011.[14]

This was followed by another consultation paper on *The Business Insured's Duty of Disclosure and the Law of Warranties*.[15] Again, we consulted widely and published a draft Bill in February 2014 to give effect to some of the recommendations in the consultation papers. This Bill was subsequently, but with certain important revisions, enacted in the Insurance Act 2015.

For reasons of space, I shall focus on one topic—damages for late payment of claims—which was included in the initial draft of the Insurance Bill, but was left out of the Act. Although this provision was widely supported on consultation, some key stakeholders—the Association of British Insurers (the ABI) and Lloyds Market Association—resisted it on the basis that it might encourage speculative litigation,

---

[10] Law Commission and Scottish Law Commission, LC CP 192 and SLC DP 134, *Misrepresentation, Non-Disclosure and Breach of Warranty by the Insured* (2007); LC CP 201 and SLC DP 152, *Insurance Contract Law: Post Contract Duties and other Issues* (2011); LC CP 204 and SLC DP 155, *The Business Insured's Duty of Disclosure and the Law of Warranties* (2012).

[11] Law Commission and Scottish Law Commission, LC 319 and SLC 219, *Consumer Insurance Law: Pre-Contract Disclosure and Misrepresentation* (2009).

[12] See particularly chapters 9 (Sir Terence Etherton) and 22 (Hector MacQueen).

[13] D Lloyd Jones, 'The Law Commission and the Implementation of Law Reform', Sir William Dale Annual Lecture (2012) 22.

[14] Law Commission and Scottish Law Commission, LC CP 201, SLC DP 152, *Insurance Contract Law: Post Contract Duties and Other Issues* (2011).

[15] Law Commission and Scottish Law Commission, LC CP 204, SLC DP 155 (2012).

and have the unwelcome effect of being used to exert undue pressure to expedite claims settlement. The ABI highlighted that claims management companies could exploit any uncertainty in the law in a bid to obtain additional income streams. The view was quite properly taken by HM Treasury that this clause was therefore controversial and was not suitable for the special Law Commission parliamentary procedure.[16] The view was further taken that not only might its inclusion threaten the passage of the Insurance Bill as a whole, but it might also jeopardise the future of the special Law Commission procedure itself. In these circumstances it was decided by HM Treasury to drop that clause of the Bill, without prejudice to its possible future enactment at some future time.

The Insurance Act 2015 received Royal Assent on 12 February 2015 and will come into effect in August 2016. Together with the Consumer Insurance Act 2012, it has brought about the most profound change in insurance contract law since the Marine Insurance Act 1906 and has, in so doing, struck a much fairer balance between the interests of the policyholder and insurers.

Overall, it can be said that the co-operation between the Law Commission and HM Treasury in the drafting and enactment of the Insurance Act 2015 represents a very good example of the successful working of the Protocol between the Lord Chancellor and the Law Commission signed in March 2010.[17]

We are still working on some of the remaining topics in insurance law such as insurable interest—as to which we published a further consultation paper in March 2015[18]—and we are still hoping for an early legislative opportunity to enact the provisions for damages for late payment for which, as I have indicated, there is widespread support.

What this chapter shows is: (1) the importance of extensive consultation with all affected stakeholders to any Law Commission project; and (2) the impact of the government's changing and evolving policy priorities on the progress of the Law Commission's work.

---

[16] See chapter 22 (Hector MacQueen).

[17] Law Commission and Ministry of Justice, LC 321, *Protocol between the Lord Chancellor (on behalf of the Government) and the Law Commission* (2010).

[18] Law Commission and Scottish Law Commission, *Reforming Insurance Contract Law, Issues Paper 10, Insurable Interest: Updated Proposals* (2015), available at www.lawcom.gov.uk/wp-content/uploads/2015/06/ICL10_insurable_interest_issues.pdf.

# Part 7

# Courts and Commissions

# 28

# *Introduction*

LORD DRUMMOND YOUNG

The relationship between courts and Commissions can be described as a continuing dialogue—an important part of the wider dialogue through which the law develops to meet changing circumstances. Clearly any law reform project by a Commission must start with the existing decisions of the courts, and consider those critically. Thus courts influence Commissions. The dialogue works in the other direction, however; the work of Commissions can have an important influence on what courts do. This is most obvious where recommendations are implemented by legislation. In that event, the reports produced by the Commission may provide valuable guidance to the courts as to the purpose and context of the legislation. Charles Harpum examines this process in 'The Refiner's Fire' (chapter 31), in relation to the Land Registration Act 2002. His contribution demonstrates how judicial consideration of the statute may be greatly assisted by Commission reports.

But Commission reports can have an impact on the decisions of the courts even in the absence of legislation. They normally provide a good exposition of the existing law, with its successes, its deficiencies and its problems. They can be helpful in providing an analytic framework for an area of law, which can serve as a basis for judicial development. Moreover, Commission reports are based on extensive consultation, and thus they provide courts with a valuable link to the economic and social considerations that bear on the law and its development. James Lee, in 'The Etiquette of Law Reform' (chapter 29), considers how far the work of the Law Commissions in the United Kingdom has influenced the UK Supreme Court in its decisions. The picture that emerges is mixed, with significant differences among the individual judges.

Of course in some areas the common law is best left to judicial development, either indefinitely or until problems emerge that seem to require legislative intervention. In those areas, work by Commissions should be circumspect. Barbara McDonald, in 'Law Reform in Private Law: The Role of Statutes in Supplementing or Supplanting the Common Law' (chapter 30), considers when it may, or may not, be appropriate for Commissions to interfere with the development of the common law. As ever, the picture that emerges is one of constant dialogue: courts and Commissions each influence what the other is doing. That dialogue is surely one of the most important benefits that have emerged in the last 50 years from the creation of the Commissions, for it is through that dialogue that the law will develop in a practical and effective manner.

# 29

# *The Etiquette of Law Reform*

JAMES LEE*

> Two Brits walk into a bar. Well, I say, 'walk into'. One holds the door open for the
> other: 'Oh! Sorry, after you'. The other demurs 'No, no, I insist, after you!'
> A stand-off of quintessentially British awkwardness ensues. To avoid
> any further embarrassment, they both go home without entering.

## I INTRODUCTION

What is the etiquette of law reform? My concern is that recent developments in the
relationship between the Law Commissions and the Supreme Court suggest either
that the scenario outlined above is applicable, or that certain issues are stuck in
a broken revolving door, unable to get out. My reason for invoking 'etiquette' is
that, even within the (shared) provinces of what the courts and law reform commissions *can* do, it is important to understand what they *should* and *should not* do.[1]
In common with other chapters in this collection, this essay will show that there is
no unanimity of view over the appropriateness of what things are for the court and
what things are for the Commissions. But I shall also demonstrate that reference to
the Law Commissions reveals aspects of the dynamics of the relationships between
the Justices.

This essay builds upon an analysis of the 404 decisions of the UK Supreme Court
by the end of the sixth year of the Supreme Court's jurisprudence, in July 2015.
Of those, 48[2] included some reference to the Law Commission or Scottish Law

* I am grateful to Matthew Dyson, Graham Gee, Simon Lee, Perry Keller, Shona Wilson Stark and
many others who attended the conference for helpful discussions. Part of section III of this essay was first
aired in an Inner Temple Academic Fellow's Lecture in April 2012. All views, and any errors, are my own.

[1] For that reason, 'etiquette' here is being used in the sense of tacit, though occasionally explicit, rules
of good conduct.

[2] From a search on bailii.org and then my own analysis. Searching for 'law commission' produces
50 cases: the two which I am not counting in the figures are *Moohan v Lord Advocate* [2014] UKSC
67, where at [64] and [82], Lord Hodge referred to work by the International Law Commission and *R
(Adams) v Secretary of State for Justice* [2011] UKSC 18, in which Lord Phillips at [47] and Lord Kerr
at [173]–[175] referred to a report of the New Zealand Law Commission (NZLC 49, *Compensating the
Wrongly Convicted* (1988)).

Commission, which is nearly exactly 12 per cent of the total, or just under one in every eight cases. Sixty-eight separate opinions within those cases refer to Law Commissions in some way or other.[3] A qualitative reflection on the bare figures demonstrates that those Justices who have been involved with the Law Commissions are more likely to refer to the Commissions in judgments.[4] It will be seen that, overall, Lady Hale is the most likely to refer to the Law Commissions, and her experience clearly informs her approach to judging.[5]

In what follows, I examine first this general judicial practice of referring to the Law Commissions. I then take three case studies, beginning with Lady Hale's contribution to the law on cohabitation. Then I consider recent Supreme Court decisions on the law of illegality, and finally the dialogue between the Supreme Court and the European Court of Human Rights over the admissibility of hearsay evidence under chapter 2 of the Criminal Justice Act 2003.

The lives of our top court and the Commissions are intertwined.[6] As Duxbury has noted, the House of Lords recognised its power to depart from previous decisions just one year after the Law Commissions Act 1965, which 'led to an increase in legislative activity, [making] the overruling of some unsatisfactory House of Lords precedents unnecessary'.[7] Then, more recently, at the time of the creation of the UK Supreme Court in 2009, the role of the Law Commission was also shaped by the Law Commission Act 2009 and attendant protocol. A new regime governs the relationship between the Law Commission and the government. The Law Commission Act 2009[8] introduces new governmental accountability for the implementation of Law Commission reports, in that an annual report must be issued by the Lord Chancellor, indicating what decisions have been made about any yet-to-be-taken-forward proposals. There is now an agreed protocol between the government and the English and Welsh Commission,[9] which requires the specific endorsement of a government department before that Commission can even begin a project.[10] There

---

[3] See section II below.

[4] Lady Hale and Lord Hodge were Commissioners at the Law Commission and Scottish Law Commission respectively; Lords Carnwath (1999–2002) and Toulson (2002–06) were successive Chairmen of the Law Commission. See the data in section IIA below. It is also noticeable that the Justices may do so in dissent: eg Lady Hale dissenting in *R (on the application of McDonald) v Royal Borough of Kensington and Chelsea* [2011] UKSC 33, [65] (a quarter of Lady Hale's opinions in which she refers to the Commissions were dissenting judgments).

[5] See section III below.

[6] An example is considered by E Cooke, 'Taking Women's Property Seriously: Mrs Boland, the House of Lords, the Law Commission and the Role of Consensus' in J Lee (ed), *From House of Lords to Supreme Court: Judges, Jurists and the Process of Judging* (Oxford, Hart Publishing, 2009).

[7] N Duxbury, *The Nature and Authority of Precedent* (Cambridge, CUP, 2008) 127. See also J Lee, 'Fides et Ratio: Precedent in the Early Jurisprudence of the United Kingdom Supreme Court' (2015) 21(1) *European Journal of Current Legal Issues*.

[8] See chapter 9 (Sir Terence Etherton). See also J Lee, '"Inconsiderate Alterations in our Laws"' in *From House of Lords to Supreme Court*, n 6 above, 95–99.

[9] Law Commission and Ministry of Justice, LC 321, *Protocol between the Lord Chancellor (on behalf of the Government) and the Law Commission* (2010).

[10] ibid paras 6–9.

is also a fast-track scheme for the passage of politically uncontroversial Bills proposed by the Law Commissions.[11] My primary focus, and the dataset, is on the Law Commissions and the Supreme Court: however, I shall also make judicious reference to some Privy Council decisions from the same period, where appropriate.

In his two seminal books,[12] Alan Paterson has vividly illustrated the importance of dialogues in understanding the work of the Supreme Court, and also the relationship between the Court and other institutions. In considering the role of Parliament and the Commission, Paterson has noted that:

> While some variants of the arguments may be thought less weighty than others nonetheless they do appear to be part of an on-going dialogue between the final court and Parliament (and the Law Commission). This dialogue, however, is almost entirely symbolic and sufficiently asynchronous as to appear more like a monologue in which Parliament appears not to hear the Court and the Court sometimes responds by developing the law where normally they would not.[13]

Other chapters in this collection consider the further variations on the argument about the line between judicial development of the law and legislation, especially those by Lady Hale[14] and Professor Burrows.[15] I consider here the ways in which those arguments are made by the Justices in their decisions. It will be seen that reflecting upon reference to the Law Commissions sheds light not only on dialogues between the Supreme Court and the Commissions, and between the Court and legislature, but also on dialogues between the Justices, and even the dialogue between the Court (and Commissions) and the European Court of Human Rights.

## II REFERENCES

### A Data

Table 1 shows the authorship of opinions to mention one or both of the Law Commissions in the 48 cases to do so: there are 68 such opinions (since in some cases more than one speech made some mention of the Law Commissions). The Justices are listed in order of seniority of appointment, and then the chronological order of joint opinions.

---

[11] These have included Law Commission proposals in the law of trusts. The reforms may alleviate somewhat the concern that 'Law Commission reports regularly gather dust, despite being ready for off-the-shelf implementation': J Morgan, 'Policy Reasoning in Tort Law: The Courts, the Law Commission and the Critics' (2009) 125 *LQR* 215, 220. See chapters 9 (Sir Terence Etherton) and 22 (Hector MacQueen).

[12] AA Paterson, *The Law Lords* (London, Macmillan, 1982) and A Paterson, *Final Judgment* (Oxford, Hart Publishing, 2013) (hereafter *Final Judgment*).

[13] *Final Judgment*, 281.

[14] See chapter 2 (Lady Hale).

[15] See chapter 20 (Andrew Burrows).

Table 1

| Justice of the Supreme Court (Lord/Lady) | Opinions with references to the Law Commission(s) |
|---|---|
| Phillips | 2 |
| Hope | 4 |
| Saville | 0 |
| Rodger | 0 |
| Walker | 3 |
| Hale | 14 |
| Brown | 0 |
| Mance | 2 |
| Collins | 4 |
| Kerr | 2 |
| Clarke | 2 |
| Dyson | 1 |
| Wilson | 4 |
| Sumption | 5 |
| Reed | 3 |
| Carnwath | 6 |
| Neuberger | 4 |
| Hughes | 1 |
| Toulson | 2 |
| Hodge | 2 |
| Lord Phillips, Lord Hope, Lord Rodger, Lord Walker, Lord Brown, Lord Collins And Lord Kerr[16] | 1 |
| Hale and Walker[17] | 1 |
| Phillips and Judge[18] | 1 |
| Neuberger and Hodge[19] | 1 |
| Toulson and Hodge[20] | 1 |
| Hale and Toulson[21] | 1 |
| Neuberger and Reed[22] | 1 |

[16] Joint majority judgment in *Radmacher (formerly Granatino) v Granatino* [2010] UKSC 4.
[17] Joint lead judgment in *Jones v Kernott* [2011] UKSC 53.
[18] Joint lead majority judgment in *R v Gnango* [2011] UKSC 59.
[19] Joint lead judgment in *R (on the application of Newhaven Port and Properties Ltd) v East Sussex County Council* [2015] UKSC 7.
[20] Joint concurring judgment in *Jetivia SA & Anor v Bilta (UK) Ltd* [2015] UKSC 23, as to which, see below, section IV.
[21] Joint lead judgment in *Rhodes v OPO* [2015] UKSC 32.
[22] Joint dissent in *Zurich Insurance PLC UK Branch v International Energy Group Ltd* [2015] UKSC 33.

Table 2 shows the number of opinions authored by a Justice, whether individually or jointly, to include a reference to the Law Commissions (including Lord Judge who has not been a permanent Justice of the Court but gave the joint judgment for the Court with Lord Phillips PSC in *Gnango*), from the most frequent referrer to the least frequent.[23]

**Table 2**

| Justice of the Supreme Court (Lord/Lady) | Opinions with references to the Law Commission(s) |
|---|---|
| Hale | 16 |
| Carnwath | 6 |
| Neuberger | 6 |
| Hope | 5 |
| Collins | 5 |
| Sumption | 5 |
| Phillips | 4 |
| Wilson | 4 |
| Reed | 4 |
| Toulson | 4 |
| Hodge | 4 |
| Walker | 3 |
| Kerr | 3 |
| Mance | 2 |
| Clarke | 2 |
| Rodger | 1 |
| Brown | 1 |
| Dyson | 1 |
| Hughes | 1 |
| Judge | 1 |
| Saville | 0 |

The most striking feature of this table is Lady Hale's clear lead. The table does not of course take into account the length of service, and Lady Hale has been on the Court for the duration of its six years, whereas by the end of the sixth year, Lord Hodge had been in post for just over two years.[24] Table 3 therefore takes into account the duration of service by 31 July 2015, to the nearest year, to give the average references per year.

---

[23] The total in this table is higher than the 68 in Table 1, because of the allocation of individual credit to joint opinions to both or all authors.

[24] Having been appointed in April 2013.

Table 3

| Justice of the Supreme Court (Lord/Lady) | Opinions with references to the Law Commission | Years of service | References per year |
|---|---|---|---|
| Hale | 16 | 6 | 2.67 |
| Collins | 5 | 2 | 2.5 |
| Carnwath | 6 | 3 | 2 |
| Neuberger | 6 | 3 | 2 |
| Toulson | 4 | 2 | 2 |
| Hodge | 4 | 2 | 2 |
| Sumption | 5 | 3 | 1.67 |
| Phillips | 4 | 3 | 1.33 |
| Reed | 4 | 3 | 1.33 |
| Hope | 5 | 4 | 1.25 |
| Wilson | 4 | 4 | 1 |
| Walker | 3 | 4 | 0.75 |
| Kerr | 3 | 6 | 0.5 |
| Rodger | 1 | 2 | 0.5 |
| Dyson | 1 | 2 | 0.5 |
| Hughes | 1 | 2 | 0.5 |
| Mance | 2 | 6 | 0.33 |
| Clarke | 2 | 6 | 0.33 |
| Brown | 1 | 3 | 0.33 |
| Judge | 1 | N/A | N/A |
| Saville | 0 | N/A | N/A |

It is here that the crude year calculation requires some elaboration. both Lord Collins and Lord Neuberger sat in cases outside of their official service on the Court, with Lord Collins as an ad hoc judge and Lord Neuberger when he was Master of the Rolls before becoming President of the Supreme Court. Indeed, they each have one reference to an opinion when they were not one of the current serving Justices of the Court.[25] Thus the picture that emerges is that the Justices who have served at the Law Commissions—Lady Hale, Lords Carnwath, Toulson and Hodge—are amongst the most frequent referrers to the Commissions in their judgments, and indeed are most likely to do so.

---

[25] Lord Neuberger in *Berrisford v Mexfield Housing Co-operative Ltd* [2011] UKSC 52, [96]; Lord Collins in *Scott v Southern Pacific Mortgages* [2014] UKSC 52, [35ff].

## B Comments

Having identified the statistics, it is then necessary to assess the *type* of references to the Commissions. Some of these references[26] are merely of recording the history of legislation (or what did not go into legislation) or other changes originating in Commission proposals,[27] and giving due credit. So in *Cart v The Upper Tribunal*,[28] Lady Hale noted that 'judicial review in its modern form' was the 'product of two developments', one of which was the clarification of procedures for relief 'in the revised Order 53 of the Rules of the Supreme Court, introduced in 1978 following the recommendations of the Law Commission's *Report on Remedies in Administrative Law* (1976, Law Com No 73)'.[29] Her Ladyship seems more willing to give credit to the Commission than other Justices.[30] Sometimes the references in an opinion involve quotation of a previous judge's reference to the Commissions in an earlier case: so when Lord Kerr mentioned the Law Commission in *Re B (A Child)*,[31] his Lordship was really only referring to Baroness Hale's judgment in the House of Lords decision *In re G (Children) (Residence: Same-sex Partner)*.[32] In a case on damages for breaches of human rights,[33] Lord Carnwath drew upon a joint report from the Commissions on *Damages under the Human Rights Act*,[34] acknowledging that he had been Chairman of the Law Commission at the time.[35]

Sometimes they can involve a critical judgement of the ultimate legislation: in *R v Gnango*,[36] Lord Phillips and Lord Judge noted that the Law Commission's *Report on Public Order*[37] had paved the way for the Public Order Act 1986, and that the government had proposed to accept the Commission's definition of

---

[26] On the use of academic opinion by the House of Lords, see K Stanton, 'Use of Scholarship by the House of Lords in Tort Cases' in *From House of Lords to Supreme Court*, n 6 above. Stanton helpfully identifies the different ways in which academic material may be used: 'Providing factual or historical background' (209); 'Summarising/collecting a list of cases' (211); 'Stating the law' (212); and 'Providing food for judicial reasoning' (213). It will be seen here that the Law Commissions' reports may be used in a similar way.

[27] See, eg, Lord Walker in *Office of Fair Trading v Abbey National plc* [2009] UKSC 6, [34].

[28] *Cart v The Upper Tribunal* [2011] UKSC 28.

[29] ibid [16].

[30] See also *Aintree University Hospitals NHS Foundation Trust v James* [2013] UKSC 67, which was 'the first case under the Mental Capacity Act 2005 to come before this Court' (at [1]), and her Ladyship noted that the Act's approach to best interests under section 4 'follows very closely the recommendations of the Law Commission in their *Report on Mental Incapacity* (1995, Law Com No 231) on which the 2005 Act is based' (at [24]). Similarly, see *Scott*, n 25 above, [35]–[36] (Lord Collins) and [103] (Lady Hale).

[31] *Re B (A Child)* [2009] UKSC 5.

[32] *In re G (Children) (Residence: Same-sex Partner)* [2006] UKHL 43, [30]. See similarly Lord Clarke, dissenting, in *VTB Capital Plc v Nutritek International Corp* [2013] UKSC 5, [206], referring to Brooke LJ in *R (Al-Jedda) v Secretary of State for Defence* [2006] EWCA Civ 327, [2007] QB 621.

[33] On the role of the Commissions in human rights case law, see section V below.

[34] LC 266 and SLC 180 (2000).

[35] *R (on the application of Faulkner) (FC) (Appellant) v Secretary of State for Justice* [2013] UKSC 23, [119]; R Carnwath, 'ECHR Remedies from a Common Law Perspective (2000) 20 *International and Comparative Law Quarterly* 517.

[36] *R v Gnango* [2011] UKSC 59.

[37] LC 123, *Offences Relating to Public Order* (1983).

affray: 'unfortunately the draftsman of what was to become the Public Order Act 1986 appears to have thought that he could improve on the drafting of the Law Commission'.[38]

More broadly, reference to Commission reports can be used as a guide to inter-pretation, by way of using *trauvaux preparatoires* (or in some cases subsequent or parallel to Commission reports).[39] Alternatively, where the Commissions are cur-rently looking at a project, it might not be appropriate for the courts to intervene by engaging in reform.[40] Where they have addressed an issue, there may be a compara-tive value in referring to a Commission report. For example, Lord Hodge offered a complementary Scots perspective, referring to yet-to-be-implemented Scottish Law Commission proposals, in an English case on rectification of wills, *Marley v Rawlings*.[41] Lord Neuberger, who gave the leading judgment, said:

> [D]uring our deliberations, we wondered what Scots law would make of the problem thrown up by this appeal. In that connection, it is instructive to read Lord Hodge's judg-ment. As frequently happens, the law north and south of the border each appear to have something to learn from the other, and to involve slightly different ways of arriving at the same outcome.[42]

Another way in which the Commissions might be invoked is in a direct appeal for review and/or reform.[43] Sometimes this is express, and sometimes more oblique.[44] An example of express recommendation is *Walton v The Scottish Ministers*,[45] which concerned a challenge to a scheme permitting the 'construction of a new road net-work in the vicinity of Aberdeen'.[46] Lord Carnwath in a concurring speech raised the issue of the precise effect of quashing an order, which would not 'necessarily invalidate the whole process' which had led to the decision.[47] His Lordship noted that the point had been omitted from the relevant Commission report,[48] and con-cluded that 'there is a strong case for statutory reform to provide a more flexible and coherent range of powers in such cases'.[49]

---

[38] *Gnango*, n 36 above, [35].
[39] See, eg, *Clyde & Co LLP v Bates van Winkelhof* [2014] UKSC 32 and (somewhat more controver-sially) *Yemshaw v London Borough of Hounslow* [2011] UKSC 3.
[40] See, eg, Lord Mance in *Teal Assurance Company Limited v W R Berkley Insurance (Europe) Limited* [2013] UKSC 57, [4]. See chapters 2 (Lady Hale) and 20 (Andrew Burrows).
[41] *Marley v Rawlings* [2014] UKSC 2, [87]–[93].
[42] ibid [85]. *David T Morrison & Co Limited v ICL Plastics Limited* [2014] UKSC 48, a case on prescription and limitation in Scotland, is a relatively rare example of the two Scottish Justices on the Supreme Court disagreeing with one another. Lord Reed gave the judgment for the majority, while Lord Hodge dissented, urging reconsideration of relevant proposals from the Scottish Law Commission: [101] (see also Lord Reed, [31]).
[43] *Scott v Southern Pacific* [2014] UKSC 52.
[44] See Lord Wilson's concurring speech in *R (Hodkin) v Registrar General of Births, Deaths and Marriages* [2013] UKSC 77, [83], seemingly approving the 'powerful recommendation' of a working party endorsed by the Law Commission that there should be reforms to the process for the solemnisation of marriages.
[45] *Walton v The Scottish Ministers* [2012] UKSC 44.
[46] ibid [1] (Lord Reed).
[47] ibid [144].
[48] LC 226, *Administrative Law: Judicial Review and Statutory Appeals* (1994).
[49] *Walton*, n 45 above, [145].

A further reason why an issue might be suited to the reform by Parliament (preferably informed by the Commissions) rather than the courts is if it requires substantial reform, especially of legislation. One area of common agreement on this point is the law of limitation, which Lady Hale has described as 'complicated and incoherent'.[50] In *Test Claimants in the FII Group Litigation v Revenue and Customs Commissioners*,[51] the Supreme Court declined to give a wider interpretation to section 32(1)(c) of the Limitation Act 1980, relating to mistake, because of the difficulty of defining the limits of a more expansive approach: 'Any such developments are a matter for the Law Commission and for Parliament, not for this court'.[52] In 2001, the Law Commission had proposed a sensible, comprehensive reform,[53] which remains unimplemented. But this is an example of where the courts feel constrained from undertaking reform because of the nature of the problem, partly born out of previous incremental changes.[54] Interestingly, in the defamation case of *Spiller v Joseph*,[55] Lord Phillips PSC raised many questions and suggested that, although some changes could be made judicially, 'the whole area merits consideration by the Law Commission, or an expert committee'.[56] There has since been substantive and substantial reform by the Defamation Act 2013, but the Act was a project of the Ministry of Justice, not the Law Commission.[57]

Finally the sort of *evidence* on which a decision for reform would be need to be made may be a factor for the courts. In particular, the question of empirical research has been identified as one for the Commissions rather than the courts.[58] In a 2015 decision[59] affirming that the police do not generally owe a duty of care in negligence to victims of crime, Lord Kerr and Lady Hale dissented. Lord Kerr argued that the reasons given for not imposing a duty of care did not withstand scrutiny, citing Law Commission papers and reports which had suggested 'a lack of empirical evidence':[60]

> Set against the poverty—or complete absence—of evidence to support the claims of dire consequences should liability for police negligence be recognised is the fundamental principle that legal wrongs should be remedied.[61]

Lady Hale has also noted that the Board of the Privy Council (and to a similar extent the Supreme Court), 'does not have the resources to research and develop the policy

---

[50] *Ministry of Defence v AB* [2012] UKSC 9, [163].
[51] *Test Claimants in the FII Group Litigation v Revenue and Customs Commissioners* [2012] UKSC 19.
[52] ibid [63].
[53] LC 270, *Limitation of Actions* (2001).
[54] As Lady Hale further explained in *Ministry of Defence v AB* [2012] UKSC 9, [163].
[55] *Spiller v Joseph* [2010] UKSC 53.
[56] ibid [117].
[57] eg Draft Defamation Bill Consultation Paper CP3/11.
[58] Lord Hoffmann in *Chartbrook v Persimmon Homes* [2009] UKHL 38, [2009] 1 AC 1101 observed at [41]: 'It is possible that empirical study (for example, by the Law Commission) may show that the alleged disadvantages of admissibility are not in practice very significant or that they are outweighed by the advantages of doing more precise justice in exceptional cases or falling into line with international conventions.'
[59] *Michael v South Wales Police* [2015] UKSC 2.
[60] ibid [185]. Lord Kerr there referred to the project which culminated LC 322, *Administrative Redress: Public Bodies and The Citizen* (2010).
[61] *Michael v South Wales Police*, n 59 above, [186].

arguments, conduct empirical research and consult the legal and general public on possible ways forward'.[62]

### III LAW OF COHABITATION

## A Lady Hale

Lady Hale was identified above as the most frequent referrer to the Commissions. Her Ladyship has sometimes considered reports from when she herself was a member of the Commission.[63] There are many studies of Lady Hale as the first woman[64] to be appointed to the House of Lords, Supreme Court and now as the Court's Deputy President. But also significant are her Ladyship's experiences as an academic and Law Commissioner. She is not the first former academic to be appointed to the House of Lords or Supreme Court, but she is the first Law Lord or Justice to have served as a non-Chair Commissioner.[65] Insofar as the influence of having a Commissioner judge has been considered, it has mainly been left to Lady Hale herself, both in and out of court.[66] For example, in one of the last decisions of the House of Lords, *Chartbrook Ltd v Persimmon Homes Ltd*,[67] Lady Hale noted that '[my] experience at the Law Commission has shown me how difficult it is to achieve flexible and nuanced reform to a rule of the common law by way of legislation'.[68]

Judicially, her Ladyship has often drawn upon her own experiences: in one employment law case,[69] Lady Hale noted in dissent that she 'should perhaps declare an interest, as the only member of this court to have spent a substantial proportion of her working life as an employee rather than as a self-employed barrister or tenured office holder'.[70] In that case, her Ladyship dissented on the basis that contract law was defective in not recognising contributory fault consistently, as the Law Commission had observed,[71] but the 'solution to problems like that is principled

---

[62] *Crawford Adjusters & Ors v Sagicor General Insurance (Cayman) Ltd & Anor (Cayman Islands)* [2013] UKPC 17, [83]. See also her Ladyship's judgment in *Radmacher*, considered at text to n 86 below.

[63] *Re A (Children)* [2013] UKSC 60, concerning the Family Law Act 1986 which followed a joint report of the Commissions: LC 138 and SLC 9, *Family Law: Custody of Children—Jurisdiction and Enforcement within the United Kingdom* (1984). Another example from the House of Lords is *R v Hasan (Aytach)* [2005] UKHL 22, [2005] 2 AC 467.

[64] Most notably, Erika Rackley's *Women, Judging and the Judiciary: From Difference to Diversity* (London, Routledge-Cavendish, 2012). H Samuels, 'Judicial Deference and Feminist Method' [2014] *PL* 512.

[65] Lord Scarman served as the Law Commission's first Chairman, and later became a Lord of Appeal in Ordinary.

[66] Baroness Hale of Richmond, 'Law Maker or Law Reformer: What is a Law Lady for?' (2005) 40 *Irish Jurist* 1; B Hale, 'Collective Responsibility: Law Reform at the Law Commission' in R Probert and C Barton (eds), *Fifty Years of Family Law: Essays for Stephen Cretney* (Cambridge, Intersentia, 2012) ch 2.

[67] *Chartbrook Ltd v Persimmon Homes Ltd* [2009] UKHL 38.

[68] ibid [99]. See also her Ladyship's judgment in *OBG v Allan* [2007] UKHL 21, [2008] 1 AC 1, [315], which she begins by observing 'Reforming the common law by statute is not an easy task ...'.

[69] *Edwards v Chesterfield Royal Hospital NHS Foundation Trust* [2011] UKSC 58.

[70] ibid [110].

[71] LC 219, *Contributory Negligence as a Defence in Contract* (1993).

and comprehensive law reform.'[72] A particularly noticeable example of Lady Hale's influence is the law of cohabitation in England and Wales.

## B  Cohabitation Case Study

The modern law begins with *Stack v Dowden*,[73] in which [Baroness] Hale gave the leading judgment for the House of Lords. The Law Commission was concluding its own report into the area at the same time.[74] It reported just after *Stack* was decided, took that case into account and concluded that reform was still needed: 'the case is far from offering, and does not purport to offer, a comprehensive solution to the hardships that can arise for cohabitants on separation'.[75] Lord Neuberger, who was in a minority in *Stack*, expressed a preference for legislative development of the law, and argued that, in the United Kingdom:

> [T]he legislature suffers from two complementary, but apparently inconsistent, problems, which renders a degree of judicial activism arguably necessary and certainly beneficial. The first problem is that of too much ill thought-out legislation; the second is … failing to legislate in controversial and sensitive areas.[76]

His Lordship nominated the law of cohabitation as an example of the latter, of Parliament 'failing to grasp the nettle'.[77] In the Supreme Court decision in *Jones v Kernott*, Lady Hale and Lord Walker delivered the joint leading majority judgment for the Court. Lord Collins lamented 'the absence of legislative intervention (which continues despite the Law Commission Report…) [which] made it necessary for the judiciary to respond to adapting old principles to new situations'.[78] Lord Wilson remarked upon 'the continued failure of Parliament to confer upon the courts limited redistributive powers in relation to the property of each party upon the breakdown of a non-marital relationship'.[79] The joint judgment noted that there were no plans for the Commission's proposals to be implemented 'in the near future'.[80] Thus the Court was fortified in its revision of the law by the lack of parliamentary enthusiasm.[81]

---

[72] *Edwards*, n 69 above, [120].

[73] *Stack v Dowden* [2007] UKHL 17.

[74] LC 307, *Cohabitation: The Financial Consequences of Relationship Breakdown* (2007).

[75] ibid para 2.14.

[76] Lord Neuberger MR, 'Has Equity Had its Day?', Hong Kong Common Law Lecture 2010, 12 October 2010 para 38.

[77] ibid para 40.

[78] *Kernott*, n 17 above, [57].

[79] ibid [78].

[80] ibid [35]. The coalition government had stated that the Commission's proposals would not be taken forward during the 2010–15 Parliament: HC Deb vol 532 col 16WS (6 September 2011). See the strong response by Professor Elizabeth Cooke, Law Commissioner, 'Statement on the Government's response to the Law Commission Report', 6 September 2011.

[81] 'In the meantime there will continue to be many difficult cases in which the court has to reach a conclusion on sparse and conflicting evidence. It is the court's duty to reach a decision on even the most difficult case': *Kernott*, n 17 above, [36].

This conclusion is supported by the subsequent Supreme Court decision in *Gow v Grant*,[82] concerning the Scottish legislation which is similar to the Law Commission's proposed reforms. Lord Hope noted that the Scottish regime had been introduced by the belated implementation of the recommendations of the Scottish Law Commission.[83] Lady Hale reaffirmed her belief in the desirability of a legislative scheme, as being 'less costly and more productive of settlements as well as achieving fairer results than the present law'.[84] The '"sufficient basis for changing the law" [has] already been amply provided by the long-standing judicial calls for reform'.[85]

We might also compare Lady Hale's approach in *Stack* and *Kernott* with her dissenting judgment in *Radmacher v Granatino*.[86] That case saw the Supreme Court recognise the validity of ante-nuptial agreements. It was a nine-member panel, and Lady Hale was the sole dissentient. Remarkably, seven of the majority jointly gave the leading judgment.[87] Her Ladyship viewed the majority's approach as inappropriate, especially because the Commission had a current project under way. The Commission 'can develop options for reform across the whole field, upon which it can consult widely. In the light of all this, it can make detailed proposals for legislative reform, which can be put before Parliament'.[88] She continued:

> [T]hat is the democratic way of achieving comprehensive and principled reform. There is some enthusiasm for reform within the judiciary and the profession, and in the media, and one can well understand why. But that does not mean that it is right.[89]

In her Ladyship's opinion, the effect of the majority's approach was to undermine the status of marriage: she concluded with the declaration that 'Marriage still counts for something in the law of this country and long may it continue to do so.'[90] What is not clear is quite why the Law Commission's competence is a factor against the judicial development of the law in *Radmacher* but was not similarly a factor in *Stack* or *Kernott*.

## C Reflections

Alan Paterson records that there is no formal line of communication between the Supreme Court and the Law Commissions.[91] If not quite a dialogue, the example of cohabitation perhaps suggests that it is more akin to the wry look of mutual, eye-rolling disapproval exchanged between British passengers on a train when someone else is talking loudly on their telephone.[92]

---

[82] *Gow v Grant* [2012] UKSC 29.
[83] The Family Law (Scotland) Act 2006 largely implemented recommendations from over a decade earlier: SLC 135, *Report on Family Law* (1992).
[84] *Gow*, n 82 above, [47].
[85] ibid [50].
[86] *Radmacher*, n 16 above.
[87] See n 16 above. Lord Mance separately concurred.
[88] *Radmacher*, n 16 above, [134].
[89] ibid [135].
[90] ibid [195].
[91] *Final Judgment*, 282.
[92] Perhaps even with tutting.

As between the Justices, I would suggest that the invocation of the Law Commissions may be an argumentative tactic on two levels. The first, as a more sophisticated objection on the basis of constitutional or institutional competence, as Paterson indicates above:[93] we shall see this argument play out in the context of illegality in the next section. As Lord Neuberger and Lord Reed have recently noted, sometimes the courts should more simply acknowledge that they cannot help: 'in some types of case, it is better for the courts to accept that common law principle precludes a fair result, and to say so, on the basis that it is then up to Parliament (often with the assistance of the Law Commission) to sort the law out'.[94]

Reference to the Law Commissions may also be of particular force when an individual Justice invokes their own particular expertise as a former Commissioner, especially where they were involved in the very report in question. But as seen above, not all of Lady Hale's references to the matters being for the Law Commission, or to existing projects, relate to her time there. So it is an individual judgement. That is not to claim that Justices like Lady Hale or Lord Carnwath or Lord Toulson or Lord Hodge should have any priority in such cases, any more than a judge in a previous case can claim a prerogative over the interpretation of their own judgments.[95] Realistically, though, it may be of especial normative force as a matter of argument, within the context of the dialogue amongst the Justices, and the fact that those with experience of Commissioning are more inclined to refer to the Commissions reinforces the point. On which point, we may turn to a broader example of judicial disagreement.

## IV ILLEGALITY

In some circumstances, it may be a defence to a civil claim that the claim arises out of illegality. As Lord Mansfield famously stated, 'no court will lend its aid to a man who founds his cause of action on an immoral or an illegal act',[96] which is often rendered in Latin as *ex turpi causa non oritur actio*. Exactly when illegality will be a defence, and when it should be, has been and remains a matter of considerable controversy. This area has been reviewed by the Law Commission in a project which was completed in 2010.[97] Having previously considered general statutory reform, the Commission decided in its final report that two decisions from the last days of the House of Lords, *Gray v Thames Trains Ltd*[98] and *Stone & Rolls Ltd v Moore Stephens*[99] showed that it was possible to develop the law in a sensible fashion

[93] *Final Judgment* quoted at text to n 13 above.
[94] *Zurich*, n 22 above, [209].
[95] I have considered that point elsewhere: J Lee, 'Fidelity in Interpretation: Lord Hoffmann and the Adventure of the Empty House' (2008) 28 *Legal Studies* 1, and together with S Lee, 'Humility in the Supreme Court' (2015) 26 *King's Law Journal* 165, 171–74.
[96] *Holman v Johnson* (1775) 1 Cowp 341, 343 (Lord Mansfield).
[97] LC 320, *The Illegality Defence* (2010), see paras 2.87–2.102. Lord Sumption described the Law Commission as having 'struggled valiantly with the issue': *Jetivia*, n 20 above, [62].
[98] *Gray v Thames Trains Ltd* [2009] UKHL 33, [2009] AC 1339.
[99] *Stone & Rolls Ltd v Moore Stephens* [2009] UKHL 39.

judicially:[100] '[in] view of these trends within the case law, we do not think that legislative reform is needed outside the area of trust law'.[101]

The one area where the Commission still thought reform was needed was in the context of title to property.[102] The case of *Tinsley v Milligan*[103] provides that title to property can be established notwithstanding illegality if the claimant does not have to 'rely' upon evidence of the illegality to succeed in their claim.[104] The House of Lords was divided on what test should be applied, but their Lordships were unanimous that it should not be a discretionary test based upon whether it would shock the public conscience to allow recovery.[105]

As Davies has noted, it was 'entirely unsurprising and eminently sensible for the Law Commission to recommend statutory intervention in order to overturn *Tinsley* and the reliance rule in this area.'[106] The Commission proposed that the court should have a discretion to decide who should be entitled to the property, for example to declare that the trustee is the legal and beneficial owner. This statutory discretion should be based on factors such as the gravity of the illegal conduct, deterrence and proportionality. The coalition government decided against implementing the reforms on illegality.[107] If there is to be reform, therefore, it would need to come from the courts.

Professor Burrows has cited illegality as a successful example of dialogue between the Commission and the courts.[108] 'Although perhaps less obviously "a success", the Law Commission's project on illegality is another example of the Law Commission being instrumental in bringing about desirable *judicial* law reform.'[109] Burrows confessed to previously having been pessimistic about the chances of judicial reform of the law but a series of decisions up to 2013 had offered him encouragement that it was possible.[110]

The Supreme Court has now considered illegality several times. In the past two years, we have had a trio of cases in which the Court has flirted with doing something about the law of illegality, but ultimately not much has happened. It is as though the saga was being considered by the Supreme Court of Tartarus, with Justices Sisyphus, Tantalus and Prometheus in a slender majority and Zeus dissenting.[111] There is a

---

[100] LC 320, n 97 above, paras 3.32–3.41.

[101] ibid para 3.40.

[102] ibid paras 1.9 and 2.22.

[103] *Tinsley v Milligan* [1994] 1 AC 340.

[104] ibid 376 (Lord Browne-Wilkinson).

[105] ibid eg, 363 (Lord Goff).

[106] PS Davies, 'The Illegality Defence? Two Steps Forward, One Step Back?' [2009] *Conveyancer* 182, 194. See also PS Davies 'The Illegality Defence: Turning Back the Clock' [2010] *Conveyancer* 282.

[107] Ministry of Justice, *Report on the Implementation of Law Commission Proposals* (HC 1900, 2012) para 52.

[108] A Burrows, 'Alternatives to Legislation: Restatements and Judicial Law Reform' in L Gullifer and S Vogenauer (eds), *English and European Perspectives on Contract and Commercial Law: Essays in Honour of Hugh Beale* (Oxford, Hart Publishing, 2014) 47–51.

[109] ibid 47.

[110] ibid 48.

[111] 'Zeus asserted that it is for the judges to make the law, and for academics to accept judicial formulations without demur': TB Smith, 'Authors and Authority' (1972–73) 12 *Journal of the Society of Public Teachers of Law (New Series)* 3, 7.

notably strident tone to the debate amongst the Justices.[112] It is not possible to review the law in full here,[113] but I wish to offer a brief survey to demonstrate the problems of law reform etiquette.

## A *Hounga*: Strike 1

In *Hounga v Allen*,[114] the claimant sought to bring a claim for the statutory tort of unlawful discrimination[115] which had led to her dismissal from her employment as an au pair. She was originally from Nigeria but was trafficked to the United Kingdom (with her knowing participation) by the family of Mrs Allen: the claimant had no right to work in the United Kingdom. The question for the Court was whether Miss Hounga could maintain her claim notwithstanding that she had been a participant in an illegal contract in the first place: 'a small claim generate[d] an important point'.[116] The Court was unanimous that the claim should succeed (though the abandoned claim in contract would not have succeeded). Lord Wilson gave the leading judgment and Lord Hughes gave a separate concurring opinion. Both referred to the Law Commission report in their opinions.[117]

Lord Wilson conceded that 'application of the defence of illegality to claims in tort is highly problematic'.[118] The *Tinsley* reliance test had been applied to tort, but it was also said that 'the concept of a need to "rely" on an unlawful act is often easier to state than to apply'.[119] Another approach—the 'inextricable link' test—had also developed. For Lord Wilson, there is a 'subjectivity inherent in the requisite value judgement'.[120] Weighing up the public policy considerations, the importance of the policy against trafficking was stronger than the policy against allowing claims in circumstances of background illegality. Lord Hughes similarly considered that the focus is 'on the position of the claimant vis-à-vis the court from which she seeks relief'[121] and suggested that it depended upon there being a close connection between the illegality and the civil claim.[122]

Interestingly Lord Hughes recognised that a general statement of the defence has 'always proved elusive', but that 'a case in which, as I understand it, all the members of this court are agreed on the outcome of the appeal is not a suitable vehicle to essay a general synthesis such as has been so difficult to formulate'.[123] Yet, as is considered in section C below, a divided court was also unable to offer a solution in the third case, *Jetivia*.

---

[112] In *Jetivia*, Lord Sumption caustically said at [105]: 'I agree with Lord Toulson and Lord Hodge that Occam's Razor is a valuable analytical tool, but only if it is correctly understood. Entia non sunt multiplicanda praeter necessitatem. Do not gratuitously multiply your postulates.'
[113] See, eg, A Loke, 'Tainting Illegality' (2014) 34 *Legal Studies* 560.
[114] *Hounga v Allen* [2014] UKSC 47.
[115] Pursuant to Race Relations Act 1976, s 4(2)(c).
[116] *Hounga*, n 114 above, [4].
[117] ibid [30] (Lord Wilson) and [54] (Lord Hughes).
[118] ibid [25].
[119] ibid [30].
[120] ibid [38].
[121] ibid [56].
[122] ibid [57]
[123] ibid [54].

## B *Apotex*: Strike 2

Lord Sumption had his turn to consider the law of illegality in *Les Laboratoires Servier v Apotex Inc*.[124] The facts were complicated but the case considered whether infringement of a foreign patent constituted relevant illegality for the purposes of the *ex turpi* defence. His Lordship noted that 'English law has a long-standing repugnance for claims which are founded on the claimant's own illegal or immoral acts'.[125] The defence will therefore often lead to 'disproportionately harsh consequences'.[126] The Court was not invited to depart from *Tinsley*,[127] though Lord Sumption noted that the test 'has had its critics', including the Law Commission.[128] But Lord Sumption disapproved of the Law Commission's suggested approval of the subsequent flexible course of case law:

> I confess that I find this difficult to justify as an approach to authority or the proper development of the law. It is directly inconsistent with the decision of the House of Lords in *Tinsley v Milligan* and the whole of the reasoning which underlies it. It makes the law uncertain, by inviting the courts to depart from existing rules of law in circumstances where it is difficult for them to acknowledge openly what they are doing or to substitute a coherent alternative structure.[129]

Lord Mance shared Lord Sumption's concern that a flexible focus on the facts[130] was inconsistent with *Tinsley*.[131] Turning to the issue in hand, the Court considered that 'illegality' only applies to criminal acts (or quasi-criminal acts).[132] Apotex was therefore able to proceed with its action.

Lord Toulson agreed with the outcome of the appeal, but did not share Lord Sumption's disapproval of consideration of public policy in a context-specific way, with reference to *Hounga v Allen* (to which Lord Sumption, surprisingly, did not refer at all). His Lordship also said that there may be occasion for the Supreme Court to review *Tinsley*, with reference to the Commission's work, but again the Court had not been invited to review it in *Apotex*.[133]

## C *Jetivia*: Three Strikes and ...

*Jetivia*[134] is our final case on the operation of the illegality defence, this time in the context of the attribution of conduct of fraudulent directors. The company had

---

[124] *Les Laboratoires Servier v Apotex Inc* [2014] UKSC 55.
[125] ibid [13].
[126] ibid [18].
[127] ibid [19].
[128] ibid [20].
[129] ibid.
[130] As Etherton LJ had suggested: *Les Laboratoires Servier v Apotex Inc* [2012] ECWA Civ 593, [75].
[131] *Apotex*, [33].
[132] ibid [28].
[133] ibid [64].
[134] *Jetivia SA & Anor v Bilta* [2015] UKSC 23.

been wound up at the petition of HMRC as a result of the appellants involving the company in a carousel fraud. The company's liquidators then sued the directors and another company involved in the scheme. The court was unanimous as to the outcome—the defence did not bar the claims as the directors' conduct cannot be attributed to the company when it comes to a claim by the company against the directors themselves. But again we have marked differences of view over the rationale for the defence and whether any cases should be departed from (in the future if not now). And again we have many references to the Law Commission's project. A seven-Justice bench was convened, and we have four separate opinions: Lord Neuberger (with whom Lord Clarke and Lord Carnwath agreed), Lord Mance, Lord Sumption and a joint opinion by Lords Toulson and Hodge. Lord Neuberger did his best to mediate:

> In my view, while the proper approach to the defence of illegality needs to be addressed by this court (certainly with a panel of seven and conceivably with a panel of nine Justices) as soon as appropriately possible, this is not the case in which it should be decided. We have had no real argument on the topic: this case is concerned with attribution, and that is the issue on which the arguments have correctly focussed. Further, in this case, as in the two recent Supreme Court decisions of *Les Laboratoires* and *Hounga*, the outcome is the same irrespective of the correct approach to the illegality defence.[135]

His Lordship did accept that there was a case for reconsideration, especially in the light of the different views in the two recent Supreme Court cases, and also in the light of the Law Commission report.[136]

Lord Sumption's trenchant judgment seems to start from the premise that he had resolved the principles in *Apotex* (his Lordship generally refers to the case without expressly mentioning that it was his own judgment):[137] 'The fact that the illegality defence is based on policy does not entitle a court to reassess the value or relevance of that policy on a case-by-case basis.'[138] Lord Sumption does refer to *Hounga* but states that 'the court was not purporting to depart from *Tinsley* ... without saying so'.[139] To adopt a more flexible approach on the facts in *Jetivia* would be both 'unnecessary and undesirable'.[140]

Lords Toulson and Hodge (again, former members of Commissions) preferred the *Hounga* approach: 'It has been stated many times that the doctrine of illegality has been developed by the courts on the ground of public policy. The context is always important.'[141] They recognised that *Tinsley* stands for the rigid reliance test, but noted that even the judges in the case thought the law was 'very unsatisfactory, but ... beyond judicial reform'.[142] Furthermore, their Lordships considered that the

---

[135] ibid [15].
[136] ibid [17].
[137] ibid [62]–[63] (although his Lordship does mention that it was his own work at [100]).
[138] ibid [99].
[139] ibid [102]: his Lordship later said that he had sympathy with Arden LJ's 'scepticism about [*Hounga*'s] significance as a statement of principle of general application'.
[140] ibid [105].
[141] ibid [129].
[142] ibid [168].

Law Commission's work,[143] coupled with the decision in *Hounga*, may, however, point the way forward.[144]

*Tinsley* was then left formally untouched, as the Court was not invited to depart from it. But the previous authority of *Stone & Rolls* did not fare so well. Lord Neuberger said that 'it is very hard to seek to derive much in the way of reliable principle from it',[145] and would confine it to its facts.[146] Lords Hodge and Toulson concluded that '*Stone & Rolls* should be regarded as a case which has no majority ratio decidendi'.[147] Lord Sumption placed great emphasis on the case being one of attribution, but Lord Mance recognised that Jonathan Sumption QC had been counsel in *Stone & Rolls* and conceded a point on which Lord Sumption now sought to rely. Lord Mance implied that counsel (and judges) do not establish precedents in that way.[148]

## D Next Innings?

To conclude this example, the Supreme Court has certainly seemed to accept that the defence of illegality is ripe for reform, and the persistent undertone of opinions appears to be that *Tinsley* is not safe. Yet it still stands as a precedent, perhaps because the 'right' set of facts has not yet come before or the Court (or the courts).

We may therefore pause to wonder why it was necessary to have a seven-Justice bench in *Jetivia*, and consider illegality again for the third time in two years, if not to consider the defence properly, but only to have another argument about it. It is both notable and noticeable that no single Justice sat on all three appeals. Lords Neuberger, Carnwath and Toulson were the panel which granted permission to appeal in *Jetivia*.[149] The main problem is clearly that the Justices are themselves divided on what the law is and should be. As Professor Buckley commented in a note on both *Hounga* and *Apotex*: 'the concept of illegality, when deployed to resist the enforcement of a civil obligation, has an extraordinary propensity to cause confusion and to generate judicial opinions of striking diversity'.[150]

Indeed, two of the most prominent Justices on this issue, Lord Sumption[151] and Lord Mance,[152] have each written extra-curially about it, and even Lords Toulson and Hodge recognised in *Jetivia* the need to resolve matters.[153] But currently matching

---

[143] ibid [169].

[144] ibid [173].

[145] ibid [23].

[146] ibid [30]: 'the time has come in my view for us to hold that the decision in *Stone & Rolls* should, as Lord Denning MR graphically put it in relation to another case in *In re King* [1963] Ch 459, 483, be "put on one side and marked 'not to be looked at again'"'.

[147] *Jetivia*, n 134 above, [154].

[148] ibid [48].

[149] Permission to Appeal Results—February 2014 (www.supremecourt.uk/docs/permission-to-appeal-2014-02.pdf).

[150] RA Buckley, 'Illegality in the Supreme Court' (2015) 131 *LQR* 341, 341.

[151] Lord Sumption, 'Reflections on the Law of Illegality' [2012] 20 *Restitution Law Review* 1.

[152] J Mance, 'Ex Turpi Causa—When Latin Avoids Liability' (2014) 18 *Edinburgh Law Review* 175.

[153] *Jetivia*, n 134 above, [174]: 'The Law Commission report has not so far been considered in any detail by this court, nor has this court been invited to review the decision in *Tinsley v Milligan*. The differences between Lord Sumption and us suggest to us that there is a pressing need for both.'

up Justices to discern a view as to what *ratio* each decision has (and in fact revisiting the *ratio* of earlier decisions) is very difficult. It all makes for an interesting parlour game at a legal academics' dinner party, but it leaves the law in a considerable state of uncertainty. We have suggestions of a variable, 'each case turns on its own facts' approach to illegality, but *Tinsley* still stands. Perhaps it is time for the Law Commission to consider taking up the baton of reform again, since the Supreme Court is divided and continues to prevaricate. As it is, lower courts can only hope for further guidance from the Supreme Court: Sir Terence Etherton has recently stated that 'the proper approach to the defence of illegality needs to be addressed by the Supreme Court (conceivably with a panel of nine Justices) as soon as appropriately possible'.[154]

## V HEARSAY HERESIES

My final example of utility of reference to the Law Commission[155] in Supreme Court judgments concerns the Court's dialogue with the European Court of Human Rights (ECtHR). As Paterson has noted, there is a factual personal dialogue between judges of each of these courts,[156] but we can see that there is also an institutional dialogue.

One of the key cases in the story of dialogue is the *Al-Khawaja* saga over hearsay evidence.[157] The hearsay rule in criminal proceedings was altered by part 2 of the Criminal Justice Act 2003 to allow the admission of such evidence in limited circumstances. In *R v Al-Khawaja*[158] and *R v Tahery*,[159] the Court of Appeal held that this rule did not infringe the right to a fair trial under article 6 of the Convention. When those two cases went to the Fourth Section Chamber of the ECtHR, the Court held that, because hearsay witness statements were the sole or decisive factor in conviction, the applicants' trials had been unfair, contrary to article 6.[160]

The Supreme Court responded in *R v Horncastle*,[161] in which Lord Phillips gave the judgment for the Court. In his judgment, his Lordship noted[162] that the changes to the rule were largely the result of the relevant Law Commission report.[163] It was not just any Law Commission report, however: it was a response to a recommendation from a Royal Commission on Criminal Justice in 1993.[164] Furthermore, his Lordship

---

[154] *Sharma v Top Brands Ltd & Ors* [2015] EWCA Civ 1140, [38]. See also Popplewell J in *Molton Street Capital LLP v Shooters Hill Capital Partners LLP & Anor* [2015] EWHC 3419 (Comm), [177]–[181].

[155] I regret that I cannot find any reference to the Scottish Law Commission in judgments of the Strasbourg Court (again, based on a bailii.org search).

[156] *Final Judgment*, 224.

[157] The general context is more fully considered by B Dickson, *Human Rights and the United Kingdom Supreme Court* (Oxford, OUP, 2013) 212–16; F Stark, 'Reconciling the Irreconcilable?' (2012) 71 *CLJ* 475; L Heffernan, 'Hearsay in Criminal Trials: The Strasbourg Perspective' [2013] 49 *Irish Jurist* 132; M Redmayne, 'Hearsay and Human Rights: Al-Khawaja in the Grand Chamber' (2012) 75 *MLR* 865.

[158] *R v Al-Khawaja* [2005] EWCA Crim 2697.

[159] *R v Tahery* [2006] EWCA Crim 529.

[160] *Al-Khawaja and Tahery v UK* (2009) 49 EHRR 1.

[161] *R v Horncastle* [2009] UKSC 14.

[162] ibid [29].

[163] LC 245, *Evidence in Criminal Proceedings: Hearsay and Related Topics* (1997).

[164] ibid.

then quoted the Court of Appeal, who had observed that the report came 'after several years of wide consultation with judges, practitioners, academic lawyers and other experts'.[165] The Court of Appeal then pointedly observed that the legislative scheme was:

> informed by experience accumulated over generations and represents the product of concentrated consideration by experts of how the balance should be struck between the many competing interests affected. It also represents democratically enacted legislation substantially endorsing the conclusions of the expert consideration.[166]

Lord Phillips later engaged with the specific conclusions of the Law Commission:

> It is significant … that the Law Commission gave special consideration to whether there should be a requirement that hearsay should not be capable of proving an essential element of an offence unless supported by other evidence. The Commission was persuaded by the responses to consultation that this would not be desirable … The Commission concluded that the danger of a defendant being unfairly convicted on the basis of hearsay evidence alone would be met by the safeguards that it proposed, in particular that which was subsequently adopted as section 125 of the CJA 2003.[167]

Dickson has noted that the *Horncastle* judgment 'was a conscious attempt to enter into a dialogue with the Strasbourg Court, although to some it may have seemed more like a salvo in a shouting match'.[168] Similarly, Paterson has said that it 'was written consciously as a form of advocacy'.[169] That advocacy is significantly buttressed[170] by the reference to the Law Commission. The judgment seeks to make clear that it is not just the English (UK) courts taking a different or nationalistic view of the law: part of that 'shouting-match'. Nor is it a partisan or political statement of defiance from the legislature. Rather, Lord Phillips presents this as considered, balanced reform, supported by the imprimatur of Law Commission involvement.

The Chamber (Fourth Section) judgment had not referred to the Law Commission at all,[171] and Lord Phillips suggested that that was a flaw in the reasoning in addition to other errors:

> Nor, I suspect, can the Strasbourg Court have given detailed consideration to the English law of admissibility of evidence, and the changes made to that law, after consideration by the Law Commission, intended to ensure that English law complies with the requirements of article 6(1) and (3)(d) [of the European Convention].[172]

---

[165] *R v Horncastle* [2009] EWCA Crim 964, [10].

[166] ibid.

[167] *Horncastle* (SC), n 161 above, [37].

[168] Dickson, n 157 above, 214. Dickson further observes, ibid, that *Horncastle* was one of 'the most determined [efforts] ever made by the United Kingdom's top court to convince European Court of Human Rights that it must not find a principle of English law to be in violation of the Convention'.

[169] *Final Judgment*, 226.

[170] Lord Hope and Lord Carnwath have both hinted at this point: Lord Hope, 'The Role of the Supreme Court of the United Kingdom' Lord Rodger of Earlsferry Memorial Lecture, 19 November 2011 (www.supremecourt.uk/docs/speech_111119.pdf) 15; and Lord Carnwath, 'Il Ruolo Sussidario del CEDU nel Sistema Judiciario Britannico', Rome, 20 September 2013 (www.supremecourt.uk/docs/speech-130920.pdf) 5.

[171] *Al-Khawaja and Tahery v UK* (2009) 49 EHRR 1; there is no mention in the judgment, whether in the account of the parties' submissions or the Court's reasons.

[172] *Horncastle* (SC), n 161 above, [107].

Significantly, when the Grand Chamber picked up the invitation to respond to the issue in the *Al-Khawaja* appeal,[173] the ECtHR not only engaged with the reasoning in *Horncastle*, but also referred to the Law Commission's work.[174] Indeed, the submissions of the parties addressed the Commission report, with the government praying it in aid[175] and even one of the interveners, JUSTICE, which was critical of the Supreme Court's position in *Horncastle*, specifically engaged with the relevance of the Commission's report.[176] The judgment also referred to reports from the Commissions in Hong Kong[177] and New Zealand.[178] And then the ECtHR responded to the Supreme Court by confirming that 'the safeguards contained in the 1988 and 2003 Acts, supported by those contained in section 78 of the Police and Criminal Evidence Act and the common law, are, in principle, strong safeguards designed to ensure fairness'.[179] It must be accepted that the findings on the facts of the particular cases did find a violation in the *Tahery* appeal, but that does not detract from the overall success in the Supreme Court's dialogue.[180] Clearly, the Grand Chamber 'took a more nuanced and favourable attitude towards hearsay evidence',[181] and Judge Bratza, the then UK judge on the Strasbourg Court (who had sat on both decisions in the *Al-Khawaja* appeals), called it a 'good example of the judicial dialogue' between the courts.[182]

We can take several points from this analysis. First, there is a strategic question for the Supreme Court[183] in its ongoing debate over its relationship with the European Court of Human Rights.[184] Lord Kerr has suggested that the Supreme Court might be able to pre-empt Strasbourg and persuade them in advance:

> There is no reason to suppose that a pre-emptive, properly reasoned opinion by our courts should not have the same effect. For a dialogue to be effective, both speakers should be prepared, when the occasion demands it, to utter the first word.[185]

---

[173] *Al-Khawaja and Tahery v UK* (2012) 54 EHRR 23.
[174] ibid eg, [42].
[175] ibid [101].
[176] ibid [114].
[177] ibid [81].
[178] ibid [82].
[179] ibid [151]. Albeit the concession was not in a wholly supine fashion: see, eg, ibid [139].
[180] ibid [165].
[181] Lord Mance, 'The Interface between National and European Law' 1 February 2013, (www.supremecourt.uk/docs/speech-130201.pdf) para 17; Lord Neuberger called it a 'realistic' approach by Strasbourg: 'The British and Europe', 12 February 2014 (www.supremecourt.uk/docs/speech-140212.pdf) para 36. See also Lord Neuberger, 'The Supreme Court and the Rule of Law' The Conkerton Lecture 2014, 9 October 2014 (www.supremecourt.uk/docs/speech-141009-lord-neuberger.pdf).
[182] *Al-Khawaja (GC)*, [2] (Judge Bratza).
[183] See generally Dickson, n 157 above, but esp 56–59 and ch 13.
[184] B Hale, 'Argentoratum Locutum: is Strasbourg or the Supreme Court Supreme?' (2012) 12 *Human Rights Law Review* 65; Lord Kerr, 'The UK Supreme Court: The Modest Underworker of Strasbourg?' Clifford Chance Lecture, 25 January 2012 (www.supremecourt.gov.uk/docs/speech_120125.pdf); Lord Neuberger, 'The Role of Judges in Human Rights Jurisprudence: A Comparison of the Australian and UK Experience' Supreme Court of Victoria, 8 August 2014 (www.supremecourt.uk/docs/speech-140808.pdf); Lady Hale, 'What's the Point of Human Rights?', Warwick Law Lecture 2013 (www.supremecourt.uk/docs/speech-131128.pdf); Lord Dyson, 'What's Wrong with Human Rights?', 3 November 2011, (www.supremecourt.uk/docs/speech_111103.pdf). Lord Kerr, 'The Conversation between Strasbourg and National Courts—Dialogue or Dictation?' [2009] 44 *Irish Jurist* 1.
[185] Lord Kerr, n 184 above, 14.

When picking its battles, the broader the base of evidence from the jurisdiction, the better. But it is also another significant way in which the work of the Law Commission can be understood as having a demonstrable impact. *Horncastle* is not an isolated example. The Fourth Section of the Court has also considered the influence of the Law Commission, albeit on a decision of the House of Lords.[186] Earlier in 2011, in *Hoare v United Kingdom*,[187] the ECtHR declared inadmissible a challenge by a convicted rapist who had been found liable in tort to his victim, despite case law on the Limitation Act 1980 previously having barred such a claim. The Court noted that the English courts had referred to the Law Commission's *Limitation of Actions* report, and that the Commission had described the previous law as 'anomalous'.[188] Further, the Commission's analysis had informed the House of Lords' decision in *Hoare*[189] to depart from *Stubbings v Webb*[190] exercising the Practice Statement, and this for the Court added to the cogent reasons given by their Lordships. The law in *Stubbings* had itself previously been challenged in Strasbourg.[191] The change in the law was thus neither arbitrary nor inappropriate.

In June 2015, in *Ali v The United Kingdom*,[192] an applicant challenged his conviction after a retrial on the basis that there had been widespread prejudicial media coverage of the original trial and this was a violation of article 6. The ECtHR ruled the application inadmissible, and quoted at length from the Law Commission's consultation on *Contempt of Court*.[193] The applicant suggested that the consultation paper supported his argument,[194] but the Court disagreed:

> In cases involving trial by jury, what is an appropriate lapse of time and what are suitable directions will vary depending on the specific facts of the case. It is for the national courts to address these matters—which, as the Law Commission observed in its 2012 consultation paper …, are essentially value judgments—having regard to the extent and content of the published material and the nature of the commentary, subject to review by this Court of the relevance and sufficiency of the steps taken and the reasons given.[195]

Thus, Law Commission-informed legislation, or even consultations, may then have an enduring intellectual heft worthy of respect from judges in Strasbourg (or possibly even Luxembourg). And indeed, at a time of intense scrutiny of our relationship with the Strasbourg court,[196] the Law Commission's role in the hearsay success story, and in *Hoare* and *Ali*, could be noted by government. That said, no mention

---

[186] *A v Hoare* [2008] UKHL 6; [2008] 1 AC 844.
[187] *Hoare v United Kingdom* (2011) 53 EHRR SE1.
[188] ibid [55].
[189] *Hoare (HL)*, n 186 above, [24]–[25] (Lord Hoffmann). For Lord Hoffmann's view of the Fourth Section judgment in *Al-Khawaja*, see L Hoffmann, 'The Universality of Human Rights' (2009) 125 *LQR* 416.
[190] *Stubbings v Webb* [1993] AC 498.
[191] *SW v United Kingdom* (1996) 21 EHRR 363.
[192] *Ali v The United Kingdom* [2015] ECHR 628 (30 June 2015).
[193] LC CP 209 (2012), quoted in *Ali*, [63]–[67].
[194] *Ali*, [78].
[195] ibid [91].
[196] The current Conservative government was elected in May 2015 with a manifesto commitment to replace the Human Rights Act 1998 with a British Bill of Rights.

of *Horncastle* was made in the Law Commission's evidence to its 2013 Triennial Review.[197] If I may be so bold, I nominate this feature for the next review in 2016.

## VI CONCLUSION

This essay has shown that there is a dialogue between the Supreme Court and the Law Commissions, and between the Justices about the Commissions. Although we can see that the Court and the Law Commissions have a relationship of civility, it is not clear what the rules of etiquette are: the result is a high risk of faux-pas, as we continue to see in the law relating to the illegality, until the Supreme Court sheds its British reticence. Reference to the Law Commissions within judgments of the Supreme Court can be understood to have particular rhetorical force, and it illuminates the individual reasoning styles of particular Justices, especially Lady Hale. And indeed, the *Horncastle* saga shows us that it can buttress the Court's position in other institutional dialogues as well. That is not to suggest that the Law Commissions' significance, or the significance of reference to them by Justices, is only symbolic: rather, *Horncastle* is a clear example of the Supreme Court deliberately using the work of the Law Commissions with a definite purpose. The judicial engagement with the Commissions represents another dimension to the way in which the Commissions' work can have an impact.

For the Justices, it ought to be considered similarly carefully whether they should refer to the Commissions, and why they are doing so. As a conclusion, let us turn to Debrett's arch guide to British behaviour, which can offer advice to the Law Commissions and the Supreme Court, as well as to the British generally:

> If being polite and opening a door for someone means that you have to wrestle your way past them in the first place, almost knocking them flying, then why not stand back, relax and with good manners acknowledge their own kindness in holding the door open for you[?][198]

---

[197] Evidence from the Law Commission, *Triennial Review of The Law Commission* (February 2013) (www.lawcom.gov.uk/wp-content/uploads/2015/05/Law_Commission_triennial_review_evidence.pdf).

[198] 'Politeness' in *British Etiquette: British Behaviour* (www.debretts.com/british-etiquette/british-behaviour/p-q/politeness).

# 30

# Law Reform in Private Law: The Role of Statutes in Supplementing or Supplanting the Common Law

BARBARA MCDONALD

## I INTRODUCTION

This chapter is informed by my recent experience as Commissioner at the Australian Law Reform Commission (ALRC), heading its inquiry into *Serious Invasions of Privacy in the Digital Era*.[1] We were charged primarily with the 'detailed legal design of a statutory cause of action for serious invasions of privacy'. We were not asked to consider whether or not such a statutory cause of action should be enacted but, nevertheless, many submissions and stakeholders commented, some vehemently, on that issue. The relative merits of changing the law by statute or by development of the common law should be considered by anyone urging for legal change.[2] To say 'there ought to be a law about it' is only a starting point. For the law reformer, the question is how best that legal change should come about.

This chapter will consider the variety of ways in which statute and common law may interact in law reform, and highlight some of the respective limitations and benefits of each in achieving change. It will become obvious that neither is necessarily a more reliable path to settled law reform than the other, and that society must depend on both the courts and Parliament to ensure that modern law meets the challenges of changing social conditions and perennial problems. Others too have a role in shaping and driving change. The chapter concludes with an example of law reform that, by omission, starkly illustrates the proper role of law reform Commissions, with their processes for community consultation and careful independent analysis, in considering and recommending fair and effective options for reform.

---

[1] ALRC 123 (2014).
[2] ibid paras 1.34–1.40.

## II TO LEGISLATE OR NOT

Law reformers are asked to deal with a wide range of legal problems. Sometimes they are asked to construct a legislative scheme for a new scientific or social phenomenon—for example, how the law should deal with gene patenting or commercial surrogacy. More often, law reformers are asked to consider a problem with existing laws. A common law principle may produce injustice or not sit well with contemporary standards or other laws. An existing statute may produce unintended, absurd, outdated or unjust consequences. There may be a gap in the coverage of existing laws, or a conflict or inconsistency between statutes. Or a particular field of the common law may have become such a morass of rules that some sort of legislative reordering is seen as desirable.

In any context where an immediate change in the law is seen as desirable, the question will arise as to whether legislation is the best way to remedy the mischief. We are often now told that we live in an 'age of statutes',[3] but the phrase can be taken too literally. There is barely a field of law where 'the law' is not a complex and symbiotic mix of statute and common law, the latter comprised of principles which pre-date or exist independently of statute: some of which inform and supplement the operation of particular statutes and others which interpret and apply statutes.[4] Trust law and tort law are both obvious examples. Because of this, it makes little sense to regard legislation and common law as completely separate sources of law. Rather, they are co-dependent, and legislation will never entirely supplant the common law in a common law system:

> Over time, the meaning of a statutory text is reinforced by the accumulated experience of courts in the application of the law to the facts in a succession of cases. The meaning of a statutory text is also informed, and reinformed, by the need for the courts to apply the text each time, not in isolation, but as part of the totality of the common lawn and statute law as it then exists.[5]

One consequence (or cause) of the plethora of statute law may be that it is too readily assumed that legislation is *the* solution to any legal problem. Certainly, we might expect legislators to think this, and there are examples of this somewhat naive view. Surprisingly, however, there are some occasions where even legislators would prefer to leave matters to the common law, and this may not be because they lack the political will to effect change. Rather, they may perceive that the common law already provides an appropriate level of protection for the interests at stake or that legislation will not help resolve matters that would remain

---

[3] See, eg, G Calabresi, *A Common Law for the Age of Statutes* (Oliver Wendell Holmes Lectures) (Cambridge, Harvard University Press, 1985).

[4] See generally W Gummow, 'Lecture One: The Common Law and Statute' in W Gummow, *Change and Continuity: Statute, Equity and Federalism* (Oxford, OUP, 1999); TT Arvind and J Steele (eds), *Tort Law and the Legislature* (Oxford, Hart Publishing, 2013); M Leeming, 'Theories and Principles Underlying the Development of the Common law: The Statutory Elephant in the Room' (2013) 36 *University of New South Wales Law Journal* 1002, esp n 2; S McLeish, 'Challenges to the Survival of the Common Law' (2014) 38 *Melbourne University Law Review* 818.

[5] S Gageler, 'Common Law Statutes and Judicial Legislation: Statutory Interpretation as a Common Law Process' (2011) 37(2) *Monash University Law Review* 1, 1–2.

inherently uncertain or difficult to define with precision. There may be little to gain from laborious attempts at statutory clarification or codification, as the Law Commission of England and Wales wisely decided in its 2014 report on *Fiduciary Duties of Investment Intermediaries*.[6]

In 2012, a Joint Committee of the House of Lords and the House of Commons recommended *against* the introduction of a statutory action for breach of privacy.[7] Whilst a number of factors contributed to this, the key reason given by the Committee was that a statute would not clarify the existing (albeit nascent) law that had emerged since the House of Lords recognised an action for invasion of privacy in *Campbell v MGN Ltd*.[8] Many key concepts inherent in the action are essentially matters of judgement, so that, even if reduced to statute, the action would still require the courts to balance competing interests and come to a conclusion on a case-by-case basis. The two concepts that seem to be inherently incapable of precise definition in any form of action for invasion of privacy are, first, what is or is not 'private' and, second, what falls within or outside 'the public interest'.[9] The Joint Committee did, however, make other recommendations to supplement the common law, including that courts be empowered to award exemplary damages in privacy cases. The New Zealand Law Commission also recommended that development of further protection of privacy be left to the common law, noting that this had the 'great advantage that in a fast moving area judges can make informed decisions on actual cases as they arrive'.[10] That confidence has been borne out in New Zealand.[11]

The case for a new statutory cause of action is clearly less pressing in jurisdictions where the courts have developed a cause of action for invasion of privacy and where there are statutes giving protection against or remedies for harassment, as is the case in both the United Kingdom and New Zealand. This is not however the case in Australia: despite the opening of the door to further common law development by the High Court of Australia in *Australian Broadcasting Corporation v Lenah Game Meats Pty Ltd*,[12] development has been desultory and cautious, with reliance mainly on the ordinary equitable action of breach of confidence as the source of protection.[13] Further, Australian law does not give the same weight to a general concept of public interest as a defence to breach of confidence as is given in the United Kingdom and New Zealand, so that there is arguably a case for legislative intervention, even if the action of breach of confidence adopts an extended role in protecting privacy.[14]

---

[6] LC 350 (2014) para 7.37.
[7] Joint Committee on Privacy and Injunctions, *Privacy and Injunctions* (2010–12, HL 273, HC 1443).
[8] *Campbell v MGN Ltd* [2004] UKHL 22, [2004] 2 AC 457.
[9] See also ibid [148] (Baroness Hale).
[10] New Zealand Law Commission, NZLC 113, *Invasion of Privacy: Penalties and Remedies* (2010) para 7.9.
[11] See, eg, *Hosking v Runting* [2005] 1 NZLR 1; *C v Holland* [2012] 3 NZLR 672.
[12] *Australian Broadcasting Corporation v Lenah Game Meats Pty Ltd* (2001) 208 CLR 199.
[13] See, eg, *Giller v Procopets* (2008) 24 VR 1; *Wilson v Ferguson* [2015] WASC 15.
[14] ALRC 123, n 1 above, ch 13.

One year on from the tabling of the ALRC privacy report, there is no indication that the government of the day is interested in privacy law reform. It joins other reports that await a government that becomes interested, perhaps because a politically sensitive situation will arise, prompting someone influential to say 'why don't we have a law about it?'

Even where Law Commissions have put forward cogent arguments to justify change, law reformers cannot necessarily rely on legislative intervention. There may be no political consensus for a particular reform proposal, or powerful lobby groups may hold sway. There may be little political interest in changing the law, especially in the case of 'lawyers' law', and even less to fix up errors, infelicities or absurdities in earlier attempts at law reform. Some statutory law reforms themselves 'call somewhat urgently for reform'.[15] However, there are many examples where the inertia of the legislature has not prevented the courts from developing the common law as best they can, and indeed as they must: '[i]t is not open to judges, faced with a difficult question to say "pass"'.[16]

In this spirit, the House of Lords changed the common law rule on the effect of a mistake of law, in the absence of the legislative change suggested by the Law Commission.[17] More recently, Parliament having failed to follow the recommendations of the Law Commission on ownership after cohabitation,[18] the UK Supreme Court has (somewhat controversially) developed concepts of trust law to provide some solution.[19] Such a development does not of course preclude Parliament from stepping in to reverse a controversial change, as it did promptly to restore (or impose) joint and several liability after the majority decision in *Barker v Corus UK Ltd*.[20] But it does highlight the capacity for courts to make radical change.

For those impatient for change, the common law can be frustrating to watch. Development is necessarily incremental, dependent on external factors, such as relevant situations arising; the willingness and capacity of litigants to bring claims and pursue and defend appeals; and the issues put in dispute by the parties themselves. Only decisions on those live issues will effect change in the common law.[21] The capacity of the common law to effect change is also dependent on two other, related, internal factors. First is the willingness and degree of freedom of courts to

---

[15] *Bitumen & Oil Refineries (Australia) Ltd v Commissioner for Government Transport* (1955) 92 CLR 200, 211 on the contribution provision in Law Reform (Miscellaneous Provisions) Act 1946 (NSW), s 5, modelled on the 1935 predecessor to the current Civil Liability (Contribution) Act 1978 (UK), s 6, and still unreformed. Proportionate liability reforms in Australia also meet this description. See also J Glister, 'Section 199 of the Equality Act 2010: How Not to Abolish the Presumption of Advancement' (2010) 73 *MLR* 807 for a possible further example.

[16] R Walker, 'Developing the Common Law: How Far is Too Far?' (2013–14) 37 *Melbourne University Law Review* 232, 251.

[17] *Kleinwort Benson Ltd v Lincoln City Council* [1999] 2 AC 349 (HL) on which see chapter 17 (Laura Dunlop).

[18] Law Commission, LC 307, *Co-Habitation: The Financial Consequences of Relationship Breakdown* (2007).

[19] *Jones v Kernott* [2011] UKSC 53, [2012] 1 AC 776. See Walker, n 16 above, 251.

[20] *Barker v Corus UK Ltd* [2006] UKHL 20, [2006] 2 AC 572; Compensation Act 2006 (UK), s 3.

[21] See *Tabet v Gett* (2010) 240 CLR 537, [97]–[98] (Heydon J) on the dangers of appellate courts indulging too readily in obiter dicta. But see *Farah Constructions Pty Ltd v Say-Dee Pty Ltd* (2007) 230 CLR 89, [134]–[135] on the duty of lower courts to follow 'seriously considered dicta' of the High Court.

depart from their own and others' previous decisions.[22] It would not be conducive to public confidence in the common law system if judicial changes of mind were a common occurrence, but the law cannot be frozen. As Brennan J noted: 'The greater the authority accorded to precedent by an ultimate court of appeal, the slower the pace of change.'[23] Second is the judges' degree of caution about engaging in what some might describe as 'judicial legislation', and their view that some issues are solely for the legislature. This is particularly so on issues that are controversial in society such as euthanasia or assisted suicide.[24] Yet controversy alone has not prevented courts overturning long-established rules or fictions, such as the doctrine of *terra nullius* in Australia.[25] Our highest courts are certainly now more inclined than in the past to disturb settled precedents,[26] or to modify or overturn even recent appellate decisions, as *FHR European Ventures LLP v Cedar Capital Partners LLC* shows.[27] In negligence law, certain long-established immunities have been held out-of-step with modern general principles of liability,[28] yet other common law rules remain firmly entrenched against judicial disturbance.[29]

## III PARTICULAR TYPES OF LEGISLATIVE REFORM

### A Codification

The most overarching method by which statute may supplant the common law is by the entire codification of a field of law. While codification shares some features and benefits with consolidation of existing statutes, it is a 'rather more polemical

---

[22] See M Leeming, '*Farah* and its Progeny: Comity among Intermediate Appellate Courts' (2015) 12 *The Judicial Review* 165 on intermediate appellate courts.

[23] *Dietrich v The Queen* (1992) 177 CLR 292, 320. His Honour continued at 320–21: '[i]n practical terms, the Courts are aware that rejection or discounting of the authority of precedent not only disturbs the law established by a particular precedent but infuses some uncertainty into the general body of the common law. The tension between legal development and legal certainty is continuous and it has to be resolved from case to case by a prudence derived from experience and governed by judicial methods of reasoning.'

[24] Walker, n 16 above, 253.

[25] *Mabo v Queensland (No 2)* (1992) 175 CLR 1.

[26] See generally G Lindsay, 'Building a Nation: The Doctrine of Precedent in Australian Legal History' in JT Gleeson, JA Watson and RCA Higgins (eds), *Historical Foundations of Australian Law*, vol 1 (Sydney, Federation Press, 2013); Walker, n 16 above.

[27] *FHR European Ventures LLP v Cedar Capital Partners LLC* [2014] UKSC 45, [2015] AC 250, overruling *Sinclair Investments (UK) Ltd v Versailles Trade Finance Ltd* [2011] EWCA Civ 347, [2011] 3 WLR 1153 and *Lister v Stubbs* (1890) 45 Ch D 1 (CA), and bringing English law into line with *Attorney-Gen for Hong Kong v Reid* [1994] 1 AC 324 (PC). See D Neuberger: 'Equity—The Soul and Spirit of All Law or a Roguish Thing?' John Lehane Memorial Lecture at the Supreme Court of New South Wales (2014) para 9 ff.

[28] See *Arthur JS Hall & Co (a firm) v Simons (AP), Barratt v Ansell (trading as Woolf Seddon (a firm))* [2002] 1 AC 615 (HL), abolishing advocates' immunity, not followed in Australia: *D'Orta-Ekenaike v Victoria Legal Aid* (2005) 223 CLR 1. Note impending appeal in *Attwells v Jackson Lalic Lawyers Pty Ltd* [2015] HCATrans 176. See also *Brodie v Singleton Shire Council* (2001) 206 CLR 512 abolishing non-feasance immunity of highway authorities.

[29] See, eg, *Barclay v Penberthy* (2012) 246 CLR 258 on the rule in *Baker v Bolton* (1808) 1 Camp 493 that no action arises out of the death of a third party.

topic',[30] and has been since Bacon and Bentham,[31] the latter famously saying that codification would make 'every man his own lawyer'.[32]

The pros and cons of codification is a topic of its own, but briefly and in general codes are said to have a number of advantages:[33] they can bring otherwise disparate principles of law together into a single document; they can be a comprehensive statement of the law on a particular matter, filling gaps and modernising the law; they promote accessibility and therefore knowledge of the law; they promote coherence and consistency, particularly as this is easier to achieve where the law is in one document; and they bring greater certainty to the law.

Some statutes affecting private law can more easily be identified as codes[34] than others: Sale of Goods Acts, Partnership Acts and, until 2005, Defamation Acts in some Australian states codified the law in those fields. Perhaps the single most important recent legislation in Australia approaching a code and affecting a wide range of legal arrangements is the Personal Property Securities Act 2009 (Cth), which replaces many existing legislative schemes and applies nationwide. Criminal codes are more commonly identified as such and with good reason: as Lord Bingham said in a 1998 speech, 'the arguments for incremental development of the law, persuasive elsewhere, have no application' to the criminal law, where everyone is assumed to know the law and the relevant law is that at the date of the offence.[35] Lord Bingham noted that the Law Commission's 1989 draft criminal code had not been enacted,[36] 'not for want of confidence in its objects or its contents, but for lack of parliamentary time, a powerful but not, surely, an insuperable obstacle'.[37] The only alternative has been painstaking, piecemeal reform, with an aim to eventual consolidation.

However, in private law, it is rare that a code is the sole and comprehensive statement of the field of law that must be applied. It may only partially codify the law. Other consumer protection statutes regulate liability in respect of goods; partners are subject to other common law obligations and liabilities in tort, contract and as fiduciaries; and criminal codes may be supplemented by other statutory offences. Further, the enactment of a code in a common law system does not end the role of the common law. The statutory code must be interpreted just like any other statutory measure, so that a body of common law will quickly accumulate on the meaning and application of the code.

There may be many reasons why codes have not been more widely used for law reform, apart from the influence of the common law tradition. The hurdles

---

[30] JH Farrar, *Law Reform and the Law Commission* (London, Sweet & Maxwell, 1974) 57.

[31] ibid 4.

[32] J Bentham, 'Papers Relative to Codification and Public Instruction' in P Schofield and J Harris (eds), *Legislator of the World: Writings on Codification, Law and Education* (Oxford, Clarendon Press, 1998) 137.

[33] T Bingham, 'A Criminal Code: Must We Wait for Ever?' in T Bingham, *The Business of Judging: Selected Essays and Speeches* (Oxford, OUP, 2000) 293–95. See Farrar, n 30 above, 57 ff for arguments for and against codification.

[34] Or 'mini-codes' as suggested by Ian Dennis in his contribution (chapter 12).

[35] Bingham, n 33 above, 294.

[36] Law Commission, LC 177, *A Criminal Code for England and Wales* (1989).

[37] Bingham, n 33 above, 296.

for achieving legislative reform are amplified where the aim is a comprehensive statement of the law rather than reform of a discrete issue. Usually, codification is a painstaking and massive task.[38] It requires a high degree of consensus on the substance of the codification among stakeholders. Even if that is achieved, many will doubt the capacity of legislators and drafters to find a statement that will be clear and unambiguous, and not lead to more problems or uncertainties than it solves. None of this is impossible to achieve, but codification, like other reforms,[39] often depends on the dogged persistence of powerful advocates, and the capacity to isolate for resolution a particular field of law. Many aspects of private law, with its intersections between the law of torts, contract, trusts and other equitable obligations, commercial law, consumer law, securities law, and even criminal and administrative law are not apt for complete codification, and are more suited to legislative reform of particular issues. This does not stop calls for codification, particularly in contract law, but it may be that calls for national codifications will in the long term give way to other initiatives, such as the promotion of greater uniformity with internationally recognised models for contract law, such as the UNIDROIT principles.

Restatements on the law, such as those of the American Law Institute (ALI), are also a useful way to collate common law and statutory principles into a cohesive whole, albeit without legislative effect. Their authority depends on both the standing of the appointed reporter and the degree of consensus on the final text among the judicial, professional and academic lawyers involved in the process. To some extent, the reports of law reform Commissions play a role similar to the ALI's Restatements, in the sense that they provide a valuable, careful and authoritative statement of the law at the time, usually setting out its history, its sources and the key areas of controversy.[40]

## B Reform of Specific Issues of the Common Law

Legislative reform overriding specific rules of the common law or filling important gaps has been significant in shaping the modern law in all fields of private law.

In Australia, the single most important legislative overlay on the common law has been liability for misleading or deceptive conduct in trade or commerce under the Trade Practices Act 1974 (Cth), now replaced by the Australian Consumer Law (2010).[41] It imposes strict liability, supplementing, not replacing, the common law.

---

[38] SM Cretney, 'The Programmes: Milestones or Millstones?' in G Zellick (ed), *The Law Commission and Law Reform* (London, Sweet & Maxwell, 1988) 17.

[39] See SH Bailey, 'Occupiers' Liability' in TT Arvind and J Steele (eds), *Tort Law and the Legislature* (Oxford, Hart Publishing, 2013) 211 on the key contributions of Jenkins LJ and draftsmen John Fiennes and Euan Sutherland to the Occupiers' Liability Acts 1957 and 1984 (UK). For a US example, see WD Lewis, 'The Uniform Partnership Act' (1915) 24 *Yale Law Journal* 617 on the role of the Conference of Commissioners on Uniform State Laws.

[40] See further chapter 38 (Matthew Dyson).

[41] Contained in Competition and Consumer Act 2010 (Cth), sch 2.

It has become a ubiquitous component of claims for loss in many contexts that would once rest on the common law of deceit, negligent misstatement, contract or fiduciary obligation.[42]

The Contracts (Rights of Third Parties) Act 1999 (UK), based on the 1996 report of the Law Commission,[43] is an obvious example of important legislative intervention in contract law. In relation to the former, McKendrick notes that despite numerous expressions of disquiet in the House of Lords about the state of the law restricting the rights of a third party beneficiary to sue on the contract, 'the difficulty was that the judiciary showed little inclination to act on their expressions of disquiet'.[44] The Act is only a partial reform. Because the privity rule and its exceptions remain, McKendrick agrees with Chitty that 'it has scarcely simplified the law', but concedes that it is an improvement.[45]

Also notable in reshaping liability and rights was the Unfair Contract Terms Act 1977 (UK), an important but curiously named piece of legislation given its application to non-contractual terms such as notices.[46] Australia has only recently followed this lead with unfair terms provisions and only in respect of standard form contracts.[47]

It has always been curious to this writer that the common law, including the law created in the equitable jurisdiction, has had such difficulty in invalidating attempts by parties to exclude, by contract, liabilities imposed on them by law, such as tort liability for personal injury.[48] The notion of an irreducible core of obligation of reasonable care, to avoid personal injury at least, seems a logical component of the common law and defensible in many contexts. However, because this is not a notion that has been accepted at common law, which has tended to deal more easily with procedural unfairness—by duress or unconscionable conduct—than with substantive unfairness,[49] legislation regulating unfair terms plays a unique role. Why could not the common law develop notions and criteria for dealing with a level of unfairness that would justify intervention, without upsetting the certainty that contract law requires and inspires? Why should a judge be better equipped to decide unfairness simply because she or he is directed to do so by a statute?

The issue of whether there is an irreducible core of obligation on a trustee, liability for breach of which trustees, especially professional trustees, should not be able to

---

[42] See *ABN Amro Bank NV v Bathurst Regional Council* (2014) 224 FCR 1 for a recent example of a successful claim by local government councils against credit ratings agencies in the wake of the 2008 global financial crisis.
[43] Law Commission, LC 242, *Privity of Contract: Contracts for the Benefit of Third Parties* (1996).
[44] E McKendrick, *Contract Law*, 9th edn (London, Palgrave MacMillan, 2011) 115.
[45] ibid 120, quoting H Beale (ed), *Chitty on Contracts*, 30th edn (London, Sweet & Maxwell, 2008) para 18-002.
[46] See also now Consumer Rights Act 2015 (UK).
[47] Australian Consumer Law, ss 23–24. See further JW Carter, *Contract Law in Australia*, 6th edn (Sydney, LexisNexis Butterworths, 2012) ch 24.
[48] The common law has tended to use the tools for construing contracts to restrict the operation of exclusion clauses, which has meant that a clearly drafted clause could be effective. See *Canada Steamship Lines Ltd The King* [1952] AC 192 (PC); *HIH Casualty and General Insurance Ltd v Chase Manhattan Bank* [2003] UKHL 6, [2003] 1 All ER (Comm) 349.
[49] See, eg, *National Westminster plc v Morgan* [1985] AC 686 (HL).

exclude, was the subject of a Law Commission Report in 2006.[50] The concept of the irreducible core had been expressed in *Armitage v Nurse* by Millet LJ,[51] but only with respect to the duty to act honestly and in good faith. It appeared that even gross negligence might be validly excluded. Millet LJ was obviously uneasy with this:

> At the same time, it must be acknowledged that the view is widely held that these clauses have gone too far, and that trustees who charge for their services and who, as professional men, would not dream of excluding liability for ordinary professional negligence should not be able to rely on a trustee exemption clause excluding liability for gross negligence ... The subject is presently under consideration in this country by the Trust Law Committee ... If clauses such as clause 15 of the settlement are to be denied effect, then in my opinion this should be done by Parliament, which will have the advantage of wide consultation with interested bodies and the advice of the Trust Law Committee.[52]

The issue was considered by the Law Commission which, in brief, decided that the issue was too hard for legislative reform: it was too difficult to formulate a proposal that was either sufficiently comprehensive or sufficiently defined to be useful. The whole issue was controversial: there was widespread consensus that 'something should be done'[53] but not what that should be. Apart from the fear of the effect that over-regulation might have on the administration of trusts and the willingness of people to be trustees, there was the problem of the impact on duty modification clauses—which are often used instead of exemption clauses to restrict duties—and the near impossibility of creating certainty about which clauses would be affected by any statutory prohibition. In the end, the preferred approach was merely to recommend that steps be taken to ensure that settlors of trusts were made aware of exemption clauses or clauses that would exclude or limit liability for negligence of any *paid* trustee, so that if they went ahead with the trust on this basis it would be with full information.[54] The non-legislative approach was welcomed by the Better Regulation Executive who commented:

> [W]ith complex and important issues such as trustee exemption clauses it is all too easy to play it safe and regulate. I'm glad to see that the Law Commission has listened to people on all sides of the debate and developed a proportionate risk-based approach to the issue.[55]

However, it must nevertheless be questioned why a paid professional trustee should be able to rely on an exemption for gross negligence, regardless of the sophistication of the other party.

In tort law, many legislative reforms have softened the harsh impact of particular common law rules, which counters the view held by some commentators and industry groups that it has been judges who have allowed tort liability to expand so considerably. Lord Campbell's Fatal Accidents Act 1846 (UK), surely one of the

---

[50] Law Commission, LC 301, *Trustee Exemption Clauses* (2006).

[51] *Armitage v Nurse* [1998] Ch 241 (CA).

[52] ibid 256.

[53] S Bridge, 'Trustees Exemption Clauses Report' (Speech at Launch Event for LC 301, n 50 above, 2006).

[54] ibid.

[55] As quoted on the Law Commission's website: www.lawcom.gov.uk/project/trustee-exemption-clauses/.

greatest and most socially important pieces of legislative reform, provided a statutory exception to the still existing common law rule of *Baker v Bolton* that no action could arise from the death of a third party.[56] Other legislation provided for the survival of actions, while the apportionment legislation for contributory negligence and contribution legislation have all transformed the structure of tort claims, and allowed for a much broader and fairer allocation of responsibility for negligent harm than was the case under the common law.[57] The Torts (Interference with Goods) Act 1977 (UK) and Occupiers' Liability Acts 1957 and 1984 (UK) are examples of important broader legislative reforms that fall short of codification.[58] Notably, the Australian common law reformed the law of occupiers' liability, in the absence of statutory intervention in most states.[59]

Law reform Commissions have not always favoured legislation to clarify or restructure the common law of tort. For example, the law on liability for negligently inflicted psychiatric injury has always been purely a matter of common law in the United Kingdom, with the limits of liability a troublesome issue—especially when cases arising out of the Hillsborough football disaster challenged the courts' ability to set logical and justifiable limits.[60] The Law Commission recommended against wholesale codification as it would 'result in a freezing of the law at a time before it is ready'.[61] Nor was a statutory definition of recognisable psychiatric illness practicable in the light of expert medical opinion.[62] Further, the Commission recommended against the statutory extension of liability for psychiatric injury to certain classes of close relative of the primary victim without requiring them to establish a duty of care, as was then found in New South Wales legislation (since repealed).[63] While the Law Commission felt that the development of liability should broadly be left to the common law, it did recommend 'minimal legislative intervention curing serious defects in the present law', saying 'to wait for the House of Lords to reverse *Alcock* may be to wait for a very long time'.[64] That remark was prescient.

In the ALRC privacy inquiry, the detailed legal design was explicitly required to include a large range of matters well beyond the elements of the cause of action for invasion of privacy. We were asked to make recommendations on thresholds, jurisdiction, exemptions, defences, remedies, caps on damages, limitation periods

---

[56] *Baker v Bolton* (1808) 1 Camp 493.
[57] J Steele, 'Law Reform (Contributory Negligence) Act 1945: Collision of a Different Sort' in TT Arvind and J Steele (eds), *Tort Law and the Legislature* (Oxford, Hart Publishing, 2013) 166.
[58] On the latter, see SH Bailey, 'Occupiers' Liability' in Arvind and Steele, ibid 211.
[59] See *Hackshaw v Shaw* (1984) 155 CLR 614 on liability to trespassers; *Australian Safeway Stores v Zaluzna* (1987) 162 CLR 479 on liability to lawful entrants.
[60] See, eg, *Alcock v Chief Constable South Yorkshire Police* [1992] 1 AC 310 (HL).
[61] Law Commission, LC 249, *Liability for Psychiatric Illness* (1998) para 4.1.
[62] ibid para 5.2.
[63] Law Reform (Miscellaneous Provisions) Act 1944 (NSW), s 4. That legislation was prompted by Evatt J's stirring dissent in the tragic case of *Chester v Waverley Corporation* (1939) 62 CLR 1, where a mother failed to recover for her illness from witnessing the body of her young son dragged from a water-filled trench, negligently left unguarded by the local council, because she did not see him drown. The 'immediate aftermath' extension was not developed at common law until the 1980s. Tort 'reforms' in 2002 repealed the New South Wales legislation.
[64] LC 249, n 61 above, para 4.2.

and 'access to justice'. This is a useful reminder that the legislature is not bound by precedent and historical factors, for example, as to what remedies might be awarded by the court. An advantage of creating new law by statute is that a wide range of issues can be dealt with explicitly and immediately, reducing the need for litigation to sort out ancillary matters. So that any new action would fit more obviously and coherently into existing law, including statute law, we recommended that the action be explicitly described as a tort, a point noted by Court of Appeal of England and Wales in *Google v Vidal-Hall* recently[65] when it considered how privacy actions in the United Kingdom should now be classified.[66]

## C  Legislative 'Restatements' and 'Reformulations' of Common Law Principles

Increasingly, we come across examples of legislative *restatements* of common law rules. By 'restatement' is meant a legislative provision that is an *exact* replica of the common law principle or rule. Alternatively, rather than restating a common law rule, or replacing it entirely, legislation may *reformulate* an existing common law principle in a way that is close but not identical. The statutory language and content will for the most part reflect the existing common law, but with some deliberate and key differences.

Recent examples of restatement in the United Kingdom include section 1 of the Compensation Act 2006 (UK), which sets out the principles clearly enunciated by Lord Hoffmann (with whom others agreed) in the House of Lords in *Tomlinson v Congleton Borough Council*.[67] These principles are that, in determining whether a defendant breached a duty of care, the court may consider the deterrent effect that imposing liability might have on socially desirable activities. Lord Hoffmann did not appear to regard the principles he set out as new. Indeed he referred to *Bolton v Stone*,[68] as an illustration that the social utility of the defendant's activity is a relevant factor.

Arguably, the Social Action, Responsibility and Heroism Act 2015 (UK)[69] (SARAH Act) is another example of such a statute. This Act provides that when a court is determining whether a person was negligent, the court must consider whether the alleged negligence occurred when the person was acting for the benefit of society or any of its members, whether the person demonstrated a predominantly responsible approach towards protecting the safety or other interests of others, and whether the

---

[65] *Google v Vidal-Hall* [2015] EWCA Civ 311, [2015] 3 WLR 409, [44]. Permission to appeal to the United Kingdom Supreme Court was granted in part on 28 July 2015, but the Court refused permission on 'the issue whether the claim is in tort ... because this ground does not raise an arguable point of law': www.supremecourt.uk/news/permission-to-appeal-decisions-28-july-2015.html.

[66] See generally B McDonald, 'Privacy Claims: Transformation, Fault and the Public Interest Defence' in A Dyson, J Goudkamp and F Wilmot-Smith (eds), *Defences in Tort* (Oxford, Hart Publishing, 2015).

[67] *Tomlinson v Congleton Borough Council* [2003] UKHL 47, [2004] 1 AC 46.

[68] *Bolton v Stone* [1951] AC 850 (HL).

[69] The Act is an Act of the UK Parliament, but extends only to England and Wales: SARAH Act, s 5(1).

person was acting heroically by intervening in an emergency to assist an individual in danger. It is strongly arguable that a court has always been able to take such matters into account when determining whether the defendant acted reasonably in the circumstances he or she was in. *Tomlinson* reflected a concern with social benefit, as was also seen, in another form, in *Watt v Hertfordshire County Council* (acting in an emergency 'to save life or limb' such as the fire officers).[70]

What is the purpose or rationale of legislative restatements? What is the point of a statute if the law already exists in another, common law, form?

A number of beneficial purposes for a restatement could be suggested:

— it may consolidate principles which are somewhat scattered in case law;
— it may extend the application of the rule more generally than the fact-specific instance of a decision;
— it may enhance the authority of the common law rule by the legislative recognition of its correctness, dispelling doubts as to the rule's validity; and
— it may make Parliament look busy and pro-active.

There is a more powerful justification if a certain result is desired: a restatement certainly entrenches the common law rule and later courts from overturning it or formulating exceptions which erode its efficacy. While this may seem beneficial to some, to others it may represent a freezing of the law at a particular time, when only certain perspectives or social conditions are known. A provision of the Australian states' Civil Liability Acts—that in a negligence case a plaintiff always bears the onus of proving, on the balance of probabilities, any fact relevant to the issue of causation[71]—reflects the current Australian rule on the legal onus of proof. But it does more than this: it entrenches the rule. Many industry groups or potential defendants would be comforted to think that courts could not change the legal onus nor formulate exceptions to it as some other countries have done.

Notably, civil liability legislation in Australia attempts a reformulation of the fundamental principles of negligence as to the test for breach of duty and the principles of causation. The attempt to reformulate principles was kindly or tactfully described as 'heroic' by Lord Walker,[72] but perhaps that description shows an issue that will arise with the SARAH Act, described above: what is heroic to one may be foolhardy to another.

The civil liability provisions were said not be intended as a code, but as a guide for judges.[73]

There is no doubt that putting the test for determining breach of duty in a statute[74] makes this part of negligence law more 'accessible' for judges, litigants and their lawyers, students and the public, who would otherwise have to find the relevant

---

[70] *Watt v Hertfordshire County Council* [1954] 1 WLR 835 (CA), 838 (Denning LJ).
[71] eg Civil Liability Act 2002 (NSW), s 5E; see also s 5C restating common law principles on breach of duty.
[72] Walker, n 16 above, 245.
[73] R Carr, NSW Legislative Assembly, *Parliamentary Debates (Hansard)* 23 October 200, 5764.
[74] eg Civil Liability Act 2002 (NSW), s 5B.

passages in case law.[75] This accessibility is a key advantage of statute over the common law. However accessibility also assumes other attributes such as comprehensibility and logic. It assumes general application too, yet requiring judges to work through a statutory test in every case arguably prolongs litigation and is often unnecessary. It would not, for example, require a detailed cost–benefit analysis to find that leaving a gate open at an early childcare centre near a busy road is negligence to the children. The succinct general principle from *Blyth v Birmingham Waterworks Co* will do the job.[76]

There is a more serious problem with the reformulation of general common law principles on causation.[77] Professor Stapleton concludes that it does little more than tell judges to give reasons for their decisions on causation, leaving the High Court free to develop the common law.[78] Many questions of interpretation remain unanswered, creating uncertainty and spawning litigation. This may be because of infelicities in drafting and gaps in content, but it may be because even if perfectly or correctly drafted, legislative formulations *cannot* provide a solution to the sort of complex matters of judgment about legal responsibility that are inevitably involved in causation and related issues.

## IV CONCLUSION

If ever there was an illustration of the need for and role of law reform Commissions, it is the 'civil liability' statutes of most Australian states. In an influential speech on the modern law of negligence, New South Wales Chief Justice Spigelman suggested that various issues for reform should be allocated to law reform Commissions throughout the country to consider.[79] This did not happen. The legislation that was rushed through state legislatures is still regularly the subject of appeals to the High Court of Australia, and countless intermediate appellate decisions. Even where interpretation is settled, there is a very real question of whether certain reforms are appropriate, just, or even useful, or whether they reflect a political response to the urgings of powerful lobby groups, where lobbying occurs behind closed doors.

A law reform inquiry provides an open forum for the submissions of all groups in society to be heard and seen.[80] Further, consideration of reform proposals by a properly funded law reform Commission is an investment in the stability, accessibility and integrity of the law that will repay dividends in the future.

---

[75] *Shirt v Wyong Shire Council* (1980) 146 CLR 40, 47 (Mason J).

[76] *Blyth v Birmingham Waterworks Co* (1856) 11 Ex 781. cf *Uniting Church in Australia Property Trust (NSW) v Miller* [2015] NSWCA 320, [105].

[77] eg Civil Liability Act 2002 (NSW), s 5D.

[78] J Stapleton, 'Factual Causation' (2010) 38 *Federal Law Review* 467, 483–84.

[79] J Spigelman, 'Negligence: The Last Outpost of the Welfare State' (2002) 76 *Australian Law Journal* 432.

[80] As noted by Kathryn Cronin in her contribution (chapter 6).

# 31

# *The Refiner's Fire*

## CHARLES HARPUM

### I INTRODUCTION

The purpose of this chapter is to examine, by way of a case study, how legislation that enacts Law Commission recommendations has fared when it is tested in the refining furnace of litigation. It is necessarily descriptive rather than analytical. I examine the following questions:

(1) To what extent are Law Commission reports admissible in court proceedings and for what purpose?

(2) How, in practice, do the courts employ Law Commission reports when they are called upon to interpret legislation that enacted the Commission's recommendations?

As regards the second of those two questions, it would require a series of books to examine the judicial treatment of all the Law Commission reports since the two Law Commissions were founded 50 years ago. I have confined myself to the judicial treatment of just one Act, the Land Registration Act 2002,[1] and even then only to the leading cases.[2] Before considering these questions, there are three preliminary points.

## A The Way in which the Law Commission Conducts Law Reform Projects

The way in which the Law Commission conducts law reform projects owes much to its first Chairman, Sir Leslie Scarman. It was during his Chairmanship that the Law Commission developed the system of Green Papers and White Papers, now widely

---

[1] As Commissioner, I was involved with the Land Registration Act 2002 from its inception and assisted with its passage through Parliament.

[2] Constraints of space have meant that it has been necessary to omit treatment of the adverse possession provisions of the 2002 Act.

employed by government generally when proposing new or reformed law. In most Law Commission law reform projects there are two stages:

(1) The first is the publication of a consultation paper (originally called a 'working paper').[3] That paper provides a detailed statement of the existing law. Its preparation involves a great deal of research and prior consultation with significant stakeholders. The Commission's proposals are only provisional: the Commission has always listened carefully to those who responded to its proposals. The proposals may be abandoned or modified in the light of consultation. Furthermore, consultation invariably exposes issues that the Commission had not addressed.

(2) The second stage is the publication of the final report that reflects the Commission's considered view following consultation and further consideration. That final report is usually accompanied by a draft Bill, with explanatory notes. The process of instructing Parliamentary Counsel, and his subsequent testing of the Commission's proposals in drafting the Bill, often have significant effects on the final form of the draft legislation.

The proposals for reform in the initial consultation paper are not therefore necessarily any guide to the recommendations in the final report.

## B Repealing Obsolete Legislation and Consolidation

The Law Commission does not just produce law reform Bills in the manner explained above. It has two other important functions.

The first is to purge the statute book of obsolete legislation, which it does through its Statute Law Repeal reports.[4] These reports, which appear on average once every four years, comprise a draft Statute Law (Repeals) Bill with a commentary, the contents of which are very scholarly and often fascinating. Such Bills are intended, in the words of the long titles of the Statute Law (Repeals) Acts:

> [T]o promote the reform of the statute law by the repeal, in accordance with recommendations of the Law Commission and the Scottish Law Commission, of certain enactments which (except in so far as their effect is preserved) are no longer of practical utility.

The second function is the consolidation of enactments. The background to this was explained by Carnwath LJ (a former Chairman of the Law Commission) in his judgment in *Isle of Anglesey County Council v Welsh Ministers and others*.[5] Before the Law Commissions were created in 1965, the consolidation of legislation was by means of a shortened procedure, through a special joint committee under the Consolidation of Enactments (Procedure) Act 1949. Changes were limited to

---

[3] The earliest working papers put out provisional recommendations for reform rather than asking specific questions on which views were sought, as tends to happen nowadays.

[4] For this function, see the Law Commissions Act 1965, s 3(1)(d).

[5] *Isle of Anglesey County Council v Welsh Ministers and others* [2009] EWCA Civ 94, [2010] QB 163, [47].

'corrections and minor amendments' as defined by that Act. When the Law Commissions were created, they took primary responsibility for preparing consolidation Bills. One of the first of those consolidation Bills was enacted as the Sea Fisheries (Shellfish) Act 1967, an Act which was in issue in the *Isle of Anglesey* case. As a result of the passage of that Bill before the Joint Consolidation Committee (JCC) in Parliament, a practice evolved in relation to amendments.[6] The JCC indicated that Law Commission amendments should be 'necessary in order to produce a satisfactory consolidation' and should be for the purpose of tidying up errors of the past, removing ambiguities, and generally to introduce common sense in the drafting where it had been absent in the past, but not to introduce any substantial or controversial changes in the law.

## C The Function of Legislation

The third preliminary point is that the function of legislation is to change the law. Accordingly, to the extent that a law reform Act says nothing about existing rules of law and does not impinge on them, the law remains unchanged. Parliamentary Counsel are, in my experience, very reluctant to codify existing rules of law.[7] A corollary of this is that if, as part of a reform project, the Law Commission leaves untouched some aspect of the law that it has reviewed, the existing law will continue to operate unless it is inconsistent with the other changes that are made.[8]

### II THE ADMISSIBILITY OF LAW COMMISSION REPORTS

The extent to which the courts may have recourse to a Law Commission report as an aid to interpreting legislation that enacted the recommendations in that report was considered in some detail by the Court of Appeal in *Yaxley v Gotts* in 2000 and the comments in that case have thereafter been accepted as defining the correct approach.[9]

One issue in that case concerned the interpretation of section 2(5) of the Law of Property (Miscellaneous Provisions) Act 1989 and the extent to which a person might be estopped from relying upon the provisions of section 2. Section 2 prescribes the formal requirements for contracts for the sale or other disposition of an interest in land and it enacted, in modified form, the recommendations of the Law Commission in its report, *Formalities for Contracts for Sale etc of Land*.[10] The judges included Beldam LJ, the Chairman of the Law Commission at the time of the report.

---

[6] ibid [50].

[7] The Land Registration Act 2002 contains just one codificatory provision. Section 116, which is concerned with the status of estoppel rights and mere equities, begins with the words 'It is hereby declared for the avoidance of doubt...'

[8] See, eg, *Nugent v Nugent* [2013] EWHC 4095 (Ch), [2015] Ch 121. Morgan J was perplexed by the silence of the final Law Commission report on the issue in question. However, a final report will generally only comment on changes to the law, because that is the function of the legislation.

[9] *Yaxley v Gotts* [2000] Ch 162 (CA).

[10] LC 164 (1987).

In considering the arguments on the true interpretation of section 2, Robert Walker LJ said:

> None of the recent authorities referred to by counsel is determinative of this appeal ... Nor can anything in the Law Commission's report (or its earlier working paper) be decisive. The report and the working paper are invaluable guides to the old law and to the problems which constituted the 'mischief' at which section 2 of the Act of 1989 is directed, but they cannot be conclusive as to how section 2, as enacted, is to be construed and applied.[11]

Both Clarke LJ[12] and Beldam LJ[13] took a wider view of the role of Law Commission reports than did Robert Walker LJ. They considered that Law Commission reports could be relied upon to identify both the mischief to which the legislation was directed, *and* the policy which the Law Commission had adopted to address that mischief. As Beldam LJ explained, 'it is unrealistic to divorce the defect in the law from the policy adopted to correct it'.[14] The wider view of Clarke and Beldam LJJ has in practice prevailed.[15]

In *R v Secretary of State for the Environment, ex p Spath Holme Ltd*, Lord Nicholls considered generally the use by courts of external aids to construction, including Law Commission reports.[16] He explained that the use of non-statutory materials as an aid to interpretation had a long history, originally in identifying the mischief that the statute was intended to cure, but nowadays to identify and give effect to the purpose of the legislation. That analysis supports the wider view of the role of Law Commission reports that was taken by Clarke and Beldam LJJ in *Yaxley*. However, Lord Nicholls cautioned that such external aids to construction were not found within the body of the statute and citizens should be able to rely upon what they read in an Act of Parliament. Such aids should not overturn the clear and unambiguous language of the statute. I know of no case in which the courts have overturned the plain words of a statutory provision by reference to any statement of policy and intent in the Law Commission's report from which it derived.

### III LAW COMMISSION REPORTS BEFORE THE COURTS: A CASE STUDY

#### A Introduction

As I have indicated, I have undertaken a case study of the way in which the courts have interpreted the Land Registration Act 2002 (LRA 2002), which enacted, largely unamended, proposals contained in a Law Commission report. The purpose of this study is to examine how the courts have employed the report in interpreting the LRA 2002 and the extent to which they depart from the conclusions expressed in it.

---

[11] *Yaxley*, n 9 above, 175–76.
[12] ibid 182.
[13] ibid 189–90.
[14] ibid 190.
[15] See, eg, *Knights Construction (March) Ltd v Roberto Mac Ltd* [2011] 2 EGLR 123, [69].
[16] *R v Secretary of State for the Environment, ex p Spath Holme Ltd* [2001] 2 AC 349 (HL), 397–99.

There were in fact two reports that preceded the LRA 2002. The first was a consultative document, *Land Registration for the Twenty-First Century: A Consultative Document* (hereafter LC 254).[17] The second was the final report that accompanied the draft Land Registration Bill, *Land Registration for the Twenty-First Century: A Conveyancing Revolution* (hereafter LC 271).[18] Both reports were prepared jointly with the Land Registry. The reform of land registration was based upon the recognition that registration of title was something more than mere machinery, a view that had been in vogue at one time, but which could never have been true.[19] Recent authority in fact suggests that the courts are coming to accept that registration of title is driven by its own logic.

## B  The Register as a Mirror to the Title

One of the main functions of the LRA 2002 was to introduce a system of electronic transfer of registered land. A drawback of any system of registered conveyancing is the so-called 'registration gap'. There is a hiatus between the execution of a registrable disposition and its submission to the Land Registry for registration. Registration is effective from the date upon which the application for registration is received,[20] but until such receipt, there is a risk that a further disposition of the land may take place which could detrimentally affect the title. Devices exist, such as official priority searches, which minimise but do not eliminate this risk. The scheme of electronic conveyancing that was devised and enacted by the LRA 2002 was intended to achieve the simultaneous registration of a disposition and so eliminate the 'gap'. However, the recession put an end to the introduction of that scheme of electronic conveyancing and it will not now be implemented in the form then visualised. As part of the review of the LRA 2002, which the Law Commission is to carry out, a new scheme of electronic conveyancing will be devised.

The original scheme for electronic conveyancing drove much of the logic of the LRA 2002. In a world of electronic conveyancing, the register should necessarily be paramount. In paragraph 1.5 of LC 271, it was explained that:

> The fundamental objective of the Bill is that, under the system of electronic dealing with land that it seeks to create, the register should be a complete and accurate reflection of the state of the title of the land at any given time, so that it is possible to investigate title to land on line, with the absolute minimum of additional enquiries and inspections.[21]

---

[17] LC 254 (1998).
[18] LC 271 (2001).
[19] See LC 254, n 17 above, paras 1.5–1.6; LC 271, n 18 above, para 1.5. Even after the reforms brought about by LRA 2002, there are apparently those who still take the view that 'the system of land registration is merely conveyancing machinery': see *Southern Pacific Mortgages Ltd v Scott* [2014] UKSC 52, [2015] AC 385, [96] (Lady Hale). That dictum has been criticised: see M Dixon, 'Why?' [2014] *Conveyancer and Property Lawyer* 461, 464; N Hopkins, 'Priorities and Sale and Lease Back: A Wrong Question, Much Ado about Nothing and a Story of Tails and Dogs' [2015] *Conveyancer and Property Lawyer* 245, 252.
[20] See LRA 2002, s 74.
[21] LC 271, n 18 above, para 1.5.

What underpins that principle is that in any coherent system of registered title, it should be possible to rely upon the register. That should be a fundamental principle regardless of whether or how electronic conveyancing is introduced and implemented.

There is no doubt that this principle that the register should be an accurate mirror of the title has been understood by the courts. Thus, for example, in *Franks v Bedward*, Rimer LJ, without referring explicitly to paragraph 1.5 of LC 271,[22] said that:

> Subject to exceptions, the register is intended to provide a comprehensive and accurate reflection of the state of the title to registered land at any given time, so that it is possible to investigate title to land online with the minimum of additional inquiries and inspections.[23]

There are a number of important concomitants of that principle and these have been explored in a number of cases on the LRA 2002, of which I shall consider three:

(1) Those who deal with registered land should be entitled to rely upon what is in the register as a reliable record of the information that they require to inform their decision to proceed with a registrable disposition.
(2) The categories of overriding interests, certain unregistered interests affecting registered land that bind the land any anyone who acquires it, would have to be significantly reduced.
(3) It ought not to be possible to rectify the register retrospectively, because that would undermine the principle set out in paragraph 1.5 of LC 271 quoted above.

*i The Register as a Reliable Record*

As regards issue 1, there is a striking illustrative decision of the Court of Appeal, *Cherry Tree Investments Ltd v Landmain Ltd*.[24] Was it permissible to construe a registered legal charge by reference to extrinsic evidence, namely, a facility letter that modified the chargee's power of sale? Although the registered charge had been registered, there was no reference in the register to the facility letter. By a majority, the Court of Appeal held that it was not possible to construe the registered charge by reference to such extrinsic evidence. Lewison LJ referred expressly to paragraph 1.5 of LC 271, and other relevant paragraphs of that report,[25] to show that an essential part of the scheme of the LRA 2002 was to create a system under which there should be easy and open access to information held by the Land Registry. The particular provisions of the LRA 2002 that implemented those paragraphs were part of the background against which the registered charge was to be construed.[26]

[22] The judgments did not refer to LC 271. However, at first instance, Briggs J had referred to and paraphrased para 1.5 of that report: see *Franks v Bedward* [2010] EWHC 1650 (Ch), [2010] 3 EGLR 29, [17].
[23] *Franks v Bedward* [2011] EWCA Civ 772, [2012] 1 WLR 2428, [25].
[24] *Cherry Tree Investments Ltd v Landmain Ltd* [2012] EWCA Civ 736, [2013] Ch 305.
[25] ibid [105] ff.
[26] ibid [130].

*ii Curtailing Overriding Interests*

As already explained, overriding interests are unregistered proprietary rights affecting registered land which bind any disponee of the land affected, whether that disposition is for valuable consideration or not and in some cases regardless of the knowledge or means of knowledge of the disponee. Overriding interests are necessarily incompatible with the objective that the register should be as comprehensive a record of the title as possible. Because these interests existed under the LRA 1925 their overriding status could not simply be abolished. Indeed it is inevitable that some such rights should not be on the *land* register, because, for example, as in the case of local land charges,[27] they are recorded in another register.[28] The LRA 2002 adopted a number of strategies to limit the effect of overriding interests, including:

(i)    Provisions that were intended to ensure that overriding interests are disclosed, whether on first registration or on a disposal where title is already registered. The disclosed interests are registered and cease to be overriding interests.[29]
(ii)   The removal of overriding status from a group of more obscure overriding interests on 13 October 2013, ten years after the LRA 2002 came into force.[30] The purpose of the legislation was to encourage the registration of such rights prior to that date. If such rights were not registered by then, they would be defeated by any subsequent disposition for valuable consideration of the land affected.[31]
(iii)  The scope of a number of overriding interests which were retained, was cut back.

It is primarily the third strategy that has to date come before the courts. The two major categories of overriding interests that were cut back were: (a) the protection given to the rights of persons in actual occupation; and (b) easements.[32] The protection of the property rights of persons in actual occupation had been the most litigated aspect of the LRA 1925.[33] In the light of that litigation, it was unsurprising that the balance between purchasers and occupiers was changed by the LRA 2002 so that it was more in favour of purchasers.

As regards the rights of persons in actual occupation of registered land, the LRA 2002 cut back the protection to occupiers in a number of ways.[34] In particular,

---

[27] See LRA 2002, sch 1, para 6 and sch 3, para 6.
[28] The local land charges register: see the Local Land Charges Act 1975. Responsibility for local land charges is to be transferred from local authorities to the Land Registry pursuant to the Infrastructure Act 2015.
[29] LRA 2002, s 71.
[30] See the five overriding interests listed in LRA 2002, s 117(1), to which chancel repair liability was added by the Land Registration Act 2002 (Transitional Provisions) Order 2003, SI 2003/2431, following the decision in *Aston Cantlow and Wilmcote with Billesley Parochial Church Council v Wallbank* [2003] UKHL 37, [2004] 1 AC 546.
[31] Under LRA 2002, s 29.
[32] Expressly granted but unregistered easements, which only take effect in equity, were excluded, because only legal easements could be overriding interests: see LRA 2002, sch 3, para 3.
[33] The relevant provision was LRA 1925, s 70(1)(g).
[34] The relevant provision is LRA 2002, sch 3, para 2.

protection was limited to the land actually occupied, and no longer included other land within the same title, and the burden of enquiry on purchasers was mitigated. The restrictions imposed by the LRA 2002 have come before the courts on a handful of occasions.[35] The most high-profile discussion was in the Supreme Court in *Southern Pacific Mortgages Ltd v Scott*,[36] where the changes made by the LRA 2002 were in fact irrelevant to the issue before the court. That issue was whether X, who was in occupation under what appears to have been a fraudulent sale and lease back arrangement, had an interest in the land at the moment when the freehold was sold to Y and simultaneously mortgaged. It was held that X had no interest, but that had nothing whatever to do with the law on title registration. The outcome would not have been different had the LRA 1925 been applicable. Lord Collins gave the principal judgment and set out the stated intentions of the LRA 2002 as the Law Commission had explained them. Lady Hale was somewhat critical of the provisions of the LRA 2002,[37] even though they did not impinge on the outcome. She was compelled to accept that, under the law, the persons in actual occupation did not have any proprietary interest which could be overriding. While sympathising with the plight of those who have agreed to the sale and lease back of their homes and then found themselves evicted as a result of fraud, the answer to that problem, if there is an answer, does not lie in any change to the law on title registration. Title registration can only protect property rights.

The other notable case, in which there was a more sympathetic consideration of the changes to the scope of overriding interests, was the decision of the Court of Appeal in *Chaudhary v Yavuz*.[38] One of the principal issues in that case was whether the claimant respondent had an overriding interest in a metal staircase over the defendant's land, which provided access to the first floor of the claimant's adjacent property. That staircase had been erected in 2006 by oral agreement between the claimant and the then owners of the neighbouring property. The adjoining land was purchased by the defendant, who removed the staircase. The claimant could not assert any legal easement over the staircase in those circumstances[39] and alleged instead (amongst other things) that he was in actual occupation of the staircase, and had an overriding interest on that basis. That argument found no favour with the Court of Appeal. Lloyd LJ pointed out that 'it seems counter-intuitive, to say the least, to assert that the owner of dominant land ... is in occupation of other land ... over which he asserts an easement'.[40] The Court of Appeal quoted paragraph 1.5 of LC 271 as set out above and explained the workings of the scheme of priority under the LRA 2002.

---

[35] See, eg, *Thomas v Clydesdale Bank Ltd* [2010] EWHC 2755 (QB) (which arose on an application to set aside a judgment given in default); *Mehra v Mehra* [2008] 3 EGLR 153. In neither case was there any reference to LC 271.
[36] *Southern Pacific Mortgages Ltd v Scott* [2014] UKSC 52, [2015] AC 385.
[37] As Law Commissioner, Lady Hale had been party to earlier proposals to reform land registration which had not been accepted, not least because the Land Registry strongly opposed them.
[38] *Chaudhary v Yavuz* [2011] EWCA Civ 1314, [2013] Ch 249.
[39] Only a legal easement can be an overriding interest. The claimant unsuccessfully claimed equitable rights arising under a constructive trust.
[40] *Chaudhary*, n 38 above, [28].

### iii  Can Rectification be Retrospective?

The third aspect of the principle set out in LC 271 at paragraph 1.5, that the register should accurately reflect the state of the title, goes to the issue of rectification. The LRA 2002, like the LRA 1925 before it, makes provision for the correction of errors in the register. The alteration of the register to correct a mistake in circumstances where that alteration prejudicially affects the title of a registered proprietor is called 'rectification' by the LRA 2002.[41] If a person suffers loss by reason of rectification, which he is almost bound to do because his title will be prejudicially affected, he will be entitled to recovery indemnity from the Land Registry under schedule 8 paragraph 1 of the LRA 2002.

If the register should so far as possible accurately reflect the state of the title, can rectification ever be retrospective? If rectification can be retrospective, derivative interests created between the date upon which the mistake in the register is made and the date of its eventual rectification may be affected. If rectification *can* retrospectively affect such a derivative interest, it undermines the principle that the register should be treated as an accurate reflection of the title.

Under the LRA 1925, the courts had held the register could be rectified, but, as regards derivative interests, only prospectively. If, therefore, the register of a freehold title was rectified to restore a note of a restrictive covenant that had been removed by mistake, that rectification would not affect a person who had been granted a lease after the mistaken removal of the notice but before the rectification of the register.[42] Those cases had been criticised as a matter of authority because they were decided without reference to the LRA 1925, section 82(2), which appeared to suggest that the register could be rectified retrospectively, even as regards derivative interests. In LC 254, the Law Commission's initial reaction had been to endorse those criticisms. However, by the time that LC 271 was published, the proposals for reform had significantly developed and had crystallised around the principle set out in LC 271, paragraph 1.5 that the register should reflect the title. In the light of that principle, the judicial decisions mentioned above were seen as much more in line with the principles of title registration than was a literal application of the LRA 1925, section 82(2). This was one of those situations in which the Law Commission changed its views between consultation and the final report and draft Bill. Although the fact that there had been a change of heart was not made explicit in LC 271, the intention of the provision, the LRA 2002, schedule 4, paragraph 8, was made explicit. It was intended 'to accord with the manner in which the analogous provisions of [LRA 1925] have been interpreted'.[43] The wording of the provision is somewhat Delphic:

> The powers under this Schedule to alter the register, so far as relating to rectification, extend to changing for the future the priority of any interest affecting the registered estate or charge concerned.

---

[41] LRA 2002, sch 4, para 1.

[42] See *Freer v Unwins Ltd* [1976] Ch 288 (Ch); and *Clark v Chief Land Registrar* [1993] Ch 294 (Ch), 317–18.

[43] Law Commission, LC 271, *Land Registration for the Twenty-First Century: A Conveyancing Revolution* (2001) para 10.8.

On two occasions, the Adjudicator had interpreted this provision in accordance with the explanation given in LC 271.[44] However, when the matter came before the Court of Appeal in *MacLeod v Gold Harp Properties Ltd*,[45] this interpretation was rejected. It was a classic instance of hard cases making bad law. It was a wholly unmeritorious appeal. The issue was whether two leases, which the registrar had been fraudulently induced to remove from the register, could be retrospectively reinstated so as to have priority over a subsequent lease that had been granted in favour of Gold Harp Properties Ltd, a company owned by the perpetrator of the fraud. The claimants, who owned the leases, were not actually living on the property, which is how the fraud came to be perpetrated. The trial judge retrospectively reinstated the leases and the Court of Appeal dismissed an appeal from his decision. There was a simple answer to the case, which was discussed by the Court of Appeal. It was accepted by Gold Harp's counsel that the subsequent lease to Gold Harp was not granted for valuable consideration.[46] On that basis, even if the prior leases had been prospectively restored to the register, they would have taken effect in possession and Gold Harp's lease would have taken effect as a lease of the reversion. The reason for this is that the general rule in the LRA 2002, section 28, that priority is determined by the date of creation of the interest, would have applied. Accordingly, as a matter of priority, Gold Harp's lease would have been subject to the prior leases, which continued to subsist in equity, even though the legal title to them had been removed from the register. The Court of Appeal considered that there was real substance in this point,[47] though Underhill LJ did observe that 'I am not wholly comfortable that the analysis is as straightforward as may appear at first sight'.[48] However, as this point had not been raised by a respondent's notice, the Court of Appeal considered that it could not decide the case on that ground.

The Court of Appeal decided that, under the LRA 2002, schedule 4, paragraph 8, rectification could be retrospective but when it was, it conferred no rights of action for anything done prior to the court order. In consequence, the leases were restored and had priority over the subsequent lease to Gold Harp, but the lessees had no claim in damages for mesne profits against Gold Harp for the period prior to the judgment ordering rectification, whilst they were out of possession.

The Court of Appeal comprehensively examined every aspect of the case, relevant authority and published commentary. The point that Underhill LJ did not fully appreciate was that the Law Commission had changed its view between the consultative report in 1998, LC 254 and the final report of 2001, LC 271.[49] It had done so

---

[44] *Piper Trust Ltd v Caruso (UK) Ltd* [2010] EWLandRA 2009/0623 and *DB UK Bank Ltd v Santander UK plc* [2012] EWLandRA 2011/1169. I successfully argued the point in the latter case.

[45] *MacLeod v Gold Harp Properties Ltd* [2014] EWCA Civ 1084, [2015] 1 WLR 1249. No member of the Court was a chancery lawyer. Underhill LJ gave the only reasoned judgment.

[46] ibid [18].

[47] ibid [34].

[48] If it was not as straightforward as it appeared on that basis, the reason has eluded me.

[49] The statement by Underhill LJ, *Gold Harp*, n 45 above, [65], that '[t]here is nothing in the drafting of the bill or its exposition in the 2001 report to suggest any change from the thinking in the 1998 consultation paper' is, with great respect, simply incorrect. The statement in LC 271, n 43 above, para 10.8 shows clearly that there had been a change of heart.

precisely because of the fundamental principle, set out in LC 271 at paragraph 1.5, that the register should mirror the title, so far as possible. Underhill LJ quoted that passage, but dismissed it as being 'very general in character'.[50] Underhill LJ rejected the concern that retrospective rectification would do violence to the integrity of the register on the ground that 'the guarantee of title conferred by registration is well understood not to be absolute'.[51]

While it is very easy to see why the Court of Appeal wished in that case to reach the conclusion that it did, I would respectfully suggest that the decision was incorrect and that it may have unfortunate consequences. Had the Court of Appeal decided the case the other way and held that the leases could not be reinstated with priority over the later lease, the result might have been appeared to be unjust. However, a closer analysis shows that it would not have been in practice. For these purposes, it has to be assumed that Gold Harp: (a) was not privy to the fraud; and (b) gave valuable consideration for its lease. Of those assumptions, (a) is questionable and (b) was admitted not to be the case. On those assumptions, the claimants' leases would have been restored to the register, but they would have been reversionary on Gold Harp's lease.[52] The claimants would have recovered indemnity from the Land Registry because of the consequent diminution in value of their leases to virtually nil. However, the Land Registry would have had its extensive statutory rights of recourse against the perpetrators of the fraud to recover what it had had to pay by way of indemnity.[53]

The *Gold Harp* case is, so far as I can ascertain, unique amongst the reported cases in not interpreting the LRA 2002 in the manner that was set out in LC 271.[54] As I have explained, a court is rightly *not* in any sense bound to adopt the Law Commission's own view of what it intended to do. However, *Gold Harp* is already causing difficulties in practice because it is inconsistent with other aspects of the LRA 2002 and it seems unlikely that the last has been heard of it.[55]

## C Fraud, Mistake and Registration

The effect of registering a person with a registered estate or charge where that person should not have been so registered has given rise to a number of issues and, in particular, the following:

(1)    If X, a person acting in good faith and for valuable consideration, is registered as proprietor under a forged disposition, does that registration vest both the

---

[50]    *Gold Harp*, n 45 above, [78].

[51]    ibid [99].

[52]    The claimants were not living at the property. If they had been, Gold Harp's lease would have been subject to their overriding interest as the rights as persons in actual occupation.

[53]    For those rights, see LRA 2002, sch 8, para 10.

[54]    In most of the cases in which a point of principle on LRA 2002 has arisen, the court has considered what was said in LC 271.

[55]    The difficulties that I have encountered are practically important, but technical. It is unnecessary to consider them here.

legal and the beneficial title in that person, or does it merely vest the bare legal title?

(2)   If X is registered as proprietor, either pursuant to a forged disposition or in circumstances in which X should not have been registered, and, before the rightful owner seeks rectification of the register, X makes a further disposition of the land to Y, can the register be rectified against Y as well?

Both issues have been contentious, but have been resolved in a satisfactory way that reflects the underlying principles of title registration.

### i The Vesting Effect of Registration

On 22 February 2002, four days before the LRA 2002 received Royal Assent, the Court of Appeal gave judgment in *Malory Enterprises Ltd v Cheshire Homes (UK) Ltd.*[56] In that case, the innocent purchaser under a forged transfer was registered as proprietor. The true owner, who, on the findings of fact, had remained in actual occupation of the land in question (a derelict block of flats), successfully sought rectification of the register against the purchaser. The Court of Appeal held that the registration of the forged transfer only vested the bare legal title in the innocent purchaser. The former registered proprietor remained the beneficial owner. Furthermore, the protective priority provisions of the LRA 1925 that applied to disponees for valuable consideration[57] did not apply to forged transfers. The result was that the innocent purchaser took subject to the overriding interest of the former registered proprietor, who was still in actual occupation, to have the title rectified so as to be restored as the owner.

The issue of whether the innocent purchaser was entitled to indemnity was not considered or decided. However, earlier authority suggested that where the register was rectified to give effect to an overriding interest, no indemnity was payable, because the purchaser was always bound by the overriding interest.[58] That was certainly the Land Registry's view. It limited the circumstances in which the Registry had to pay indemnity in cases of forged transfers.

*Malory* was much criticised, because it effectively undermined the scheme of land registration. Where the guarantee of title was most required, it was absent. Nevertheless, the case was followed and applied to the LRA 2002 by Newey J in *Fitzwilliam v Richall Holdings Services Ltd.*[59]

In what is probably the most important decision to date on the LRA 2002, *Swift 1st Limited v The Chief Land Registrar*,[60] the Court of Appeal rejected *Malory*. The Court gave effect to the principles of a title registration system and, in particular, to the principle that, in a registered system, it is the fact of registration that confers title. A fraudster forged a legal charge over the property of an innocent landowner in favour of Swift. The owner occupied the property at the time of the forged charge.

---

[56]   *Malory Enterprises Ltd v Cheshire Homes (UK) Ltd* [2002] EWCA Civ 151, [2002] Ch 216.
[57]   That is LRA 1925, ss 20 and 23.
[58]   See *Re Chowood's Registered Land* [1933] Ch 574 (Ch).
[59]   *Fitzwilliam v Richall Holdings Services Ltd* [2013] EWHC 86 (Ch), [2013] 1 P & CR 19.
[60]   *Swift 1st Limited v The Chief Land Registrar* [2015] EWCA Civ 330, [2015] 3 WLR 239.

When the fraud came to light, Swift accepted that the register had to be rectified and its charge removed. It then sought indemnity from the Land Registry, which was refused on the basis that Swift had suffered no loss. The Court of Appeal rejected the Land Registry's contention and held that Swift was entitled to an indemnity. There are several important elements in the one reasoned judgment that was given by Patten LJ.

First, the Court refused to follow *Malory* on the ground that it was decided *per incuriam*, principally because section 114 of the LRA 1925 had not been cited. That section made it clear that, where a fraudulent disposition was made for valuable consideration, the disponee was entitled to the benefit of the provisions of the LRA 1925 both on indemnity and on the priority of registered dispositions for valuable consideration. It necessarily followed that where there was a forged disposition, but the disponee was registered, that registration vested both the legal and beneficial ownership in him.

Secondly, the indemnity provisions of the LRA 2002, like those of the LRA 1925 before them, made express provision for the payment of indemnity in respect of forged dispositions. The LRA 2002, schedule 8, paragraph 1(2)(b) provides that:

[T]he proprietor of a registered estate or charge claiming in good faith under a forged disposition is, where the register is rectified, to be regarded as having suffered loss by reason of such rectification as if the disposition had not been forged.[61]

The Court of Appeal held that this provision overrode the principle that indemnity was not payable in a case where the register was altered to give effect to an overriding interest. In *Swift*, the owner of the property which had been charged by Swift, did have an overriding interest at the time of the charge. She was in actual occupation of the property and had a property right, namely a right to seek rectification of the register. Notwithstanding this overriding interest, because of the LRA 2002, schedule 8, paragraph 1(2)(b), Swift was entitled to indemnity from the Land Registry. As Patten LJ explained, paragraph 1(2)(b) was 'consistent with the principle that registration confers substantive rights on the proprietor even under the forged disposition and that its loss is to be regarded as prejudicial to the title notwithstanding that the transfer or charge was void'.[62]

## *ii Void Dispositions and Rectification*

A further question that has troubled the courts and tribunals[63] concerns the power of the court or registrar to rectify the register in the following circumstances:

(a) X is registered as the proprietor of Blackacre or of a charge over Blackacre in circumstances in which X should not have been so registered. That may be because the disposition of, or charge over Blackacre was a forgery, and therefore

[61] This replicated the effect of LRA 1925, s 83(4), which had reversed the effect of *Attorney-General v Odell* [1906] 2 Ch 47 (CA).
[62] *Swift*, n 60 above, [51].
[63] Originally the Adjudicator to the Land Registry, but now the First Tier Tribunal Property Chamber (Land Registration).

void, or because disposition was never meant to include Blackacre, because, for example, the disponor did not in fact own it.[64]

(b) X then makes a disposal of Blackacre to Y, whether by way of an outright disposition, or by way of a charge over Blackacre.

(c) At this point, the true owner of Blackacre, Z, discovers what has happened and seeks rectification of the register against either Y alone (if X has made an outright disposition to Y) or against both X and Y (if X still has an interest, as where he or she has charged Blackacre to Y).

It is clear that the registration of X was a mistake. In those circumstances, the court or registrar has the power to rectify the register against X.[65] But does the court or registrar have power to order rectification against Y? Was the registration of Y a mistake?

These issues had arisen under the LRA 1925 and they had been answered in two related cases. In *Argyle Building Society v Hammond*,[66] the Court of Appeal held that if the transfer to X was wholly void, as it would have been on the facts set out above, any disposition to Y would also be treated as void. This followed from the provision in the LRA 1925, section 82(2), by which the power to rectify could be exercised even though it affected derivative estates and interests.

By contrast, it was held by the Court of Appeal in a sequel to the *Argyle* case, *Norwich and Peterborough Building Society v Steed*,[67] that where the initial transfer to X was not void but merely voidable, as where it was induced by fraud, and X then made the disposition to Y before Z had avoided the disposition, the registration of Y was not a mistake and there was no ground for rectification of the register against Y.

Did similar principles apply under the LRA 2002? The principles and authorities under the LRA 1925 were discussed in LC 254,[68] but not in LC 271. LC 271 was intended to explain the operation of the draft Land Registration Bill that was annexed to it, rather than to consider afresh matters that had been reviewed in LC 254.

It is unnecessary to chart the tortuous path in which this issue was explored by the courts and tribunals, because the matter was finally resolved by a very impressive decision of the Deputy Adjudicator, Mr Michael Mark, which has since received the approval of the Court of Appeal.

In *Knights Construction (March) Ltd v Roberto Mac Ltd*,[69] on the first registration of certain land, the Salvation Army was mistakenly registered with a parcel of land (the disputed land) that was owned and in the possession of Knights Construction. In 2009, Roberto Mac purchased land from the Salvation Army, including the disputed land, and attempted to enclose the disputed land. The mistake was

---

[64] This was the situation in *Knights Construction (March) Ltd v Roberto Mac Ltd* [2011] 2 EGLR 123.

[65] See LRA 2002, sch 4, paras 2(1)(a) and 5(a).

[66] *Argyle Building Society v Hammond* (1985) 49 P & CR 148 (CA).

[67] *Norwich and Peterborough Building Society v Steed* [1993] Ch 116 (CA).

[68] Law Commission, LC 254, *Land Registration for the Twenty-First Century: A Consultative Document* (1998) paras 8.15 and 8.32.

[69] *Knights Construction (March) Ltd v Roberto Mac Ltd* [2011] 2 EGLR 123.

discovered and Knights Construction applied to have the disputed land removed from Roberto Mac's registered title.

The register can be altered by the court or registrar for the purposes of correcting a mistake.[70] The registration of the Salvation Army as proprietor was plainly a 'mistake' for these purposes. Had it still been the registered proprietor, it would have had no answer to any claim by Knights Construction for the removal of the land from its title.[71] But what of Roberto Mac, which derived title from the Salvation Army?

The Deputy Adjudicator sought to determine whether the LRA 2002 had been intended to change the law as it had been under the LRA 1925 in relation to void and voidable dispositions, which I have set out above. He made extensive reference to both LC 254 and LC 271 and concluded that:

(a)  the Law Commission and Land Registry were perfectly aware of the previous decisions;
(b)  they did not intend to alter the law as set out in them except in the relatively minor respects identified by them; but
(c)  their efforts to achieve clarity by the redrafting of the provisions had had the opposite effect.[72]

He held that Knights Construction was entitled to have the register altered as against Roberto Mac on any one of three possible bases that had been canvassed in the cases, namely:

(1)  The original registration of the Salvation Army was a mistake, and, to correct that mistake, which persisted, the disputed land should be removed from Roberto Mac's title.
(2)  The registration of Roberto Mac as proprietor of the land flowed from the mistake of including the land in the original title, and therefore should be treated as part and parcel of that mistake.
(3)  The registration of the second transfer to Roberto Mas was itself a mistake.[73]

I consider that the third explanation was the correct one.[74] Although 'mistake' is not defined in the LRA 2002, it is obvious what it must mean in the context of a mistake *in the register*. If the registrar had known the true facts, what would he have done? If he would have done something different from what he actually did, there is a mistake in the register. In relation to Roberto Mac, if the registrar had been asked to register Roberto Mac, knowing that the vendor of the disputed land, the Salvation Army, should not have been the registered proprietor of it, he would not have registered the transfer.

---

[70]  LRA 2002, sch 4, paras 2(1)(a) and 5(a).
[71]  *Knights Construction*, n 69 above, [40] and [81].
[72]  ibid [89].
[73]  ibid [132].
[74]  It was derived from Blackburne J's judgment in *Pinto v Lim* [2005] EWHC 630 (Ch): see *Knights Construction*, n 69 above, [93].

This point matters because in *MacLeod v Gold Harp Properties Ltd*, Underhill LJ approved the analysis in *Knights Construction* and relied upon it as a justification for retrospective rectification. He said:

> If the law is that a derivative interest registered during a period where a relevant freehold interest is wrongly omitted from the Register may be lost as a result of the reinstatement of that interest, I can see no relevant difference of principle or policy in the case where the conflict is between two derivative interests. In both cases the essential issue is the same, namely whether an interest created during the period of mistaken deregistration may be prejudiced by the reinstatement of an interest to which it would have been subject but for that mistake.[75]

With all due respect, I do not agree with that analysis. If the registration of Roberto Mac's interest was itself a mistake, as it would be on the test that I have set out above, there is no question of retrospective rectification. Rectification is always effective against the person whose estate is rectified.[76]

The decision in *Knights Construction* is consistent with the principles of registered land. The disponee in the position of Roberto Mac will be entitled to indemnity from the Land Registry if he can show that he has suffered loss by reason of the rectification of the register. If it had been held that there was no mistake, Knights Construction would have had no grounds for claiming indemnity under the LRA 2002, schedule 8.

## IV CONCLUSIONS

There are no profound conclusions to be drawn from this case study. The cases suggest that courts and tribunals will often refer to Law Commission reports by way of guidance if they are placed before them. The mischief that the legislation addressed and the policy that was adopted in addressing it will usually be relevant. The cases on the LRA 2002 suggest that the courts will usually interpret the legislation as the Law Commission intended. The only case in which that has not happened of which I am aware is *Gold Harp*,[77] where the appellant's complete lack of merits undoubtedly influenced the outcome. The weight that is given to Law Commission reports undoubtedly reflects the thoroughness with which they are prepared. We should celebrate Lord Scarman's vision.

[75] *MacLeod v Gold Harp Properties Ltd* [2014] EWCA Civ 1084, [2015] 1 WLR 1249, [97].
[76] *Sainsbury's Supermarkets Ltd v Olympia Homes Ltd* [2005] EWHC 1235 (Ch), [2006] 1 P & CR 289, [96].
[77] See n 75 above.

# 32

# *Reflections on the Courts and the Commission*

## DAVID ORMEROD[*]

I would like to make a few short comments in response to the detailed and fascinating chapters arising from the panel in which I took part, and some even briefer points in relation to other aspects of the views expressed during the course of the panel, about the way the Commission and the courts interact. In short, I would suggest that the Law Commission of England and Wales has a strong relationship with the courts, and one that presents opportunities for mutual benefits.

### I  THE ETIQUETTE OF LAW REFORM

James Lee's chapter raises a raft of interesting issues.[1] His statistics demonstrate a healthy citation rate for Law Commission papers, and his analysis of the different ways in which the Supreme Court has engaged with the Commission's work offers useful insights. I think he would agree that the courts and the Commission are engaged in a dynamic interrelationship. Whereas he views the dialogue as being punctuated by awkward stand-offs, I see it as one in which the conversation can include pregnant pauses and interjections from third parties (such as Parliament) at appropriate points without rendering the exchange any less meaningful.

One of his concerns is that there is no clarity around the circumstances in which the Supreme Court will adopt the Law Commission's work nor when the courts will suggest a project be taken on by the Commission. It is highly unlikely that any single litmus test could be devised given the very many variables which influence these decisions: the case, the subject-matter, the likelihood of parliamentary action, etc. Rather than attempt to regard this as a formal arrangement of cross referrals of work, it may be viewed as a more flexible, longer-term collaborative exercise in which the courts and Commission are engaged: refining the law. Indeed, as Lord Hoffmann has observed, 'the development of the law is not solely the province of one branch of Government, but ought to be a partnership between all three'.[2]

---

[*] I am grateful to Vincent Scully and Sarah Taylor for excellent research assistance.
[1] See chapter 29 (James Lee).
[2] L Hoffmann, '*Fairchild* and After' in A Burrows, D Johnston and R Zimmermann (eds), *Judge and Jurist: Essays in Memory of Lord Rodger of Earlsferry* (Oxford, OUP, 2013) 69.

Summarising what has been said repeatedly during the course of the conference, it is possible to see the courts as: a reliable and valuable supplier of work to the Commission; offering excellent opportunities for reviewing and promoting Commission work; as well as occasional adopters of its recommendations. In return, the Commission can accept projects on aspects of law in which the courts are unable, or prefer not, to advance reform either because of democratic deference or issues associated with institutional competence. It also provides a source of high quality materials to assist the courts in their decision making—particularly when interpreting enactments based on Law Commission reports.

## A The Courts as Suppliers of Work to the Commission

The courts are often responsible for projects being referred to the Commission. Although they have no power to refer an issue to the Commission directly, they can have a strong influence on whether the Commission undertakes a project. In a general sense the courts have a constant influence on the Commission's reform agenda by exposing the deficiencies in the law creating the opportunity for others to suggest projects for the Commission.[3] More relevant to this debate are those occasions when a judgment makes explicit reference to the need for the Commission to take on a project. It has been suggested that, since the judiciary receives no formal response from government when they suggest an area of law ought to be reformed, the Law Commission ought to develop a formal mechanism for doing so. Indeed, Brice Dickson goes so far as to suggest that the Law Commission 'could maintain an on-going register of such judicial calls and make a public response regarding the desirability and possible shape of the required reforms'.[4] I would suggest, however, that experience shows that the Law Commission is sufficiently responsive to calls from the judiciary to reform the law that the institution of such a formal mechanism would be superfluous.

A recent example is that in relation to misconduct in public office, which is one of the projects in which the criminal team is currently engaged. Lord Justice Leveson, as he then was, in *R v DL* concluded his judgment by stating that:

> It is no part of the purpose of this judgment to seek to revisit the formulation of the offence as enunciated in *Attorney General's Reference (No 3 of 2003)* although that might, in the future, become necessary; *indeed, consideration of the offence by the Law Commission would be of value.* [Emphasis added.][5]

Very shortly thereafter the project on reform of the crime of misconduct in public office was adopted in the Law Commission's *Eleventh Programme of Law Reform.*[6]

---

[3] Some would no doubt say that the courts also provide work for the Commission by themselves *creating* the deficiencies in the law.

[4] B Dickson, 'Judicial Activism in the House of Lords' in B Dickson (ed), *Judicial Activism in Common Law Supreme Courts* (Oxford, OUP, 2007) 398.

[5] *R v DL* [2011] EWCA Crim 1259, [2011] 2 Cr App R 14, [21].

[6] LC 330 (2011).

We have heard many other examples of calls for the Commission to take on work, but that one stands out as it was potentially so influential, being timed as it was when the *Eleventh Programme* was being finalised.

Precisely *why* the courts might choose to recommend a project will differ from case to case. I would respectfully agree with Lady Hale[7] that the courts' willingness to recommend that the Law Commission undertake reform may stem from, amongst other things:

— a realisation that the issues are ill-suited to judicial determination constrained by the adversarial processes of litigation;
— the courts being ill-equipped and ill-placed to conduct research and consultation;
— the issues involved being too policy-laden for a judicial body;
— and perhaps, dare I say it, on occasion the court being daunted by the task even if it did feel qualified. That is not a flippant comment—I suspect most former Commissioners and Chairmen would agree that projects can look beguilingly simple before they are started but often, if not always, turn out to be much more complicated than anticipated.

The practical reality is that not every topic which the courts identify as potentially worthy of consideration by the Commission will be adopted as a project, but that does not detract from the fact that the courts' willingness to refer to the Commission is entirely appropriate.

When the courts do explicitly suggest that the Commission takes on reform in an area of law I would venture that, for several reasons, it is usually welcomed. First, if the courts are recommending a project it is clearly one that poses a real problem in practice. It is not just a pure theoretical legal nicety dreamt up in an 'ivory tower'. A government is therefore more likely to agree to such a project forming part of a programme of law reform. Secondly, the legal problem is also one which is likely to have already been subjected to substantial scrutiny. The courts are unlikely to recommend an area of dispute for the Commission to resolve unless it has posed a persistent and serious problem. There will, therefore, be a wealth of material—judicial and academic—from which the Commission can launch its work. The advantage this offers is not to be undervalued, as the start-up costs of a project in even identifying the scope of a problem can be demanding. When that task has been largely performed by the courts in advance the project launches more quickly and on strong foundations. Finally, the provenance of a project can influence the prospects of implementation. What better provenance for a reform project than the Supreme Court or indeed the Court of Appeal? If the courts say that a real problem arises in practice and the Commission has produced a solution there is a likelihood that government will listen. Admittedly, some of these projects nominated by the courts are not going to have the 'high sex appeal' to which Sir Grant Hammond referred,[8] but not all Law Commission projects do or should. The Commission serves a vital

---

[7] See chapter 2 (Lady Hale).
[8] See chapter 19 (Sir Grant Hammond) (quoting G Drewry, 'The Legislative Implementation of Law Reform Proposals' (1986) 7 *Statute Law Review* 161, 163).

role in technical and challenging law reform work that no one else is equipped to undertake.

Arguably then, in taking on referrals from the courts—albeit indirectly—it may be that the Commission is fulfilling a critical role as a bridge between the three limbs of the state. This point is well made by Alan Paterson, who suggests that the Law Commission can facilitate a serious dialogue between Parliament, the executive and the judiciary.[9]

James Lee referred to the 'monologue' delivered by the courts to Parliament. I prefer to see it as the Law Commission serving as an important medium through which, in some instances, the government, courts and Parliament have a dialogue.

## B  The Courts as Promoters and Reviewers of the Commission's Reform

James Lee's chapter refers to very clear examples of cases in which the courts have relied on, or referred to, Law Commission proposals or recommendations whether in endorsing them, using them to set the record straight,[10] or as a plank in an argument to persuade Parliament to act. Equally important can be the judicial feedback the Commission receives during the lifetime of a project. Our consultation and engagement process is a dynamic one that runs throughout the entire project and the judiciary are actively engaged throughout. The label may be inelegant and one some may find distasteful, but they are 'key stakeholders'. On every criminal project, for example, the team engages with the senior judiciary, the Council of HM Circuit Judges, HM Council of District Judges and Magistrates' Association members. In some projects we can go further: for example, in the sentencing codification project we will be conducting qualitative interviews with judges on the possible structures for the new sentencing code. The courts can serve as superb reviewers and sometimes promoters of our work.

As noted above, I believe this is a symbiotic relationship: we are providing high-quality, reliable, accessible sources of law for the courts to draw upon. There can be no doubt that the courts see our consultations as a fruitful source of information and ideas. As a very recent example, in *O (A Child) v Rhodes*, the Supreme Court cited the Commission's *Reform of Offences against the Person: A Scoping Consultation Paper*[11] in relation to the definition of recklessness.[12] A more unusual example arose in the Court of Appeal in *R v Williams*.[13] In considering the approach to causation in an offence of causing death by driving while disqualified, Sir John Thomas P referred to:

[t]he report of the Law Commission Working Party referred to in the Bench Book [although it] was never published. However, as it had been referred to in a public document and

---

[9]  AA Paterson, *Final Judgment: The Last Law Lords and the Supreme Court* (Oxford, Hart Publishing, 2013) 281–82.
[10]  *R v Gnango* [2011] UKSC 59, [2012] 1 AC 827.
[11]  LC CP 217 (2014).
[12]  *O (A Child) v Rhodes* [2015] UKSC 32, [2015] 2 WLR 1373, [84].
[13]  *R v Williams* [2010] EWCA Crim 2552, [2011] 1 WLR 588.

was strongly relied on by Miss Evans QC for the appellant, we are grateful to the Law Commission for making available to the parties and to the court a draft report of 2003 containing the wording referred to in the Bench Book.[14]

Shona Wilson Stark's confession in the discussion in an earlier panel that as an undergraduate she would use the Law Commission papers as an accessible and reliable source of law is one I suspect many judges would be prepared to adopt.

## C  The Courts' Adoption of Commission Work

The adoption of Commission work can come about in a variety of ways. Three seem obvious:

— the courts being influenced by reports;
— wholesale judicial reform based on a Law Commission recommendation; and
— judicial use of the reports as a means of interpreting the Acts based on Law Commission recommendations.

At the conference, we heard countless powerful examples of the influence that Law Commission work has on judicial decision making at all levels. We also heard numerous examples of the courts going so far as to adopt Commission work to create new law. In some instances this will be by the court adopting recommendations of the Commission that were addressed to the courts. In others instances it may be that the court is brave enough to adopt recommendations that were addressed to Parliament. Lady Hale cited marital rape as such an example.[15] Of course we cannot expect these to be commonplace. By definition, when the subject-matter has been referred to Law Commission it is one of some considerable complexity and/or technicality. The Commission's solution is unlikely to be the only one possible. There can be no expectation that the courts will adopt it. They are, and should be, more cautious than Parliament in this manner. However, it is worth returning here to what Lady Hale emphasised in her introduction: the sound justifications for judicial avoidance of direct proactive law reform present less of an obstacle when the judges are 'adopting' the work of the Commission: provided the point of law arising in the case allows for it.[16]

Much less has been said about the third category: the value that Law Commission reports provide in enriching the courts' interpretative function.

## II  THE REFINER'S FIRE

Charles Harpum's chapter treats us to a comprehensive and scholarly account on the Land Registration Act delivered from his unique perspective on that legislation.[17]

---

[14] ibid [25].
[15] See chapter 2 (Lady Hale).
[16] ibid.
[17] See chapter 31 (Charles Harpum).

It is particularly valuable in its analysis of one underdeveloped issue: the Commission's influence on the courts' interpretative function. It is gratifying to hear that from his encyclopaedic knowledge of Land Registration, there is only one instance— *Gold Harp*[18]—of the court failing to adopt an interpretation consistent with the Commission's position in the report. His presentation was, and resulting chapter is, so rich in discussion of this use of Law Commission reports that I need say no more on that particular topic.

I do however want to pick up a point which he makes with vigour when endorsing the general convention in parliamentary drafting that a clause should only be included in a Bill if it changes the law.[19] I am far less convinced that this should be an absolute rule. Sometimes a statutory provision might prove useful to a reader simply by referring the reader to other legislative provisions.

To take a concrete example, in our recent work on codification of sentencing law, the draft Bill will clearly have to include all of the ancillary orders that a judge might impose on conviction. There is a growing list of such orders and they derive from very many diverse statutes. One is the power to disqualify a director. The provision empowering the sentencing court to do so is found in the Company Directors Disqualification Act 1986.[20] Taking that provision and inserting it into the code would produce a more coherent sentencing code, but would leave a gap in the Companies Act that may seem odd. This is particularly the case where, as here, the power is not limited to cases that would involve the imposition of a sentence after a criminal trial. One solution is to leave the provision in the Companies Act, but to include in the sentencing code a 'flag' to the reader that a further power is available to disqualify a director, and where to find it. And why should a statutory provision not say 'the power available to a judge to make a disqualification order is in the Company Directors Disqualification Act 1986'?

I recognise that this would take us into a much wider debate well beyond the current conference agenda and into the question of the role of parliamentary drafters and their intended audiences for legislation.

## III  THE ROLE OF LEGISLATION IN SUPPLEMENTING OR SUPPLANTING THE COMMON LAW

We have been treated to some refreshing insights into the importance of the common law as a feature of good law reform by Barbara McDonald.[21] As her examples demonstrate, it may take considerable time for the Supreme Court to be persuaded of the merits of particular proposals.

On the question of the value of labouring over codification, her chapter may paint a picture which it too pessimistic. Clearly, there are a variety of specific examples

---

[18] *MacLeod v Gold Harp Properties Ltd* [2014] EWCA Civ 1084, [2015] 1 WLR 1249.
[19] See chapter 31 (Charles Harpum).
[20] Company Directors Disqualification Act 1986, s 2 applies to conviction of indictable offences; s 5 applies to conviction of summary offences.
[21] See chapter 30 (Barbara McDonald).

that could be taken, but I have reason to hope that the Law Commission of England and Wales is proving that there is substantial value in this field. I do not want to revisit the much broader debate about codification on which Ian Dennis provides an excellent analysis.[22] There are, however, much narrower forms of activity on the spectrum of codification including, if not 'codifying' a whole discipline, then at least codifying groups of offences which are worth considering. One recent example of the Commission's work on this is the creation of a new criminal offence to replace the common law of contempt applicable when jurors engage in misconduct. In a report on contempt of court,[23] we recommended a statutory offence of jury misconduct for jurors who search for information related to the trial. The recommendation has now been implemented in the Criminal Justice and Courts Act 2015.

Prior to the statutory offences in the 2015 Act, the limits of the conduct a juror was permitted to engage in were defined by each judge on a case-by-case basis at the beginning of each trial. Although the judges followed guidelines in the Crown Court Bench Book and elsewhere, there was no specific form of words to make clear to the juror what exactly was forbidden as contempt of court carrying a two-year maximum sentence of imprisonment. Several high-profile cases have led to jurors being imprisoned in such circumstances.[24] Despite the best efforts of judges in their directions, jurors remained confused about what they were permitted to do on the internet during the trial. In a survey almost a quarter of jurors were unsure of what internet use was permitted during their jury service and 7 per cent of those surveyed admitted to having used the internet in an impermissible manner while serving as jurors.[25] This lack of clarity was unsatisfactory for defendants, because while jurors remain confused there is a risk that they will search for (and find) prejudicial material, thereby jeopardising the fairness of the trial. The lack of clarity was also unsatisfactory for the jurors themselves, who were at risk of imprisonment without understanding the boundary of what is forbidden. Furthermore, there were serious practical consequences when jurors do engage in such conduct: it risks the trial being stopped, with all the consequent delay and distress to the complainant, the defendant and any witnesses, not to mention the cost to the public purse.

The recommendations in our report for a statutory offence as implemented in the 2015 Act mean that all jurors will know that it is a crime to engage in this form of conduct—there will be greater clarity. Creating a new criminal offence is not a matter to be taken lightly. But in this case it did seem necessary to legislate or, better yet, to codify: if behaviour can result in someone being imprisoned for up to two years then it ought to be defined in clear terms by Parliament.

There are several other benefits from introducing a statutory crime to deal with such behaviour: a more consistent approach will result, with all jurors being subject to the same rules, as defined by Parliament. Further, the symbolic effect of Parliament creating a specific offence will underline the seriousness of the conduct and

---

[22] See chapter 12 (Ian Dennis).
[23] LC 340, *Juror Misconduct and Internet Publications* (2013).
[24] *Attorney General v Davey and A-G v Beard* [2013] EWHC 2317 (Admin), [2014] 1 Cr App R 1 (combined judgment).
[25] C Thomas, 'Avoiding the Perfect Storm of Juror Contempt' [2013] *Crim LR* 483.

give enhanced legitimacy to the criminalisation of the behaviour of those jurors. Creating a new offence will also add to the deterrent effect, as jurors will be clearer about what is forbidden.[26] Sometimes codifying small pockets of law can therefore serve a valuable purpose.

The Supreme Court has recently recognised the limitations of the common law as a means of remedying particular problems. As Lord Neuberger PSC and Lord Reed stated recently in *International Energy Group Ltd v Zurich Insurance Plc*:

> However, in some types of case, it is better for the courts to accept that common law principle precludes a fair result, and to say so, on the basis that it is then up to Parliament (often with the assistance of the Law Commission) to sort the law out. In particular, the courts need to recognise that, unlike Parliament, they cannot legislate in the public interest for special cases, and they risk sowing confusion in the common law if they attempt to do so.[27]

Judicial recognition of the limitations of the common law presents a further opportunity for the Law Commission to facilitate the type of dialogue that was alluded to earlier. The Law Commission is particularly suited to examining polycentric issues that are simply too complex to be left to the common law and can assist Parliament in crafting a suitable solution to them. This is especially the case where the problems are technical and legally complex.

## IV THE COMMISSION INFLUENCING JUDICIAL PRACTICE DIRECTIONS

I hope it is not too much of a stretch to include a brief section on the impact the Commission can have on the courts' Practice Directions. One of the most innovative instances of the adoption of Law Commission recommendations is the recent adoption of the expert evidence recommendations.

The expert evidence project came to the Commission as a result of a recommendation from a parliamentary committee with, I might add, endorsement from the criminal courts. In 2009 we produced a consultation paper,[28] and a final report followed in 2011 with an 11-clause Bill.[29] Disappointingly the government chose, in 2013, not to implement the recommendations, primarily on the grounds of cost. The government was not confident that sufficient savings could be made quickly enough! A series of discussions were had with the Criminal Procedure Rules Committee as to whether any of the recommendations might be implemented in the Criminal Procedure Rules. I attended that committee and various versions of the Criminal Procedure Rules were debated to ensure that what was being proposed was within the vires of

---

[26] An additional benefit is that any juror who does carry out searches about a trial will then face prosecution in the usual way in the Crown Court with all the usual criminal procedural protections, legal aid, bail, appeals etc. Jurors who engage in this type of behaviour are dealt with for contempt using an unusual process in the Divisional Court.

[27] *International Energy Group Ltd v Zurich Insurance Plc* [2015] UKSC 33, [2015] 2 WLR 1471, [209].

[28] LC CP 190, *Expert Evidence in Criminal Proceedings* (2009).

[29] LC 325, *Expert Evidence in Criminal Proceedings* (2011).

the committee.[30] A solution was found by using both the Criminal Procedure Rules and the Criminal Practice Directions.

The Lord Chief Justice incorporated the core recommendations from the Law Commission draft Bill in the Criminal Practice Direction in 2014 and the 2014 Criminal Procedure Rules correlate to those directions.[31] His Kalisher Lecture at the Central Criminal Court last year described the process:

> This is plainly a novel way of implementing an excellent Report. With the changes in the common law that paralleled the Report, the Rules and the Practice Direction together with the work under taken by the Advocacy Training Council, the Report has been nearly implemented.[32]

Almost immediately the Court of Appeal recognised that fact and endorsed the approach as a matter of common law. In *R v H*:

> Before leaving an examination of the principles governing admissibility of this type of evidence, it is appropriate to note the general concern about expert witnesses. Whilst legislative reform has not been taken forward, following the Law Commission Report on Expert Evidence in Criminal Proceedings, there is real concern about the use of unreliable or inappropriate expert evidence. As a result, Part 33 of the Criminal Procedure Rules has been revised (with effect from 1 October 2014) and a new Practice Direction is to be published which will incorporate the reliability factors recommended by the Law Commission for the admission of expert evidence ... When these changes occur, a new and more rigorous approach on the part of advocates and the courts to the handling of expert evidence must be adopted. That should avoid misunderstandings about what is (and what is not) appropriately included in an expert's report and so either avoid, or at least render far more straightforward, submissions on admissibility such as those made in this case.[33]

## V THE COURTS' ROLE AS A BAROMETER OF OUR SUCCESS

Finally, if the frequency of citations serves as one measure of success then there is a tangential benefit to the Commission from the courts' reliance on our work. Professor Burrows raises a very important issue about the correct measure of success being focused on the quality of the Commission's output not the quantity of citations of its work.[34] The Commission could search commercial databases of case law for frequency of citations, but that number will not reveal anything about the impact the Commission's work had on the decision making. We could, of course, examine more closely the judicial comments, or even engage in more thorough qualitative research interviews with judges to assess the impact Law Commission work has on judicial decision making. This may prove fruitful in many ways. I would be particularly interested in discovering whether judges, as experienced 'users' of legislation, could

---

[30] As prescribed in the Courts Act 2003, s 69.
[31] See what is now CrimPR, rule 19.
[32] J Thomas, 'Expert Evidence: The Future of Forensic Science in Criminal Trials' (2014) para 17.
[33] *R v H* [2014] EWCA Crim 1555, (2014) 140 BMLR 59, [43]–[44] (Sir Brian Leveson P).
[34] See chapter 20 (Andrew Burrows).

offer views on the relative merits of Law Commission legislation in contrast to that drafted without Law Commission involvement.

I believe there is considerably more mileage in Professor Burrows' plan, but it needs some careful planning. If we are measuring the quality of legislation we need to be clear about precisely what we are measuring and how. Taking a criminal law Act for example, are we measuring the success of that legislation in terms of:

(1)  academic reviews on its merits, clarity, etc;
(2)  the number of appeals generated compared to appeals under equivalent prede-cessor provisions[35] as an indicator of the number of ambiguities;[36]
(3)  whether judges feel that the offences work 'effectively for courts';
(4)  whether the proportion of cases prosecuted leading to convictions is high, thereby indicating that the offences work well in court in attacking their intended 'mischief';[37] and
(5)  whether the offence is cost effective—by hearings being shorter, leading to more guilty pleas, fewer appeals and so on.

I suspect that very different views on 'success' and 'quality' would be presented depending on these different factors.

## VI CONCLUSION

As I have argued, the courts and Commissions have a symbiotic relationship. Commissions take the work the courts cannot do (or do not relish doing), we wel-come their reviews of and feedback on our work. If they adopt our work we are both beneficiaries—as is the law and society generally.

---

[35]  Acknowledging what is possibly an inevitable spike for new legislation.
[36]  The danger is obvious since there may be many other factors leading to a rise in appeals.
[37]  The dangers are again obvious: there are so many other variables.

# Part 8

# Commissioning the Future

# 33

# *Introduction*

ELIZABETH COOKE

It was a great pleasure for me to chair this conference panel, very shortly after leaving the Law Commission of England and Wales. The change in flavour and scope of the Commissions' work in the 50 years since they were founded is well illustrated by the resultant papers, and I am struck by the way each Commission has become, over 50 years, a pervasive force in the law, respectively, of England and Wales and of Scotland. It has not been an easy process, and it is not going to get any easier; both Commissions have learned, and are still learning, the art of the possible in their relationships with successive governments, and we can see that reflected in different ways in the papers presented by two Chairs and two Chief Executives in this session.

The pervasive nature of the reform effected by the two Commissions is illustrated in my own journey. I was the Commissioner with responsibility for projects relating to land law and family law in England and Wales from July 2008; I left the Law Commission at the end of May 2015 to take up the post of Principal Judge of the Land Registration Division of the First Tier Tribunal (Property Chamber). That post was created in the Land Registration Act 2002, albeit then under the more succinct title of 'The Adjudicator to HM Land Registry'. And the Land Registration Act 2002 itself was an enactment—with very little amendment—of the Law Commission's recommendations in its 2001 report, *Land Registration for the Twenty-first Century: A Conveyancing Revolution*.[1] So in my daily work, in a job effectively created by the Law Commission, I deal constantly with a statute embodying the Commission's recommendations, and I look frequently at its 2001 report for assistance.

The future is a foreign country, as Matthew Dyson reminds us in his very perceptive and wide-ranging chapter.[2] I was conscious throughout my time at the Commission of the privilege of working there, of the value of all that has been done there so far, and of the need to do things differently in the future in order to preserve what is good in our work. I wish the present and future members of both Commissions the perseverance to continue the tradition of both institutions but also to grasp good change when it is possible.

---

[1] LC 271 (2001), details of which can be found in the contribution of its principal author and my predecessor-but-two, Charles Harpum (chapter 31).

[2] See chapter 38 (Matthew Dyson).

# 34

# The Scottish Law Commission and the Future of Law Reform in Scotland

## LORD PENTLAND[*]

### I INTRODUCTION

In this chapter, I want to set out some ideas about the future of law reform in Scotland prompted by the fiftieth anniversary of the creation of the Scottish Law Commission. Before doing that, I will take the opportunity to look back briefly at the origins of the Scottish Commission; these were in certain respects rather different (and interestingly so) from those of the Law Commission for England and Wales. I will go on to examine some of the challenges the Commission faced in establishing itself as an independent law reform agency in the face of scepticism and, in some quarters, outright hostility. I will then briefly survey the work of the Commission over the past half-century and say a few words about the impact of the changes in the constitutional landscape in which it has operated. Finally, I will venture a few suggestions as to where the future direction of Scottish travel might lie.

### II ORIGINS

Let me look first then at the origins of the Scottish Law Commission.[1] As every law reformer knows, Law Commissions for Scotland and for England and Wales were set up in 1965 under the Law Commissions Act passed in that year by the

[*] I am grateful to my fellow Commissioners, Hector MacQueen, Andrew Steven, Caroline Drummond and David Johnston, each of whom read and valuably commented on earlier versions. I also thank our chief executive, Malcolm McMillan, for his input and advice. The views expressed are my own and not necessarily those of the Scottish Law Commission.

[1] For more detail on the origins of the Scottish Law Commission, see SW Stark, 'The Longer You Can Look Back, the Further You Can Look Forward: The Origins of the Scottish Law Commission' (2014) 18 *Edinburgh Law Review* 59.

UK Parliament. These bodies came to be the basic model for law reform agencies subsequently established in many Commonwealth countries and further afield. A key feature of this model is that the law reform agency is set up with a guarantee (usually, but not always, enshrined in its constituting statute)[2] that it enjoys institutional independence from the state it is designed to serve. Alongside that guarantee (and constantly rubbing up against it) there is the harsh reality that the law reform agency depends for financial support, usually extending to the provision of staff and other resources, on the state. The state retains the power to dissolve the law reform agency or to withdraw its funding.

The Commonwealth Secretariat has observed that '[a]n essential feature and a key advantage of [a law reform agency] is its independence, especially from government but also from all others'.[3] In Malawi, section 136 of the Constitution provides for independence of its Law Commission, although what exactly is meant by independence in this context is not defined. On its website, the Kenya Law Reform Commission goes a little further by stating that independence refers to the Commission's intellectual independence, that is 'the willingness to make findings and offer non-partisan advice and recommendations to government without fear or favor'.[4] In the United Kingdom, there is no statutory guarantee of independence, although I believe that the principle is now so widely accepted as to have become constitutionally entrenched by convention.

There are other possible models for law reform agencies, under which they are essentially private organisations; these are found mainly in the United States. And there are some half-way houses. In the Canadian province of Manitoba, the Law Reform Commission functions with the help of grants from the provincial Department of Justice and the Manitoba Law Foundation. The British Columbia Law Institute is a not-for-profit charitable society. The Malawi Commission is permitted to receive donations of funds from other institutions or organisations apart from government.

When considering the history and achievements of the United Kingdom Commissions, it is, I think, worth recalling that they were created at a time when life in the United Kingdom and elsewhere was changing rapidly. The Law Commissions owe their existence to that changing world. By the 1960s, the grey and dreary post-war years of food rationing and conscription lay behind us. Most homes had a new television set and even a refrigerator, or so Wikipedia tells me. But more importantly, there were seismic shifts in the ways people thought and behaved. Rebellion was in the air and deference to established authority was on the wane. It was the age of swinging London, Carnaby Street, Twiggy and the Beatles. In 1964, a Labour government had been narrowly elected under the technocratic leadership of Harold Wilson on a manifesto entitled, 'The New Britain'; at 48 he was the youngest

---

[2] There is no such guarantee in the Law Commissions Act 1965.
[3] Commonwealth Secretariat, 'Law Reform Agencies: Their Role and Effectiveness' (2005) para 13.
[4] Kenya Law Reform Commission, 'Mission, Vision, Core Values' www.klrc.go.ke/index.php/about-klrc/mission-and-vision.

prime minister of this country for 70 years. Within a few years many of the old taboos would be dismantled. Restrictive laws on censorship, divorce, homosexuality, immigration and abortion were relaxed, and capital punishment was abolished.

As part of this tidal wave of social change, the view gathered force amongst some lawyers in England, that the law had fallen badly behind the times and that the machinery for reforming it had become ossified. The new Lord Chancellor in the Labour government, Gerald Gardiner, believed that effective law reform demanded a standing body with general responsibility for keeping the whole of the law under review. The new agency would be independent of government. Its head (originally conceived as a Minister of State) would preside over a committee of at least five highly qualified lawyers to be known as law commissioners. That was the ambitious vision behind the 1965 Act. It was largely the brainchild of English lawyers and its mission was focused on the reform of the law of England and Wales.[5]

It is well known that Scots law developed from its Roman law origins along a separate path from the common law of England and Wales. It is a mix of native law, Roman law and English law. Its continued independence is guaranteed by the Acts of Union of 1706 and 1707, the effect of which was that the Parliaments of Scotland and England united to form the Parliament of Great Britain based in the Palace of Westminster in London. Between then and 1999, Scotland continued to have (and jealously to guard) its own distinct legal system and a separate legal profession, but there was no Scottish legislature as such. Legislation to reform Scots law did not have a high political priority and often struggled to find parliamentary time at Westminster.

Despite Scots law being a legal system without its own dedicated legislature, there was in the 1960s no real drive for new law reform machinery in Scotland. The legal establishment in Edinburgh appears to have been content with the existing ad hoc and part-time law reform committees. The Lord Advocate in the new Labour government of 1964, the formidable Gordon Stott QC, was distinctly underwhelmed by Lord Gardiner's vision of law reform, remarking in his diary that he did not think that the Lord Chancellor had a clear idea of what he wanted, and arguing at a Cabinet Committee that the Commission might turn out to be a source of delay rather than expedition.[6]

Initially, Lord Gardiner thought that it would be sufficient to have an English Law Commission, which if it proved to be successful, could be extended to Scotland. Scottish Ministers in the Labour government, including the Secretary of State[7] and the Lord Advocate eventually took the view that a new body for England alone would be politically unacceptable in Scotland. After some hesitation it was, therefore, decided that if there was to be a Law Commission for England and Wales then the Scots had better be given one too.

[5] See chapter 4 (Paul Mitchell).
[6] G Stott, *Lord Advocate's Diary 1961–66* (Aberdeen, Aberdeen University Press, 1991) 143–44.
[7] The Rt Hon William Ross MP.

## III  THE 1965 ACT AND THE EARLY DAYS
## OF THE SCOTTISH LAW COMMISSION

Under section 2(1) of the 1965 Act, which remains largely unamended as to the powers and duties it confers (at least insofar as the Scottish Law Commission is concerned), the Commission is responsible for promoting reform of the whole of the law of Scotland. The Act goes on to say, at section 3(1), that this is to be done with a view to the systematic development and reform of the law (ie the whole of the law). And if that were not daunting enough, the same section adds, for good measure, that this duty is to include, in particular, codification of the law, the elimination of anomalies, the repeal of obsolete and unnecessary enactments, the reduction of the number of separate enactments and generally the simplification and modernisation of the law. Undoubtedly, a tall order.

Read literally, all this was unrealistically ambitious. Writing about the Scottish Law Commission as Lord Advocate some 30 years after the passing of the 1965 Act, Alan Rodger (Lord Rodger of Earlsferry), an experienced politician and parliamentarian as well as distinguished judge and jurist, was struck by the naivety of the debates in Parliament about what the new law reform bodies would achieve.[8] Sir Geoffrey Palmer in his recent Scarman Lecture detected what he described as a 'crusading sense of legal renewal' in the early literature on law reform agencies, although he acknowledged that 'the great expectations of 1965 have not been realised'.[9]

In Scotland, there was scepticism and even outright hostility in some important and influential quarters towards the establishment of the Scottish Law Commission, not least from Scotland's most senior judge, the Lord President of the Court of Session, the former Conservative Lord Advocate, Lord Clyde. Notwithstanding this somewhat shaky start, the first Scottish Law Commissioners, under the chairmanship of Lord Kilbrandon, were determined that the new body should not be strangled at birth, nor should it operate as a mere branch of government. Lord Kilbrandon was a man of principle with a strong sense of public duty. He accepted chairmanship of the new body despite the fact that the Lord President had threatened that any judge rash enough to do so would lose his seniority and that his prospects of promotion to an appellate level would be terminally damaged.

The new Commissioners made it clear from the beginning that they were not disposed to adopt an unduly narrow view of their functions. In their *First Annual Report* they said this:

> We are concerned with all the law of Scotland, and we do not consider that we are in any way confined to what is loosely referred to as 'lawyers' law'. All law has social implications, and it is impossible to draw any dividing line between 'social law' and 'lawyers' law'. We interpret the terms of the Act as imposing on us a duty to see to the development and reform of *all* the law systematically. Our intention is that when any question of social policy arises in connection with any branch of law with which we are dealing, we shall draw attention to

---

[8]  A Rodger, 'The Bell of Law Reform' 1993 *Scots Law Times (News)* 339.
[9]  G Palmer, 'The Law Reform Enterprise: Evaluating the Past and Charting the Future' (2015) 131 *LQR* 402, 420.

it and express our views upon it so far as it affects the legal point under consideration. The decision upon it will be a matter for others—ultimately for the Government of the day.[10]

It is of some interest to note that Lord Kilbrandon's thinking about the role of the new body seems to have developed significantly during its first year of operations. In a newspaper interview at the time the Commission was set up, he had observed that questions of how society lived were not matters for a Law Commission consisting of lawyers only.[11]

In the final paragraph of the *First Annual Report*, three key points were made. First, it was stated that the Commission's work had to be intelligible and acceptable to the general public, in whose interests, fundamentally, all the Commission's work was done. Secondly, the Commission stressed that it had to be accessible to the public (in its first year the Commission had received 49 proposals from members of the public out of a total of 193 proposals; a large majority of those from the public were said to have contained suggestions for reform that were well worth consideration). Thirdly, the Commission had to be independent; constitutionally this was thought to be the most important of its attributes.

Intelligibility, accessibility and independence. These have been guiding principles throughout the past half-century.

The independent-minded stance that the Commission adopted was quickly tested. The Commission's first project considered whether the evidential rule requiring corroboration in civil proceedings should be abolished. As will be seen, three pillars of the Scottish legal establishment strongly opposed the idea. Corroboration of evidence was a sacred icon of Scots law and had to be preserved; otherwise the walls of the temple would come crashing down. Many years later a debate, conducted just as passionately and intensely, would rage around a law reform proposal to abolish the requirement for corroboration in Scots criminal law; perhaps this goes to show that legal history really does repeat itself. I shall return to the subject of reforming the doctrine of corroboration in criminal cases later in this chapter.

Staying for the time being with the events of 1965 and 1966, the Lord President of the Court of Session, the Faculty of Advocates (the Scottish Bar) and the Law Society of Scotland each urged that abolition of corroboration in civil actions would have dire consequences for Scots law. The Commission did not agree. In its conclusion it said:

> The rule requiring corroboration is a survival from the early history of Scots law. It is no longer justified in the class of case in which we recommend its abolition. It is unknown or has long been abandoned in most other systems of jurisprudence. We are not convinced by any of the reasons which have been advanced for its retention. It is causing real hardship to individuals in Scotland today.[12]

It cannot have been easy for the newly appointed Scottish Law Commissioners to face down the *ancien regime* in this way. By doing so, they marked out the

---

[10] Scottish Law Commission, SLC 3, *First Annual Report* (1967) para 9.
[11] 'Aim Will Be to Bring Law Up to Date' *The Scotsman* (Edinburgh, 17 June 1965).
[12] Scottish Law Commission, SLC 4, *Proposal for Reform of the Law of Evidence Relating to Corroboration* (1967) para 23.

independence[13] of the new body and they set the standard for their successors. The recommendation was promptly implemented, but only to the extent of abolishing corroboration in personal injury cases.[14] It took until 1988 for it to be swept away in the case of civil actions in general.[15]

That report was quickly followed by others tackling issues with societal implications. The Commission's second report recommended that the law should be changed to permit the legitimation of children by the subsequent marriage of their parents, notwithstanding that the parents had not been free to marry at the time of the child's conception or birth.[16] Then there was a report proposing extension of the grounds for divorce to include separation for two years with consent.[17] At the time these proposals would undoubtedly have been socially controversial.

So I think it can be said that the Scottish Law Commission understood from its earliest days that it had to operate as a truly independent advisory body beholden to no external interest. It understood also that its work would not always be limited to technical aspects of the law, but could extend to socially controversial areas.

Independence from government has remained a key principle throughout our existence and it is one to which we remain strongly committed today. The principle has become so firmly entrenched that it would be unthinkable for the government to seek to influence the approach we resolve to take towards reform of any branch of the law; whether they choose to accept our recommendations is, of course, another matter altogether.

## IV THE WORK OF THE SCOTTISH LAW COMMISSION

Over the past 50 years the Scottish Law Commission has been responsible for reforming the law of Scotland in a vast number of areas. Many of our projects have involved systemic reforms to fundamental principles of Scots law—the sort of law reform that is particularly suited to a specialist law reform agency, which has built up substantial knowledge and expertise in comparative analysis, in conducting comprehensive public consultations, in policy development and in the preparation of legislation. For various reasons, a government department may find it difficult to undertake this type of law reform work—amongst the difficulties may be a lack of resources (especially in times of economic difficulty), and more pressing political priorities. It is not realistic to expect such reforms to emanate from decisions of the courts, especially in a small system such as ours.

We have published about 240 reports recommending reforms. Most we have produced ourselves, although there has been important joint work with the Law Commission for England and Wales, with whom we have always enjoyed an

---

[13] For further reflection on 'independence', see chapter 16 (William Binchy).

[14] Law Reform (Miscellaneous Provisions) (Scotland) Act 1968, s 9.

[15] Civil Evidence (Scotland) Act 1988, s 1.

[16] Scottish Law Commission, SLC 5, *Reform of the Law Relating to Legitimation* per Subsequens Matrimonium (1967).

[17] Scottish Law Commission, SLC 6, *Divorce: The Grounds Considered* (1967).

extremely strong and positive relationship. More recently, we have worked also with the Northern Ireland Law Commission, which was established in April 2007; it is a matter of regret that the Northern Ireland Government has decided to withdraw funding from that body.[18] In addition to reports recommending reform of the law, we have issued around 160 consultation documents.

Space permits me to mention just a few major themes. From the early 1980s, the Commission embarked on a series of studies of family law, beginning with a report on financial provision.[19] Then we looked at outdated rules in the law of husband and wife;[20] illegitimacy;[21] occupancy rights in the marital home;[22] matrimonial property;[23] the recognition of foreign nullity decrees;[24] jurisdiction and enforcement in child custody cases;[25] and child abduction.[26] Much of this work resulted in modernising legislation.

The Commission's work on reform of property law is also worth highlighting. For centuries, almost all land in Scotland had been held on feudal tenure, under which multiple rights of ownership co-existed in the same piece of land. The Commission's ambitious aim was to abolish that system, erected on the foundation of the ancient feudal relationship of superior and vassal, and to replace it with a modern system based on the principle of absolute ownership of land.[27] As a result of the Commission's work, the feudal system was dismantled. There were related reforms to title conditions, long leases, tenements and land registration.

The Commission has examined many other areas of private law; they are too numerous to list in full; they include: the law relating to companies and partnerships;[28] the law of succession;[29] the law affecting adults with incapacity;[30] many aspects of the law relating to contracts;[31] and the law of negligence.[32]

The final area I want to touch on is criminal law. Here the Commission has been very active over the years. I would mention, in particular, the work done on sexual

[18] See chapter 5 (Neil Faris).
[19] Scottish Law Commission, SLC 67, *Report on Aliment and Financial Provision* (1981).
[20] Scottish Law Commission, SLC 76, *Report on Outdated Rules in the Law of Husband and Wife* (1983).
[21] Scottish Law Commission, SLC 82, *Report on Illegitimacy* (1984).
[22] Scottish Law Commission, SLC 60, *Report on Occupancy Rights in the Matrimonial Home and Domestic Violence* (1980).
[23] Scottish Law Commission, SLC 86, *Report on Matrimonial Property* (1984).
[24] Law Commission and Scottish Law Commission, LC 137 and SLC 88, *Recognition of Foreign Nullity Decrees and Related Matters* (1984).
[25] Law Commission and Scottish Law Commission, LC 138 and SLC 91, *Custody of Children—Jurisdiction and Enforcement within the United Kingdom* (1985).
[26] Scottish Law Commission, SLC 102, *Child Abduction* (1987).
[27] Scottish Law Commission, SLC 168, *Abolition of the Feudal System* (1999).
[28] Law Commission and Scottish Law Commission, LC 283 and SLC 192, *Partnership Law* (2003).
[29] Scottish Law Commission, SLC 124, *Report on Succession* (1990) and SLC 215, *Report on Succession* (2009).
[30] Scottish Law Commission, SLC 240, *Report on Adults with Incapacity* (2014).
[31] eg Scottish Law Commission, SLC 152, *Report on Three Bad Rules in Contract Law* (1996); SLC 174, *Report on Remedies for Breach of Contract* (1999).
[32] eg Scottish Law Commission, SLC 31, *The Law Relating to Damages for Injuries Causing Death* (1973); SLC 196, *Report on Damages for Psychiatric Injury* (2004).

offences, resulting in a comprehensive new statute passed by the Scottish Parliament in 2009.[33] We have recently considered other sensitive and topical aspects of the criminal law, including the rules on double jeopardy,[34] and on similar fact evidence.[35]

Bringing matters up to date, our *Ninth Programme of Law Reform*[36] includes projects on the law of defamation and on aspects of the law of prescription. We are continuing with projects on compulsory purchase, on moveable transactions and on the law of contract in the light of the Draft Common Frame of Reference. We are involved in joint projects on insurance law and on electoral law.

We have five commissioners drawn from the judiciary, private legal practice and the universities (some of whom are part-time). They are supported by an experienced team of solicitors seconded from the Scottish Government legal service and a small number of legal assistants, who are normally recent law graduates. Our programme work is carried out by project teams, usually comprising a lead commissioner, a project manager and a legal assistant. We are also fortunate in having the services of an experienced parliamentary draftsman. Our reports are normally accompanied by a draft Bill.

The Chairman of the Commission has always been a serving Senator of the College of Justice. In the early days, the appointment was on a full-time basis, but for some years the Chairman has spent 40 per cent of his or her time on the bench and 60 per cent at the Commission. I am convinced that it is of the greatest importance that the Chairman should continue to be a Senator. It means that the Commission has strong practical contacts with the senior judiciary and is in touch with the daily work of the courts.

In addition to our programme work, Scottish Ministers will from time to time refer to the Commission specific law reform issues which have, for one reason or another, arisen. We are not obliged to accept such references, but we invariably try to do so, although this may sometimes mean that our programme work has to be re-prioritised.

I should not overlook the important work that the Commission carries out, in partnership with the Law Commission for England and Wales, on statute law repeals. This work involves repealing statutes that are no longer of practical utility. The purpose is to modernise and simplify the statute book, thereby reducing its size and thus saving the time of lawyers and others who use it. This work has resulted in 20 statute law repeal Bills since 1965 repealing more than 3,000 whole Acts and achieving partial repeals in thousands of others. The most recent report and draft Bill were published in June 2015.[37]

---

[33] Scottish Law Commission, SLC 209, *Rape and Other Sexual Offences* (2007), which resulted in the Sexual Offences (Scotland) Act 2009.
[34] Scottish Law Commission, SLC 218, *Double Jeopardy* (2009).
[35] Scottish Law Commission, SLC 229, *Similar Fact Evidence and the* Moorov *Doctrine* (2012).
[36] SLC 242 (2015).
[37] Law Commission and Scottish Law Commission, LC 357 and SLC 243, *Statute Law Repeals: Twentieth Report* (2015).

## V  THE CHANGING CONSTITUTIONAL FRAMEWORK

No survey of the past 50 years touching on legal and political life in Scotland would be complete without reference to devolution and the growth of Scottish nationalism. The New Labour government elected in 1997, under the leadership of Tony Blair, was in favour of devolving some powers from the Westminster Parliament to a Scottish Parliament to be established in Edinburgh. Following a referendum vote in Scotland in favour of devolution, the Westminster Parliament passed the Scotland Act 1998. This created a Scottish Parliament (now based in Holyrood, Edinburgh) and a Scottish Government. The Act does not spell out which areas are devolved to the Scottish Parliament; rather it specifies those matters that are reserved to the United Kingdom Parliament. Subjects not reserved are devolved to the Scottish Parliament. The Scottish Parliament has primary legislative competence, that is, the power to enact statutes on devolved issues. Reserved matters include the constitution, foreign affairs, defence, international development and financial and economic issues. Consequently, devolved matters extend to areas such as health and social work, education and training, local government and housing, justice and policing, the environment and economic development and internal transport.

Until these constitutional changes took effect in 1999, the Scottish Law Commission reported with recommendations for reform of Scots law to the government of the United Kingdom, which was, as I have explained, responsible for the whole of Scots law; implementation of law reform recommendations was a matter for the UK Government and the UK Parliament at Westminster.

With responsibility for Scots law divided under the devolution scheme between Holyrood and Westminster, sensitive questions arose about the future of the Scottish Law Commission. Would we continue to be responsible for all of Scots law, as was previously the case, or would the constitutional changes mean that the Scottish Commission would deal only with the devolved areas? There were siren voices urging that we should just cover devolved issues. In my view, that would have emasculated the role of the Scottish Commission. It would have left a gaping hole insofar as reserved aspects of Scots law were concerned; it would have worsened the position for law reform in Scotland. Fortunately, good sense prevailed and it was decided that the Scottish Law Commission would continue to be responsible for the whole breadth of Scots law, extending to reserved and devolved matters.

What this has meant in practice is that the Scottish Law Commission now has to navigate the corridors of power both in Edinburgh and in London. We have positive relationships with the UK Government and the UK Parliament on reserved areas of Scots law. So far as projects within devolved areas go (and they account for most of our work), we have also had to develop strong relationships with the Scottish Government and the Scottish Parliament. It is the Scottish Government which is solely responsible for sponsoring the Commission, and for providing funding for us.

In the early years following devolution, the Scottish Law Commission seized the opportunities presented for law reform by the creation of the Scottish Parliament. It persuaded the new Scottish Government and the Scottish Parliament to adopt a number of our pre-devolution reports and to implement important legislative reforms based on them. There were, for example, sweeping reforms to land and property law, as I have already mentioned, and to areas such as incapacity law. After the first few years, however, the pace of change slowed. Somewhat ironically, the implementation rate for Law Commission measures at Holyrood started to decline, despite the advent of the new legislature.

In order to drive Scottish law reform back up the Scottish political agenda the Commission has made major efforts to reach out to the new institutions to ensure that the need for systematic law reform is fully appreciated.

The outcome has been the introduction of a new Scottish parliamentary procedure for Commission Bills complying with criteria set by the Scottish Parliament's Presiding Officer—the main one being a requirement that there should be a wide consensus on the need for reform and on the approach recommended. There is a similar procedure for law reform measures in the Westminster Parliament; this has worked well in regard to some recent reforms in reserved areas.[38]

By this decision in 2013, the Scottish Parliament expressly acknowledged the importance of the contribution of the Scottish Law Commission to the promotion and delivery of effective law reform; and the need to improve the rate of implementation of law reform Bills.

The first Commission Bill to go through the new process successfully passed its parliamentary stages and came into force on 1 July 2015: it is called the Legal Writings (Counterparts and Delivery) (Scotland) Act 2015. The Committee has recently completed consideration of a second Commission measure on aspects of the law of succession.[39] The Commission is working hard to provide further Bills for the process. The Committee has dealt with a Commission Bill consolidating bankruptcy law.[40]

Still on the constitutional front, in 2014 the United Kingdom and Scotland faced the possibility of a further shift in the tectonic plates. A referendum on independence was held in Scotland. The majority voted against independence—55 per cent to 45 per cent. Had the vote gone the other way, new horizons for law reform and the Commission might have opened up. There was discussion about a written constitution for Scotland. We noted with interest the Constitution for Malawi (to which I have already referred) with provision in the Constitution about the Malawi Law Commission and its role. A precedent for a Scottish constitution perhaps?

VI THE FUTURE

There have been a number of recent important contributions to the debate about the future of the United Kingdom Law Commissions.

Sir Geoffrey Palmer[41] has called for the Law Commissions to be entrusted with wider responsibilities and for their remits to be broadened to include big projects

---

[38] See chapters 9 (Sir Terence Etherton), 22 (Hector MacQueen) and 37 (Malcolm McMillan).
[39] The Succession (Scotland) Act 2016.
[40] The Bankruptcy (Scotland) Act 2016.
[41] G Palmer, 'The Law Reform Enterprise: Evaluating the Past and Charting the Future' (2015) 131 *LQR* 402.

with social implications. He believes that law reform agencies must become central to legislative activities. And he has argued strongly and persuasively for codification to be restored to the agenda and pursued with determination, with the Law Commissions being allowed to take the lead. Lord Neuberger, now the President of the UK Supreme Court, has expressed the view in a public lecture that serious consideration should be given to pursuing systematic codification of areas of the law.[42] Lord Carloway, the (then) Lord Justice Clerk,[43] in his keynote address to the biennial conference of the Commonwealth Association of Law Reform Agencies in Edinburgh in 2015, acknowledged that the Scottish Law Commission was the 'standard bearer for substantive law reform in Scotland'.[44] He observed, however, that it was the duty of every lawyer to be 'pro-active in evaluating and maintaining a legal system that is fit for purpose; that purpose being to meet the constantly evolving needs of the society which it serves'.[45] His answer to the question he posed about who the law reformers are in the legal community was what he described as the obvious one: 'all of us'.[46]

In recent times, there have been important law reform projects in Scotland carried out by ad hoc committees, including two chaired by Lord Carloway.[47] In his review of the Supreme Court's ruling in the case of *Cadder v HM Advocate*,[48] Lord Carloway recommended that the requirement for corroboration in criminal cases should be abolished. The recommendation, like the Scottish Law Commission's recommendation on corroboration in civil cases nearly half a century earlier, proved to be highly controversial. It gave rise to a political furore in Scotland. Once again the proposal was vigorously opposed by the legal profession, although it had the support of victims' groups, the prosecution service and (after some hesitation) the police. After a further review chaired by a retired judge, Lord Bonomy, on the scope of compensatory safeguards in the event of abolition,[49] the Scottish Government announced that it proposed to amend its Criminal Justice Bill to remove the proposal to abolish the requirement. Of course, it is a matter for government to decide as to how and by whom it wishes law reform work to be handled. One might legitimately ask, however, whether this type of project would not have been particularly well-suited for consideration by the Scottish Law Commission since it involved review of a fundamental aspect of Scots law. As I have mentioned, there are distinct advantages (including cost) in systematic law reform projects being carried out by independent law reform agencies, not just for the legal system but for government as well.

---

[42] D Neuberger, 'General, Equal and Certain: Law Reform Today and Tomorrow', Statute Law Society, 2011 Lord Renton Lecture (2012) 33 *Statute Law Review* 323 (Lord Neuberger was Master of the Rolls at the time of this Lecture).

[43] Lord Carloway is now the Lord President of the Court of Session.

[44] C Sutherland, 'To "Mend the Lawes, That Neids Mendement": A Scottish Perspective on Lawyers as Law Reformers' Commonwealth Association of Law Reform Agencies Conference (2015) 3.

[45] ibid 4.

[46] ibid 29.

[47] *The Carloway Review* (2011) (on *Cadder v HM Advocate* [2010] UKSC 43, [2010] 1 WLR 2601) and Scottish Court Service, *Evidence and Procedure Review Report* (2015).

[48] *Cadder*, n 47 above.

[49] *The Post-corroboration Safeguards Review* (2015).

In order to ensure that such advantages are properly understood and taken into account, it is an important part of the law reform agency's job to develop and maintain strong working relationships with government and to make sure that it stays on the government's radar at all times.

At the Scottish Law Commission we are not complacent about our place in the legal fabric of the country. We fully understand that we must continuously justify our value to Scots law and to Scottish society. Particularly in times of pressure on public spending, we need to be flexible and forward-thinking in our outlook and approach. We must ensure that we communicate effectively with the Westminster and Holyrood governments, the two legislatures, the legal profession and with all other relevant interests in the community we serve. We must work hard to explain who we are, what we do and how we go about our work. Amongst other things, we must take full advantage of modern technologies to reach the widest possible audience. Consultation exercises must be carried out in a way that allows for maximum engagement with civil society; this should extend to creative use of social media. We need to continue to be accessible and to produce work that is intelligible, as was noted in our first annual report, and we must jealously protect our independence as the first Scottish Law Commissioners recognised.

At the same time as doing all this, we must ensure that we do not compromise on the high quality of our work. Worthwhile law reform, particularly when it involves major structural changes to established principles of law, takes time. It has to be thought through rigorously and developed carefully, in close consultation with stakeholders. In this regard, the input of our project advisory groups has been crucial, as naturally our knowledge of day-to-day experience in particular areas is sometimes limited. However, we also have to accept that if we are perceived to take too long with major projects then this can affect our reputation, particularly among stakeholders who seek change at the earliest opportunity.

Is it possible then to articulate a clear vision for the Scottish Law Commission in the modern era? I do not myself think that it is necessary to amend the 1965 Act in order to achieve this or to replace it with a new piece of legislation. No doubt it can be said that in some respects the 1965 Act is expressed in language that is of wide and general reach and that, compared with many modern statutes, an exhaustively detailed specification of administrative matters does not feature; some may think there are advantages in that. The core responsibilities of the Law Commissions are not, however, left in any doubt by the terms of the 1965 Act and the values and principles underlying the Commissions are entirely clear.

I would make two suggestions for possible improvements in the way the Scottish Law Commission works.

First, I believe that the cause of systematic law reform in Scotland would benefit from a re-examination of the relationship between the Scottish Government and the Scottish Law Commission. If such an exercise has ever been carried out, it has not been done for some time. I do not suggest that the constitutional independence of the Commission from government should be weakened. Rather, the emphasis should be on improving the system for planning and carrying out our work in a way that seeks to promote a more concrete assurance of government support for our legislative proposals from an earlier stage. There should also, I think, be closer contact and stronger mutual engagement between the Commission and the relevant directorates of the Scottish Government during the currency of projects. The basic objective is to improve the prospects for earlier legislative implementation of the Commission's recommendations. Earlier implementation must, I think, be an important aim. It may reduce the need for further consultation and for reworking of our proposals.

With these ideas in mind, the following points occur to me as a possible outline for a new scheme; they are not, in any sense, intended to be exhaustive or prescriptive. Others may well have different and better ideas; my purpose is to stimulate debate with a view to improving how we and the Scottish Government take forward the work of law reform. A number of my suggestions have been influenced by the system in New Zealand.[50]

— There is, I believe, a need to align the planning of our work more closely with government directorates when projects are being considered for inclusion in our programmes of law reform. The Commission needs to take full account of the Scottish Government's strategic objectives when deciding on our proposed work programme. The government, for its part, must be cognisant of the Commission's considered views on the areas of Scots law that are in need of reform.

— Of course, ideas for law reform cannot be the sole preserve or responsibility of government; they can come from many directions, not least from within the Law Commission itself or from stakeholders in the context of a public consultation exercise on the content of each programme. It is ultimately up to the Commission to select its proposed projects on the basis of transparent criteria—that much flows from the principle of independence. And it is, at the end of the day, for the government to approve the Commission's proposed programme.

— I believe that the selection of projects needs to take full and careful account of the prospects for legislative implementation; so there should be real and meaningful engagement between the government and the Commission focused on this issue when projects are being considered for inclusion.

— To promote orderly and systematic planning, there should be a specific requirement for each directorate of the Scottish Government to consider, sufficiently far in advance of the formulation of each new programme of law reform, whether to propose law reform projects for the Commission from within their areas of responsibility.

— Ministers who intend to propose a project should identify how the project aligns with the government's priorities and strategic objectives and why it would be a suitable project for the Commission to undertake.

— It would remain the responsibility of the Commission to decide whether to include any project nominated by the government in its proposed programme of law reform. There would, however, be an understanding that government-nominated projects would be treated seriously as candidates for inclusion in the programme.

---

[50] See New Zealand Cabinet Office Circular (CO(09)1), 24 April 2009, and also chapter 19 (Sir Grant Hammond).

— In the event that a project nominated by a Minister is accepted by the Commission for inclusion in the programme, the government directorate would be bound to support the Commission's work during the course of the project and to provide advice to the government in responding promptly to the final report of the Commission on the project. The nature and level of the support would vary as between projects and would have to be worked out on a case by case basis. It might in some instances extend to the secondment of officials to the Commission for a project or some part of it.

— The relevant portfolio Minister, whose directorate has promoted and supported a law reform project, would be responsible for preparing an analysis of the Law Commission's report and draft Bill within a period to be agreed; in general a period of six months would seem reasonable. Under current arrangements the Scottish Government has agreed to provide a public response to Commission reports within three months of their publication, but this system is not working adequately. The three-month time limit is too short to allow for a properly considered response to be provided.

— If the government accepts a ministerial recommendation for legislation, it would be under a responsibility to introduce a Bill to the Scottish Parliament as soon as practicable. Many Bills would be suitable for the new parliamentary process.

— If a Commission recommendation for legislation is rejected, the government would be bound to submit a report explaining the reasons for its decision to the Scottish Parliament within a period to be agreed; three months would appear to be reasonable. Any MSP would then be able to call for a parliamentary debate on the matter.[51]

In my opinion, arrangements along these lines would assist in trying to ensure that the work of the Commission is in tune with the Scottish Government's strategic objectives and, therefore, stands an improved prospect of being implemented within a reasonable time. To some these proposals may appear unduly ambitious. I acknowledge that they would involve changes in established practices and that the fine details would require refinement and careful thinking through. There are always problems and negative points that can be identified with any new system of this type. The attraction of such a scheme, however, is that it provides a framework for addressing the difficulties that are liable to arise where too great a distance develops between government and the Commission during our project work; the result of such a distancing effect can be that valuable law reform work is wasted or becomes out of date or has to be redone.

The second area where I consider that there may be scope for developing the way in which we go about our business relates to the harnessing of legal expertise for our projects. Greater flexibility may have some attractions. Partnership or some form of collaborative arrangements between the Commission and the University Law Schools might be one possible option; thus allowing for academic staff to be sec-

---

[51] Douglas Cusine has suggested that there should be a convention that SLC reports are at least debated in the Scottish Parliament: see D Cusine, 'Civil Law Reform: Where We Are and Where We Are Going' 2015 *Scots Law Times (News)* 27.

onded to the Commission to work on projects in which they have particular expertise and to which they can bring the benefit of their research. I would have thought that the type of intensive analytical work carried out in the course of a law reform project would be recognised as having scholarly merit and practical impact for the purposes of receiving funding and accreditation as acceptable published academic work.

In voicing these thoughts, I do not for one moment intend to imply any criticism of the Commission's current legal staff, all of whom are (as I have mentioned) solicitors seconded from the Scottish Government legal service; they do an excellent job in demanding and challenging circumstances. It seems to me, however, that there may be advantages, in the case of some projects, in considering whether the engagement of academic or other consultants (perhaps even from the private sector) with established knowledge in particular areas would allow for projects to be progressed more quickly and efficiently.[52] It would not be necessary for such suitably qualified experts to spend time reading into a subject.

All public bodies should constantly be looking critically at how they operate to ensure that they deliver value for public money in times of great economic pressure. The Scottish Law Commission is no exception and we need to think creatively about how we utilise our limited budget and small staff.

[52] There have been some instances in the past where the Commission engaged the assistance of outside experts, but this has not happened for a good number of years.

# 35

# *Looking to the Future*

## SIR DAVID LLOYD JONES

Speaking towards the end of this conference provided an excellent opportunity to take up some of the themes raised by other speakers in their assessment of the progress of law reform over the last 50 years and to make some observations about how law reform might develop in future. I am also writing at the end of my term as Chairman of the Law Commission of England and Wales and I hope I may be forgiven, therefore, if there is an element of stocktaking about what follows.

## I CONSOLIDATION AND CODIFICATION

Consolidation and codification both appear within the statutory functions of the Law Commission of England and Wales.[1] Neither is a precise term of art. In general, however, a consolidation draws together a number of existing enactments on the same subject, usually in one Bill, to form a rational structure and to make the cumulative effect of different layers of amendment more intelligible and accessible. Codification was described in 1966 by Sir Leslie Scarman as 'a species of enacted law which purports so to formulate the law that it becomes within its field the authoritative, comprehensive and exclusive source of that law'.[2] It is appropriate to ask to what extent the Law Commission has succeeded in performing its statutory duty to secure the systematic development and reform of the law, including in particular, its codification, simplification and modernisation.

Over the last 50 years the Law Commission of England and Wales has been responsible for over 220 consolidated statutes, but this function has declined significantly in recent years. This is certainly not because there is a reduced need for such consolidation; on the contrary, the massive increase in the volume of primary

---

[1] Law Commissions Act, 1965, s 3(1): 'to take and keep under review all the law [of England and Wales] ... with a view to its systematic development and reform, including in particular the codification of such law, the elimination of anomalies, the repeal of obsolete and unnecessary enactments, the reduction of the number of separate enactments and generally the simplification and modernisation of the law'. For further scrutiny of codification, see chapters 12 (Ian Dennis) and 32 (David Ormerod).

[2] L Scarman, 'Codification and Judge-Made Law: A Problem of Co-existence' (1966–67) 42 *Indiana Law Journal* 355, 358. Law Commission, LC CP 223, *Form and Accessibility of the Law Applicable in Wales* (2015) includes a detailed discussion of consolidation and codification in chs 7 and 8 respectively.

and secondary legislation in recent years makes this work all the more important. (Nor do I believe that access to legislation online is any substitute for a proper consolidation. This may have reduced the pressure to consolidate simply to take account of amendments, but a true consolidation performs a wider function, in particular where successive amending statutes have distorted the structure of the original Act.) This falling off has been due principally to a lack of interest on the part of government, an unwillingness by departments to provide the support and commitment which such a project requires and, in certain areas, an inability to leave the law alone for long enough to permit consolidation. A particularly unhappy experience over an attempted consolidation of statutes on private pensions from which the Department for Work and Pensions withdrew its support in 2010[3] led my predecessor, Sir James Munby, once to observe that 'it is hard work to get a consolidation project off the ground; and then it is hard work to keep it flying'.[4] In 2011, the Commission announced that it would not in future seek out consolidation projects and would only undertake one if there were a governmental commitment to seeing it through to the passing of a consolidation Act. As a result, the only consolidation statute for which we were responsible in my three years as Chairman was the Co-operatives and Community Benefit Societies Act 2014—the fact that it was requested by No 10 may have had something to do with that—although we hope soon to resume work on a consolidated Bail Bill. This is disappointing as parliamentarians have voiced their desire to see more rather than fewer consolidation Bills. Moreover, the Law Commission has a statutory responsibility in this field and it is anxious to discharge it.

By contrast, there seems to be a real appetite in Wales for consolidation.[5] The need here is even greater than in England. The grant of primary legislative powers to the National Assembly following the implementation of Part 4 of the Government of Wales Act 2006 means that some Westminster Acts are now being amended both in Westminster and by the National Assembly. In addition to the usual benefits, a consolidating Act of the Welsh Assembly would have the significant additional value of disentangling Welsh from English and UK legislation, making both more accessible. The Counsel General has spoken of the need to develop a Welsh statute book by a programme of consolidating legislation.[6] This will take a long time to achieve. A start has been made in that, when drafting reforming legislation, the Office of Legislative Counsel usually produces a Bill which restates the law separately as it applies to Wales. The demand for consolidation of legislation in Wales was one of

---

[3] In 2006, the Commission began a consolidation of the legislation on private pensions at the request of the Department for Work and Pensions. That department decided in October 2010 that it would no longer support the project. The work therefore had to be abandoned, as the Law Commission did not have the resources to complete it itself. It was a huge exercise, and by October 2010 the Commission was within less than five months of the planned date for publishing a draft Bill for consultation. At that time, the draft Bill ran to 848 clauses and 21 schedules. The whole exercise was an enormous waste of time and resources. See, generally, Law Commission, LC 328, *Annual Report 2010–11* (2011) para 2.83.

[4] ibid para 2.84.

[5] LC CP 223, n 2 above, ch 7.

[6] Theodore Huckle QC, 'Access to Legislation' www.gov.wales/docs/caecd/publications/130114welsh districtjudgesspeech260912.pdf.

the reasons why the Law Commission undertook its current project on the *Form and Accessibility of the Law Applicable in Wales*. It may be that there is a future role for the Commission in relation to consolidation in Wales.

Early in the Commission's history, great emphasis was placed on the need for the codification of the law.[7] Looking back over the last 50 years it does seem that very little has been achieved in that direction. The Commission's first programme of law reform proposed, inter alia, the codification of the law of contract and the law of landlord and tenant.[8] These have not been achieved.[9] Similarly, the Commission's project on the codification of the criminal law was suspended, because the Commission came to the view that codification had to be preceded by a process of simplification of the law. That process continues with the publication in November 2014 of our report on *Kidnapping and Related Offences*[10] and our recent report on *Public Nuisance and Outraging Public Decency*.[11] The experience of the Law Commission in this regard confirms the good sense shown by Gardiner and Martin in *Law Reform Now* where they wrote that codification should not be given too high a priority, for the sole reason that the condition of English law was so encumbered with obsolete and unjust law that codification would have to be preceded by reform.[12]

I do not think that we should despair over this, however. Codification may well be a desirable ultimate objective, but there can also be real value in the reforms which are achieved along the way. Moreover, I believe that codification is coming back into fashion. The Lord Chief Justice is a prominent exponent of the virtues of codification and has called for the Welsh Assembly to abandon the Westminster model and to develop its own innovative style of legislation, starting with a sensible organisation of Welsh law into a code.[13]

More immediately, the Commission has undertaken a major project on the reform and codification of the law of sentencing procedure which is due to report in 2017. This is an area of the law crying out for codification. The current confused state of the law—in which hundreds of separate provisions are scattered across dozens of different statutes—is leading to serious error.[14] In 2011, the then Lord Chancellor declined to approve its inclusion in the Law Commission's eleventh programme of law reform, notwithstanding that it had widespread support from the judiciary, the professions and academic lawyers. I am glad to say that a great deal of further activity by the Commission on different fronts, in which David Ormerod has played an inspirational part, has led to the inclusion of the project in the Commission's current twelfth programme of law reform.[15] The project will produce a single

[7] See, eg, Scarman, n 2 above. On the Commission's attempts at codification see, generally, LC CP 223, n 2 above, ch 8.

[8] Law Commission, LC 1, *First Programme of Law Reform* (1965).

[9] M Kerr, 'Law Reform in Changing Times' (1980) 96 *LQR* 515. See also P North, 'Problems of Codification in a Common Law System' (1982) 46 *Rabels Zeitschrift* 490.

[10] LC 355 (2014).

[11] LC 358 (2015).

[12] G Gardiner and A Martin (eds), *Law Reform Now* (London, Victor Gollancz, 1963) 11–12.

[13] J Thomas, 'The Role of the Judiciary in a Rapidly Changing Wales', Legal Wales Conference, Cardiff (2013).

[14] R Banks and L Harris, *Banks on Sentence*, 8th edn (Burwash, R Banks, 2013) vol 1, xii.

[15] Law Commission, LC 354, *Twelfth Programme of Law Reform* (2014).

sentencing Bill which, if implemented by Parliament, will be the single port of call for sentencing tribunals. It will set out the relevant provisions in a clear, simple and logical way and will allow for all updates to sentencing procedure thereafter to be made in a single place.[16] Moreover, the Commission has recently published a scoping consultation paper on firearms law in which it not only identifies urgent amendment of the existing statute law but also provisionally proposes that the entire legislative framework regulating firearms is so seriously flawed as to require a wider reform project to codify the law.[17]

## II  WHAT SORT OF PROJECTS SHOULD THE LAW COMMISSION UNDERTAKE?

A number of chapters in this volume address the issue of which projects are suitable to be undertaken by Law Commissions. Sir Geoffrey Palmer in his Scarman Lecture in March 2015 also addressed this issue, which he described in terms of lawyers' law versus big policy.[18] He quoted Lord Denning in the parliamentary debate on the Law Commissions Bill in 1965: 'I am sure it would be wrong for a Commission of this kind to take over broad questions of policy in the law, which must be the province of Parliament.'[19] Palmer, while accepting that there are areas in which lawyers will have more to contribute than in others, found this unconvincing. He argued that big projects including heavy social policy can be successfully completed by Law Commissions. He referred to the observation of Sir Ivor Richardson that the New Zealand Law Commission was 'the statutory equivalent of a semi-permanent Royal Commission with a roving function'.[20]

I have to say that I have a very different view from Geoffrey Palmer as to what is the appropriate role of a Law Commission—at least in this jurisdiction. Here, I believe that the Commission has succeeded to the extent that it has because it has concentrated its activities in the field of lawyers' law and has, unlike Law Commissions in some other Commonwealth states, generally avoided projects which have at their heart major issues of social policy, morality or political controversy.[21]

That is not to say that the Law Commission of England and Wales only takes on projects which are not controversial. That is certainly not the case. A few examples demonstrate that we are not being timid about this. In our recent work on contempt of court and juror misconduct we have had to address issues of freedom of expression and permissible limitations on reporting in the media.[22] Our current

---

[16] The first issues paper in this project was published on 1 July 2015: Law Commission, *Sentencing Procedure: Issues Paper 1: Transition* (2015).

[17] Law Commission, LC CP 224, *Firearms Law: A Scoping Consultation Paper* (2015).

[18] G Palmer, 'The Law Reform Enterprise: Evaluating the Past and Charting the Future' (2015) 131 *LQR* 402, 414.

[19] HL Deb 1 April 1965, vol 264, col 1213.

[20] I Richardson, 'FW Guest Memorial Lecture 1989: Commissions of Inquiry' (1989–92) 7 *Otago Law Review* 1, 3.

[21] See chapter 11 (Yves Le Bouthillier) for the contrasting approach in Canada.

[22] Law Commission, LC 340, *Contempt of Court (1): Juror Misconduct and Internet Publications* (2013).

work includes projects on fitness to plead,[23] and misconduct in public office, both issues which have become highly controversial in this country in recent months. It is important that we should be addressing such legal issues which have excited so much public interest.

In our project on electoral law, we have ruled out of scope issues which, after consultation, we considered to be matters of political policy such as reform of the franchise, the voting system in use at any election and electoral boundaries.[24] We do not have the expertise to make recommendations in these areas. However, we are also finding that it is often difficult to demarcate matters involving judgements of political policy from technical aspects of electoral administration law reform, for example in relation to postal votes.

We have recently undertaken a scoping project on marriage, that is, getting married. One reason why this is, at this stage, only a scoping project is that we need to consider whether it may throw up issues on which we, as lawyers, are not well placed to make judgements: for example, whether the Church of England as the established church in England should enjoy special treatment in this matter.

There can be no bright line dividing projects appropriate for the Commission from those which are not. However, I doubt that the Law Commission would be the appropriate body to address reform of the law relating, for example, to assisted suicide.[25] Here, the central issues are essentially issues of morality and, in my view, matters for Parliament. To my mind, the great strength of the Law Commission is in its legal expertise. It excels in dealing with projects where, after thorough research and consultation, defects in the law are capable of being remedied as a result of lawyers finding lawyers' solutions. We should stick to what we are good at.

## III WALES

The Law Commission is, of course, the Law Commission of England and Wales. Devolution brings new responsibilities for the Commission and will open up many new opportunities in the future. In particular, we are already seeing a divergence of English law and Welsh law in the devolved areas within the shared legal system of England and Wales and this divergence is now accelerating rapidly.

From the start of devolution, the Commission has worked very closely with the Welsh Government, in its various forms, and the National Assembly for Wales. We have often had to run very hard to keep up with the rapidity of change in Wales. Wales is now on its third devolution settlement and, in March 2015, the UK Government announced its intention to introduce legislation which would establish a fourth, the first on a reserved powers model.

The fact that the National Assembly now enjoys primary legislative powers in the devolved areas has opened up new possibilities for the Commission so far as

[23] Law Commission, LC CP 197, *Unfitness to Plead* (2010).
[24] Law Commission, Scottish Law Commission and Northern Ireland Law Commission, LC CP 218, SLC DP 158 and NILC 20, *Electoral Law: A Joint Consultation Paper* (2014).
[25] See chapter 26 (Sir Jack Beatson).

implementation is concerned.[26] The Law Commission's report on adult social care has been implemented, in rather different ways, by separate legislation in England and in Wales.[27] Its 2006 report on renting homes[28] has not been implemented in England. However, at the request of the Welsh Government, the Law Commission has updated this report,[29] and on 9 February 2015 the Renting Homes (Wales) Bill was introduced into the Welsh Assembly. As a result of the Renting Homes (Wales) Act 2016, Wales now has a modern law of residential tenancies which is fit for purpose. It is to be hoped that England may, in due course, follow its example.

Nevertheless, it became clear to us at the Commission that there were deficiencies in the machinery of law reform in relation to Wales. In particular, under the Law Commissions Act 1965 it was not possible for the Welsh Government to refer a law reform project to the Law Commission directly. This lacuna has now been remedied by the Wales Act 2014 which amends the Law Commissions Act 1965. It also imposes on the Welsh Ministers an obligation to report annually to the National Assembly on the implementation of Law Commission recommendations and provides for a Protocol between the Welsh Government and the Law Commission setting out our joint working practices.[30]

In addition, and entirely outside the statutory structure, we created in 2013 a Welsh Advisory Committee to advise the Law Commission on the exercise of its statutory functions in relation to Wales, to help it identify the law reform needs of Wales within both the devolved and non-devolved areas and to identify and take into account specific Welsh issues in all of its law reform projects.

We are currently undertaking two projects which are 'Welsh projects' in the sense that they fall within the devolved areas. One is on *Planning Law in Wales*. The other is on the *Form and Accessibility of the Law Applicable in Wales*,[31] a project which is necessitated by the difficulties which are currently being experienced in identifying the applicable law, difficulties which are greatly exacerbated by the incremental nature of successive devolution settlements.

There have, in recent years, been calls in some quarters for the creation of a separate Law Commission for Wales and various models have been proposed. If that were to take place, it is likely that it would, entirely understandably, concentrate on law reform projects within the devolved field. It might be necessary to guard against a situation in which reform of the law in the retained fields—the great majority of the law applicable in Wales—would not in those circumstances receive the attention it needs. A number of different models have been suggested. However, the Welsh Government has made clear in its evidence to the Silk Commission that it is not at present calling for a separate Law Commission for Wales and that it is content with

---

[26] Government of Wales Act 2006, part 4.

[27] Recommendations in Law Commission, Scottish Law Commission and Northern Ireland Law Commission, LC 345, SLC 237 and NILC 18, *Regulation of Health Care Professionals: Regulation of Social Care Professionals in England* (2014) have been implemented in England by Parliament in the Care Act 2014 and in Wales by the Welsh Assembly in the Social Services and Well-being (Wales) Act 2014.

[28] Law Commission, LC 297, *Renting Homes: The Final Report* (2006).

[29] Law Commission, LC 337, *Renting Homes in Wales/Rhentu Cartrefi yng Nghymru* (2013).

[30] Law Commission and Welsh Ministers, *Protocol between the Welsh Ministers and the Law Commission* (2015), Gen-LD10290.

[31] Law Commission, LC CP 223, *Form and Accessibility of the Law Applicable in Wales* (2015).

the current arrangements. I consider it likely that, for the foreseeable future at least, the present Commission will continue to perform its present roles for both nations within the shared jurisdiction. This does mean, however, that the Commission will have to ensure that it remains an effective law reform body for Wales in both devolved and retained areas.

## IV THE FUTURE OF THE LAW COMMISSION

What might the future hold for the Law Commission as an institution? In its first 50 years the Law Commission has more than proved its worth. It has published 203 law reform reports of which approximately two thirds have been implemented in whole or in part. It has also been responsible for 222 consolidation Acts of Parliament and 19 Statute Law Repeal Acts. It has survived the bonfire of the quangos in the Public Bodies Act 2011 and has recently emerged successfully from a Triennial Review which confirmed that there is a continuing need for a Law Commission and that the present model is the most appropriate for maintaining its independence from government.

In 2014 it enjoyed its busiest and most productive year publishing 14 law reform reports.[32] Also, in the year to April 2015, eight Law Commission reports were implemented in Westminster[33] and one in Wales.[34] Westminster also passed a Law

---

[32] Law Commission, LC 342, *Wildlife Law: Control of Invasive Non-native Species* (2014); LC 343, *Matrimonial Property, Needs and Agreements* (2014); LC 344, *Contempt of Court (2): Court Reporting* (2014); Law Commission, Scottish Law Commission and Northern Ireland Law Commission, LC 345, SLC 237 and NILC 18, *Regulation of Health Care Professionals: Regulation of Social Care Professionals in England* (2014); Law Commission, LC 346, *Patents, Trade Marks and Design Rights: Groundless Threats* (2014); LC 347, *Taxi and Private Hire Services* (2014); LC 348, *Hate Crime: Should the Current Offences be Extended?* (2014); LC 349, *Conservation Covenants* (2014); LC 350, *Fiduciary Duties of Investment Intermediaries* (2014); LC 351, *Data Sharing between Public Bodies* (2014); Law Commission and Scottish Law Commission, LC 353 and SLC 238, *Insurance Contract Law: Business Disclosure, Warranties, Insurers' Remedies for Fraudulent Claims and Late Payment* (2014); Law Commission, *Social Investment by Charities* (Recommendations Paper) (2014); LC 355, *Simplification of Criminal Law: Kidnapping and Related Offences* (2014); LC 356, *Rights to Light* (2014).

[33] The Inheritance and Trustees' Powers Act 2014 implemented Law Commission, LC 331, *Intestacy and Family Provision Claims on Death* (2011); the Care Act 2014 implemented recommendations on adult social care (n 27 above); the Consumer Rights Act 2015 implemented Law Commission recommendations in three joint reports with the Scottish Law Commission: LC 292 and SLC 199, *Unfair Terms in Contracts* (2005), LC 332 and SLC 226, *Consumer Redress for Misleading and Aggressive Practices* (2012); and LC 317 and SLC 216, *Consumer Remedies for Faulty Goods* (2009); the Infrastructure Act 2015 implemented Law Commission recommendations on *Control of Invasive Non-native Species* (LC 342 (2014)); the Criminal Justice and Courts Act 2015 implemented recommendations in relation to juror misconduct and internet publications (n 22 above); the Insurance Act 2015 implemented recommendations in the Law Commission's most recent report (with the Scottish Law Commission) on *Insurance Contract Law* (LC 353 and SLC 238 (2014)). In addition, in the same period, the recommendations in LC 350, *Fiduciary Duties of Investment Intermediaries* (2014) were adopted by the government and recommendations in LC 325, *Expert Evidence in Criminal Proceedings* (2011) were implemented in the Criminal Procedure Rules. More recently, the Charities (Protection and Social Investment) Bill will implement Law Commission proposals on *Social Investment by Charities* (n 32 above).

[34] The Social Services and Well-being (Wales) Act 2014 implements in Wales Law Commission proposals on adult social care (n 27 above). This is the first occasion on which Law Commission recommendations have been implemented by the National Assembly using its powers under Government of Wales Act 2006, part 4.

Commission consolidation Bill, the Co-operative and Community Benefit Societies Act 2014.

There is no shortage of demand for the services of the Law Commission in the field of law reform. Our consultation on our twelfth programme of law reform produced over 250 proposals for law reform projects. In the event we have taken on nine new projects as part of that programme.[35] Since then, the Justice Committee has proposed that we look at manorial rights and at complicity in the criminal law,[36] and we have taken on a project on transfer fees in residential leases and a scoping project on marriage. There are other fascinating projects waiting in the wings. So we have a full order book.

It would appear therefore that, at the moment at least, the standing of the Law Commission is high. However, we cannot afford to be complacent about this—not least as we are not and cannot expect to be insulated from the chilly financial winds currently blowing through Whitehall. I believe that it is remarkable that such a small organisation can produce the quantity and quality of work that it does. Moreover, the Law Commission represents extremely good value for money, especially when compared with the cost of recent public inquiries. Over the life of the last Parliament, our core funding received through the Ministry of Justice, which is currently just under £3million per annum, has been cut by 25 per cent.[37] To date, we have been able to continue to function at the same level of activity as a result of skilful budgeting by our Chief Executive and by charging other government departments for particular projects. However, these departments are themselves likely to be in line for further savings. Any further cuts will inevitably force us to reduce the number of our staff, the scale of our operations and the number of law reform projects which we can undertake. This is problematic for us because it is only by producing high quality proposals for law reform across the whole of the law that we can demonstrate the need for law reform and the advantages of an independent Law Commission.

Moreover, Law Commissions, as some recent examples show, are often considered disposable luxuries. Over the years Canada has had a number of provincial Commissions including the Law Commission of Ontario which was established in 1964 (a year before the Law Commission and the Scottish Law Commission) and which lost its funding in 1996. A federal law reform body, the Law Reform Commission of Canada, was established in 1971. It was disbanded in 1993 and its successor, the Law Commission of Canada, although created by statute in 1997 did not have its funding renewed in 2006.

---

[35] Bills of sale; protecting consumer prepayments on retailer insolvency; land registration; wills; mental capacity and detention; firearms; sentencing procedure; planning law in Wales; and the form and accessibility of the law applicable in Wales: Law Commission, LC 354, *Twelfth Programme of Law Reform* (2014).

[36] See the appeal in *R v Jogee* [2016] UKSC 8, [2016] 2 WLR 681 where the Law Commission's work was cited by counsel.

[37] See too chapters 26 (Sir Jack Beatson) and 36 (Elaine Lorimer).

Much closer to home is the current position of the Northern Ireland Law Commission, as discussed in Neil Faris' contribution to this volume (chapter 5). The Northern Ireland Commission was created by the Justice (Northern Ireland) Act 2002.[38] For some time it had been operating in a limited manner and in November 2014 the Minister of Justice in the Northern Ireland executive announced that the Commission would close on 31 March 2015. The reason the Minister of Justice has given for its closure is simply that there is no available funding. The closing of the Northern Ireland Law Commission is troubling at a number of different levels. It is troubling that a Law Commission can be considered to be so readily disposable. It also poses practical problems for the other Law Commissions in the United Kingdom. In the past, the Law Commission of England and Wales has undertaken certain law reform projects on a UK-wide basis jointly with the Scottish Law Commission and the Northern Ireland Law Commission. These may concern subjects within a devolved area, for example our recent project on *Regulation of Health Care Professionals*,[39] or in a reserved area, for example our current project on *Electoral Law*.[40] The elections project is a good example of a law reform project that can sensibly be undertaken only on a UK-wide basis. Yet, such a project requires the expert input of an independent law reform body in each of the jurisdictions concerned. I am glad to say that a temporary solution has been found under which the Northern Ireland Law Commission will remain in existence as a shell and the Cabinet Office will fund a limited participation by it in the elections project. However, there remain concerns as to the ability to conduct law reform in the future on a UK-wide basis.

I am anxious not to be misunderstood. I am not suggesting that there is any current threat to the continued existence of the Law Commission of England and Wales or to the Scottish Law Commission. It is, however, important that we should remain aware of the continuing need to justify our role by the quality and scope of the work we produce.

## V CONCLUSION

To my mind, the model of a Law Commission as developed in England and Wales and in Scotland works well as an effective means of delivering law reform. The Law Commission and the Scottish Law Commission both enjoy a number of huge advantages.[41] Within the Commissions, there is great legal expertise in many

---

[38] Justice (Northern Ireland) Act 2002, ss 50–52.

[39] Law Commission, Scottish Law Commission and Northern Ireland Law Commission, LC 345, SLC 237 and NILC 18, *Regulation of Health Care Professionals: Regulation of Social Care Professionals in England* (2014).

[40] Law Commission, Scottish Law Commission and Northern Ireland Law Commission, LC CP 218, SLC DP 158 and NILC 20, *Electoral Law: A Joint Consultation Paper* (2014).

[41] See generally, House of Commons Political and Constitutional Reform Committee, *Ensuring Standards in the Quality of Legislation* (2013–14, HC 85) ev 69–76.

different fields. We are in a position to consult widely and thoroughly on the state of the existing law, on perceived deficiencies and proposals for reform. Our independence from government and our reputation for independence permit engagement with a wide range of parties who value our objectivity and our impartiality. Our system of peer review, involving rigorous expert scrutiny of reports and draft legislation, is a sound quality assurance system. We have our own in house Parliamentary Counsel. We have the advantage of special parliamentary procedures, which are particularly suited to law reform measures. We have time within which to consider law reform and draft legislation in depth. We have remarkable teams of professionals, both lawyers and administrative staff, who are dedicated to the cause of law reform. There may be choppy waters ahead, but I am confident that with all these advantages the Commissions will come through with flying colours.

# 36

# *Commissioning the Future—A Chief Executive's Perspective*

## ELAINE LORIMER

In his chapter, David Lloyd Jones,[1] has discussed the achievements of the Law Commission and has provided some insight into possible future challenges and opportunities. What follows is the view from the Chief Executive's desk about the current context within which the Law Commission is operating and what this means for the organisation from an administrative perspective.

The current context is, without doubt, a challenging one: there is still severe budgetary constraint across the public service, which is set to continue; the legal landscape is changing rapidly, with devolution in particular impacting on our work as it affects Wales; arm's-length bodies are subject to constant challenge to demonstrate their continued relevance and value; there is pressure to deliver more quickly, make our publications more accessible and technologically friendly; good quality law, of itself, is not the key priority of government with economic growth being the main imperative; an assessment of the economic impact of reforms is now required as part of the package of law reform by government together with compliance with their 'one in, three out' rule in relation to regulation; there is ever-increasing pressure on parliamentary time.

What impact has this had on the Law Commission? The Law Commission has not been immune from the budgetary cuts, having its funding cut by 25 per cent over the period of the last government.[2] Yet it has continued to function and has delivered a large number of projects through its *Eleventh Programme of Law Reform* and other projects which have come to us via Ministerial reference. We have managed to maintain our size and basic structure.

The Law Commission has adapted to the changing environment through adopting a more flexible resourcing and funding model. Government departments are now expected to offer funding to cover the marginal costs of taking on a project if there is no internal Law Commission resource available to do it. This has allowed us to build up a smaller core permanent organisation, staffed by lawyers who are expert in

---

[1] See chapter 35 (Sir David Lloyd Jones).
[2] For a look further back, and a comparison across other forms of government inquiry, see chapter 26 (Sir Jack Beatson).

the craft of law reform and to supplement this with subject experts who are recruited to work on specific projects.

The future challenge for us is to make sure that this funding model is not too heavily skewed towards project-specific funding as the Commission then runs the risk of being purely demand-led and, essentially, a service provider. We must also not lose sight of areas of law in need of reform which have a significant impact on business and citizens but 'fall through the cracks' as they are not priorities for any particular department. The Law Commission's ability to deal with issues that will not otherwise be addressed by government has been an important part of the Commission's contribution to law reform. Our statutory duty is to keep all of the law of England and Wales under review. We must therefore remain vigilant to make sure that we are given sufficient funding to have a core permanent organisation to support the work of a Chairman and four Commissioners.

This financial model is underpinned by the Protocol the Law Commission has with the Lord Chancellor,[3] and now also with the Welsh Government.[4] These Protocols set out the principles which will apply to law reform projects and, in particular, the undertaking by government that there is a reasonable prospect of implementation of the Law Commission's law reform recommendations.

The Protocols and funding mechanism require greater project management discipline on the part of the Law Commission. Milestones are set and regular updates are provided to the relevant government department for the project. There are much more structured discussions about the product the Law Commission will produce, how long it will take, and whether a Bill is expected or not. This is all, of course, in addition to the substance of the problem that the law reform project is attempting to solve! Given the pressure on legislative drafting resources we now have to be certain that a Bill is absolutely necessary and expected by government rather than assuming that it is.

All of this context requires a different skill set from before—we must retain our core expertise in the craft of law reform, but also have a firm handle on our costs; how long projects take; and be accountable for their successful completion.

We know from our recent *Triennial Review*[5] that we are still considered to be relevant and have expertise that is respected. We have built up a strong reputation for the integrity with which we approach our work and for our independence of thought. We know (because stakeholders have said so) that one of our core strengths is the objective way in which we consult and arrive at our conclusions. This is the heart of our value. If we lose our reputation for this, we lose what is one of our most valuable assets.

In the economic context I have described, this means that the way in which we operate is of fundamental importance to our continued success. We strive to be a

---

[3] Law Commission and Ministry of Justice, LC 321, *Protocol between the Lord Chancellor (on behalf of the Government) and the Law Commission* (2010).
[4] Law Commission and Welsh Ministers, *Protocol between the Welsh Ministers and the Law Commission* (2015), Gen-LD10290.
[5] Ministry of Justice, *Triennial Review: Law Commission, Report of Stage One* (2013) and *Report of Stage Two* (2014).

listening organisation—one which is learned but also one which is keen to make sure that its reforms will work on the ground in society and make a positive difference. The areas covered by our current work are a good example of this. We will have to prioritise reforms which are relevant to current societal need.

Added to this, our success is mostly measured by the level of acceptance by government of our reforms. We also now have a growing role to play in supporting the implementation of our reforms as we hold the expertise in the area.[6] Having worked on it in such detail, we know the key stakeholders, their points of view and the policy behind our reforms. This is particularly true where the reforms are being taken into legislation. Where the Law Commission's special legislative procedure is being used, our Commissioner gives expert evidence to the committee, and to date, our staff have also supported the Bill team with the technicalities of the policy. We have found that the Law Commission must be the guardians of this legislative procedure, in terms of assessing what is suitable for the procedure and what is not. We also have to be expert in the intricacies of the procedure and the requirements at every stage. We cannot expect officials in government or Parliament to be our corporate memory.

In the main legislative programme, we also provide input for relevant Bills, where our Commissioner may be expected to give evidence as part of pre-legislative scrutiny, and our staff provide expert support to the Bill team for the provisions which are based on our reforms. Gone are the days where the Commission produced its report and the work ended there. In many cases, a new stage in the project begins.

Our Commissioners and staff therefore are key to our continued success. We need to have access to real expertise in the areas of law we are reforming, but we need much more than that. We have to be excellent communicators—to be able to engage positively across the whole spectrum of stakeholders we deal with: from members of the public through to the leading experts in the field; from powerful highly organised commercial bodies to small community groups.

Our organisation therefore now has expertise in communication skills, media handling, social media and the use of technology, for example. We need to keep up to date, insofar as resources allow, with new technology. And so we are looking at what further opportunities social media and our website provide for how we conduct our work.

We also require social research expertise (for surveys and data gathering) and, now, for every project, economic input to assess the economic impact of our reforms. This last point should not be underestimated. This is technical work, operating in an area where, by its nature, data may be non-existent or patchy. Yet we have to provide this for our reforms to be taken seriously and pass through the various levels of governmental scrutiny that precede legislative implementation.

The way in which we conduct our research and how we engage therefore requires us to access a whole range of skills to be able to function professionally. We not only need lawyers, we require other professionals to support the project work. And we need professional support to keep the organisational wheels turning efficiently too.

---

[6] See chapters 15 (Shona Wilson Stark), 20 (Andrew Burrows) and 37 (Malcolm McMillan).

I suspect this is quite a change from what was envisaged in the 1960s by the architects of our organisation! To reflect this, we recognised the desirability for further expertise to be brought into the leadership of the Law Commission and in September 2015 we appointed a non-executive board member to provide challenge and advice to the Commissioners and the Chief Executive when they meet as the management board.

Turning now to the legal landscape. Much has happened since 1965, with the creation and membership of the EU; the impact of the Human Rights Act 1998; and the jurisdiction of Strasbourg to name but a few; and of course devolution. For the Law Commission in England and Wales, we have sought in recent times to respond to the changing landscape in Wales by advocating reforms to the 1965 Act to place Welsh Ministers in a similar position to their counterparts in Whitehall and therefore being able to refer projects to the Law Commission for matters within their devolved competence. This is a significant step, and means that the Law Commission now has to build up expertise in the devolution settlement in Wales and the growing body of Welsh law.[7] We have new relationships to forge with a different set of Ministers and officials and the National Assembly to respond to.

Our relationships with parliamentarians in Whitehall have been key over the years in assisting in raising the profile of the Law Commission's work and in supporting our reforms as they have been brought forward by government. The Chairman and Commissioners have all given evidence to various committees over the years and the trend has already started with the National Assembly in Wales with the Chairman, Chief Executive and one of our Commissioners all giving evidence to committees in recent months.

Given that the devolution settlements are under further revision, what is certain is that the constitutional framework within which the Law Commission operates is going to continue to evolve, and we will need to keep up with the changes as they happen to be able to adapt accordingly. It would be sensible for us to expect Wales-only projects to become a regular feature of our work programme, and we will need to see what scope will remain for future UK-wide projects—run jointly, of course, with the Scottish and Northern Ireland Law Commissions.

So what about the future? I think it is bright for our Law Commission. Provided we do not lose sight of our core value, and continue to deliver excellence, we stand in a good place to make a positive difference to the law of England and Wales, and therefore to society as a whole. We have demonstrated our ability to respond to major changes in the context in which we operate and so we should feel confident that we are ready for whatever challenges and opportunities the future holds for us.

---

[7] See particularly, chapter 35 (Sir David Lloyd Jones).

# 37

# Implementation of Law Reform Reports: Developments in Scotland

## MALCOLM MCMILLAN

### I INTRODUCTION

In commissioning the future, to what extent should a law reform body such as the Scottish Law Commission devote time and attention to the implementation of Commission recommendations for reform of the law? This raises the issue of what has been referred to at times as an 'after-sales' service—namely what work the Commission does or should do further to submission of a report to Ministers.

Under the Law Commissions Act 1965, the Scottish Law Commission and the Law Commission are advisory bodies, with a statutory remit to give recommendations to Ministers on law reform. They are not executive or legislative bodies. Further, the Commissions' resources are limited, and so any diversion of their resources into implementation issues may detract from making progress with their current workload of law reform projects. So on one view, the Commissions should stick to their statutory remit and make proposals for law reform to Ministers. On that view, following submission of a report to Ministers, the Commissions are largely *functus officio*.

Yet the overall aim of the law reform body is to see improvements in the law. The advisory law reformer no doubt will be very satisfied by completing a project and publishing a report with recommendations. But a deeper satisfaction may lie in seeing these recommendations taken forward and enacted into law. The best law reformers are arguably practical people, interested in seeing improvements to the law take effect and so meeting the needs of society.

Law reform bodies may also take the view that they owe it to their consultees, to their advisory groups of experts, and to the investment in law reform from the public purse generally, to do what they can to encourage and assist with implementation of their recommendations. The law reform body after all will be amongst those most interested in implementation.

The success of a law reform body, and its value to society, may also be measured largely—though by no means wholly—by the rate of implementation of its reports.

Many (though not all) law reform bodies therefore have taken an increasing interest in what happens to their recommendations—in how governments and Parliaments respond to and act upon their law reform reports. Some law reform bodies have devoted resources to assisting with the process of implementation.

To take this route is not of course a new phenomenon for the Scottish Law Commission. In 1976, the Commission discussed one route to implementation in the UK Parliament prior to devolution in 1999, namely the use of Private Members' Bills. The Commission referred to what had been 'an annual and somewhat substantial employment of resources in affording technical assistance to the sponsors of Private Members' Bills designed to give effect to the reforms originally proposed by us'.[1]

In recent years, the Scottish Law Commission has taken a strategic approach to the issue of implementation by the Scottish Government and the Scottish Parliament.[2] As a result, there have been significant developments in the implementation of law reform reports in Scotland. There may be further developments lying ahead in the near future.

A new process for certain Scottish Law Commission Bills has been established in the Scottish Parliament,[3] and used successfully twice. The process was specially designed to increase capacity within the Scottish Parliament for addressing law reform measures, and thereby improve the rate of implementation of Commission recommendations. So this new procedure has opened up another route for implementation of law reform for Scotland, as the Commission celebrated its golden anniversary in 2015.

## II THE SCOTTISH PARLIAMENT: THE DELEGATED POWERS AND LAW REFORM COMMITTEE

The new process in the Scottish Parliament involves a Committee with a specific remit on law reform: the Delegated Powers and Law Reform Committee. The Parliament also made special provision for a 'Scottish Law Commission Bill': a Bill which implements all or part of a report of the Scottish Law Commission, and which meets certain criteria laid down by the Presiding Office of the Parliament. Such Bills are within the remit of the Delegated Powers and Law Reform Committee.

---

[1] Scottish Law Commission, SLC 43, *Eleventh Annual Report* (1977) para 10. See also SLC 41, *Tenth Annual Report* (1976) para 13.

[2] The Scottish Law Commission's remit covers all of Scots law, both areas of law reserved to the UK Parliament under the Scotland Act 1998, and those devolved to the Scottish Parliament. The Commission therefore works with both the UK and Scottish Governments, and the UK and Scottish Parliaments, on implementation of recommendations for reform of Scots law. Most of the Commission's work, however, is on devolved areas of Scots law. So implementation in the devolved context is the focus of this chapter.

[3] See chapter 22 (Hector MacQueen).

## A  Background: The Scottish Parliament

It may be useful to recap briefly[4] on the structure and processes of the Scottish Parliament, in particular as regards the role of Committees.

The Scottish Parliament was established by an Act of the UK Parliament at Westminster: the Scotland Act 1998; with devolved powers to legislate for Scotland on a wide range of matters.

It is a single-chamber Parliament; it has no upper house or second chamber. The Committees of the Parliament therefore play an important role. Each Committee is chaired by a convener, and most Committees have between five and nine Members of the Scottish Parliament as members. The members are selected with regard to the balance of the various political parties and groupings in the Parliament.

A Committee can invite any person to attend a meeting as a witness. Witnesses give evidence or provide documents related to the business of the Committee. The Parliament has a number of mandatory Committees, and sets up subject Committees to look at areas of policy, such as justice.

There are usually three stages of a Bill introduced to the Parliament:

Stage 1:   the Parliamentary Committee or Committees take evidence on the Bill and produce a report on its general principles. If the Parliament agrees, the Bill goes on to Stage 2. If it does not agree, the Bill falls.

Stage 2:   the Bill is considered in detail by a Committee, or occasionally by a Committee of the whole Parliament. Amendments to the Bill can be made at this stage.

Stage 3:   the Bill is again considered at a meeting of the Parliament. Further amendments can be made and the Parliament then debates, and decides whether to pass the Bill in its final form.

Once the Bill has been passed, there is a four-week period during which it may be challenged if it is believed to be outwith the legislative competence (ie outwith the powers) of the Scottish Parliament. If the Bill is not challenged by a reference by a UK Law Officer or a Scottish Law Officer to the UK Supreme Court, it is then submitted by the Presiding Officer to the Queen for Royal Assent. On receiving the Royal Assent, the Bill becomes an Act of the Scottish Parliament.

## B  Implementation of Commission Reports

Returning to the relationship between the Commission, and the Scottish Government and the Scottish Parliament, the record on the implementation of Commission recommendations[5] in areas devolved to the Scottish Parliament has been under scrutiny in recent years. This was initiated by the Commission.

---

[4]  For further detail, see chapter 34 (Lord Pentland).
[5]  See chapter 15 (Shona Wilson Stark).

During the early years following devolution under the Scotland Act 1998, the new Scottish Parliament passed a number of substantial enactments based on Commission reports in various fields including incapacity, debt arrangement and attachment, land law and property law. As the years passed, however, the rate of implementation of Commission reports began to fall overall, even as regards reports on projects which had been referred to the Commission by Ministers themselves. There were no doubt various factors that brought about this trend—heavy government legislative programmes, reflecting the government's political priorities, with insufficient room for Commission Bills in the programmes; together with many competing pressures of business on Scottish parliamentary time, in particular on the Justice Committee within whose remit most of the Commission's devolved law reform work fell.

## C  The Commission's Concerns

Whatever the reasons, the situation emerging on implementation of Commission reports in devolved areas of Scots law was sufficient to set the alarm bells ringing, within the Commission at least, for the fate of the Commission's work, and on the pace of modernisation and development of Scots law.

The Commission's concerns were expressed publicly. In his foreword to the Commission's annual report for 2008, the then Chairman of the Commission, Lord Drummond Young, said:

> It is a matter of some concern that the number of Commission reports that remain unimplemented has risen significantly since devolution. Many of these reports result from Ministerial references, and in nearly all cases the report has not received any official reaction. The rate of implementation of Scottish Law Commission reports now compares unfavourably with other jurisdictions of similar size such as New Zealand and the larger Australian states. The work of law reform bodies is particularly important in such jurisdictions because the opportunities to develop the law through court decisions are not as numerous as in larger jurisdictions. The danger is that Scots law will fall behind the rest of the world's legal systems in responding to the challenges of an era marked by rapid technological and economic change.[6]

## D  Exploring Ways Forward

Lord Drummond Young's statement aroused interest and concern in Scotland. There was a favourable response from Ministers, government officials, Members of the Scottish Parliament and parliamentary officials, and from legal bodies in Scotland with an interest in law reform such as the Law Society of Scotland. There emerged a willingness to work together to find ways to improve the position on the implementation of Commission reports, in order to support the overall aim of modernising the law of Scotland for the benefit of Scottish people and businesses.

---

[6] Scottish Law Commission, SLC 214, *Annual Report 2008* (2009) 5.

Ways in which the situation could be improved at a structural level were considered. These included new procedures in the Parliament, and in the government's planning process for legislation, so as to regularly include law reform measures, and further, increasing government accountability for Commission reports. One result was that the Cabinet Secretary for Justice undertook that Ministers would issue a response to a Commission report within three months of its submission. The responses are made public on the Commission's website. Other methods of implementing particular Commission Bills in the Scottish Parliament were also considered, for example by way of a Member's Bill or a Committee Bill.

Given the pressure of business on the Committees, especially the Justice Committee at this stage, one key way forward to improve the track record on implementation lay in examining ways in which the capacity of the Parliament to consider Commission Bills could be enhanced. That was the focus of the initial work on the issue of improving implementation. Work continues however on other fronts to address the issue of implementation.

In April 2009, and in June 2012, Commission events for Ministers, Members of the Scottish Parliament and officials were held at the Scottish Parliament to discuss the work of the Commission.[7] For the purposes of the discussions, it was helpful to bear in mind a precedent of a special legislative process for law reform in the UK Parliament, the House of Lords procedure for Law Commission Bills.[8] This procedure was introduced on a trial basis in 2008, and reviewed after two Bills passed through it, in 2009 and 2010.[9] The House of Lords adopted the procedure in 2010.[10] The procedure is available for Scottish Law Commission Bills, as well as for Bills from the Law Commission for England and Wales and Bills from both Commissions working jointly.[11]

The willingness of all concerned to address the issue of implementation of Commission reports led to the establishment of working groups, comprising officials from the government, the Parliament and the Commission, to consider the issues and possible ways to address them. The Parliament's Standards, Procedures and Public Appointments (SPPA) Committee considered a report from the working groups; carried out their own review including consultation with other Committees of the Parliament; and then made recommendations to the Parliament.[12]

---

[7] The April 2009 event was hosted by Ian McKee, MSP. The June 2012 event was hosted by Roderick Campbell MSP.

[8] House of Lords Procedure Committee, *Law Commission Bills* (2010–11, HL 30).

[9] One of the Bills, resulting in the Third Parties (Rights Against Insurers) Act 2010, was based on a joint report from the Commissions: Law Commission and Scottish Law Commission, LC 272 and SLC 184, *Third Parties—Rights Against Insurers* (2001).

[10] HL Deb 7 October 2010, vol 721 col 224.

[11] The procedure has now been used for a Bill for Scotland based on a Scottish Law Commission report: the Partnerships (Prosecutions) (Scotland) Act 2013 based on SLC 224, *Report on Criminal Liability of Partnerships* (2011).

[12] This process is described in more detail in M McMillan, 'Law Reform in the Scottish Parliament: A New Process—A New Era?' (2014) 3 *Scottish Parliamentary Review* 95.

## III  SCOTTISH PARLIAMENT DECISION ON THE NEW PROCESS

The Scottish Parliament accepted the recommendations from the SPPA Committee. The Parliament decided on 28 May 2013[13] to make changes to its Standing Orders,[14] to provide a new process for law reform. An existing Committee of the Parliament, the Subordinate Legislation Committee, was re-named the Delegated Powers and Law Reform Committee; and the remit of the Committee was extended to include scrutiny of certain types of Scottish Law Commission Bills.

The Parliamentary Bureau (which organises the business of the Parliament) were given the power, after introduction of a Commission Bill meeting criteria set by the Presiding Officer of the Parliament, to refer the Bill to the Delegated Powers and Law Reform Committee. This Committee would then take the lead in scrutinising the Bill.

The Delegated Powers and Law Reform Committee was given the power to refer such a Bill back to the Parliamentary Bureau if it becomes clear that the Bill does not in fact meet the criteria for such a Bill. The Parliament can then designate another Committee as the new lead Committee, which can take into account any evidence gathered and any views submitted to it by the Delegated Powers and Law Reform Committee. These changes took effect on 5 June 2013.

## IV  CRITERIA FOR SUCH BILLS

The Presiding Officer of the Parliament made a determination on 6 June 2013 setting out the criteria for Commission Bills for this process:

> As well as implementing all or part of a report of the Scottish Law Commission, the definition of a Scottish Law Commission Bill includes criteria to be determined by the Presiding Officer. The Presiding Officer has determined under Rule 9.17A.1 (b) that a Scottish Law Commission Bill is a Bill within the legislative competence of the Scottish Parliament—
>
> (a)  where there is a wide degree of consensus amongst key stakeholders about the need for reform and the approach recommended;
> (b)  which does not relate directly to criminal law reform;
> (c)  which does not have significant financial implications;
> (d)  which does not have significant European Convention on Human Rights (ECHR) implications; and
> (e)  where the Scottish Government is not planning wider work in that particular subject area.[15]

The criteria reflect concerns raised in Parliament that the remit of any new Committee is not extended so as to affect the remit of the existing Justice Committee, or in effect create a second Justice Committee (given an unsatisfactory experience previously in the Parliament of having two Justice Committees in place at the same time in one

---

[13]  Scottish Parliament Official Report 28 May 2013 cols 20374–79.
[14]  Standing Orders of the Scottish Parliament, 4th edn (2014) ch 9.
[15]  Scottish Parliament Business Bulletin (93/2013) 1.

session). The focus of the Parliament was on finding a way forward to address law reform Bills of a certain type: ones that reform the law to reflect changes in society or develop the common law; rather than Bills that are contentious or have a political profile.

Many Commission Bills, emanating from useful law reform projects designed to address a variety of technical legal issues, will qualify for the process. This is subject to the proviso that consultees generally agree that the reform is needed, and on the approach to reform put forward. This process is therefore not a route for implementation of Commission Bills that require decisions by the Parliament on sensitive issues on which there may be a range of views within the country, and across political parties.

## V  FIRST ACT THROUGH THE NEW PROCESS

The first Commission Bill put into the new parliamentary process has now successfully been enacted, following scrutiny by the Delegated Powers and Law Reform Committee. This is the Legal Writings (Counterparts and Delivery) (Scotland) Act 2015. The Bill received Royal Assent on 1 April 2015. It came into effect on 1 July 2015.

The Act makes two significant improvements to Scots law and practice when executing documents. It provides that a document which is to be signed by two or more parties can be executed in counterpart—that is, that each party can sign its own copy of the document, which will then be delivered to other party or parties (or their nominee where there are several of them). The Act also permits delivery of paper legal documents by electronic means, meaning that the document will take legal effect upon such delivery, thus resolving a doubt as to whether faxing or emailing a copy of the signed paper document can make it legally effective.

As a Bill, it qualified for the process on the basis that it would implement recommendations 1–20 of the Commission's *Report on Formation of Contract: Execution in Counterpart*,[16] and that it met the criteria set by the Presiding Officer. The Minister for Energy, Enterprise and Tourism, Fergus Ewing MSP, wrote to the Chairman of the Commission on 28 February 2014,[17] noting that government officials and the Commission team responsible for the Bill gave joint consideration to the matter and came to the shared conclusion that the Bill met the criteria. The annex to his letter set out the detailed reasoning for this conclusion. The Minister arranged for the letter to be laid formally in the Parliament.

In preparing the Bill, the Commission carried out extensive consultation, as is its usual practice. This established that there was a widespread support for the Bill, as required by the first of the criteria set by the Presiding Officer. The Commission published a discussion paper, part 3 of which was devoted to the topic of execution in

---

[16]  SLC 231 (2013).
[17]  The letter can be viewed on the Commission's website at www.scotlawcom.gov.uk/law-reform/law-reform-projects/contract-law-light-draft-common-frame-reference-dcf/.

counterpart.[18] The Commission, jointly with the University of Edinburgh's Centres for Private and Commercial Law, hosted a seminar on execution in counterpart on 29 November 2012, and the Commission published a draft Bill for discussion on its website. Following the seminar, the Commission released a revised draft of the Bill for further comment in January 2013, coinciding with publication of an article on the topic written by a legal practitioner.[19] All responses expressed support for the Bill.

As regards the other specific criteria for such a Bill to qualify for the process, it was agreed that the Bill relates to civil law reform and not to criminal law reform; that no significant cost implications arise, only relatively minor costs in making lawyers aware of the changes; that the Bill does not have implications under the European Convention on Human Rights; and the government confirmed that it was not planning wider work in the area of execution in counterpart.

## VI SECOND ACT THROUGH THE PROCESS

The Scottish Government's *Programme for Scotland 2014–15* stated that the government 'will continue to identify opportunities to make use of the new legislative procedure which was established to improve the rate of implementation of reports from the Scottish Law Commission'.[20] A second Bill, the Succession (Scotland) Bill, was introduced in June 2015 and was dealt with by the Delegated Powers and Law Reform Committee. It covered technical aspects of succession law and was enacted on 3 March 2016. The Act implements a number of recommendations made by the Commission in its *Report on Succession* in 2009.[21]

## VII CONSIDERATION OF THE PROCESS

Questions may arise as to which Bills meet the criteria set and qualify for the process. It could be argued that the criteria are unduly restrictive in effect. It may be noted, however, that criteria set out in a determination by the Presiding Officer can be adjusted more easily in the light of experience than can the Parliament's Standing Orders.

A question was raised in the Parliament by the convener of the Delegated Powers and Law Reform Committee on whether thinking should start about a wider remit for the Committee, in order to look after the maintenance of Scots law. As the process beds in, and confidence in it grows in light of successful experience, it may be that the criteria can be interpreted broadly, or the terms of the criteria can be

---

[18] Scottish Law Commission, SLC DP 154, *Discussion Paper on Formation of Contract* (2012).
[19] P Hally, 'Separate But Legal' (2013) 58(1) *Journal of the Law Society of Scotland* 22. The consultative process is described in the letter from the Minister referred to at n 17 above.
[20] Scottish Government, *One Scotland: The Government's Programme for Scotland 2014–15* (2014) para 223.
[21] SLC 215 (2009).

adjusted in the light of experience. If the latter, there would be a further increase in parliamentary capacity to deal with Commission Bills. Pending any such developments, there are already a number of benefits to law reform as a result of the new process.

The profile of the Commission and of law reform has been raised considerably, within the Scottish Parliament and beyond. The Parliament's Standing Orders provide for a new type of Bill—a 'Scottish Law Commission Bill'; giving recognition to the valuable role and status of the Commission. More parliamentary time and capacity is available to deal with Commission Bills. This will, over time, increase the rate of implementation of Commission reports. Further, within the parliamentary context, an enhanced responsibility has been provided for a Committee which had the expertise to address this type of work, and also some capacity to take on a new area of work.

As a result, improvements can be made to Scots law in order to make the law more efficient and up-to-date, and so make things easier for people, and for businesses and their advisers; as with the first Act through the process. The establishment of the process in the Scottish Parliament has had a further effect on the Scottish Law Commission. Now, and in the future, the Commission must continue to adapt in order to respond to the opportunities that the process offers. Now there may be an onus on the Commission to identify law reform projects that will result in a Bill suitable for the process. The Commission has adapted its methodology for this purpose. In consulting on the content of the next programme of law reform, the Commission specifically asked consultees for suggested projects that would be suitable for the new process. The Commission will also carry out work on current projects with an eye on identifying any reforms that might be put forward as suitable candidates for the process.

These developments also have a resource implication for the Commission in the future. Where a Bill is chosen by the government as a candidate for the process, the Commission needs to support the government Bill team in preparing the Bill for introduction. The Parliament's Standing Orders provide that such a Bill is a 'Scottish Law Commission Bill'. This brings the government and the Commission into a co-operative way of working for the purpose of introducing and handling the Bill. If the Commission and the government did not agree that the government Bill was a 'Scottish Law Commission Bill', in reflecting Commission recommendations, the Bill may not meet the parliamentary requirements for the process.

Once such a Bill has been introduced to the Parliament, a Commissioner supported by a Commission team would also brief the Committee about the Bill, if requested to do so, and give evidence on the Bill to the Committee on behalf of the Commission.

## VIII SUMMARY AND THE FUTURE

It took some years of steady work to achieve an increase in the capacity of the Scottish Parliament to deal with Commission Bills. This involved the Commission in highlighting the need to increase implementation; and for this purpose engaging with Ministers, government and the Parliament through a series of meetings and events.

The welcome result, a new parliamentary process for law reform, reflected the common understanding amongst Ministers, government officials, parliamentarians and the Commission that it is important to find opportunities for Parliament to consider Bills implementing Commission recommendations. The process recognises the valuable role of the Scottish Law Commission in making recommendations to improve, simplify and update the law of Scotland. This has raised the profile of the Scottish Law Commission and of law reform in Scotland, in particular with the Scottish Government and the Scottish Parliament.

With the new process in place and used successfully, another door to the implementation of law reform reports has opened in Scotland. Overall however, it is recognised that the new process is but a partial answer to the issue of finding parliamentary time to implement Commission recommendations.[22]

Given a free hand to commission the future for law reform, the Commission no doubt would seek a seamless process: a law reform project agreed with the government at the outset; the completed law reform report with a Bill submitted by the Commission to Ministers; closely followed by introduction of the Bill to Parliament as a government Bill, following careful legislative planning by the government; and consideration of the Bill by a Parliament with the time and capacity to consider the measure. This would all happen while the lead Commissioner and team who produced the report and Bill were still in place at the Commission, to offer their expertise to assist with the introduction and passage of the Bill by explaining the context and the policies recommended. This would represent the ideal and most efficient model, to a law reform body at least.

Given the realities of political and administrative life, however, the realistic expectation for the future may be that most Commission Bills, including Bills on difficult and complex areas of policy and law, would in due course be taken forward as government Bills in the Scottish Parliament; and that many of these would be considered by lead policy Committees, such as the Justice Committee, alongside a steady flow of other Commission Bills that meet the criteria of being implemented via the Delegated Powers and Law Reform Committee process. This will involve the Commission in continuing to work with the government and the Parliament on law reform project planning, on legislative planning, and on parliamentary capacity for law reform.

---

[22] See, eg, the statement to the Scottish Parliament by Dave Thompson MSP on behalf of the Standards, Procedures and Public Appointments Committee in moving the motion that the Parliament agree to the changes to Standing Orders set out in the Annex to the Report by the Committee: Scottish Parliament Official Report 28 May 2013, col 20375.

So in practice, commissioning the future for the Scottish Law Commission involves the Commission in continuing to work with the government and with Parliament on implementation, at both a strategic level and in relation to individual Commission Bills, and having adequate resources for that as well as for current law reform projects. The work of the law reform body in this day and age does not end with the submission of a report to Ministers.

# 38

# *The Future is a Foreign Country, They Do Things Differently There*

## I INTRODUCTION

LP Hartley began his well-known book, *The Go-Between*, with the words 'The past is a foreign country: they do things differently there.'[1] This served as an introduction to one of the themes in that work: that the past has a rich and misunderstood relationship with the present. On the one hand, we should know our past was lived differently to today, as differently as in another country. On the other hand, the past that actually defines us is one that we do not remember correctly. *The Go-Between* is in part a novel about identity, of how the past shapes a person, whether he realises it or not.

This chapter redirects that opening phrase slightly, to ask how our present relates to our future. What must the law be in the future and how can we make it so? Are we thinking enough about the *future* of law, which will almost certainly be lived differently to today? Or are we trying always to fix the present, doomed to aim for a target that has already passed? If our memory tricks us into thinking we know where we have come from, what determines our perspective on the future?

The chapter therefore addresses two issues in English and Welsh[2] law:

(1)  the distinctive *identity* of the Law Commission; and
(2)  how to understand the 'law' of *tomorrow*.

By looking at law reform outside of just England, the chapter also asks whether, if the past is a different country, might the future be one too? If so, are there other countries today which can help us understand that future and what kind of law reform bodies we will need for it?

---

[*] Particular thanks to Jamie Lee, Shona Wilson Stark and Albert Ruda.
[1] LP Hartley, *The Go-Between* (London, Hamish Hamilton, 1953) 5.
[2] For convenience, but not accuracy, the test will hereafter refer to 'English law'. The chapter focuses on English law, but much of the reasoning will apply to Scotland as well.

## II DISTINCTIVE IDENTITY OF THE LAW COMMISSION

### A National Identity

The Commission is a very particular creature. It has at least *five* characteristics which set it aside from other English bodies today: independence, expertise, collective responsibility, consultation mechanisms and scope.[3]

The first characteristic of the Commission is that it is *independent* (and apolitical). It was designed to be a Commission without ties of loyalty or influence to the executive, judiciary or Parliament but still able to work with them and/or under them to achieve law reform. Similarly, the Commission itself is largely free from political allegiances. Its recommendations are not overtly justified by political motives, and it does not appear that they are covertly so motivated on a significant scale, which is part of their call to be authoritative. It also distinguishes it from the government departments and Ministries who, prior to the 1965 Act, had been the default drafters of reform within their sphere of operations and who continue to do so in some areas, like tax. In a way, the Commission is also more independent than a court, since the court has obligations to the case in front of it, which the Commission does not have. One aspect of independence and lack of political animus has shifted recently: following the new Protocol in 2010,[4] the projects the Commission are *permitted* to undertake now entirely depend on the initial willingness of a government Minister to support reform in that field. This independence and lack of political animus may make the Commission best suited to 'lawyers' law reform' rather than to the policy-driven reform that characterises most government Bills.[5] That said, where conditions are right, policy-based reform has been achieved successfully, such as in family law.[6]

Second, the Commission clearly has distinctive *expertise*. It is chaired by a judge of the High Court, or more recently, of the Court of Appeal, and its Commissioners must have distinguished themselves by holding judicial office, by practising law or as an academic.[7] Commissioners have been enticed by, for instance, opportunities for promotion, such as at the Bench, or by effecting important reforms or by a salary increase. The Commission does not have any lay members,[8] but can have ad hoc appointments,[9] though they do not seem to have been utilised extensively as yet.

---

[3] Similar to the slightly different five noted by Lady Hale in her contribution to this volume (chapter 2): independence, diversity of legal expertise, mission, implementation and methods; *cf* too Kathryn Cronin's five features of the Australian Commission: permanence, wide consultation, public and parliamentary presence, independence and bearing some democratic legitimacy (chapter 6). See also chapter 34 (Lord Pentland), noting 'Intelligibility, accessibility and independence' as guiding principles, and chapter 16 (William Binchy).

[4] Law Commission and Ministry of Justice, LC 321, *Protocol between the Lord Chancellor (on behalf of the Government) and the Law Commission* (2010).

[5] See, eg, A Burrows, 'Some Reflections on Law Reform in England and Canada' (2004) 39 *Canadian Business Law Journal* 320, 330–31.

[6] See also chapters 2 (Lady Hale) and 7 (Eric Clive).

[7] See the Law Commissions Act 1965, s 1. See also, particularly, chapter 9 (Sir Terence Etherton) for an explanation of how to attract senior judges, but the knock-on effect in attracting those already in the Court of Appeal is less clear.

[8] Compare the Northern Ireland Law Commission: Justice (Northern Ireland) Act 2002, s 50(4)(d).

[9] 1965 Act, s 5(1).

One particularly important addition to the Commission is the availability, on second-ment or through the lending of services, of Parliamentary Counsel.[10] The experience on the Commission also shapes those who serve on it. This includes its judicial chairs, its academics and practitioners and its research assistants, all typically going on to even higher office bearing their appreciation for the methods and achievements of the Commission. This expertise distinguishes the Commission from other law reform and law assessment bodies, such as the Judicial College.

The third aspect of the distinctiveness of the Law Commission is the *collective responsibility* of all the Commissioners for the publications of the Commission. It should be admitted that not everyone has the same august view of the Commission. Tony Weir, not noted for obfuscation, omitted the 'emanations' of the Law Commission from his *Casebook on Tort*:

> [B]ecause so many of their proposals in this area are daft: the courts' deference to it is perplexing, for after all, it is not as if a professor or solicitor gained in either wisdom or authority by being appointed to a committee staffed by recent graduates, even if it is presided over by a High Court judge, who will be rewarded for his furlough from sensible decision-making by promotion to the Court of Appeal.[11]

While caustic, Weir's comments neatly raise the fundamental question of how much the members of the Commission can work together to produce a body greater in wisdom or authority than the sum of its parts. The key to that is collective responsibility. The 'microcosm'[12] of the legal world should be represented in the Commission and each report it produces. This is a distinctive characteristic for a law reform body, though it falls short of the obligations of the codification commissions that many civil law countries use.

Fourth, the Commission acts as a clearing-house for the full range of legal actors in England and Wales through its effective *consultation mechanisms*.[13] Those mechanisms are necessarily limited to who is asked, and who otherwise finds the time, to read the lengthy reports and then reply. This will normally be lawyers, reflecting the role of lawyers more generally and raising the risk of a divide between the working of ordinary people and the lawyers writing their laws.

Fifth and finally, the Commission has a vast *scope* of projects which can be investigated, more than previous law reform bodies. The pithiest explanation of this is perhaps still Lord Scarman's, when he chaired the first Law Commission, in reference to the wide obligation in section 3(1) of the 1965 Act to keep all the law under review:

> This comprehensive approach is important; the Act gives the Law Commission wider terms of reference than any previous law reform agency has ever had and enables it to consider proposals against the background of the law as a whole. A patchwork quilt of improvements unrelated to the whole pattern of the law is apt to create as many problems as it solves.[14]

[10] See chapter 20 (Andrew Burrows).
[11] T Weir, *A Casebook on Tort*, 10th edn, (London, Thomson Sweet and Maxwell, 2004) vii.
[12] C Sutherland, 'To "Mend the Lawes, That Neids Mendement": A Scottish Perspective on Lawyers as Law Reformers' Commonwealth Association of Law Reform Agencies Conference (2015) 11 *cf* 19.
[13] See particularly, chapter 4 (Paul Mitchell) sections V–VI.
[14] L Scarman, 'The Law Commission' (1972) 1 *Anglo-American Law Review* 31, 33. On Lord Scarman's vision, see further chapter 4 (Paul Mitchell).

## B International Peers

These five characteristics make the Law Commission distinctive in England, and a similar statement could be made of the Scottish Commission, but can the Commission learn something from law reform and law reform bodies in other foreign countries? A brief introduction to some foreign law reform bodies provides some interesting perspectives.

### i American Law Institute

The American Law Institute's (ALI) Restatements are extensive collections of the rules on a given topic, such as restitution or intentional torts, where the reporters have attempted to identify the majority rule and any significant minority rule, amongst the 50 states. The Restatements' approach to law reform is distinct from that of a Law Commission. The ALI's purpose was to assist in the development of the law in America, in the face of federal complexity and a disinclination on the part of legislators to getting 'lawyers' law' right. A Restatement does not need enacting, indeed it is not written in a form which is amenable to legislation without further work. The work presents a rule, followed by a commentary on that rule. Legislation based on template provisions is well known in the USA, such as the Model Penal Code and the Uniform Commercial Code (UCC). Rather, the Restatements rely on their authority and utility to persuade individual legal actors to use them. Their target audience is trial judges, aiming to equip them with the research to sort out how to analyse the issues in front of them and work towards a well-informed answer.[15] Reporters vary in how much they promote the 'best' solution while working in the grey area of what is a majority rule and what is a minority rule. The law is certainly clearer and more accessible having been through the process of being restated, the reporters having sacrificed five to ten years on the project. The Restatements also occupy a distinctive place in academic careers. For many years the reporters were some of the most famous law professors and they worked on clearly doctrinal material based on a close reading of vast numbers of cases from different states. Even from the creation of the ALI in 1923, that kind of doctrinal work was not as valued in the USA as in England, and the position is not clearly different today. The reporter's work is still valued, but anecdotally it is increasingly undertaken by significant scholars of perhaps less renown and at what may previously have been less prestigious law schools. The work is onerous and lengthy, affording as recompense the opportunity to master an area of law and become a distinguished commentator on that field for the future.

What makes the ALI process so distinctive is the combination of meticulous, lengthy investigation in the hands of one or two reporters and assistants, combined

---

[15] See, eg, B Cardozo, *The Growth of the Law* (New Haven, Yale University Press, 1924) 9: 'it will be something less than a code and something more than a treatise. It will be invested with unique authority, not to command, but to persuade. It will embody a composite thought and speak a composite voice. Universities and bench and bar will have had a part in its creation. I have great faith in the power of such a restatement to unify our law.'

with a gruelling review process. A series of drafts must be presented to the ALI Council, their working groups and any members who choose to review that particular Restatement. The membership of the ALI encompasses judges, practitioners and academics, and the drafts are subjected to detailed critique before they are approved. This collegiate responsibility is far more demanding than any process of consultation. At times, each sentence in a book-length, sometimes multi-volume, work has to be justified. The process produces a honed and fully reasoned product, designed to last a decade or more. The review process in the ALI does not detract from the ownership the ALI as a body has. Members of the ALI contribute their time and effort to review a draft Restatement because it is intellectually demanding, they recognise its value and because there is prestige in contributing in this way. At the same time, each edition of the Restatement is commonly linked to the names of its reporters, even if technically only the accompanying Reporter's Notes are their exclusive work.

An institute like the ALI was the model that the European Law Institute favoured, since its creation in 2011.[16] This endeavour was led within continental Europe, but featured significant UK membership, such as Sir Francis Jacobs as its first President, and Diana Wallis its second, other leading members include Lord Thomas, John Sorabji, Hugh Beale and others.

Can England and Wales benefit from understanding the ALI and its relative, the ELI? An 'institute' of this kind might not be an English national model yet, and a significant shift in funding and research profiles would be necessary first. Nonetheless, it is a model which, with the right parties, can lead to significant success. Indeed, it has already had some success in private hands: two 'restatements' of English law has already been published,[17] with a distinguished advisory group albeit one less elaborate than that which the ALI uses.

In part, the ALI fulfils a particular niche in a federal system lacking a Supreme Court unifying its common law.[18] It seeks to find consensus where the law is not exactly 'common', which is not the same problem as English law always faces. There is a single line of authority in England but it is practical limits of time and money which prevent many cases from following it up to its apogee, the Supreme Court, and thus in effect, the Court of Appeal is often the last court in England, dealing with thousands of cases a year to the Supreme Court's hundred or so; indeed, many important questions do not even proceed past the High Court. In England, staying updated in the face of the mass of new cases at a level lower than the Supreme Court is difficult, a task professional bodies and subscription services attempt to ease. By comparison, the ALI works slowly to collect a vast resource which is only up to date at the point of publication (if then). However, this mechanism highlights that individual decisions can be put into a more or less coherent pattern which can be

---

[16]  *cf* this question in reverse, in chapter 24 (Hugh Beale).

[17]  A Burrows, *A Restatement of the English Law of Unjust Enrichment* (Oxford, OUP, 2012); A Burrows, *A Restatement of the English Law of Contract* (Oxford, OUP, 2016).

[18]  As opposed to a Supreme Court for federal matters and a Supreme Constitutional Court, subject to which states have granted wider jurisdiction to the Courts: 28 USC §1251 et seq, and various special statutes.

useful for years, even decades afterwards. English law itself is a testament to this, seen in the Law Commission's own reports, which can be cited for a significant period after their publication. Particularly for England to consider is how the ALI draws on a range of legal actors and skills in honing its reports, providing a level of 'ownership' for practitioners and judges. This could extend beyond even the rational force that the Law Commission builds for its reports through careful reasoning and its consultation mechanisms. Finally, the ALI focuses on 'lawyers' law', and particularly that law which trial judges most use; it is also more focused on private law topics, also in part a function of the institutional structures other fields of law have, as well as the interests of the academics who do most of the research going into the Restatements. English law would likely wish a wider field of reform, but that does not deny the value in understanding the merits dedicated academics or practitioners, appointed ad hoc, could bring to specific projects.

Perhaps an interim step is a hybrid model, since we already possess a full-time Law Commission, as opposed to the part-time ALI reporters. Such a step would be a prestigious advisory body being added to the Commission's structures.[19] The cost would be minimal, but the body could be large enough to have constituencies, such as judicial, legislative, practitioner and academic, filled with members selected on the basis of their experience and expertise. The body need not formally be part of the Law Commission, and would not detract from the consultation exercise itself. The reports from the Law Commission could be honed even further by such a body. It would also allow for recognition of the work that those outside the Commission do to assist in the honing of the reports, recognition greater than merely noting that a particular person has replied to the consultation. Individually useful replies from the consultation can still be referred to in later reports.

## ii Uniform Code Commissioners

The benefits of the ALI can also be contrasted with the US Uniform Code Commissioners. The Commissioners create, and consider amendments to, articles within the UCC. The Commissioners are exclusively practising attorneys, rather than from a range of backgrounds within the study and use of commercial law. They also produce the Official Comments of the UCC Permanent Editorial Board (PEB) and the Permanent Editorial Board Commentaries, as authoritative explorations of the text. There is an extensive body of case law from jurisdictions which have accepted the UCC. The idea of having a Uniform Code is well understood where there are different legal systems to be made uniform, just as there once was a clear need for a 'common' law in England. Other attempts, such as the Lando Commission for contract law, or the Principles of European Tort Law, have had modest success in other countries in Europe, though they are hardly even taught in law faculties in England. The most advanced European form of this proposal was the Draft Common Frame of Reference, an ambitious project which produced significant scholarship on what the law was, but perhaps less successfully sought to argue what the law across

---

[19] *cf* the lay advisory body that had existed in Canada: discussed in chapter 11 (Yves Le Bouthillier).

Europe should be. The idea of 'uniform' law would be to take the idea of a restatement too far for the English and Welsh jurisdiction, but there is something to be said for an advisory body, or for a way to manage the morass of legal material that is being generated within England and Wales.

### iii German Reformers

Having considered the common law and pan-European law reform bodies, we might turn to consider others, in particular, those from the civil law traditions. Some of these create ad hoc bodies to deal with particular issues once those issues have attained sufficient attention to be deemed worthy of reform, ironically in a process not dissimilar to how a committee of academics led the work on the Draft Criminal Code, under the aegis of the Law Commission. Germany appears to be in this category, as is France.[20] Taking Germany as an example, for a moment, Law Reform Commissions, howsoever called, are not common in German legal thinking.[21] That is not to say that commissions have not played a key role in drafting successive codes, including the civil code (Bürgerliches Gesetzbuch or BGB), as they have. But each commission is largely ad hoc. Barring creation, and some subsequent amendment, the nature of the legal system is that of an established code, leading to judicial interpretation of that code. German courts feel able, in appropriate cases at least, to creatively interpret these rules, rather than wait for their form to be changed. One of the most famous examples is the development of contractual good faith in German law.[22] The civil code in particular, the, has undergone significant reform only rarely since 1900 when it was enacted, the most significant being the *Schuldrechtsmodernisierung* or *Shuldrechtsreform* of 2001. The trigger for these reforms was the European Community Directive on the Sale of Consumer Goods dating from 1999 which had to take place by the end of 2001. However, the scale of the changes, amendments to over 300 provisions, represents a German use of this opportunity to make thorough changes to the law.[23] These reforms were based initially on an earlier reform proposal drafted by a committee of scholars in 1992, which had attracted little interest since 1994; the hasty process of revision undertaken in 2001 then ignored ten years of scholarly debate and such projects as the new Dutch civil code, the Lando Commission's Principles of European Contract Law, and the UNIDROIT Principles.[24] Interestingly, also in 2001, a purely government-directed reform of the law of damages took place with little to no wider involvement.[25]

---

[20]  And Quebec, see chapter 11 (Yves Le Bouthillier) n 1.

[21]  See, in English, JA Bargenda, 'The Grass is (a Bit) Greener on the Other Side: Praising the Idea of Law Reform' (2015) 40 *Australian Bar Review* 136.

[22]  Especially §§242 and 157; see esp S Whittaker and R Zimmermann, 'Good Faith in European Contract Law: Surveying the Landscape' in S Whittaker and R Zimmermann (eds), *Good Faith In European Contract Law* (Cambridge, CUP, 2000) 18–31.

[23]  See generally, R Zimmermann, *The New German Law of Obligations: Historical and Comparative Perspectives* (Oxford, OUP, 2005).

[24]  See, eg, J Gordley, 'Review of The New German Law of Obligations by Reinhard Zimmermann' [2006] *German Law Journal* 729.

[25]  See generally, G Wagner, *Das Neue Schadensersatzrecht* (Baden-Baden, Nomos, 2002).

By comparison with the 30-year gestation period of the BGB itself, the reform was sudden and did not involve an independent law reform body. Ad hoc committees of lawyers were the prime method for the first reforms, typically involving significant academics, as well as representatives from the Ministry of Justice, the judiciary and practitioners. Such a method was, in fact, just how the BGB and other historic provisions were created.[26] The key step is having a well-resourced pool for each committee, drawn often from a well-funded academic sphere on the one hand and practitioners and judges on the other, with prestige and honour for all those who take part. The German system of two extensive state-based examinations and the two year internship rota undertaken by all lawyers requires significant time and effort from many established lawyers, so contributing to law reform is only one more form of public service, one with even more widely acknowledged value than in England.

*iv La Comisión General de Codificación (CGC)*

So much for Germany, but it should not be forgotten that civilian legal systems are also very diverse and complex. There are a number of Codification Commissions in civil law countries, a leading example of which is Spain.[27] Spanish law adopted its first criminal code in 1822, and its first civil code in 1889. From 1843,[28] the CGC has been its leading body to shape and reshape the codes. That said, Spanish law has also used ad hoc commissions, often within Ministries and across Ministries, to drive reform, particularly large-scale reform. The CGC can be requested by the Minister of Justice to review a particular area of law and present recommendations, but it can also elect to review legal questions on its own motion. The body is divided into five sections: civil, commercial, public, criminal and procedural. Notice at once that there is an entire section devoted to procedural law, mirroring the greater academic attention paid on the continent to a specific category of procedure, including evidence and remedies, rather than the English tendency to bundle them up with substantive law. Having achieved codification, the work of the CGC is focused on keeping the law up to date, clear and open to appropriate improvements. However, the terms 'post-codification' and indeed 'de-codification' are well known in Spain, capturing the idea of movements away from the unificatory pull of a code.[29] The Spanish codes, perhaps some more than others, are still open to politically driven amendment, though perhaps on a lesser scale than in England. This process can lead to a fragmentation of the law, and the CGC resists this. It does so through careful and detailed law reform proposals, scrutinised by academics and other lawyers.

---

[26] S Vogenauer, 'An Empire of Light? Learning and Lawmaking in the History of German Law' [2005] *CLJ* 481, 492–93.

[27] For this purpose, essentially the historically delimited kingdom of Castille. See generally, C Jerez Delgado and MJ Pérez García, 'La Comisión General De Codificación y su Labor en la Modernización del Derecho de Obligaciones' *Revista Jurídica de la Universidad Autónoma de Madrid*, no 19, 2009-I, 155; EI Pastor, 'La Comisión General de Codificación (1843–1997): de la Codificación Moderna a la Descodificación Contemporánea' *Anuario de Historia del Derecho Español*, tomo LXXXiii, 2013, 65.

[28] Real Decreto de 19 de agosto de 1843. See now Real Decreto 160/1997, de 7 de febrero.

[29] See, eg, JA Escartín Ipiéns, 'Política y Sociedad en los Procesos de Elaboración de las Leyes Civiles' *Revista de Derecho Civil*, vol I, núm 2 (abril–junio 2014) 1, 3.

Its Commissioners are significant legal actors, often senior professors. Thus, even those states with codified law can embrace the need to review those codes.

We can see that 'law reform commissions' are in fact known to codified legal systems, or systems from the civil law tradition, as the Spanish example shows. In addition, many of the workings of those Commissions are not obviously different from that known to the common law. There is then a delicate balance with the courts' interpretation of the law, including in those systems where judges cannot formally *make* law, such as the Spanish. According to the Spanish civil code, article 1(1) and (6), the sources of the Spanish legal system are statutes, customs and general legal principles, and the repeated doctrine only of the Supreme Court can complement those primary sources. That is, courts lower than the Supreme Court cannot give judgments which are sources of law, and only the *established* jurisprudence of the Supreme Court, not a single or even a few decisions, can do more than supplement the primary sources of law. It would be in practice be possible for legal principles to be creatively interpreted, but certainly by this stage, the civil code having been in force for over 125 years, that is rare. At the same time, the Spanish,[30] just like the French,[31] legal system requires judges to resolve the cases in front of them so an answer must be found somewhere. Ultimately, the role of the CGC is to make sure that judges do not have to extend themselves too far from the plain wording of the code. Indeed, in September 2015 the Spanish Council of Ministers reaffirmed the wide role of the CGC in promoting legal certainty, clarity of law for citizens, simplification of legal rules and precise language.[32] At the same time, it affirmed their independence and key role in bringing together legal voices from across Spain. Interestingly, it also extended their role from pre-legislative measures to merely regulatory ones, increasing the reach of its 'softer' power. These purposes may provide further ways of looking at English law, and the Law Commission and its work.

### v  Swedish Parliamentary Processes

It might also be worthwhile to consider more generally how legislation should be carried out. Parliament has many conscientious legislators but much of the content and sadly too often the form of that legislation comes nowhere close to the standard of the Law Commissions' work. One matter for the future is to consider how the legislation not related to the Commission could be improved. Sweden provides a fascinating comparison here.[33] Generally governed through consensus without a single party having an overall majority, the Swedish legislature reforms carefully and after meaningful consultation with political groups and civil society. Any issue of upcoming legislation is examined by a commission of inquiry.[34] These typically involve

---

[30]  Código Civil, art 1(7).
[31]  Code Civil, art 4.
[32]  Diario La Ley, No 8615, Sección Hoy es Noticia, 29 de Septiembre de 2015.
[33]  See generally, T Bull and I Cameron, 'Legislative Review for Human Rights Compatibility: A View from Sweden' in M Hunt, H Hooper and P Yowell (eds), *Parliament and Human Rights: Redressing the Democratic Deficit* (Oxford, Hart Publishing, 2015).
[34]  Based on a constitutional requirement (IG 7:2) that government business should be well prepared before a decision is taken. More technical issues might go before a departmental inquiry.

parliamentarians, former judges of the Supreme Court and/or law professors as well as governmental and academic experts. After the Commission's report and the consultations on it are concluded, the matter goes before the Law Council, a six-person panel of Supreme Court judges, four active and two retired. The membership of the Council is nominated by the courts, not the government. The Council's influential and public advice covers matters of logic and legal quality as well as being a constitutional safeguard. These two stages are significant, in parliamentary discussions and throughout public debate, in how the government approaches law reform. There are even categories for protecting certain rights, potential legislation about which receives even greater scrutiny. Against a background of culturally valued and robust legislative processes, Law Commissions themselves will have different, often narrower, roles.

### vi Swiss Semi-Direct Democracy

Similarly, law reform informed by the general populace is a useful comparison. In its most extreme form, this could encompass a function like the 'semi-direct' democracy in Switzerland.[35] There, draft federal legislation is made available for comment by cantonal governments, political parties and civil society in a formalised opinion poll which also offers the opportunity for changes to be proposed. The results are considered by a dedicated parliamentary committee and then debated in Parliament. Parliament, and its committee, pay attention to the public consultation particularly because should they not, and 50,000 citizens sign a petition, a referendum on the legislation must be held. It is not uncommon for there to be referenda on a dozen pieces of legislation a year, often grouped together into sets of three or four. Voting in the referenda largely takes place by post, and is not obligatory, save in the particular example of a 'popular initiative', where 100,000 citizens demand a change in the Constitution. This process clearly has significant risks. In 2014 a referendum led to 50.3 per cent of votes in favour of imposing quotas on immigration, and thus jeopardising Swiss access to the European single market.[36] The implications of this vote are still not clear, with a three-year deadline to resolve the apparent inconsistency between the constitutional obligation to abide by the vote and the treaty obligations with the EU. The proposal had only been supported by one of the governing parties and any 'wriggle room' in the referendum question's formulation will now be key for the other parties.

### III  WHAT IS THE 'LAW' OF TOMORROW?

Understanding the identity of the Law Commission today helps to ask what Commission, and other reform bodies, must be for the future. The first question is what 'law'

---

[35] W Haller, *The Swiss Constitution in Comparative Context* (Zürich/St. Galen, Dike, 2009) 221–37.
[36] See, eg, www.bfs.admin.ch/bfs/portal/de/index/themen/17/03/blank/key/2014/013.html in German or French.

it should reform, the second is by what means the reform should take place. After that we can consider the shape and accessibility of the law itself. Other questions, particularly about how to maintain the commitment of government and Parliament to law reform in the face of the ever growing pressures on the legislative timetable and on the Ministry of Justice, deserve to be reconsidered once the impact of the new Protocol is clearer.[37]

## A  What Law Should Be Reformed?

The work of the Commission has focused on *legislation* to reform rules of *substantive law*, including remedies. However, there is significant benefit in addressing other forms of law, particularly the creation and reform of *legal reasoning* as well as *procedural and evidential rules*. That benefit could be particularly felt in the future, especially a future of decreased government spending where legal process is even less available to the average person.[38] Since it is not clear that these areas are being developed entirely satisfactorily by other means, there is a clear need for a body like the Commission to contribute. It may be that an alternative non-governmental body would have to take on this task in an age of austerity but the Law Commission could still play a role in creating and assisting that body.

There is little guidance in the relevant statutory materials about what idea of law the Law Commission should employ. Indeed, it is ironic that the two statutes affecting the English and Welsh Law Commission are so short, when the legislative output from that Commission has been so large. The obligations of the English and Welsh and Scottish Commissions do not themselves state that substantive or procedural rules are the focus of the Commissions. Section 3(1) of the 1965 Act imposes on those Commissions a duty to:

> take and keep under review all the law with which they are respectively concerned with a view to its systematic development and reform, including in particular the codification of such law, the elimination of anomalies, the repeal of obsolete and unnecessary enactments, the reduction of the number of separate enactments and generally the simplification and modernisation of the law.

This does not actually refer to 'reform', nor does the title of the Commissions: a subtle reminder that the line between 'law reform' and 'law making' is hard to draw and can be fiercely debated.[39]

Section 3(1) does not only concern substantive law. A code could just as easily be of procedure, evidence, or of an institution or legal actor. Similarly, anomalies

---

[37]  See chapter 9 (Sir Terence Etherton) for an analysis of the historical decline in governmental support for Law Commission work, and the attempts made to correct that course.

[38]  For a radical view on the substantive shift which might be necessary, see N McBride, 'Tort Law and Criminal Law in an Age of Austerity' in M Dyson (ed), *Unravelling Tort and Crime* (Cambridge, CUP, 2014).

[39]  eg C Sutherland, 'To "Mend the Lawes, That Neids Mendement": A Scottish Perspective on Lawyers as Law Reformers' Commonwealth Association of Law Reform Agencies Conference (2015) 7–8.

(to be eliminated) are not only substantive. For instance, surely it would be anomalous for one area of law to claim that statutes in its field required a special form of statutory interpretation? And yet, it took repeated decisions of the House of Lords before tax law was subjected to the same rules of statutory interpretation.[40]

Indeed, as regards *legal reasoning*, the Commission could perform a vital role in providing new ways of thinking about law as much as of thinking through problems within the law.[41] This function is partly carried out by the scoping and consultation papers the Commission puts out, introducing their reasoning and, through the process of effective consultation, pooling and combining different ways of thinking about the law. The Commissions' 'pre-consultation', with stakeholders, is another layer of the process. However, both processes are indirect and clearly treated as a stepping stone to substantive law reforms. The same is true of the effort (and word count) taken to explain the proposals when they come out in reports, since that understanding is typically focused on the proposal itself. Something close to reforming legal reasoning occurs when the Commission analyses a 'rule', which really means a principle with effects in multiple discrete substantive areas, such as *The Forfeiture Rule and the Law of Succession*.[42] Dame Mary Arden has noted the important function of the Law Commission in pushing forward the use of explanatory notes: they developed a practice that went on to become standard across all forms of legislation.[43]

The most notable attempt (and failure) from the Commissions occurred very early in their existence, the joint report on *The Interpretation of Statutes*.[44] The report was presaged in the Law Commission's *First Programme of Law Reform*, Item XVII of which said:

> It is evident that a programme of law reform, which must necessarily use the instrument of legislation, depends for its successful realisation on the interpretation given by the courts to the enactments in which the programme is embodied.[45]

The Programme accepted that many problems of interpretation were often originally problems of drafting, one of the key roles of the Commission itself.[46] The resulting statute was very simple, one page long with four simple clauses. It clarified the materials to be admissible, but continued the exclusion of Hansard and other reports of Parliament as guides to interpretation. This was on practical grounds, for instance that they were likely to be inaccessible to those who would need to live their lives in accordance with the statutes. However, the Commissions proposed that the work of any committee or Royal Commission (and indeed the Law Commission) which had

---

[40] *Barclays Mercantile Business Finance Ltd v Mawson (Inspector of Taxes)* [2004] UKHL 51, [2005] 1 AC 684; see esp [29] and [34].

[41] *cf* the last Federal Law Commission in Canada which, until its abolition, included the task of developing new approaches and new concepts of law: chapter 11 (Yves Le Bouthillier) explains this history.

[42] LC 295 (2005).

[43] Chair's conference introduction to panel 5.

[44] LC 21 and SLC 11 (1969).

[45] LC 1 (1965).

[46] LC 21 and SLC 11, n 44 above, para 5.

preceded the Act be admissible. Ultimately this report was cited in *Pepper v Hart*[47] where the House of Lords admitted Hansard in an effort to assess a tax dispute, but the 1969 report was overshadowed by the more recent (1990) and permissive report of the New Zealand Law Commission in favour of allowing parliamentary reports to be admissible as evidence.[48] The irony is that *Pepper v Hart* was a tax dispute, like a few of the other examples in the Law Commission paper.[49] A further irony is that the Law Commission does not now report on legal methods but, after *Pepper v Hart*, its reports *are* admissible evidence for statutory interpretation.

In fact, a process to integrate, promulgate and retrain is an important part of legal change. To quote John Bell:

> In a sense, the argument that simply enacting a text will not make a significant change in the law is not a new insight. Public lawyers have known this for a long time. For example, in the Glorious Revolution of 1688, Parliament not merely passed an Act acknowledging William and Mary to be the lawful sovereigns, but also made the judges swear an oath of allegiance to the new monarchs. In more recent times, the reunification of Germany was followed by a very substantial purge of the East German judiciary. When incorporating the European Convention, not merely did Parliament pass the text of the Human Rights Act 1998, but its entry into force was delayed until 2000 in order that the Judicial Studies Board could conduct a re-education of the judiciary at all levels in how to implement it ... change in the law is as much a matter of winning hearts and minds of lawyers, as it is in enacting texts. The conception of law that underpins this public law understanding is that law is essentially a social institution, a set of norms by which a community operates. Accordingly, merely changing certain rules without altering the social attitudes and practices is bound to fail.[50]

The Law Commission is actually well placed to bring together different important perspectives on the nature of legal reasoning and thereby 'win', through persuasion and enlightenment. As noted above, few other bodies have the range of judicial, practitioner and academic strength, nor the ability to consult effectively and widely. There is no other body which effectively develops issues of legal reasoning in an accessible way for all. Academics specialised in jurisprudence do, but that is only one corner of a diverse but important set of issues, from statutory interpretation to epistemology and statistics, from the drafting and interpretation of contracts through to the extent of judicial authority to create law, from the principles of precedent and distinguishing cases to how to read historical or comparative materials. These are not irrelevant matters. Some could be the subject of legislation, but even a consultation or scoping paper could bring significant assistance to those using the law. Surely continuing professional development is not only about substantive law, but also about how to be lawyers.

---

[47] *Pepper v Hart* [1993] AC 593 (HL).

[48] New Zealand Law Commission, NZLC 17, *A New Interpretation Act: To Avoid 'Prolixity and Tautology'* (1990).

[49] See, eg, LC 21 and SLC 11 (1969), n 44 above, fn 87, para 50 and fn 166.

[50] J Bell, 'Review of N Jansen, "The Making of Legal Authority"' (2011) 74 *MLR* 150, 151. Indeed, in the age of both top-down and bottom-up harmonisation, can we meaningfully harmonise or unify the law if there are processes underneath it which will draw it apart again?

As regards *procedural and evidential rules*, the Law Commission has played a bit part in reform.[51] For example, the most significant shift in decades in rules on police procedure and evidence came without input from the Law Commission: the Police and Criminal Evidence Act 1984 (PACE).[52] In the climate of the 1981 Brixton Riots and the Scarman report into the those riots,[53] the Act was the direct result of the Royal Commission on Criminal Procedure in 1981 chaired by Sir Cyril Philips.[54] It is unclear why a Royal Commission particularly was better suited to undertake the work, rather than, for instance, asking the Law Commission, then over a decade old and with codification a key goal. There are apparently no official records explaining the decision.[55] When the Royal Commission was engaged, it instead built upon a number of earlier works, particularly the ill-fated eleventh report of the Criminal Law Revision Committee from 1972.[56] That report had foundered largely on the proposal that adverse inferences could be drawn from a suspect's silence in the police station, a change that actually took a further decade to be implemented.[57]

The Civil Procedure Rules Committee and the Criminal Procedure Rules Committee now in practice lead in their respective fields. First, the Civil Procedure Rules represent a single, uniform procedural code applicable across not only the High Court but also the County Court, each of which had previously operated under its own set of rules.[58] The reasons for the review of the former rules, presided over by Lord Woolf, which led to his *Access to Justice* report of 1996, and in due course the preparation and adoption of the 1998 Civil Procedure Rules,[59] were to improve access to justice and reduce the costs of litigation; to reduce the complexity of the rules and modernise terminology; and to remove unnecessary distinctions of practice and procedure. These mirror the obligations of the Law Commissions quite well. The Criminal Procedure Rules 2005 were the first unified set of rules of English criminal procedure, and came into force on 4 April 2005.[60] Rather than spend '3 or 4 years preparing a complete code', the Rule Committee 'decided to draft the overriding objectives and that part of the code relating to case management, and consolidate and tidy up the some 500 individual rules which it had inherited', then turn to replace individual inherited rules over time.[61] In this way the

---

[51] Perhaps the earliest was LC 16, *Blood Tests and Proof of Paternity in Civil Proceedings* (1968), implemented in the Family Law Reform Act 1969, since amended. Other than that, the leading examples to 2001 are perhaps LC 216, *The Hearsay Rule in Civil Proceedings* (1993); LC 245, *Evidence in Criminal Proceedings: Hearsay* (1997); LC 267, *Double Jeopardy and Prosecution Appeals* (2001); LC 270, *Limitation of Actions* (2001); LC 273, *Evidence of Bad Character in Criminal Proceedings* (2001).

[52] M Zander, 'PACE (The Police and Criminal Evidence Act 1984): Past, Present, and Future', LSE Law, Society and Economy Working Papers 1/2012.

[53] L Scarman, *The Brixton Disorders, 10–12 April 1981* (Cmnd 8427, 1981).

[54] See, eg, R Munday, 'The Royal Commission on Criminal Procedure' (1981) 40 *CLJ* 193.

[55] Zander, n 52 above, fn 2.

[56] Criminal Law Revision Committee, *Evidence (General)* (Cmnd 499, 1972).

[57] Criminal Justice and Public Order Act 1994, ss 34–37; see, eg, *R v Argent* [1997] 2 Cr App R 27 (CA).

[58] Respectively the Rules of the Supreme Court 1965, and the County Court Rules 1981.

[59] Under the Civil Procedure Act 1997.

[60] The groundwork had been laid by the Courts Act 2003, ss 68–74.

[61] Judicial Studies Board, Criminal Justice Reforms Handbook, November 2004. There is also a Consolidated Criminal Practice Direction issued by the LCJ (as provided for by Courts Act 2003, s 74) sitting alongside the rules.

rules are incomplete in a sense and they also do not deal with all of the law of procedure.[62] The purpose behind this Committee was also strikingly similar to that of the Law Commissions, as a result of Auld LJ's *Review of the Criminal Courts of England and Wales*.[63] Auld LJ was much exercised by the complexity of the task facing those involved in the workings of criminal law, and called first for the Law Commission to draft a Bill consolidating primary and secondary legislation, and then for a rules committee to be formed.[64] Yet the Law Commission was not so asked, the government's White Paper, *Justice for All*,[65] accepted Auld LJ's findings, but moved straightaway to creating the Criminal Procedure Rules Committee in sections 69–73 of the Courts Act 2003. It also amended the Civil Procedure Rules Committee and created the Family Procedure Rules and Family Procedure Rules Committee,[66] which Auld LJ had not addressed but which the government argued would necessarily be affected.[67] These new rules and bodies can achieve a great deal, and have already done so, but until they can amend primary legislation, the Law Commission still has a role to play. As Ian Dennis' contribution to this volume notes, the Law Commission's latest plan to codify sentencing represents an interesting twist for the future.[68]

The common law has often found changing remedies easier than substantive law, and this may have played some role in addressing sentencing now. However, the common law has also focused more generally on procedure more than substance, so it is harder to see why procedural and evidential rules were not easier to change than substantive rules of law. For the Commission in particular, having the right personnel seems to be particularly important to reforming the law. There have hitherto been few who specialised in evidence and procedure, though remedies are things that most common[69] lawyers should be able to turn their hands to. However, a possible remedy, the ability to appoint ad hoc Commissioners, perhaps as part-time, seems not to have been given much use in practice.

## B  What Means Should be Used to Reform the Law?

Other sections of this volume explore in detail the different means of law reform so only a passing note will be made here, touching on techniques and content.

The Commission has long known that attitudes towards the law, and a lack of understanding of the law, can be significant and important. Two good examples of this are the *Data Sharing between Public Bodies* report from July 2014,[70] which

---

[62] The Law Commission's most recent paper on evidence was the LC 325, *Expert Evidence in Criminal Procedure in England and Wales* (2011), which is being given effect, at least in part, by CPD V (Evidence) Pt 33A.3–33A.5.

[63] See, eg, www.justice.gov.uk/courts/procedure-rules/criminal/notes.

[64] London, HMSO, 2001, 271–80.

[65] Cm 5563, 2002, para 4.51.

[66] Courts Act 2003, ss 75–79.

[67] Courts Act 2003, explanatory notes, paras 170–71.

[68] See chapter 12 (Ian Dennis).

[69] For this purpose, including Chancery lawyers.

[70] LC 351 (2014).

assessed a range of hurdles to effective data sharing, and two reports on housing in 2008, dealing with *Proportionate Dispute Resolution*,[71] and on *Encouraging Responsible Letting*.[72] Its report into *Post-legislative Scrutiny* in 2006 is a prime example of the merit in assessing more than simply the content of legal rules.[73]

Statutory change is clearly important but it is not uncommon for the changes recommended to be implemented by non-legislative means, such as through executive power by the making of regulations, by written parliamentary answer or changes to guidelines or associated rules.[74] Yet even here, its (pre-legislative) reports are important as tools for understanding the draft law, should it prove uncertain in practice. Significant legal change and clarity has been brought about by these reports.[75]

Yet it is abundantly clear that Commission reports are often cited by courts even in areas of law where it is difficult to legislate. For example, the Draft Criminal Code of 1989,[76] has been cited by courts extensively. That Draft Code was only achieved through the work of an academic team headed by JC Smith.[77] The Draft Code provisions have been adopted by courts in a number of instances, famously in the leading case on the meaning of recklessness in the Criminal Damage Act 1971, *R v G*.[78] There Lord Bingham led the House of Lords in expressly adopting Draft Code clause 18(c).[79] Prior to the replacement and extension of inchoate criminal liability for incitement in the Serious Crime Act 2007, Part II, itself originally a Law Commission recommendation, judges had already adopted clause 47 of the Commission's Draft Code, dealing with incitement.[80] On occasion other areas of law have adopted, typically only partially, the Law Commission's recommendations, such as in *Restitution: Mistakes of Law*[81] through *Kleinwort Benson v Lincoln City Council* in 1999,[82] and *Damages for Personal Injury: Non-Pecuniary Loss*[83] in *Heil v Rankin* in 2000; in both cases significant criticism of the recommendations were made and the

---

[71] LC 309 (2008).

[72] LC 312 (2008).

[73] LC 302 (2006). See further chapter 20 (Andrew Burrows).

[74] eg Law Commission and Scottish Law Commission, LC 332 and SLC 226, *Consumer Redress for Misleading and Aggressive Practices* (2012) in the Consumer Protection (Amendment) Regulations 2014; LC 302, n 73 above, in Office of the Leader of the House of Commons, *Post-Legislative Scrutiny: The Government's Approach* (Cm 7320, 2008); Law Commission, LC 301, *Trustee Exemption Clauses* (2006) in HC Deb 14 September 2010, vol 515, col 38WS.

[75] Even just as a matter of process: Andrew Burrows has noted 'Lord Scarman, the first Chairman of the Law Commission, considered that [the] idea of a working, or consultation, paper was the greatest contribution to the public life of the nation made by the Law Commission. This was because, subsequently, all government departments borrowed the idea in developing the now wide-scale practice of producing "green papers" foreshadowing white papers and legislation': Burrows, n 5 above, 324.

[76] Law Commission, LC 177, *A Criminal Code* (1989). See also chapter 12 (Ian Dennis).

[77] Law Commission, LC 143, *Codification of the Criminal Law: A Report to the Law Commission* (1985).

[78] *R v G* [2003] UKHL 50, [2004] 1 AC 1034.

[79] ibid [41]. See also LC 177, n 76 above, app B, examples 18 (iii)–(v).

[80] *DPP v Armstrong* [2000] Crim LR 379 (QB); *R v Goldman* [2001] EWCA Crim 1684, [2001] Crim LR 822.

[81] LC 227 (1994).

[82] *Kleinwort Benson v Lincoln City Council* [1999] 2 AC 349 (HL).

[83] LC 257 (1999).

appropriateness of the courts implementing Commission proposals was questioned.[84] That the matters at hand had been thoroughly examined by the Commission was clearly a factor in their eventual reform. Certainly in the case of the *Damages* report, it was intended from the start that the report be implemented through a change in judicial practice, rather than through legislation.[85] A rare example of a 'soft law' recommendation was the advisory report *Consents to Prosecution* in 1998.[86]

## C  Shape

The Law Commission can play an important role in shaping the law for the future. English law currently faces a crisis of *size* and *fragmentation*.

The *size* of the legal sources has accelerated significantly in the last 20 years. Academic work has been cited in judicial decisions more readily, and the number of outputs for that academic work has increased significantly, from book publications to new and expanded journals and online publishing of completed works and of drafts, such as on the Social Science Research Network (SSRN). Commercial legal databases have for some years been collecting cases that were not selected to be reported by the established law reports. From 2002, court decisions taken at the level of the High Court or higher have been reported electronically in the form of a neutral citation, and for free, on www.bailii.org. With neutral citation, a decision can be read and referenced immediately upon being handed down; however there is no filter for cases. The obligation to check for a contrasting case is now borne by the barrister, solicitor, academic and/or judge, not first by law reporters. This might be thought to be more intellectually honest, but it has significant limitations, since the pace of research would slow dramatically if everyone were to rely on this level of detail. Yet that is the level of detail required for unofficial reports to be cited before the courts.[87]

English law has historically relied on practitioners, and more recently, academics, to write texts which collect together the leading cases and make sense of the complex collection of cases and statutory materials of which the common law is made up. These have always been private and chargeable and are increasingly having to be online databases to stay up to date.

The law has also become more *fragmented*.[88] It is unclear where the appropriate categories for understanding the law are, with regular skirmishes between traditional categories like tort law or the law or real property and newer conceptualisations of the law like human rights. Some categories morph, such as employment law becoming labour law. New categories arise, such as construction law, medical law, data protection law, public procurement law and others. The growth of these

---

[84] *Heil v Rankin* [2001] QB 272 (CA), raising the levels of awards for general damages following the Commission in part.
[85] Burrows, n 5 above, 328.
[86] LC 255 (1998).
[87] Practice Direction (Citation of Authorities) [2012] 1 WLR 780, [6]–[10].
[88] Note also, the aspect of devolution, as discussed in chapter 35 (Sir David Lloyd Jones).

areas of law seems to be based on their functional characteristics: the actions being regulated are related rather than the traditional way the law has grouped actions or principles. The purpose seems to be to collect and tailor the legal principles and rules for the particular task to be regulated. One result is greater specialisation of legal rules and legal actors, leading to the loss of common principles. Another is a growth in alternative dispute resolution. Disputes can be channelled away from the courts, leaving the substantive law itself less rich and slower to develop.[89]

The Law Commission reflects this reality of fragmentation. The Commission's work is rarely able to approach the scale and comprehensiveness of that undertaken by continental codification commissions and as suggested above, if the Law Commission cannot, no one else will. This explosion of size and complexity threatens any remaining coherence in English law and the Commission is not currently funded in a way to cope (nor, indeed, are the universities or research councils, who could otherwise assist in some ways). This fragmentation is one of the things the ALI restatements have worked against, albeit not across the whole range of legal fields.

## D  Accessibility

Finally, the Law Commission can help to make the law of the future more accessible and three ways will be noted here.[90] This is particularly urgent in light of the growth and fragmentation just noted.

First, this means making the texts which explain the rules easily available, to lay people as much as to the legally trained. The governmental website for accessing legislation, www.legislation.gov.uk appears to be astoundingly out of date, a vast number of pages refer to unincorporated changes from legislation over the last few years. It also compares poorly with its peers. The Supreme Court has developed a number of tools for such accessibility, developing the distinctive character of that court a little more within the hierarchy of courts in the United Kingdom. English accessibility is particularly bad compared with our international peers. The French have a detailed site, www.legifrance.gouv.fr, covering legislation and case law, and many of the key texts, like the civil and criminal substantive and procedure codes have been translated into English with the assistance of, for instance, JR Spencer. In Spain, the Bolétin Oficial del Estado publishes all legislation and maintains an extensive online database, in the fine tradition of the continental approach to the promulgation of laws.[91] Similarly, the Spanish Supreme Court website has case law going back decades.[92] Even the Chilean National Congress Library site, www.leychile.cl/Consulta, makes the material available in England laughable, since the Chilean site features detailed historical material, scans of original documents and

---

[89] As noted by Beverley McLachlin, Chief Justice of Canada in an address at the Obligations VI conference at Western University, Ontario, Canada, July 2012.

[90] See, particularly, chapters 10 (George Gretton) and 14 (Lord Toulson).

[91] www.boe.es/legislacion/legislacion.php.

[92] www.poderjudicial.es/cgpj/es/Poder-Judicial/Tribunal-Supremo/Jurisprudencia/Jurisprudencia-del-TS.

other supplementary material, let alone the texts of legislative provisions (the Chilean Supreme Court website is similarly helpful). While the Law Commission may not be the best body to host such a database, it certainly feels this burden since it must plan reform of law inaccessible to the majority of the population.

Second, accessibility means helping to make the texts intelligible, in the nature of how they are written and explained. Here the Law Commission can and does already do well. The Good Law project is one example. The project includes making the law accessible online, but more generally for those interested in reform to 'come together with a shared objective of making legislation work well for the users of today and tomorrow'.[93] This includes, in particular, making law necessary, clear, coherent, effective and accessible. The aim is clearly laudable, but it is to be feared that the achievement of its goals requires time and effort on each occasion of drafting and promulgation, time that political manoeuvring rarely allows for the majority of legislation.[94] Andrew Burrows made this point quite neatly:

> Another example, which I will not name so as to avoid embarrassing anyone, was not a Law Commission Bill but one that Parliamentary Counsel in the Law Commission was drafting. I found a letter left in the photocopier. It said something like this: 'I have had 36 hours to draft this complex bill. The policy instructions I was given were very sketchy. In consequence I have sometimes had to resort to making up the details of the policy. I have had to do so under extreme time pressure.'[95]

This embarrassing note, a call for improved general legislative methods, underlies a more recent paper by a leading law reformer, judge and politician in New Zealand, Sir Geoffrey Palmer.[96] He argued just last year that the level of scrutiny and care which the Law Commissions undertake should be the model for all legislation. This approach is clearly more attainable than currently imagined, since other countries, like Sweden noted above, already have procedures much further down that line than in the United Kingdom.

Third, the Law Commission could be even more significant as a force for making *law reform*, not just *law*, more accessible. This is currently attempted through well publicised and explained (albeit long) reports. It may even be that evidence of popular support for a *proposed* project, might encourage Ministerial support sufficient for the 2010 Protocol conditions to be met. By comparison, the newest way for Americans to express their constitutional right to petition their government is via an online petition form.[97] Similarly, attitudes to law reform could be gauged through surveys such as the Hansard Society use to gauge political engagement.[98] The Australian Law Reform Commission has experimented with public hearings for their projects.[99] As yet, no play or other artistic work on the Law Commission's

---

[93] www.gov.uk/good-law.
[94] The discussion of trends in and approaches to legal drafting are sadly outside the scope of this paper.
[95] Burrows, n 5 above, 329. See, eg, on the need for transitional arrangements, *R v Newbon* [2005] Crim LR 738.
[96] G Palmer, 'The Law Reform Enterprise: Evaluating the Past and Charting the Future' (2015) 131 *LQR* 402, 420–421; see further chapter 14 (Lord Toulson).
[97] www.petitions.whitehouse.gov/.
[98] www.auditofpoliticalengagement.org/.
[99] See chapter 6 (Kathryn Cronin).

works has come to light in England and Wales and it does not seem likely that that particular form of increasing accessibility attempted in Canada will be adopted soon, but one never knows.[100]

## IV CONCLUSION

In one scene in *The Go-Between*, the protagonist seeks to effect change through arcane and almost meaningless words on a page. Bullied at school for the contents of his diary, he decides to use that same diary to seek revenge. He writes gibberish as curses but spells out the potentially fatal effects on his tormentors should they not desist. The spells appear effective when those targets happen to suffer accidents, and he is feted by pupil and teacher alike.

An author can easily seek to, and after the writing, be tempted to believe, that his words have changed the world. This is no less true even though, as Lord Sumption has recently pointed out, it is difficult to predict the future.[101] Even so, when we reform the law today we must be trying to predict something about the future. We make decisions about what factors in society will be the same, and which will change. The identity, and distinctiveness, of the Law Commission is one facet in the calculation of what it should seek to do for the future. Another is what 'law' we should be seeking to reform. The purpose of the Commission cannot only be *statutory reform* of *substantive* law. There are also significant difficulties to face in the shape and accessibility of the law. Clearly the Law Commission has a difficult task, with funding short and scrutiny high. The author is amongst those who value its role today. What is the best law reform body or networks of bodies for the future? It may be that the Commission can excel best with partners and allies in law reform, as much as it does when it has the support of government, Parliament and others today. There is much to consider from the experience of law reform in other countries. Ways to foster greater skill and knowledge sharing are valuable not just within the United Kingdom. Perhaps there could be greater links between national Law Commissions, like the links ever growing between judges of different legal systems. Secondments for staff to and from the different Commissions could be as common as secondments for practitioners to assist judges in the Court of Appeal and Supreme Court. Indeed, is the future of any given area of law actually another country, and if so, will the English ever accept that?

---

[100] See chapter 11 (Yves Le Bouthillier).
[101] *R (on the application of Lord Carlile of Berriew QC and others) v Secretary of State for the Home Department* [2014] UKSC 60, [2015] AC 945, [46]; adapting Hartley's phrase independently of the present author.

# 39

# *Making Law—Who,*
# *How and What?*

> Why, Prime Minister, do you waste all this time by setting up a Royal Commission
> on the Electoral System? You have the votes in Parliament. Use them to establish the
> electoral system you want!

> The PM: Getting politicians to design an electoral system is like
> getting panel beaters to design intersections!

The place was Turangawaewae on the banks of the Waikato River, then the residence
of the Maori Queen, now the Maori King. The year was 1985, some 30 years ago,
the Prime Minister was David Lange and the five members of the Commission, me
included, were in attendance. As I listened to the question, I was formulating in my
head a dense, boring sentence or two, more likely a boring paragraph or two about
the importance of having an independent body, in this case an experienced judge, a
political scientist, a Māori sociologist, a statistician and an academic lawyer, following a broadly consultative process and a deep study of alternative systems, producing
a set of proposals based on principle and New Zealand values and circumstances.[1]
But David Lange got all that in one quick quip! That was the beginning of one process for law reform, really for fundamental constitutional reform, a process which
did not reach the point of popular acceptance until ten years later, following much
public debate, legislation[2] and two referendums, and which continues, recently
with a further referendum supporting the system.[3] That was followed by a valuable
report based on wide public consultation recommending important changes of detail
prepared by the independent standing Electoral Commission.[4] Unfortunately, there
was not the political will to implement them.

---

[*] In speaking at the conference, I recalled that it was nearly 20 years since I had been involved in the
detail of many of the matters described over the two days, a discussion from which I had greatly benefitted. I saw my task at the end of those two valuable days as taking a wider view. Many thanks to Monique
van Alphen Fyfe for excellent editorial work.
[1] Royal Commission on the Electoral System, *Report of the Royal Commission on the Electoral
System: Towards a Better Democracy* (Wellington, Government Printer, 1986).
[2] Electoral Referendum Acts of 1991 and 1993 (New Zealand).
[3] Electoral Referendum Act 2010 (New Zealand).
[4] The Electoral Commission, *Report of the Electoral Commission on the Review of the MMP Voting
System* (Wellington, 2012).

A second area of law reform or principle on which I will be drawing is the prohibition of discrimination and the principle of equality. Fifty years ago, the initial Race Relations Act of this country was enacted. That legislation was marked by another seminar at the same weekend of this conference,[5] legislation which has continued to be the subject of reform and extension notably in the Sex Discrimination Act 1975, the Equality Act 2000 and the Marriage (Same Sex Couples) Act 2013.

My third area is the law of piracy and other maritime crimes where in the nature of things the process of law making will be international as well as national and where there is one recent piece of rhetoric to match David Lange's: 'You don't need a peg leg or an eye patch ... to be a pirate'.[6] That is from the pen of an American judge, Alex Kozinski CJ of the Ninth Federal Circuit Court of Appeals. In preparing its judgment, his Court was able to depend on widely accepted treaty texts which were the product of state practice occurring over centuries, scholarly writing, national legislation, judicial decisions, unofficial and official international codification efforts and two diplomatic conferences leading to widely accepted treaties.

My fourth and final area is the law of interpretation, where again nationally and internationally the actors are scholars, judges, law reform bodies, public and private, and legislators and treaty makers.

As I have indicated, I will be commenting on some of the choices which are made and which will continue to be made in codifying, developing and reforming the law and the broader constitutional system. Those choices involve three questions: who—the participants; how—the processes they follow; and what—the principles they apply and the product of the work, including its form. Of necessity, I will be very selective and I will be roaming widely.

## I ELECTORAL SYSTEMS AND EQUALITY

I begin with electoral systems and in particular with the New Zealand one, but then move, in terms of the principle of equality, to Western Samoa and the United States. Since 1893, New Zealand has had universal adult suffrage. It can claim to be the oldest democracy in the world. From that time it has also had a method for determining electoral boundaries through a body which does have political party representatives but which is chaired by a member, usually a judge, chosen by the other members, and includes the Government Statistician, the Surveyor-General and the Chief Electoral Officer. It engages in extensive public consultation and operates within tight substantive and numerical constraints. Since 1956, that method and other fundamental matters, including the voting age and the term of Parliament, can be amended only by a referendum or by a three quarters vote in the House which essentially requires agreement between the major political parties.[7] Until 1956 major

---

[5] 'The Race Relations Act at 50' British Academy Conference, Thursday 9 & Friday 10 July 2015; see I Solanke, 'The Race Relations Act @ 50 conference Where were you?' 26 *British Academy Review* (Summer 2015) 20.

[6] *Institute of Cetacean Research v Sea Shepherd Conservation Society* 725 F 3d 940 (9th Cir 2013).

[7] Electoral Act 1956 (New Zealand), s 189, replaced by the Electoral Act 1993 (New Zealand), s 268.

changes, including the introduction of women's suffrage in 1893, were made by Parliament using its regular processes, but since then proposals for changes to the voting age, the number of members of Parliament and the term of Parliament have been adopted or rejected in accordance with the processes just indicated. And, as I have mentioned, the major change to a proportional system introduced in 1993, was adopted following two referendums and has recently been confirmed by another one. At the heart of that change were important principles: in the interests of fairness and equality, said the Commission, the number of seats gained by a political party should be proportional to the number of voters who support that party; and the votes of all electors should be of equal value.

I have mentioned just two of the ten criteria stated by the Commission; other important interests had to be considered. As the Commission and the existing limits on electoral changes recognised, the answers in governing cannot always lie with simple majority decision making. The nature and basis of Māori representation, a major term of reference, similarly indicate limits on majority decision making. That matter, particular in many respects to New Zealand, was the subject of lengthy consultation and consideration in that Commission's work and report and subsequently in important executive, legislative and judicial actions. Universal principles, to the extent that they are recognised, for instance in the International Covenant on Civil and Political Rights, will often have to be balanced against such local values. That is to be seen, to move from legislative and popular processes to the courts, in a challenge made 30 years ago to the Samoan parliamentary electoral system.[8] In the years before its independence in 1960 and for the next 20 years only Matai, the chiefs, could vote and could be candidates. There were some exceptions. That limit had been the subject of lengthy debates through the 1950s in the United Nations, particularly the Trusteeship Council (Western Samoa was a Trust Territory), at the conference which prepared the Constitution and then in the process which led to a popular referendum which adopted the Constitution. Late in its preparation, a Bill of Rights was included in the Constitution at the urging of the UN. It was essentially based on the Universal Declaration of Human Rights and included the proposition that 'All persons are equal before the law and entitled to equal protection under the law'.[9]

In the Supreme Court, the Chief Justice, an Australian, ruled that the limits on the suffrage and candidacy breached that guarantee.[10] The Attorney-General appealed to the Court of Appeal, consisting of three New Zealand lawyers. The appeal succeeded. I recall six points made by the Court. It recorded the UN accounts of the debates on the matter which demonstrated consistent Samoan opposition to universal suffrage; it noted that the universal franchise provisions of the Universal Declaration had not been included in the Constitution, a deliberate omission the Court thought; it also noted that, by contrast, other recent Pacific Island constitutions

---

[8] *Attorney-General v Saipa'ia Olomalu* [1980–93] WSLR 41 (Court of Appeal of Western Samoa). I was a member of that Court.
[9] Constitution of the Independent State of Samoa 1960, art 15(1).
[10] *Saipa'ia Olomalu v Attorney-General* [1980–93] WSLR 26 (Supreme Court of Western Samoa).

did expressly provide for universal suffrage; further, the constitution emphasised Samoan custom and traditions; next, momentous constitutional changes are not to be brought about by a side wind or loose and ambiguous general words; and finally it recalled that in the debates in the Constitutional Convention in 1960 the proposal that universal suffrage be included in the Constitution was rejected. I come back to that last matter when I consider the law of interpretation. In the final part of the judgment, the Court makes it clear that it is not implying a view about whether the limited suffrage was in the long-term interests of the country; that issue and related matters were to be decided by Parliament and not by the courts. In fact in 1990 the suffrage was made universal by the legislators following a positive result from a universal suffrage referendum, but candidacy remains limited to the Matai.[11]

Those supporting the argument for universal suffrage based on the guarantee of equal protection referred to the great case of *Baker v Carr* in the US Supreme Court and to related rulings.[12] The Western Samoan Court of Appeal dismissed their relevance on the basis that they came later than the preparation of the Western Samoan Constitution and that US equal protection jurisprudence had some special characteristics.

The central question in *Baker v Carr* was about the allocation of decision-making power. The Court rejected the contention that the claim was non-justiciable and presented a political question: it was not a matter to be resolved only by other branches of government (here the Tennessee legislature had in fact not reapportioned the electorates in 60 years, although the voting population had increased four-fold); and the claim did not depend on the very broadly stated guarantee of 'a republican form of government'[13] which is seen as involving a lack of judicially discoverable and manageable standards for resolving the dispute. Accordingly, the claim based on equal protection continued, and courts began to exercise extensive powers to reapportion legislatures. They were and are however continuing to apply broadly stated standards: the right of a citizen to vote for members of the legislature is unconstitutionally impaired when its weight is in a substantial fashion diluted when compared with the votes of citizens living in other parts of the state. (The differences in proportion in that case went as far as 40:1 and 16:1, in another over 1000:1!)[14]

Divergences from a strict population standard, the courts have said, may be allowed to give effect to a rational state policy. But 'citizens, not history or economic interests, cast votes ... people, not land or trees or pastures, vote'.[15] The challenges arising from those broadly articulated standards continue. Fully 50 years after *Baker v Carr*, for instance, the Supreme Court is being asked to determine in the next year whether apportionment is to be calculated on the basis of those qualified to vote or the total population.[16]

---

[11] Electoral Amendment Act 1990 (Western Samoa).
[12] *Baker v Carr* 369 US 186 (1962).
[13] Constitution of the United States of America, art 4(4).
[14] See *Reynolds v Sims* 377 US 533 (1964).
[15] ibid 579–80.
[16] *Evenwel v Abbott* (US, No 14-940, pending).

A better choice of method might be to have a regular, principled and largely independent process like that which has operated in New Zealand for more than a century. The US Supreme Court has indeed just upheld the establishment of such a body in Arizona by referendum.[17]

## II EQUALITY LEGISLATION

I mentioned above UK legislation concerned with promoting equality and opposing discrimination. That legislation and similar legislation elsewhere was prepared in many cases through regular departmental and legislative processes, in some cases, with significant expert input. Thus in February 1965, Sir Frank Soskice, the Home Secretary, proposed to his Cabinet colleagues legislation to give effect to the undertaking in the Queen's speech at the opening of Parliament 'to take action against racial discrimination and promote full integration into the community of immigrants who have come here from the Commonwealth'.[18] He had discussed the form of the legislation with the Lord Chancellor and the law officers and the proposals had been discussed in the House Affairs Committee which had expressed general agreement with them but, in view of their political importance and inevitably controversial nature, it thought that they should be brought to Cabinet. The paper proposed the creation of offences in refusing to provide defined public services on racial grounds, racial incitement and stirring up racial hatred. The parliamentary and public debate following the introduction of the Bill led to a Cabinet decision to introduce a conciliation process to help implement civil rights and obligations set out in the proposed legislation.[19] That change was made. The legislation was soon seen as unsatisfactory and was replaced and, as indicated, legislative change, some of it major, has continued.

In those contests over discrimination the UK courts have had some role, sometimes an important one, but the major actor appears to me to be the legislator;[20] that is so in New Zealand as well.[21] The role of courts in the United States has provided a major contrast over the last 50 years. That is most recently demonstrated by the gay marriage decision of the Supreme Court based on the guarantees of due process and equal protection and on the liberty of the person.[22] A further actor in the area of discrimination appeared in the late 1960s—multilateral treaty making, initially with the International Convention on the Elimination of All Forms of Racial Discrimination which came into force in 1969. The New Zealand Race Relations Act made

---

[17] *Arizona State Legislature v Arizona Independent Redistricting Commission* (US, No 13-1314, 29 June 2015).

[18] Home Office, *Racial Discrimination and Incitement to Racial Hatred*, CAB 129/120 C(65)23, 17 February 1965.

[19] Race Relations Act 1965 (United Kingdom).

[20] See, eg, Sex Discrimination Act 1975, Equality Act 2000 and Marriage (Same Sex Couples) Act 2013 (all United Kingdom); cf *Gammans v Ekins* [1950] 2 KB 328 (CA); *Dyson Holdings v Fox* [1976] QB 503 (CA); and *Fitzpatrick v Sterling Housing Association Ltd* [2001] 1 AC 27 (HL).

[21] See, eg, Civil Union Act 2004 (New Zealand) and Marriage (Definition of Marriage) Amendment Act 2013 (New Zealand); cf *Quilter v Attorney-General* [1998] 1 NZLR 523 (CA).

[22] *Obergefell v Hodges* 576 (US, No 14-556, 26 June 2015).

the treaty element explicit: it was an Act to affirm and promote racial equality in New Zealand and to implement the International Convention.[23]

## III A CASE STUDY IN CODIFICATION: PIRACY

The international element is a major feature of the law of piracy. At least since Cicero's time, pirates have been referred as *hostes humani generis*, enemies of the human race. The crime is committed in the open seas and all states have criminal jurisdiction over it—or so it is said. The list of piratical acts maintained by the International Maritime Board shows 126 attacks on ships in 2015, the last four at Mombasa, in Indonesian waters, in the Philippines and in Lome, Togo.[24] It is a significant practical problem and has been over the centuries.

The practice identifies five principal legal questions:

(1)  Is piracy limited to the high seas?
(2)  Must it involve an attack from outside the ship? The 'two ships' rule.
(3)  How is the purpose and act to be defined? Is it limited to acts of private plunder or purpose or can it extend to public purposes?
(4)  Which states have the power to seize the vessel and arrest the alleged offenders and prosecute them?
(5)  May slave traders be treated as pirates?

States in their practice, including their legal advisers, judges, law reformers, national and international, private and official, legislators and treaty makers have addressed the issues over the centuries.

The material is rich. I take three points from it, the first and second recognising the limits of codification by courts and even national legislatures and the third the challenge presented in the course of codification by the balance between principle and detail. In 1879 in the United Kingdom, the Criminal Code Commissioners including Sir James Fitzjames Stephen reported their proposals for the codification of the criminal law of England and Wales.[25] This was a time of great confidence in the various codification efforts. Think back over the nineteenth century to Napoleon and the various continental codes, to David Dudley Field in New York, to the setting up of the Institut de droit international and the International Law Association, to the Indian codes and the UK commercial codes. But on piracy, there was disagreement on basic questions, including the possible high seas limit, the two ships rule and the relevance of private or public purpose. The Bill on which the Commissioners were reporting in 1879 contained a definition of 'Piracy by the Law of Nations' but they thought

> it better to leave this offence undefined ... as no definition of it would be satisfactory which is not recognised as such by other nations: and after careful consideration, we have not been

---

[23]  Race Relations Act 1971 (New Zealand), preamble.
[24]  International Chamber of Commerce Commercial Crime Services, 'Live Piracy & Armed Robbery Report 2015' www.icc-ccs.org/piracy-reporting-centre/live-piracy-report.
[25]  See chapter 12 (Ian Dennis).

able to discover a definition fulfilling such a condition. We may observe as to this that the subject has been much discussed in the courts of the United Sates, and the result appears to justify the course which we have adopted. We do not think it will lead to practical inconvenience.[26]

Accordingly, the relevant provision of the Draft Code said simply:

Piracy by the Law of Nations

Everyone shall be guilty of an indictable offence, and shall be liable upon conviction thereof to penal servitude for life, who does any act which amounts to piracy by the law of nations.[27]

That approach was adopted in the New Zealand Criminal Code of 1893 at section 104, followed by section 121 of the Crimes Act 1908 and section 92 of the Crimes Act 1961.

In terms of the Commissioners' reference to the United States, the US Supreme Court had upheld an attack on the constitutionality of the US statute of 1819 which was written in essentially the same terms. Piracy, it said, was defined with reasonable certainty by the law of nations.[28]

Fifty years later, the Privy Council was asked on a reference from Hong Kong whether robbery was an essential element of piracy.[29] No, was the answer. Viscount Sankey LC, in a masterly opinion, drawing, as he said, on a wider range of authority than when a municipal law question is under examination, cast some doubt on the two ships rule; he emphasised that pirates placed themselves outside the allegiance of their state; they were no longer nationals but *hostes humani generis*; he emphasised the continuing development of international law—it is a living and expanding code, instancing aerial warfare and aerial transport; but rejected the suggestions that it restate the whole law of piracy:

[T]heir Lordships do not themselves propose to hazard a definition of piracy. They remember the words of M Portalis, one of Napoleon's commissioners, who said: 'We have guarded against the dangerous ambition of wishing to regulate and to foresee everything ... A new question springs up. Then how is it to be decided? To this question it is replied that the office of the law is to fix by enlarged rules the general maxims of right and wrong, to establish firm principles fruitful in consequences, and not to descend to the detail of all questions which may arise upon each topic.' (Quoted by Halsbury LC in *Halsbury's Laws of England*, Introduction, ccxi.) A careful examination of the subject shows a gradual widening of the earlier definition of piracy to bring it from time to time more in consonance with situations either not thought of or not in existence when the older jurisconsults were expressing their opinions.[30]

As the Privy Council mentions in the course of its opinion, the restatement role that was being urged on it had been taken up shortly before in the League of Nations and

---

[26] Criminal Code Bill Commission, *Report of the Royal Commission appointed to consider the Law Relating to Indictable Offences* (C 2345, 1879) 20.

[27] ibid 85.

[28] *United States v Smith* (1820) 18 US (5 Wheat) 153.

[29] *Re Piracy Jure Gentium* [1934] AC 586 (PC).

[30] ibid 600. The passage from Portalis is included in Lord Hailsham LC's preface to the 1972 version of the first volume of the fourth edition, but unfortunately not in the reissue.

at the Harvard Law School.[31] The Harvard Law School research elaborated a draft convention with comments.[32] It is a most thorough, carefully researched text, incorporating 250 pages of relevant authority. That piece of non-governmental scholarship greatly assisted the UN International Law Commission 20 years later when it prepared its 1956 draft articles on the high seas.[33] In general, said the Commission, it was able to endorse the findings of that research.[34]

Unlike the Harvard study, the Commission's work was subject to governmental comment, first, as it was being prepared[35]—including for instance the question of state piracy—and, second, in the diplomatic conference which prepared the 1958 conventions.[36] Essentially, the same text has been included in the 1982 United Nations Convention on the Law of the Sea (UNCLOS).[37]

Accordingly there is now much greater certainty. The Australian Crimes Act since 1992 has in fact incorporated that treaty language. While the New Zealand Act has not, it may be assumed that the treaty language would be read into the general reference to the law of nations if the case arose.

My remaining point concerning piracy relates to the balance between precision and broader drafting. The treaty text requires private ends or purposes, a standard which Kozinski CJ of the Ninth Circuit addressed in the peg leg/eye patch case I mentioned. It can be compared with the political offence limit placed on the duty to extradite. What is a 'political offence'? In 1891 the issue came before a court which included the now Mr Justice Stephen.[38] (He provides one example of the changing-of-hats scholar, codifier and judge; to take a more recent instance, three of the five original members of the New Zealand Supreme Court established in 2004 had been members of the New Zealand Law Commission.) The argument that the offence alleged in that case was such an offence and accordingly exempted from extradition was based in part on what Stephen had said in his *History of Criminal Law*. That judge said this about his earlier discussion:

I gave what appeared to me to be the true interpretation of the expression 'political character.' It is very easy to give it too wide an explanation. I think that my late friend Mr [John Stuart] Mill [in a debate in Parliament] made a mistake upon the subject, probably because he was not accustomed to use language with that degree of precision which is essential to everyone who has ever had, as I have had on many occasions, to draft Acts of Parliament, which, although they may be easy to understand, people continually try to

---

[31] ibid 599.

[32] Harvard Research in International Law, 'Draft Convention on Piracy with Comments' (1932) 26 *American Journal of International Law Sup* 739.

[33] The text was originally prepared in French and was titled *Regime of the High Seas* (1954) 2 *Yearbook of the International Law Commission* 7, UN Doc A/CN4/79.

[34] *Report of the International Law Commission to the General Assembly* (1956) 2 *Yearbook of the International Law Commission* 253, 282, UN Doc A/3159.

[35] *Comments by Governments on the Provisional Articles Concerning the Regime of the High Seas* (1956) 2 *Yearbook of the International Law Commission* 37, UN Doc A/CN4/99/Addl-9.

[36] Convention on the High Seas (adopted 20 April 1958, entered into force 30 September 1962) 450 UNTS 11.

[37] United Nations Convention on the Law of the Sea (adopted 10 December 1982, 16 November 1994) 1833 UNTS 3 (UNCLOS), arts 100–07.

[38] *Re Castioni* [1891] 1 QB 149 (QB).

misunderstand, and in which therefore it is not enough to attain to a degree of precision which a person reading in good faith can understand; but it is necessary to attain if possible to a degree of precision which a person reading in bad faith cannot misunderstand. It is all the better if he cannot pretend to misunderstand it. Having given my view upon that subject, I shall say no more with regard to the interpretation of the Act of Parliament.[39]

## IV THE LAW OF INTERPRETATION

The reference to what John Stuart Mill said in the House of Commons, to the use of which no objection was made, leads into my final topic—the law of interpretation, not just of statutes but also of contracts, constitutions and treaties.

That law has been stated over the years by scholars, individually and in groups, judges, legislatures and treaty makers, acting with or without independent advice.[40] Over the last two centuries, for instance, the Napoleonic Code of 1804 and later continental codes have included rules for the interpretation of contracts but not of statutes, from mid-nineteenth century legislatures in North America and New Zealand have enacted Interpretation Acts requiring the purposive interpretation of statutes. The New Zealand Interpretation Ordinance of 1851, for instance, added to the routine provisions about time, distance, singular and plural, repeals, etc, to be found in Lord Brougham's Act of the previous year, a direction that where the meaning of an enactment was doubtful it was to be construed according to its purpose.[41] In the 1930s, the Harvard research project on the law of treaties included, if with hesitation, rules on the interpretation of treaties, a matter which was taken up in the 1950s and 1960s by the Institut de droit international, the International Law Commission and the American Law Institute and the diplomatic conference which adopted the Vienna Convention on the law of treaties in 1969.[42] In that year the British Law Commissions similarly proposed a purposive direction, a provision calling for interpretation consistent with international obligations, and a provision allowing limited access to the drafting history but prohibiting access to parliamentary materials. Those proposals were not adopted, although the purposive proposal was influential in Australia at the federal and state level. Those Australian statutes also regulated the use of the drafting history, including Hansard, in a manner similar to the Vienna Convention. The New Zealand Law Commission in 1990 proposed

---

[39] ibid 167–68. It is interesting that no point was taken about the fact that John Stuart Mill had expressed his opinion in a debate in the House of Commons. The views of the relevant Minister, also stated in the House, were cited by counsel. Like the judge, counsel were helped in this reference by those speeches being included in a leading text on extradition.

[40] See KJ Keith, *Interpreting Treaties, Statutes and Contracts* (Occasional Paper No 19, New Zealand Centre for Public Law, Wellington, 2009).

[41] New Zealand Interpretation Ordinance 1851 16 Vict 3 (New Zealand), cl 3; *cf* Interpretation Act 1850 (United Kingdom).

[42] Harvard Research in International Law, 'Law of Treaties' (1935) 29 *American Journal of International Law Sup* 653, 937; see, eg, H Lauterpaucht, 'De l'interprétation des Traités' (1950) 43 *Annuaire de l'Institut de Droit International* 366 and H Waldock, 'Sixth Report on the Law of Treaties' (1966) *Yearbook of the International Law Commission* 51.

a redrafted purposive provision (the existing provision, copied originally from Canada, had been in essentially the same form for 100 years). It did not make any proposal about the drafting history. The courts were already using that material, an action which the Commission supported for reasons set out in some detail, and they should be left to develop the practice, without the kind of guidance provided by the Australian legislation and the Vienna Convention. Two years later the House of Lords in *Pepper v Hart* essentially adopted that New Zealand position, in effect preferring the New Zealand Commission's view to that of the British Commissions.[43] Debates on the Law Commissions' Bill had doubted whether statutory interpretation was a genuine subject for the Commissions. Was it, asked Lord Wilberforce, a real subject?[44] Those doubts are enhanced by the absence or near absence of references to the legislation in American, Canadian and Australian judgments and writings on interpretation. But the experience in New Zealand and internationally is flatly to the contrary.

## V CONCLUSIONS

I should try to draw some conclusions. The first is obvious. Choices of method of law making in terms of who, how and what are being made and have been made at all times. More than one body will often be involved in a process of law making which may well be continuous. Consider my first and last topics. In Westminster systems the politicians through legislative process have often exercised total control over change over the electoral system. The New Zealand experience is something of an exception. In the United States, the legislative and executive monopolies, highlighted by Governor Elbridge Gerry of Massachusetts with his salamander shaped electorate, has been considerably reduced by the US Supreme Court over the last 50 years with its willingness to intervene in what had been seen as the 'political thicket' on the basis of the principle of equality. At the risk of appearing chauvinistic I would suggest that 30 years ago the Lange government got it right and David Lange captured the principle which should govern the allocation of functions in this fundamental area in a single sentence with that great quip. There must be a very strong, even compelling, case for major constitutional change being made only by broad agreement among the major political parties or by the people through a referendum. In this country the Blair government headed a little way down that track with the Jenkins Commission but nothing came of that.[45]

---

[43] *Pepper v Hart* [1993] AC 593 (HL) at 599–601. A proposal to that effect had been made by members of the Donoughmore Committee 60 years earlier, see *Report of the (Donoughmore) Committee on Ministers' Powers* (Cmd 4060, 1932) at 135–37. For generous acknowledgements of the borrowing see A Lester, '*Pepper v Hart* Revisited' (1994) 15 *Statute Law Review* 10 and A Lester, 'English Judges as Law Makers' [1993] *PL* 269, 275.

[44] HL Deb 16 November 1966, vol 277, col 1294. See also chapter 38 (Matthew Dyson).

[45] *The Report of the Independent Commission on the Voting System* (Cm 4090, 1998).

The differing processes in respect of interpretation to be found even in the common law world demonstrate that in the area of what is often thought of as 'lawyers' law' a deliberate, consultative process is to be preferred to judicial clarification or development. The New Zealand Supreme Court has supported the proposition that post-contractual practice may be relevant to the interpretation of a written contract[46]—a view which Lord Wilberforce had said was the 'refuge of the desperate'.[47] An eminent New Zealand commercial lawyer, Jack Hodder QC, has criticised this approach on two process grounds: this was a decision of legislative scope on which few were able to make submissions, and the decision had increased the cost of much contract litigation. How, he asked, can the court be adequately informed in argument about the wider costs of a decision it may make?[48] There is a parallel here with the position Lord Reid took in rejecting the admissibility of business records in *Myers v DPP*. He took that cautious position although he had never taken a narrow view of the functions of the House of Lords as an appellate tribunal.[49]

On what basis are the choices to be made? I have already mentioned one—the constitutional importance of the issue. Another, as with piracy and a high number of other issues in this increasingly interdependent globalised world, is that international processes may be a critical feature; consider the preamble, from almost 100 years ago, to the Constitution of the International Labour Organisation, which recognised that the failure of one nation to introduce humane conditions of work would be an obstacle to other nations taking that action.

Another broader basis for choice is functional: which body or combination of bodies, is best qualified, following what procedures and with what principles and product in mind to undertake the task? Consider the positions taken by Jack Hodder and Lord Reid.

In some cases the answer might be to leave the matter to practice. Any attempt to codify, clarify, or develop the law may be counterproductive. Non-binding guidelines or codes of practice may be the answer. The Economist, in a recent leader and briefing called for doctor-assisted dying to be made lawful. In arguing that case it indicated it is opposed to the existing 'fudge'.[50]

My final thought goes to the roles of those Law Commissions, national and international, which have a responsibility to keep the whole of the law for which they are responsible under review. Should they not be in the business every so often of looking not just at the areas of the law in need of review—in itself a massive task—but also of which bodies might undertake their review, the processes they might follow, the principles they might consider and the form the product might take?

---

[46] *Wholesale Distributors Limited v Gibbons Holdings Limited* [2007] NZSC 37, [2008] 1 NZLR 277; see also *Vector Gas Limited v Bay of Plenty Energy Limited* [2010] NZSC 5, [2010] 2 NZLR 444.

[47] *L Schuler AG v Wickman Machine Tool Sales Ltd* [1974] AC 235 (HL), 261, referring to *Watcham v Attorney-General of the East Africa Protectorate* [1919] AC 533 (PC).

[48] J Hodder, 'Commentary: The Supreme Court—A Brief Introduction to a Long Conversation' in C Geiringer and DR Knight (eds), *Seeing the World Whole: Essays in Honour of Sir Kenneth Keith* (Wellington, Victoria University Press, 2008) 347.

[49] *Myers v Director of Public Prosecutions* [1965] AC 1001 (HL), 1021.

[50] 'Doctor-assisted Dying: The Right to Die' *The Economist* (London, 27 June 2015).

I might have given greater attention to principle. I have the excuse that at a recent international law conference I addressed the essential role of the principle of humanitarianism balanced against military necessity underlying the law of armed conflict and the role there of the dictates of the public conscience. I also considered other principles that were recognised in practice in the Battle of Agincourt 600 years back and fair trial in Magna Carta 200 years earlier.[51] Recall too the Shelley proposition that 'Poets are the unacknowledged legislators of the world'.[52]

[51] KJ Keith, 'International Humanitarian Law: Principles, Problems and Prospects' International Law-making at a Crossroads: Participants, Processes and Principles, 23rd Annual Conference of the Australian and New Zealand Society of International Law (2015).

[52] PB Shelley, 'A Defence of Poetry' in PB Shelley, *Essays, Letters from Abroad, Translations and Fragments* (London, Edward Moxon, 1840) 1, 57.

# Index

accessibility, principle of
  criminal law   110, 115–16
  generally   129–30, 138, 344
  increasing accessibility   90–2, 397–9
  Law Commission publications   241
  legal databases   115–16, 131, 142, 396
    error rate   92
  miscarriages of justice   130–1
  secondary legislation   131
  statute law   131, 247, 308–9
Alberta Law Reform Commission   178
American Law Institute *see* United States
Anton, AE   248
Archer, Peter   26
Arden, Dame Mary   4, 9, 391
Ashton, Baroness   79–80, 81
assisted suicide   196n, 253, 255, 301, 359
asylum and immigration legislation   132
Auld LJ (Sir Robin Auld)   394
Australia
  federal system   55–63, 184
  law reform agencies   55–6, 55n, 61
Australian Law Reform Commission
  Aboriginal laws   58–9, 61
  consultants and advisers   58–9
  delegated legislation   62–3
  establishment   55, 57
  funding   62
  human rights   58
  implementation rate   61, 178
  independence   56, 57
  operation   57–63
  President and Commissioners   57
  public hearings   59, 398
  referral of projects to   57
  remit   57–8, 62
  reports and recommendations   58–60, 60n
  *Serious Invasions of Privacy in the Digital
    Era*   10, 297, 299–300, 306–7
  technical law reform   60
  threat of closure   62

Baker, Richard   206
Beale, Hugh   4, 15, 140, 384
Bean, David   26
Beatson, Sir Jack   4, 5, 7, 8, 9, 10, 15, 22, 199,
  266
Beith, Lord   4, 5
Beldam, Sir Roy   248, 312, 313
Bell, John   392
Bentham, Jeremy   302, 302n
Bill of Rights, proposed   127, 137–8

Binchy, William   4, 10, 126, 187, 199
Bingham, Lord   129, 131, 136, 194, 195, 302,
  395
Blair, Tony   348
Bonomy, Lord   350
Bratza, Judge (Sir Nicholas Bratza)   294
Brennan J (Sir Gerard Brennan)   301
British Columbia Law Commission   341
Bromley, Peter   20
Brooke, Sir Henry   21, 247
Buckley, Richard   291
Burrows, Andrew   4, 6, 12, 173, 186n, 199, 251,
  276, 287, 395n, 398
  'Alternatives to Legislation'   135, 136
  restatements of English law   384, 384n

Canada
  constitution repatriated   98
  Law Commission *see* Law Commission of
    Canada
  Law Reform Commission of Canada   98, 106,
    362
    closure   10, 98, 106
    remit   98–9
  provincial law commissions   75, 97, 97n, 99,
    99n, 341, 362
  Truth and Reconciliation Commission   101,
    101n
Cardozo, Benjamin   18, 24, 173
Carloway, Lord   350
Carnwath, Lord   4, 6, 22, 279, 280, 281, 286,
  290, 291, 311
Channon, Paul   267
Charleton J (Mr Justice Peter Charleton)   157
Chinese Communist Party   127–8, 129
Chorley, Leo   31
Civil Procedure Rules Committee   393–4
clarity, principle of   129–30
Clark of Calton, Lady   148
Clarke, Lord   87, 290, 313
Clive, Eric   4, 13, 15, 94n, 230
Clyde, Lord   343
Codes of Practice   26, 119–20, 135
codification
  arguments against   113–14
  common law   93, 108, 113–14, 141, 302–9,
    331–3
  contract law   303
  criminal law   108–22, 302
  economic efficiency   94–5
  generally   12–15, 19, 20, 72, 299, 301–3,
    355–6

government disinterest in  75, 93, 95–6
Law Commissions' remit  25, 65, 89–90,
  93–4, 108, 129, 246, 343, 355–8
meaning  93
'mini-codes'  118–19
piracy  405–8
restatement  93
Scottish Law Commission  108, 343, 350
Spain  387–8
United States  303, 383–6
Welsh law  357
Coke, Sir Edward  128
Collins, Lord  279, 284, 317
Commissioners
  ad hoc appointments  381
  changes of  251
  collective responsibility  381, 382
  diversity of expertise  18–19, 25, 381–2
  generally  7, 18–19, 25, 31–2, 154, 381
  independence of mind  153
  international projects  67
  judges as  154
  Law Commission of Canada  102–3
  recruitment  19
common law
  codification  93, 108, 113–14, 141, 301–9,
    331–3
  contract law  136
  criminal liability  112, 113, 114–15
  damages for personal injury  136, 144–5
  democracy and the rule of law  128
  England and Wales  342
  European Convention on Human Rights  113
  flexibility  114, 394
  historical consciousness  128
  law development and reform via  128, 135–6,
    139, 141, 144–6, 155–6, 201
    implementation of Commissions'
      proposals  144–5, 189, 193–7
    influencing  155–7, 199
    limits of  333
    objections to  145
  legislative restatements  307–9
  Lord Scarman's view  141
  review  140–1, 155–6
  revision  175, 343
  rights  128, 129
  Scotland  6, 202
  statute law, interaction with  297–309, 331–3
  *see also* courts; judiciary
Commonwealth Secretariat
  'Law Reform Agencies: Their Role and
    Effectiveness'  151
comparative law  72, 383–389, 392
consolidation
  duplicative legislation  132–4
  economic efficiency  94–5
  government disinterest in  75, 95–6, 356
  Law Commissions' remit  19, 66, 89–90,
    92–3, 129, 133–4, 140, 175, 199–200,
    311–12, 355–7, 361, 362
  obsolete legislation  19, 66, 133, 311–12, 343

statute law  66, 92
Welsh law  356–7
consultation papers
  generally  240–3, 311
consultation process
  changing priorities  257
  electronic media  235
  European Union  226–7
  generally  7–8, 29–30, 39–43, 154, 154n, 217,
    244, 297
  Law Commission of Canada  103–4
  public accessibility  398–9
  Scottish Law Commission  238–43
contract law
  arguments for codification  303
  common law development  136
Cooke, Elizabeth  4, 7
Cotton, Arthur Stapleton  19
Court of Appeal
  'single or collective' judgments  141
Court Rules
  implementation by  144
courts
  development of the law  6–7, 23, 26, 113–114,
    145, 173, 213, 276, 284–285, 326
  interpretation of the law  128
    citation of Commission reports  149, 242,
      276–96, 310, 312–25, 327, 395
    influence of Commission  331, 333–4
  Practice Directions  333–4
  relationship with Law Commissions  4, 6–7,
    273, 326–35
  referral of projects to Commission  327–9
  review and promotion of Commission
    reforms  329–30
  Supreme Court  6–7, 273, 274–96,
    300, 326
  *see also* common law; judiciary
Cretney, Stephen  147, 257
criminal law
  accessibility  110, 115–16
  attempts at codification  108–22, 302
  comprehensibility  110, 116–17
  consistency and certainty  110, 117–21
  European Convention on Human Rights  113
  evidence  119
  hearsay evidence  275, 292–6
  liability  112, 113, 114–15
  proliferation of legislation  132–3, 264
  Royal Commission report  114, 114n
Criminal Law Revision Committee  111, 393
Criminal Procedure Rules  119–20, 144
Criminal Procedure Rules Committee  393–4
Cronin, Kathryn  4, 5
Croucher, Rosalind  62

Davenport, Brian  251
Davidson, Lord  8
Davies, Paul S  287
defamation
  planned Scottish legislation  211
delegated legislation

federal systems   5, 62–3
implementation of Law Commission proposals
    by   143–4
Delegated Powers and Law Reform Committee
    Scotland   185–6, 206–13, 370–9
    criteria for Commission Bills   374–5, 376
    membership   212
    remit   374
democratic legitimacy   56
Denning, Lord   4, 13, 14, 358
Dennis, Ian   332, 394
Department for Constitutional Affairs
    former role with the Law Commission   78
    *see also* executive; Ministry of Justice
Des Rosiers, Nathalie   103
Dickson, Brice   48, 293, 327
Don, Nigel   207–8, 211, 212
draft Bills
    generally   311
    Law Commission remit   66, 140–1, 140n,
        175, 243
drafting
    EU legislation   220, 229–30
    time pressures   398
Drummond Young, Lord   4, 6, 372
Duff, RA   110
Dunlop, Laura   4, 10, 125, 199
Duxbury, Neil   275
Dworkin, Gerald   31
Dyson, Matthew   4, 6, 10, 15, 339

equality, principle of   137
Etherton, Sir Terence   4, 5, 11, 22, 75, 199, 202,
    248, 261, 292
European Convention on Human Rights   113
European Court of Human Rights
    generally   368
    hearsay evidence   275, 292–6
    relationship with Supreme Court   275, 276,
        292–6, 326
European Law Institute   231–4, 384
European Union
    *Action Plan on Contract Law*   220–1
    'chapeau' rules   223–4, 230, 233
    Common European Sales law   223–6, 230,
        386
        consultation process   226–7
        *Feasibility Study*   223, 223n, 224–5, 227,
            229, 233
        *Statement on...*   232–3
    Common Frame of Reference   94n, 220–1,
        226, 347, 385–6
    *Communication on Contract Law*   230
    Consumer Rights Directive   220–2, 223, 230
    cross-border sales   221–2
    'European Contract Law'   220, 220n
    generally   368
    *Green Paper on Review of the Consumer
        Acquis*   221
    law
        drafting   220, 229–30

harmonisation   221–2
    potential for use of Law Commission
        methods   219, 229–34
    problems with   219–20
    review by Law Commissions   140
    use of legal terms   220
legislative process   227–8
off-premises contracts   221
*The Principles of European Contract
    Law*   225, 225n, 230
'Rome I' problem   221, 223
Rome II   252n
*The Way Forward*   221n, 222
euthanasia   9, 253, 255, 301, 410
Ewing, Fergus   207, 208, 213, 375
executive
    delegated legislative powers   128
    relationship with Law Commissions   29,
        153–4
    subject to the law   128
    *see also* government

fairness, principle of   129
Family Procedure Rules   394
Family Procedure Rules Committee   394
Faris, Neil   4, 15, 29, 75, 363
Frost, Robert   97
Fuller, Lon L   129

Gardiner, Lord   7, 17–18, 19, 29, 33, 46, 75,
    77–8, 125, 142, 175, 342, 357
Garrett, Brian   48n
Genn, Hazel   249
German Civil Code   93
Ghana Law Reform Commission   178
Gibson, Sir Peter   258
Goff, Lord   163, 164–5, 194
Goldie, Annabel   207, 213
Good Law project   398
Goodman, Arnold   17–18
government
    changing priorities   245, 251–62
    relationship with Law Commissions   4, 5, 26,
        29, 76–7, 153–4
        enhancing   80, 85
    Scottish   348–9, 351–3
    *see also* executive
Gower, LCB   33, 35, 39, 43
Gray, Charles   128
Grayling, Chris   181
Green Papers   310–11, 395n
Gretton, George L   4, 13, 75, 166

Haldane Society   17
Hale, Lady   4, 6, 9, 198, 200, 257, 264, 275,
    276, 278, 279, 282, 283–6, 296, 317,
    328, 330
Hale, Sir Matthew   3, 128
Halliday, John   83
Hamilton, Adrian   267
Hamilton, Michael   48

Hammond, Sir Grant   4, 6, 10, 12, 173, 174, 189, 191, 198, 202–3, 328
Hardiman J (Mr Justice Adrian Hardiman)   156
Harpum, Charles   4, 6, 257, 273, 330–1
Hart, HLA   111
Hartley, LP   380, 399
Harvey, CP   135
Hegel, Georg   236, 236n
Hobbes, Thomas   242, 242n, 243
Hodder, Jack   410
Hodge, Lord   4, 8, 279, 281, 286, 290–1
Hoffmann, Lord   137, 326–7
Hogan, Brian   111
Hope, Lord   285
Horace   159
House of Lords
    Practice Statement   7, 141
Hughes, Lord   288
human rights
    assisted suicide   196n
    Australian Law Reform Commission   58
    concept of   396
    European Convention on Human Rights   137
    national human rights institutions   157–8
    normative content of law reform   152–3
    Paris Principles   157, 157n
    protection generally   136–8, 368

illegality, Supreme Court decisions   275, 286–92
implementation *see* reports and recommendations
independence of Law Commissions
    European Law Commission, potential for   231
    funding   341
    generally   10, 18, 56
    Law Commission of England and Wales   25, 26, 87, 151–8, 341
    lobbying by Commissions   187
    Lord Chancellor/Commission protocol   257, 381
    principle of   101, 104, 151–8, 187, 341, 344, 351
    relations with executive   153–5
    relations with human rights institutions   157–8
    relations with judiciary   154–7
    relations with legislature   153–5
    relations with philanthropists   158
inquiries
    single-issue   246, 264
    cost   254
insurance contract reform   266–9
intelligibility, principle of   344
international law   401, 405–8
international projects, Commissioners representing UK   67
interpretation, law of   401, 408–9
Irvine, Lord   250

Jacobs, Sir Francis   232, 384
Jellicoe Committees   247, 257
Johnston, David   4, 8, 12, 15

Joint Committee on Privacy and Injunctions   299, 299n
Judge, Lord   280
Judicial Appointments Commission   85–6
judiciary
    collegiate decision-making   141
    Law Commission reports
        admissibility   312–13
        citation   149, 242, 274–96, 310, 312–25, 327, 395
        as guides to interpretation   281
        implementation   189, 193–7, 199, 201
    law reform by   23–5, 26, 35, 141–2, 144–6, 189, 301
        Commissions influencing   155–7, 159–69, 173, 175, 199, 217, 242
        Scots law   202
        statute law reform compared   193–7
    Practice Directions   333–4
    proposing changes to remit   155–6
    relationship with Law Commissions   77, 154–7
        enhancing   80, 85
    *see also* common law; courts
Juncker, Jean-Claude   233
*Justice for All* White Paper   394
Justinian   242n

Keith, Sir Kenneth   4, 6, 9, 15
Kenya Law Reform Commission   341
Kerr, Lord   280, 282, 294
Kerr, Sir Michael   266
Kilbrandon, Lord   32, 343, 344
Kirby, Michael   58
Kötz, Hein   93
Kozinski, Alex   401, 407

Lange, David   400, 409
Law Commission of Canada
    Advisory Committee   102, 103
    budget   102–3
    closure   75, 98, 362
    Commissioners   102–3
    expertise   103–4
    generally   97–107, 362, 391n
    independence   101, 104, 381
    partnerships   103
    President   102–3
    public input   103–4
    regional and linguistic balance   102, 105
    relationships, studies of   99, 104–6
    remit   98–100, 106
    structure   101–3
Law Commission of England and Wales
    accessibility   241, 397–9
    achieving consensus   251
    advisory function   65, 66, 175, 369
    annual reports   34, 34n
    Chairman   7, 18, 19, 85–8, 154
    characteristics   380–2
    collective responsibility   381, 382

Commissioners 7, 18–19, 25, 31–2, 154, 381
  ad hoc appointments 381
  changes of 251
  collective responsibility 381, 382
  recruitment 19
consultation papers
  generally 240–3, 311
  reports compared 241–2
consultation process 7–8, 29–30, 39–43, 134,
    238, 239, 244, 381, 382
core practices 134
criminal law codification project 108–22
Draft Criminal Code Bill 108, 110–11, 113
  achievements and failures 111–15, 120–2
  conception of criminal law 110
  objective 109–11
  orthodox subjectivism 110–11, 113
  *see also* codification of criminal law
establishment 17–18, 33–5, 127, 340–2
expertise 18–19, 25, 381–2
funding/budget 76, 77, 253–5, 264, 362,
    365–6, 369, 399
future role 396–9, 400–11
holding government to account 80–1
House of Lords special procedure 81–3,
    184–5, 203–5, 248, 250, 261–62, 276, 373
  Bills impacting on Scots law 205, 373
  Bills subject to amendment 204–5
  Bills which have undergone 204, 261n
  criminal law reform 211
  success 206
independence 10, 18, 25, 26, 87, 151–8, 341
  Lord Chancellor/Commission protocol 5,
    80, 83–5, 257, 381
initiatives to improve effectiveness 80–3
Lord Chancellor/Commission protocol 5, 11,
    22, 69–70, 248, 248n, 256–8, 269,
    275, 366
Lord Chancellor's reports to Parliament 11,
    22, 147–8, 181–2
ministerial responsibility for 78
Northern Ireland 48
Parliamentary Counsel 19–20, 134, 140n,
    189, 192–3, 199, 230, 382
parliamentary oversight 11, 22, 80, 147–8,
    181–2
professionalism 33–4
programmes 20–6, 34, 65, 66
  approval 65, 66, 68
quinquennial review 83
referral of projects to 9, 327–9, 362
reforms proposed by 9–10, 26
reforms proposed to 66
relationship with courts 4, 6–7, 273,
    326–35
  Supreme Court 273, 274–96, 300
relationship with government 4, 5, 26, 29,
    76–7
  enhancing 80, 85
relationship with the judiciary 23–5, 77
relationship with Parliament 4, 5–6

remit 19, 25, 64, 65–9, 108, 129, 140, 175,
    246–7, 369, 390
  'branches of the law' 66, 67–8
  codification 12–15, 19, 20, 25, 65, 72,
    89–90, 93–4, 108, 299, 331–3, 355–8
  consolidation 19, 66, 133–4, 175, 199–200,
    261–2, 311–12, 355–7, 361, 362
  EU law 140
  substantive law reform 140
reports and recommendations
  admissibility in court 312–25
  consultation papers compared 241–2
  draft Bills 66, 140–1, 140n, 175, 192–3,
    243, 311
  explanatory notes 311
  generally 311
  impact assessments 239, 239n
  implementation generally 10–12,
    19–20
  implementation methods 143–5
  implementation rate 23, 32, 77–8, 134,
    139, 142–3, 149–50, 177, 198–9, 361
  joint reports 363
  number published 134, 361
  parliamentary time available 5, 79, 81–2,
    131–2, 142, 176, 181, 302
  reports on implementation 253, 259–60
  submission 176
  unimplemented 148–50, 198–9
research 367
scope 381, 382
sentencing procedure, initiative on 109,
    120–1, 120n, 133–4, 262, 331
social policy issues 64–72
staffing 264
state's power to dissolve 341
subjects covered by 358–9
Triennial Review 16, 361, 366, 366n
Wales 15
  devolution 356–7, 359–61, 365, 368
  protocol with Welsh ministers 11, 360,
    360n, 366
  Welsh Advisory Committee 360
weakened position 199
Law Commission of India 154n, 178
law reform
  accessibility 398–9
  areas for 9–10, 26
  comparative law 72
  controversial subjects 9, 65, 253, 255, 301,
    359
  financial constraints 253–5, 264
  France 386
  Germany 386–7
  Law Commissions' remit 19, 25, 64, 65–9,
    175, 343
  law making generally 400–11
  lawyers' law 9, 19, 32, 66–7, 107, 197, 300,
    343–4, 381, 385, 410
  legal reasoning 390, 391–2
  normative content 152–3

origins   3, 340–1
political   381
procedural and evidential rules   390, 393–4
social policy issues   64–72
Spain   387–8
substantive law   390
Sweden   388–9, 398
Switzerland   389
law reform agencies
  academic studies   76
  achieving consensus   251
  Australia   55–6, 55n, 61
  balancing principle and pragmatism   217
  changing priorities   245, 251–62
  common features   76–7
  consultation process   297
  democratic legitimacy   56
  funding   341
  future role   396–9, 400–11
  independence *see* independence
  lobbying by   187
  models for   340–1, 383–9
  objective valuation   77
  state's power to dissolve   341
  time issues *see* time issues
  United States   383–6
Law Reform Commission of Hong Kong   178
Law Reform Commission of the Republic of
  Ireland   156, 156n, 177
Law Reform Committee   17
Lawyers' law
  human rights rhetoric   152–3
  law reform   9, 19, 32, 66–7, 107, 197, 300,
    343–4, 381, 385
Le Bouthillier, Yves   4, 10, 15, 75
Lee, James   4, 6, 273, 329
legality, principle of   137
legislation, function   312
Legislative Reform Order (LRO)   143–4
Leveson LJ (Sir Brian Leveson)   327–8
Lewis, Stephen   4, 8, 12, 200
Lewison LJ (Sir Kim Lewison)   315
Llewellyn, Karl   95
Lloyd of Berwick, Lord   80–1, 84
Lloyd Jones, Sir David (Lloyd Jones LJ)   4, 5, 9,
    13, 15, 16, 87, 247, 256, 256n, 365
Lloyd LJ (Sir Timothy Lloyd)   317
Longmore LJ (Sir Andrew)   266, 267
Lord Chancellor
  changing role   78
  Lord Chancellor/Commission protocol   5, 11,
    22, 69–70, 248, 248n, 256–8, 269, 275, 366
  Ministry of Justice   78
  reports on Commission proposals   11, 22,
    147–8, 181–2
  submission of Commission programmes
    to   65, 66
Lorimer, Elaine   4, 12, 202

McCluskey, Lord   143
MacDermott, Lord   47

McDonald, Barbara   4, 10, 13, 273, 331
MacDonald, Lewis   207
MacDonald, Roderick   99–100
Mackay, Lord   173, 264–5
McKendrick, Ewan   304
McMillan, Malcolm   4, 5, 11, 12, 202
MacQueen, Hector   4, 5, 6, 11, 173–4
Magna Carta   128
Maguire, Mr Justice   52
Major, John   260
Malawi Law Commission
  Constitutional provision   349
  funding   341
  implementation rate   178
  independence   341
Malcolm, Lord   166
Mance, Lord   267, 289, 290–1
Manitoba Law Reform Commission   178, 341
Mansfield, Lord   286
Mark, Michael   323
Marsh, Norman   35, 39
Marshall, Chief Justice   137
Martin, Andrew   18, 19, 26, 357
Mason, John   206
Michael, James   148–9
Mill, John Stuart   407, 408
Miller, Kenneth   140
Ministry of Justice
  expansion of remit   78
  *see also* Department for Constitutional Affairs
miscarriages of justice, principles of good
  law   130–1
Mitchell, Paul   4, 10, 29, 70, 199
Munby, Sir James   4, 8, 13, 84, 87, 245–6, 245n,
    259, 356

Napier, Sir Oliver   47
Neuberger, Lord   15, 279, 281, 284, 286, 290–1,
    333, 350
Newey J (Sir Guy Newey)   321
New Zealand Evidence Act 2006
  five-yearly reviews   180, 189, 191
New Zealand Law Commission
  *Contract Statutes Review*   191, 191n
  draft Cabinet papers   182–3
  generally   9, 352
  implementation rate of reports   179–81
  *Invasion of Privacy: Penalties and
    Remedies*   299, 299n
  Judicature Modernisation Bill   187
  mandatory Cabinet responses   180
  Minister responsible for   176
  *A New Interpretation Act*   392, 392n
  remit   175–6
  submission of reports   176, 180
Nicholls, Lord   24, 313
North, Sir Peter   187, 248, 251, 266
  *Report of the Review of Drink and Drug
    Driving Law*   263, 263n
Northern Ireland Director and Office of Law
  Reform   47–8

Northern Ireland Law Commission
British–Irish Agreement 53
current projects 52
establishment 49, 53
funding 51
joint reports 363
operation 46–50
remit 49
suspension 29, 51–4, 75, 346, 363

O'Brien, Sheriff Principal 160
obsolete legislation 19, 66, 133, 311–12, 343, 357
O'Higgins CJ (Chief Justice Thomas Francis O'Higgins) 157
Ormerod, David 4, 13, 200, 357

Paines, Nicholas 4, 12, 173
Palmer, Sir Geoffrey 9, 13, 16, 64, 134, 182, 186, 190, 192, 246n, 247, 262, 265, 343, 349–50, 358, 398
Paris Principles 157, 157n
Parliament
changing government priorities 245, 251–62
holding government to account 80–1
legality, principle of 137
parallel chambers 183–5
pre-emption of 53
relationship with Law Commissions 4, 5–6
cross-party support 87
enhancing 80, 85
oversight of Commission 80, 176
reports to, on Commission proposals 181–2
securing parliamentary support 235
securing parliamentary time 5, 79, 81–2, 131–2, 142, 176, 181, 253
subject to the law 128
as supreme law maker 128–9
Parliamentary Business and Legislation Committee 79, 83
Parliamentary Counsel (office of Parliamentary Draftsmen)
codifying existing law 312
and the Law Commission 19–20, 134, 140n, 189, 192–3, 199, 230, 382
time pressures 398
*When Laws Become Too Complex* 129–30
Paterson, Alan 276, 285, 292, 293, 329
Patten LJ (Sir Nicholas Patten) 322
Pen, Justin 62
Pentland, Lord 4, 6, 10
Philips, Sir Cyril 393
Phillips, Lord 86–7, 280, 282, 292–3
Prentice, Dan 258
primary legislation
law reform via 139–43
resulting from Commission proposals 142

Queensland Law Reform Commission 178

reasonable chastisement 113
Reed, Lord 236, 281, 286, 333
Regulatory Reform Order, delegated legislation 143–4
Reid, Lord 4, 16, 95, 145, 410
Renton Report 92
repeals
Law Commissions' remit 19, 66, 140, 311–12, 343, 361
necessity for 93n, 129
reports and recommendations
*for individual reports see separate table of Law Commission reports*
explanatory notes 311
generally 311
House of Lords special procedure 5–6, 15, 81–3, 184–5, 356–7, 359–61, 365, 368
implementation
Australia 61, 178
by judiciary 26, 189, 193–7
defining implementation 146–8
generally 10–12, 19–20
implementation units 183
large projects 186–7
Law Commission input 367
length of process 173, 174
Lord Chancellor's reports 11, 22, 147–8, 181–2
methods 143–5, 193–7
parallel chambers 183–5
practical difficulties 79, 81, 176–7, 186–7
rates 23, 32, 77–8, 77n, 134, 139, 142–8, 149–50, 173, 177–81, 198–9, 361, 372
reports on 253n, 259–60
Scotland 177, 369–80
techniques to encourage 181–8, 369–70
Lord Chancellor/Commission protocol 11, 22, 69–70, 80, 83–5, 248, 248n, 256–8, 269, 275, 366, 381
parliamentary support 235
parliamentary time available 5, 79, 81, 142, 176, 181, 302
submission 176
unimplemented 125–6, 148–50, 198–9
contribution made by 77, 142–3, 148–50, 160–9
judicial citation 149, 199, 242, 395
rights
common law 128, 129
equality of treatment 137
principle of legality 137
rule of law 136–8
*see also* human rights
Rimer LJ (Sir Colin Rimer) 315
Ritchie, Iain 159
Rix LJ (Sir Bernard Rix) 267
Rodger of Earlsferry, Lord 163–4, 343
Royal Commissions 72, 393

rule of law
  core principles   129–30
  democracy, law reform and   127–38
  fundamental rights   136–8
  Law Commissions, generally   138
  repeals   93n, 129
  systematic development and reform   129

Sackville J (Justice Ronald Sackville)   56
Salisbury, Lord   127
Sankey, Lord   406
Scarman, Lord   32, 33, 41–3
  on codification   14, 355
  Law Commission system   310, 325, 382, 395n
  proposed Bill of Rights   137–8
  view of common law   141
Scotland
  devolution   368, 371
  law reform bodies   3
  Roman law as model   342
  Scottish Law Commission Bills   377
Scottish Civil Courts Review   168
Scottish Law Commission
  accessibility   241, 344
  advisory function   65, 66, 369
  Chairman   7, 347
  Commissioners   7, 18–19
  consultation/discussion papers
    generally   240–3
    reports compared   241–2
  consultation process   7–8, 238–43, 244
  Delegated Powers and Law Reform
    Committee   185–6, 206–13, 370–9
    criteria for Commission Bills   374–5, 376
    membership   212
    remit   374
  see also Scottish Law Commission Bill
    Procedure
  establishment   127, 340–2
    initial scepticism   343
  funding   341, 348, 369
  harnessing legal expertise   353–4
  House of Lords special procedure for Law
    Commission Bills   5–6, 15, 81–3, 184–5,
    356–7, 359–61, 365, 368
    introduction   82
    statutes enacted using   82–3
  independence   10, 341, 344, 345, 351
  programmes, approval of   65, 66, 68
  referral of projects to   9, 347
  reforms proposed by   9
  reforms proposed to   66
  relationship with Scottish government   5
  remit   32, 64, 65–9, 108, 129, 140, 343–4,
    349–50, 369, 370n, 390
    codification   12–15, 65, 72, 108, 343, 350
    consolidation   66, 92, 133, 261–2, 311–12
    EU law   140
  reports and recommendations
    draft Bills   66, 243, 311, 347
    impact assessments   239, 239n
    implementation   10–12, 177, 369–80
    joint reports   345–6, 347, 363
    number published   345
    reports and consultation papers
      compared   241–2
    submission   176
  Scottish Law Commission Bill procedure   11,
    206–12, 349
    criminal law   211
    review   209
    see also Delegated Powers and Law Reform
      Committee
  social policy issues   66–7, 69
  see also Delegated Powers of Law Reform
    Committee
  staffing   347
  state's power to dissolve   341
Scottish Parliament
  Bills, stages of   371
  establishment   371
  referral of projects to Commission   347
  relationship with Scottish Law Commission   4,
    5–6, 348–9, 351–3
Second Reading Committee see also House of
  Lords special procedure
secondary legislation
  accessibility compromised   131
  review by Law Commissions   140
sentencing procedure
  initiative on   109, 120–1, 133–4, 262, 331,
    357–8
  Sentencing Guidelines   75
Shelley, Percy Bysshe   411
Smith, JC   21, 111, 395
Smith, TB   7
social policy, reform   64–72
Society of Labour Lawyers   26
Sorabji, John   384
Soskice, Sir Frank   404
South African Law Reform Commission   9, 173,
  173n, 177
Sparrow, John   43
Special Public Bill Committee see also House of
  Lords special procedure
  Scottish Law Commission reports   203, 204
Spencer, JR   397
Spigelman James   309
Stapleton, Jane   309
Stark, Shona Wilson   4, 9, 10, 125–6,
  198, 330
statute databases
  accessibility   115–16, 131, 142, 396
  amendments to   247
  error rate   92
statute law
  accessibility   131, 138, 247, 308–9
  accuracy   247
  alternatives to   125, 193–7
  common law, interaction with   297–309,
    331–3
  legislative restatements   307–9

consolidation  66, 92, 133–4, 175
drafting  132, 192–3
duplicative  132–4
function of legislation  312
implementation by
    generally  198–200, 201–3
    Law Commission reports  217
interpretation  242, 243
judicial law reform compared  193–7
Law Commission input  367
post-legislative scrutiny  6, 12, 131, 134–5, 189–92
pre-legislative scrutiny  134, 367
    Special Public Bill procedure  203
reform and revision  66, 175, 343
    obsolete legislation  19, 66, 133, 311–12, 343
    *see also* codification; consolidation
repeals  66, 93n, 140, 311–12, 343, 347, 361
securing parliamentary time  79, 81–2, 131–2, 142, 176, 181
volume of legislation passed  131–2
Stephen J (Sir James Fitzjames Stephen)  111, 111n, 114, 405, 407–8
Stevenson, Stewart  208
Stott, Gordon  342
Straw, Jack  80, 84
subjectivism  110–11, 113
Sumption, Lord  289, 290–1, 399
Supreme Court
    collegiate decision-making  141n
    decisions on law of illegality  275, 286–92
    judgments on hearsay evidence  275, 292–6
    Practice Statement  7, 141
    relationship with ECHR  275, 276, 292–6
    relationship with Law Commissions  6–7, 273, 274–96, 300, 326

Thomas, Sir John  329–30
Thomas of Cymgiedd, Lord (earlier, Thomas LJ)  119, 120, 334, 334n, 357, 384
Thornberry, Emily  80
time issues
    changing priorities  245, 251–62
    consolidations  262

parliamentary time available  5, 79, 81–2, 131–2, 142, 176, 181, 253, 302
    shortening timescales  262–5
    timescales generally  245–65
Toulson, Lord  4, 6, 9–10, 22, 81, 86, 125, 126, 279, 286, 289, 290–1
transparency, principle of  129–30
Tranter, Kieran  60, 61, 63
Treacy LJ (Sir Colman Treacy)  120–1
Trudeau, Pierre-Elliott  98
Tyldesley, Peter  266

UNCITRAL *Model Law on International Commercial Arbitration*  255n
Underhill LJ (Sir Nicholas Underhill)  319–20, 325
United States
    American Law Institute
        codification  303
        generally  341, 383–5
        Restatements  383
    Uniform Code Commissioners  385–6
    Uniform Commercial Code  94–5, 383
unjust enrichment, development of law  125, 162–6, 163n, 201–2

Walker, Lord  284, 313
Wallis, Diana  232, 384
Weir, Tony  382
Wells, WT (William Wells QC MP)  31–2
Welsh devolution
    Law Commission of England and Wales  5–6, 15, 356–7, 359–61, 365, 368
    protocol with Welsh ministers  360, 360n, 366
    Welsh Advisory Committee  360
White Papers  310–11, 395n
Wigg, George  18
Wilberforce, Lord  250, 410
Williams, Glanville  17, 18, 111
Wills, Michael  80
Wilson, Harold  18, 33–4, 64, 341
Wilson, Lord  284, 288
Woodhouse, Sir Owen  176
Woolf, Lord  125, 136, 393

Lightning Source UK Ltd.
Milton Keynes UK
UKHW031406070519
342241UK00005B/452/P